APPLIED OPERATING SYSTEM CONCEPTS

FIRST EDITION

WINDOWS XP UPDATE

APPLIED OPERATING SYSTEM CONCEPTS

FIRST EDITION

WINDOWS XP UPDATE

Avi
Silberschatz

Peter
Galvin

Greg
Gagne

John Wiley & Sons, Inc.

COVER ILLUSTRATION: Susan Cyr

This book was set in LaTeX by Avi Silberschatz and printed and bound by Quebecor Fairfield. The cover was printed by Phoenix Color Corp.

This book is printed on acid-free paper. ∞

ISBN 0-471-26314-1

Printed in the United States of America

10 9 8 7 6 5 4 3 2 1

PREFACE

Operating systems are an essential part of any computer system. Similarly, a course in operating systems is an essential part of any computer-science education. This book is intended to serve as a text for an introductory course in operating systems at the junior or senior undergraduate level, or at the first-year graduate level. It provides a clear description of the *concepts* that underlie operating systems.

We discuss fundamental concepts that are applicable to a variety of systems. We use Java to present many of these ideas, and we include numerous examples that pertain specifically to UNIX and to other popular operating systems. In particular, we use Sun Microsystems' Solaris 2 operating system, in addition to Microsoft Windows, Windows NT, Windows 2000 and Windows XP. Other operating systems discussed are Linux, IBM OS/2, the Apple Macintosh Operating System, and Mach.

Contents of This Book

The text is organized in seven major parts:

- **Overview** (Chapters 1 through 3). In these chapters, we explain what operating systems *are*, what they *do*, and how they are *designed* and *constructed*. We explain how the concept of an operating system has developed, what the common features of an operating system are, what an operating system does for the user, and what it does for the computer-system operator. The presentation is motivational, historical, and explanatory; we avoid discussing how the ideas are carried out within the computer system. Therefore, these chapters are suitable for individuals, or for students in lower-level classes, who want to learn what an operating system is without studying the details of the internal algorithms. Chapter 2 covers the hardware topics that are important to operating systems. Readers well versed in such topics (for example, I/O, DMA, and hard-disk operation) may choose to skim or skip this chapter.

- **Process management** (Chapters 4 through 8). At the heart of modern operating systems are *processes*, the units of work, which execute *concurrently*. There are operating-system processes, which execute system code, and user processes, which execute user code. These chapters cover various methods for process scheduling, interprocess communication, process synchronization, and deadlock handling. Also included under this topic is a discussion of threads.

- **Memory and storage management** (Chapters 9 through 13). A process must be (at least partially) in main memory during execution. To ensure good utilization of and response speed of the CPU, the computer must keep several processes in memory. The many different memory-management schemes reflect various approaches; their effectiveness depends on the particular situation. Since main memory is usually too small to accommodate all data and programs, and since it cannot store data permanently, the computer system must provide secondary storage to back up main memory. Most modern computer systems use disks as the primary on-line storage medium for information (both programs and data). The file system provides the mechanism for on-line storage of and access to both data and programs that reside on the disks. These chapters deal with the classic internal algorithms and structures of storage management. They provide a firm practical understanding of the properties, advantages, and disadvantages of the algorithms used. The devices that attach to a computer vary in multiple dimensions. In many ways, they are the slowest major components of the computer. Because devices vary so widely, the operating system needs to provide a wide range of functionality to allow applications to control all aspects of the devices. These chapters discuss system I/O in depth, including I/O system design, interfaces, and internal system structures and functions. Because devices create a performance bottleneck, we examine other influences on performance. Matters related to secondary and tertiary storage are explained as well.

- **Distributed systems** (Chapters 14 through 17). A *distributed system* is a collection of processors that do not share memory or a clock. Such a system gives the user access to the various resources that the system maintains. Access to a shared resource allows computation speedup and improved data availability and reliability. Such a system also gives the user a distributed file system, which is a file-service system whose users, servers, and storage devices are dispersed among the various sites of a distributed system. A distributed system must provide various mechanisms for process synchronization and communication, so that we can deal with the deadlock problem and the variety of failures that are not encountered in a centralized system.

- **Protection and security** (Chapters 18 and 19). The various processes in an operating system must be protected from one another's activities. For that purpose, we use mechanisms to ensure that the files, memory segments, CPU, and other resources can be operated on by only those processes that have gained proper authorization from the operating system. Protection is a mechanism for controlling the access of programs, processes, or users to the resources defined by a computer system. This mechanism must provide a means for specification of the controls to be imposed, as well as a means of enforcement. Security protects the information stored in the system (both data and code), as well as the physical resources of the computer system, from unauthorized access, malicious destruction or alteration, and accidental introduction of inconsistency.

- **Case studies** (Chapters 20 through 24). We present detailed case studies of five operating systems: UNIX Berkeley 4.3BSD, Linux, Microsoft Windows NT, Windows 2000, and Windows XP. We chose Berkeley 4.3BSD and Linux because UNIX at one time was almost small enough to understand, and yet was not a toy operating system. Most of its internal algorithms were selected for *simplicity,* rather than for speed or sophistication. Both Berkeley 4.3BSD and Linux are readily available to computer-science departments, so many students have access to these systems. We chose Windows NT, Windows 2000, and Windows XP, because these are a modern operating systems whose design and implementation are drastically different from those of UNIX.

Java

This book uses Java to illustrate many operating-system concepts, such as multitasking, CPU scheduling, process synchronization, deadlock, security, and distributed systems. Java is more a technology than a programming language, so it is an excellent vehicle for demonstrations.

Java was originally developed as a language to program microprocessors in consumer devices such as cellular telephones and set-top boxes. The advent of the Web in the mid-1990s showed the Java team at Sun Microsystems the language's potential usefulness across the Internet: Programmers can use Java to write applications and *applets*—programs that run on web pages. Java also provides support for development of database applications, graphical user interfaces (GUIs), reusable objects, and two-dimensional and three-dimensional modeling, to name a few. All such programs can run on a single computer or on a distributed system across the Internet.

We provide an overview of Java technology in Chapter 3, and illustrate the creation and coordination of multitasking Java programs in Chapters 5 and 7. In Chapter 4, we use Java to demonstrate how different processes can communicate using shared memory and message passing. In Chapter 6, we use Java to demonstrate CPU-scheduling algorithms; in Chapter 8, we illustrate deadlock and deadlock-recovery methods using Java. In Chapter 15, we show how Java can apply many of these concepts to a distributed system. To a lesser extent, we also use Java to illustrate a virtual machine as well as memory management and computer security.

Much of the Java-related material in this text has been developed and class tested in undergraduate operating-systems classes. Students typically entered these classes with knowledge of C++ and of basic object-oriented principles, but they were not familiar with Java. They had no trouble with the syntax of Java; their difficulties lay in understanding such concepts as multithreading and multiple concurrently running threads sharing data. These concepts are more operating-system than Java issues; even students with a sound knowledge of Java are likely to have difficulty with them. We emphasize concurrency and passing of object references to several threads, rather than concentrating on syntax.

Java is an especially fast-moving technology; however, we use Java examples that are core to the language and are unlikely to change in the near future. All the Java programs in this text compile with the Java Development Kit (JDK), Release 1.2. Although you do not need a thorough knowledge of Java to understand the examples in the text, if you do not know Java, you should read the Java Primer in Appendix A.

Relationship to OSC

This text is based on the Fifth Edition of *Operating System Concepts* (OSC). Much of the material in this text was derived from OSC; the texts differ in how the material is presented. OSC presented concepts fundamental to all operating systems, rather than particular implementations of systems. This text discusses applied knowledge. We present the concepts using examples from Java and from many contemporary operating systems, such as Solaris 2 and Windows NT.

The applied nature of this text and the addition of Java material resulted in the need to remove material from OSC in memory management, process management, mass-storage systems, and distributed systems.

Mailing List and Supplements

For information about teaching supplements and on-line material, which complement this book, visit our web site at

http://www.wiley.com/college/silberschatz

To obtain restricted supplements, you should contact your local sales representative. You can find the local Wiley representative at the "Who's My Rep?" webpage: http://www.wiley.com/college/rep/index.html

We also provide an environment where users can communicate with one another and with us. Our mailing list, consisting of users of our book, has the address aos-book@research.bell-labs.com. If you want to be on the list, please send a message to avi@bell-labs.com indicating the title of the book, your name, your affiliation, and your e-mail address.

Home Page

A World Wide Web home page for the book is available at

http://www.bell-labs.com/topic/books/aos-book

The home page contains information about the book, such as the set of slides that accompanies the book, model course syllabi, Java source code, and up-to-date errata.

Errata

We have attempted to fix every error in this new edition, but—as happens with operating systems—a few obscure bugs will remain. We would appreciate it if you would notify us of any errors or omissions that you identify in the book. Also, if you would like to suggest improvements or to contribute exercises, we would be glad to hear from you. Send your suggestions to Avi Silberschatz, Director, Information Sciences Research Center, MH 2T-310, Bell Laboratories, 600 Mountain Ave., Murray Hill, NJ 07974 (avi@bell-labs.com).

Acknowledgments

This book is derived from Operating Systems Concepts, the first three editions of which were coauthored by James Peterson. Other people who helped us with the previous editions are Randy Bentson, David Black, Joseph Boykin, Jeff Brumfield, Gael Buckley, P. C. Capon, John Carpenter, Thomas Casavant, Ajoy Kumar Datta, Joe Deck, Thomas Doeppner, Caleb Drake, M. Raşit Eskicioğlu,

Hans Flack, Robert Fowler, G. Scott Graham, Rebecca Hartman, Wayne Hathaway, Christopher Haynes, Bruce Hillyer, Mark Holliday, Richard Kieburtz, Carol Kroll, Thomas LeBlanc, John Leggett, Jerrold Leichter, Ted Leung, Gary Lippman, Carolyn Miller, Michael Molloy, Yoichi Muraoka, Jim M. Ng, Ed Posnak, Boris Putanec, Charles Qualline, John Quarterman, John Stankovic, Adam Stauffer, Steven Stepanek, Hal Stern, Louis Stevens, David Umbaugh, Steve Vinoski, John Werth, and J. S. Weston. Hamid Arabnia, Sudarshan K. Dhall, Steven Stepanek, Pete Thomas, L. David Umbaugh, Tommy Wagner.

The idea of creating an applied version of the Operating System Concepts book came from Maite Suarez-Rivas. The cover illustrator was Susan Cyr while the cover designer was Lynne Reed. Michael Hirsch, executive marketing manager, has done all the promotions in preparation for the release of the text. Patricia Unubun was helpful with book production. Lyn Dupré edited the book; Barbara Pendergast did the proofreading. Marilyn Turnamian updated the text, Instructors Manual and the slides.

Michael Shapiro reviewed the Solaris information. Chapter 13 was partially derived from a paper by Hillyer and Silberschatz [1996]. Chapter 17 was derived from a paper by Levy and Silberschatz [1990]. Chapter 21 was derived from an unpublished manuscript by Stephen Tweedie. Chapter 22 was derived from an unpublished manuscript by Cliff Martin; Chapter 23 was derived from an unpublished manuscript by Cliff Martin. Chapter 24 was derived from an unpublished manuscript by Dave Probert, Cliff Martin, and Avi Silberschatz. additional editing on that chapter was done by Bruce Hillyer.

We thank the following people, who reviewed this book: Bil Lewis, Bob Erickson, Robert Gann, Chris Armen, Anthony J. Duben, Kadathur Lakshmanan, Boleslaw K. Szymanski, David Binkley, Arun Ektare, John R. Graham, Henning Schulzrinne, Robert Kline, Stephen J. Hartley, Paul W. Ross, Mike Dahlin, John Norton, James Heliotis, and Ruknet Cezzar.

Abraham Silberschatz, Murray Hill, NJ, 1999
Peter Baer Galvin, Norton MA, 1999
Greg Gagne, Salt Lake City, UT, 1999

CONTENTS

PART TWO   ■   PROCESS MANAGEMENT

Chapter 7   Process Synchronization

Chapter 8   Deadlocks

PART THREE   ■   STORAGE MANAGEMENT

Chapter 9   Memory Management

Chapter 10   Virtual Memory

PART FIVE   ■   PROTECTION AND SECURITY

PART SIX ■ CASE STUDIES

Chapter 24   Windows XP

Appendix A   Java Primer

Bibliography   891

Credits   915

Index   917

Part One

OVERVIEW

An *operating system* is a program that acts as an intermediary between a user of a computer and the computer hardware. The purpose of an operating system is to provide an environment in which a user can execute programs in a *convenient* and *efficient* manner.

We trace the development of operating systems from the first hands-on systems to current multiprogrammed and time-shared systems. Understanding the reasons behind the development of operating systems gives us an appreciation for what an operating system does and how it does it.

The operating system must ensure the correct operation of the computer system. To prevent user programs from interfering with the proper operation of the system, the hardware must provide appropriate mechanisms to ensure such proper behavior. We describe the basic computer architecture that allows us to write a correct operating system.

To ease the programming task, the operating system provides certain services to programs and to the users of those programs. The specific services provided, of course, differ from one operating system to another, but we identify and explore common classes.

Chapter 1

INTRODUCTION

An **operating system** is a program that acts as an intermediary between a user of a computer and the computer hardware. The purpose of an operating system is to provide an environment in which a user can execute programs. The primary goal of an operating system is thus to make the computer system **convenient** to use. A secondary goal is to use the computer hardware in an **efficient** manner.

To understand what operating systems are, we must first understand how they have developed. In this chapter, we trace the development of operating systems from the first hands-on systems to current multiprogrammed and time-shared systems. As we move through the various stages, we see how the components of operating systems evolved as natural solutions to problems in early computer systems. Understanding the reasons behind the development of operating systems gives us an appreciation for what tasks an operating system does and how it does them.

1.1 ■ What Is an Operating System?

An operating system is an important part of almost every computer system. A computer system can be divided roughly into four components: the **hardware,** the **operating system,** the **application programs,** and the **users** (Figure 1.1).

The hardware—the central processing unit (CPU), the memory, and the input/output (I/O) devices—provides the basic computing resources. The application programs—such as word processors, spreadsheets, compilers, and

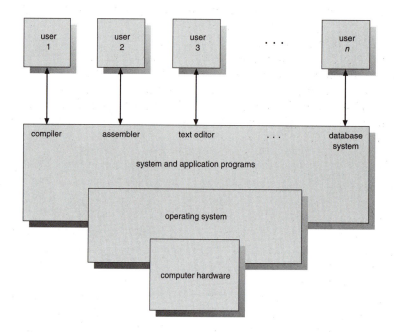

Figure 1.1   Abstract view of the components of a computer system.

web browsers —define the ways in which these resources are used to solve the computing problems of the users. There may be many different users (people, machines, other computers) trying to solve different problems. Accordingly, there may be many different application programs. The operating system controls and coordinates the use of the hardware among the various application programs for the various users.

An operating system is similar to a *government*. The components of a computer system are its hardware, software, and data. The operating system provides the means for the proper use of these resources in the operation of the computer system. Like a government, the operating system performs no useful function by itself. It simply provides an *environment* within which other programs can do useful work.

We can view an operating system as a **resource allocator**. A computer system has many resources (hardware and software) that may be required to solve a problem: CPU time, memory space, file-storage space, I/O devices, and so on. The operating system acts as the manager of these resources and allocates them to specific programs and users as necessary for tasks. Since there may be many—possibly conflicting—requests for resources, the operating system must decide which requests are allocated resources so that it can operate the computer system efficiently and fairly.

A slightly different view of an operating system emphasizes the need to control the various I/O devices and user programs. An operating system is a

control program. A control program controls the execution of user programs to prevent errors and improper use of the computer. It is especially concerned with the operation and control of I/O devices.

In general, however, there is no completely adequate definition of an operating system. Operating systems exist because they are a reasonable way to solve the problem of creating a usable computing system. The fundamental goal of computer systems is to execute user programs and to make solving user problems easier. Toward this goal, computer hardware is constructed. Since bare hardware alone is not particularly easy to use, application programs are developed. These various programs require certain common operations, such as those controlling the I/O devices. The common functions of controlling and allocating resources are then brought together into one piece of software: the operating system.

There is also no universally accepted definition of what is and what is not part of the operating system. A simple viewpoint is that everything a vendor ships when you order "the operating system" should be considered. The memory requirements and features included, however, vary greatly across systems. Some take up less than 1 megabyte of space and lack even a full-screen editor, whereas others require hundreds of megabytes of space and are entirely based on graphical windowing systems. A more common definition is that the operating system is the one program running at all times on the computer (usually called the *kernel*), with all else being application programs. This last definition is the one that we generally follow. The matter of what constitutes an operating system is becoming important. In 1998, the United States Department of Justice filed suit against Microsoft, in essence claiming that Microsoft included too much functionality in its operating systems and thus prevented competition from application vendors.

It is easier to define an operating system by what it *does* than by what it *is*. The primary goal of an operating system is *convenience for the user*. Operating systems exist because they are supposed to make it easier to compute with them than without them. This view is particularly clear when you look at operating systems for small personal computers (PCs).

A secondary goal is *efficient* operation of the computer system. This goal is particularly important for large, shared multiuser systems. These systems are typically expensive, so it is desirable to make them as efficient as possible. These two goals—convenience and efficiency—are sometimes contradictory. In the past, efficiency was often more important than convenience. Thus, much of operating-system theory concentrates on optimal use of computing resources.

To see what operating systems are and what they do, let us consider how they have developed over the past 35 years. By tracing that evolution, we can identify what are the common elements of operating systems, and see how and why these systems have developed as they have.

Operating systems and computer architecture have had a great deal of influence on each other. To facilitate the use of the hardware, researchers developed operating systems. As operating systems were designed and used, it became obvious that changes in the design of the hardware could simplify them. In this short historical review, notice how identification of operating-system problems led to the introduction of new hardware features.

1.2 ■ Batch Systems

Early computers were (physically) enormously large machines run from a console. The common input devices were card readers and tape drives. The common output devices were line printers, tape drives, and card punches. The user did not interact directly with the computer systems. Rather, the user prepared a job—which consisted of the program, the data, and some control information about the nature of the job (control cards)—and submitted it to the computer operator. The job was usually in the form of punch cards. At some later time (after minutes, hours, or days), the output appeared. The output consisted of the result of the program, as well as a dump of memory and registers in case of program error.

The operating system in these early computers was fairly simple. Its major task was to transfer control automatically from one job to the next. The operating system was always resident in memory (Figure 1.2).

To speed up processing, operators **batched** together jobs with similar needs and ran them through the computer as a group. Thus, the programmers would leave their programs with the operator. The operator would sort programs into batches with similar requirements and, as the computer became available, would run each batch. The output from each job would be sent back to the appropriate programmer.

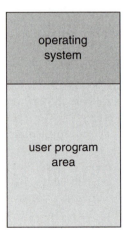

Figure 1.2   Memory layout for a simple batch system.

In this execution environment, the CPU is often idle, because the speeds of the mechanical I/O devices are intrinsically slower than are those of electronic devices. Even a slow CPU works in the microsecond range, with thousands of instructions executed per second. A fast card reader, on the other hand, might read 1200 cards per minute (20 cards per second). Thus, the difference in speed between the CPU and its I/O devices may be three orders of magnitude or more. Over time, of course, improvements in technology and the introduction of disks resulted in faster I/O devices. However, CPU speeds increased even faster, so the problem was not only unresolved, but also exacerbated.

The introduction of disk technology allowed the operating system to keep all jobs on a disk, rather than in a serial card reader. With direct access to several jobs, it could do **job scheduling** to use resources and perform tasks efficiently. We discuss job and CPU scheduling in detail in Chapter 6; a few important aspects are covered here.

The most important aspect of job scheduling is the ability to multiprogram. A single user cannot, in general, keep either the CPU or the I/O devices busy at all times. **Multiprogramming** increases CPU utilization by organizing jobs such that the CPU always has one to execute.

The idea is as follows. The operating system keeps several jobs in memory simultaneously (Figure 1.3). This set of jobs is a subset of the jobs kept in the job pool (since the number of jobs that can be kept simultaneously in memory is usually much smaller than the number of jobs that can be in the job pool). The operating system picks and begins to execute one of the jobs in the memory. Eventually, the job may have to wait for some task, such as an I/O operation, to complete. In a nonmultiprogrammed system, the CPU would sit idle. In

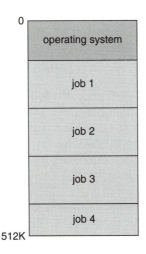

Figure 1.3   Memory layout for a multiprogramming system.

a multiprogramming system, the operating system simply switches to and executes another job. When *that* job needs to wait, the CPU is switched to another job, and so on. Eventually, the first job finishes waiting and gets the CPU back. As long as there is always at least one job to execute, the CPU is never idle.

This idea is common in other life situations. A lawyer does not work for only one client at a time. Rather, several clients may be being served at the same time. While one case is waiting to go to trial or to have papers typed, the lawyer can work on another case. If she has enough clients, the lawyer never will be idle for lack of work to do. (Idle lawyers tend to become politicians, so there is a certain social value in keeping lawyers busy.)

Multiprogramming is the first instance where the operating system must make decisions for the users. Multiprogrammed operating systems are therefore fairly sophisticated. All the jobs that enter the system are kept in the job pool. This pool consists of all processes residing on disk awaiting allocation of main memory. If several jobs are ready to be brought into memory, and if there is not enough room for all of them, then the system must choose among them. Making this decision is *job scheduling*, which is discussed in Chapter 6. When the operating system selects a job from the job pool, it loads that job into memory for execution. Having several programs in memory at the same time requires some form of memory management, which is covered in Chapters 9 and 10. In addition, if several jobs are ready to run at the same time, the system must choose among them. Making this decision is *CPU scheduling*, which is discussed in Chapter 6. Finally, multiple jobs running concurrently require that their ability to affect one another be limited in all phases of the operating system, including process scheduling, disk storage, and memory management. These considerations are discussed throughout the text.

1.3 ■ Time-Sharing Systems

Multiprogrammed batched systems provided an environment where the various system resources (for example, CPU, memory, peripheral devices) were utilized effectively, but it did not provide for user interaction with the computer system. **Time sharing**, or **multitasking,** is a logical extension of multiprogramming. The CPU executes multiple jobs by switching among them, but the switches occur so frequently that the users can interact with each program while it is running.

An **interactive,** or **hands-on, computer system** provides direct communication between the user and the system. The user gives instructions to the operating system or to a program directly, using either a keyboard or a mouse, and waits for immediate results. Accordingly, the **response time** should be short—typically within 1 second or so.

A time-shared operating system allows the many users to share the computer simultaneously. Since each action or command in a time-shared system tends to be short, only a little CPU time is needed for each user. As the system switches rapidly from one user to the next, each user is given the impression that the entire computer system is dedicated to her use, whereas actually one computer is being shared among many users.

A time-shared operating system uses CPU scheduling and multiprogramming to provide each user with a small portion of a time-shared computer. Each user has at least one separate program in memory. A program that is loaded into memory and is executing is commonly referred to as a **process**. When a process executes, it typically executes for only a short time before it either finishes or needs to perform I/O. I/O may be interactive; that is, output is to a display for the user and input is from a user keyboard, mouse, or other device. Since interactive I/O typically runs at people speeds, it may take a long time to complete. Input, for example, may be bounded by the user's typing speed; seven characters per second is fast for people, but is incredibly slow for computers. Rather than let the CPU sit idle when this interactive input takes place, the operating system will rapidly switch the CPU to the program of some other user.

Time-sharing operating systems are even more complex than are multiprogrammed operating systems. In both, several jobs must be kept simultaneously in memory, so the system must have memory management and protection (Chapter 9). So that a reasonable response time can be obtained, jobs may have to be swapped in and out of main memory to the disk that now serves as a backing store for main memory. A common method for achieving this goal is *virtual memory*, which is a technique that allows the execution of a job that may not be completely in memory (Chapter 10). The main obvious advantage of this scheme is that programs can be larger than physical memory. Further, it abstracts main memory into a large, uniform array of storage, separating logical memory as viewed by the user from physical memory. This arrangement frees programmers from concern over memory-storage limitations. Time-sharing systems must also provide a file system (Chapter 11). The file system resides on a collection of disks; hence, disk management must be provided (Chapter 13). Also, time-sharing systems provide a mechanism for concurrent execution, which requires sophisticated CPU-scheduling schemes (Chapter 6). To ensure orderly execution, the system must provide mechanisms for job synchronization and communication, and it may ensure that jobs do not get stuck in a deadlock, forever waiting for one another (Chapter 7).

The idea of time sharing was demonstrated as early as 1960, but since time-shared systems are difficult and expensive to build, they did not become common until the early 1970s. Although some batch processing is still done, most systems today are time sharing. Accordingly, multiprogramming and time sharing are the central themes of modern operating systems, and they are the central themes of this book.

1.4 ■ Personal-Computer Systems

Personal computers (PCs) appeared in the 1970s. During their first decade, the CPUs in PCs lacked the features needed to protect an operating system from user programs. PC operating systems therefore were neither multiuser nor multitasking. However, the goals of these operating systems have changed with time; instead of maximizing CPU and peripheral utilization, the systems opt for maximizing user convenience and responsiveness. These systems include PCs running Microsoft Windows, and the Apple Macintosh. The MS-DOS operating system from Microsoft has been superseded by multiple flavors of Microsoft Windows, and IBM has upgraded MS-DOS to the OS/2 multitasking system. The Apple Macintosh operating system has been ported to more advanced hardware, and now includes new features, such as virtual memory and multitasking. Linux, a UNIX-like operating system available for PCs, has also become popular recently.

Operating systems for these computers have benefited in several ways from the development of operating systems for mainframes. Microcomputers were immediately able to adopt some of the technology developed for larger operating systems. On the other hand, the hardware costs for microcomputers are sufficiently low that individuals have sole use of the computer, and CPU utilization is no longer a prime concern. Thus, some of the design decisions that are made in operating systems for mainframes may not be appropriate for smaller systems. Other design decisions still apply. For example, file protection was at first not necessary on a personal machine. However, these computers are now often tied into other computers over local-area networks or other Internet connections. When other computers and other users can access the files on a PC, file protection again becomes a necessary feature of an operating system. The lack of such protection has made it easy for malicious programs to destroy data on systems such as MS-DOS and the Macintosh operating system. These programs may be self-replicating, and may spread rapidly via *worm* or *virus* mechanisms to disrupt entire companies or even worldwide networks.

Overall, an examination of operating systems for mainframes and micro-computers shows that features that were at one time available on only mainframes have been adopted by microcomputers. The same concepts are appropriate for the various different classes of computers: mainframes, minicomputers, and microcomputers (Figure 1.4).

A good example of this movement occurred with the MULTICS operating system. MULTICS was developed from 1965 to 1970 at the Massachusetts Institute of Technology (MIT) as a computing *utility*. It ran on a large and complex mainframe computer (the GE 645). Many of the ideas that were developed for MULTICS were subsequently used at Bell Laboratories (one of the original partners in the development of MULTICS) in the design of UNIX. The UNIX operating system was designed circa 1970 for a PDP-11 minicomputer. Around 1980, the features of UNIX became the basis for UNIX-like operating

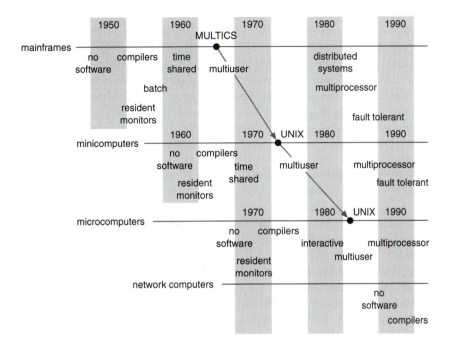

Figure 1.4 Migration of operating-system concepts and features.

systems on microcomputer systems, and they are being included in more recent operating systems such as Microsoft Windows NT, IBM OS/2, and the Macintosh Operating System. Thus, the features developed for a large mainframe system have moved to microcomputers, over time.

At the same time that features of large operating systems were being scaled down to fit PCs, more powerful, faster, and more sophisticated hardware systems were being developed. The **personal workstation** is a large PC—for example, the Sun SPARCstation, the HP/Apollo, the IBM RS/6000 computer, or the Intel Pentium class system running Windows NT or a UNIX derivative. Many universities and businesses have large numbers of workstations tied together with local-area networks. As PCs gain more sophisticated hardware and software, the line dividing the two categories is blurring.

1.5 ■ Parallel Systems

Most systems to date are single-processor systems; that is, they have only one main CPU. However, there is a trend toward **multiprocessor systems**. Such systems have more than one processor in close communication, sharing the computer bus, the clock, and sometimes memory and peripheral devices. These systems are referred to as **tightly coupled** systems.

There are several reasons for building such systems. One advantage is increased **throughput**. By increasing the number of processors, we hope to get more work done in less time. The speed-up ratio with n processors is not n, however, but rather is less than n. When multiple processors cooperate on a task, a certain amount of overhead is incurred in keeping all the parts working correctly. This overhead, plus contention for shared resources, lowers the expected gain from additional processors. Similarly, a group of n programmers working closely together does not result in n times the amount of work being accomplished.

Multiprocessor systems can also save money compared to multiple single-processor systems because the processors can share peripherals, mass storage, and power supplies. If several programs are to operate on the same set of data, it is cheaper to store those data on one disk and to have all the processors share them, rather than to have many computers with local disks and many copies of the data.

Another reason for multiprocessor systems is that they increase reliability. If functions can be distributed properly among several processors, then the failure of one processor will not halt the system, but rather will only slow it down. If we have ten processors and one fails, then each of the remaining nine processors must pick up a share of the work of the failed processor. Thus, the entire system runs only 10 percent slower, rather than failing altogether. This ability to continue providing service proportional to the level of surviving hardware is called **graceful degradation**. Systems that are designed for graceful degradation are also called **fault tolerant**.

Continued operation in the presence of failures requires a mechanism to allow the failure to be detected, diagnosed, and corrected (if possible). The Tandem system uses both hardware and software duplication to ensure continued operation despite faults. The system consists of two identical processors, each with its own local memory. The processors are connected by a bus. One processor is the primary, and the other is the backup. Two copies are kept of each process: one on the primary processor and the other on the backup. At fixed checkpoints in the execution of the system, the state information of each job (including a copy of the memory image) is copied from the primary machine to the backup. If a failure is detected, the backup copy is activated, and is restarted from the most recent checkpoint. This solution is obviously an expensive one, since there is considerable hardware duplication.

The most common multiple-processor systems now use **symmetric multiprocessing**, in which each processor runs an identical copy of the operating system, and these copies communicate with one another as needed. Some systems use **asymmetric multiprocessing,** in which each processor is assigned a specific task. A master processor controls the system; the other processors either look to the master for instruction or have predefined tasks. This scheme defines a master–slave relationship. The master processor schedules and allocates work to the slave processors.

Symmetric multiprocessing (SMP) means that all processors are peers; there is no master–slave relationship between processors. Each processor concurrently runs a copy of the operating system. Figure 1.5 illustrates a typical SMP architecture. An example of the SMP system is Encore's version of UNIX for the Multimax computer. This computer can be configured such that it employs dozens of processors, all running copies of UNIX. The benefit of this model is that many processes can run simultaneously—(N processes can run if there are N CPUs)—without causing a significant deterioration of performance. However, we must carefully control I/O to ensure that the data reach the appropriate processor. Also, since the CPUs are separate, one may be sitting idle while another is overloaded, resulting in inefficiencies. These inefficiencies can be avoided if the processors share certain data structures. A multiprocessor system of this form will allow processes and resources—such as memory—to be shared dynamically among the various processors, and can lower the variance among the processors. Such a system must be written carefully, as we shall see in Chapter 7. Virtually all modern operating systems—including Windows NT, Solaris, Digital UNIX, OS/2, and Linux—now provide support for SMP.

The difference between symmetric and asymmetric multiprocessing may be the result of either hardware or software. Special hardware can differentiate the multiple processors, or the software can be written to allow only one master and multiple slaves. For instance, Sun's operating system SunOS Version 4 provides asymmetric multiprocessing, whereas Version 5 (Solaris 2) is symmetric on the same hardware.

As microprocessors become less expensive and more powerful, additional operating-system functions are off-loaded to slave processors, or *back-ends*. For example, it is fairly easy to add a microprocessor with its own memory to manage a disk system. The microprocessor could receive a sequence of requests from the main CPU and implement its own disk queue and scheduling algorithm. This arrangement relieves the main CPU of the overhead of disk scheduling. PCs contain a microprocessor in the keyboard to convert the key strokes into codes to be sent to the CPU. In fact, this use of microprocessors has become so common that it is no longer considered multiprocessing.

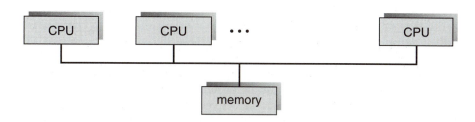

Figure 1.5   Symmetric multiprocessing architecture.

1.6 ■ Real-Time Systems

Another form of a special-purpose operating system is the **real-time system**. A real-time system is used when there are rigid time requirements on the operation of a processor or the flow of data; thus, it is often used as a control device in a dedicated application. Sensors bring data to the computer. The computer must analyze the data and possibly adjust controls to modify the sensor inputs. Systems that control scientific experiments, medical imaging systems, industrial control systems, and certain display systems are real-time systems. Also included are some automobile-engine fuel-injection systems, home-appliance controllers, and weapon systems. A real-time system has well-defined, fixed time constraints. Processing *must* be done within the defined constraints, or the system will fail. For instance, it would not do for a robot arm to be instructed to halt *after* it had smashed into the car that it was building. A real-time system is considered to function correctly only if it returns the correct result within any time constraints. Contrast this requirement to a time-sharing system, where it is desirable (but not mandatory) to respond quickly, or to a batch system, where there may be no time constraints at all.

There are two flavors of real-time systems. A **hard real-time system** guarantees that critical tasks be completed on time. This goal requires that all delays in the system be bounded, from the retrieval of stored data to the time that it takes the operating system to finish any request made of it. Such time constraints dictate the facilities that are available in hard real-time systems. Secondary storage of any sort is usually limited or missing, with data instead being stored in short-term memory, or in read-only memory (ROM). ROM is located on nonvolatile storage devices that retain their contents even in the case of electric outage; most other types of memory are volatile. Most advanced operating-system features are absent too, since they tend to separate the user from the hardware, and that separation results in uncertainty about the amount of time an operation will take. For instance, virtual memory (discussed in Chapter 10) is almost never found on real-time systems. Therefore, hard real-time systems conflict with the operation of time-sharing systems, and the two cannot be mixed. Since none of the existing general-purpose operating systems support hard real-time functionality, we do not concern ourselves with this type of system in this text.

A less restrictive type of real-time system is a **soft real-time system,** where a critical real-time task gets priority over other tasks, and retains that priority until it completes. As in hard real-time systems, kernel delays need to be bounded: A real-time task cannot be kept waiting indefinitely for the kernel to run it. Soft real time is an achievable goal that is amenable to mixing with other types of systems. Soft real-time systems, however, have more limited utility than do hard real-time systems. Given their lack of deadline support, they are risky to use for industrial control and robotics. There are several areas in which they are useful, however, including multimedia, virtual reality, and advanced scientific projects such as undersea exploration and planetary rovers. These systems need advanced operating-system features that cannot be supported by hard real-time systems. Because of the expanded uses for soft real-time functionality, it is finding its way into most current operating systems, including major versions of UNIX.

In Chapter 6, we consider the scheduling facility needed to implement soft real-time functionality in an operating system. In Chapter 10, we describe the design of memory management for real-time computing. Finally, in Chapter 22, we describe the real-time components of the Windows NT operating system.

1.7 ■ Distributed Systems

The growth of computer networks—especially the Internet and World Wide Web (WWW)—has had a profound influence on the recent development of operating systems. When PCs were first introduced in the 1970s, they were designed for "personal" use and were generally considered as standalone computers. With the beginning of widespread public use of the Internet in the 1980s for electronic mail, ftp, and gopher, many PCs became connected to computer networks. With the introduction of the Web in the mid–1990s, network connectivity came to be considered an essential component of a computer system.

Virtually all modern PCs and workstations are capable of running a web browser for accessing *hypertext* documents on the Web. Operating systems such as Windows, OS/2, MacOS, and UNIX now also include the system software (such as TCP/IP and PPP) that enables a computer to access the Internet via a local-area network or telephone connection. Several include the web browser itself, as well as electronic mail, remote login, and file-transfer clients and servers.

In contrast to the tightly coupled systems discussed in Section 1.5, the computer networks used in these type of applications consist of a collection of processors that do not share memory or a clock. Instead, each processor has its own local memory. The processors communicate with one another through various communication lines, such as high-speed buses or telephone lines. These systems are usually referred to as *loosely coupled* systems, or *distributed* systems.

Some operating systems have taken the concept of networks and distributed systems further than the notion of providing network connectivity. A **network operating system** is an operating system that provides features such as file sharing across the network, and that includes a communication scheme that allows different processes on different computers to exchange messages. A computer running a network operating system acts autonomously from all other computers on the network, although it is aware of the network and is able to communicate with other networked computers. A **distributed operating system** is a less autonomous environment: The different operating systems communicate closely enough to provide the illusion that there is only a single operating system controlling the network. We cover computer networks and distributed systems in Chapters 14 through 16.

1.8 ■ Summary

Operating systems have been developed over the past 40 years for two main purposes. First, the operating system attempts to schedule computational activities to ensure good performance of the computing system. Second, it provides a convenient environment for the development and execution of programs.

Initially, computer systems were used from the front console. Software such as assemblers, loaders, linkers, and compilers improved the convenience of programming the system, but also required substantial set-up time. To reduce the set-up time, facilities hired operators and batched similar jobs.

Batch systems allowed automatic job sequencing by a resident operating system and greatly improved the overall utilization of the computer. The computer no longer had to wait for human operation. CPU utilization was still low, however, because of the slow speed of the I/O devices relative to that of the CPU. Off-line operation of slow devices provides a means to use multiple reader-to-tape and tape-to-printer systems for one CPU.

To improve the overall performance of the computer system, developers introduced the concept of *multiprogramming*. With multiprogramming, several jobs are kept in memory at one time; the CPU is switched back and forth among them to increase CPU utilization and to decrease the total time needed to execute the jobs.

Multiprogramming, which was developed to improve performance, also allows time sharing. Time-shared operating systems allow many users (from one to several hundred) to use a computer system interactively at the same time.

PCs are microcomputers that are considerably smaller and less expensive than are mainframe systems. Operating systems for these computers have benefited from the development of operating systems for mainframes in several ways. However, since individuals have sole use of the computer, CPU utilization is no longer a prime concern. Hence, some of the design decisions that are made in operating systems for mainframes may not be appropriate for smaller systems.

Parallel systems have more than one CPU in close communication; the CPUs share the computer bus, and sometimes share memory and peripheral devices. Such systems can provide increased throughput and enhanced reliability.

A hard real-time system is often used as a control device in a dedicated application. A hard real-time operating system has well-defined, fixed time constraints. Processing *must* be done within the defined constraints, or the system will fail. Soft real-time systems have less stringent timing constraints, and do not support deadline scheduling.

Recently, the influence of the Internet and the World Wide Web has encouraged the development of modern operating systems that include web browsers and networking and communication software as integral features. Paralleling the growth of the Web is the increasing use of Java, a combined programming language and technology that provides many features that make it a suitable example for us to present as an applied study of many operating-system concepts.

We have shown the logical progression of operating-system development, driven by inclusion of features in the CPU hardware that are needed for advanced functionality. This trend can be seen today in the evolution of PCs, with inexpensive hardware being improved sufficiently to allow, in turn, improved characteristics.

■ Exercises

1.1 What are the three main purposes of an operating system?

1.2 List the four steps that are necessary to run a program on a completely dedicated machine.

1.3 What is the main advantage of multiprogramming?

1.4 What are the main differences between operating systems for mainframe computers and personal computers?

1.5 In a multiprogramming and time-sharing environment, several users share the system simultaneously. This situation can result in various security problems.

    a. What are two such problems?

    b. Can we ensure the same degree of security in a time-shared machine as we have in a dedicated machine? Explain your answer.

1.6 Define the essential properties of the following types of operating systems:

    a. Batch

    b. Interactive

    c. Time sharing

    d. Real time

    e. Network

    f. Distributed

1.7 We have stressed the need for an operating system to make efficient use of the computing hardware. When is it appropriate for the operating system to forsake this principle and to "waste" resources? Why is such a system not really wasteful?

1.8 Under what circumstances would a user be better off using a time-sharing system, rather than a PC or single-user workstation?

1.9 Describe the differences between symmetric and asymmetric multiprocessing. What are three advantages and one disadvantage of multiprocessor systems?

1.10 What is the main difficulty that a programmer must overcome in writing an operating system for a real-time environment?

1.11 Consider the various definitions of *operating system*. Consider whether the operating system should include applications such as web browsers and mail programs. Argue both that it should and that it should not, and support your answer.

Bibliographical Notes

Time-sharing systems were proposed first by Strachey [1959]. The earliest time-sharing systems were the Compatible Time-Sharing System (CTSS) developed at MIT [Corbato et al. 1962] and the SDC Q-32 system, built by the System Development Corporation [Schwartz et al. 1964, Schwartz and Weissman 1967]. Other early, but more sophisticated, systems include the MULTIplexed Information and Computing Services (MULTICS) system developed at MIT [Corbato and Vyssotsky 1965], the XDS-940 system developed at the University of California at Berkeley [Lichtenberger and Pirtle 1965], and the IBM TSS/360 system [Lett and Konigsford 1968].

A survey of distributed operating systems was presented by Tanenbaum and van Renesse [1985]. Real-time operating systems are discussed by Stankovic and Ramamrithan [1989]. A special issue of Operating System Review on real-time operating systems is edited by Zhao [1989].

MS-DOS and PCs are described by Norton [1986], and by Norton and Wilton [1988]. An overview of the Apple Macintosh hardware and software is presented in [Apple 1987]. The OS/2 operating system is covered in [Microsoft 1989]. More OS/2 information can be found in Letwin [1988] and in Deitel and Kogan [1992]. Solomon [1998] discusses the structure of Microsoft Windows NT operating system.

There are numerous up-to-date general textbooks on operating systems [Finkel 1988, Krakowiak 1988, Pinkert and Wear 1989, Deitel 1990, Stallings 1992, Tanenbaum 1992].

Chapter 2

COMPUTER-SYSTEM STRUCTURES

We need to have a general knowledge of the structure of a computer system before we can explore the details of system operation. In this chapter, we look at several disparate parts of this structure to round out our background knowledge. This chapter is mostly concerned with computer-system architecture, so you can skim or skip it if you already understand the concepts. Because an operating system is intimately tied to the I/O mechanisms of a computer, I/O is discussed first. The subsequent sections examine the data-storage structure.

The operating system must also ensure the correct operation of the computer system. So that user programs will not interfere with the proper operation of the system, the hardware must provide appropriate mechanisms to ensure correct behavior. Later in this chapter, we describe the basic computer architecture that makes it possible to write a functional operating system.

2.1 ■ Computer-System Operation

A modern, general-purpose computer system consists of a CPU and a number of device controllers that are connected through a common bus that provides access to shared memory (Figure 2.1). Each device controller is in charge of a specific type of device (for example, disk drives, audio devices, and video displays). The CPU and the device controllers can execute concurrently, competing for memory cycles. To ensure orderly access to the shared memory, a memory controller is provided whose function is to synchronize access to the memory.

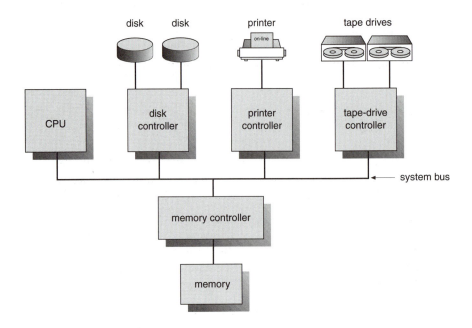

Figure 2.1   A modern computer system.

For a computer to start running—for instance, when it is powered up or rebooted—it needs to have an initial program to run. This initial program, or **bootstrap program,** tends to be simple. It initializes all aspects of the system, from CPU registers to device controllers to memory contents. The bootstrap program must know how to load the operating system and to start executing that system. To accomplish this goal, the bootstrap program must locate and load into memory the operating-system kernel. The operating system then starts executing the first process, such as "init," and waits for some event to occur. The occurrence of an event is usually signaled by an **interrupt** from either the hardware or the software. Hardware may trigger an interrupt at any time by sending a signal to the CPU, usually by way of the system bus. Software may trigger an interrupt by executing a special operation called a **system call** (also called a *monitor call*).

There are many different types of events that may trigger an interrupt—for example, the completion of an I/O operation, division by zero, invalid memory access, and a request for some operating-system service. For each such interrupt, a service routine is provided that is responsible for dealing with the interrupt.

When the CPU is interrupted, it stops what it is doing and immediately transfers execution to a fixed location. The fixed location usually contains the starting address where the service routine for the interrupt is located.

The interrupt service routine executes; on completion, the CPU resumes the interrupted computation. A time line of this operation is shown in Figure 2.2.

Interrupts are an important part of a computer architecture. Each computer design has its own interrupt mechanism, but several functions are common. The interrupt must transfer control to the appropriate interrupt service routine. The straightforward method for handling this transfer would be to invoke a generic routine to examine the interrupt information; the routine, in turn, would call the interrupt-specific handler. However, interrupts must be handled quickly, and, given that there is a predefined number of possible interrupts, a table of pointers to interrupt routines can be used instead. The interrupt routine is then called indirectly through the table, with no intermediate routine needed. Generally, the table of pointers is stored in low memory (the first 100 or so locations). These locations hold the addresses of the interrupt service routines for the various devices. This array, or **interrupt vector**, of addresses is then indexed by a unique device number, given with the interrupt request, to provide the address of the interrupt service routine for the interrupting device. Operating systems as different as MS-DOS and UNIX dispatch interrupts in this manner.

The interrupt architecture must also save the address of the interrupted instruction. Many old designs simply stored the interrupt address in a fixed location or in a location indexed by the device number. More recent architectures store the return address on the system stack. If the interrupt routine needs to modify the processor state—for instance, by modifying register values—it must explicitly save the current state and then restore that state before returning. After the interrupt is serviced, the saved return address is loaded into the program counter, and the interrupted computation resumes as though the interrupt had not occurred.

Modern operating systems are **interrupt driven**. If there are no processes to execute, no I/O devices to service, and no users to whom to respond, an

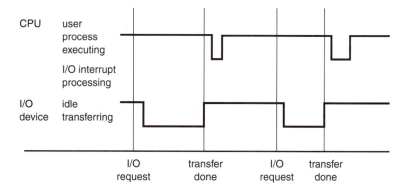

Figure 2.2 Interrupt time line for a single process doing output.

operating system will sit quietly, waiting for something to happen. Events are almost always signaled by the occurrence of an interrupt, or a trap. A **trap** (or an exception) is a software-generated interrupt caused either by an error (for example, division by zero or invalid memory access), or by a specific request from a user program that an operating-system service be performed. The interrupt-driven nature of an operating system defines that system's general structure. For each type of interrupt, separate segments of code in the operating system determine what action should be taken.

2.2 ■ I/O Structure

As we discussed in Section 2.1, a general-purpose computer system consists of a CPU and multiple device controllers that are connected through a common bus. Each device controller is in charge of a specific type of device. Depending on the controller, there may be more than one attached device. For instance, the **small computer-systems interface (SCSI)** controller, found on many small-to medium-sized computers, can have seven or more devices attached to it. A device controller maintains some local buffer storage and a set of special-purpose registers. The device controller is responsible for moving the data between the peripheral devices that it controls and its local buffer storage. The size of the local buffer within a device controller varies from one controller to another, depending on the particular device being controlled. For example, the size of the buffer of a disk controller is the same as or a multiple of the size of the smallest addressable portion of a disk, called a **sector,** which is usually 512 bytes.

2.2.1 I/O Interrupts

To start an I/O operation, the CPU loads the appropriate registers within the device controller. The device controller, in turn, examines the contents of these registers to determine what action to take. For example, if it finds a read request, the controller will start the transfer of data from the device to its local buffer. Once the transfer of data is complete, the device controller informs the CPU that it has finished its operation. It accomplishes this communication by triggering an interrupt.

This situation will occur, in general, as the result of a user process requesting I/O. Once the I/O is started, two courses of action are possible. In the simplest case, the I/O is started; then, at I/O completion, control is returned to the user process. This case is known as **synchronous** I/O. The other possibility, called **asynchronous** I/O, returns control to the user program without waiting for the I/O to complete. The I/O then can continue while other system operations occur (Figure 2.3).

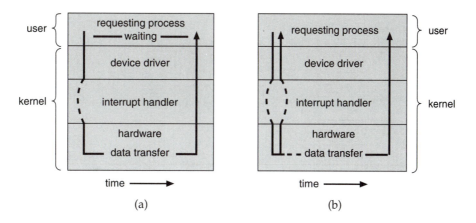

Figure 2.3   Two I/O methods: (a) synchronous, and (b) asynchronous.

Waiting for I/O completion may be accomplished in one of two ways. Some computers have a special `wait` instruction that idles the CPU until the next interrupt. Machines that do not have such an instruction may have a wait loop:

Loop: `jmp` *Loop*

This tight loop simply continues until an interrupt occurs, transferring control to another part of the operating system. Such a loop might also need to poll any I/O devices that do not support the interrupt structure; instead, these devices simply set a flag in one of their registers and expect the operating system to notice that flag.

If the CPU always waits for I/O completion, at most one I/O request is outstanding at a time. Thus, whenever an I/O interrupt occurs, the operating system knows exactly which device is interrupting. On the other hand, this approach excludes concurrent I/O operations to several devices, and also excludes the possibility of overlapping useful computation with I/O.

A better alternative is to start the I/O and then to continue processing other operating-system or user program code. A system call (a request to the operating system) is then needed to allow the user program to wait for I/O completion, if desired. If no user programs are ready to run, and the operating system has no other work to do, we still require the `wait` instruction or idle loop, as before. We also need to be able to keep track of many I/O requests at the same time. For this purpose, the operating system uses a table containing an entry for each I/O device: the **device-status table** (Figure 2.4). Each table entry indicates the device's type, address, and state (not functioning, idle, or busy). If the device is busy with a request, the type of request and other parameters will be stored in the table entry for that device. Since it is possible for other processes to issue requests to the same device, the operating system will also maintain a wait queue—a list of waiting requests—for each I/O device.

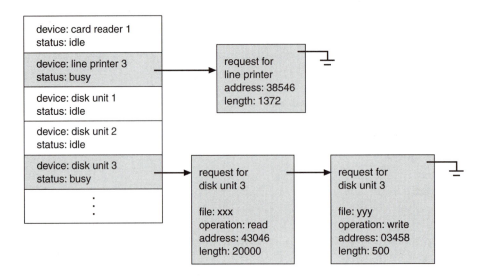

Figure 2.4   Device-status table.

An I/O device interrupts when it needs service. When an interrupt occurs, the operating system first determines which I/O device caused the interrupt. It then indexes into the I/O device table to determine the status of that device, and modifies the table entry to reflect the occurrence of the interrupt. For most devices, an interrupt signals completion of an I/O request. If there are additional requests waiting in the queue for this device, the operating system starts processing the next request.

Finally, control is returned from the I/O interrupt. If a process was waiting for this request to complete (as recorded in the device-status table), we can now return control to it. Otherwise, we return to whatever we were doing before the I/O interrupt: to the execution of the user program (the program started an I/O operation and that operation has now finished, but the program has not yet waited for the operation to complete) or to the wait loop (the program started two or more I/O operations and is waiting for a particular one to finish, but this interrupt was from one of the other operations). In a time-sharing system, the operating system could switch to another ready-to-run process.

The schemes used by specific input devices may vary from this one. Many interactive systems allow users to type ahead—to enter data before the data are requested—on the terminals. In this case, interrupts may occur, signaling the arrival of characters from the terminal, while the device-status block indicates that no program has requested input from this device. If typeahead is to be allowed, then a buffer must be provided to store the typeahead characters until some program wants them. In general, we may need a buffer for each input terminal.

The main advantage of asynchronous I/O is increased system efficiency. While I/O is taking place, the system CPU can be used for processing or starting I/Os to other devices. Because I/O can be slow compared to processor speed, the system makes efficient use of its facilities. In Section 2.2.2, we describe another mechanism for improving system performance.

2.2.2 DMA Structure

Consider a simple terminal-input driver. When a line is to be read from the terminal, the first character typed is sent to the computer. When that character is received, the asynchronous-communication (or serial-port) device to which the terminal line is connected interrupts the CPU. When the interrupt request from the terminal arrives, the CPU is about to execute some instruction. (If the CPU is in the middle of executing an instruction, the interrupt is normally held pending the completion of instruction execution.) The address of this interrupted instruction is saved, and control is transferred to the interrupt service routine for the appropriate device.

The interrupt service routine saves the contents of any CPU registers that it will need to use. It checks for any error conditions that might have resulted from the most recent input operation. It then takes the character from the device, and stores that character in a buffer. The interrupt routine must also adjust pointer and counter variables, to be sure that the next input character will be stored at the next location in the buffer. The interrupt routine next sets a flag in memory indicating to the other parts of the operating system that new input has been received. The other parts are responsible for processing the data in the buffer, and for transferring the characters to the program that is requesting input (see Section 2.5). Then, the interrupt service routine restores the contents of any saved registers, and transfers control back to the interrupted instruction.

If characters are being typed to a 9600-baud terminal, the terminal can accept and transfer one character approximately every 1 millisecond, or 1000 microseconds. A well-written interrupt service routine to input characters into a buffer may require 2 microseconds per character, leaving 998 microseconds out of every 1000 for CPU computation (and for servicing of other interrupts). Given this disparity, asynchronous I/O is usually assigned a low interrupt priority, allowing other, more important interrupts to be processed first, or even to preempt the current interrupt for another. A high-speed device, however—such as a tape, disk, or communications network—may be able to transmit information at close to memory speeds; the CPU would need 2 microseconds to respond to each interrupt, with interrupts arriving every 4 microseconds (for example). That would not leave much time for process execution.

To solve this problem, **direct memory access (DMA)** is used for high-speed I/O devices. After setting up buffers, pointers, and counters for the I/O device, the device controller transfers an entire block of data directly to or from its own buffer storage to memory, with no intervention by the CPU. Only one interrupt is generated per block, rather than the one interrupt per byte (or word) generated for low-speed devices.

The basic operation of the CPU is the same. A user program, or the operating system itself, may request data transfer. The operating system finds a buffer (an empty buffer for input, or a full buffer for output) from a pool of buffers for the transfer. (A buffer is typically 128 to 4,096 bytes, depending on the device type.) Next, a portion of the operating system called a **device driver** sets the DMA controller registers to use appropriate source and destination addresses, and transfer length. The DMA controller is then instructed to start the I/O operation. While the DMA controller is performing the data transfer, the CPU is free to perform other tasks. Since the memory generally can transfer only one word at a time, the DMA controller "steals" memory cycles from the CPU. This cycle stealing can slow down the CPU execution while a DMA transfer is in progress. The DMA controller interrupts the CPU when the transfer has been completed.

2.3 ■ Storage Structure

Computer programs must be in main memory (also called **Random-Access Memory,** or **RAM**) to be executed. Main memory is the only large storage area (millions to billions of bytes) that the processor can access directly. It is implemented in a semiconductor technology called **Dynamic Random-Access Memory (DRAM)**, which forms an array of memory words. Each word has its own address. Interaction is achieved through a sequence of load or store instructions to specific memory addresses. The load instruction moves a word from main memory to an internal register within the CPU, whereas the store instruction moves the content of a register to main memory. Aside from explicit loads and stores, the CPU automatically loads instructions from main memory for execution.

A typical instruction-execution cycle, as executed on a system with a **von Neumann** architecture, will first fetch an instruction from memory and will store that instruction in the **instruction register**. The instruction is then decoded and may cause operands to be fetched from memory and stored in some internal register. After the instruction on the operands has been executed, the result may be stored back in memory. Notice that the memory unit sees only a stream of memory addresses; it does not know how they are generated (the instruction counter, indexing, indirection, literal addresses, and so on) or what they are for (instructions or data). Accordingly, we can ignore *how* a memory address is generated by a program. We are interested in only the sequence of memory addresses generated by the running program.

Ideally, we would want the programs and data to reside in main memory permanently. This arrangement is not possible for the following two reasons:

1. Main memory is usually too small to store all needed programs and data permanently.

2. Main memory is a *volatile* storage device that loses its contents when power is turned off or otherwise lost.

Thus, most computer systems provide **secondary storage** as an extension of main memory. The main requirement for secondary storage is that it be able to hold large quantities of data permanently.

The most common secondary-storage device is a **magnetic disk,** which provides storage of both programs and data. Most programs (web browsers, compilers, word processors, spreadsheets, and so on) are stored on a disk until they are loaded into memory. Many programs then use the disk as both a source and a destination of the information for their processing. Hence, the proper management of disk storage is of central importance to a computer system, as we discuss in Chapter 13.

In a larger sense, however, the storage structure that we have described—consisting of registers, main memory, and magnetic disks—is only one of many possible storage systems. There are also cache memory, CD-ROM, magnetic tapes, and so on. Each storage system provides the basic functions of storing a datum, and of holding that datum until it is retrieved at a later time. The main differences among the various storage systems lie in speed, cost, size, and volatility. In Sections 2.3.1 through 2.3.3, we describe main memory, magnetic disks, and magnetic tapes, because they illustrate the general properties of all commercially important storage devices. In Chapter 13, we discuss the specific properties of many particular devices, such as floppy disks, hard disks, CD-ROMs, and DVDs.

2.3.1 Main Memory

Main memory and the registers built into the processor itself are the only storage that the CPU can access directly. (Consider that there are machine instructions that take memory addresses as arguments, but none that take disk addresses.) Therefore, any instructions in execution, and any data being used by the instructions, must be in one of these direct-access storage devices. If the data are not in memory, they must be moved there before the CPU can operate on them.

In the case of I/O, as mentioned in Section 2.1, each I/O controller includes registers to hold commands and the data being transferred. Usually, special I/O instructions allow data transfers between these registers and system memory. To allow more convenient access to I/O devices, many computer architectures provide **memory-mapped I/O.** In this case, ranges of memory addresses are set aside, and are mapped to the device registers. Reads and writes to these memory addresses cause the data to be transferred to and from the device registers. This method is appropriate for devices that have fast response times, such as video controllers. In the IBM PC, each location on the screen is mapped to a memory location. Displaying text on the screen is almost as easy as writing the text into the appropriate memory-mapped locations.

Memory-mapped I/O is also convenient for other devices, such as the serial and parallel ports used to connect modems and printers to a computer. The CPU transfers data through these kinds of devices by reading and writing a few device registers, called an I/O **port**. To send out a long string of bytes through a memory-mapped serial port, the CPU writes one data byte to the data register, then sets a bit in the control register to signal that the byte is available. The device takes the data byte, and then clears the bit in the control register to signal that it is ready for the next byte. Then, the CPU can transfer the next byte. If the CPU uses polling to watch the control bit, constantly looping to see whether the device is ready, this method of operation is called **programmed I/O (PIO)**. If the CPU does not poll the control bit, but instead receives an interrupt when the device is ready for the next byte, the data transfer is said to be **interrupt driven**.

Registers that are built into the CPU are generally accessible within one cycle of the CPU clock. Most CPUs can decode instructions and perform simple operations on register contents at the rate of one or more operations per clock tick. The same cannot be said for main memory, which is accessed via a transaction on the memory bus. Memory access may take many cycles to complete, in which case the processor normally needs to **stall,** since it does not have the data required to complete the instruction that it is executing. This situation is intolerable because of the frequency of memory accesses. The remedy is to add fast memory between the CPU and main memory. A memory buffer used to accommodate a speed differential, called a **cache,** is described in Section 2.4.1.

2.3.2 Magnetic Disks

Magnetic disks provide the bulk of secondary storage for modern computer systems. Conceptually, disks are relatively simple (Figure 2.5). Each disk **platter** has a flat circular shape, like a CD. Common platter diameters range from 1.8 to 5.25 inches. The two surfaces of a platter are covered with a magnetic material, similar to magnetic tape. We store information by recording it magnetically on the platters.

A read–write head flies just above each surface of every platter. The heads are attached to a **disk arm,** which moves all the heads as a unit. The surface of a platter is logically divided into circular **tracks,** which are subdivided into **sectors**. The set of tracks that are at one arm position forms a **cylinder**. There may be thousands of concentric cylinders in a disk drive, and each track may contain hundreds of sectors. The storage capacity of common disk drives is measured in gigabytes. (A kilobyte is 1,024 bytes, a megabyte is $1,024^2$ bytes, and a gigabyte is $1,024^3$ bytes, but disk manufacturers often round off these

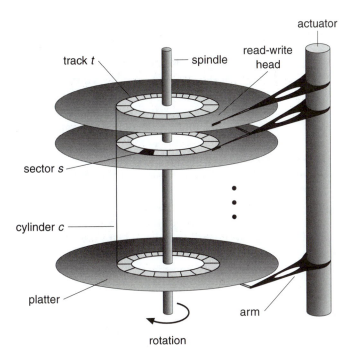

Figure 2.5   Moving-head disk mechanism.

numbers and say that a megabyte is 1 million bytes, and a gigabyte is 1 billion bytes.)

When the disk is in use, a drive motor spins it at high speed. Most drives rotate 60 to 150 times per second. Disk speed has two parts. The **transfer rate** is the rate at which data flow between the drive and the computer. The **positioning time,** sometimes called the **random-access time,** consists of the time to move the disk arm to the desired cylinder, called the **seek time,** and the time for the desired sector to rotate to the disk head, called the **rotational latency**. Typical disks can transfer several megabytes of data per second, and they have seek times and rotational latencies of several milliseconds.

Because the disk head flies on an extremely thin (measured in microns) cushion of air, there is a danger of the head contacting the disk surface. Although the disk platters are coated with a thin protective layer, sometimes the head will damage the magnetic surface. This accident is called a **head crash**. A head crash normally cannot be repaired; the entire disk must be replaced.

A disk can be **removable,** allowing different disks to be mounted as needed. Removable magnetic disks generally consist of one platter, held in a plastic case to prevent damage while not in the disk drive. **Floppy disks** are inexpensive removable magnetic disks that have a soft plastic case containing a flexible platter. The head of a floppy-disk drive generally sits directly on the disk surface, so the drive is designed to rotate more slowly than a hard-disk drive, which reduces the wear on the disk surface. The storage capacity of a floppy disk is typically only 1 megabyte or so. Removable disks are available that work much like normal hard disks, and that have capacities measured in gigabytes.

A disk drive is attached to a computer by a set of wires called an **I/O bus**. Several kinds of buses are available, including EIDE and SCSI buses. The data transfers on a bus are carried out by special electronic processors called **controllers**. The **host controller** is the controller at the computer end of the bus. A **disk controller** is built into each disk drive. To perform a disk I/O operation, the computer places a command into the host controller, typically using memory-mapped I/O ports, as described in Section 2.3.1. The host controller then sends the command via messages to the disk controller, and the disk controller operates the disk-drive hardware to carry out the command. Disk controllers usually have a built-in cache. Data transfer at the disk drive happens between the cache and the disk surface, and data transfer to the host, at fast electronic speeds, occurs between the cache and the host controller.

2.3.3 Magnetic Tapes

Magnetic tape was used as an early secondary-storage medium. Although it is relatively permanent, and can hold large quantities of data, its access time is slow in comparison to that of main memory. Random access to magnetic tape is about a thousand times slower than random access to magnetic disk, so tapes are not useful for secondary storage. Tapes are used mainly for backup, for storage of infrequently used information, and as a medium for transferring information from one system to another.

A tape is kept in a spool, and is wound or rewound past a read–write head. Moving to the correct spot on a tape can take minutes, but once positioned, tape drives can write data at speeds comparable to disk drives. Tape capacities vary greatly, depending on the particular kind of tape drive. Some tapes hold 20 times more data than does a large disk drive. Tapes and their drivers are usually categorized by width, including 4, 8, and 19 millimeter, 1/4 and 1/2 inch.

2.4 ■ Storage Hierarchy

The wide variety of storage systems in a computer system can be organized in a hierarchy (Figure 2.6) according to speed and cost. The higher levels are expensive, but they are fast. As we move down the hierarchy, the cost per bit generally decreases, whereas the access time generally increases. This tradeoff is reasonable; if a given storage system were both faster and less expensive than another—other properties being the same—then there would be no reason to use the slower, more expensive memory. In fact, many early storage devices,

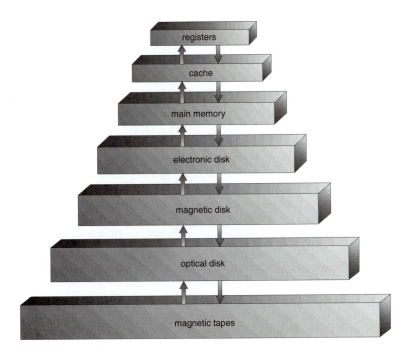

Figure 2.6 Storage-device hierarchy.

including paper tape and core memories, are relegated to museums now that magnetic tape and semiconductor memory have become faster and cheaper.

In addition to having differing speed and cost, the various storage systems are either volatile or nonvolatile. **Volatile storage** loses its contents when the power to the device is removed. In the absence of expensive battery and generator backup systems, data must be written to **nonvolatile storage** for safekeeping. In the hierarchy shown in Figure 2.6, the storage systems above the various disks are volatile, whereas those below the electronic disk are nonvolatile. An electronic disk can be designed to be either volatile or nonvolatile. During normal operation, the electronic disk stores data in a large DRAM array, which is volatile. But many electronic-disk devices contain a hidden magnetic hard disk and a battery for backup power. If external power is interrupted, the electronic-disk controller copies the data from RAM to the magnetic disk. When external power is restored, the controller copies the data back into the RAM.

The design of a complete memory system must balance all these factors: It uses only as much expensive memory as necessary, while providing as much inexpensive, nonvolatile memory as possible. Caches can be installed to ameliorate performance deficits where there is a large access-time or transfer-rate disparity between two components.

2.4.1 Caching

Caching is an important principle of computer systems. Information is normally kept in some storage system (such as main memory). As it is used, it is copied into a faster storage system—the **cache**—on a temporary basis. When we need a particular piece of information, we first check whether it is in the cache. If it is, we use the information directly from the cache; if it is not, we use the information from the main storage system, putting a copy in the cache under the assumption that there is a high probability that it will be needed again soon.

Extending this view, internal programmable registers, such as index registers, provide a high-speed cache for main memory. The programmer (or compiler) implements the register-allocation and register-replacement algorithms to decide which information to keep in registers and which to keep in main memory. There are also caches that are implemented totally in hardware. For instance, most systems have an instruction cache to hold the next instructions expected to be executed. Without this cache, the CPU would have to wait several cycles while an instruction was fetched from main memory. For similar reasons, most systems have one or more high-speed data caches in the memory hierarchy. We are not concerned with these hardware-only caches in this text, since they are outside of the control of the operating system.

Since caches have limited size, **cache management** is an important design problem. Careful selection of the cache size and of a replacement policy can result in 80 to 99 percent of all accesses being in the cache, causing extremely high performance. Various replacement algorithms for software-controlled caches are discussed in Chapter 10.

Main memory can be viewed as a fast cache for secondary memory, since data on secondary storage must be copied into main memory for use, and data must be in main memory before being moved to secondary storage for safekeeping. The file-system data may appear on several levels in the storage hierarchy. At the highest level, the operating system may maintain a cache of file-system data in main memory. Also, electronic RAM disks (also known as solid-state disks) may be used for high-speed storage that is accessed through the file-system interface. The bulk of secondary storage is on magnetic disks. The magnetic-disk storage, in turn, is often backed up onto tapes or removable disks to protect against data loss in case of a hard-disk failure. Some systems automatically archive old file data from secondary storage to tertiary storage, such as tape jukeboxes, to lower the storage cost (see Section 13.7.2).

The movement of information between levels of a storage hierarchy may be either explicit or implicit, depending on the hardware design and the controlling operating-system software. For instance, data transfer from cache to CPU and registers is usually a hardware function, with no operating-system intervention. On the other hand, transfer of data from disk to memory is usually controlled by the operating system.

2.4.2 Coherency and Consistency

In a hierarchical storage structure, the same data may appear in different levels of the storage system. For example, consider an integer A located in file B that is to be incremented by 1. Suppose that file B resides on magnetic disk. The increment operation proceeds by first issuing an I/O operation to copy the disk block on which A resides to main memory. This operation is followed by a possible copying of A to the cache, and by a copying of A to an internal register. Thus, the copy of A appears in several places. Once the increment takes place in the internal register, the value of A differs in the various storage systems. The value of A becomes the same only after the new value of A is written back to the magnetic disk.

In an environment where there is only one process executing at a time, this arrangement poses no difficulties, since an access to integer A will always be to the copy at the highest level of the hierarchy. However, in a multitasking environment, where the CPU is switched back and forth among various processes, extreme care must be taken to ensure that, if several processes wish to access A, then each of these processes will obtain the most recently updated value of A.

The situation becomes more complicated in a multiprocessor environment where, in addition to maintaining internal registers, the CPU also contains a local cache. In such an environment, a copy of A may exist simultaneously in several caches. Since the various CPUs can all execute concurrently, we must make sure that an update to the value of A in one cache is immediately reflected in all other caches where A resides. This situation is called **cache coherency,** and it is usually a hardware problem (handled below the operating-system level).

In a distributed environment, the situation becomes even more complex. In such an environment, several copies (replicas) of the same file can be kept on different computers that are distributed in space. Since the various replicas may be accessed and updated concurrently, we must ensure that, when a replica is updated in one place, all other replicas are brought up to date as soon as possible. There are various ways to achieve this guarantee, as we discuss in Chapter 17.

2.5 ■ Hardware Protection

Early computer systems were single-user programmer-operated systems. When the programmers operated the computer from the console, they had complete control over the system. As operating systems developed, however, this control was given to the operating system. Starting with the resident monitor, the operating system began to perform many of the functions, especially I/O, for which the programmer had been responsible previously.

In addition, to improve system utilization, the operating system began to *share* system resources among several programs simultaneously. With spooling, one program might have been executing while I/O occurred for other processes;

the disk simultaneously held data for many processes. Multiprogramming put several programs in memory at the same time.

This sharing both improved utilization and increased problems. When the system was run without sharing, an error in a program could cause problems for only the one program that was running. With sharing, many processes could be adversely affected by a bug in one program.

For example, consider the simple batch operating system (Section 1.2), which provides nothing more than automatic job sequencing. Suppose that a program gets stuck in a loop reading input cards. The program will read through all its data and, unless something stops it, will continue reading the cards of the next job, and the next, and so on. This loop could prevent the correct operation of many jobs.

Even more subtle errors can occur in a multiprogramming system, where one erroneous program might modify the program or data of another program, or even the resident monitor itself. MS-DOS and the Macintosh OS both allow this kind of error.

Without protection against these sorts of errors, either the computer must execute only one process at a time, or all output must be suspect. A properly designed operating system must ensure that an incorrect (or malicious) program cannot cause other programs to execute incorrectly.

Many programming errors are detected by the hardware. These errors are normally handled by the operating system. If a user program fails in some way —such as by making an attempt either to execute an illegal instruction, or to access memory that is not in the user's address space—then the hardware will trap to the operating system. The trap transfers control through the interrupt vector to the operating system, just like an interrupt. Whenever a program error occurs, the operating system must abnormally terminate the program. This situation is handled by the same code as is a user-requested abnormal termination. An appropriate error message is given, and the memory of the program may be dumped. The memory dump is usually written to a file so that the user or programmer can examine it, and perhaps can correct and restart the program.

2.5.1 Dual-Mode Operation

To ensure proper operation, we must protect the operating system and all other programs and their data from any malfunctioning program. Protection is needed for any shared resource. The approach taken by many operating systems provides hardware support that allows us to differentiate among various modes of execution.

At the very least, we need two separate **modes** of operation: **user mode** and **monitor mode** (also called **supervisor mode**, **system mode**, or **privileged mode**). A bit, called the **mode bit**, is added to the hardware of the computer to indicate the current mode: monitor (0) or user (1). With the mode bit, we are able to distinguish between a task that is executed on behalf of the operating system, and of one that is executed on behalf of the user. As we shall see, this architectural enhancement is useful for many other aspects of system operation.

At system boot time, the hardware starts in monitor mode. The operating system is then loaded, and starts user processes in user mode. Whenever a trap or interrupt occurs, the hardware switches from user mode to monitor mode (that is, changes the state of the mode bit to 0). Thus, whenever the operating system gains control of the computer, it is in monitor mode. The system always switches to user mode (by setting the mode bit to 1) before passing control to a user program.

The dual mode of operation provides us with the means for protecting the operating system from errant users, and errant users from one another. We accomplish this protection by designating some of the machine instructions that may cause harm as **privileged instructions**. The hardware allows privileged instructions to be executed in only monitor mode. If an attempt is made to execute a privileged instruction in user mode, the hardware does not execute the instruction, but rather treats the instruction as illegal and traps to the operating system.

The lack of a hardware-supported dual mode can cause serious shortcomings in an operating system. For instance, MS-DOS was written for the Intel 8088 architecture, which has no mode bit, and therefore no dual mode. A user program running awry can wipe out the operating system by writing over it with data, and multiple programs are able to write to a device at the same time, with possibly disastrous results. More recent and advanced versions of the Intel CPU, such as the Pentium, do provide dual-mode operation. As a result, more recent operating systems, such as Microsoft Windows NT and IBM OS/2, take advantage of this feature and provide greater protection for the operating system.

2.5.2 I/O Protection

A user program may disrupt the normal operation of the system by issuing illegal I/O instructions, by accessing memory locations within the operating system itself, or by refusing to relinquish the CPU. We can use various mechanisms to ensure that such disruptions cannot take place in the system.

To prevent a user from performing illegal I/O, we define all I/O instructions to be privileged instructions. Thus, users cannot issue I/O instructions directly; they must do it through the operating system. For I/O protection to be complete, we must be sure that a user program can never gain control of the computer in monitor mode. If it could, I/O protection could be compromised.

Consider the computer executing in user mode. It will switch to monitor mode whenever an interrupt or trap occurs, jumping to the address determined from the interrupt vector. Suppose that a user program, as part of its execution, stores a new address in the interrupt vector. This new address could overwrite the previous address with an address in the user program. Then, when a corresponding trap or interrupt occurred, the hardware would switch to monitor mode, and would transfer control through the (modified) interrupt vector to the user program! The user program could gain control of the computer in monitor mode.

2.5.3 Memory Protection

To ensure correct operation, we must protect the interrupt vector from modification by a user program. In addition, we must also protect the interrupt service routines in the operating system from modification. Otherwise, a user program might overwrite instructions in the interrupt service routine with jumps to the user program, thus gaining control from the interrupt service routine that was executing in monitor mode. Even if the user did not gain unauthorized control of the computer, modifying the interrupt service routines would probably disrupt the proper operation of the computer system and of its spooling and buffering.

We see then that we must provide memory protection at least for the interrupt vector and the interrupt service routines of the operating system. In general, we want to protect the operating system from access by user programs, and, in addition, to protect user programs from one another. This protection must be provided by the hardware. It can be implemented in several ways, as we describe in Chapter 9. Here, we outline one such possible implementation.

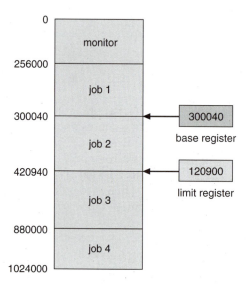

Figure 2.7   A base and a limit register define a logical address space.

What we need to separate each program's memory space is the ability to determine the range of legal addresses that the program may access, and to protect the memory outside that space. We can provide this protection by using two registers, usually a base and a limit, as illustrated in Figure 2.7. The **base register** holds the smallest legal physical memory address; the **limit register** contains the size of the range. For example, if the base register holds 300040 and limit register is 120900, then the program can legally access all addresses from 300040 through 420940 inclusive.

This protection is accomplished by the CPU hardware comparing *every* address generated in user mode with the registers. Any attempt by a program executing in user mode to access monitor memory or other users' memory results in a trap to the monitor, which treats the attempt as a fatal error (Figure 2.8). This scheme prevents the user program from (accidentally or deliberately) modifying the code or data structures of either the operating system or other users.

The base and limit registers can be loaded by only the operating system, which uses a special privileged instruction. Since privileged instructions can be executed in only monitor mode, and since only the operating system executes in monitor mode, only the operating system can load the base and limit registers. This scheme allows the monitor to change the value of the registers, but prevents user programs from changing the registers' contents.

The operating system, executing in monitor mode, is given unrestricted access to both monitor and users' memory. This provision allows the operating system to load users' programs into users' memory, to dump out those programs in case of errors, to access and modify parameters of system calls, and so on.

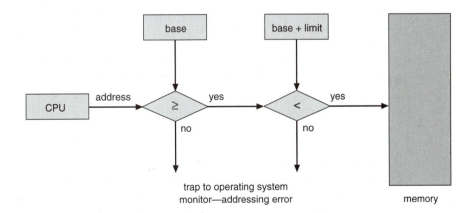

Figure 2.8   Hardware address protection with base and limit registers.

2.5.4 CPU Protection

The third piece of the protection puzzle is ensuring that the operating system maintains control. We must prevent a user program from getting stuck in an infinite loop, and never returning control to the operating system. To accomplish this goal, we can use a **timer**. A timer can be set to interrupt the computer after a specified period. The period may be fixed (for example, 1/60 second) or variable (for example, from 1 millisecond to 1 second, in increments of 1 millisecond). A variable timer is generally implemented by a fixed-rate clock and a counter. The operating system sets the counter. Every time the clock ticks, the counter is decremented. When the counter reaches 0, an interrupt occurs. For instance, a 10-bit counter with a 1-millisecond clock would allow interrupts at intervals from 1 millisecond to 1,024 milliseconds, in steps of 1 millisecond.

Before turning over control to the user, the operating system ensures that the timer is set to interrupt. If the timer interrupts, control transfers automatically to the operating system, which may treat the interrupt as a fatal error or may give the program more time. Instructions that modify the operation of the timer are clearly privileged.

Thus, we can use the timer to prevent a user program from running too long. A simple technique is to initialize a counter with the amount of time that a program is allowed to run. A program with a 7-minute time limit, for example, would have its counter initialized to 420. Every second, the timer interrupts and the counter is decremented by 1. As long as the counter is positive, control is returned to the user program. When the counter becomes negative, the operating system terminates the program for exceeding the assigned time limit.

A more common use of a timer is to implement time sharing. In the most straightforward case, the timer could be set to interrupt every N milliseconds, where N is the **time slice** that each user is allowed to execute before the next user gets control of the CPU. The operating system is invoked at the end of each time slice to perform various housekeeping tasks, such as adding the value N to the record that specifies (for accounting purposes) the amount of time the user program has executed thus far. The operating system also resets registers, internal variables, and buffers, and changes several other parameters to prepare for the next program to run. (This procedure is known as a *context switch*; it is explored in Chapter 4.) Following a context switch, the next program continues with its execution from the point at which it left off (when its previous time slice ran out).

Another use of the timer is to compute the current time. A timer interrupt signals the passage of some period, allowing the operating system to compute the current time in reference to some initial time. If we have interrupts every 1 second, and we have had 1427 interrupts since we were told that it was 1:00 P.M., then we can compute that the current time is 1:23:47 P.M. Some computers determine the current time in this manner, but the calculations must be done carefully for the time to be kept accurately, since the interrupt-processing time (and other times when interrupts are disabled) tends to cause the software clock to slow down. Most computers have a separate hardware time-of-day clock that is independent of the operating system.

2.6 ■ General System Architecture

The desire to improve the utilization of the computer system led to the development of multiprogramming and time sharing, where the resources of the computer system are shared among many different programs and processes. Sharing led directly to modifications of the basic computer architecture, to allow the operating system to maintain control over the computer system, especially over I/O. Control must be maintained if we are to provide continuous, consistent, and correct operation.

To maintain control, developers introduced a dual mode of execution (user mode and monitor mode). This scheme supports the concept of privileged instructions, which can be executed in only monitor mode. I/O instructions and instructions to modify the memory-management registers or the timer are privileged instructions.

As you can imagine, several other instructions are also classified as privileged. For instance, the `halt` instruction is privileged; a user program should never be able to halt the computer. The instructions to turn the interrupt system on and off also are privileged, since proper operation of the timer and I/O depends on the ability to respond to interrupts correctly. The instruction to change from user mode to monitor mode is privileged, and on many machines any change to the mode bit is privileged.

Because I/O instructions are privileged, they can be executed by only the operating system. Then how does the user program perform I/O? By making I/O instructions privileged, we have prevented user programs from doing any I/O, either valid or invalid. The solution to this problem is that, because only the monitor can do I/O, the user must *ask* the monitor to do I/O on the user's behalf.

Such a request is known as a **system call** (also called a **monitor call** or an **operating-system function call**). A system call is invoked in a variety of ways, depending on the functionality provided by the underlying processor. In all forms, it is the method used by a process to request action by the operating system. A system call usually takes the form of a trap to a specific location in the interrupt vector. This trap can be executed by a generic `trap` instruction, although some systems (such as the MIPS R2000 family) have a specific `syscall` instruction.

When a system call is executed, it is treated by the hardware as a software interrupt. Control passes through the interrupt vector to a service routine in the operating system, and the mode bit is set to monitor mode. The system-call service routine is a part of the operating system. The monitor examines the

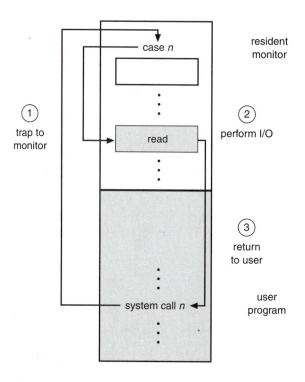

Figure 2.9   Use of a system call to perform I/O.

interrupting instruction to determine what system call has occurred; a parameter indicates what type of service the user program is requesting. Additional information needed for the request may be passed in registers, on the stack, or in memory (with pointers to the memory locations passed in registers). The monitor verifies that the parameters are correct and legal, executes the request, and returns control to the instruction following the system call.

Thus, to do I/O, a user program executes a system call to request that the operating system perform I/O on its behalf (Figure 2.9). The operating system, executing in monitor mode, checks that the request is valid, and (if the request is valid) does the I/O requested. The operating system then returns to the user.

2.7 ■ Summary

Multiprogramming and time-sharing systems improve performance by overlapping CPU and I/O operations on a single machine. Such an overlap requires that data transfer between the CPU and an I/O device be handled either by polled or interrupt-driven access to an I/O port, or by a DMA data transfer.

For a computer to do its job of executing programs, the programs must be in main memory. Main memory is the only large storage area that the processor can access directly. It is an array of words or bytes, ranging in size from hundreds of thousands to hundreds of millions. Each word has its own address. The main memory is a volatile storage device that loses its contents when power is turned off or lost. Most computer systems provide secondary storage as an extension of main memory. The main requirement of secondary storage is to be able to hold large quantities of data permanently. The most common secondary-storage device is a magnetic disk, which provides storage of both programs and data. A magnetic disk is a nonvolatile storage device that also provides random access. Magnetic tapes are used mainly for backup, for storage of infrequently used information, and as a medium for transferring information from one system to another.

The wide variety of storage systems in a computer system can be organized in a hierarchy according to their speed and their cost. The higher levels are expensive, but they are fast. As we move down the hierarchy, the cost per bit generally decreases, whereas the access time generally increases.

The operating system must ensure correct operation of the computer system. To prevent user programs from interfering with the proper operation of the system, the hardware has two modes: user mode and monitor mode. Various instructions (such as I/O instructions and halt instructions) are privileged, and can be executed in only monitor mode. The memory in which the operating system resides must also be protected from modification by the user. A timer prevents infinite loops. These facilities (dual mode, privileged instructions, memory protection, timer interrupt) are basic building blocks used by operating systems to achieve correct operation. Chapter 3 continues this discussion with details of the facilities that operating systems provide.

■ Exercises

2.1 *Prefetching* is a method of overlapping the I/O of a job with that job's own computation. The idea is simple. After a read operation completes and the job is about to start operating on the data, the input device is instructed to begin the next read immediately. The CPU and input device are then both busy. With luck, by the time that the job is ready for the next data item, the input device will have finished reading that data item. The CPU can then begin processing the newly read data, while the input device starts to read the following data. A similar idea can be used for output. In this case, the job creates data that are put into a buffer until an output device can accept them.

Compare the prefetching scheme with *spooling*, where the CPU overlaps the input of one job with the computation and output of other jobs.

2.2 How does the distinction between monitor mode and user mode function as a rudimentary form of protection (security) system?

2.3 What are the differences between a trap and an interrupt? What is the use of each function?

2.4 For what types of operations is DMA useful? Explain your answer.

2.5 Which of the following instructions should be privileged?

   a. Set value of timer.

   b. Read the clock.

   c. Clear memory.

   d. Turn off interrupts.

   e. Switch from user to monitor mode.

2.6 Some computer systems do not provide a privileged mode of operation in hardware. Consider whether it is possible to construct a secure operating system for these computers. Give arguments both that it is and that it is not possible.

2.7 Some early computers protected the operating system by placing it in a memory partition that could not be modified by either the user job or the operating system itself. Describe two difficulties that you think could arise with such a scheme.

2.8 Protecting the operating system is crucial to ensuring that the computer system operates correctly. Provision of this protection is the reason for dual-mode operation, memory protection, and the timer. To allow maximum flexibility, however, we would also like to place minimal constraints on the user.

   The following is a list of instructions that are normally protected. What is the *minimal* set of instructions that must be protected?

   a. Change to user mode.

   b. Change to monitor mode.

   c. Read from monitor memory.

   d. Write into monitor memory.

   e. Fetch an instruction from monitor memory.

   f. Turn on timer interrupt.

   g. Turn off timer interrupt.

2.9 Give two reasons why caches are useful. What problems do they solve? What problems do they cause? If a cache can be made as large as the device for which it is caching (for instance, a cache as large as a disk), why not make it that large and eliminate the device?

2.10 Writing an operating system that can operate without interference from malicious or undebugged user programs requires hardware assistance. Name three hardware aids for writing an operating system, and describe how they could be used together to protect the operating system.

2.11 Some CPUs provide for more than two modes of operation. What are two possible uses of these multiple modes?

Bibliographical Notes

Hennessy and Patterson [1996] provide coverage of I/O systems and buses, and of system architecture in general. Tanenbaum [1990] describes the architecture of microcomputers, starting at a detailed hardware level.

Discussions concerning magnetic-disk technology are presented by Freedman [1983] and by Harker and colleagues [1981]. Optical disks are covered by Kenville [1982], Fujitani [1984], O'Leary and Kitts [1985], Gait [1988], and Olsen and Kenley [1989]. Discussions of floppy disks are offered by Pechura and Schoeffler [1983] and by Sarisky [1983].

Cache memories, including associative memory, are described and analyzed by Smith [1982]. That paper also includes an extensive bibliography on the subject. Hennessy and Patterson [1996] discuss the hardware aspects of TLBs, caches, and MMUs.

General discussions concerning mass-storage technology are offered by Chi [1982] and by Hoagland [1985].

Chapter 3

OPERATING-SYSTEM STRUCTURES

An operating system provides the environment within which programs are executed. Internally, operating systems vary greatly in their makeup, being organized along many different lines. The design of a new operating system is a major task. It is important that the goals of the system be well defined before the design begins. The type of system desired is the basis for choices among various algorithms and strategies.

There are several vantage points from which to view an operating system. One is by examining the services that it provides. Another is by looking at the interface that it makes available to users and programmers. A third is by disassembling the system into its components and their interconnections. In this chapter, we explore all three aspects of operating systems, showing the viewpoints of users, programmers, and operating-system designers. We consider what services an operating system provides, how they are provided, and what the various methodologies are for designing such systems.

3.1 ■ System Components

We can create a system as large and complex as an operating system only by partitioning it into smaller pieces. Each of these pieces should be a well-delineated portion of the system, with carefully defined inputs, outputs, and functions. Obviously, not all systems have the same structure. However, many modern systems share the goal of supporting the system components outlined in Sections 3.1.1 through 3.1.8.

3.1.1 Process Management

A program does nothing unless its instructions are executed by a CPU. A **process** can be thought of as a program in execution, but its definition will broaden as we explore it further. A time-shared user program such as a compiler is a process. A word-processing program being run by an individual user on a PC is a process. A system task, such as sending output to a printer, also is a process. For now, you can consider a process to be a job or a time-shared program, but later you will learn that the concept is more general. As we shall see in Chapter 4, it is possible to provide system calls that allow processes to create subprocesses to execute concurrently.

A process needs certain resources—including CPU time, memory, files, and I/O devices—to accomplish its task. These resources are either given to the process when it is created, or allocated to it while it is running. In addition to the various physical and logical resources that a process obtains when it is created, various initialization data (input) may be passed along. For example, consider a process whose function is to display the status of a file on the screen of a terminal. The process will be given as an input the name of the file, and will execute the appropriate instructions and system calls to obtain and display on the terminal the desired information. When the process terminates, the operating system will reclaim any reusable resources.

We emphasize that a program by itself is not a process; a program is a *passive* entity, such as the contents of a file stored on disk, whereas a process is an *active* entity, with a **program counter** specifying the next instruction to execute. The execution of a process must be sequential. The CPU executes one instruction of the process after another, until the process completes. Further, at any time, at most one instruction is executed on behalf of the process. Thus, although two processes may be associated with the same program, they are nevertheless considered two separate execution sequences. It is common to have a program that spawns many processes as it runs.

A process is the unit of work in a system. Such a system consists of a collection of processes, some of which are operating-system processes (those that execute system code) and the rest of which are user processes (those that execute user code). All these processes can potentially execute concurrently, by multiplexing the CPU among them.

The operating system is responsible for the following activities in connection with process management:

- Creating and deleting both user and system processes
- Suspending and resuming processes
- Providing mechanisms for process synchronization
- Providing mechanisms for process communication
- Providing mechanisms for deadlock handling

We discuss process-management techniques in Chapters 4 through 7.

3.1.2 Main-Memory Management

As we discussed in Chapter 1, the main memory is central to the operation of a modern computer system. Main memory is a large array of words or bytes, ranging in size from hundreds of thousands to billions. Each word or byte has its own address. Main memory is a repository of quickly accessible data shared by the CPU and I/O devices. The central processor reads instructions from main memory during the instruction-fetch cycle, and both reads and writes data from main memory during the data-fetch cycle. The I/O operations implemented via DMA also read and write data in main memory. The main memory is generally the only large storage device that the CPU is able to address and access directly. For example, for the CPU to process data from disk, those data must first be transferred to main memory by CPU-generated I/O calls. Equivalently, instructions must be in memory for the CPU to execute them.

For a program to be executed, it must be mapped to absolute addresses and loaded into memory. As the program executes, it accesses program instructions and data from memory by generating these absolute addresses. Eventually, the program terminates, its memory space is declared available, and the next program can be loaded and executed.

To improve both the utilization of the CPU and the speed of the computer's response to its users, we must keep several programs in memory. There are many different memory-management schemes. These schemes reflect various approaches to memory management, and the effectiveness of the different algorithms depends on the particular situation. Selection of a memory-management scheme for a specific system depends on many factors—especially on the *hardware* design of the system. Each algorithm requires its own hardware support.

The operating system is responsible for the following activities in connection with memory management:

- Keeping track of which parts of memory are currently being used and by whom

- Deciding which processes are to be loaded into memory when memory space becomes available

- Allocating and deallocating memory space as needed

Memory-management techniques will be discussed in Chapters 9 and 10.

3.1.3 File Management

File management is one of the most visible components of an operating system. Computers can store information on several different types of physical media. Magnetic tape, magnetic disk, and optical disk are the most common media. Each of these media has its own characteristics and physical organization. Each medium is controlled by a device, such as a disk drive or tape drive, that also has its own unique characteristics. These properties include access speed, capacity, data-transfer rate, and access method (sequential or random).

For convenient use of the computer system, the operating system provides a uniform logical view of information storage. The operating system abstracts from the physical properties of its storage devices to define a logical storage unit, the file. The operating system maps files onto physical media, and accesses these files via the storage devices.

A **file** is a collection of related information defined by its creator. Commonly, files represent programs (both source and object forms) and data. Data files may be numeric, alphabetic, or alphanumeric. Files may be free-form (for example, text files), or may be formatted rigidly (for example, fixed fields). A file consists of a sequence of bits, bytes, lines, or records whose meanings are defined by their creators. The concept of a file is an extremely general one.

The operating system implements the abstract concept of a file by managing mass storage media, such as tapes and disks, and the devices that control them. Also, files are normally organized into directories to ease their use. Finally, when multiple users have access to files, it may be desirable to control by whom and in what ways (for example, read, write, append) files may be accessed.

The operating system is responsible for the following activities in connection with file management:

- Creating and deleting files

- Creating and deleting directories

- Supporting primitives for manipulating files and directories

- Mapping files onto secondary storage

- Backing up files on stable (nonvolatile) storage media

File-management techniques will be discussed in Chapter 11.

3.1.4 I/O-System Management

One of the purposes of an operating system is to hide the peculiarities of specific hardware devices from the user. For example, in UNIX, the peculiarities of I/O devices are hidden from the bulk of the operating system itself by the **I/O subsystem**. The I/O subsystem consists of

- A memory-management component that includes buffering, caching, and spooling

- A general device-driver interface

- Drivers for specific hardware devices

Only the device driver knows the peculiarities of the specific device to which it is assigned.

We discussed in Chapter 2 how interrupt handlers and device drivers are used in the construction of efficient I/O subsystems. In Chapter 12, we discuss how the I/O subsystem interfaces to the other system components, manages devices, transfers data, and detects I/O completion.

3.1.5 Secondary-Storage Management

The main purpose of a computer system is to execute programs. These programs, with the data they access, must be in main memory, or **primary storage,** during execution. Because main memory is too small to accommodate all data and programs, and because the data that it holds are lost when power is lost, the computer system must provide **secondary storage** to back up main memory. Most modern computer systems use disks as the principal on-line storage medium, for both programs and data. Most programs—including compilers, assemblers, sort routines, editors, and formatters—are stored on a disk until loaded into memory, and then use the disk as both the source and destination of their processing. Hence, the proper management of disk storage is of central importance to a computer system. The operating system is responsible for the following activities in connection with disk management:

- Free-space management

- Storage allocation

- Disk scheduling

Because secondary storage is used frequently, it must be used efficiently. The entire speed of operation of a computer may hinge on the speeds of the disk subsystem and of the algorithms that manipulate that subsystem. Techniques for secondary-storage management will be discussed in Chapter 13.

3.1.6 Networking

A **distributed system** is a collection of processors that do not share memory, peripheral devices, or a clock. Instead, each processor has its own local memory and clock, and the processors communicate with one another through various communication lines, such as high-speed buses or networks. The processors in a distributed system vary in size and function. They may include small microprocessors, workstations, minicomputers, and large, general-purpose computer systems.

The processors in the system are connected through a **communication network,** which can be configured in a number of different ways. The network may be fully or partially connected. The communication-network design must consider message routing and connection strategies, and the problems of contention and security.

A distributed system collects physically separate, possibly heterogeneous, systems into a single coherent system, providing the user with access to the various resources that the system maintains. Access to a shared resource allows computation speedup, increased functionality, increased data availability, and enhanced reliability. Operating systems usually generalize network access as a form of file access, with the details of networking being contained in the network interface's device driver. The protocols that create a distributed system can have a great effect on that system's utility and popularity. The innovation of the World Wide Web was to create a new access method for information sharing. It improved on the existing file-transfer protocol (FTP) and network file-system (NFS) protocol by removing the need for a user to log in before she is allowed to use a remote resource. It defined a new protocol, **http**, for use in communication between a web server and a web browser. A web browser then just needs to send a request for information to a remote machine's web server, and the information (text, graphics, links to other information) is returned. This increase in convenience fostered huge growth in the use of http, and of the Web in general.

We discuss networks and distributed systems, with particular focus on distributed computing using Java, in Chapters 14 through 17.

3.1.7 Protection System

If a computer system has multiple users and allows the concurrent execution of multiple processes, then the various processes must be protected from one another's activities. For that purpose, mechanisms ensure that the files, memory segments, CPU, and other resources can be operated on by only those processes that have gained proper authorization from the operating system.

For example, memory-addressing hardware ensures that a process can execute only within its own address space. The timer ensures that no process can gain control of the CPU without eventually relinquishing control. Device-control registers are not accessible to users, so that the integrity of the various peripheral devices is protected.

Protection is any mechanism for controlling the access of programs, processes, or users to the resources defined by a computer system. This mechanism must provide means for specification of the controls to be imposed and means for enforcement.

Protection can improve reliability by detecting latent errors at the interfaces between component subsystems. Early detection of interface errors can often prevent contamination of a healthy subsystem by another subsystem that is malfunctioning. An unprotected resource cannot defend against use (or misuse) by an unauthorized or incompetent user. A protection-oriented system provides a means to distinguish between authorized and unauthorized usage, as we discuss in Chapter 18.

3.1.8 Command-Interpreter System

One of the most important systems programs for an operating system is the **command interpreter,** which is the interface between the user and the operating system. Some operating systems include the command interpreter in the kernel. Other operating systems, such as MS-DOS and UNIX, treat the command interpreter as a special program that is running when a job is initiated, or when a user first logs on (on time-sharing systems).

Many commands are given to the operating system by **control statements**. When a new job is started in a batch system, or when a user logs on to a time-shared system, a program that reads and interprets control statements is executed automatically. This program is sometimes called the **control-card interpreter,** or the **command-line interpreter,** and is often known as the **shell**. Its function is simple: To get the next command statement and execute it.

Operating systems are frequently differentiated in the area of the shell, with a user-friendly command interpreter making the system more agreeable to some users. One style of user-friendly interface is the mouse-based window and menu system used in the Macintosh and in Microsoft Windows. The mouse is moved to position the mouse pointer on images, or **icons,** on the screen that represent programs, files, and system functions. Depending on the mouse pointer's location, clicking a button on the mouse can invoke a program, select a file or directory—known as a **folder**—or pull down a menu that contains commands. More powerful, complex, and difficult-to-learn shells are appreciated by other users. In some of these shells, commands are typed on a keyboard and displayed on a screen or printing terminal, with the enter (or return) key signaling that a command is complete and is ready to be executed. The MS-DOS and UNIX shells operate in this way.

The command statements themselves deal with process creation and management, I/O handling, secondary-storage management, main-memory management, file-system access, protection, and networking.

3.2 ■ Operating-System Services

An operating system provides an environment for the execution of programs. It provides certain services to programs and to the users of those programs. The specific services provided, of course, differ from one operating system to another, but we can identify common classes. These operating-system services are provided for the convenience of the programmer, to make the programming task easier.

- *Program execution:* The system must be able to load a program into memory and to run that program. The program must be able to end its execution, either normally or abnormally (indicating error).

- *I/O operations:* A running program may require I/O. This I/O may involve a file or an I/O device. For specific devices, special functions may be desired (such as to rewind a tape drive, or to blank a CRT screen). For efficiency and protection, users usually cannot control I/O devices directly. Therefore, the operating system must provide a means to do I/O.

- *File-system manipulation:* The file system is of particular interest. Obviously, programs need to read and write files. They also need to create and delete files by name.

- *Communications:* There are many circumstances in which one process needs to exchange information with another process. There are two major ways in which such communication can occur. The first takes place between processes that are executing on the same computer; the second takes place between processes that are executing on different computer systems that are tied together by a computer network. Communications may be implemented via *shared memory,* or by the technique of *message passing,* in which packets of information are moved between processes by the operating system.

- *Error detection:* The operating system constantly needs to be aware of possible errors. Errors may occur in the CPU and memory hardware (such as a memory error or a power failure), in I/O devices (such as a parity error on tape, a connection failure on a network, or lack of paper in the printer), and in the user program (such as an arithmetic overflow, an attempt to access an illegal memory location, or a too-great use of CPU time). For each type of error, the operating system should take the appropriate action to ensure correct and consistent computing.

In addition, another set of operating-system functions exists not for helping the user, but rather for ensuring the efficient operation of the system itself. Systems with multiple users can gain efficiency by sharing the computer resources among the users.

- *Resource allocation:* When there are multiple users or multiple jobs running at the same time, resources must be allocated to each of them. Many different types of resources are managed by the operating system. Some (such as CPU cycles, main memory, and file storage) may have special allocation code, whereas others (such as I/O devices) may have much more general request and release code. For instance, in determining how best to use the CPU, operating systems have CPU-scheduling routines that take into account the speed of the CPU, the jobs that must be executed, the number of registers available, and other factors. There might also be routines to allocate a tape drive for use by a job. One such routine locates an unused tape drive and marks an internal table to record the drive's new user. Another routine is used to clear that table. These routines may also allocate plotters, modems, and other peripheral devices.

- *Accounting:* We want to keep track of which users use how much and what kinds of computer resources. This record keeping may be used for accounting (so that users can be billed) or simply for accumulating usage statistics. Usage statistics may be a valuable tool for researchers who wish to reconfigure the system to improve computing services.

- *Protection:* The owners of information stored in a multiuser computer system may want to control use of that information. When several disjoint processes execute concurrently, it should not be possible for one process to interfere with the others, or with the operating system itself. Protection involves ensuring that all access to system resources is controlled. *Security* of the system from outsiders is also important. Such security starts with each user having to authenticate himself to the system, usually by means of a password, to be allowed access to the resources. It extends to defending external I/O devices, including modems and network adapters, from invalid access attempts, and to recording all such connections for detection of breakins. If a system is to be protected and secure, precautions must be instituted throughout it. A chain is only as strong as its weakest link.

3.3 ■ System Calls

System calls provide the interface between a process and the operating system. These calls are generally available as assembly-language instructions, and are usually listed in the manuals used by assembly-language programmers.

Certain systems allow system calls to be made directly from a higher-level language program, in which case the calls normally resemble predefined function or subroutine calls. They may generate a call to a special run-time routine that makes the system call, or the system call may be generated directly in-line.

Several languages—such as C, C++, and Perl—have been defined to replace assembly language for systems programming. These languages allow system calls to be made directly. For example, UNIX system calls may be invoked directly from a C or C++ program. System calls for modern Microsoft Windows platforms are part of the Win32 API, which is available for use by all the compilers written for Microsoft Windows.

Java does not allow system calls to be made directly, because a system call is specific to an operating system and results in platform-specific code. However, if an application requires system-specific features, a Java program can call a method that has been written in another language—typically C or C++—that can make the system call. Such methods are known as "native" methods.

As an example of how system calls are used, consider writing a simple program to read data from one file and to copy them to another file. The first input that the program will need is the names of the two files: the input file and the output file. These names can be specified in many ways, depending on the operating-system design. One approach is for the program to ask the user for the names of the two files. In an interactive system, this approach will require a sequence of system calls, first to write a prompting message on the screen, and then to read from the keyboard the characters that define the two files. On mouse-based and icon-based systems, a menu of file names is usually displayed in a window. The user can then use the mouse to select the source name, and a window can be opened for the destination name to be specified.

Once the two file names are obtained, the program must open the input file and create the output file. Each of these operations requires another system call. There are also possible error conditions for each operation. When the program tries to open the input file, it may find that there is no file of that name or that the file is protected against access. In these cases, the program should print a message on the console (another sequence of system calls), and then terminate abnormally (another system call). If the input file exists, then we must create a new output file. We may find that there is already an output file with the same name. This situation may cause the program to abort (a system call), or we may delete the existing file (another system call) and create a new one (another system call). Another option, in an interactive system, is to ask the user (a sequence of system calls to output the prompting message and to read the response from the terminal) whether to replace the existing file or to abort the program.

Now that both files are set up, we enter a loop that reads from the input file (a system call) and writes to the output file (another system call). Each read and write must return status information regarding various possible error conditions. On input, the program may find that the end of the file has been reached, or that there was a hardware failure in the read (such as a parity error). The write operation may encounter various errors, depending on the output device (no more disk space, physical end of tape, printer out of paper, and so on).

Finally, after the entire file is copied, the program may close both files (another system call), write a message to the console (more system calls), and finally terminate normally (the final system call). As we can see, programs may make heavy use of the operating system.

Most users never see this level of detail, however. The run-time support system (the set of functions built into libraries included with a compiler) for most programming languages provides a much simpler interface. For example, the cout statement in C++ is probably compiled into a call to a run-time support routine that issues the necessary system calls, checks for errors, and finally returns to the user program. Thus, most of the details of the operating-system interface are hidden from the programmer by the compiler and by the run-time support package.

System calls occur in different ways, depending on the computer in use. Often, more information is required than simply the identity of the desired system call. The exact type and amount of information vary according to the particular operating system and call. For example, to get input, we may need to specify the file or device to use as the source, and the address and length of the memory buffer into which the input should be read. Of course, the device or file and length may be implicit in the call.

Three general methods are used to pass parameters to the operating system. The simplest approach is to pass the parameters in *registers*. In some cases, however, there may be more parameters than registers. In these cases, the parameters are generally stored in a *block* or table in memory, and the address of the block is passed as a parameter in a register (Figure 3.1). Parameters also can be placed, or *pushed*, onto the *stack* by the program, and *popped* off the stack by the operating system. Some operating systems prefer the block or stack methods, because those approaches do not limit the number or length of parameters being passed.

System calls can be grouped roughly into five major categories: **process control, file manipulation, device manipulation, information maintenance,** and **communications**. In Sections 3.3.1 through 3.3.5, we discuss briefly the types of system calls that may be provided by an operating system. Most of these system calls support, or are supported by, concepts and functions that are discussed in later chapters. Figure 3.2 summarizes the types of system calls normally provided by an operating system.

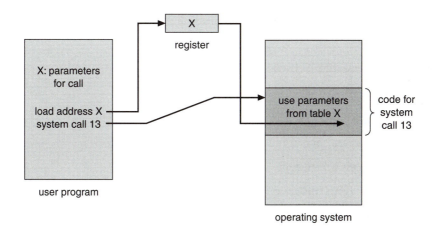

Figure 3.1 Passing of parameters as a table.

- Process control
    - end, abort
    - load, execute
    - create process, terminate process
    - get process attributes, set process attributes
    - wait for time
    - wait event, signal event
    - allocate and free memory

- File management
    - create file, delete file
    - open, close
    - read, write, reposition
    - get file attributes, set file attributes

- Device management
    - request device, release device
    - read, write, reposition
    - get device attributes, set device attributes
    - logically attach or detach devices

- Information maintenance
    - get time or date, set time or date
    - get system data, set system data
    - get process, file, or device attributes
    - set process, file, or device attributes

- Communications
    - create, delete communication connection
    - send, receive messages
    - transfer status information
    - attach or detach remote devices

Figure 3.2   Types of system calls.

3.3.1 Process Control

A running program needs to be able to halt its execution either normally (end) or abnormally (abort). If a system call is made to terminate the currently running program abnormally, or if the program runs into a problem and causes an error trap, a dump of memory is sometimes taken and an error message generated. The dump is written to disk and may be examined by a *debugger* to determine the cause of the problem. Under either normal or abnormal circumstances, the operating system must transfer control to the command interpreter. The command interpreter then reads the next command. In an interactive system, the command interpreter simply continues with the next command; it is assumed that the user will issue an appropriate command to respond to any error. In a batch system, the command interpreter usually terminates the entire job and continues with the next job. Some systems allow control cards to indicate special recovery actions in case an error occurs. If the program discovers an error in its input and wants to terminate abnormally, it may also want to define an error level. More severe errors can be indicated by a higher-level error parameter. It is then possible to combine normal and abnormal termination by defining a normal termination as error at level 0. The command interpreter or a following program can use this error level to determine the next action automatically.

A process or job executing one program may want to load and execute another program. This feature allows the command interpreter to execute a program as directed by, for example, a user command, the click of a mouse, or a batch command. An interesting question is where to return control when the loaded program terminates. This question is related to the problem of whether the existing program is lost, saved, or allowed to continue execution concurrently with the new program.

If control returns to the existing program when the new program terminates, we must save the memory image of the existing program; thus, we have effectively created a mechanism for one program to call another program. If both programs continue concurrently, we have created a new job or process to be multiprogrammed. Often, there is a system call specifically for this purpose (create process or submit job).

If we create a new job or process, or perhaps even a set of jobs or processes, we should be able to control its execution. This control requires the ability to determine and reset the attributes of a job or process, including the job's priority, its maximum allowable execution time, and so on (get process attributes and set process attributes). We may also want to terminate a job or process that we created (terminate process) if we find that it is incorrect or is no longer needed.

Having created new jobs or processes, we may need to wait for them to finish their execution. We may want to wait for a certain amount of time (wait time); more probably, we may want to wait for a specific event to occur (wait event). The jobs or processes should then signal when that event has occurred (signal event). System calls of this type, dealing with the coordination of concurrent processes, are discussed in great detail in Chapter 7.

Another set of system calls is helpful in debugging a program. Many systems provide system calls to dump memory. This provision is useful for debugging. A program trace lists each instruction as it is executed; it is provided by fewer systems. Even microprocessors provide a CPU mode known as *single step,* in which a trap is executed by the CPU after every instruction. The trap is usually caught by a debugger, which is a system program designed to aid the programmer in finding and correcting bugs.

Many operating systems provide a time profile of a program. It indicates the amount of time that the program executes at a particular location or set of locations. A time profile requires either a tracing facility or regular timer interrupts. At every occurrence of the timer interrupt, the value of the program counter is recorded. With sufficiently frequent timer interrupts, a statistical picture of the time spent on various parts of the program can be obtained.

There are so many facets of and variations in process and job control that we shall use examples to clarify these concepts. The MS-DOS operating system is an example of a single-tasking system, which has a command interpreter that is invoked when the computer is started (Figure 3.3(a)). Because MS-DOS is single-tasking, it uses a simple method to run a program, and does not create a new process. It loads the program into memory, writing over most of itself to give the program as much memory as possible (Figure 3.3(b)). It then sets the instruction pointer to the first instruction of the program. The program then runs and either an error causes a trap, or the program executes a system call to terminate. In either case, the error code is saved in the system memory for later

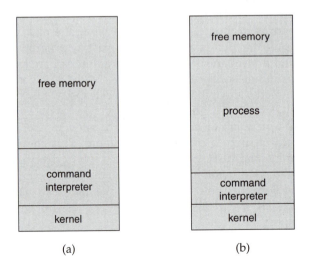

(a)   (b)

Figure 3.3   MS-DOS execution. (a) At system startup. (b) Running a program.

use. Following this action, the small portion of the command interpreter that was not overwritten resumes execution. Its first task is to reload the rest of the command interpreter from disk. Once this task is accomplished, the command interpreter makes the previous error code available to the user or to the next program.

Although the MS-DOS operating system does not have general multitasking capabilities, it does provide a method for limited concurrent execution. A TSR program is a program that "hooks an interrupt" and then exits with the terminate and stay resident system call. For instance, it can hook the clock interrupt by placing the address of one of its subroutines into the list of interrupt routines to be called when the system timer is triggered. This way, the TSR routine will be executed several times per second, at each clock tick. The terminate and stay resident system call causes MS-DOS to reserve the space occupied by the TSR, so it will not be overwritten when the command interpreter is reloaded.

Berkeley UNIX is an example of a multitasking system. When a user logs on to the system, the *shell* (command interpreter) of the user's choice is run. This shell is similar to the MS-DOS shell in that it accepts commands and executes programs that the user requests. However, since UNIX is a multitasking system, the command interpreter may continue running while another program is executed (Figure 3.4). To start a new process, the shell executes a fork system call. Then, the selected program is loaded into memory via an exec system call, and the program is then executed. Depending on the way the command was issued, the shell then either waits for the process to finish, or runs the process "in the background." In the latter case, the shell immediately requests another command. When a process is running in the background, it cannot receive input directly from the keyboard, because the shell is using this resource. I/O

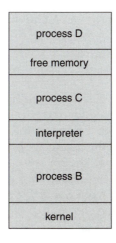

Figure 3.4   UNIX running multiple programs.

is therefore done through files, or through a mouse and windows interface. Meanwhile, the user is free to ask the shell to run other programs, to monitor the progress of the running process, to change that program's priority, and so on. When the process is done, it executes an exit system call to terminate, returning to the invoking process a status code of 0, or a nonzero error code. This status or error code is then available to the shell or other programs. Processes are discussed in Chapter 4.

3.3.2 File Management

The file system will be discussed in more detail in Chapter 11. We can identify several common system calls dealing with files, however.

We first need to be able to create and delete files. Either system call requires the name of the file and perhaps some of the file's attributes. Once the file is created, we need to open it and to use it. We may also read, write, or reposition (rewinding or skipping to the end of the file, for example). Finally, we need to close the file, indicating that we are no longer using it.

We may need these same sets of operations for directories if we have a directory structure for organizing files in the file system. In addition, for either files or directories, we need to be able to determine the values of various attributes, and perhaps to reset them if necessary. File attributes include the file name, a file type, protection codes, accounting information, and so on. At least two system calls, get file attribute and set file attribute, are required for this function. Some operating systems provide many more calls.

3.3.3 Device Management

A program, as it is running, may need additional resources to proceed. Additional resources may be more memory, tape drives, access to files, and so on. If the resources are available, they can be granted, and control can be returned to the user program; otherwise, the program will have to wait until sufficient resources are available.

Files can be thought of as abstract or virtual devices. Thus, many of the system calls for files are also needed for devices. If there are multiple users of the system, however, we must first request the device, to ensure exclusive use of it. After we are finished with the device, we must release it. These functions are similar to the open and close system calls for files.

Once the device has been requested (and allocated to us), we can read, write, and (possibly) reposition the device, just as we can with ordinary files. In fact, the similarity between I/O devices and files is so great that many operating systems, including UNIX and MS-DOS, merge the two into a combined file–device structure. In this case, I/O devices are identified by special file names.

3.3.4 Information Maintenance

Many system calls exist simply for the purpose of transferring information between the user program and the operating system. For example, most systems have a system call to return the current time and date. Other system calls may return information about the system, such as the number of current users, the version number of the operating system, the amount of free memory or disk space, and so on.

In addition, the operating system keeps information about all its processes, and there are system calls to access this information. Generally, there are also calls to reset the process information (get process attributes and set process attributes). In Section 4.1.3, we discuss what information is normally kept.

3.3.5 Communication

There are two common models of communication. In the **message-passing model,** information is exchanged through an interprocess-communication facility provided by the operating system. Before communication can take place, a connection must be opened. The name of the other communicator must be known, be it another process on the same CPU, or a process on another computer connected by a communications network. Each computer in a network has a *host name*, such as an IP name, by which it is commonly known. Similarly, each process has a *process name*, which is translated into an equivalent identifier by which the operating system can refer to it. The get hostid, and get processid system calls do this translation. These identifiers are then passed to the general-purpose open and close calls provided by the file system, or to specific open connection and close connection system calls, depending on the system's model of communications. The recipient process usually must give its permission for communication to take place with an accept connection call. Most processes that will be receiving connections are special-purpose *daemons*, which are systems programs provided for that purpose. They execute a wait for connection call and are awakened when a connection is made. The source of the communication, known as the *client*, and the receiving daemon, known as a *server*, then exchange messages by read message and write message system calls. The close connection call terminates the communication.

In the **shared-memory model,** processes use map memory system calls to gain access to regions of memory owned by other processes. Recall that, normally, the operating system tries to prevent one process from accessing another process' memory. Shared memory requires that two or more processes agree to remove this restriction. They may then exchange information by reading and writing data in these shared areas. The form of the data and the location are determined by these processes and are not under the operating system's control. The processes are also responsible for ensuring that

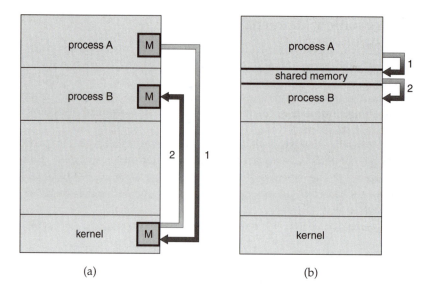

Figure 3.5   Communications models. (a) Msg passing. (b) Shared memory.

they are not writing to the same location simultaneously. Such mechanisms are discussed in Chapter 7. We will also look at a variation of the process model—threads—that shares memory by default. Threads will be covered in Chapter 5.

Both of these methods are common in operating systems, and some systems even implement both. Message passing is useful when smaller numbers of data need to be exchanged, because no conflicts need to be avoided. It is also easier to implement than is shared memory for intercomputer communication. Shared memory allows maximum speed and convenience of communication, as it can be done at memory speeds when within a computer. Problems exist, however, in the areas of protection and synchronization. The two communications models are contrasted in Figure 3.5. In Chapter 4, we will look at a Java implementation of each model.

3.4 ■ System Programs

Another aspect of a modern system is the collection of system programs. Recall Figure 1.1, which depicted the logical computer hierarchy. At the lowest level is hardware. Next is the operating system, then the system programs, and finally the application programs. System programs provide a convenient environment for program development and execution. Some of them are simply user interfaces to system calls; others are considerably more complex. They can be divided into these categories:

- *File management:* These programs create, delete, copy, rename, print, dump, list, and generally manipulate files and directories.

- *Status information:* Some programs simply ask the system for the date, time, amount of available memory or disk space, number of users, or similar status information. That information is then formatted, and is printed to the terminal or other output device or file.

- *File modification:* Several text editors may be available to create and modify the content of files stored on disk or tape.

- *Programming-language support:* Compilers, assemblers, and interpreters for common programming languages (such as C, C++, Java, Visual Basic, and PERL) are often provided to the user with the operating system. Most of these programs are now priced and provided separately.

- *Program loading and execution:* Once a program is assembled or compiled, it must be loaded into memory to be executed. The system may provide absolute loaders, relocatable loaders, linkage editors, and overlay loaders. Debugging systems for either higher-level languages or machine language are needed also.

- *Communications:* These programs provide the mechanism for creating virtual connections among processes, users, and different computer systems. They allow users to send messages to one another's screens, to browse web pages, to send electronic-mail messages, to log in remotely, or to transfer files from one machine to another.

Most operating systems are supplied with programs that are useful in solving common problems, or in performing common operations. Such programs include web browsers, word processors and text formatters, spreadsheets, database systems, compiler compilers, plotting and statistical-analysis packages, and games. These programs are known as **system utilities** or **application programs**.

Perhaps the most important system program for an operating system is the **command interpreter,** the main function of which is to get and execute the next user-specified command.

Many of the commands given at this level manipulate files: create, delete, list, print, copy, execute, and so on. There are two general ways in which these commands can be implemented. In one approach, the command interpreter itself contains the code to execute the command. For example, a command to delete a file may cause the command interpreter to jump to a section of its code that sets up the parameters and makes the appropriate system call. In this case, the number of commands that can be given determines the size of the command interpreter, since each command requires its own implementing code.

An alternative approach—used by UNIX, among other operating systems—implements most commands by system programs. In this case, the command interpreter does not understand the command in any way; it merely uses the command to identify a file to be loaded into memory and executed. Thus, the UNIX command to delete a file

$$rm\ G$$

would search for a file called *rm*, load the file into memory, and execute it with the parameter G. The function associated with the rm command would be defined completely by the code in the file *rm*. In this way, programmers can add new commands to the system easily by creating new files with the proper names. The command-interpreter program, which can be small, does not have to be changed for new commands to be added.

There are problems with this approach to the design of a command interpreter. Notice first that, because the code to execute a command is a separate system program, the operating system must provide a mechanism for passing parameters from the command interpreter to the system program. This task can often be clumsy, because the command interpreter and the system program may not both be in memory at the same time, and the parameter list can be extensive. Also, it is slower to load a program and to execute it than simply to jump to another section of code within the current program.

Another problem is that the interpretation of the parameters is left up to the programmer of the system program. Thus, parameters may be provided inconsistently across programs that appear similar to the user, but that were written at different times by different programmers.

The view of the operating system seen by most users is thus defined by the system programs, rather than by the actual system calls. Consider PCs. When her computer is running the Microsoft Windows operating system, a user might see a command-line MS-DOS shell, or the graphical mouse and windows interface. Both use the same set of system calls, but the system calls look different and act in different ways. Consequently, this user view may be substantially removed from the actual system structure. The design of a useful and friendly user interface is therefore not a direct function of the operating system. In this book, we shall concentrate on the fundamental problems of providing adequate service to user programs. From the point of view of the operating system, we do not distinguish between user programs and system programs.

3.5 ■ System Structure

A system as large and complex as a modern operating system must be engineered carefully if it is to function properly and be modified easily. A common approach is to partition the task into small components, rather than have one monolithic system. Each of these modules should be a well-defined portion of the system, with carefully defined inputs, outputs, and function. We have already discussed briefly the common components of operating systems (Section 3.1). In this section, we discuss the way that these components are interconnected and melded into a kernel.

3.5.1 Simple Structure

There are numerous commercial systems that do not have a well-defined structure. Frequently, such operating systems started as small, simple, and limited systems, and then grew beyond their original scope. MS-DOS is an example of such a system. It was originally designed and implemented by a few people who had no idea that it would become so popular. It was written to provide the most functionality in the least space (because of the limited hardware on which it ran), so it was not divided into modules carefully. Figure 3.6 shows its structure.

In MS-DOS, the interfaces and levels of functionality are not well separated. For instance, application programs are able to access the basic I/O routines to write directly to the display and disk drives. Such freedom leaves MS-DOS vulnerable to errant (or malicious) programs, causing entire system crashes when user programs fail. Of course, MS-DOS was also limited by the hardware of its era. Because the Intel 8088 for which it was written provides no dual mode and no hardware protection, the designers of MS-DOS had no choice but to leave the base hardware accessible.

Another example of limited structuring is the original UNIX operating system. UNIX is another system that initially was limited by hardware functionality. It consists of two separable parts: the kernel and the system programs.

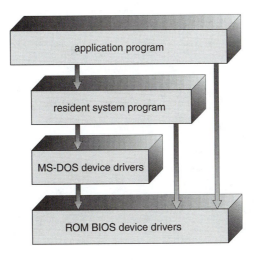

Figure 3.6   MS-DOS layer structure.

The kernel is further separated into a series of interfaces and device drivers, which have been added and expanded over the years as UNIX has evolved. We can view the traditional UNIX operating system as being layered as shown in Figure 3.7. Everything below the system-call interface and above the physical hardware is the kernel. The kernel provides the file system, CPU scheduling, memory management, and other operating-system functions through system calls. Taken in sum, that is an enormous amount of functionality to be combined into one level. System programs use the kernel-supported system calls to provide useful functions, such as compilation and file manipulation.

System calls define the **application programmer interface (API)** to UNIX; the set of system programs commonly available defines the **user interface**. The programmer and user interfaces define the context that the kernel must support.

New versions of UNIX are designed to use more advanced hardware. Given proper hardware support, operating systems may be broken into pieces that are smaller and more appropriate than are those allowed by the original MS-DOS or UNIX systems. The operating system can then retain much greater control over the computer and over the applications that make use of that computer. Implementors have more freedom to make changes to the inner workings of the system and in the creation of modular operating systems. Under the top-down approach, the overall functionality and features are determined and are separated into components. Information hiding is also important, because it leaves programmers free to implement the low-level routines as they see fit, provided that the external interface of the routine stays unchanged and that the routine itself performs the advertised task.

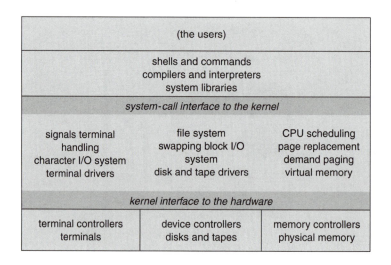

Figure 3.7   UNIX system structure.

3.5.2 Layered Approach

The modularization of a system can be done in many ways; one method is the **layered approach**, in which the operating system is broken up into a number of layers (levels), each built on top of lower layers. The bottom layer (layer 0) is the hardware; the highest (layer N) is the user interface.

An operating-system layer is an implementation of an abstract object that is the encapsulation of data, and of the operations that can manipulate those data. A typical operating-system layer—say layer M—is depicted in Figure 3.8. It consists of data structures and a set of routines that can be invoked by higher-level layers. Layer M, in turn, can invoke operations on lower-level layers.

The main advantage of the layered approach is **modularity**. The layers are selected such that each uses functions (operations) and services of only lower-level layers. This approach simplifies debugging and system verification. The first layer can be debugged without any concern for the rest of the system, because, by definition, it uses only the basic hardware (which is assumed correct) to implement its functions. Once the first layer is debugged, its correct functioning can be assumed while the second layer is debugged, and so on. If an error is found during the debugging of a particular layer, the error must be on that layer, because the layers below it are already debugged. Thus, the design and implementation of the system is simplified when the system is broken down into layers.

Each layer is implemented with only those operations provided by lower-level layers. A layer does not need to know how these operations are implemented; it needs to know only what these operations do. Hence, each layer hides the existence of certain data structures, operations, and hardware from higher-level layers.

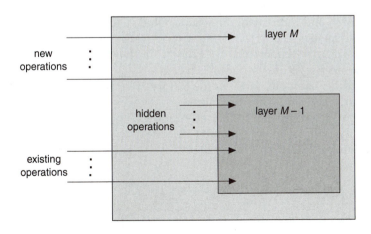

Figure 3.8   An operating-system layer.

The major difficulty with the layered approach involves the appropriate definition of the various layers. Because a layer can use only those layers that are at a lower level, careful planning is necessary. For example, the device driver for the backing store (disk space used by virtual-memory algorithms) must be at a level lower than that of the memory-management routines, because memory management requires the ability to use the backing store.

Other requirements may not be so obvious. The backing-store driver would normally be above the CPU scheduler, because the driver may need to wait for I/O and the CPU can be rescheduled during this time. However, on a large system, the CPU scheduler may have more information about all the active processes than can fit in memory. Therefore, this information may need to be swapped in and out of memory, requiring the backing-store driver routine to be below the CPU scheduler.

A final problem with layered implementations is that they tend to be less efficient than other types. For instance, when a user program executes an I/O operation, it executes a system call that is trapped to the I/O layer, which calls the memory-management layer, which in turn calls the CPU-scheduling layer, which is then passed to the hardware. At each layer, the parameters may be modified, data may need to be passed, and so on. Each layer adds overhead to the system call; the net result is a system call that takes longer than does one on a nonlayered system.

These limitations have caused a small backlash against layering in recent years. Fewer layers with more functionality are being designed, providing most of the advantages of modularized code while avoiding the difficult problems of layer definition and interaction. For instance, OS/2 is a descendant of MS-DOS that adds multitasking and dual-mode operation, as well as other new features. Because of this added complexity and the more powerful hardware for which OS/2 was designed, the system was implemented in a more layered fashion. Contrast the MS-DOS structure to that shown in Figure 3.9; from both the system-design and implementation standpoints, OS/2 has the advantage. For instance, direct user access to low-level facilities is not allowed, providing the operating system with more control over the hardware and more knowledge of which resources each user program is using.

As a further example, consider the history of Windows NT. The first release had a highly layer-oriented organization. However, this version delivered low performance compared to that of Windows 95. Windows NT 4.0 partially redressed the performance problem by moving layers from user space to kernel space and more closely integrating them.

3.5.3 Microkernels

As UNIX expanded, the kernel became large and difficult to manage. In the mid-1980s, researchers at Carnegie Mellon University developed an operating system called **Mach** that modularized the kernel using the **microkernel** approach.

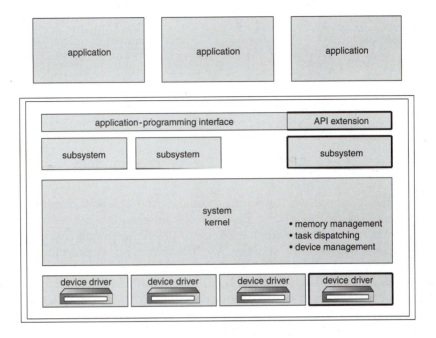

Figure 3.9 OS/2 layer structure.

This method structures the operating system by removing all nonessential components from the kernel, and implementing them as system and user-level programs. The result is a smaller kernel. There is little consensus regarding which services should remain in the kernel and which should be implemented in user space. In general, however, microkernels typically provide minimal process and memory management, in addition to a communication facility.

The main function of the microkernel is to provide a communication facility between the client program and the various services that are also running in user space. Communication is provided by *message passing*, which was described in Section 3.3.5. For example, if the client program wishes to access a file, it must interact with the file server. The client program and service never interact directly. Rather, they communicate indirectly by exchanging messages with the microkernel.

The benefits of the microkernel approach include the ease of extending the operating system. All new services are added to user space and consequently do not require modification of the kernel. When the kernel does have to be modified, the changes tend to be fewer, because the microkernel is a smaller kernel. The resulting operating system is easier to port from one hardware design to another. The microkernel also provides more security and reliability, since most services are running as user—rather than kernel—processes. If a service fails, the rest of the operating system remains untouched.

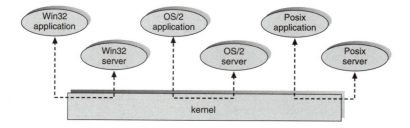

Figure 3.10   Windows NT client–server structure.

Several contemporary operating systems have used the microkernel approach. Digital UNIX provides a UNIX interface to the user, but is implemented with a Mach kernel. Mach maps UNIX system calls into messages to the appropriate user-level services. Apple MacOS X Server operating system is based on the Mach kernel. Windows NT uses a hybrid structure. We have already mentioned that part of the Windows NT architecture uses layering. Windows NT is designed to run various applications, including Win32 (native Windows applications), OS/2, and POSIX. It provides a server that runs in user space for each application type. Client programs for each application type also run in user space. The kernel coordinates the message passing between client applications and application servers. The client–server structure of Windows NT is depicted in Figure 3.10.

3.6 ■ Virtual Machines

Conceptually, a computer system is made up of layers. The hardware is the lowest level in all such systems. The kernel running at the next level uses the hardware instructions to create a set of system calls for use by outer layers. The system programs above the kernel are therefore able to use either system calls or hardware instructions, and in some ways these programs do not differentiate between these two. Thus, although they are accessed differently, they both provide functionality that the program can use to create even more advanced functions. System programs, in turn, treat the hardware and the system calls as though they both are at the same level.

Some systems carry this scheme a step further by allowing the system programs to be called easily by the application programs. As before, although the system programs are at a level higher than that of the other routines, the application programs may view everything under them in the hierarchy as though the latter were part of the machine itself. This layered approach is taken to its logical conclusion in the concept of a **virtual machine**. The VM operating system for IBM systems is the best example of the virtual-machine concept, because IBM pioneered the work in this area.

By using CPU scheduling (Chapter 6) and virtual-memory techniques (Chapter 10), an operating system can create the illusion that a process has its own processor with its own (virtual) memory. Of course, normally, the process has additional features, such as system calls and a file system, which are not provided by the bare hardware. The virtual-machine approach, on the other hand, does not provide any additional functionality, but rather provides an interface that is *identical* to the underlying bare hardware. Each process is provided with a (virtual) copy of the underlying computer (Figure 3.11).

The physical computer shares resources to create the virtual machines. CPU scheduling can share out the CPU to create the appearance that users have their own processors. Spooling and a file system can provide virtual card readers and virtual line printers. A normal user time-sharing terminal provides the function of the virtual-machine operator's console.

A major difficulty with the virtual-machine approach involves disk systems. Suppose that the physical machine has three disk drives but wants to support seven virtual machines. Clearly, it cannot allocate a disk drive to each virtual machine. Remember that the virtual-machine software itself will need substantial disk space to provide virtual memory and spooling. The solution is to provide virtual disks, which are identical in all respects except size—termed *minidisks* in IBM's VM operating system. The system implements each minidisk by allocating as many tracks on the physical disks as the minidisk needs. Obviously, the sum of the sizes of all minidisks must be smaller than the size of the physical disk space available.

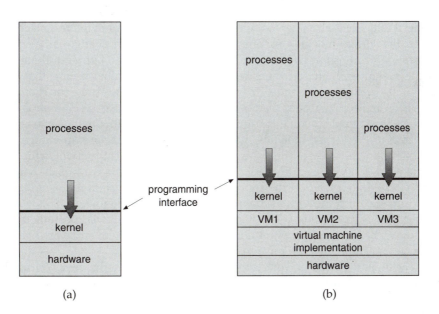

Figure 3.11   System models. (a) Nonvirtual machine. (b) Virtual machine.

Users thus are given their own virtual machines. They can then run any of the operating systems or software packages that are available on the underlying machine. For the IBM VM system, a user normally runs CMS— a single-user interactive operating system. The virtual-machine software is concerned with multiprogramming multiple virtual machines onto a physical machine, but does not need to consider any user-support software. This arrangement may provide a useful partitioning into two smaller pieces of the problem of designing a multiuser interactive system.

3.6.1 Implementation

Although the virtual-machine concept is useful, it is difficult to implement. Much work is required to provide an *exact* duplicate of the underlying machine. Remember that the underlying machine has two modes: user mode and monitor mode. The virtual-machine software can run in monitor mode, since it is the operating system. The virtual machine itself can execute in only user mode. Just as the physical machine has two modes, however, so must the virtual machine. Consequently, we must have a virtual user mode and a virtual monitor mode, both of which run in a physical user mode. Those actions that cause a transfer from user mode to monitor mode on a real machine (such as a system call or an attempt to execute a privileged instruction) must also cause a transfer from virtual user mode to virtual monitor mode on a virtual machine.

This transfer can generally be done fairly easily. When a system call, for example, is made by a program running on a virtual machine, in virtual user mode, it will cause a transfer to the virtual-machine monitor in the real machine. When the virtual-machine monitor gains control, it can change the register contents and program counter for the virtual machine to simulate the effect of the system call. It can then restart the virtual machine, noting that it is now in virtual monitor mode. If the virtual machine then tries, for example, to read from its virtual card reader, it will execute a privileged I/O instruction. Because the virtual machine is running in physical user mode, this instruction will trap to the virtual-machine monitor. The virtual-machine monitor must then simulate the effect of the I/O instruction. First, it finds the spooled file that implements the virtual card reader. Then, it translates the read of the virtual card reader into a read on the spooled disk file, and transfers the next virtual "card image" into the virtual memory of the virtual machine. Finally, it can restart the virtual machine. The state of the virtual machine has been modified exactly as though the I/O instruction had been executed with a real card reader for a real machine executing in a real monitor mode.

The major difference, of course, is time. Whereas the real I/O might have taken 100 milliseconds, the virtual I/O might take less time (because it is spooled) or more time (because it is interpreted). In addition, the CPU is being multiprogrammed among many virtual machines, further slowing down the virtual machines in unpredictable ways. In the extreme case, it may be necessary to simulate all instructions to provide a true virtual machine. VM works for IBM machines because normal instructions for the virtual machines can execute directly on the hardware. Only the privileged instructions (needed mainly for I/O) must be simulated and hence execute more slowly.

3.6.2 Benefits

The virtual-machine concept has several advantages. Notice that, in this environment, there is complete protection of the various system resources. Each virtual machine is completely isolated from all other virtual machines, so there are no security problems. On the other hand, there is no direct sharing of resources. Two approaches to provide sharing have been implemented. First, it is possible to share a minidisk. This scheme is modeled after a physical shared disk, but is implemented by software. With this technique, files can be shared. Second, it is possible to define a network of virtual machines, each of which can send information over the virtual communications network. Again, the network is modeled after physical communication networks, but is implemented in software.

Such a virtual-machine system is a perfect vehicle for operating-systems research and development. Normally, changing an operating system is a difficult task. Because operating systems are large and complex programs, it is difficult to be sure that a change in one part will not cause obscure bugs in some other part. This situation can be particularly dangerous because of the power of the operating system. Because the operating system executes in monitor mode, a wrong change in a pointer could cause an error that would destroy the entire file system. Thus, it is necessary to test all changes to the operating system carefully.

The operating system, however, runs on and controls the entire machine. Therefore, the current system must be stopped and taken out of use while changes are made and tested. This period is commonly called *system-development time*. Since it makes the system unavailable to users, system-development time is often scheduled late at night or on weekends, when system load is low.

A virtual-machine system can eliminate much of this problem. System programmers are given their own virtual machine, and system development is done on the virtual machine, instead of on a physical machine. Normal system operation seldom needs to be disrupted for system development.

Despite these advantages, little improvement on the technique had been made until recently. Virtual machines are coming back into fashion as a means of solving system compatibility problems. For instance, there are thousands of programs available for MS-DOS on Intel CPU-based systems. Computer vendors such as Sun Microsystems and Digital Equipment Corporation (DEC) use other, faster processors, but would like their customers to be able to run these MS-DOS programs. The solution is to create a virtual Intel machine on top of the native processor. An MS-DOS program is run in this environment, and its Intel instructions are translated into the native instruction set. MS-DOS is also run in this virtual machine, so the program can make its system calls as usual. The net result is a program that appears to be running on an Intel-based system but is really executing on a different processor. If the processor is sufficiently fast, the MS-DOS program will run quickly, even though every instruction is being translated into several native instructions for execution. Similarly, the PowerPC-based Apple Macintosh includes a Motorola 68000 virtual machine to allow execution of binary codes that were written for the older 68000-based Macintosh. Unfortunately, the more complex the machine being emulated, the more difficult it is to build an accurate virtual machine and the slower that virtual machine runs. One of the key features of the Java platform is that it runs on a virtual machine. We discuss Java and the Java virtual machine in the following section.

3.7 ■ Java

Java is a technology introduced by Sun Microsystems in late 1995. We refer to it as a *technology* rather than just a programming language because it provides more than a conventional programming language. Java technology consists of three essential components:

1. Programming-language specification

2. Application-programming interface (API)

3. Virtual-machine specification

We shall provide an overview of these three components.

3.7.1 Programming Language

The Java language can best be characterized as an object-oriented, architecture-neutral, distributed, and multithreaded programming language. Java objects are specified with the `class` construct; a Java program consists of one or more classes. For each Java class, the Java compiler produces an architecture-neutral *bytecode* output (`.class`) file that will run on any implementation of the Java virtual machine (JVM). Java was originally favored by the Internet programming community because of its support for **applets,** which are programs with limited resource access that run within a web browser. Java also provides high-level support for networking and distributed objects. It is a multithreaded language, meaning that a Java program may have several different threads, or flows, of control. We cover distributed objects using Java's remote method invocation (RMI) in Chapter 15, and we discuss multithreaded Java programs in Chapter 5.

Java is considered a secure language. This feature is especially important considering that a Java program may be executing across a distributed network. We look at Java security in Chapter 19. Java also automatically manages memory by performing **garbage collection**: the practice of reclaiming memory from objects no longer in use and returning it to the system.

3.7.2 API

The API for Java consists of a base API and a standard extension API. The base API provides basic language support for graphics, I/O, utilities, and networking. Examples of the base API are java.lang, java.awt, java.io, and java.net. The standard extension API includes support for enterprise, commerce, security, and media. As the language evolves, many packages that were once part of the standard extension API are becoming part of the base API.

3.7.3 Virtual Machine

The JVM is a specification for an abstract computer. The JVM consists of a **class loader** and a Java interpreter that executes the architecture-neutral bytecodes. The class loader loads .class files from both the Java program and the Java API for execution by the Java interpreter. The Java interpreter may be a software interpreter that interprets the bytecodes one at a time, or it may be a **just-in-time (JIT)** compiler that turns the architecture–neutral bytecodes into native machine language for the host computer. In other instances, the interpreter may be implemented in a hardware chip that executes Java bytecodes natively. The JVM is presented in Figure 3.12.

The **Java platform** consists of the JVM and Java API; it is displayed in Figure 3.13. The Java platform may be implemented on top of a host operating system, such as UNIX or Windows; as part of a web browser; or in hardware.

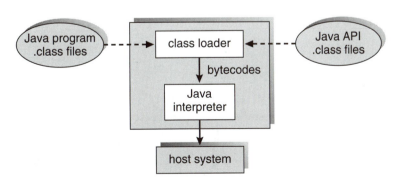

Figure 3.12   The Java virtual machine.

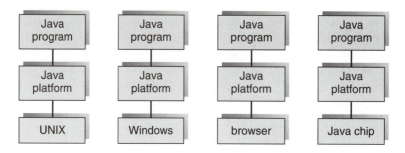

Figure 3.13   The Java platform.

An instance of the JVM is created whenever a Java application or applet is run. This instance of the JVM starts running when the main() method of a program is invoked. This is also true for applets even though the programmer does not define a main(). In this case, the browser executes the main() method before creating the applet. If we simultaneously run two Java programs and a Java applet on the same computer, we will have three instances of the JVM.

It is the Java platform that makes it possible to develop programs that are architecture neutral and portable. The platform implementation is system specific, and it abstracts the system in a standard way to the Java program, providing a clean, architecture-neutral interface. This interface allows a .class file to run on any system that has implemented the JVM and API; it is shown in Figure 3.14. Implementing the Java platform consists of developing a JVM and Java API for a specific system (such as Windows or UNIX) according to the specification for the JVM.

We use the JVM throughout this text to illustrate operating-system concepts. We refer to the specification of the JVM, rather than to any particular implementation.

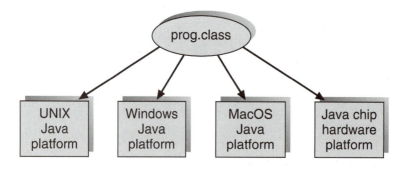

Figure 3.14   Java .class file on cross platforms.

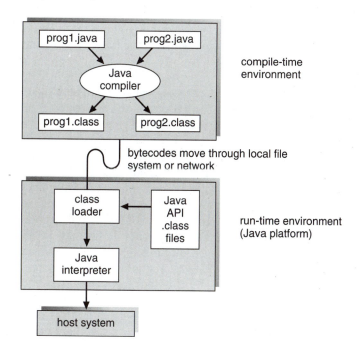

Figure 3.15   Java development environment.

3.7.4 Java Development Environment

The Java development environment consists of a compile-time environment and a run-time environment. The compile-time environment turns a Java source file into a bytecode (.class file). The Java source file may be either a Java program or applet. The run-time environment is the Java platform for the host system. The development environment is portrayed in Figure 3.15.

3.8 ■ System Design and Implementation

In this section, we discuss problems we face when designing and implementing a system. There are, of course, no complete solutions to the design problems, but there are approaches that have been successful.

3.8.1 Design Goals

The first problem in designing a system is to define the goals and specifications of the system. At the highest level, the design of the system will be affected by the choice of hardware and type of system: batch, time shared, single user, multiuser, distributed, real time, or general purpose.

Beyond this highest design level, the requirements may be much harder to specify. The requirements can be divided into two basic groups: *user* goals and *system* goals.

Users desire certain obvious properties in a system: The system should be convenient to use, easy to learn, easy to use, reliable, safe, and fast. Of course, these specifications are not particularly useful in the system design, since there is no general agreement on how to achieve these goals.

A similar set of requirements can be defined by those people who must design, create, maintain, and operate the system: The operating system should be easy to design, implement, and maintain; it should be flexible, reliable, error free, and efficient. Again, these requirements are vague and have no general solution.

There is no unique solution to the problem of defining the requirements for an operating system. The wide range of systems shows that different requirements can result in a large variety of solutions for different environments. For example, the requirements for MS-DOS, a single-user system for microcomputers, must have been substantially different from those for MVS, the large multiuser, multiaccess operating system for IBM mainframes.

The specification and design of an operating system is a highly creative task. Although no textbook can tell you how to do it, there do exist general principles, developed by the field of **software engineering**, that are especially applicable to operating systems.

3.8.2 Mechanisms and Policies

One important principle is the separation of **policy** from **mechanism**. Mechanisms determine *how* to do something; policies determine *what* will be done. For example, the timer construct (see Section 2.5) is a mechanism for ensuring CPU protection, but deciding how long the timer is to be set for a particular user is a policy decision.

The separation of policy and mechanism is important for flexibility. Policies are likely to change across places or over time. In the worst case, each change in policy would require a change in the underlying mechanism. A general mechanism would be more desirable. A change in policy would then require redefinition of only certain parameters of the system. For instance, if, in one computer system, a policy decision is made that I/O-intensive programs should have priority over CPU-intensive ones, then the opposite policy could be instituted easily on some other computer system if the mechanism were properly separated and were policy independent.

Microkernel-based operating systems take the separation of mechanism and policy to one extreme, by implementing a basic set of primitive building blocks. These blocks are almost policy free, allowing more advanced mechanisms and policies to be added via user-created kernel modules, or via user programs themselves. At the other extreme is a system such as the Apple Macintosh operating system, in which both mechanism and policy are encoded in the system to enforce a global look and feel to the system. All applications have similar interfaces, because the interface itself is built into the kernel.

Policy decisions are important for all resource-allocation and scheduling problems. Whenever it is necessary to decide whether or not to allocate a resource, a policy decision must be made. Whenever the question is *how* rather than *what*, it is a mechanism that must be determined.

3.8.3 Implementation

Once an operating system is designed, it must be implemented. Traditionally, operating systems have been written in assembly language. Now, however, they often are written in higher-level languages. For instance, an implementation of the JVM was written in Java at Sun Microsystems.

The first system that was not written in assembly language was probably the Master Control Program (MCP) for Burroughs computers. MCP was written in a variant of ALGOL. MULTICS, developed at MIT, was written mainly in PL/1. The Primos operating system for Prime computers is written in a dialect of Fortran. The UNIX operating system, OS/2, and Windows NT are mainly written in C. Only some 900 lines of code of the original UNIX were in assembly language, most of which constituted the scheduler and device drivers.

The advantages of using a higher-level language, or at least a systems-implementation language, for implementing operating systems are the same as those accrued when the language is used for application programs: The code can be written faster, is more compact, and is easier to understand and debug. In addition, improvements in compiler technology will improve the generated code for the entire operating system by simple recompilation. Finally, an operating system is far easier to *port*—to move to some other hardware—if it is written in a high-level language. For example, MS-DOS was written in Intel 8088 assembly language. Consequently, it is available on only the Intel family of CPUs. The UNIX operating system, on the other hand, which is written mostly in C, is available on a number of different CPUs, including Intel 80X86, Motorola 680X0, SPARC, and MIPS RX000.

The major claimed disadvantages of implementing an operating system in a higher-level language are reduced speed and increased storage requirements. Although an expert assembly-language programmer can produce efficient small routines, for large programs a modern compiler can perform complex analysis and apply sophisticated optimizations that produce excellent code. Modern processors have deep pipelining and multiple functional units, which can handle complex dependencies that can overwhelm the limited ability of the human mind to keep track of details.

As is true in other systems, major performance improvements in operating systems are more likely to be the result of better data structures and algorithms than of excellent assembly-language code. In addition, although operating systems are large, only a small amount of the code is critical to high performance;

the memory manager and the CPU scheduler are probably the most critical routines. After the system is written and is working correctly, bottleneck routines can be identified, and can be replaced with assembly-language equivalents.

To identify bottlenecks, we must be able to monitor system performance. Code must be added to compute and display measures of system behavior. In a number of systems, the operating system does this task by producing trace listings of system behavior. All interesting events are logged with their time and important parameters, and are written to a file. Later, an analysis program can process the log file to determine system performance and to identify bottlenecks and inefficiencies. These same traces can be run as input for a simulation of a suggested improved system. Traces also can help people to find errors in operating-system behavior.

An alternative is to compute and display the performance measures in real time. For example, a timer can trigger a routine to store the current instruction pointer value. The result is a statistical picture of the program locations most frequently used within the program. This approach may allow system operators to become familiar with system behavior and to modify system operation in real time.

3.9 ■ System Generation

It is possible to design, code, and implement an operating system specifically for one machine at one site. More commonly, however, operating systems are designed to run on any of a class of machines at a variety of sites with a variety of peripheral configurations. The system must then be configured or generated for each specific computer site, a process sometimes known as **system generation (SYSGEN)**.

The operating system is normally distributed on disk or tape. To generate a system, we use a special program. The SYSGEN program reads from a given file or asks the operator of the system for information concerning the specific configuration of the hardware system, or probes the hardware directly to determine what components are there. The following kinds of information must be determined.

- What CPU is to be used? What options (extended instruction sets, floating-point arithmetic, and so on) are installed? For multiple CPU systems, each CPU must be described.

- How much memory is available? Some systems will determine this value themselves by referencing memory location after memory location until an "illegal address" fault is generated. This procedure defines the final legal address and hence the amount of available memory.

- What devices are available? The system will need to know how to address each device (the device number), the device interrupt number, the device's type and model, and any special device characteristics.

- What operating-system options are desired, or what parameter values are to be used? These options or values might include how many buffers of which sizes should be used, what type of CPU-scheduling algorithm is desired, what the maximum number of processes to be supported is, and so on.

Once this information is determined, it can be used in several ways. At one extreme, a system administrator can use it to modify a copy of the source code of the operating system. The operating system then is completely compiled. Data declarations, initializations, and constants, along with conditional compilation, produce an output object version of the operating system that is tailored to the system described.

At a slightly less tailored level, the system description can cause the creation of tables and the selection of modules from a precompiled library. These modules are linked together to form the generated operating system. Selection allows the library to contain the device drivers for all supported I/O devices, but only those needed are linked into the operating system. Because the system is not recompiled, system generation is faster, but the resulting system may be overly general.

At the other extreme, it is possible to construct a system that is completely table driven. All the code is always part of the system, and selection occurs at execution time, rather than at compile or link time. System generation involves simply creating the appropriate tables to describe the system.

The major differences among these approaches are the size and generality of the generated system and the ease of modification as the hardware configuration changes. Consider the cost of modifying the system to support a newly acquired graphics terminal or another disk drive. Balanced against that cost, of course, is the frequency (or infrequency) of such changes.

After an operating system is generated, it must be made available for use by the hardware. But how does the hardware know where the kernel is, or how to load that kernel? The procedure of starting a computer by loading the kernel is known as *booting* the system. On most computer systems, there is a small piece of code, stored in ROM, known as the *bootstrap program* or *bootstrap loader*. This code is able to locate the kernel, load it into main memory, and start its execution. Some computer systems, such as PCs, use a two-step process in which a simple bootstrap loader fetches a more complex boot program from disk, which in turn loads the kernel. Booting a system is discussed in Section 13.3.2 and in Chapter 20.

3.10 ■ Summary

Operating systems provide a number of services. At the lowest level, system calls allow a running program to make requests from the operating system directly. At a higher level, the command interpreter or shell provides a mechanism for a user to issue a request without writing a program. Commands may come from files during batch-mode execution, or directly from a terminal when in an interactive or time-shared mode. System programs are provided to satisfy many common user requests.

The types of requests vary according to the level of the request. The system-call level must provide the basic functions, such as process control and file and device manipulation. Higher-level requests, satisfied by the command interpreter or system programs, are translated into a sequence of system calls. System services can be classified into several categories: program control, status requests, and I/O requests. Program errors can be considered implicit requests for service.

Once the system services are defined, the structure of the operating system can be developed. Various tables are needed to record the information that defines the state of the computer system and the status of the system's jobs.

The design of a new operating system is a major task. It is important that the goals of the system be well defined before the design begins. The type of system desired is the foundation for choices among various algorithms and strategies that will be necessary.

Since an operating system is large, modularity is important. Designing a system as a sequence of layers or using a microkernel is considered a good technique. The virtual-machine concept takes the layered approach and treats both the kernel of the operating system and the hardware as though they were all hardware. Even other operating systems may be loaded on top of this virtual machine.

Any operating system that has implemented the JVM is able to run all Java programs, because the JVM abstracts the underlying system to the Java program, providing an architecture-neutral interface.

Throughout the entire operating-system design cycle, we must be careful to separate policy decisions from implementation details (mechanisms). This separation allows maximum flexibility if policy decisions are to be changed later.

Operating systems are now almost always written in a systems-implementation language or in a higher-level language. This feature improves their implementation, maintenance, and portability. To create an operating system for a particular machine configuration, we must perform system generation.

■ Exercises

3.1 What are the five major activities of an operating system in regard to process management?

3.2 What are the three major activities of an operating system in regard to memory management?

3.3 What are the three major activities of an operating system in regard to secondary-storage management?

3.4 What are the five major activities of an operating system in regard to file management?

3.5 What is the purpose of the command interpreter? Why is it usually separate from the kernel?

3.6 List five services provided by an operating system. Explain how each provides convenience to the users. Explain in which cases it would be impossible for user-level programs to provide these services.

3.7 What is the purpose of system calls?

3.8 Using system calls, write a program in either C or C++ that reads data from one file and copies it to another file. Such a program was described in Section 3.3.

3.9 Why does Java provide the ability to call from a Java program native methods that are written in, say, C or C++? Provide an example where a native method is useful.

3.10 What is the purpose of system programs?

3.11 What is the main advantage of the layered approach to system design?

3.12 What is the main advantage of the microkernel approach to system design?

3.13 What is the main advantage for an operating-system designer of using a virtual-machine architecture? What is the main advantage for a user?

3.14 Why is a just-in-time compiler useful for executing Java programs?

3.15 Why is the separation of mechanism and policy a desirable property?

3.16 The experimental Synthesis operating system has an assembler incorporated within the kernel. To optimize system-call performance, the kernel assembles routines within kernel space to minimize the path that the system call must take through the kernel. This approach is the antithesis of the layered approach, in which the path through the kernel is extended so that building the operating system is made easier. Discuss the pros and cons of the Synthesis approach to kernel design and to system-performance optimization.

Bibliographical Notes

Dijkstra [1968] advocated the layered approach to operating-system design. Brinch Hansen [1970] was an early proponent of the construction of an operating system as a kernel (or nucleus) on which can be built more complete systems.

The first operating system to provide a virtual machine was the CP/67 on an IBM 360/67. The commercially available IBM VM/370 operating system was derived from CP/67. General discussions concerning virtual machines have been presented by Hendricks and Hartmann [1979], by MacKinnon [1979], and by Schultz [1988]. Cheung and Loong [1995] explored issues of operating systems structuring from microkernel to extensible systems.

MS-DOS, Version 3.1, is described in [Microsoft 1986]. Windows NT is described by Solomon [1998]. The Apple Macintosh operating system is described in [Apple 1987]. Berkeley UNIX is described in [CSRG 1986]. The standard AT&T UNIX system V is described in [AT&T 1986]. A good description of OS/2 is given by Iacobucci [1988]. Mach is introduced by Accetta and colleagues [1986], and AIX is presented by Loucks and Sauer [1987]. The experimental Synthesis operating system is discussed by Massalin and Pu [1989].

The specification for the Java language and the Java virtual machine is presented by Gosling and colleagues [1996] and by Lindholm and Yellin [1998], respectively. The internal workings of the Java virtual machine are described by Venners [1998] and by Meyer and Downing [1997]. There are several good general-purpose books on programming in Java [Flanagan 1997, Horstmann and Cornell 1998a, Niemeyer and Peck 1997]. More information on Java is available on the Web at http://www.javasoft.com.

Part Two

PROCESS MANAGEMENT

A *process* can be thought of as a program in execution. A process needs resources—such as CPU time, memory, files, and I/O devices—to accomplish its task. These resources are allocated either when the process is created or while it is executing.

A process is the unit of work in most systems. Such a system consists of a collection of processes: Operating-system processes execute system code, and user processes execute user code. All these processes can potentially execute concurrently.

The operating system is responsible for the following activities in connection with process management: the creation and deletion of both user and system processes; the scheduling of processes; and the provision of mechanisms for synchronization, communication, and deadlock handling for processes.

Although traditionally a process contained a single *thread* of control as it ran, most modern operating systems now support processes that have multiple threads.

Chapter 4

PROCESSES

Early computer systems allowed only one program to be executed at a time. This program had complete control of the system, and had access to all the system's resources. Current-day computer systems allow multiple programs to be loaded into memory and to be executed concurrently. This evolution required firmer control and more compartmentalization of the various programs. These needs resulted in the notion of a **process,** which is a program in execution. A process is the unit of work in a modern time-sharing system.

The more complex the operating system is, the more it is expected to do on behalf of its users. Although its main concern is the execution of user programs, it also needs to take care of various system tasks that are better left outside the kernel itself. A system therefore consists of a collection of processes: Operating-system processes executing system code, and user processes executing user code. All these processes can potentially execute concurrently, with the CPU (or CPUs) multiplexed among them. By switching the CPU between processes, the operating system can make the computer more productive.

4.1 ■ Process Concept

One hindrance to our discussion of operating systems is that there is a question of what to call all the CPU activities. A batch system executes *jobs*, whereas a time-shared system has *user programs*, or *tasks*. Even on a single-user system, such as Microsoft Windows and Macintosh OS, a user may be able to run several programs at one time: a word processor, web browser, and e-mail package.

Even if the user can execute only one program at a time, the operating system may need to support its own internal programmed activities, such as memory management. In many respects, all these activities are similar, so we call all of them *processes.*

The terms *job* and *process* are used almost interchangeably in this text. Although we personally prefer the term *process,* much of operating-system theory and terminology was developed during a time when the major activity of operating systems was job processing. It would be misleading to avoid the use of commonly accepted terms that include the word *job* (such as *job scheduling*) simply because *process* has superseded *job.*

4.1.1 The Process

Informally, a process is a program in execution. A process is more than the program code, which is sometimes known as the **text section**. It also includes the current activity, as represented by the value of the **program counter** and the contents of the processor's registers. A process generally also includes the process **stack,** which contains temporary data (such as method parameters, return addresses, and local variables), and a **data section,** which contains global variables.

We emphasize that a program by itself is not a process; a program is a *passive* entity, such as the contents of a file stored on disk, whereas a process is an *active* entity, with a program counter specifying the next instruction to execute and a set of associated resources.

Although two processes may be associated with the same program, they are nevertheless considered two separate execution sequences. For instance, several users may be running different copies of the mail program, or the same user may invoke many copies of the editor program. Each of these is a separate process, and, although the text sections are equivalent, the data sections vary. It is also common to have a process that spawns many processes as it runs. We discuss such matters in Section 4.4.

4.1.2 Process State

As a process executes, it changes **state**. The state of a process is defined in part by the current activity of that process. Each process may be in one of the following states:

- **New:** The process is being created.

- **Running:** Instructions are being executed.

- **Waiting:** The process is waiting for some event to occur (such as an I/O completion or reception of a signal).

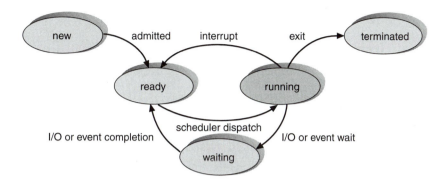

Figure 4.1   Diagram of process state.

- **Ready:** The process is waiting to be assigned to a processor.

- **Terminated:** The process has finished execution.

These names are arbitrary, and they vary across operating systems. The states that they represent are found on all systems, however. Certain operating systems also more finely delineate process states. It is important to realize that only one process can be *running* on any processor at any instant. Many processes may be *ready* and *waiting,* however. The state diagram corresponding to these states is presented in Figure 4.1.

4.1.3 Process Control Block

Each process is represented in the operating system by a **process control block** (**PCB**)—also called a task control block. A PCB is shown in Figure 4.2. It contains many pieces of information associated with a specific process, including these:

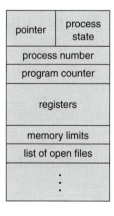

Figure 4.2   Process control block (PCB).

- *Process state:* The state may be new, ready, running, waiting, halted, and so on.

- *Program counter:* The counter indicates the address of the next instruction to be executed for this process.

- *CPU registers:* The registers vary in number and type, depending on the computer architecture. They include accumulators, index registers, stack pointers, and general-purpose registers, plus any condition-code information. Along with the program counter, this state information must be saved when an interrupt occurs, to allow the process to be continued correctly afterward (Figure 4.3).

- *CPU-scheduling information:* This information includes a process priority, pointers to scheduling queues, and any other scheduling parameters. (Chapter 6 describes process scheduling.)

- *Memory-management information:* This information may include such information as the value of the base and limit registers, the page tables, or the segment tables depending on the memory system used by the operating system (Chapter 9).

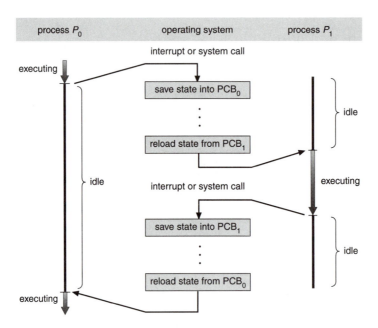

Figure 4.3   Diagram showing CPU switch from process to process.

- *Accounting information:* This information includes the amount of CPU and real time used, time limits, account numbers, job or process numbers, and so on.

- *I/O status information:* The information includes the list of I/O devices allocated to this process, a list of open files, and so on.

The PCB simply serves as the repository for any information that may vary from process to process.

4.1.4 Threads

The process model discussed so far has implied that a process is a program that performs a single **thread** of execution. For example, if a process is running a word processor program, there is a single thread of instructions being executed. This single thread of control only allows the process to perform one task at one time. The user could not simultaneously type in characters and run the spell checker within the same process. Many modern operating systems have extended the process concept to allow a process to have multiple threads of execution. They thus allow the process to perform more than one task at a time. Chapter 5 explores multithreaded processes.

4.2 ▪ Process Scheduling

The objective of multiprogramming is to have some process running at all times, to maximize CPU utilization. The objective of time sharing is to switch the CPU among processes so frequently that users can interact with each program while it is running. For a uniprocessor system, there will never be more than one running process. If there are more processes, the rest will have to wait until the CPU is free and can be rescheduled.

4.2.1 Scheduling Queues

As processes enter the system, they are put into a **job queue.** This queue consists of all processes in the system. The processes that are residing in main memory and are ready and waiting to execute are kept on a list called the **ready queue.** This queue is generally stored as a linked list. A ready-queue header contains pointers to the first and final PCBs in the list. We extend each PCB to include a pointer field that points to the next PCB in the ready queue.

There are also other queues in the system. When a process is allocated the CPU, it executes for a while and eventually quits, is interrupted, or waits for the occurrence of a particular event, such as the completion of an I/O request. In the case of an I/O request, such a request may be to a dedicated tape drive, or to a shared device, such as a disk. Since there are many processes in the

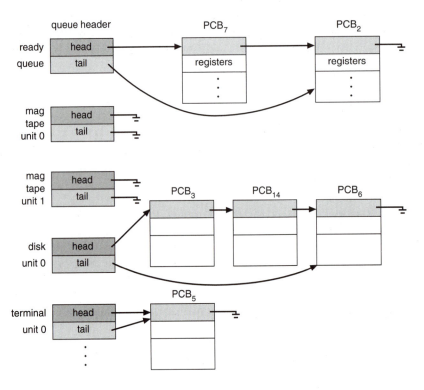

Figure 4.4   The ready queue and various I/O device queues.

system, the disk may be busy with the I/O request of some other process. The process therefore may have to wait for the disk. The list of processes waiting for a particular I/O device is called a **device queue**. Each device has its own device queue (Figure 4.4).

A common representation for a discussion of process scheduling is a **queueing diagram,** such as that in Figure 4.5. Each rectangular box represents a queue. Two types of queues are present: the ready queue and a set of device queues. The circles represent the resources that serve the queues, and the arrows indicate the flow of processes in the system.

A new process is initially put in the ready queue. It waits in the ready queue until it is selected for execution or is **dispatched**. Once the process is allocated the CPU and is executing, one of several events could occur:

- The process could issue an I/O request, and then be placed in an I/O queue.

- The process could create a new subprocess and wait for its termination.

- The process could be removed forcibly from the CPU, as a result of an interrupt, and be put back in the ready queue.

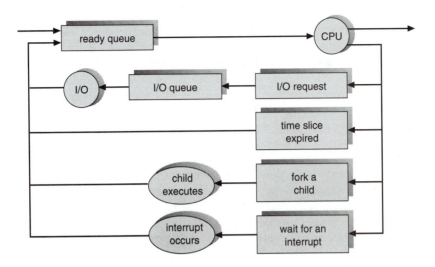

Figure 4.5   Queueing-diagram representation of process scheduling.

In the first two cases, the process eventually switches from the waiting state to the ready state, and is then put back in the ready queue. A process continues this cycle until it terminates, at which time it is removed from all queues and has its PCB and resources deallocated.

4.2.2 Schedulers

A process migrates between the various scheduling queues throughout its lifetime. The operating system must select, for scheduling purposes, processes from these queues in some fashion. The selection process is carried out by the appropriate **scheduler**.

In a batch system, there are often more processes submitted than can be executed immediately. These processes are spooled to a mass-storage device (typically a disk), where they are kept for later execution. The **long-term scheduler,** or **job scheduler,** selects processes from this pool and loads them into memory for execution. The **short-term scheduler,** or **CPU scheduler,** selects from among the processes that are ready to execute, and allocates the CPU to one of them.

The primary distinction between these two schedulers is the frequency of their execution. The short-term scheduler must select a new process for the CPU frequently. A process may execute for only a few milliseconds before waiting for an I/O request. Often, the short-term scheduler executes at least once every 100 milliseconds. Because of the short duration of time between executions, the short-term scheduler must be fast. If it takes 10 milliseconds to decide to execute a process for 100 milliseconds, then $10/(100 + 10) = 9$ percent of the CPU is being used (wasted) simply for scheduling the work.

The long-term scheduler, on the other hand, executes much less frequently. There may be minutes between the creation of new processes in the system. The long-term scheduler controls the **degree of multiprogramming** (the number of processes in memory). If the degree of multiprogramming is stable, then the average rate of process creation must be equal to the average departure rate of processes leaving the system. Thus, the long-term scheduler may need to be invoked only when a process leaves the system. Because of the longer interval between executions, the long-term scheduler can afford to take more time to decide which process should be selected for execution.

It is important that the long-term scheduler make a careful selection. In general, most processes can be described as either I/O bound or CPU bound. An **I/O-bound process** is one that spends more of its time doing I/O than it spends doing computations. A **CPU-bound process,** on the other hand, is one that generates I/O requests infrequently, using more of its time doing computation than an I/O-bound process uses. It is important that the long-term scheduler select a good **process mix** of I/O-bound and CPU-bound processes. If all processes are I/O bound, the ready queue will almost always be empty, and the short-term scheduler will have little to do. If all processes are CPU bound, the I/O waiting queue will almost always be empty, devices will go unused, and again the system will be unbalanced. The system with the best performance will have a combination of CPU-bound and I/O-bound processes.

On some systems, the long-term scheduler may be absent or minimal. For example, time-sharing systems such as UNIX often have no long-term scheduler, but simply put every new process in memory for the short-term scheduler. The stability of these systems depends either on a physical limitation (such as the number of available terminals) or on the self-adjusting nature of human users. If the performance declines to unacceptable levels, some users will simply quit.

Some operating systems, such as time-sharing systems, may introduce an additional, intermediate level of scheduling. This **medium-term scheduler** is diagrammed in Figure 4.6. The key idea behind a medium-term scheduler is that sometimes it can be advantageous to remove processes from memory

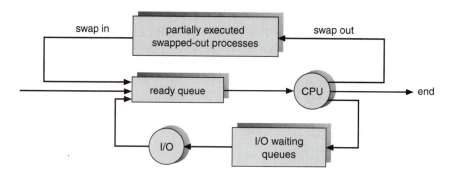

Figure 4.6   Addition of medium-term scheduling to the queueing diagram.

(and from active contention for the CPU), and thus to reduce the degree of multiprogramming. At some later time, the process can be reintroduced into memory and its execution can be continued where it left off. This scheme is called **swapping**. The process is swapped out, and is later swapped in, by the medium-term scheduler. Swapping may be necessary to improve the process mix, or because a change in memory requirements has overcommitted available memory, requiring memory to be freed up. Swapping is discussed in Chapter 9.

4.2.3 Context Switch

Switching the CPU to another process requires saving the state of the old process and loading the saved state for the new process. This task is known as a **context switch**. The **context** of a process is represented in the PCB of a process; it includes the value of the CPU registers, the process state (see Figure 4.1), and memory-management information. When a context switch occurs, the kernel saves the context of the old process in its PCB and loads the saved context of the new process scheduled to run. Context-switch time is pure overhead, because the system does no useful work while switching. Its speed varies from machine to machine, depending on the memory speed, the number of registers that must be copied, and the existence of special instructions (such as a single instruction to load or store all registers). Typical speeds range from 1 to 1000 microseconds.

Context-switch times are highly dependent on hardware support. For instance, some processors (such as the Sun UltraSPARC) provide multiple sets of registers. A context switch simply includes changing the pointer to the current register set. Of course, if there are more active processes than there are register sets, the system resorts to copying register data to and from memory, as before. Also, the more complex the operating system, the more work must be done during a context switch. As we will see in Chapter 9, advanced memory-management techniques may require extra data to be switched with each context. For instance, the address space of the current process must be preserved as the space of the next task is prepared for use. How the address space is preserved, and what amount of work is needed to preserve it, depend on the memory-management method of the operating system. As we will see in Chapter 5, context switching has become such a performance bottleneck that programmers are using new structures (threads) to avoid it whenever possible.

4.3 ■ Operations on Processes

The processes in the system can execute concurrently, and they must be created and deleted dynamically. Thus, the operating system must provide a mechanism for process creation and termination.

4.3.1 Process Creation

A process may create several new processes, via a create-process system call, during the course of execution. The creating process is called a **parent** process, whereas the new processes are called the **children** of that process. Each of these new processes may in turn create other processes, forming a **tree** of processes (Figure 4.7).

In general, a process will need certain resources (CPU time, memory, files, I/O devices) to accomplish its task. When a process creates a subprocess, that subprocess may be able to obtain its resources directly from the operating system, or it may be constrained to a subset of the resources of the parent process. The parent may have to partition its resources among its children, or it may be able to share some resources (such as memory or files) among several of its children. Restricting a child process to a subset of the parent's resources prevents any process from overloading the system by creating too many subprocesses.

In addition to the various physical and logical resources that a process obtains when it is created, initialization data (input) may be passed along by the parent process to the child process. For example, consider a process whose function is to display the status of a file, say *F1*, on the screen of a terminal. When it is created, it will get, as an input from its parent process, the name of the file *F1*, and it will execute using that datum to obtain the desired information. It may also get the name of the output device. Some operating systems pass

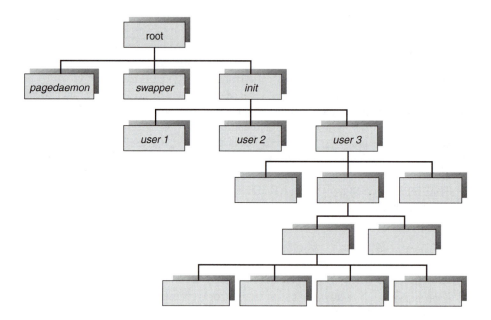

Figure 4.7   A tree of processes on a typical UNIX system.

resources to child processes. On such a system, the new process may get two open files, *F1* and the terminal device, and may just need to transfer the datum between the two.

When a process creates a new process, two possibilities exist in terms of execution:

1. The parent continues to execute concurrently with its children.

2. The parent waits until some or all of its children have terminated.

There are also two possibilities in terms of the address space of the new process:

1. The child process is a duplicate of the parent process.

2. The child process has a program loaded into it.

To illustrate these different implementations, let us consider the UNIX operating system. In UNIX, each process is identified by its **process identifier,** which is a unique integer. A new process is created by the fork system call. The new process consists of a copy of the address space of the original process. This mechanism allows the parent process to communicate easily with its child process. Both processes (the parent and the child) continue execution at the instruction after the fork with one difference: The return code for the fork is zero for the new (child) process, whereas the (nonzero) process identifier of the child is returned to the parent.

Typically, the execlp system call is used after a fork system call by one of the two processes to replace the process' memory space with a new program. The execlp system call loads a binary file into memory (destroying the memory image of the program containing the execlp system call) and starts its execution. In this manner, the two processes are able to communicate, and then to go their separate ways. The parent can then create more children, or, if it has nothing else to do while the child runs, it can issue a wait system call to move itself off the ready queue until the termination of the child. The C program shown in Figure 4.8 illustrates the UNIX system calls previously described. The parent creates a child process using the fork() system call. We now have two different processes running a copy of the same program. The value of *pid* for the child process is zero; that for the parent is an integer value greater than zero. The child process overlays its address space with the UNIX command /bin/ls (used to get a directory listing) using the execlp() system call. The parent waits for the child process to complete with the wait() system call. When the child process completes, the parent process resumes from the call to wait() where it completes using the exit() system call.

The DEC VMS operating system, in contrast, creates a new process, loads a specified program into that process, and starts it running. The Microsoft Windows NT operating system supports both models: The parent's address

```
#include <stdio.h>

void main(int argc, char *argv[])
{
int pid;

    /* fork another process */
    pid = fork();

    if (pid < 0) { /* error occurred */
        fprintf(stderr, "Fork Failed");
        exit(-1);
    }
    else if (pid == 0) { /* child process */
        execlp("/bin/ls","ls",NULL);
    }
    else { /* parent process */
        /* parent will wait for the child to complete */
        wait(NULL);
        printf("Child Complete");
        exit(0);
    }
}
```

Figure 4.8   C program forking a separate process.

space may be duplicated, or the parent may specify the name of a program for the operating system to load into the address space of the new process.

4.3.2 Process Termination

A process terminates when it finishes executing its final statement and asks the operating system to delete it by using the exit system call. At that point, the process may return data (output) to its parent process (via the wait system call). All the resources of the process—including physical and virtual memory, open files, and I/O buffers—are deallocated by the operating system.

There are additional circumstances when termination occurs. A process can cause the termination of another process via an appropriate system call (for example, abort). Usually, such a system call can be invoked by only the parent of the process that is to be terminated. Otherwise, users could arbitrarily kill each other's jobs. Note that a parent needs to know the identities of its children. Thus, when one process creates a new process, the identity of the newly created process is passed to the parent.

A parent may terminate the execution of one of its children for a variety of reasons, such as these:

- The child has exceeded its usage of some of the resources that it has been allocated.

- The task assigned to the child is no longer required.

- The parent is exiting, and the operating system does not allow a child to continue if its parent terminates.

To determine the first case, the parent must have a mechanism to inspect the state of its children.

Many systems, including VMS, do not allow a child to exist if its parent has terminated. In such systems, if a process terminates (either normally or abnormally), then all its children must also be terminated. This phenomenon, referred to as **cascading termination,** is normally initiated by the operating system.

To illustrate process execution and termination, we consider that, in UNIX, we can terminate a process by using the `exit` system call; its parent process may wait for the termination of a child process by using the `wait` system call. The `wait` system call returns the process identifier of a terminated child, so that the parent can tell which of its possibly many children has terminated. If the parent terminates, however, all its children have assigned as their new parent the *init* process. Thus, the children still have a parent to collect their status and execution statistics.

4.4 ■ Cooperating Processes

The concurrent processes executing in the operating system may be either independent processes or cooperating processes. A process is **independent** if it cannot affect or be affected by the other processes executing in the system. Clearly, any process that does not share any data (temporary or persistent) with any other process is independent. On the other hand, a process is **cooperating** if it can affect or be affected by the other processes executing in the system. Clearly, any process that shares data with other processes is a cooperating process.

There are several reasons for providing an environment that allows process cooperation:

- *Information sharing:* Since several users may be interested in the same piece of information (for instance, a shared file), we must provide an environment to allow concurrent access to these types of resources.

- *Computation speedup:* If we want a particular task to run faster, we must break it into subtasks, each of which will be executing in parallel with the others. Notice that such a speedup can be achieved only if the computer has multiple processing elements (such as CPUs or I/O channels).

- *Modularity:* We may want to construct the system in a modular fashion, dividing the system functions into separate processes or threads, as we discussed in Chapter 3.

- *Convenience:* Even an individual user may have many tasks on which to work at one time. For instance, a user may be editing, printing, and compiling in parallel.

Concurrent execution that requires cooperation among the processes requires mechanisms to allow processes to communicate with one another (Section 4.5), and to synchronize their actions (Chapter 7).

```java
import java.util.*;

public class BoundedBuffer
{
    public BoundedBuffer() {
        // buffer is initially empty
        count = 0;
        in = 0;
        out = 0;

        buffer = new Object[BUFFER_SIZE];
    }

    // producer calls this method
    public void enter(Object item) {
        // Figure 4.10
    }
    // consumer calls this method
    public Object remove() {
        // Figure 4.11
    }

    public static final int NAP_TIME = 5;
    private static final int BUFFER_SIZE = 5;

    private volatile int count;
    private int in; // points to the next free position
    private int out; // points to the next full position
    private Object[] buffer;
}
```

Figure 4.9   Shared-memory solution to the producer–consumer problem.

To illustrate the concept of cooperating processes, let us consider the producer–consumer problem, which is a common paradigm for cooperating processes. A **producer** process produces information that is consumed by a **consumer** process. For example, a print program produces characters that are consumed by the printer driver. A compiler may produce assembly code, which is consumed by an assembler. The assembler, in turn, may produce object modules, which are consumed by the loader.

To allow producer and consumer processes to run concurrently, we must have available a buffer of items that can be filled by the producer and emptied by the consumer. A producer can produce one item while the consumer is consuming another item. The producer and consumer must be synchronized, so that the consumer does not try to consume an item that has not yet been produced. In this situation, the consumer must wait until an item is produced.

The **unbounded-buffer** producer–consumer problem places no practical limit on the size of the buffer. The consumer may have to wait for new items, but the producer can always produce new items. The **bounded-buffer** producer–consumer problem assumes that there is a fixed buffer size. In this case, the consumer must wait if the buffer is empty, and the producer must wait if the buffer is full.

The buffer may be either provided by the operating system through the use of an interprocess-communication (IPC) facility (Section 4.5), or explicitly coded by the application programmer with the use of shared memory. Let us illustrate a shared-memory solution to the bounded-buffer problem. The producer and consumer processes share an instance of the BoundedBuffer class (Figure 4.9).

The shared buffer is implemented as a circular array with two logical pointers: in and out. The variable in points to the next free position in the buffer; out points to the first full position in the buffer. count is the number of items currently in the buffer. The buffer is empty when count == 0 and is full when count == BUFFER_SIZE. The producer process invokes the enter() method (Figure 4.10) when it wishes to enter an item in the buffer, and the consumer calls the remove() method (Figure 4.11) when it wants to consume an item from the buffer. Note that both the producer and the consumer will block in the while loop if the buffer is either full or empty.

In Chapter 7, we discuss how synchronization among cooperating processes can be implemented effectively in a shared-memory environment.

4.5 ■ Interprocess Communication

In Section 4.4, we showed how cooperating processes can communicate in a shared-memory environment. The scheme requires that these processes share a common buffer pool, and that the code for implementing the buffer be written explicitly by the application programmer. Another way to achieve the same effect is for the operating system to provide the means for cooperating processes

```
public void enter(Object item) {
    while (count == BUFFER_SIZE)
        ; // do nothing

    // add an item to the buffer
    ++count;
    buffer[in] = item;
    in = (in + 1) % BUFFER_SIZE;

    if (count == BUFFER_SIZE)
        System.out.println("Producer Entered " +
            item + " Buffer FULL");
    else
        System.out.println("Producer Entered " +
            item + " Buffer Size = " + count);
}
```

Figure 4.10   The `enter()` method.

to communicate with each other via an **interprocess communication** (IPC) facility.

IPC provides a mechanism to allow processes to communicate and to synchronize their actions without sharing the same address space. IPC is particularly useful in a distributed environment where the communicating processes may reside on different computers connected with a network. An example is a **chat** program used on the World Wide Web. In Chapter 15, we look at distributed computing using Java.

IPC is best provided by a message-passing system, and message systems can be defined in many different ways. We look at different design issues and present a Java solution to the producer–consumer problem that uses message passing.

4.5.1 Message-Passing System

The function of a message system is to allow processes to communicate with one another without the need to resort to shared data. An IPC facility provides at least the two operations: `send`(message) and `receive`(message).

Messages sent by a process can be of either fixed or variable size. If only fixed-sized messages can be sent, the system-level implementation is straightforward. This restriction, however, makes the task of programming more difficult. On the other hand, variable-sized messages require a more complex system-level implementation, but the programming task becomes simpler.

```
public Object remove() {
    Object item;

    while (count == 0)
        ; // do nothing

    // remove an item from the buffer
    --count;
    item = buffer[out];
    out = (out + 1) % BUFFER_SIZE;

    if (count == 0)
        System.out.println("Consumer Consumed " +
            item + " Buffer EMPTY");
    else
        System.out.println("Consumer Consumed " +
            item + " Buffer Size = " + count);

    return item;
}
```

Figure 4.11   The `remove()` method.

If processes P and Q want to communicate, they must send messages to and receive messages from each other; a **communication link** must exist between them. This link can be implemented in a variety of ways. We are concerned here not with the link's physical implementation (such as shared memory, hardware bus, or network, which are covered in Chapter 14), but rather with its logical implementation. Here are several methods for logically implementing a link and the `send/receive` operations:

- Direct or indirect communication

- Symmetric or asymmetric communication

- Automatic or explicit buffering

- Send by copy or send by reference

- Fixed-sized or variable-sized messages

We look at each of these types of message systems next.

4.5.2 Naming

Processes that want to communicate must have a way to refer to each other. They can use either direct or indirect communication.

4.5.2.1 Direct Communication

Under **direct communication,** each process that wants to communicate must explicitly name the recipient or sender of the communication. In this scheme, the send and receive primitives are defined as:

- send(P, message) – Send a message to process P.

- receive(Q, message) – Receive a message from process Q.

A communication link in this scheme has the following properties:

- A link is established automatically between every pair of processes that want to communicate. The processes need to know only each other's identity to communicate.

- A link is associated with exactly two processes.

- Between each pair of processes, there exists exactly one link.

This scheme exhibits a symmetry in addressing; that is, both the sender and the receiver processes have to name the other to communicate. A variant of this scheme employs asymmetry in addressing. Only the sender names the recipient; the recipient is not required to name the sender. In this scheme, the send and receive primitives are defined as follows:

- send(P, message) – Send a message to process P.

- receive(id, message) – Receive a message from any process; the variable *id* is set to the name of the process with which communication has taken place.

The disadvantage in both of these schemes (symmetric and asymmetric) is the limited modularity of the resulting process definitions. Changing the name of a process may necessitate examining all other process definitions. All references to the old name must be found, so that they can be modified to the new name. This situation is not desirable from the viewpoint of separate compilation.

4.5.2.2 Indirect Communication

With **indirect communication,** the messages are sent to and received from **mailboxes,** or **ports**. A mailbox can be viewed abstractly as an object into which messages can be placed by processes and from which messages can be removed. Each mailbox has a unique identification. In this scheme, a process can communicate with some other process via a number of different mailboxes. Two processes can communicate only if the processes have a shared mailbox. The send and receive primitives are defined as follows:

- send(A, message) – Send a message to mailbox A.

- receive(A, message) – Receive a message from mailbox A.

In this scheme, a communication link has the following properties:

- A link is established between a pair of processes only if both members of the pair have a shared mailbox.

- A link may be associated with more than two processes.

- Between each pair of communicating processes, there may be a number of different links, with each link corresponding to one mailbox.

Now suppose that processes P_1, P_2, and P_3 all share mailbox A. Process P_1 sends a message to A, while P_2 and P_3 each execute a receive from A. Which process will receive the message sent by P_1? The answer depends on the scheme that we choose:

- Allow a link to be associated with at most two processes.

- Allow at most one process at a time to execute a receive operation.

- Allow the system to select arbitrarily which process will receive the message (that is, either P_2 or P_3, but not both, will receive the message). The system may identify the receiver to the sender.

A mailbox may be owned either by a process or by the operating system. If the mailbox is owned by a process (that is, the mailbox is part of the address space of the process), then we distinguish between the owner (who can only receive messages through this mailbox) and the user of the mailbox (who can only send messages to the mailbox). Since each mailbox has a unique owner, there can be no confusion about who should receive a message sent to this mailbox. When a process that owns a mailbox terminates, the mailbox disappears. Any process that subsequently sends a message to this mailbox must be notified that the mailbox no longer exists.

On the other hand, a mailbox that is owned by the operating system has an existence of its own. It is independent, and is not attached to any particular process. The operating system then must provide a mechanism that allows a process to do the following:

- Create a new mailbox

- Send and receive messages through the mailbox

- Delete a mailbox

The process that creates a new mailbox is that mailbox's owner by default. Initially, the owner is the only process that can receive messages through this mailbox. However, the ownership and receive privilege may be passed to other processes through appropriate system calls. Of course, this provision could result in multiple receivers for each mailbox.

4.5.3 Synchronization

Communication between processes takes place by calls to send and receive primitives. There are different design options for implementing each primitive. Message passing may be either **blocking** or **nonblocking**—also known as **synchronous** and **asynchronous**.

- **Blocking send:** The sending process is blocked until the message is received by the receiving process or by the mailbox.

- **Nonblocking send:** The sending process sends the message and resumes operation.

- **Blocking receive:** The receiver blocks until a message is available.

- **Nonblocking receive:** The receiver retrieves either a valid message or a null.

Different combinations of send and receive are possible. When both the send and receive are blocking, we have a **rendezvous** between the sender and the receiver.

4.5.4 Buffering

Whether the communication is direct or indirect, messages exchanged by communicating processes reside in a temporary queue. Basically, there are three ways that such a queue can be implemented:

- **Zero capacity:** The queue has maximum length 0; thus, the link cannot have any messages waiting in it. In this case, the sender must block until the recipient receives the message.

- **Bounded capacity:** The queue has finite length n; thus, at most n messages can reside in it. If the queue is not full when a new message is sent, the latter is placed in the queue (either the message is copied or a pointer to the message is kept), and the sender can continue execution without waiting. The link has a finite capacity, however. If the link is full, the sender must block until space is available in the queue.

- **Unbounded capacity:** The queue has potentially infinite length; thus, any number of messages can wait in it. The sender never blocks.

The zero-capacity case is sometimes referred to as a message system with no buffering; the other cases are referred to as automatic buffering.

4.5.5 Producer–Consumer Example

We can now present a solution to the producer–consumer problem that uses message passing. The producer and consumer will communicate indirectly using the shared mailbox illustrated in Figure 4.12.

The buffer is implemented using the java.util.Vector class, meaning that it will be a buffer of unbounded capacity. Also note that both the send() and receive() methods are nonblocking.

When the producer generates an item, it places that item in the mailbox via the send() method. The code for the producer is shown in Figure 4.13.

The consumer obtains an item from the mailbox using the receive() method. Because receive() is nonblocking, the consumer must evaluate the value of the Object returned from receive(). If it is null, the mailbox is empty. The code for the consumer is shown in Figure 4.14.

Chapter 5 shows you how to implement the producer and consumer as separate threads of control, and how to allow the mailbox to be shared between the threads.

4.5.6 An Example: Mach

As an example of a message-based operating system, consider the Mach operating system, developed at Carnegie Mellon University. The Mach kernel supports the creation and destruction of multiple tasks, which are similar to processes but have multiple threads of control. Most communication in Mach —including most of the system calls and all intertask information—is carried out by *messages*. Messages are sent to and received from mailboxes, called *ports* in Mach.

```
import java.util.*;

public class MessageQueue
{
    public MessageQueue() {
      queue = new Vector();
    }

    // This implements a nonblocking send
    public void send(Object item) {
      queue.addElement(item);
    }

    // This implements a nonblocking receive
    public Object receive() {
      Object item;

      if (queue.size() == 0)
          return null;
      else {
          item = queue.firstElement();
          queue.removeElementAt(0);

          return item;
      }
    }

    private Vector queue;
}
```

Figure 4.12   Mailbox for message passing.

Even system calls are made by messages. When each task is created, two special mailboxes—the Kernel mailbox and the Notify mailbox—are also created. The Kernel mailbox is used by the kernel to communicate with the

```
MessageQueue mailBox;

while (true) {
    Date message = new Date();
    mailBox.send(message);
}
```

Figure 4.13   The producer process.

```
MessageQueue mailBox;

while (true) {
   Date message = (Date) mailBox.receive();
   if (message != null)
      // consume the message
}
```

Figure 4.14   The consumer process.

task. The kernel sends notification of event occurrences to the Notify port. Only three system calls are needed for message transfer. The msg_send call sends a message to a mailbox. A message is received via msg_receive. Remote Procedure Calls (RPCs) are executed via msg_rpc, which sends a message and waits for exactly one return message from the sender. In this way, RPC models a typical subroutine procedure call, but can work between systems.

The port_allocate system call creates a new mailbox and allocates space for its queue of messages. The maximum size of the message queue defaults to eight messages. The task that creates the mailbox is that mailbox's owner. The owner also is given receive access to the mailbox. Only one task at a time can either own or receive from a mailbox, but these rights can be sent to other tasks if desired.

The mailbox has an initially empty queue of messages. As messages are sent to the mailbox, the messages are copied into the mailbox. All messages have the same priority. Mach guarantees that multiple messages from the same sender are queued in first-in, first-out (FIFO) order, but does not guarantee an absolute ordering. For instance, messages sent from each of two senders may be queued in any order.

The messages themselves consist of a fixed-length header, followed by a variable-length data portion. The header includes the length of the message and two mailbox names. When a message is sent, one mailbox name is the mailbox to which the message is being sent. Commonly, the sending thread expects a reply; the mailbox name of the sender is passed on to the receiving task, which may use it as a "return address" to send messages back.

The variable part of a message is a list of typed data items. Each entry in the list has a type, size, and value. The type of the objects specified in the message is important, since operating-system–defined objects—such as the ownership or receive access rights, task states, and memory segments—may be sent in messages.

The send and receive operations themselves are flexible. For instance, when a message is sent to a mailbox, the mailbox may be full. If the mailbox is not full, the message is copied to the mailbox and the sending thread continues. If the mailbox is full, the sending thread has four options:

1. Wait indefinitely until there is room in the mailbox.

2. Wait at most n milliseconds.

3. Do not wait at all, but rather return immediately.

4. Temporarily cache a message. One message can be given to the operating system to keep, even though the mailbox to which it is being sent is full. When the message can be put in the mailbox, a message is sent back to the sender; only one such message to a full mailbox can be pending at any time for a given sending thread.

The final option is meant for server tasks, such as a line-printer driver. After finishing a request, these tasks may need to send a one-time reply to the task that had requested service, but must also continue with other service requests, even if the reply mailbox for a client is full.

The receive operation must specify from which mailbox or mailbox set to receive a message. A **mailbox set** is a collection of mailboxes, as declared by the task, which can be grouped together and treated as one mailbox for the purposes of the task. Threads in a task can receive from only a mailbox or mailbox set for which that task has receive access. A port_status system call returns the number of messages in a given mailbox. The receive operation attempts to receive from (1) any mailbox in a mailbox set, or (2) a specific (named) mailbox. If no message is waiting to be received, the receiving thread may wait, wait at most n milliseconds, or not wait.

The Mach system was especially designed for distributed systems, which we discuss in Chapters 14 through 16, but Mach is also suitable for single-processor systems. The major problem with message systems has generally been poor performance caused by copying the message first from the sender to the mailbox, and then from the mailbox to the receiver. The Mach message system attempts to avoid double copy operations by using virtual-memory management techniques (Chapter 10). Essentially, Mach maps the address space containing the sender's message into the receiver's address space. The message itself is never actually copied. This message-management technique provides a large performance boost, but works for only intrasystem messages. The Mach operating system is discussed in the extra chapter that is posted on our web site (http://www.bell-labs.com/topic/books/os-book).

4.5.7 An Example: Windows NT

The Windows NT operating system is an example of modern design that employs modularity to increase functionality and to decrease the time needed to implement new features. NT provides support for multiple operating environments or *subsystems,* with which application programs communicate via a message-passing mechanism. The application programs can be considered to be clients of the NT subsystem server.

The message-passing facility in NT is called the **local procedure-call facility (LPC)**. The LPC in Windows NT communicates between two processes that are on the same machine. It is similar to the standard RPC mechanism that is widely used, but it is optimized for and specific to NT. Windows NT, like Mach, uses a port object to establish and maintain a connection between two processes. Every client that calls a subsystem needs a communication channel, which is provided by a port object and is never inherited. NT uses two types of ports: connection ports and communication ports. They are really the same, but are given different names according to how they are used. Connection ports are named objects (see Chapter 22 for more information about NT objects), visible to all processes; they give applications a way to set up a communication channel. This communication works as follows:

- The client opens a handle to the subsystem's connection port object.

- The client sends a connection request.

- The server creates two private communication ports, and returns the handle to one of them to the client.

- The client and server use the corresponding port handle to send messages or callbacks and to listen for replies.

NT uses three types of message-passing techniques over a port that the client specifies when it establishes the channel. The simplest, which is used for small messages, uses the port's message queue as intermediate storage and copies the message from one process to the other. Under this method, messages of up to 256 bytes can be sent.

If a client needs to send a larger message, it passes the message through a section object (shared memory). The client has to decide, when it sets up the channel, whether or not it will need to send a large message. If the client determines that it does want to send large messages, it asks for a section object to be created. Likewise, if the server decides that replies will be large, it creates a section object. So that the section object can be used, a small message is sent that contains a pointer and size information about that section object. This method is more complicated than the first method, but it avoids the data copying. In both cases, a callback mechanism can be used when either the client or the server cannot respond immediately to a request. The callback mechanism allows them to perform asynchronous message handling.

One of the drawbacks of using message passing to perform rudimentary functions, such as graphics functions, is that the performance may not be as good as that in a non–message-passing (that is, shared-memory) system. To increase performance, the native NT environment (Win32) uses a third method of message passing, called **quick LPC**. A client sends to the server's connection port a connection request indicating that it will be using quick LPC. The server sets up a dedicated server thread to handle requests, a 64-kilobyte section object, and an event-pair object. From then on, messages are passed in the section object, and synchronization is performed by the event-pair object. This scheme eliminates message copying, the overhead of using the port object, and the overhead of determining which client thread is calling it, since there is one server thread per client thread. The kernel also gives the dedicated thread scheduling preference. The drawback is that this method uses more resources than do the other two methods. Since there is overhead involved in passing messages, NT may batch several messages into a single message to reduce that overhead. For more information about Windows NT, see Chapter 22.

4.6 ■ Summary

A process is a program in execution. As a process executes, it changes state. The state of a process is defined by that process's current activity. Each process may be in one of the following states: new, ready, running, waiting, or terminated. Each process is represented in the operating system by its own process-control block (PCB).

A process, when it is not executing, is placed in some waiting queue. There are two major classes of queues in an operating system: I/O request queues and the ready queue. The ready queue contains all the processes that are ready to execute and are waiting for the CPU. Each process is represented by a PCB, and the PCBs can be linked together to form a ready queue. Long-term (job) scheduling is the selection of processes to be allowed to contend for the CPU. Normally, long-term scheduling is heavily influenced by resource-allocation considerations, especially memory management. Short-term (CPU) scheduling is the selection of one process from the ready queue.

The processes in the system can execute concurrently. There are several reasons for allowing concurrent execution: information sharing, computation speedup, modularity, and convenience. Concurrent execution requires a mechanism for process creation and deletion.

The processes executing in the operating system may be either independent processes or cooperating processes. Cooperating processes must have the means to communicate with each other. Principally, there exist two complementary communication schemes: shared memory and message systems. The shared-memory method requires communicating processes to share some variables. The processes are expected to exchange information through the use of these shared variables. In a shared-memory system, the responsibility for providing communication rests with the application programmers; the operating system needs to provide only the shared memory. The message-system method allows the processes to exchange messages. The responsibility for providing communication may rest with the operating system itself. These two schemes are not mutually exclusive, and can be used simultaneously within a single operating system.

We can implement either shared memory or message passing using Java. Separate threads of control can be created and can communicate using either method.

■ Exercises

4.1 MS-DOS provided no means of concurrent processing. Discuss three major complications that concurrent processing adds to an operating system.

4.2 Describe the differences among short-term, medium-term, and long-term scheduling.

4.3 A DECSYSTEM-20 computer has multiple register sets. Describe the actions of a context switch if the new context is already loaded into one of the register sets. What else must happen if the new context is in memory rather than in a register set, and all the register sets are in use?

4.4 Describe the actions taken by a kernel to context switch between processes.

4.5 What are the benefits and the detriments of each of the following? Consider both the systems and the programmers' levels.

    a. Symmetric and asymmetric communication

    b. Automatic and explicit buffering

    c. Send by copy and send by reference

    d. Fixed-sized and variable-sized messages

4.6 Consider the interprocess-communication scheme where mailboxes are used.

    a. Suppose a process P wants to wait for two messages, one from mailbox A and one from mailbox B. What sequence of send and receive should it execute?

    b. What sequence of send and receive should P execute if P wants to wait for one message from mailbox A or from mailbox B (or from both)?

    c. A receive operation makes a process wait until the mailbox is nonempty. Either devise a scheme that allows a process to wait until a mailbox is empty, or explain why such a scheme cannot exist.

Bibliographical Notes

The subject of interprocess communication was discussed by Brinch Hansen [1970] with respect to the RC 4000 system. Schlichting and Schneider [1982] discussed asynchronous message-passing primitives. The IPC facility implemented at the user level was described by Bershad and colleagues [1990].

Details of interprocess communication in UNIX systems were presented by Gray [1997]. Barrera [1991] and Vahalia [1996] presented interprocess communication in the Mach system. Solomon [1998] outlined interprocess communication in Windows NT.

Discussions concerning the implementation of RPCs were presented by Birrell and Nelson [1984]. A design of a reliable RPC mechanism was presented by Shrivastava and Panzieri [1982]. A survey of RPCs was presented by Tay and Ananda [1990]. Stankovic [1982] and Staunstrup [1982] discussed procedure calls versus message-passing communication.

Chapter 5

THREADS

The process model introduced in Chapter 4 assumed that a process was an executing program with a single thread of control. Many modern operating systems now provide features for a process to contain multiple threads of control. This chapter introduces many concepts associated with multithreaded computer systems and covers how to use Java to create and manipulate threads.

5.1 ■ Overview

A thread, sometimes called a **lightweight process**, is a basic unit of CPU utilization; it comprises a thread ID, a program counter, a register set, and a stack. It shares with other threads belonging to the same process its code section, data section, and other operating-system resources, such as open files and signals. A traditional, or **heavyweight**, process has a single thread of control. Because the process has multiple threads of control, the process can do more than one task at a time. Figure 5.1 illustrates the difference between a traditional single-threaded process and a multithreaded process.

Many software packages that run on modern desktop PCs are multithreaded. An application is typically implemented as a separate process with several threads of control. A web browser might have one thread display images or text while another thread retrieves data from the network. A word processor may have a thread for displaying graphics, another thread for reading keystrokes from the user, and a third thread for performing spelling and grammar checking in the background.

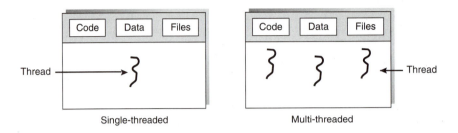

Figure 5.1   Single- and multithreaded processes.

There are also situations where a single application may be required to perform several similar tasks. For example, a web server accepts client requests for web pages, images, sound, and so forth. A busy web server may have several (perhaps hundreds) of clients concurrently accessing it. If the web server ran as a traditional single-threaded process, it would be able to service only one client at a time with its single process. The amount of time that a client might have to wait for its request to be serviced could be enormous. One solution is to have the server run as a single process that accepts requests. When the server receives a request, it creates a separate process to service that request. However, rather than incurring the overhead of creating a new process to service each request, it may be more efficient for one process that contains multiple threads to serve the same purpose. This approach would multithread the web-server process. The server would create a separate thread that would listen for client requests; when a request was made, rather than creating another process, it would create another thread to service the request.

Java has other uses for threads. For one, Java has no concept of asynchronous behavior. For example, when it attempts to telnet to a server, the client is blocked until either the connection is made or a timeout has occurred. A timeout is an example of an asynchronous event and Java has no direct support for asynchronous events. If a Java program attempts to connect to a server, it will block until the connection is made. (Consider what will happen if the server is down!) The Java solution is to set up a thread that will attempt to make a connection to the server and another thread that will initially sleep for the timeout duration (say, 60 seconds) and then awaken. When this timer thread awakens, it will check to see whether the connection thread is still trying to connect to the server. If that thread is still trying, it will interrupt and prevent the thread from continuing to try.

5.2 ■ Benefits

The benefits of multithreaded programming can be broken down into four major categories:

1. *Responsiveness*: Multithreading an interactive application may allow a program to continue running even if part of it is blocked or is performing a lengthy operation, thereby increasing responsiveness to the user. For instance, a multithreaded web browser could still allow user interaction in one thread while an image is being loaded in another thread.

2. *Resource sharing*: By default, threads share the memory and the resources of the process to which they belong. The benefit of code sharing allows an application to have several different threads of activity all within the same address space.

3. *Economy*: Allocating memory and resources for process creation is costly. Alternatively, because threads share resources of the process to which they belong, it is more economical to create and context switch threads. It can be difficult to gauge empirically the difference in overhead for creating and maintaining a process rather than a thread, but in general it is much more time consuming to create and manage processes than threads. In Solaris, creating a process is about 30 times slower than is creating a thread, and context switching is about five times slower.

4. *Utilization of multiprocessor architectures*: The benefits of multithreading can be greatly increased in a multiprocessor architecture, where each thread may be running in parallel on a different processor. In a single-processor architecture, the CPU generally moves between each thread so quickly that there is an illusion of parallelism, but in reality only one thread is running at a time.

5.3 ■ User and Kernel Threads

Our discussion so far has treated threads in a generic sense. However, support for threads may be provided at either the user level, for **user threads**, or by the kernel, for **kernel threads**. We discuss the distinction next.

5.3.1 User Threads

User threads are supported above the kernel and are implemented by a thread library at the user level. The library provides support for thread creation, scheduling, and management with no support from the kernel. Because the kernel is unaware of user-level threads, all thread creation and scheduling are done in user space without the need for kernel intervention. Therefore, user-level threads are generally fast to create and manage; they have drawbacks, however. For instance, if the kernel is single threaded, then any user-level thread performing a blocking system call will cause the entire process to block, even if there are other threads available to run within the application. User-thread libraries include POSIX *Pthreads*, Mach *C-threads*, and Solaris *threads*.

5.3.2 Kernel Threads

Kernel threads are supported directly by the operating system: Thread creation, scheduling, and management are done by the kernel in kernel space. Because thread management is done by the operating system, kernel threads are generally slower to create and manage than are user threads. However, since the kernel is managing the threads, if a thread performs a blocking system call, the kernel can schedule another thread in the application for execution. Also, in a multiprocessor environment, the kernel can schedule threads on different processors. Windows NT, Solaris, and Digital UNIX are operating systems that support kernel threads.

5.4 ■ Multithreading Models

Many systems provide support for both user and kernel threads, resulting in different multithreading models. We look at three common types of threading implementation.

5.4.1 Many-to-One Model

The many-to-one model (Figure 5.2) maps many user-level threads to one kernel thread. Thread management is done in user space, so it is efficient, but the entire process will block if a thread makes a blocking system call. Also, because only one thread can access the kernel at a time, multiple threads are unable to run in parallel on multiprocessors. User-level thread libraries implemented on operating systems that do not support kernel threads use the many-to-one model.

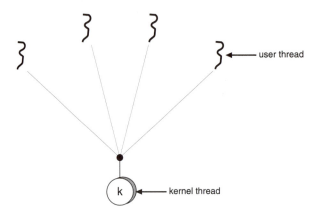

Figure 5.2   Many-to-one model.

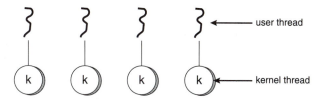

Figure 5.3   One-to-one model.

5.4.2 One-to-One Model

The one-to-one model (Figure 5.3) maps each user thread to a kernel thread. It provides more concurrency than the many-to-one model by allowing another thread to run when a thread makes a blocking system call; it also allows multiple threads to run in parallel on multiprocessors. The only drawback to this model is that creating a user thread requires creating the corresponding kernel thread. Because the overhead of creating kernel threads can burden the performance of an application, most implementations of this model restrict the number of threads supported by the system. Windows NT and OS/2 implement the one-to-one model.

5.4.3 Many-to-Many Model

The many-to-many model (Figure 5.4) multiplexes many user-level threads to a smaller or equal number of kernel threads. The number of kernel threads may be specific for either a particular application or a particular machine (an application may be allocated more kernel threads on a multiprocessor than on a uniprocessor.) Whereas the many-to-one model allows the developer to create as many user threads as she wishes, true concurrency is not gained because

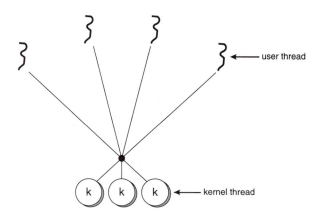

Figure 5.4   Many-to-many model.

only one thread can be scheduled by the kernel at a time. The one-to-one model allows for greater concurrency, but the developer has to be careful not to create too many threads within an application (and in some instances may be limited in the number of threads that she can create). The many-to-many model suffers from neither of these shortcomings: Developers can create as many user threads as necessary, and the corresponding kernel threads can run in parallel on a multiprocessor. Also, when a thread performs a blocking system call, the kernel can schedule another thread for execution. Solaris, IRIX, and Digital UNIX support this model.

5.5 ▪ Solaris 2 Threads

Solaris 2 is a version of UNIX that until 1992 supported only traditional heavy-weight processes with a single thread of control. It has been transformed into a modern operating system with support for threads at the kernel and user levels, symmetric multiprocessing (SMP), and real-time scheduling.

Solaris 2 supports user-level threads with a library containing APIs for thread creation and management. Solaris 2 defines an intermediate level of threads as well. Between user-level threads and kernel-level threads are lightweight processes (LWP.) Each process contains at least one LWP. The thread library multiplexes user-level threads on the pool of LWPs for the process, and only user-level threads currently connected to an LWP accomplish work. The rest are either blocked or waiting for an LWP on which they can run.

All operations within the kernel are executed by standard kernel-level threads. There is a kernel-level thread for each LWP, and there are some kernel-level threads that run on the kernel's behalf and have no associated LWP (for instance, a thread to service disk requests). Kernel-level threads are the only objects scheduled within the system (see Chapter 6 for a discussion of scheduling). Solaris implements the many-to-many model; its entire thread system is depicted in Figure 5.5.

User-level threads may be either bound or unbound. A **bound** user-level thread is permanently attached to a LWP. Only that thread runs on the LWP, and by request the LWP can be dedicated to a single processor (see the rightmost thread in Figure 5.5). Binding a thread is useful in situations that require quick response time, such as a real-time application. An **unbound** thread is not permanently attached to any LWP. All unbound threads in an application are multiplexed onto the pool of available LWPs for the application. Threads are unbound by default.

Consider the system in operation. Any one process may have many user-level threads. These user-level threads may be scheduled and switched among the LWPs by the thread library without kernel intervention. User-level threads are extremely efficient because no kernel support is required for the thread library to context switch from one user-level thread to another.

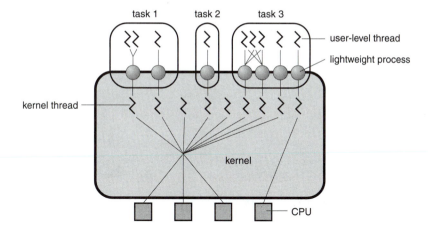

Figure 5.5   Solaris 2 threads.

Each LWP is connected to exactly one kernel-level thread, whereas each user-level thread is independent of the kernel. There may be many LWPs in a process, but they are needed only when the thread needs to communicate with the kernel. For instance, one LWP is needed for every thread that may block concurrently in system calls. Consider five different file-read requests that could be occurring simultaneously. Then, five LWPs would be needed, because they could all be waiting for I/O completion in the kernel. If a task had only four LWPs, then the fifth request would have to wait for one of the LWPs to return from the kernel. Adding a sixth LWP would gain nothing if there were only enough work for five.

The kernel threads are scheduled by the kernel's scheduler and execute on the CPU or CPUs in the system. If a kernel thread blocks (such as while waiting for an I/O operation to complete), the processor is free to run another kernel thread. If the thread that blocked was running on behalf of an LWP, the LWP blocks as well. Up the chain, the user-level thread currently attached to the LWP also blocks. If a process has more than one LWP, another LWP can be scheduled by the kernel.

The threads library dynamically adjusts the number of LWPs in the pool to ensure the best performance for the application. For example, if all the LWPs in a process are blocked and there are other threads that are able to run, the threads library automatically creates another LWP to be assigned to a waiting thread. A program is thus prevented from being blocked by a lack of unblocked LWPs. Also, LWPs are kernel resources that are expensive to maintain if they are not being used. The threads library ages LWPs and deletes them when they are unused for a long time, typically about 5 minutes.

The developers used the following data structures to implement threads on Solaris 2:

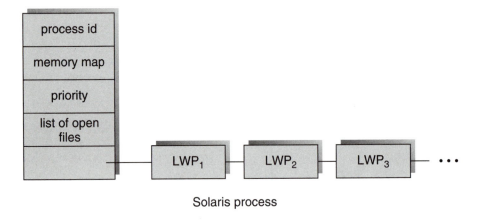

Solaris process

Figure 5.6   Solaris process.

- A user-level thread contains a thread ID, register set (including a PC and stack pointer), stack, and priority (used by the threads library for scheduling purposes.) None of these data structures are kernel resources; all exist within user space.

- An LWP has a register set for the user-level thread it is running, as well as memory and accounting information. An LWP is a kernel data structure, and it resides in kernel space.

- A kernel thread has only a small data structure and a stack. The data structure includes a copy of the kernel registers, a pointer to the LWP to which it is attached, and priority and scheduling information.

Each process in Solaris 2 contains much of the information described in the process control block (PCB), which was discussed in Section 4.1.3. In particular, a Solaris process contains a process id (PID), memory map, list of open files, priority, and a pointer to a list of LWPs associated with the process (see Figure 5.6).

5.6 ■ Java Threads

As we have already seen, support for threads is provided either by the operating system or by a threads library package. For example, the Win32 library provides a set of APIs for multithreading native Windows applications, and Pthreads provides a library of thread-management functions for POSIX–compliant systems. Java is unique in that it provides support at the language level for creation and management of threads.

All Java programs comprise at least a single thread of control. Even a simple Java program consisting of only a main() method runs as a single thread in the JVM. In addition, Java provides commands that allow the developer to create and manipulate additional threads of control within the program.

5.6.1 Thread Creation

One way to create a thread explicitly is to create a new class that is derived from the Thread class, and to override the run() method of the Thread class. This aproach is shown in Figure 5.7.

An object of this derived class will run as a separate thread of control in the JVM. However, creating an object that is derived from the Thread class does not specifically create the new thread; rather, it is the start() method that actually creates the new thread. Calling the start() method for the new object (1) allocates memory and initializes a new thread in the JVM and (2) calls the run() method making the thread eligible to be run by the JVM. (Note: Do not ever call the run() method directly. Call the start() method, and it will call the run() method on your behalf.)

When this program runs, two threads are created by the JVM. The first is the thread associated with the application—the thread that starts execution at the main() method. The second thread is the runner thread that is created explicitly with the start() method. The runner thread begins execution in its run() method.

```
class Worker1 extends Thread
{
    public void run() {
        System.out.println("I Am a Worker Thread");
    }
}

public class First
{
    public static void main(String args[]) {
        Worker1 runner = new Worker1();

        runner.start();

        System.out.println("I Am The Main Thread");
    }
}
```

Figure 5.7   Thread creation by extending the Thread class.

Another option to create a separate thread is to define a class that implements the Runnable interface. The Runnable interface is defined as follows:

```
public interface Runnable
{
    public abstract void run();
}
```

Therefore, when a class implements Runnable, it must define a run() method. (The Thread class, in addition to defining static and instance methods, also implements the Runnable interface. That explains why a class derived from Thread must define a run() method.)

Implementing the Runnable interface is similar to extending the Thread class, the only change being substituting "extends Thread" for "implements Runnable":

```
class Worker2 implements Runnable
{
    public void run() {
        System.out.println("I am a worker thread.   ");
    }
}
```

Creating a new thread from a class that implements Runnable is slightly different from creating a thread from a class extending Thread. Since the new class does not extend Thread, it does not have access to the static or instance methods—such as the start() method—of the Thread class. However, an object of the Thread class is still needed because it is the start() method that creates a new thread of control. Figure 5.8 shows how thread creation using the Runnable interface can be achieved.

```
public class Second
{
    public static void main(String args[]) {
        Runnable runner = new Worker2();

        Thread thrd = new Thread(runner);

        thrd.start();

        System.out.println("I Am The Main Thread");
    }
}
```

Figure 5.8   Thread creation implementing the Runnable interface.

In the class Second, a new Thread object is created that is passed a Runnable object in its constructor. When the thread is created with the start() method, the new thread begins execution in the run() method of the Runnable object.

Both methods of thread creation are equally popular. Why does Java support two approaches for creating threads? Which approach is more appropriate to use in what situations?

The first question is easy to answer. Since Java does not support multiple inheritance, if a class is already derived from another class, it will not also be able to extend the Thread class. A good example is that an applet already extends the Applet class. To multithread an applet, you extend the Applet class and implement the Runnable interface:

```
public class ThreadedApplet extends Applet
      implements Runnable
{
          .   .   .
}
```

The answer to the second question is less obvious. Object-oriented purists might say that, unless you are enhancing the Thread class, the class should not be extended. (Although this point may be moot, as many of the methods in the Thread class are defined as final.) However, if the new class implements the Runnable interface and does not extend Thread, none of the Thread instance methods can be called from inside that class. We will not attempt to determine the correct answer in this debate. For clarity of code, unless a class requires multithreading and is already extended, we will adopt the approach of extending the Thread class.

5.6.2   Thread Management

Java provides several APIs for managing threads, including:

- suspend(): Supends execution of the currently running thread

- sleep(): Puts the currently running thread to sleep for a specified amount of time

- resume(): Resumes execution of a thread that had been suspended

- stop(): Stops execution of a thread; once a thread has been stopped, it cannot be resumed or started

Each of the different methods for controlling the state of a thread may be useful in certain situations. For instance, applets are natural examples for multithreading because they commonly have graphics, animation, and audio

—all good candidates for managing as separate threads. However, it may not make sense for an applet to run while it is not being displayed, particularly if the applet is performing a CPU-intensive task. A way of handling this latter situation is to have the applet run as a separate thread of control, suspending the thread when the applet is not being displayed and resuming it when the applet is displayed again.

You can do that by noting that the start() method of an applet is called when an applet is first displayed. If the user leaves the web page or the applet scrolls off the screen, the applet's stop() method is called. (It is unfortunate that both a different start() and stop() are associated both with threads and applets.) If the user returns to the applet's web page, the latter's start() method is called again. The destroy() method of an applet is called when the applet is removed from the browser's cache. It is possible to prevent an applet from running while it is not being displayed in a web browser by having the stop() method of the applet suspend the thread and resume execution of the thread in the applet's start() method.

The applet ClockApplet (shown in Figure 5.9) displays the date and time in a browser. If the applet is being displayed for the first time, the start() method creates a new thread; otherwise, it resumes execution of the thread. The stop() method of the applet suspends execution of the thread. The destroy() method of the applet stops execution of the thread. The run() method of the thread has a forever loop that alternates between sleeping for 1 second and then calling the repaint() method. The repaint() method ultimately calls the paint() method that displays the date in the browser's window.

With the release of Java 2, the suspend(), resume(), and stop() methods are **deprecated**. Deprecated methods are still implemented in the current API; however, their use is discouraged. The reasons for deprecating these methods are covered in Chapter 8. Note that, despite being deprecated, these methods still provide a reasonable alternative (see Figure 5.9, for example).

5.6.3 Thread States

A Java thread can be in one of four possible states:

1. *New*: A thread is in this state when an object for the thread is created (that is, the new statement.)

2. *Runnable*: Calling the start() method allocates memory for the new thread in the JVM and calls the run() method for the thread object. When a thread's run() method is invoked, the thread moves from the New to the Runnable state. A thread in the Runnable state is eligible to be run by the JVM. Note that Java does not distinguish between a thread that is eligible to run and a thread that is currently running by the JVM. A running thread is still in the Runnable state.

```
import java.applet.*;
import java.awt.*;
public class ClockApplet extends Applet
     implements Runnable
{
   public void run() {
      while (true) {
         try {
            Thread.sleep(1000);
         }
         catch (InterruptedException e) { }
         repaint();
      }
   }

   public void start() {
      if ( clockThread == null ) {
         clockThread = new Thread(this);
         clockThread.start();
      }
      else
         clockThread.resume();
   }

   public void stop() {
      if (clockThread != null)
         clockThread.suspend();
   }

   public void destroy() {
      if (clockThread != null) {
         clockThread.stop();
         clockThread = null;
      }
   }

   public void paint(Graphics g) {
      g.drawString(new java.util.Date().toString(),10,30);
   }

   private Thread clockThread;
}
```

Figure 5.9 Applet that displays the date and time of day.

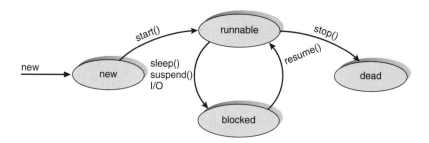

Figure 5.10   Java thread states.

3. *Blocked*: A thread becomes Blocked if it performs a blocking statement, such as by doing I/O, or if it invokes certain Java `Thread` methods, such as `sleep()` or `suspend()`.

4. *Dead*: A thread moves to the Dead state when its `run()` method terminates or when its `stop()` method is called.

It is not possible to determine the exact state of a thread, although the `isAlive()` method returns a `boolean` value that a program can use to determine whether or not a thread is in the Dead state. Figure 5.10 illustrates the different thread states, and labels several possible transitions.

5.6.4 Threads and the JVM

In addition to a Java program containing several different threads of control, there are several threads running asynchronously on behalf of the JVM handling system-level tasks such as memory management and graphics controls. Such threads include a garbage-collector thread. The garbage collector evaluates objects within the JVM to see whether they are still in use. If they are not, it returns the memory to the system. Among the other threads is one that handles timer events, such as calls to the `sleep()` method, one that handles events from graphics controls, such as pressing a button, and one that updates the screen. Thus, a typical Java application contains several different threads of control in the JVM. Certain threads are created explicitly by the program; other threads are system-level tasks running on behalf of the JVM.

5.6.5 The JVM and Host Operating System

The typical implementation of the JVM is on top of a host operating system. This setup allows the JVM to hide the implementation details of the underlying operating system and to provide a consistent, abstract environment that allows Java programs to operate on any platform that supports a JVM. The specification for the JVM does not indicate how Java threads are to be mapped to the underlying operating system, instead leaving that decision to the particular implementation of the JVM. Typically, a Java thread is considered a user-level thread, and the JVM is responsible for thread management. Windows NT uses the one-to-one model; therefore, each Java thread for a JVM running on NT maps to a kernel thread. Solaris 2 initially implemented the JVM using the many-to-one model (called *green threads* by Sun). However, as of Version 1.1 of the JVM with Solaris 2.6, the JVM was implemented using the many-to-many model.

5.6.6 Multithreaded Solution Example

In this section, we present a complete multithreaded solution to the producer–consumer problem that uses message passing. The class Server in Figure 5.11 first creates a mailbox for buffering messages, using the MessageQueue class developed in Chapter 4. It then creates separate producer and consumer threads (Figures 5.12 and 5.13, respectively), and passes each thread a reference to the shared mailbox. The producer thread alternates among sleeping for a while, producing an item, and entering that item into the mailbox. The consumer alternates between sleeping and then retrieving an item from the mailbox and consuming it. Because the receive() method of the MessageQueue class is nonblocking, the consumer must check to see whether the message that it retrieved is null.

```
public class Server
{
    public Server() {
        // first create the message buffer
        MessageQueue mailBox = new MessageQueue();

        // now create the producer and consumer threads
        Producer producerThread = new Producer(mailBox);
        Consumer consumerThread = new Consumer(mailBox);

        producerThread.start();
        consumerThread.start();
    }

    public static void main(String args[]) {
        Server server = new Server();
    }

    public static final int NAP_TIME = 5;
}
```

Figure 5.11   The class Server.

```
import java.util.*;

class Producer extends Thread
{
    public Producer(MessageQueue m) {
        mbox = m;
    }

    public void run() {
        Date message;

        while (true) {
            int sleeptime = (int) (Server.NAP_TIME *
                Math.random() );
            System.out.println("Producer sleeping for " +
                sleeptime + " seconds");
            try {
                Thread.sleep(sleeptime*1000);
            }
            catch(InterruptedException e) { }

            // produce an item and enter
            // it into the buffer
            message = new Date();
            System.out.println("Producer produced " +
                message);
            mbox.send(message);
        }
    }

    private MessageQueue mbox;
}
```

Figure 5.12   Producer thread.

5.7 ▪ Summary

A thread is a flow of control within a process. A multithreaded process contains several different flows of control within the same address space. The benefits of multithreading include increased responsiveness to the user, resource sharing within the process, economy, and the ability to take advantage of multiprocessor architectures. User-level threads are threads that are visible to the programmer and are unknown to the kernel. User-level threads are typically managed by a threads library in user space. Kernel-level threads are

```java
import java.util.*;

class Consumer extends Thread
{
    public Consumer(MessageQueue m) {
        mbox = m;
    }

    public void run() {
        Date message;

        while (true) {
            int sleeptime = (int) (Server.NAP_TIME * Math.random());
            System.out.println("Consumer sleeping for " +
                sleeptime + " seconds");
            try {
                Thread.sleep(sleeptime*1000);
            }
            catch(InterruptedException e) { }

            // consume an item from the buffer
            message = (Date)mbox.receive();

            if (message != null)
                System.out.println("Consumer consumed " + message);
        }
    }

    private MessageQueue mbox;
}
```

Figure 5.13 Consumer thread.

supported and managed by the operating-system kernel. In general, user-level threads are faster to create and manage than are kernel threads. There are three different types of models relating user and kernel threads: The many-to-one model maps many user threads to a single kernel thread. The one-to-one model maps each user thread to a corresponding kernel thread. The many-to-many model multiplexes many user threads to a smaller or equal number of kernel threads.

Java is unique because it provides support for threads at the language level. All Java programs consist of at least a single thread of control, and it is easy to create multiple threads of control within the same program. Java also provides a set of APIs to manage threads, including methods to suspend and resume a thread, to put a thread to sleep for a period of time, and to stop a running thread. A Java thread may also be in one of four possible states: New, Runnable, Blocked, and Dead. The different APIs for managing threads often change the state of the thread. A multithreaded Java solution to the producer–consumer problem provided an example.

■ Exercises

5.1 Provide two programming examples of multithreading giving improved performance over a single-threaded solution.

5.2 Provide two programming examples of multithreading that would *not* improve performance over a single-threaded solution.

5.3 What are two differences between user-level threads and kernel-level threads? Under what circumstances is one type better than the other?

5.4 Describe the actions taken by a kernel to context switch between kernel-level threads.

5.5 Describe the actions taken by a thread library to context switch between user-level threads.

5.6 What resources are used when a thread is created? How do they differ from those used when a process is created?

5.7 Modify the messageQueue class such that the receive() method blocks until there is a message available in the queue.

5.8 Implement the send() and receive() methods for a message-passing system that has zero capacity. Implement the send() method such that the sender blocks until the receiver accepts the message. Implement the receive() method such that the receiver blocks until there is a message available in the queue.

5.9 Implement the send() and receive() methods for a message-passing system with bounded capacity. Implement the send() method such that the sender will block until there is space available in the queue. Implement the receive() method such that the receiver will block until there is a messager available in the queue.

5.10 Write a multithreaded Java program that generates the Fibonacci series. The operation of this program should be as follows: The user will run the program and will enter on the command line the number of Fibonacci numbers that the program is to generate. The program will then create a separate thread that will generate the Fibonacci numbers.

5.11 Write a multithreaded Java program that outputs prime numbers. This program should work as follows: The user will run the program and will enter a number on the command line. The program will then create a separate thread that outputs all the prime numbers less than or equal to the number that the user entered.

Bibliographical Notes

Thread performance issues were discussed by Anderson and colleagues [1989], who continued their work [1991] by evaluating the performance of user-level threads with kernel support. Marsh and associates [1991] discussed first-class user-level threads. Bershad and colleagues [1990] described combining threads with RPC. Draves and colleagues [1991] discussed the use of continuations to implement thread management and communication in operating systems.

The IBM OS/2 operating system is a multithreaded operating system that runs on personal computers [Kogan and Rawson 1988]. Sun Microsystems' Solaris 2 thread structure was described by Eykholt and colleagues [1992]. The user-level threads were detailed in Stein and Shaw [1992]. Peacock [1992] discussed the multithreading of the file system in Solaris 2.

Information on multithreaded programming is given in Lewis and Berg [1998], in Sunsoft [1995], and in Kleiman and colleagues [1996], although these references tend to be biased toward Pthreads. Oaks and Wong [1999], Lea [1997], and Hartley [1998] discuss multithreading in Java. Solomon [1998] describes how threads are implemented in Windows NT; Beveridge and Wiener [1997] discuss multithreading using Win32, and Pham and Garg [1996] describe multithreading programming using Windows NT. Vahalia [1996] and Graham [1995] describe how Solaris implements multithreading.

Chapter 6

CPU SCHEDULING

CPU scheduling is the basis of multiprogrammed operating systems. By switching the CPU among processes, the operating system can make the computer productive. In this chapter, we introduce the basic scheduling concepts and present several different CPU scheduling algorithms. We also consider the problem of selecting an algorithm for a particular system. In Chapter 5, we introduced threads to the process model. On operating systems that support them, it is kernel-level threads—not processes—that are being scheduled by the operating system. However, the terms **process scheduling** and **thread scheduling** are often used interchangeably. In this chapter, we use *process scheduling* when discussing general scheduling concepts, and *thread scheduling* to refer to thread-specific ideas.

6.1 ■ Basic Concepts

The objective of multiprogramming is to have some process running at all times, to maximize CPU utilization. For a uniprocessor system, there will never be more than one running process. If there are more processes, the rest will have to wait until the CPU is free and can be rescheduled.

The idea of multiprogramming is relatively simple. A process is executed until it must wait, typically for the completion of some I/O request. In a simple computer system, the CPU would then just sit idle. All this waiting time is wasted; no useful work is accomplished. With multiprogramming, we try to use this time productively. Several processes are kept in memory at one time.

When one process has to wait, the operating system takes the CPU away from that process and gives the CPU to another process. This pattern continues. Every time that one process has to wait, another process may take over the use of the CPU.

Scheduling is a fundamental operating-system function. Almost all computer resources are scheduled before use. The CPU is, of course, one of the primary computer resources. Thus, its scheduling is central to operating-system design.

6.1.1 CPU–I/O Burst Cycle

The success of CPU scheduling depends on the following observed property of processes: Process execution consists of a **cycle** of CPU execution and I/O wait. Processes alternate back and forth between these two states. Process execution begins with a **CPU burst**. That is followed by an **I/O burst,** which is followed

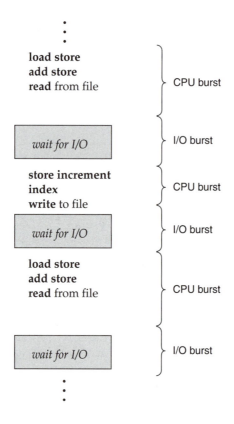

Figure 6.1   Alternating sequence of CPU and I/O bursts.

by another CPU burst, then another I/O burst, and so on. Eventually, the final CPU burst ends with a system request to terminate execution, rather than with another I/O burst (Figure 6.1).

The durations of these CPU bursts have been measured extensively. Although they vary greatly from process to process and from computer to computer, they tend to have a frequency curve similar to that shown in Figure 6.2. The curve is generally characterized as exponential or hyperexponential. There is a large number of short CPU bursts, and there is a small number of long CPU bursts. An I/O-bound program typically will have many short CPU bursts. A CPU-bound program might have a few long CPU bursts. This distribution can be important in the selection of an appropriate CPU scheduling algorithm.

6.1.2 CPU Scheduler

Whenever the CPU becomes idle, the operating system must select one of the processes in the ready queue to be executed. The selection process is carried out by the **short-term scheduler** (or CPU scheduler). The scheduler selects from among the processes in memory that are ready to execute, and allocates the CPU to one of them.

Note that the ready queue is not necessarily a first-in, first-out (FIFO) queue. As we shall see when we consider the various scheduling algorithms, a ready

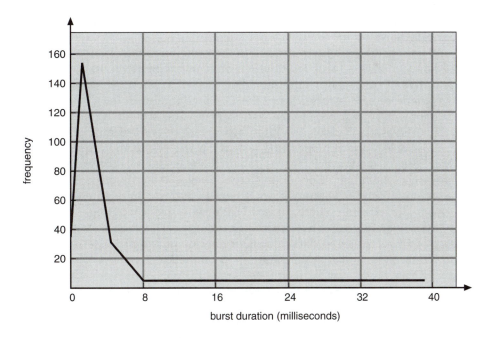

Figure 6.2   Histogram of CPU-burst times.

queue may be implemented as a FIFO queue, a priority queue, a tree, or simply an unordered linked list. Conceptually, however, all the processes in the ready queue are lined up waiting for a chance to run on the CPU. The records in the queues are generally PCBs of the processes.

6.1.3 Preemptive Scheduling

CPU scheduling decisions may take place under the following four circumstances:

1. When a process switches from the running state to the waiting state (for example, I/O request, or invocation of wait for the termination of one of the child processes)

2. When a process switches from the running state to the ready state (for example, when an interrupt occurs)

3. When a process switches from the waiting state to the ready state (for example, completion of I/O)

4. When a process terminates

For circumstances 1 and 4, there is no choice in terms of scheduling. A new process (if one exists in the ready queue) must be selected for execution. There is a choice, however, for circumstances 2 and 3.

When scheduling takes place only under circumstances 1 and 4, we say that the scheduling scheme is **nonpreemptive** or **cooperative**; otherwise, it is **preemptive**. Under nonpreemptive scheduling, once the CPU has been allocated to a process, the process keeps the CPU until it releases the CPU either by terminating or by switching to the waiting state. This scheduling method was used by Microsoft Windows 3.x; Windows 95 introduced preemptive scheduling. The Apple Macintosh operating system introduced preemptive scheduling in MacOS 8 for the PowerPC platform. Previous versions of the MacOS used cooperative scheduling. Cooperative scheduling is the only method that can be used on certain hardware platforms, because it does not require the special hardware (for example, a timer) needed for preemptive scheduling.

Unfortunately, preemptive scheduling incurs a cost associated with coordination of access to shared data. Consider the case of two processes that share data. While one is updating the data, it is preempted so that the second process can run. The second process then tries to read the data, which are in an inconsistent state. Thus, we need new mechanisms to coordinate access to shared data; we discuss this topic in Chapter 7.

Preemption also has an effect on the design of the operating-system kernel. During the processing of a system call, the kernel may be busy with an activity on behalf of a process. Such activities may involve changing important kernel data (for instance, I/O queues). What happens if the process is preempted in the middle of these changes, and the kernel (or the device driver) needs to read or modify the same structure? Chaos ensues. Certain operating systems, including most versions of UNIX, deal with this problem by waiting either for a system call to complete, or for an I/O block to take place, before doing a context switch. This scheme ensures that the kernel structure is simple, since the kernel will not preempt a process while the kernel data structures are in an inconsistent state. Unfortunately, this kernel-execution model is a poor one for supporting real-time computing and multiprocessing. These problems, and their solutions, are described in Sections 6.4 and 6.5.

In the case of UNIX, there are still sections of code at risk. Because interrupts can, by definition, occur at any time, and because interrupts cannot always be ignored by the kernel, the sections of code affected by interrupts must be guarded from simultaneous use. The operating system needs to accept interrupts at almost all times; otherwise, input might be lost or output overwritten. So that these sections of code are not accessed concurrently by several processes, they disable interrupts at entry and reenable interrupts at exit.

6.1.4 Dispatcher

Another component involved in the CPU scheduling function is the **dispatcher**. The dispatcher is the module that gives control of the CPU to the process selected by the short-term scheduler. This function involves the following:

- Switching context

- Switching to user mode

- Jumping to the proper location in the user program to restart that program

The dispatcher should be as fast as possible, given that it is invoked during every process switch. The time that it takes for the dispatcher to stop one process and to start another running is known as the **dispatch latency**.

6.2 ■ Scheduling Criteria

Different CPU scheduling algorithms have different properties and may favor one class of processes over another. In choosing which algorithm to use in a particular situation, we must consider the different properties of the various algorithms.

Many criteria have been suggested for comparing CPU scheduling algorithms. Which characteristics are used for comparison can make a substantial difference in the determination of the best algorithm. Criteria that are used include the following:

- *CPU utilization*: We want to keep the CPU as busy as possible. CPU utilization may range from 0 to 100 percent. In a real system, it should range from 40 percent (for a lightly loaded system) to 90 percent (for a heavily used system).

- *Throughput*: If the CPU is busy executing processes, then work is being done. One measure of work is the number of processes that are completed per time unit, called throughput. For long processes, this rate may be one process per hour; for short transactions, throughput might be 10 processes per second.

- *Turnaround time*: From the point of view of a particular process, the important criterion is how long it takes to execute that process. The interval from the time of submission of a process to the time of completion is the turnaround time. Turnaround time is the sum of the periods spent waiting to get into memory, waiting in the ready queue, executing on the CPU, and doing I/O.

- *Waiting time*: The CPU scheduling algorithm does not affect the amount of time during which a process executes or does I/O; it affects only the amount of time that a process spends waiting in the ready queue. Waiting time is the sum of the periods spent waiting in the ready queue.

- *Response time*: In an interactive system, turnaround time may not be the best criterion. Often, a process can produce some output fairly early, and can continue computing new results while previous results are being output to the user. Thus, another measure is the time from the submission of a request until the first response is produced. This measure, called response time, is the time that it takes to start responding, but not the time that it takes to output that response. The turnaround time is generally limited by the speed of the output device.

It is desirable to maximize CPU utilization and throughput, and to minimize turnaround time, waiting time, and response time. In most cases, we optimize the average measure. However, there are circumstances under which it is desirable to optimize the minimum or maximum values, rather than the average. For example, to guarantee that all users get good service, we may want to minimize the maximum response time.

Investigators have suggested that, for interactive systems (such as time-sharing systems), it is more important to minimize the *variance* in the response time than it is to minimize the average response time. A system with reasonable and *predictable* response time may be considered more desirable than a system that is faster on the average, but is highly variable. However, little work has been done on CPU scheduling algorithms that minimize variance.

As we discuss various CPU scheduling algorithms, we want to illustrate their operation. An accurate illustration should involve many processes, each being a sequence of several hundred CPU bursts and I/O bursts. For simplicity of illustration, we consider only one CPU burst (in milliseconds) per process in our examples. Our measure of comparison is the average waiting time. More elaborate evaluation mechanisms are discussed in Section 6.8.

6.3 ■ Scheduling Algorithms

CPU scheduling deals with the problem of deciding which of the processes in the ready queue is to be allocated the CPU. There are many different CPU scheduling algorithms. In this section, we describe several of these algorithms.

6.3.1 First-Come, First-Served Scheduling

By far the simplest CPU scheduling algorithm is the **first-come, first-served scheduling** (**FCFS**) algorithm. With this scheme, the process that requests the CPU first is allocated the CPU first. The implementation of the FCFS policy is easily managed with a FIFO queue. When a process enters the ready queue, its PCB is linked onto the tail of the queue. When the CPU is free, it is allocated to the process at the head of the queue. The running process is then removed from the queue. The code for FCFS scheduling is simple to write and understand.

The average waiting time under the FCFS policy, however, is often quite long. Consider the following set of processes that arrive at time 0, with the length of the CPU-burst time given in milliseconds:

Process	Burst Time
P_1	24
P_2	3
P_3	3

If the processes arrive in the order P_1, P_2, P_3, and are served in FCFS order, we get the result shown in the following **Gantt chart**:

P_1		P_2	P_3

0   24   27   30

The waiting time is 0 milliseconds for process P_1, 24 milliseconds for process P_2, and 27 milliseconds for process P_3. Thus, the average waiting time is (0 + 24 + 27)/3 = 17 milliseconds. If the processes arrive in the order P_2, P_3, P_1, however, the results will be as shown in the following Gantt chart:

The average waiting time is now $(6 + 0 + 3)/3 = 3$ milliseconds. This reduction is substantial. Thus, the average waiting time under a FCFS policy is generally not minimal, and may vary substantially if the process CPU-burst times vary greatly.

In addition, consider the performance of FCFS scheduling in a dynamic situation. Assume we have one CPU-bound process and many I/O-bound processes. As the processes flow around the system, the following scenario may result. The CPU-bound process will get and hold the CPU. During this time, all the other processes will finish their I/O and will move into the ready queue, waiting for the CPU. While the processes wait in the ready queue, the I/O devices are idle. Eventually, the CPU-bound process finishes its CPU burst and moves to an I/O device. All the I/O-bound processes, which have short CPU bursts, execute quickly and move back to the I/O queues. At this point, the CPU sits idle. The CPU-bound process will then move back to the ready queue and be allocated the CPU. Again, all the I/O processes end up waiting in the ready queue until the CPU-bound process is done. There is a **convoy effect,** as all the other processes wait for the one big process to get off the CPU. This effect results in lower CPU and device utilization than might be possible if the shorter processes were allowed to go first.

The FCFS scheduling algorithm is nonpreemptive. Once the CPU has been allocated to a process, that process keeps the CPU until it releases the CPU, either by terminating or by requesting I/O. The FCFS algorithm is particularly troublesome for time-sharing systems, where it is important that each user get a share of the CPU at regular intervals. It would be disastrous to allow one process to keep the CPU for an extended period.

6.3.2 Shortest-Job-First Scheduling

A different approach to CPU scheduling is the **shortest-job-first** (SJF) algorithm. This algorithm associates with each process the length of the latter's next CPU burst. When the CPU is available, it is assigned to the process that has the smallest next CPU burst. If two processes have the same-length next CPU burst, FCFS scheduling is used to break the tie. Note that a more appropriate term would be the **shortest next CPU burst**, because the scheduling is done by examining the length of the next CPU-burst of a process, rather than its total length. We use the term SJF because most people and textbooks refer to this type of scheduling discipline as SJF.

As an example, consider the following set of processes, with the length of the CPU burst time given in milliseconds:

Process	Burst Time
P_1	6
P_2	8
P_3	7
P_4	3

Using SJF scheduling, we would schedule these processes according to the following Gantt chart:

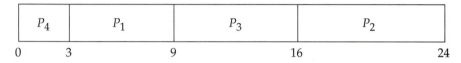

The waiting time is 3 milliseconds for process P_1, 16 milliseconds for process P_2, 9 milliseconds for process P_3, and 0 milliseconds for process P_4. Thus, the average waiting time is $(3 + 16 + 9 + 0)/4 = 7$ milliseconds. If we were using the FCFS scheduling scheme, then the average waiting time would be 10.25 milliseconds.

The SJF scheduling algorithm is provably *optimal*, in that it gives the minimum average waiting time for a given set of processes. By moving a short process before a long one the waiting time of the short process decreases more than it increases the waiting time of the long process. Consequently, the *average* waiting time decreases.

The real difficulty with the SJF algorithm is knowing the length of the next CPU request. For long-term (job) scheduling in a batch system, we can use as the length the process time limit that a user specifies when he submits the job. Thus, users are motivated to estimate the process time limit accurately, since a lower value may mean faster response. (Too low a value will cause a time-limit-exceeded error and require resubmission.) SJF scheduling is used frequently in long-term scheduling.

Although the SJF algorithm is optimal, it cannot be implemented at the level of short-term CPU scheduling. There is no way to know the length of the next CPU burst. One approach is to try to approximate SJF scheduling. We may not *know* the length of the next CPU burst, but we may be able to *predict* its value. We expect that the next CPU burst will be similar in length to the previous ones. Thus, by computing an approximation of the length of the next CPU burst, we can pick the process with the shortest predicted CPU burst.

The next CPU burst is generally predicted as an exponential average of the measured lengths of previous CPU bursts. Let t_n be the length of the nth CPU burst, and let τ_{n+1} be our predicted value for the next CPU burst. Then, for α, $0 \le \alpha \le 1$, define

$$\tau_{n+1} = \alpha\, t_n + (1 - \alpha)\tau_n.$$

This formula defines an **exponential average**. The value of t_n contains our most recent information; τ_n stores the past history. The parameter α controls the relative weight of recent and past history in our prediction. If $\alpha = 0$, then $\tau_{n+1} = \tau_n$, and recent history has no effect (current conditions are assumed to be transient); if $\alpha = 1$, then $\tau_{n+1} = t_n$, and only the most recent CPU burst matters (history is assumed to be old and irrelevant). More commonly, $\alpha = 1/2$, so recent history and past history are equally weighted. The initial τ_0 can be defined as a constant or as an overall system average. Figure 6.3 shows an exponential average with $\alpha = 1/2$ and $\tau_0 = 10$.

To understand the behavior of the exponential average, we can expand the formula for τ_{n+1} by substituting for τ_n, to find

$$\tau_{n+1} = \alpha t_n + (1 - \alpha)\alpha t_{n-1} + \cdots + (1 - \alpha)^j \alpha t_{n-j} + \cdots + (1 - \alpha)^{n+1}\tau_0.$$

Since both α and $(1 - \alpha)$ are less than or equal to 1, each successive term has less weight than its predecessor.

The SJF algorithm may be either preemptive or nonpreemptive. The choice arises when a new process arrives at the ready queue while a previous process is executing. The new process may have a shorter next CPU burst than what is left of the currently executing process. A preemptive SJF algorithm will preempt the currently executing process, whereas a nonpreemptive SJF algorithm will allow

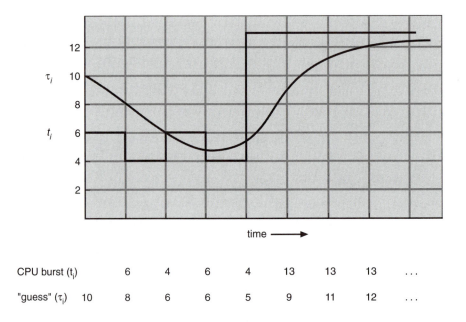

CPU burst (t_i)		6	4	6	4	13	13	13	. . .
"guess" (τ_i)	10	8	6	6	5	9	11	12	. . .

Figure 6.3   Prediction of the length of the next CPU burst.

the currently running process to finish its CPU burst. Preemptive SJF scheduling is sometimes called **shortest-remaining-time-first** scheduling.

As an example, consider the following four processes, with the length of the CPU-burst time given in milliseconds:

Process	Arrival Time	Burst Time
P_1	0	8
P_2	1	4
P_3	2	9
P_4	3	5

If the processes arrive at the ready queue at the times shown and need the indicated burst times, then the resulting preemptive SJF schedule is as depicted in the following Gantt chart:

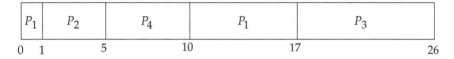

Process P_1 is started at time 0, since it is the only process in the queue. Process P_2 arrives at time 1. The remaining time for process P_1 (7 milliseconds) is larger than the time required by process P_2 (4 milliseconds), so process P_1 is preempted, and process P_2 is scheduled. The average waiting time for this example is $((10-1)+(1-1)+(17-2)+(5-3))/4 = 26/4 = 6.5$ milliseconds. A nonpreemptive SJF scheduling would result in an average waiting time of 7.75 milliseconds.

6.3.3 Priority Scheduling

The SJF algorithm is a special case of the general **priority** scheduling algorithm. A priority is associated with each process, and the CPU is allocated to the process with the highest priority. Equal-priority processes are scheduled in FCFS order.

An SJF algorithm is simply a priority algorithm where the priority (p) is the inverse of the (predicted) next CPU burst. The larger the CPU burst, the lower the priority, and vice versa.

Note that we discuss scheduling in terms of *high* priority and *low* priority. Priorities are generally some fixed range of numbers, such as 0 to 7, or 0 to 4095. However, there is no general agreement on whether 0 is the highest or lowest priority. Some systems use low numbers to represent low priority; others use low numbers for high priority. This difference can lead to confusion. In this text, we assume that low numbers represent high priority.

As an example, consider the following set of processes, assumed to have arrived at time 0, in the order $P_1, P_2, \cdots, P_5$, with the length of the CPU-burst time given in milliseconds:

Process	Burst Time	Priority
P_1	10	3
P_2	1	1
P_3	2	4
P_4	1	5
P_5	5	2

Using priority scheduling, we would schedule these processes according to the following Gantt chart:

P_2	P_5	P_1	P_3	P_4

0   1   6   16   18 19

The average waiting time is 8.2 milliseconds.

Priorities can be defined either internally or externally. Internally defined priorities use some measurable quantity or quantities to compute the priority of a process. For example, time limits, memory requirements, the number of open files, and the ratio of average I/O burst to average CPU burst have been used in computing priorities. External priorities are set by criteria that are external to the operating system, such as the importance of the process, the type and amount of funds being paid for computer use, the department sponsoring the work, and other, often political, factors.

Priority scheduling can be either preemptive or nonpreemptive. When a process arrives at the ready queue, its priority is compared with the priority of the currently running process. A preemptive priority scheduling algorithm will preempt the CPU if the priority of the newly arrived process is higher than the priority of the currently running process. A nonpreemptive priority scheduling algorithm will simply put the new process at the head of the ready queue.

A major problem with priority scheduling algorithms is **indefinite blocking** or **starvation**. A process that is ready to run but lacking the CPU can be considered blocked, waiting for the CPU. A priority scheduling algorithm can leave some low-priority processes waiting indefinitely for the CPU. In a heavily loaded computer system, a steady stream of higher-priority processes can prevent a low-priority process from ever getting the CPU. Generally, one of two things will happen. Either the process will eventually be run (at 2 A.M. Sunday, when the system is finally lightly loaded), or the computer system will eventually crash and lose all unfinished low-priority processes. (Rumor has it that, when they shut down the IBM 7094 at MIT in 1973, they found a low-priority process that had been submitted in 1967 and had not yet been run.)

A solution to the problem of indefinite blockage of low-priority processes is **aging**. Aging is a technique of gradually increasing the priority of processes that wait in the system for a long time. For example, if priorities range from 127 (low) to 0 (high), we could increment the priority of a waiting process by 1 every 15 minutes. Eventually, even a process with an initial priority of 127 would have the highest priority in the system and would be executed. In fact, it would take no more than 32 hours for a priority 127 process to age to a priority 0 process.

6.3.4 Round-Robin Scheduling

The **round-robin** (**RR**) scheduling algorithm is designed especially for time-sharing systems. It is similar to FCFS scheduling, but preemption is added to switch between processes. A small unit of time, called a **time quantum**, or time slice, is defined. A time quantum is generally from 10 to 100 milliseconds. The ready queue is treated as a circular queue. The CPU scheduler goes around the ready queue, allocating the CPU to each process for a time interval of up to 1 time quantum.

To implement RR scheduling, we keep the ready queue as a FIFO queue of processes. New processes are added to the tail of the ready queue. The CPU scheduler picks the first process from the ready queue, sets a timer to interrupt after 1 time quantum, and dispatches the process.

One of two things will then happen. The process may have a CPU burst of less than 1 time quantum. In this case, the process itself will release the CPU voluntarily. The scheduler will then proceed to the next process in the ready queue. Otherwise, if the CPU burst of the currently running process is longer than 1 time quantum, the timer will go off and will cause an interrupt to the operating system. A context switch will be executed, and the process will be put at the **tail** of the ready queue. The CPU scheduler will then select the next process in the ready queue.

The average waiting time under the RR policy, however, is often long. Consider the following set of processes that arrive at time 0, with the length of the CPU-burst time given in milliseconds:

Process	Burst Time
P_1	24
P_2	3
P_3	3

If we use a time quantum of 4 milliseconds, then process P_1 gets the first 4 milliseconds. Since it requires another 20 milliseconds, it is preempted after the first time quantum, and the CPU is given to the next process in the queue, process P_2. Since process P_2 does not need 4 milliseconds, it quits before its time quantum expires. The CPU is then given to the next process, process P_3. Once each process has received 1 time quantum, the CPU is returned to process P_1 for an additional time quantum. The resulting RR schedule is

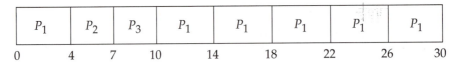

The average waiting time is $17/3 = 5.66$ milliseconds.

In the RR scheduling algorithm, no process is allocated the CPU for more than 1 time quantum in a row (unless it is the only runnable process). If a process' CPU burst exceeds 1 time quantum, that process is *preempted* and is put back in the ready queue. The RR scheduling algorithm is preemptive.

If there are n processes in the ready queue and the time quantum is q, then each process gets $1/n$ of the CPU time in chunks of at most q time units. Each process must wait no longer than $(n - 1) \times q$ time units until its next time quantum. For example, if there are five processes, with a time quantum of 20 milliseconds, then each process will get up to 20 milliseconds every 100 milliseconds.

The performance of the RR algorithm depends heavily on the size of the time quantum. At one extreme, if the time quantum is extremely large, the RR policy is the same as the FCFS policy. If the time quantum is extremely small (say 1 microsecond), the RR approach is called **processor sharing,** and appears (in theory) to the users as though each of n processes has its own processor running at $1/n$ the speed of the real processor. This approach was used in Control Data Corporation (CDC) hardware to implement 10 peripheral processors with

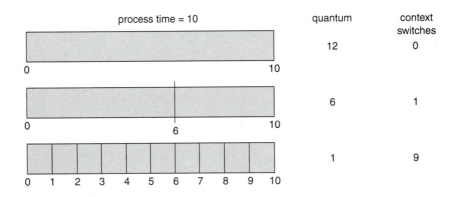

Figure 6.4   The way in which a smaller time quantum increases context switches.

only one set of hardware and 10 sets of registers. The hardware executes one instruction for one set of registers, then goes on to the next. This cycle continues, resulting in 10 slow processors rather than one fast one.   (Actually, since the processor was much faster than memory and each instruction referenced memory, the processors were not much slower than 10 real processors would have been.)

In software, however, we need also to consider the effect of context switching on the performance of RR scheduling. Let us assume that we have only one process of 10 time units. If the quantum is 12 time units, the process finishes in less than 1 time quantum, with no overhead. If the quantum is 6 time units, however, the process requires 2 quanta, resulting in a context switch. If the time quantum is 1 time unit, then nine context switches will occur, slowing the execution of the process accordingly (Figure 6.4).

Thus, we want the time quantum to be large with respect to the context-switch time. If the context-switch time is approximately 10 percent of the time quantum, then about 10 percent of the CPU time will be spent in context switch.

Turnaround time also depends on the size of the time quantum. As we can see from Figure 6.5, the average turnaround time of a set of processes does not necessarily improve as the time-quantum size increases. In general, the average turnaround time can be improved if most processes finish their next CPU burst in a single time quantum. For example, given three processes of 10

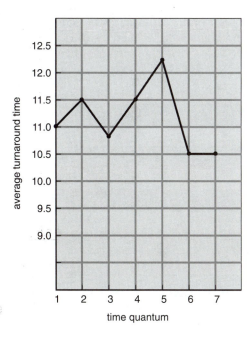

process	time
P_1	6
P_2	3
P_3	1
P_4	7

Figure 6.5   The way in which turnaround time varies with the time quantum.

time units each and a quantum of 1 time unit, the average turnaround time is 29. If the time quantum is 10, however, the average turnaround time drops to 20. If context-switch time is added in, the average turnaround time increases for a smaller time quantum, since more context switches will be required.

On the other hand, if the time quantum is too large, RR scheduling degenerates to FCFS policy. A rule of thumb is that 80 percent of the CPU bursts should be shorter than the time quantum.

6.3.5 Multilevel Queue Scheduling

Another class of scheduling algorithms has been created for situations in which processes are easily classified into different groups. For example, a common division is made between **foreground** (interactive) processes and **background** (batch) processes. These two types of processes have different response-time requirements, and so might have different scheduling needs. In addition, foreground processes may have priority (externally defined) over background processes.

A **multilevel queue-scheduling algorithm** partitions the ready queue into several separate queues (Figure 6.6). The processes are permanently assigned to one queue, generally based on some property of the process, such as memory size, process priority, or process type. Each queue has its own scheduling algorithm. For example, separate queues might be used for foreground and background processes. The foreground queue might be scheduled by an RR algorithm, while the background queue is scheduled by an FCFS algorithm.

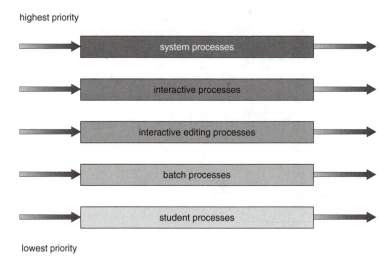

Figure 6.6   Multilevel queue scheduling.

In addition, there must be scheduling between the queues, which is commonly implemented as fixed-priority preemptive scheduling. For example, the foreground queue may have absolute priority over the background queue.

Let us look at an example of a multilevel-queue-scheduling algorithm with five queues:

1. System processes

2. Interactive processes

3. Interactive editing processes

4. Batch processes

5. Student processes

Each queue has absolute priority over lower-priority queues. No process in the batch queue, for example, could run unless the queues for system processes, interactive processes, and interactive editing processes were all empty. If an interactive editing process entered the ready queue while a batch process was running, the batch process would be preempted.

Another possibility is to time slice between the queues. Each queue gets a certain portion of the CPU time, which it can then schedule among the various processes in its queue. For instance, in the foreground-background queue example, the foreground queue can be given 80 percent of the CPU time for RR scheduling among its processes, whereas the background queue receives 20 percent of the CPU to give to its processes in a FCFS manner.

6.3.6 Multilevel Feedback-Queue Scheduling

Normally, in a multilevel queue-scheduling algorithm, processes are permanently assigned to a queue on entry to the system. Processes do not move between queues. If there are separate queues for foreground and background processes, for example, processes do not move from one queue to the other, since processes do not change their foreground or background nature. This setup has the advantage of low scheduling overhead, but is inflexible.

Multilevel feedback-queue scheduling, however, allows a process to move between queues. The idea is to separate processes with different CPU-burst characteristics. If a process uses too much CPU time, it will be moved to a lower-priority queue. This scheme leaves I/O-bound and interactive processes in the higher-priority queues. Similarly, a process that waits too long in a lower-priority queue may be moved to a higher-priority queue. This form of aging prevents starvation.

For example, consider a multilevel feedback-queue scheduler with three queues, numbered from 0 to 2 (Figure 6.7). The scheduler first executes all processes in queue 0. Only when queue 0 is empty will it execute processes

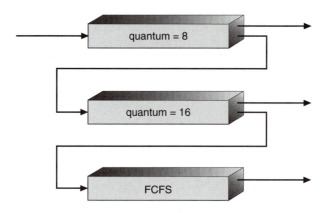

Figure 6.7   Multilevel feedback queues.

in queue 1. Similarly, processes in queue 2 will only be executed if queues 0 and 1 are empty. A process that arrives for queue 1 will preempt a process in queue 2. A process in queue 1 will in turn be preempted by a process arriving for queue 0.

A process entering the ready queue is put in queue 0. A process in queue 0 is given a time quantum of 8 milliseconds. If it does not finish within this time, it is moved to the tail of queue 1. If queue 0 is empty, the process at the head of queue 1 is given a quantum of 16 milliseconds. If it does not complete, it is preempted and is put into queue 2. Processes in queue 2 are run on an FCFS basis, only when queues 0 and 1 are empty.

This scheduling algorithm gives highest priority to any process with a CPU burst of 8 milliseconds or less. Such a process will quickly get the CPU, finish its CPU burst, and go off to its next I/O burst. Processes that need more than 8, but less than 24, milliseconds are also served quickly, although with lower priority than shorter processes. Long processes automatically sink to queue 2 and are served in FCFS order with any CPU cycles left over from queues 0 and 1.

In general, a multilevel feedback queue scheduler is defined by the following parameters:

- The number of queues

- The scheduling algorithm for each queue

- The method used to determine when to upgrade a process to a higher-priority queue

- The method used to determine when to demote a process to a lower-priority queue

- The method used to determine which queue a process will enter when that process needs service

The definition of a multilevel feedback queue scheduler makes it the most general CPU scheduling algorithm. It can be configured to match a specific system under design. Unfortunately, it requires some means by which to select values for all the parameters to define the best scheduler. Although a multilevel feedback queue is the most general scheme, it is also the most complex.

6.4 ■ Multiple-Processor Scheduling

Our discussion thus far has focused on the problems of scheduling the CPU in a system with a single processor. If multiple CPUs are available, the scheduling problem is correspondingly more complex. Many possibilities have been tried, and, as we saw with single-processor CPU scheduling, there is no one best solution. We discuss briefly concerns in multiprocessor scheduling. We concentrate on systems in which the processors are identical—**homogeneous**—in terms of their functionality; we can then use any available processor to run any processes in the queue.

Even within homogeneous multiprocessors, there are sometimes limitations on scheduling. Consider a system with an I/O device attached to a private bus of one processor. Processes that wish to use that device must be scheduled to run on that processor.

If several identical processors are available, then **load sharing** can occur. We could provide a separate queue for each processor. In this case, however, one processor could be idle, with an empty queue, while another processor is extremely busy. To prevent this situation, we use a common ready queue. All processes go into one queue and are scheduled onto any available processor.

In such a scheme, one of two scheduling approaches may be used. One approach uses **symmetric multiprocessing** (**SMP**), where each processor is self-scheduling. Each processor examines the common ready queue and selects a process to execute. As we shall see in Chapter 7, if we have multiple processors trying to access and update a common data structure, each processor must be programmed carefully: We must ensure that two processors do not choose the same process, and that processes are not lost from the queue.

Some systems carry this structure one step further, by having all scheduling decisions, I/O processing, and other system activities handled by one single processor—the master server. The other processors execute only user code. This **asymmetric multiprocessing** is far simpler than symmetric multiprocessing, because only one processor accesses the system data structures, alleviating the need for data sharing.

6.5 ■ Real-Time Scheduling

In Chapter 1, we discussed the growing importance of real-time operating systems. Here, we describe the scheduling facility needed to support real-time computing within a general-purpose computer system.

Real-time computing is of two types. **Hard real-time** systems are required to complete a critical task within a guaranteed amount of time. Generally, a process is submitted along with a statement of the amount of time in which it needs to complete or perform I/O. The scheduler then either admits the process, guaranteeing that the process will complete on time, or rejects the request as impossible. Such a guarantee, made under **resource reservation,** requires that the scheduler know exactly how long it takes to perform each type of operating-system function; therefore, each operation must be guaranteed to take a maximum amount of time. Such a guarantee is impossible in a system with secondary storage or virtual memory, as we show in Chapters 9 through 13, because these subsystems cause unavoidable and unforeseeable variation in the amount of time to execute a particular process. Therefore, hard real-time systems are composed of special-purpose software running on hardware dedicated to their critical process, and lack the full functionality of modern computers and operating systems.

Soft real-time computing is less restrictive. It requires that critical processes receive priority over less fortunate ones. Although adding soft real-time functionality to a time-sharing system may cause an unfair allocation of resources and may result in longer delays, or even starvation, for some processes, it is at least possible to achieve. The result is a general-purpose system that can also support multimedia, high-speed interactive graphics, and a variety of tasks that would not function acceptably in an environment that does not support soft real-time computing.

Implementing soft real-time functionality requires careful design of the scheduler and related aspects of the operating system. First, the system must have priority scheduling, and real-time processes must have the highest priority. The priority of real-time processes must not degrade over time, even though the priority of non–real-time processes may. Second, the dispatch latency must be small. The smaller the latency, the faster a real-time process can start executing once it is runnable.

It is relatively simple to ensure that the former property holds. For example, we can disallow process aging on real-time processes, thereby guaranteeing that the priority of the various processes does not change. However, ensuring the latter property is much more involved. The problem is that many operating systems, including most versions of UNIX, are forced to wait either for a system call to complete or for an I/O block to take place before they can do a context switch. The dispatch latency in such systems can be long, since some system calls are complex and some I/O devices are slow.

To keep dispatch latency low, we need to allow system calls to be pre-emptible. There are several ways to achieve this goal. One is to insert **pre-emption points** in long-duration system calls, which check to see whether a high-priority process needs to be run. If one does, a context switch takes place; when the high-priority process terminates, the interrupted process continues with the system call. Preemption points can be placed at only *safe* locations in

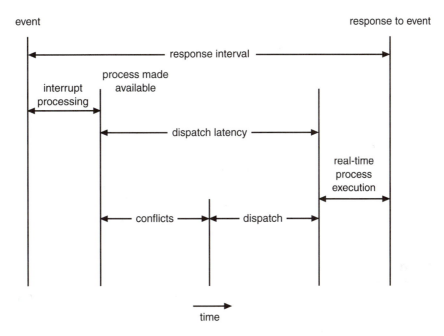

Figure 6.8   Dispatch latency.

the kernel—only where kernel data structures are not being modified. Even with preemption points, dispatch latency can be large, because it is practical to add only a few preemption points to a kernel.

Another method for dealing with preemption is to make the entire kernel preemptible. So that correct operation is ensured, all kernel data structures must be protected through the use of various synchronization mechanisms that we discuss in Chapter 7. With this method, the kernel can always be preemptible, because any kernel data being updated are protected from modification by the high-priority process. This method is used in Solaris 2.

What happens if the higher-priority process needs to read or modify kernel data that are currently being accessed by another, lower-priority process? The high-priority process would be waiting for a lower-priority one to finish. This situation is known as **priority inversion**. In fact, there could be a chain of processes, all accessing resources that the high-priority process needs. This problem can be solved via the **priority-inheritance protocol,** in which all these processes (the processes that are accessing resources that the high-priority process needs) inherit the high priority until they are done with the resource in question. When they are finished, their priority reverts to its original value.

In Figure 6.8, we show the makeup of dispatch latency. The **conflict phase** of dispatch latency has two components:

1. Preemption of any process running in the kernel

2. Release by low-priority processes of resources needed by the high-priority process

As an example, in Solaris 2 with preemption disabled, the dispatch latency is over 100 milliseconds; with preemption enabled, it is usually reduced to 2 milliseconds.

6.6 ■ Thread Scheduling

In Chapter 5, we introduced threads to the process model, thus allowing a single process to have multiple threads of control. Furthermore, we distinguished between *user-level* and *kernel-level* threads. User-level threads are managed by a thread library, and the kernel is unaware of them. To run on a CPU, user-level threads are ultimately mapped to an associated kernel-level thread, although this mapping may be indirect and use a lightweight process (LWP) . One distinction between user-level and kernel-level threads lies in how they are scheduled. The threads library schedules user-level threads to run on an available LWP, a scheme known as **process local scheduling** (thread scheduling is done local to the application). Conversely, the kernel uses **system global scheduling** to decide which kernel thread to schedule. We do not cover in detail how different threads libraries locally schedule threads—that is more a software-library than an operating-system concern. We cover global scheduling because it is performed by the operating system. We look next at how Solaris 2 schedules threads.

6.6.1 Solaris 2 Scheduling

Solaris 2 uses priority-based process scheduling. It has defined four classes of scheduling, which are, in order of priority, real time, system, time sharing, and interactive. Within each class there are different priorities and different scheduling algorithms (time sharing and interactive use the same scheduling policies). Solaris 2 scheduling is illustrated in Figure 6.9.

A process starts with one LWP and is able to create new LWPs as needed. Each LWP inherits the scheduling class and priority of the parent process. The default scheduling class for a process is time sharing. The scheduling policy for time sharing dynamically alters priorities and assigns time slices of different lengths using a multilevel feedback queue. By default, there is an inverse relationship between priorities and time slices: The higher the priority, the smaller the time slice, and the lower the priority, the larger the time slice. Interactive processes typically have a higher priority; CPU-bound processes a lower priority. This scheduling policy gives good response time for interactive processes and good throughput for CPU-bound processes. Solaris 2.4 introduced the interactive class to process scheduling. The interactive class uses

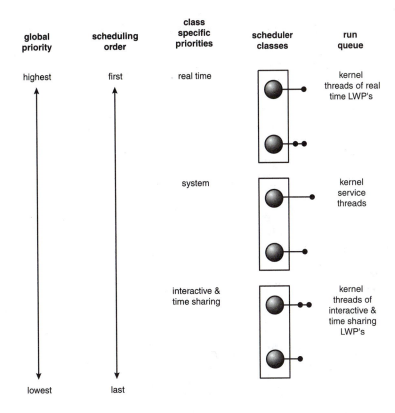

Figure 6.9   Solaris 2 scheduling.

the same scheduling policy as the time-sharing class, but it gives windowing applications a higher priority for better performance.

Solaris uses the system class to run kernel processes, such as the scheduler and paging daemon. Once established, the priority of a system process does not change. The system class is reserved for kernel use (user processes running in kernel mode are not in the systems class).

Threads in the real-time class are given the highest priority to run among all classes. This assignment allows a real-time process to have a guaranteed response from the system within a bounded period of time. A real-time process will run before a process in any other class. In general, few processes belong to the real-time class.

There is a set of priorities within each scheduling class. However, the scheduler converts the class-specific priorities into global priorities, and selects to run the thread with the highest global priority. The selected thread runs on the CPU until it (1) blocks, (2) uses its time slice, or (3) is preempted by a higher-priority thread. If there are multiple threads with the same priority, the scheduler uses a round-robin queue.

6.7 ■ Java Thread Scheduling

The JVM schedules threads using a preemptive, priority-based scheduling algorithm. All Java threads are given a priority and the JVM schedules the Runnable thread with the highest priority for execution. If two or more Runnable threads have the highest priority, the JVM will schedule the threads using a FIFO queue.

The JVM schedules a thread to run when one of the following events occur:

1. The currently running thread exits the Runnable state. A thread may leave the Runnable state several ways such as blocking for I/O, exiting its run() method, or having its suspend() or stop() method invoked.

2. A thread with a higher priority than the thread currently running enters the Runnable state. In this case, the JVM preempts the currently running thread and schedules the thread with the higher priority for execution.

6.7.1 Time Slicing

The specification for the JVM does not indicate whether or not threads are time-sliced—it is up to the particular implementation of the JVM. If threads are time sliced, then a Runnable thread is executed for its time quantum or until it exits the Runnable state or is preempted by a higher-priority thread. If threads are not time sliced, then a thread runs until one of the two events listed occurs.

So that all threads have an equal amount of CPU time on a system that does not perform time slicing, a thread may yield control of the CPU with the yield() method. By invoking the yield() method, a thread relinquishes control of the CPU allowing another thread of equal priority to run. A thread voluntarily yielding control of the CPU is called **cooperative multitasking**. The use of the yield() method appears as

```
public void run() {
    while (true) {
        // perform a CPU-intensive task
        .  .  .
        // now yield control of the CPU
        Thread.yield();
    }
}
```

6.7.2 Thread Priorities

As mentioned, the JVM schedules threads according to priority. The JVM selects to run a Runnable thread with the highest priority. All Java threads are given a priority that is a positive integer within a given range. Threads are given a default priority when they are created and—unless they are changed explicitly

```
public class HighThread extends Thread
{
    public void run() {
        this.setPriority(Thread.NORM_PRIORITY + 1);
        // remainder of run() method
    }
          .   .   .
}
```

Figure 6.10   Setting a priority using `setPriority()`.

by the program—they maintain the same priority throughout their lifetime; the JVM does not dynamically alter priorities. The Java `Thread` class identifies the following thread priorities:

Priority	Comment
`Thread.MIN_PRIORITY`	The minimum thread priority.
`Thread.MAX_PRIORITY`	The maximum thread priority.
`Thread.NORM_PRIORITY`	The default thread priority.

The value of `MIN_PRIORITY` is 1, `MAX_PRIORITY` is 10, and `NORM_PRIORITY` is 5. Every Java thread has a priority that falls somewhere within this range. When a thread is created, it is given the same priority as the thread that created it. Unless otherwise specified, the default priority for all threads is `NORM_PRIORITY`. The priority of a thread can also be set explicitly with the `setPriority()` method. The priority can be set either before a thread is started or while a thread is active. The class `HighThread` (Figure 6.10) increases the priority by 1 more than the default priority prior to performing the remainder of its `run()` method.

6.7.3 Java-Based Round-Robin Scheduler

The class `Scheduler` (Figure 6.11) implements a time-sliced, round-robin thread scheduler. The scheduler contains a single queue of threads from which it selects a thread to run. The scheduler itself runs as a separate thread with priority 6. The threads that it schedules are at either priority 2 or 4, depending on whether or not the thread has been scheduled to run.

The operation of the scheduler is as follows. When a thread is added to the scheduler's queue (with the `addThread()` method), it is given a default priority of 2. When the scheduler selects a thread to run, it sets the priority of the thread to 4. The scheduler then goes to sleep for a time quantum. Since the JVM uses a priority-based scheduling algorithm, the thread with priority 4 is the highest-priority Runnable thread, so it is allocated the CPU for the time quantum. When the time quantum expires, the scheduler wakes up. Since the

```
public class Scheduler extends Thread
{
    public Scheduler() {
       timeSlice = DEFAULT_TIME_SLICE;
       queue = new CircularList();
    }

    public Scheduler(int quantum) {
       timeSlice = quantum;
       queue = new CircularList();
    }

    public void addThread(Thread t) {
       t.setPriority(2);
       queue.addItem(t);
    }

    private void schedulerSleep() {
       try {
          Thread.sleep(timeSlice);
       } catch (InterruptedException e) { };
    }

    public void run() {
       Thread current;

       this.setPriority(6);

       while (true) {
          // get the next thread
          current = (Thread)queue.getNext();
          if ( (current != null) && (current.isAlive()) ) {
             current.setPriority(4);
             schedulerSleep();
             current.setPriority(2);
          }
       }
    }

    private CircularList queue;
    private int timeSlice;
    private static final int DEFAULT_TIME_SLICE = 1000;
}
```

Figure 6.11   Round-robin scheduler.

scheduler is running at priority 6, it preempts the currently running thread. The scheduler then sets the priority of the preempted thread back to 2, then selects a new thread to run, repeating the same process.

If there are no threads in the queue, the scheduler sits in a loop waiting to retrieve the next thread. In general, busy-wait loops are a waste of CPU resources. However, it probably does not matter in this case, since there are no threads other than the scheduler available to run. As soon as another thread is eligible to run, the scheduler will schedule it and will go to sleep. A fairly simple modification to the `CircularList` class is to add a method `isEmpty()` that indicates to the scheduler whether the queue is empty. If the queue is empty, the scheduler can go to sleep for some duration and then awaken to check the queue again. Such a modification prevents the busy-wait activity of the scheduler.

The class `TestScheduler` (Figure 6.12) illustrates how we can use the scheduler by creating an instance of the scheduler and adding three threads to the scheduler's queue. Since time slicing cannot be assumed, the `TestScheduler` class is running at the highest priority so that it remains running to start all threads.

```
public class TestScheduler
{
    public static void main(String args[]) {
        Thread.currentThread().setPriority(Thread.MAX_PRIORITY);

        Scheduler CPUScheduler = new Scheduler();
        CPUScheduler.start();

        // uses TestThread, although this
        // could be any Thread object.
        TestThread t1 = new TestThread("Thread 1");
        t1.start();
        CPUScheduler.addThread(t1);

        TestThread t2 = new TestThread("Thread 2");
        t2.start();
        CPUScheduler.addThread(t2);

        TestThread t3 = new TestThread("Thread 3");
        t3.start();
        CPUScheduler.addThread(t3);
    }
}
```

Figure 6.12   Java program that illustrates the use of the scheduler.

6.8 ■ Algorithm Evaluation

How do we select a CPU scheduling algorithm for a particular system? As we saw in Section 6.3, there are many scheduling algorithms, each with its own parameters. As a result, selecting an algorithm can be difficult.

The first problem is defining the criteria to be used in selecting an algorithm. As we saw in Section 6.2, criteria are often defined in terms of CPU utilization, response time, or throughput. To select an algorithm, we must first define the relative importance of these measures. Our criteria may include several measures, such as:

- Maximizing CPU utilization under the constraint that the maximum response time is 1 second

- Maximizing throughput such that turnaround time is (on average) linearly proportional to total execution time

Once the selection criteria have been defined, we want to evaluate the various algorithms under consideration. There are a number of different evaluation methods; we describe them in Sections 6.8.1 through 6.8.4.

6.8.1 Deterministic Modeling

One major class of evaluation methods is **analytic evaluation**. Analytic evaluation uses the given algorithm and the system workload to produce a formula or number that evaluates the performance of the algorithm for that workload.

One type of analytic evaluation is **deterministic modeling**. This method takes a particular predetermined workload and defines the performance of each algorithm for that workload.

For example, assume that we have the workload shown. All five processes arrive at time 0, in the order given, with the length of the CPU-burst time given in milliseconds:

Process	Burst Time
P_1	10
P_2	29
P_3	3
P_4	7
P_5	12

Consider the FCFS, SJF, and RR (quantum = 10 milliseconds) scheduling algorithms for this set of processes. Which algorithm would give the minimum average waiting time?

For the FCFS algorithm, we would execute the processes as

The waiting time is 0 milliseconds for process P_1, 10 milliseconds for process P_2, 39 milliseconds for process P_3, 42 milliseconds for process P_4, and 49 milliseconds for process P_5. Thus, the average waiting time is $(0 + 10 + 39 + 42 + 49)/5 = 28$ milliseconds.

With nonpreemptive SJF scheduling, we execute the processes as

The waiting time is 10 milliseconds for process P_1, 32 milliseconds for process P_2, 0 milliseconds for process P_3, 3 milliseconds for process P_4, and 20 milliseconds for process P_5. Thus, the average waiting time is $(10 + 32 + 0 + 3 + 20)/5 = 13$ milliseconds.

With the RR algorithm, we execute the processes as

The waiting time is 0 milliseconds for process P_1, 32 milliseconds for process P_2, 20 milliseconds for process P_3, 23 milliseconds for process P_4, and 40 milliseconds for process P_5. Thus, the average waiting time is $(0 + 32 + 20 + 23 + 40)/5 = 23$ milliseconds.

We see that, *in this case*, the SJF policy results in less than one-half of the average waiting time obtained with FCFS scheduling; the RR algorithm gives us an intermediate value.

Deterministic modeling is simple and fast. It gives exact numbers, allowing the algorithms to be compared. However, it requires exact numbers for input, and its answers apply to only those cases. The main uses of deterministic modeling are in describing scheduling algorithms and providing examples. In cases where we may be running the same programs over and over again and can measure the program's processing requirements exactly, we may be able to use deterministic modeling to select a scheduling algorithm. Over a set of examples, deterministic modeling may indicate trends that can then be analyzed and proved separately. For example, it can be shown that, for the environment described (all processes and their times available at time 0), the SJF policy will always result in the minimum waiting time.

In general, however, deterministic modeling is too specific, and requires too much exact knowledge, to be useful.

6.8.2 Queueing Models

The processes that are run on many systems vary from day to day, so there is no static set of processes (and times) to use for deterministic modeling. What can be determined, however, is the distribution of CPU and I/O bursts. These distributions may be measured and then approximated or simply estimated. The result is a mathematical formula describing the probability of a particular CPU burst. Commonly, this distribution is exponential and is described by its mean. Similarly, the distribution of times when processes arrive in the system (the arrival-time distribution) must be given. From these two distributions, it is possible to compute the average throughput, utilization, waiting time, and so on for most algorithms.

The computer system is described as a network of servers. Each server has a queue of waiting processes. The CPU is a server with its ready queue, as is the I/O system with its device queues. Knowing arrival rates and service rates, we can compute utilization, average queue length, average wait time, and so on. This area of study is called **queueing-network analysis**.

As an example, let n be the average queue length (excluding the process being serviced), let W be the average waiting time in the queue, and let λ be the average arrival rate for new processes in the queue (such as three processes per second). Then, we expect that during the time W that a process waits, $\lambda \times W$ new processes will arrive in the queue. If the system is in a steady state, then the number of processes leaving the queue must be equal to the number of processes that arrive. Thus,

$$n = \lambda \times W.$$

This equation, known as **Little's formula,** is particularly useful because it is valid for any scheduling algorithm and arrival distribution.

We can use Little's formula to compute one of the three variables, if we know the other two. For example, if we know that seven processes arrive every second (on average), and that there are normally 14 processes in the queue, then we can compute the average waiting time per process as 2 seconds.

Queueing analysis can be useful in comparing scheduling algorithms, but it also has limitations. At the moment, the classes of algorithms and distributions that can be handled are fairly limited. The mathematics of complicated algorithms or distributions can be difficult to work with. Thus, arrival and service distributions are often defined in unrealistic, but mathematically tractable, ways. It is also generally necessary to make a number of independent assumptions, which may not be accurate. Thus, so that they will be able to compute an answer, queueing models are often only an approximation of a real system. As a result, the accuracy of the computed results may be questionable.

6.8.3 Simulations

To get a more accurate evaluation of scheduling algorithms, we can use **simulations**. Running simulations involves programming a model of the computer system. Software data structures represent the major components of the system. The simulator has a variable representing a clock; as this variable's value is increased, the simulator modifies the system state to reflect the activities of the devices, the processes, and the scheduler. As the simulation executes, statistics that indicate algorithm performance are gathered and printed.

The data to drive the simulation can be generated in several ways. The most common method uses a random-number generator, which is programmed to generate processes, CPU-burst times, arrivals, departures, and so on, according to probability distributions. The distributions can be defined mathematically (uniform, exponential, Poisson) or empirically. If the distribution is to be defined empirically, measurements of the actual system under study are taken. The results define the actual distribution of events in the real system; this distribution can then be used to drive the simulation.

A distribution-driven simulation may be inaccurate, however, due to relationships between successive events in the real system. The frequency distribution indicates only how many of each event occur; it does not indicate anything about the order of their occurrence. To correct this problem, we can use **trace tapes**. We create a trace tape by monitoring the real system, recording the sequence of actual events (Figure 6.13). We then use this sequence to drive the simulation. Trace tapes provide an excellent way to compare two algorithms on exactly the same set of real inputs. This method can produce accurate results for its inputs.

Simulations can be expensive, often requiring hours of computer time. A more detailed simulation provides more accurate results, but also requires more computer time. In addition, trace tapes can require large amounts of storage space. Finally, the design, coding, and debugging of the simulator can be a major task.

6.8.4 Implementation

Even a simulation is of limited accuracy. The only completely accurate way to evaluate a scheduling algorithm is to code it up, to put it in the operating system, and to see how it works. This approach puts the actual algorithm in the real system for evaluation under real operating conditions.

The major difficulty of this approach is the high cost. The expense is incurred not only in coding the algorithm and modifying the operating system

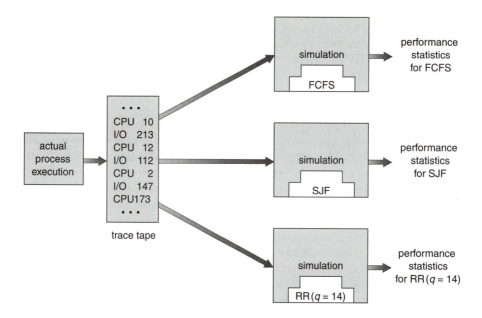

Figure 6.13   Evaluation of CPU schedulers by simulation.

to support it as well as its required data structures, but also in the reaction of the users to a constantly changing operating system. Most users are not interested in building a better operating system; they merely want to get their processes executed and to use their results. A constantly changing operating system does not help the users to get their work done.

The other difficulty with any algorithmic evaluation is that the environment in which the algorithm is used will change. The environment will change not only in the usual way, as new programs are written and the types of problems change, but also as a result of the performance of the scheduler. If short processes are given priority, then users may break larger processes into sets of smaller processes. If interactive processes are given priority over noninteractive processes, then users may switch to interactive use.

For example, researchers designed one system that classified interactive and noninteractive processes automatically by looking at the amount of terminal I/O. If a process did not input or output to the terminal in a 1-second interval, the process was classified as noninteractive and was moved to a lower-priority queue. This policy resulted in a situation where one programmer modified his programs to write an arbitrary character to the terminal at regular intervals of less than 1 second. The system gave his programs a high priority, even though the terminal output was completely meaningless.

The most flexible scheduling algorithms can be altered by the system managers or by the users so that they are tuned for a specific application or set of applications. For instance, a workstation that performs high-end graphical applications may have scheduling needs different from those of a web server or file server. Some operating systems—particularly several versions of UNIX—allow the system manager to fine tune the scheduling parameters for a particular system configuration. Another approach is to use APIs such as `yield()` and `setPriority()`, thus enabling applications to act predictably. The downfall of this approach is that performance tuning of a system or application most often does not result in improved performance in more general situations.

6.9 ■ Summary

CPU scheduling is the task of selecting a waiting process from the ready queue and allocating the CPU to it. The CPU is allocated to the selected process by the dispatcher.

First-come, first-served (FCFS) scheduling is the simplest scheduling algorithm, but it can cause short processes to wait for very long processes. Shortest-job-first (SJF) scheduling is provably optimal, providing the shortest average waiting time. Implementing SJF scheduling is difficult because predicting the length of the next CPU burst is difficult. The SJF algorithm is a special case of the general priority scheduling algorithm, which simply allocates the CPU to the highest-priority process. Both priority and SJF scheduling may suffer from starvation. Aging is a technique to prevent starvation.

Round-robin (RR) scheduling is more appropriate for a time-shared (interactive) system. RR scheduling allocates the CPU to the first process in the ready queue for q time units, where q is the time quantum. After q time units, if the process has not relinquished the CPU, it is preempted and the process is put at the tail of the ready queue. The major problem is the selection of the time quantum. If the quantum is too large, RR scheduling degenerates to FCFS scheduling; if the quantum is too small, scheduling overhead in the form of context-switch time becomes excessive.

The FCFS algorithm is nonpreemptive; the RR algorithm is preemptive. The SJF and priority algorithms may be either preemptive or nonpreemptive.

Multilevel queue algorithms allow different algorithms to be used for various classes of processes. The most common is a foreground interactive queue, which uses RR scheduling, and a background batch queue, which uses FCFS scheduling. Multilevel feedback queues allow processes to move from one queue to another.

Many contemporary computer systems now support multiple processors where each processor is scheduling itself independently. Typically, there is a queue of processes (or threads), all of which are available to run. Each processor makes a scheduling decision and selects from this queue.

The JVM uses a preemptive, priority-based thread-scheduling algorithm that selects to run the thread with the highest priority. The specification does not indicate whether the JVM should time-slice threads; that is up to the particular implementation of the JVM.

The wide variety of scheduling algorithms demands that we have methods to select among algorithms. Analytic methods use mathematical analysis to determine the performance of an algorithm. Simulation methods determine performance by imitating the scheduling algorithm on a "representative" sample of processes, and computing the resulting performance.

■ Exercises

6.1 A CPU scheduling algorithm determines an order for the execution of its scheduled processes. Given n processes to be scheduled on one processor, how many possible different schedules are there? Give a formula in terms of n.

6.2 Define the difference between preemptive and nonpreemptive scheduling. Explain why strict nonpreemptive scheduling is unlikely to be used in a computer center.

6.3 Consider the following set of processes, with the length of the CPU-burst time given in milliseconds:

Process	Burst Time	Priority
P_1	10	3
P_2	1	1
P_3	2	3
P_4	1	4
P_5	5	2

The processes are assumed to have arrived in the order P_1, P_2, P_3, P_4, P_5, all at time 0.

a. Draw four Gantt charts that illustrate the execution of these processes using FCFS, SJF, a nonpreemptive priority (a smaller priority number implies a higher priority), and RR (quantum = 1) scheduling.

b. What is the turnaround time of each process for each of the scheduling algorithms in part a?

c. What is the waiting time of each process for each of the scheduling algorithms in part a?

d. Which of the schedules in part a results in the minimal average waiting time (over all processes)?

6.4 Suppose that the following processes arrive for execution at the times indicated. Each process will run the listed amount of time. In answering the questions, use nonpreemptive scheduling and base all decisions on the information that you have at the time the decision must be made.

Process	Arrival Time	Burst Time
P_1	0.0	8
P_2	0.4	4
P_3	1.0	1

a. What is the average turnaround time for these processes with the FCFS scheduling algorithm?

b. What is the average turnaround time for these processes with the SJF scheduling algorithm?

c. The SJF algorithm is supposed to improve performance, but notice that we chose to run process P_1 at time 0 because we did not know that two shorter processes would arrive soon. Compute what the average turnaround time will be if the CPU is left idle for the first 1 unit, and then SJF scheduling is used. Remember that processes P_1 and P_2 are waiting during this idle time, so their waiting time may increase. This algorithm could be known as *future-knowledge scheduling*.

6.5 Consider a variant of the RR scheduling algorithm where the entries in the ready queue are pointers to the PCBs.

a. What would be the effect of putting two pointers to the same process in the ready queue?

b. What would be two major advantages and two disadvantages of this scheme?

c. How would you modify the basic RR algorithm to achieve the same effect without the duplicate pointers?

6.6 What advantage is there in having different time-quantum sizes on different levels of a multilevel queueing system?

6.7 Consider the following preemptive priority-scheduling algorithm that is based on dynamically changing priorities. Larger priority numbers imply higher priority. When a process is waiting for the CPU (in the ready queue, but not running), its priority changes at a rate α; when it is running, its priority changes at a rate β. All processes are given a priority of 0 when they enter the ready queue. The parameters α and β can be set to give many different scheduling algorithms.

a. What is the algorithm that results from $\beta > \alpha > 0$?

b. What is the algorithm that results from $\alpha < \beta < 0$?

6.8 Many CPU scheduling algorithms are parameterized. For example, the RR algorithm requires a parameter to indicate the time slice. Multilevel feedback queues require parameters to define the number of queues, the scheduling algorithms for each queue, the criteria used to move processes between queues, and so on.

These algorithms are thus really sets of algorithms (for example, the set of RR algorithms for all time slices, and so on). One set of algorithms may include another (for example, the FCFS algorithm is the RR algorithm with an infinite time quantum). What (if any) relation holds between the following pairs of sets of algorithms?

a. Priority and SJF

b. Multilevel feedback queues and FCFS

c. Priority and FCFS

d. RR and SJF

6.9 Suppose that a scheduling algorithm (at the level of short-term CPU scheduling) favors those processes that have used the least processor time in the recent past. Why will this algorithm favor I/O-bound programs and yet not permanently starve CPU-bound programs?

6.10 Explain the differences in the degree to which the following scheduling algorithms discriminate in favor of short processes:

a. FCFS

b. RR

c. Multilevel feedback queues

6.11 The following questions refer to the Java-based round-robin scheduler described in Section 6.7.3.

a. If there is currently a thread T_1 in the queue for the Scheduler running at priority 4 and another thread T_2 with priority 2, is it possible for thread T_2 to run during the time quantum for T_1? Explain.

b. Explain what happens if the currently running thread has its stop() method invoked during its time quantum.

c. Explain what happens if the scheduler selects a thread to run that has had its suspend() method invoked.

6.12 Modify the `CircularList` class by adding a method `isEmpty()` that returns information about whether the queue is empty. Have the scheduler check whether the queue is empty. If the queue is empty, have the scheduler go to sleep for some duration and then awake to check the queue again.

6.13 Modify the Java-based scheduler such that it has multiple queues representing different priorities. For example, have three separate queues, one each for priority 2, 3, and 4. Have the scheduler select a thread from the highest-priority queue, set that thread's priority to 5, and allow the thread to run for a time quantum. When the time quantum expires, select the next thread from the highest queue and repeat the process. You should also modify the `Scheduler` class such that, when a thread is given to the scheduler, an initial thread priority is specified.

Bibliographical Notes

Feedback queues were originally implemented on the CTSS system described in Corbato and colleagues [1962]. This feedback queueing system was analyzed by Schrage [1967]. The preemptive priority-scheduling algorithm of Exercise 6.7 was suggested by Kleinrock [1975].

Anderson and colleagues [1989] and Lewis and Berg [1998] talked about thread scheduling. Discussions concerning multiprocessor scheduling were presented by Tucker and Gupta [1989], Zahorjan and McCann [1990], Feitelson and Rudolph [1990], and Leutenegger and Vernon [1990].

Discussions about scheduling in real-time systems were offered by Abbot [1984], Jensen and colleagues [1985], Hong and colleagues [1989], and Khanna and colleagues [1992]. A special issue on real-time operating systems was edited by Zhao [1989]. Eykholt and colleagues [1992] described the real-time component of Solaris 2.

Fair share schedulers were covered by Henry [1984], Woodside [1986], and Kay and Lauder [1988].

Discussion of scheduling policies used in the OS/2 operating system was presented by Iacobucci [1988]; the one for UNIX V operating system was presented by Bach [1987]; the one for UNIX BSD 4.4 was presented by McKusick and colleagues [1996]; and the one for the Mach operating system was presented by Black [1990]. Solaris 2 scheduling was described by Graham [1995]. Solomon [1998] discussed scheduling in Windows NT.

Java thread scheduling according to the specification of the JVM is described by Lindholm and Yellin [1998]. The idea for the Java-based round-robin scheduler was provided by Oaks and Wong [1999].

Chapter 7

PROCESS SYNCHRONIZATION

A **cooperating** process is one that can affect or be affected by the other processes that are executing in the system. Cooperating processes may either directly share a logical address space (that is, both code and data), or be allowed to share data only through files. The former case is achieved through the use of threads, which were discussed in Chapter 5. Concurrent access to shared data may result in data inconsistency. In this chapter, we discuss various mechanisms to ensure the orderly execution of cooperating processes or threads that share a logical address space, allowing data consistency to be maintained.

7.1 ■ Background

In Chapter 4, we developed a model of a system consisting of cooperating sequential processes or threads, all running asynchronously and possibly sharing data. We illustrated this model with the bounded-buffer scheme, which is representative of operating systems. The code for the producer thread is as follows:

```
while (count == BUFFER_SIZE)
    ; // no-op
// add an item to the buffer
++count;
buffer[in] = item;
in = (in + 1) % BUFFER_SIZE;
```

The code for the consumer is

```
while (count == 0)
    ; // no-op
// remove an item from the buffer
--count;
item = buffer[out];
out = (out + 1) % BUFFER_SIZE;
```

Although both the producer and the consumer routines are correct separately, they may not function correctly when executed concurrently. The reason is that the threads share the variable count, which serves as the count for the number of items in the buffer. As an illustration, suppose that the value of the variable count is currently 5, and that the producer and consumer threads execute the statements ++count and --count concurrently. Following the execution of these two statements, the value of the variable count might be 4, 5, or 6! The only correct result for count is 5, which is generated correctly only if the producer and consumer execute sequentially.

We can show how the resulting value of count may be incorrect, as follows. Note that the statement ++count may be implemented in machine language (on a typical machine) as

$$register_1 = count;$$
$$register_1 = register_1 + 1;$$
$$count = register_1;$$

where $register_1$ is a local CPU register. Similarly, the statement --count is implemented as follows:

$$register_2 = count;$$
$$register_2 = register_2 - 1;$$
$$count = register_2;$$

where again $register_2$ is a local CPU register. Remember that, even though $register_1$ and $register_2$ may be the same physical registers (an accumulator, say), the contents of this register will be saved and restored by the interrupt handler (Section 2.1).

The concurrent execution of the statements ++count and --count is equivalent to a sequential execution where the lower-level statements presented previously are interleaved in some arbitrary order (but the order within each high-level statement is preserved). One such interleaving is

$$
\begin{array}{llll}
S_0: & \textit{producer} & \text{execute} & register_1 = \text{count} & \{register_1 = 5\} \\
S_1: & \textit{producer} & \text{execute} & register_1 = register_1 + 1 & \{register_1 = 6\} \\
S_2: & \textit{consumer} & \text{execute} & register_2 = \text{count} & \{register_2 = 5\} \\
S_3: & \textit{consumer} & \text{execute} & register_2 = register_2 - 1 & \{register_2 = 4\} \\
S_4: & \textit{producer} & \text{execute} & \text{count} = register_1 & \{\text{count} = 6\ \} \\
S_5: & \textit{consumer} & \text{execute} & \text{count} = register_2 & \{\text{count} = 4\} \\
\end{array}
$$

Notice that we have arrived at the incorrect state "*count* = 4," recording that there are four full buffers, when, in fact, there are five full buffers. If we reversed the order of the statements at S_4 and S_5, we would arrive at the incorrect state "*count* = 6."

We would arrive at this incorrect state because we allowed both threads to manipulate the variable count concurrently. This situation, where several threads access and manipulate the same data concurrently, and where the outcome of the execution depends on the particular order in which the access takes place, is called a **race condition**. To guard against the race condition, we need to ensure that only one thread at a time can be manipulating the variable count. To make such a guarantee, we require some form of synchronization of the threads. Such situations occur frequently in operating systems as different parts of the system manipulate resources, and we want the changes not to interfere with one another. A major portion of this chapter is concerned with thread synchronization and coordination.

7.2 ■ Critical-Section Problem

As a first method of controlling access to a shared resource, we declare a section of code to be *critical;* we then regulate access to that section. Consider a system consisting of n threads $\{T_0, T_1, ..., T_{n-1}\}$. Each thread has a segment of code, called a **critical section,** in which the thread may be changing common variables, updating a table, writing a file, and so on. The important feature of the system is that, when one thread is executing in its critical section, no other thread is to be allowed to execute in its critical section. Thus, the execution of critical sections by the threads is *mutually exclusive* in time. The critical-section problem is how to choose a protocol that the threads can use to cooperate.

A solution to the critical-section problem must satisfy the following three requirements:

1. *Mutual exclusion:* If thread T_i is executing in its critical section, then no other threads can be executing in their critical sections.

2. *Progress:* If no thread is executing in its critical section and there exist some threads that wish to enter their critical sections, then only those threads that are not executing in their noncritical section can participate in the decision

of which will enter its critical section next, and this selection cannot be postponed indefinitely.

3. *Bounded waiting:* There exists a bound on the number of times that other threads are allowed to enter their critical sections after a thread has made a request to enter its critical section and before that request is granted. This bound prevents **starvation** of any single thread.

We assume that each thread is executing at a nonzero speed. However, we can make no assumption concerning the *relative* speed of the n threads. In Section 7.3, we examine the critical-section problem and develop a solution that satisfies these three requirements. The solutions do not rely on any assumptions concerning the hardware instructions or the number of processors that the hardware supports. We do assume, however, that the basic machine-language instructions (the primitive instructions such as load, store, and test) are executed atomically. That is, if two such instructions are executed concurrently, the result is equivalent to their sequential execution in some unknown order. Thus, if a load and a store are executed concurrently, the load will get either the old value or the new value, but not some combination of the two.

```
public class Worker extends Thread
{
    public Worker(String n, int i, MutualExclusion s) {
        name = n;
        id = i;
        shared = s;
    }

    public void run() {
        while (true) {
            shared.enteringCriticalSection(id);
            System.out.println(name + " is in critical section");
            MutualExclusion.criticalSection();
            shared.leavingCriticalSection(id);
            System.out.println(name + " is out of critical section");
            MutualExclusion.nonCriticalSection();
        }
    }

    private String name;
    private int id;
    private MutualExclusion shared;
}
```

Figure 7.1   Worker thread.

7.3 ■ Two-Tasks Solutions

In this section, we consider three different Java implementations to coordinate the actions of two different threads. The threads are numbered T_0 and T_1. For convenience, when representing T_i, we use T_j to denote the other thread; that is, $j = 1 - i$. Prior to examining the different algorithms, we present the necessary Java class files.

We implement each thread using the Worker class shown in Figure 7.1. A call to the methods criticalSection() and nonCriticalSection() represents the places where each thread performs its critical and noncritical sections. Prior to calling its critical section, each thread will call the method enteringCriticalSection(), passing its thread id (which will be either 0 or 1). A thread will not return from enteringCriticalSection() until it is able to enter its critical section. On finishing its critical section, a thread will call the method leavingCriticalSection().

The abstract class MutualExclusion.java (Figure 7.2) will serve as a template for the three different algorithms.

```java
public abstract class MutualExclusion
{
    public static void criticalSection() {
        try {
            Thread.sleep( (int) (Math.random() * TIME) );
        }
        catch (InterruptedException e) { }
    }

    public static void nonCriticalSection() {
        try {
            Thread.sleep( (int) (Math.random() * TIME) );
        }
        catch (InterruptedException e) { }
    }

    public abstract void enteringCriticalSection(int t);
    public abstract void leavingCriticalSection(int t);

    public static final int TURN_0 = 0;
    public static final int TURN_1 = 1;
    private static final int TIME = 3000;
}
```

Figure 7.2 MutualExclusion abstract class.

```
public class TestAlgorithm
{
    public static void main(String args[]) {
        MutualExclusion alg = new Algorithm_1();

        Worker first = new Worker("Runner 0", 0, alg);
        Worker second = new Worker("Runner 1", 1, alg);

        first.start();
        second.start();
    }
}
```

Figure 7.3   The TestAlgorithm class.

The static methods criticalSection() and nonCriticalSection() are invoked by each thread. We represent the three different algorithms by extending the MutualExclusion class and implementing the abstract methods enteringCriticalSection() and leavingCriticalSection().

We use the TestAlgorithm class (Figure 7.3) to create the two threads and to test each algorithm.

7.3.1 Algorithm 1

Our first approach is to let the threads share a common integer variable turn, initialized to either 0 or 1. If turn = i, then thread T_i is allowed to execute its critical section. A complete Java solution is shown in Figure 7.4.

This solution ensures that only one thread at a time can be in its critical section. However, it does not satisfy the progress requirement, since it requires strict alternation of threads in the execution of their critical section. For example, if turn = 0 and thread T_1 is ready to enter its critical section, then T_1 cannot do so, even though T_0 may be in its noncritical section.

Algorithm 1 uses the yield() method introduced in Section 6.7.1. Invoking the yield() method keeps the thread in the Runnable state, but also allows the JVM to select another Runnable thread of equal priority to run.

This solution also introduces a new Java keyword: volatile. The Java Language Specification allows a compiler to make certain optimizations, such as caching the value of a variable in a machine register rather than continually updating that value from main memory. Such optimizations occur when the compiler recognizes that the value of the variable will remain unchanged, such as in the statement

```
while (turn != t)
    Thread.yield();
```

```
public class Algorithm_1 extends MutualExclusion
{
    public Algorithm_1() {
        turn = TURN_0;
    }

    public void enteringCriticalSection(int t) {
        while (turn != t)
            Thread.yield();
    }

    public void leavingCriticalSection(int t) {
        turn = 1 - t;
    }

    private volatile int turn;
}
```

Figure 7.4   Algorithm 1.

However, if another thread can change the value of turn—as happens in algorithm 1—then it is desirable that the value of turn be refreshed from main memory during every iteration. Declaring a variable as volatile prevents the compiler from making such optimizations.

7.3.2 Algorithm 2

The problem with algorithm 1 is that it does not retain sufficient information about the state of each thread; it remembers only which thread is allowed to enter its critical section. To remedy this problem, we can replace the variable turn with the following array:

```
boolean[] flag = new boolean[2];
```

The elements of the array are initialized to false. If flag[i] is true, this value indicates that thread T_i is ready to enter its critical section. The complete Java solution is shown in Figure 7.5.

In this algorithm, thread T_i first sets flag[i] to be true, signaling that it is ready to enter its critical section. Then, T_i checks to verify that thread T_j is not also ready to enter its critical section. If T_j were ready, then T_i would wait until T_j had indicated that it no longer needed to be in the critical section (that is, until flag[j] was false). At that point, T_i would enter its critical section. On exiting the critical section, T_i would set its flag to false, allowing the other thread (if it is waiting) to enter its critical section.

```
public class Algorithm_2 extends MutualExclusion
{
    public Algorithm_2() {
        flag[0] = false;
        flag[1] = false;
    }

    public void enteringCriticalSection(int t) {
        int other;

        other = 1 - t;

        flag[t] = true;

        while (flag[other] == true)
            Thread.yield();
    }

    public void leavingCriticalSection(int t) {
        flag[t] = false;
    }

    private volatile boolean[] flag = new boolean[2];
}
```

Figure 7.5   Algorithm 2.

In this solution, the mutual-exclusion requirement is satisfied. Unfortunately, the progress requirement is still not met. To illustrate this problem, consider the following execution sequence: Suppose that thread T_0 sets flag[0] to true, indicating that it wishes to enter its critical section. Before it can begin executing the while loop, a context switch takes place and thread T_1 sets flag[1] also to true. When both threads perform the while statement, they will loop forever as the value of flag for the other thread is true.

7.3.3 Algorithm 3

By combining the key ideas of algorithm 1 and algorithm 2, we obtain a correct solution to the critical-section problem, where all three requirements are met. The threads share two variables:

```
boolean[] flag = new boolean[2];
int turn;
```

Initially, each array element is set to false, and the value of turn is immaterial (it is either 0 or 1). Figure 7.6 displays the complete Java solution.

```
public class Algorithm_3 extends MutualExclusion
{
    public Algorithm_3() {
        flag[0] = false;
        flag[1] = false;
        turn = TURN_0;
    }

    public void enteringCriticalSection(int t) {
        int other;

        other = 1 - t;

        flag[t] = true;
        turn = other;

        while ( (flag[other] == true) && (turn == other) )
            Thread.yield();
    }

    public void leavingCriticalSection(int t) {
        flag[t] = false;
    }

    private volatile int turn;
    private volatile boolean[] flag = new boolean[2];
}
```

Figure 7.6 Algorithm 3.

To enter its critical section, thread T_i first sets flag[i] to be true, and then asserts that it is the other thread's turn to enter if appropriate (turn == j). If both threads try to enter at the same time, turn is set to both i and j at roughly the same time. Only one of these assignments lasts; the other will occur, but will be overwritten immediately. The eventual value of turn decides which of the two threads is allowed to enter its critical section first.

7.4 ▪ Synchronization Hardware

As is true of other aspects of software, features of the hardware can make the programming task easier and improve system efficiency. In this section, we present simple hardware instructions that are available on many systems, and show how they can be used effectively in solving the critical-section problem.

```
public class HardwareData
{
    public HardwareData(boolean v) {
        data = v;
    }

    public boolean get() {
        return data;
    }

    public void set(boolean v) {
        data = v;
    }

    private boolean data;
}
```

Figure 7.7   Data structure for hardware solutions.

The critical-section problem could be solved simply in a uniprocessor environment if we could disallow interrupts to occur while a shared variable is being modified. In this manner, we could be sure that the current sequence of instructions would be allowed to execute in order without preemption. No other instructions would be run, so no unexpected modifications could be made to the shared variable. Unfortunately, this solution is not feasible in a multiprocessor environment. Disabling interrupts on a multiprocessor can be time consuming, as the message is passed to all the processors. This message passing delays entry into each critical section, and system efficiency decreases. Also, consider the effect on a system's clock, if the clock is kept updated by interrupts.

Many machines therefore provide special hardware instructions that allow us either to test and modify the content of a word, or to swap the contents of two words, atomically. We can use these special instructions to solve the

```
public class HardwareSolution
{
    public static boolean testAndSet(HardwareData target) {
        HardwareData temp = new HardwareData(target.get());

        target.set(true);
        return temp.get();
    }
}
```

Figure 7.8   *Test-and-Set* instruction.

```
HardwareData lock = new HardwareData(false);

while (true) {
    while (HardwareSolution.testAndSet(lock))
        Thread.yield();

    criticalSection();
    lock.set(false);
    nonCriticalSection();
}
```

Figure 7.9 Thread using *Test-and-Set* lock.

critical-section problem in a relatively simple manner. Rather than discussing one specific instruction for one specific machine, let us use Java to abstract the main concepts behind these types of instructions. The HardwareData class shown in Figure 7.7 will illustrate the instructions.

A method implementing the *Test-and-Set* instruction is shown in the HardwareSolution class in Figure 7.8. The important characteristic is that this instruction is executed atomically—that is, as one uninterruptible unit. Thus, if two *Test-and-Set* instructions are executed simultaneously (each on a different CPU), they will be executed sequentially in some arbitrary order.

If the machine supports the *Test-and-Set* instruction, then we can implement mutual exclusion by declaring lock to be an object of class HardwareData and initializing it to false. All threads will share access to lock. Figure 7.9 illustrates the structure of thread T_i.

The *Swap* instruction, defined in the swap() method in Figure 7.10, operates on the contents of two words; like the *Test-and-Set* instruction, it is executed atomically.

If the machine supports the *Swap* instruction, then mutual exclusion can be provided as follows. All threads share an object lock of class HardwareData that is initialized to false. In addition, each thread also has a local HardwareData object key. The structure of thread T_i is shown in Figure 7.11.

```
public static void swap(HardwareData a, HardwareData b) {
    HardwareData temp = new HardwareData(a.get());
    a.set(b.get());
    b.set(temp.get());
}
```

Figure 7.10 *Swap* instruction.

```
HardwareData lock = new HardwareData(false);
HardwareData key = new HardwareData(true);

while (true) {
    key.set(true);

    do {
        HardwareSolution.swap(lock,key);
    }
    while (key.get() == true);

    criticalSection();
    lock.set(false);
    nonCriticalSection();
}
```

Figure 7.11   Thread using *Swap* instruction.

7.5 ■ Semaphores

The solutions to the critical-section problem presented in Section 7.3 are not easy to generalize to more complex problems. To overcome this difficulty, we can use a synchronization tool, called a **semaphore**. A semaphore S is an integer variable that, apart from initialization, is accessed only through two standard operations: P and V. These operations were termed P from the Dutch *proberen*, meaning to test, and V from *verhogen*, meaning to increment. The definitions of P and V are as follows:

```
P(S) {
    while S <= 0
        ; // no-op
    S--;
}


V(S) {
    S++;
}
```

Modifications to the integer value of the semaphore in the P and V operations must be executed indivisibly.   That is, when one thread modifies the semaphore value, no other thread can simultaneously modify that same semaphore value. In addition, in the case of the P(S), the testing of the integer value of S (S <= 0) and of its possible modification (S--) must also be executed without interruption. We see in Section 7.5.2 how these operations can be implemented; first, let us see how semaphores can be used.

7.5.1 Usage

Operating systems often distinguish between counting and binary semaphores. The value of a **counting semaphore** can range over an unrestricted domain. The value of a **binary semaphore** can range only between 0 and 1.

The general strategy for using a binary semaphore to control access to a critical section is as follows (assume that the semaphore is initialized to 1):

```
Semaphore S;

P(S);
criticalSection();
V(S);
```

Thus, we can use the semaphore to control access to the critical section for a process or thread. A generalized solution for multiple threads is shown in the Java program in Figure 7.12. Five separate threads are created, but only one can be in its critical section at a time. The semaphore sem that is shared by all the threads controls access to the critical section.

Counting semaphores can be used to control access to a given resource consisting of only a finite number. The semaphore is initialized to the number of resources available. Each thread that wishes to use a resource would perform a P operation on the semaphore (thereby decrementing the count). When a thread releases a resource, it performs a V operation (incrementing the count). When the count for the semaphore goes to 0, all resources are being used. Subsequent threads that wish to use a resource will block until the count becomes greater than 0.

7.5.2 Implementation

The main disadvantage of the mutual-exclusion solutions of Section 7.2, and of the semaphore definition given here, is that they all require busy waiting. While a process is in its critical section, any other process that tries to enter its critical section must loop continuously in the entry code. This continual looping is clearly a problem in a multiprogramming system, where a single CPU is shared among many processes. Busy waiting wastes CPU cycles that some other process might be able to use productively. This type of semaphore is also called a **spinlock** (because the process spins while waiting for the lock). Spinlocks are useful in multiprocessor systems. The advantage of a spinlock is that no context switch is required when a process must wait on a lock, and a context switch may take considerable time. Thus, when locks are expected to be held for short times, spinlocks are useful.

To overcome the need for busy waiting, we can modify the definition of the P and V semaphore operations. When a process executes the P operation and finds that the semaphore value is not positive, it must wait. However, rather

```
public class Worker extends Thread
{
    public Worker(Semaphore s, String n) {
        name = n;
        sem = s;
    }

    public void run() {
        while (true) {
            sem.P();
            System.out.println(name + " is in critical section.");
            Runner.criticalSection();
            sem.V();
            System.out.println(name + " is out of critical
                section.");
            Runner.nonCriticalSection();
        }
    }

    private Semaphore sem;
    private String name;
}

public class FirstSemaphore
{
    public static void main(String args[]) {
        Semaphore sem = new Semaphore(1);
        Worker[] bees = new Worker[5];

        for (int i = 0; i < 5; i++)
            bees[i] = new Worker(sem, "Worker " +
                (new Integer(i)).toString() );

        for (int i = 0; i < 5; i++)
            bees[i].start();
    }
}
```

Figure 7.12   Synchronization using semaphores.

than using busy waiting, the process can *block* itself. The block operation places a process into a waiting queue associated with the semaphore, and the state of the process is switched to the waiting state. Then, control is transferred to the CPU scheduler, which selects another process to execute.

A process that is blocked, waiting on a semaphore S, should be restarted when some other process executes a V operation. The process is restarted by a *wakeup* operation, which changes the process from the waiting state to the ready state. The process is then placed in the ready queue. (The CPU may or may not be switched from the running process to the newly ready process, depending on the CPU scheduling algorithm.)

To implement semaphores under this definition, we define a semaphore as an integer value and a list of processes. When a process must wait on a semaphore, it is added to the list of processes for that semaphore. The V operation removes one process from the list of waiting processes, and awakens that process.

The semaphore operations can now be defined as

```
P(S){
    value--;
    if (value < 0) {
        add this process to list
        block;
    }
}


V(S){
    value++;
    if (value ≤ 0) {
        remove a process P from list
        wakeup(P);
    }
}
```

The block operation suspends the process that invokes it. The wakeup(P) operation resumes the execution of a blocked process P. These two operations are provided by the operating system as basic system calls.

Note that, although under the classical definition of semaphores with busy waiting the semaphore value is never negative, this implementation may have negative semaphore values. If the semaphore value is negative, its magnitude is the number of processes waiting on that semaphore. This fact is a result of the switching of the order of the decrement and the test in the implementation of the P operation.

The list of waiting processes can be easily implemented by a link field in each process control block (PCB). Each semaphore contains an integer value and a pointer to a list of PCBs. One way to add and remove processes from the list, which ensures bounded waiting, would be to use a FIFO queue, where the semaphore contains both head and tail pointers to the queue. In general, however, the list may use *any* queueing strategy. Correct use of semaphores does not depend on a particular queueing strategy for the semaphore lists.

The critical aspect of semaphores is that they are executed atomically. We must guarantee that no two processes can execute P and V operations on the same semaphore at the same time. This situation creates a critical-section problem, which can be solved in either of two ways.

In a uniprocessor environment (that is, where only one CPU exists), we can simply inhibit interrupts during the time the P and V operations are executing. Once interrupts are inhibited, instructions from different processes cannot be interleaved. Only the currently running process executes, until interrupts are reenabled and the scheduler can regain control.

In a multiprocessor environment, however, inhibiting interrupts does not work. Instructions from different processes (running on different processors) may be interleaved in some arbitrary way. If the hardware does not provide any special instructions, we can employ any of the correct software solutions for the critical-section problem (Section 7.2), where the critical sections consist of the P and V operations.

We have not completely eliminated busy waiting with this definition of the P and V operations. Rather, we have moved busy waiting to the critical sections of application programs. Furthermore, we have limited busy waiting to only the critical sections of the P and V operations, and these sections are short (if properly coded, they should be no more than about 10 instructions). Thus, the critical section is almost never occupied, and busy waiting occurs rarely, and then for only a short time. An entirely different situation exists with application programs whose critical sections may be long (minutes or even hours) or may be almost always occupied. In this case, busy waiting is extremely inefficient.

In Section 7.8.6 we see how semaphores can be implemented in Java.

7.5.3 Deadlocks and Starvation

The implementation of a semaphore with a waiting queue may result in a situation where two or more processes are waiting indefinitely for an event that can be caused by only one of the waiting processes. The event in question is the execution of a V operation. When such a state is reached, these processes are said to be **deadlocked**.

As an illustration, we consider a system consisting of two processes, P_0 and P_1, each accessing two semaphores, S and Q, set to the value 1:

```
        P0              P1

        P(S);           P(Q);
        P(Q);           P(S);

          .               .
          .               .
          .               .

        V(S);           V(Q);
        V(Q);           V(S);
```

```java
public class BoundedBuffer
{
    public BoundedBuffer() {
        // buffer is initially empty
        count = 0;
        in = 0;
        out = 0;
        buffer = new Object[BUFFER_SIZE];

        mutex = new Semaphore(1);
        empty = new Semaphore(BUFFER_SIZE);
        full = new Semaphore(0);
    }

    // producer and consumer will call this to nap
    public static void napping() {
        int sleepTime = (int)(NAP_TIME *
            Math.random());
        try {
            Thread.sleep(sleepTime*1000);
        }
        catch(InterruptedException e) { }
    }

    public void enter(Object item) {
        // Figure 7.14
    }

    public Object remove() {
        // Figure 7.15
    }

    private static final int NAP_TIME = 5;
    private static final int BUFFER_SIZE = 5;
    private Object[] buffer;
    private int count, in, out;
    // mutex controls access to count, in, out
    private Semaphore mutex;
    private Semaphore empty;
    private Semaphore full;
}
```

Figure 7.13   Solution to the bounded-buffer problem that uses semaphores.

```
public void enter(Object item) {
    empty.P();
    mutex.P();

    // add an item to the buffer
    ++count;
    buffer[in] = item;
    in = (in + 1) % BUFFER_SIZE;

    if (count == BUFFER_SIZE)
        System.out.println("Producer Entered " + item +
            " Buffer FULL");
    else
        System.out.println("Producer Entered " + item +
            "Buffer Size =" + count);

    mutex.V();
    full.V();
}
```

Figure 7.14   The enter() method.

Suppose that P_0 executes P(S), and then P_1 executes P(Q). When P_0 executes P(Q), it must wait until P_1 executes V(Q). Similarly, when P_1 executes P(S), it must wait until P_0 executes V(S). Since these signal operations cannot be executed, P_0 and P_1 are deadlocked.

We say that a set of processes is in a deadlock state when every process in the set is waiting for an event that can be caused by only another process in the set. The events with which we are mainly concerned here are resource acquisition and release; however, other types of events may result in deadlocks, as we show in Chapter 8. In that chapter, we describe various mechanisms for dealing with the deadlock problem.

Another problem related to deadlocks is **indefinite blocking** or **starvation** —a situation where processes wait indefinitely within the semaphore. Indefinite blocking may occur if we add and remove processes from the list associated with a semaphore in LIFO order.

7.6 ■ Classical Synchronization Problems

In this section, we present a number of different synchronization problems that are important mainly because they are examples for a large class of concurrency-control problems. These problems are used for testing nearly every newly proposed synchronization scheme. Semaphores are used for synchronization in our solutions.

```
public Object remove() {
    Object item;

    full.P();
    mutex.P();

    // remove an item from the buffer
    --count;
    item = buffer[out];
    out = (out + 1) % BUFFER_SIZE;

    if (count == 0)
        System.out.println("Consumer Consumed " + item +
            "Buffer EMPTY");
    else
        System.out.println("Consumer Consumed " + item +
            "Buffer Size =" + count);

    mutex.V();
    empty.V();

    return item;
}
```

Figure 7.15 The remove() method.

7.6.1 The Bounded-Buffer Problem

The bounded-buffer problem was introduced in Section 7.1; it is commonly used to illustrate the power of synchronization primitives. A solution is shown in Figure 7.13 (page 189). A producer places an item in the buffer by calling the enter() method; consumers remove items by invoking remove().

The mutex semaphore provides mutual exclusion for accesses to the buffer pool and is initialized to 1. The empty and full semaphores count the number of empty and full buffers, respectively. The semaphore empty is initialized to the capacity of the buffer—BUFFER_SIZE; the semaphore full is initialized to 0. Note that the variable count only serves the purpose of indicating whether the buffer is empty or full for output messages.

The producer thread is shown in Figure 7.16. The producer alternates between sleeping for a while, producing a message, and attempting to place that message into the buffer via the enter() method.

The consumer thread is shown in Figure 7.17. The consumer alternates between sleeping and consuming an item using the remove() method.

The BoundedBufferServer class (Figure 7.18) creates the producer and consumer threads, passing each a reference to the BoundedBuffer object.

```
import java.util.*;

public class Producer extends Thread
{
    public Producer(BoundedBuffer b) {
        buffer = b;
    }

    public void run() {
        Date message;

        while (true) {
            BoundedBuffer.napping();
            // produce an item & enter it into the buffer
            message = new Date();
            System.out.println("Producer produced " + message);
            buffer.enter(message);
        }
    }

    private BoundedBuffer buffer;
}
```

Figure 7.16   Producer thread.

7.6.2 The Readers–Writers Problem

A database is to be shared among several concurrent threads. Some of these threads may want only to read the database, whereas others may want to update (that is, to read and write) the database. We distinguish between these two types of threads by referring to the former as **readers**, and to the latter as **writers**. Obviously, if two readers access the shared data simultaneously, no adverse affects will result. However, if a writer and some other thread (either a reader or a writer) access the database simultaneously, chaos may ensue.

To ensure that these difficulties do not arise, we require that the writers have exclusive access to the shared database. This requirement leads to the **readers–writers** problem. Since it was originally stated, that problem has been used to test nearly every new synchronization primitive. The readers–writers problem has several variations, all involving priorities. The simplest one, referred to as the *first* readers–writers problem, requires that no reader will be kept waiting unless a writer has already obtained permission to use the shared database. In other words, no reader should wait for other readers to finish simply because a writer is waiting. The *second* readers–writers problem requires that, once a writer is ready, that writer performs its write as soon as

```
import java.util.*;

public class Consumer extends Thread
{
    public Consumer(BoundedBuffer b) {
        buffer = b;
    }

    public void run() {
        Date message;

        while (true) {
            BoundedBuffer.napping();
            // consume an item from the buffer
            System.out.println("Consumer wants to consume");
            message = (Date)buffer.remove();
        }
    }

    private BoundedBuffer buffer;
}
```

Figure 7.17   Consumer thread.

possible. In other words, if a writer is waiting to access the object, no new readers may start reading.

We note that a solution to either problem may result in starvation. In the first case, writers may starve; in the second case, readers may starve. For

```
public class BoundedBufferServer
{
    public static void main(String args[]) {
        BoundedBuffer server = new BoundedBuffer();

        // now create the producer and consumer threads
        Producer producerThread = new Producer(server);
        Consumer consumerThread = new Consumer(server);

        producerThread.start();
        consumerThread.start();
    }
}
```

Figure 7.18   The BoundedBufferServer class.

```
public class Reader extends Thread
{
    public Reader(int r, Database db) {
        readerNum = r;
        server = db;
    }

    public void run() {
        int c;

        while (true) {
            System.out.println("reader " + readerNum +
                " is sleeping");
            Database.napping();

            System.out.println("reader " + readerNum +
                " wants to read");
            c = server.startRead();

            // you have access to read from the database
            System.out.println("reader " + readerNum +
                " is reading.  Count =" + c);
            Database.napping();

            c = server.endRead();
            System.out.println("reader " + readerNum +
                "is done reading.  Count =" + c);
        }
    }

    private Database server;
    private int readerNum;
}
```

Figure 7.19   A reader.

this reason, other variants of the problem have been proposed. The following presents the Java class files for a solution to the first readers–writers problem. It does not address starvation. (In the exercises at the end of the chapter, you are asked to modify the solution such that it is starvation-free.) Each reader thread alternates between sleeping and reading as shown in Figure 7.19. When a reader wishes to read the database, it invokes the startRead() method; when it has finished reading, it calls endRead(). Each writer thread (Figure 7.20) performs similarly.

```
public class Writer extends Thread
{
    public Writer(int w, Database db) {
        writerNum = w;
        server = db;
    }

    public void run() {
        while (true) {
            System.out.println("writer " + writerNum +
                " is sleeping.");
            Database.napping();

            System.out.println("writer " + writerNum +
                " wants to write.");
            server.startWrite();

            // you have access to write to the database
            System.out.println("writer " + writerNum +
                " is writing.");
            Database.napping();

            server.endWrite();
            System.out.println("writer " + writerNum +
                " is done writing.");
        }
    }

    private Database server;
    private int writerNum;
}
```

Figure 7.20   A writer.

The methods called by each reader and writer thread are defined in the Database class in Figure 7.21.   The readerCount keeps track of the number of readers.   The semaphore mutex is used to ensure mutual exclusion when readerCount is updated.   The semaphore db functions as a mutual exclusion semaphore for the writers.   It also is used by the readers to prevent writers from entering the database while that database is being read.   The first reader performs a P() operation on db, thereby preventing any writers fom entering the database.   The final reader performs a V() operation on db.   Note that, if a writer is active in the database and n readers are waiting, then one reader is queued on db, and

```
public class Database
{
    public Database() {
      readerCount = 0;
      mutex = new Semaphore(1);
      db = new Semaphore(1);
    }

    // readers and writers will call this to nap
    public static void napping() {
      int sleepTime = (int)(NAP_TIME * Math.random());
      try {
         Thread.sleep(sleepTime*1000);
      }
      catch(InterruptedException e) { }
    }

    public int startRead() {
      // Figure 7.22
    }

    public int endRead() {
      // Figure 7.22
    }

    public void startWrite() {
      // Figure 7.23
    }

    public void endWrite() {
      // Figure 7.23
    }

    private static final int NUM_OF_READERS = 3;
    private static final int NUM_OF_WRITERS = 2;
    private static final int NAP_TIME = 15;

    private int readerCount;
    private Semaphore mutex;
    private Semaphore db;
}
```

Figure 7.21   The database for the readers–writers problem.

```
public int startRead() {
    mutex.P();
    ++readerCount;

    // if I am the first reader tell all others
    // that the database is being read
    if (readerCount == 1)
        db.P();

    mutex.V();

    return readerCount;
}

public int endRead() {
    mutex.P();
    --readerCount;

    // if I am the last reader tell all others
    // that the database is no longer being read
    if (readerCount == 0)
        db.V();

    mutex.V();

    return readerCount;
}
```

Figure 7.22   Methods called by readers.

$n - 1$ readers are queued on `mutex`. Also observe that, when a writer executes `db.V()`, we may resume the execution of either the waiting readers or a single waiting writer. The selection is made by the scheduler.

```
public void startWrite() {
    db.P();
}

public void endWrite() {
    db.V();
}
```

Figure 7.23   Methods called by writers.

7.6.3 The Dining-Philosophers Problem

Consider five philosophers who spend their lives thinking and eating. The philosophers share a common circular table surrounded by five chairs, each belonging to one philosopher. In the center of the table there is a bowl of rice, and the table is laid with five single chopsticks (Figure 7.24). When a philosopher thinks, she does not interact with her colleagues. From time to time, a philosopher gets hungry and tries to pick up the two chopsticks that are closest to her (the chopsticks that are between her and her left and right neighbors). A philosopher may pick up only one chopstick at a time. Obviously, she cannot pick up a chopstick that is already in the hand of a neighbor. When a hungry philosopher has both her chopsticks at the same time, she eats without releasing her chopsticks. When she is finished eating, she puts down both of her chopsticks and starts thinking again.

The **dining-philosophers problem** is considered a classic synchronization problem, not because of its practical importance, nor because computer scientists dislike philosophers, but rather because it is an example of a large class of concurrency-control problems. It is a simple representation of the need to allocate several resources among several processes in a deadlock and starvation-free manner.

One simple solution is to represent each chopstick by a semaphore. A philosopher tries to grab the chopstick by executing a P operation on that semaphore; she releases her chopsticks by executing the V operation on the appropriate semaphores. Thus, the shared data are

```
Semaphore chopStick[] = new Semaphore[5];
```

where all the elements of chopstick are initialized to 1. The structure of philosopher *i* is shown in Figure 7.25.

Figure 7.24   The situation of the dining philosophers.

```
while (true) {
    // get left chopstick
    chopStick[i].P();
    // get right chopstick
    chopStick[(i + 1) % 5].P();
    eating();
    // return left chopstick
    chopStick[i].V();
    // return right chopstick
    chopStick[(i + 1) % 5].V();
    thinking();
}
```

Figure 7.25   The structure of philosopher *i*.

Although this solution guarantees that no two neighboring philosophers are eating simultaneously, it nevertheless must be rejected because it has the possibility of creating a deadlock. Suppose that all five philosophers become hungry simultaneously, and each grabs her left chopstick. All the elements of *chopstick* will now be equal to 0. When each philosopher tries to grab her right chopstick, she will be delayed forever.

Several possible remedies to the deadlock problem are listed next. These remedies prevent deadlock by placing restrictions on the philosophers:

- Allow at most four philosophers to be sitting simultaneously at the table.

- Allow a philosopher to pick up her chopsticks only if both chopsticks are available (note that she must pick them up in a critical section).

- Use an asymmetric solution; for example, an odd philosopher picks up first her left chopstick and then her right chopstick, whereas an even philosopher picks up her right chopstick and then her left chopstick.

In Section 7.7, we present a solution to the dining-philosophers problem that ensures freedom from deadlocks. Any satisfactory solution to the dining-philosophers problem must guard against the possibility that one of the philosophers will starve to death. A deadlock-free solution does not necessarily eliminate the possibility of starvation.

7.7 ■ Monitors

Although semaphores provide a convenient and effective mechanism for process synchronization, their incorrect use can still result in timing errors that are difficult to detect, since these errors happen only if some particular execution sequences take place, and these sequences do not always occur.

We have seen an example of such types of errors in the use of counters in our solution to the producer–consumer problem (Section 7.1). In that example, the timing problem happened only rarely, and even then the counter value appeared to be reasonable—off by only 1. Nevertheless, this solution is obviously not an acceptable one. It is for this reason that semaphores were introduced in the first place.

Unfortunately, such timing errors can still occur with the use of semaphores. To illustrate how, let us review the semaphore solution to the critical-section problem. All processes share a semaphore variable `mutex`, which is initialized to 1. Each process must execute `mutex.P()` before entering the critical section, and `mutex.V()` afterward. If this sequence is not observed, two processes may be in their critical sections simultaneously. Let us examine the various difficulties that may result. Note that these difficulties will arise even if a *single* process is not well behaved. This situation may be the result of an honest programming error or of an uncooperative programmer.

- Suppose that a process interchanges the order in which the `P()` and `V()` operations on the semaphore *mutex* are executed, resulting in the following execution:

  ```
  mutex.V();
  criticalSection();
  mutex.P();
  ```

  In this situation, several processes may be executing in their critical section simultaneously, violating the mutual-exclusion requirement. This error may be discovered only if several processes are simultaneously active in their critical sections. Note that this situation may not always be reproducible.

- Suppose that a process replaces `mutex.V()` with `mutex.P()`. That is, it executes

  ```
  mutex.P();
  criticalSection();
  mutex.P();
  ```

  In this case, a deadlock will occur.

- Suppose that a process omits the `mutex.P()`, or the `mutex.V()`, or both. In this case, either mutual exclusion is violated or a deadlock will occur.

These examples illustrate that various types of errors can be generated easily when programmers use semaphores incorrectly to solve the critical-section problem. Similar problems may arise in the other synchronization models that we discussed in Section 7.6.

To deal with such errors, researchers have developed high-level language constructs. In this section, we describe one fundamental high-level synchronization construct—the *monitor* type.

Remember that a type, or abstract data type, encapsulates private data with public methods to operate on that data. A monitor presents a set of programmer-defined operations that are provided mutual exclusion within the monitor. The monitor type also contains the declaration of variables whose values define the state of an instance of that type along with the bodies of procedures or functions that operate on those variables. The Java-like pseudocode describing the syntax of a monitor is:

```
monitor monitor-name
{
    // variable declarations

    public entry p1 (. . .) {
        . . .
    }
    public entry p2 (. . .) {
        . . .
    }
}
```

The internal implementation of a monitor type cannot be accessed directly by the various threads. A procedure defined within a monitor can access only those variables that are declared locally within the monitor and any formal parameters that are passed to the procedures. The encapsulation provided by the monitor type also limits access to the local variables by only the local procedures.

The monitor construct prohibits concurrent access to all procedures defined within the monitor. Therefore, only one thread (or process) at a time can be active within the monitor at any one time. Consequently, the programmer does not need to code this synchronization explicitly; it is built into the monitor type.

Variables of type `condition` play a special role in monitors by virtue of special operations that can be invoked on them: `wait` and `signal`. A programmer who needs to write her own tailor-made synchronization scheme can define one or more variables of the `condition` type:

```
condition x,y;
```

The operation

```
x.wait;
```

means that the thread invoking this operation is suspended until another thread invokes

```
x.signal;
```

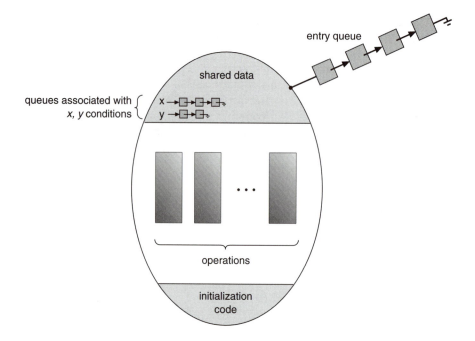

Figure 7.26   Monitor with condition variables.

The x.signal operation resumes exactly one thread. If no thread is suspended, then the signal operation has no effect; that is, the state of x is as though the operation was never executed (Figure 7.26). Contrast this scheme with the V operation with semaphores, which always affects the state of the semaphore.

Now suppose that, when the x.signal operation is invoked by a thread *P*, there is a suspended thread *Q* associated with condition x. Clearly, if the suspended thread *Q* is allowed to resume its execution, the signaling thread *P* must wait. Otherwise, both *P* and *Q* will be active simultaneously within the monitor. Note, however, that both threads can conceptually continue with their execution. Two possibilities exist:

1. *Signal-and-Wait*—*P* either waits until *Q* leaves the monitor, or waits for another condition.

2. *Signal-and-Continue*—*Q* either waits until *P* leaves the monitor, or waits for another condition.

There are reasonable arguments in favor of adopting either option. Since *P* was already executing in the monitor, *Signal-and-Continue* seems more reasonable. However, if we allow thread *P* to continue, then, by the time *Q* is resumed, the logical condition for which Q was waiting may no longer hold. *Signal-and-Wait* was advocated by Hoare, mainly because the preceding argument in favor of it translates directly to simple and elegant proof rules. A compromise between these two choices was adopted in the language Concurrent Pascal. When thread P executes the signal operation, it immediately leaves the monitor. Hence, Q is immediately resumed. This model is less powerful than Hoare's, because a thread cannot signal more than once during a single procedure call.

Let us illustrate these concepts by presenting a deadlock-free solution to the dining-philosophers problem. Recall that a philosopher is allowed to pick up her chopsticks only if both of them are available. To code this solution, we need to distinguish between three states in which a philosopher may be. For this purpose, we introduce the following data structures:

```
int[] state = new int[5];
static final int THINKING = 0;
static final int HUNGRY = 1;
static final int EATING = 2;
```

Philosopher i can set the variable `state[i]` = EATING only if her two neighbors are not eating; that is, the condition (`state[(i + 4) % 5] != EATING`) and (`state[(i + 1) % 5] != EATING`) holds.

We also need to declare

```
condition[] self = new condition[5];
```

where philosopher i can delay herself when she is hungry, but is unable to obtain the chopsticks she needs.

We are now in a position to describe our solution to the dining-philosopher problem. The distribution of the chopsticks is controlled by the monitor dp, which is an instance of the monitor type `diningPhilosophers`, whose definition using a Java-like pseudocode is shown in Figure 7.27. Each philosopher, before starting to eat, must invoke the operation `pickUp()`. This act may result in the suspension of the philosopher thread. After the successful completion of the operation, the philosopher may eat. After she eats, the philosopher invokes the `putDown()` operation, and starts to think. Thus, philosopher i must invoke the operations `pickUp()` and `putDown()` in the following sequence:

```
dp.pickUp(i);
eat();
dp.putDown(i);
```

It is easy to show that this solution ensures that no two neighboring philosophers are eating simultaneously, and that no deadlocks will occur. We note, however, that it is possible for a philosopher to starve to death. We shall not present a solution to that problem, but rather shall ask you in the exercises to develop one.

```
monitor diningPhilosophers {
    int[] state = new int[5];
    static final int THINKING = 0;
    static final int HUNGRY = 1;
    static final int EATING = 2;
    condition[] self = new condition[5];

    public diningPhilosophers {
        for (int i = 0; i < 5; i++)
            state[i] = THINKING;
    }

    public entry pickUp(int i) {
        state[i] = HUNGRY;
        test(i);
        if (state[i] != EATING)
            self[i].wait;
    }

    public entry putDown(int i) {
        state[i] = THINKING;
        // test left and right neighbors
        test((i + 4) % 5);
        test((i + 1) % 5);
    }

    private test(int i) {
        if ( (state[(i + 4) % 5] != EATING) &&
             (state[i] == HUNGRY) &&
             (state[(i + 1) % 5] != EATING) ) {
            state[i] = EATING;
            self[i].signal;
        }
    }
}
```

Figure 7.27   A monitor solution to the dining-philosophers problem.

7.8 ■ Java Synchronization

In this section, we describe how Java synchronizes the activity of threads, allowing the programmer to develop generalized solutions enforcing mutual exclusion between threads. An application that ensures data consistency even when being concurrently accessed by multiple threads is said to be **thread safe**.

7.8.1 Bounded Buffer

The shared-memory solution to the bounded-buffer problem described in Chapter 4 suffers from two problems. First, both the producer and consumer use busy-wait loops if the buffer is either full or empty. Second, as shown again in Section 7.1, the race condition on the variable count is shared by the producer and consumer. This section addresses these and other problems while developing a solution using Java synchronization mechanisms.

7.8.1.1 Busy Wait

Busy waiting was introduced in Section 7.5.2, when we examined an implementation of the P and V semaphore operations. In that section, we described how a process could block itself as an alternative to busy waiting. One way to accomplish such blocking in Java is to have a thread call the Thread.yield() method. Recall from Section 7.3.1 that, when a thread invokes the yield() method, the thread stays in the Runnable state, but it allows the JVM to select to run another Runnable thread of equal priority. The yield() method makes more effective use of the CPU than busy waiting does. However, in this instance, using *either* busy waiting or yielding could potentially lead to a deadlock.

Here is one such scenario that could cause deadlock to occur. Recall that the JVM schedules threads using a priority-based algorithm. The JVM ensures that the thread with the highest priority among all threads in the Runnable state will run before a lower-priority thread can run. If the producer has a priority higher than that of the consumer and the buffer is full, the producer will enter the while loop and either busy wait or yield() to another Runnable thread of equal priority while waiting for count to be decremented to less than BUFFER_SIZE. As long as the consumer has a priority lower than that of the producer, it will never be scheduled by the JVM to run, and therefore will never be able to consume an item and free up buffer space for the producer. In this situation, the producer and consumer are deadlocked: The producer is waiting for the consumer to free buffer space and the consumer is waiting to be scheduled by the JVM. We see shortly that there is a better alternative than busy waiting or yielding while waiting for a desired condition to occur.

7.8.1.2 Race Condition

In Section 7.1, we saw an example of the consequences of a race condition on the shared variable count. Figure 7.28 illustrates how Java prevents race conditions by handling concurrent access to shared data.

This situation introduces a new keyword: synchronized. Every object in Java has associated with it a single lock. The object that is an instance of the BoundedBuffer class has one lock associated with it. Ordinarily, when an object is being referenced (that is, its methods are being invoked), the lock is ignored. When a method is declared as synchronized, however, calling the method requires owning the lock for the object. If the lock is owned, the thread

```
public synchronized void enter(Object item) {
    while (count == BUFFER_SIZE)
        Thread.yield();

    ++count;
    buffer[in] = item;
    in = (in + 1) % BUFFER_SIZE;
}


public synchronized Object remove() {
    Object item;

    while (count == 0)
        Thread.yield();

    --count;
    item = buffer[out];
    out = (out + 1) % BUFFER_SIZE;

    return item;
}
```

Figure 7.28   Synchronized `enter()` and `remove()` methods.

calling the synchronized method blocks and is put in the *entry set* for the
object's lock. The entry set represents the set of threads waiting for the lock
to become available. If the lock is available when a synchronized method
is called, the calling thread becomes the owner of the object's lock and it can
enter the method. The lock is released when the thread exits the method. If
the entry set for the lock is not empty when the lock is released, the JVM selects
an arbitrary thread from this set as the new owner of the lock. Figure 7.29
illustrates how the entry set operates.

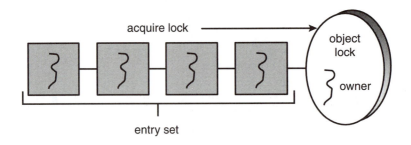

Figure 7.29   Entry set.

If the producer calls the enter() method, as shown in Figure 7.28, and the lock for the object is available, the producer becomes the owner of the lock; it can then enter the method, where it can alter the value of count and other shared data. If the consumer attempts to call the synchronized remove() method while the producer owns the lock, the consumer will block because the lock is unavailable. When the producer exits the enter() method, it releases the lock. The consumer can now acquire the lock and enter the remove() method.

At first glance, this approach appears at least to solve the problem of having a race condition on the variable count. Because both the enter() and

```java
public synchronized void enter(Object item) {
    while (count == BUFFER_SIZE) {
        try {
            wait();
        }
        catch (InterruptedException e) { }
    }
    ++count;
    buffer[in] = item;
    in = (in + 1) % BUFFER_SIZE;

    notify();
}

public synchronized Object remove() {
    Object item;

    while (count == 0) {
        try {
            wait();
        }
        catch (InterruptedException e) { }
    }
    --count;
    item = buffer[out];
    out = (out + 1) % BUFFER_SIZE;

    notify();

    return item;
}
```

Figure 7.30   enter() and remove() methods using wait() and notify().

remove() methods are declared as synchronized, we have ensured that only one thread may be active in either of these methods at a time. However, lock ownership has led to another problem. Assume that the buffer is full and the consumer is sleeping. If the producer calls the enter() method, it will be allowed to continue because the lock is available. When the producer invokes the enter() method, it sees that the buffer is full and performs the yield() method. All the while, the producer still owns the lock for the object. When the consumer awakens and tries to call the remove() method (which would ultimately free up buffer space for the producer), it will block because it does not own the lock for the object. Thus we see another example of deadlock. Both the producer and consumer are unable to proceed because (1) the producer is blocked waiting for the consumer to free space in the buffer, and (2) the consumer is blocked waiting for the producer to release the lock.

So, by declaring each method as synchronized, we have prevented the race condition on the shared variables. However, the presence of the yield() loop has led to another type of possible deadlock.

Figure 7.30 (on page 207) addresses the yield() loop by introducing two new Java methods: wait() and notify(). In addition to having a lock, every object also has associated with it a **wait set**. This wait set consists of a set of threads and is initially empty. When a thread enters a synchronized method, it owns the lock for the object. However, this thread may determine that it is unable to continue because a certain condition is not met. That will happen if the producer calls the enter() method and the buffer is full. Ideally, the thread will release the lock and will wait until the condition that will allow it to continue is met. That solution would have prevented the deadlock situation just described.

When a thread calls the wait() method, the following happens:

1. The thread releases the lock for the object.

2. The state of the thread is set to Blocked.

3. The thread is placed in the wait set for the object.

Consider the example in Figure 7.30. If the producer calls the enter() method and sees that the buffer is full, it calls the wait() method. This call releases the lock, blocks the producer, and puts the producer in the wait set

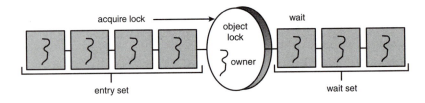

Figure 7.31   Entry and wait sets.

for the object. Releasing the lock allows the consumer ultimately to enter the
remove() method, where it frees space in the buffer for the producer. Figure
7.31 illustrates the entry and wait sets for a lock.

How then does the consumer thread signal that the producer may now
proceed? Ordinarily, when a thread exits a synchronized method, the default
action is that the departing thread releases only the lock associated with the
object, possibly removing a thread from the entry set and giving it ownership

```java
public class Bounded Buffer
{
    public BoundedBuffer() {
      // buffer is initially empty
      count = 0;
      in = 0;
      out = 0;
      buffer = new Object[BUFFER_SIZE];
    }

    // producer and consumer will call this to nap
    public static void napping() {
      int sleepTime = (int) (NAP_TIME * Math.random() );
      try {
         Thread.sleep(sleepTime*1000);
      }
      catch(InterruptedException e) { }
    }

    public synchronized void enter(Object item) {
      // Figure 7.33
    }

    public synchronized Object remove() {
      // Figure 7.34
    }

    private static final int NAP_TIME = 5;
    private static final int BUFFER_SIZE = 5;

    private int count, in, out;
    private Object[] buffer;
}
```

Figure 7.32 Bounded buffer.

of the lock. However, at the end of the synchronized `enter()` and `remove()` methods, we have a call to the method `notify()`. The call to `notify()`

1. Picks an arbitrary thread T from the list of threads in the wait set.

2. Moves T from the wait set to the entry set.

3. Sets the state of T from Blocked to Runnable.

T is now eligible to compete for the lock with the other threads. Once T has regained control of the lock, it returns from calling `wait()`, where it may check the value of `count` again.

To describe the `wait()` and `notify()` methods in terms of the program shown in Figure 7.30, we assume that the buffer is full and the lock for the object is available.

- The producer calls the `enter()` method, sees that the lock is available, and enters the method. Once in the method the producer determines that the buffer is full and calls `wait()`. The call to `wait()` (1) releases the lock for

```
public synchronized void enter(Object item) {
    while (count == BUFFER_SIZE) {
      try {
        wait();
      }
      catch (InterruptedException e) { }
    }

    // add an item to the buffer
    ++count;
    buffer[in] = item;
    in = (in + 1) % BUFFER_SIZE;

    if (count == BUFFER_SIZE)
      System.out.println("Producer Entered " + item +
        " Buffer FULL");
    else
      System.out.println("Producer Entered " + item +
        " Buffer Size = " + count);

    notify();
}
```

Figure 7.33   `enter()` method.

the object, and (2) sets the state of the producer to Blocked and puts the producer in the wait set for the object.

- The consumer ultimately calls the remove() method because the lock for the object is now available. The consumer removes an item from the buffer and calls notify(). Note that the consumer still owns the lock for the object.

- The call to notify() removes the producer from the wait set for the object, moves the producer to the entry set, and sets the producer's state to Runnable.

- The consumer exits the remove() method. Exiting this method releases the lock for the object.

- The producer tries to reacquire the lock and is successful. It resumes execution from the call to wait(). The producer tests the while loop,

```java
public synchronized Object remove() {
    Object item;

    while (count == 0) {
        try {
            wait();
        }
        catch (InterruptedException e) { }
    }

    // remove an item from the buffer
    --count;
    item = buffer[out];
    out = (out + 1) % BUFFER_SIZE;

    if (count == 0)
        System.out.println("Consumer Consumed " + item +
            " Buffer EMPTY");
    else
        System.out.println("Consumer Consumed " + item +
            " Buffer Size = " + count);

    notify();

    return item;
}
```

Figure 7.34   remove() method.

determines that there is room available in the buffer, and proceeds with the remainder of the enter() method. Since no thread is in the wait set for the object, the call to notify() is ignored. When the producer exits the method, it releases the lock for the object.

7.8.2 Complete Solution

The following represents the complete multithreaded solution, using shared memory, to the bounded-buffer problem. The BoundedBuffer class shown in Figure 7.32 (page 209) implements the synchronized methods enter() and remove(). This class may be substituted for the BoundedBuffer class that was used in the semaphore-based solution to this problem in Section 7.6.1.

7.8.3 The Readers–Writers Problem

We can now provide a solution to the first readers–writers problem by using Java synchronization. The methods called by each reader and writer thread are defined in the Database class in Figure 7.35. The readerCount keeps track of the number of readers, dbReading is set to true if the database is currently being read and to false otherwise. dbWriting indicates whether the database is currently being accessed by a writer. startRead(), endRead(), startWrite(), and endWrite() are all declared as synchronized to ensure mutual exclusion to the shared variables.

When a writer wishes to begin writing, it first checks whether the database is currently being either read or written. If the database is being read or written, the writer goes to the wait set for the object. Otherwise, it sets dbWriting to true. When a writer is finished, it sets dbWriting to false. When a reader invokes startRead(), it first checks whether the database is currently being written. If the database is available, the reader sets dbReading to true if it is the first reader. The final reader calling endRead() sets dbReading to false.

7.8.4 Multiple Notifications

As described in Section 7.8, the call to notify() selects an arbitrary thread from the list of threads in the wait set for an object. This approach works fine when there is at most one thread in the wait set, but consider the case where there are multiple threads in the wait set and more than one condition for which to wait. It is possible that a thread whose condition is still unmet may be the thread that receives the notification. For example, assume that there are five threads {$T1, T2, T3, T4, T5$} and a shared variable turn indicating which thread's turn it is. When a thread wishes to do work, it calls the doWork() method in Figure 7.38 (on page 216). Only the thread whose number matches the value of turn may proceed; all other threads must wait their turn.

```
public class Database {
    public Database() {
        readerCount = 0;
        dbReading = false;
        dbWriting = false;
    }

    // readers and writers will call this to nap
    public static void napping() {
        int sleepTime = (int)(NAP_TIME *
           Math.random());
        try {
           Thread.sleep(sleepTime*1000);
        }
        catch(InterruptedException e) { }
    }

    public synchronized int startRead() {
        // Figure 7.36
    }

    public synchronized int endRead() {
        // Figure 7.36
    }

    public synchronized void startWrite() {
        // Figure 7.37
    }

    public synchronized void endWrite() {
        // Figure 7.37
    }

    private static final int NAP_TIME = 5;

    private int readerCount;
    // flags to indicate whether the database
    // is being read or written
    private boolean dbReading;
    private boolean dbWriting;
}
```

Figure 7.35   The database.

```java
public synchronized int startRead() {
    while (dbWriting == true) {
        try {
            wait();
        }
        catch(InterruptedException e) { }
    }

    ++readerCount;

    // if I am the first reader tell all others
    // that the database is being read
    if (readerCount == 1)
        dbReading = true;

    return readerCount;
}

public synchronized int endRead() {
    --readerCount;

    // if I am the last reader tell all others
    // that the database is no longer being read
    if (readerCount == 0)
        dbReading = false;

    notifyAll();

    return readerCount;
}
```

Figure 7.36   Methods called by readers.

Assume the following:

- turn = 3.

- *T1, T2,* and *T4* are in the wait set for the object.

- *T3* is currently in the doWork() method.

When thread *T3* is done, it sets turn to 4 (indicating that it is *T4*'s turn) and calls notify(). The call to notify() picks an arbitrary thread from the wait set. If *T2* receives the notification, it resumes execution from the call to wait() and tests the condition in the while loop. *T2* sees that this is not its turn, so

```
public synchronized void startWrite() {
    while (dbReading == true || dbWriting == true) {
        try {
            wait();
        }
        catch(InterruptedException e) { }
    }

    // once there are either no readers or writers
    // indicate that the database is being written
    dbWriting = true;
}

public synchronized void endWrite() {
    dbWriting = false;

    notifyAll();
}
```

Figure 7.37 Methods called by writers.

it calls wait() again. Ultimately, T3 and T5 will call doWork() and will also invoke the wait() method, since it is the turn for neither T3 nor T5. Now, all five threads are blocked in the wait set for the object. Thus, we have another deadlock that we must handle.

Because the call to notify() picks a single thread at random from the wait set, the developer has no control over which thread gets chosen. Fortunately, Java provides a mechanism that allows all threads in the wait set to be notified. The notifyAll() method is similar to notify(), except that *every* waiting thread is removed from the wait set and is placed in the entry set. If the call to notify() in doWork() is replaced with a call to notifyAll(), when T3 finishes and sets turn to 4, it calls notifyAll(). This call has the effect of removing T1, T2, and T4 from the wait set. The three threads then compete for the object's lock once again, and ultimately T1 and T2 call wait() and only T4 proceeds with the doWork() method.

The notifyAll() method is a mechanism that wakes up all waiting threads and lets the threads decide among themselves who should run next. In general, notifyAll() is a more expensive operation than notify() because it wakes up all threads, but it is regarded as a more conservative strategy that works best when multiple threads may be in the wait set for an object.

```
// pnum is the number of the thread
// that wishes to do some work
public synchronized void doWork(int pnum) {
    while (turn != pnum) {
        try {
            wait();
        }
        catch (InterruptedException e) { }
    }

    // do some work for awhile .  .  .

    // ok, we're finished.  Now indicate to the
    // next waiting thread that it is their
    // turn to do some work.

    if (turn < 5)
        ++turn;
    else
        turn = 1;

    notify();
}
```

Figure 7.38   doWork() method.

7.8.5 Block Synchronization

In addition to declaring methods as synchronized, Java also allows blocks of code to be declared as synchronized, as illustrated in Figure 7.39.

Access to the method criticalSection() requires ownership of the lock for mutexLock. Declaring a method someMethod() as synchronized is equivalent to

```
public void someMethod() {
    synchronized(this) {
        // remainder of the method
    }
}
```

The amount of time between when a lock is assigned and when it is released is defined as the **scope** of the lock. Java provides block synchronization because a synchronized method that has only a small percentage of its code manipulating shared data may yield a scope that is too large. In such an instance, it may be better to synchronize the block of code that manipulates

```
Object mutexLock = new Object();
   .   .   .
public void someMethod() {
    nonCriticalSection();

    synchronized(mutexLock) {
        criticalSection();
    }

    nonCriticalSection();
}
```

Figure 7.39   Block synchronization.

shared data than to synchronize the entire method. Such a design results in a smaller lock scope.

We can also use the `wait()` and `notify()` methods in a synchronized block. The only difference is that they must be used with the same object that is being used for synchronization. This approach is shown in Figure 7.40.

7.8.6 Java Semaphores

Java does not provide a semaphore, but we can easily construct one using standard synchronization mechanisms. Declaring the `P()` and `V()` methods as `synchronized` ensures that each operation is performed atomically. The Semaphore class shown in Figure 7.41 implements a basic counting semaphore. We leave it as an exercise to modify the `Semaphore` class such that it acts as a binary semaphore.

```
Object mutexLock = new Object();
   .   .   .
synchronized(mutexLock) {
    try {
        mutexLock.wait();
    }
    catch (InterruptedException ie) { }
}

synchronized(mutexLock) {
    mutexLock.notify();
}
```

Figure 7.40   Block synchronization using `wait()` and `notify()`.

```
public class Semaphore
{
    public Semaphore() {
        value = 0;
    }

    public Semaphore(int v) {
        value = v;
    }

    public synchronized void P() {
        while (value <= 0) {
            try {
                wait();
            }
            catch (InterruptedException e) { }
        }

        value--;
    }

    public synchronized void V() {
        ++value;

        notify();
    }

    private int value;
}
```

Figure 7.41   Java semaphore implementation.

7.8.7 Synchronization Rules

The synchronized keyword is a straightforward construct. Just a few rules about its behavior are important to know.

1. A thread that owns the lock for an object can enter another synchronized method (or block) for the same object.

2. A thread can nest synchronized method invocations for different objects. Thus, a thread can simultaneously own the lock for several different objects.

3. If a method is not declared as synchronized, then it can be invoked regardless of lock ownership, even while another synchronized method for the same object is executing.

4. If the wait set for an object is empty, then a call to notify() or notifyAll() has no effect.

7.8.8 Java Monitors

Many programming languages have incorporated the idea of the monitor (discussed in Section 7.7), including Concurrent Pascal, Mesa, NeWs, and Java. Many other modern programming languages have provided some type of concurrency support using a mechanism similar to monitors. We now discuss the relationship of monitors in the strict sense to Java monitors.

In this section, we introduced Java synchronization using an object's lock. In many ways, this lock acts as a monitor. Every Java object has an associated monitor. A thread can acquire an object's monitor by either entering a synchronized method or blocking. However, Java does not provide support for named condition variables. With monitors, the wait and signal operations can be applied to named condition variables, allowing a thread to wait for a specific condition or to be notified when a specific condition has been met. Each Java monitor has just one unnamed condition variable associated with it. The wait(), notify(), and notifyAll() operations may apply to only this single condition variable. When a Java thread is awakened via notify() or notifyAll(), it receives no information about why it was awakened. It is up to the reactivated thread to check for itself whether the condition for which it was waiting has been met. Java monitors use the signal-and-continue approach: When a thread is signaled with the notify() method, it can acquire the lock for the monitor only when the notifying thread exits the synchronized method or block.

7.9 ■ OS Synchronization

We next describe the synchronization mechanisms provided by the Solaris and Windows NT operating systems.

7.9.1 Synchronization in Solaris 2

Solaris 2 was designed to support real-time computing, to be multithreaded, and to support multiple processors. To control access to critical sections, Solaris 2 provides adaptive mutexes, condition variables, semaphores, and reader–writer locks.

An **adaptive mutex** protects access to every critical data item. On a multiprocessor system, an adaptive mutex starts as a standard semaphore implemented as a spinlock. If the data are locked, and therefore already in use, the adaptive mutex does one of two things. If the lock is held by a thread that is currently running on another CPU, the thread spins while waiting for the lock to become available because the thread holding the lock is likely to be done soon. If the thread holding the lock is not currently in run state, the thread blocks, going to sleep until it is awakened by the lock being released. It is put to sleep so that it will avoid spinning when the lock will not be freed reasonably quickly. A lock held by a sleeping thread is likely to be in this category. On a uniprocessor system, the thread holding the lock is never running if the lock is being tested by another thread, because only one thread can run at a time. Therefore, on a uniprocessor system, threads always sleep rather than spin if they encounter a lock. We use the adaptive-mutex method to protect only those data that are accessed by short code segments. That is, a mutex is used if a lock will be held for less than a few hundred instructions. If the code segment is longer than that, spin waiting will be exceedingly inefficient. For longer code segments, condition variables and semaphores are used. If the desired lock is already held, the thread issues a wait and sleeps. When a thread frees the lock, it issues a signal to the next sleeping thread in the queue. The extra cost of putting a thread to sleep and waking it, and of the associated context switches, is less than the cost of wasting several hundred instructions waiting in a spinlock.

Note that the locking mechanisms used by the kernel are implemented for user-level threads as well, so the same types of locks are available inside and outside of the kernel. A crucial implementation difference occurs in the area of priority inheritance. Kernel-locking routines adhere to the kernel priority inheritance methods used by the scheduler, as described in Section 6.5. User-level thread-locking mechanisms do not provide this functionality, as it is kernel specific.

The readers–writers locks are used to protect data that are accessed frequently, but usually only in a read-only manner. In these circumstances, readers–writers locks are more efficient than are semaphores, because multiple threads may be reading data concurrently, whereas semaphores would always serialize access to the data. Readers–writers locks are relatively expensive to implement, so again they are used on only long sections of code.

To optimize Solaris performance, developers have refined and fine tuned the locking methods. Because locks are used frequently and typically are used for crucial kernel functions, great performance gains can be achieved by tuning their implementation and use.

7.9.2 Synchronization in Windows NT

Windows NT is a multithreaded kernel that also provides support for real-time applications and multiple processors. NT provides several types of synchronization objects to handle mutual exclusion, including mutexes, critical sections, semaphores, and event objects. We protect shared data by requiring a thread to gain ownership of a mutex to access the data and to release ownership when it is finished. A **critical-section** object behaves like a mutex with the exception that it may be used for synchronization between only those threads that belong to the same process. **Events** are synchronization objects that may be used much as are condition variables; that is, they may notify a waiting thread when a desired condition occurs.

7.10 ■ Summary

Given a collection of cooperating sequential processes or threads that share data, mutual exclusion must be provided to prevent the occurrence of a race condition on the shared data. One solution is to ensure that a critical section of code is in use by only one process or thread at a time. Different software solutions exist for solving the critical-section problem, with the assumption that only storage interlock is available.

The main disadvantage of software solutions is that they are not easy to generalize for multiple threads or for problems more complex than the critical section. Semaphores overcome this difficulty. We can use semaphores to solve various synchronization problems, and can implement them efficiently, especially if hardware support for atomic operations is available.

Various different synchronization problems (such as the bounded-buffer, readers–writers, and dining-philosophers problems) are important mainly because they are examples of a large class of concurrency-control problems. These problems are used to test nearly every newly proposed synchronization scheme.

Java provides a mechanism to coordinate the activities of multiple threads when accessing shared data through the synchronized, wait(), notify(), and notifyAll() mechanisms. Java synchronization is provided at the language level. Java synchronization is an example of a higher-level synchronization mechanism called a monitor. In addition to Java, many languages have provided support for monitors, including Concurrent Pascal and Mesa.

Operating systems also provide support for thread synchronization. For example, Solaris 2 and Windows NT provide mechanisms such as semaphores, mutexes, and condition variables to control access to shared data.

■ Exercises

7.1 The first known correct software solution to the critical-section problem for two threads was developed by Dekker; it is shown in Figure 7.42. The two threads, T_0 and T_1, coordinate activity sharing an object of class Dekker. Show that the algorithm satisfies all three requirements for the critical-section problem.

7.2 In Chapter 5, we gave a multithreaded solution to the bounded-buffer problem that used message passing. The MessageQueue class is not considered thread safe, meaning that a race condition is possible when

```
public class Dekker extends MutualExclusion
{
    public Dekker() {
        flag[0] = false;
        flag[1] = false;
        turn = TURN_0;
    }

    public void enteringCriticalSection(int t) {
        int other;

        other = 1 - t;
        flag[t] = true;

        while (flag[other] == true) {
            if (turn == other) {
                flag[t] = false;
                while (turn == other)
                        Thread.yield();

                flag[t] = true;
            }
        }
    }

    public void leavingCriticalSection(int t) {
        turn = 1 - t;
        flag[t] = false;
    }

    private volatile int turn;
    private volatile boolean[] flag = new boolean[2];
}
```

Figure 7.42   Dekker's algorithm for mutual exclusion.

multiple threads attempt to concurrently access the queue. Modify the
MessageQueue class using Java synchronization such that it is thread safe.

7.3 Create a BinarySemaphore class that implements a binary semaphore.

7.4 The wait() statement in all Java program examples was part of a while
loop. Explain why you would always need to use a while statement when
using the wait(), and why you would never use an if statement.

7.5 The solution to the readers–writers problem does not prevent waiting writers from starving: If the database is currently being read and there is a waiting writer, subsequent readers will be allowed to read the database before the writer can write. Modify the solution such that it does not starve waiting writers.

7.6 A monitor-based solution to the dining-philosophers problem, written in Java-like pseudocode and using condition variables, was given in Section 7.7. Develop a solution to the dining-philosophers problem using Java synchronization.

7.7 The solution that we gave to the dining-philosophers problem does not prevent a philosopher from starving. For example, two philosophers— say, philosopher$_1$ and philosopher$_3$—could alternate eating and thinking such that philosopher$_2$ could never eat. Using Java synchronization, develop a solution to the dining-philosophers problem that prevents a philosopher from starving.

7.8 In Section 7.4, we mentioned that disabling interrupts frequently could affect the system's clock. Explain why it could, and how such effects could be minimized.

7.9 In this chapter, we used the synchronized statement with *instance* methods. Calling an instance method requires associating the method with an object. Entering a synchronized method requires owning the object's lock. *Static* methods are unlike instance methods in that they do not require association with an object when they are called. Explain how it is possible for static methods also to be declared as synchronized.

7.10 *The Sleeping-Barber Problem.* A barbershop consists of a waiting room with n chairs, and a barber room with one barber chair. If there are no customers to be served, the barber goes to sleep. If a customer enters the barbershop and all chairs are occupied, then the customer leaves the shop. If the barber is busy, but chairs are available, then the customer sits in one of the free chairs. If the barber is asleep, the customer wakes up the barber. Write a program to coordinate the barber and the customers using Java synchronization.

7.11 *The Cigarette-Smokers Problem.* Consider a system with three *smoker* processes and one *agent* process. Each smoker continuously rolls a cigarette and then smokes it. But to roll and smoke a cigarette, the smoker needs three ingredients: tobacco, paper, and matches. One of the smoker processes has paper, another has tobacco, and the third has matches. The agent has an infinite supply of all three materials. The agent places two of the ingredients on the table. The smoker who has the remaining ingredient then makes and smokes a cigarette, signaling the agent on completion. The agent then puts out another two of the three ingredients, and the cycle repeats. Write a program to synchronize the agent and the smokers using Java synchronization.

7.12 Give the reasons why Solaris 2 and Windows NT implement multiple locking mechanisms. Describe the circumstances under which they use spinlocks, mutexes, semaphores, adaptive mutexes, and condition variables. In each case, explain why the mechanism is needed.

Bibliographical Notes

The mutual-exclusion algorithms 1 and 2 for two tasks were first discussed in the classical paper by Dijkstra [1965a]. Dekker's algorithm (Exercise 7.1)—the first correct software solution to the two-process mutual-exclusion problem— was developed by the Dutch mathematician T. Dekker. This algorithm also was discussed by Dijkstra [1965a]. A simpler solution to the two-process mutual-exclusion problem has since been presented by Peterson [1981] (algorithm 3).

Dijkstra [1965b] presented the first solution to the mutual-exclusion problem for n processes. This solution, however, does not have an upper bound on the amount of time a process must wait before that process is allowed to enter the critical section. Knuth [1966] presented the first algorithm with a bound; his bound was 2^n turns. A refinement of Knuth's algorithm by deBruijn [1967] reduced the waiting time to n^2 turns, after which Eisenberg and McGuire [1972] succeeded in reducing the time to the lower bound of $n - 1$ turns. Lamport [1974] presented a different scheme for solving the mutual-exclusion problem —the bakery algorithm; it also requires $n - 1$ turns, but it is easier to program and to understand. Burns [1978] developed the hardware-solution algorithm that satisfies the bounded waiting requirement.

General discussions concerning the mutual-exclusion problem were offered by Lamport [1986, 1991]. A collection of algorithms for mutual exclusion was given by Raynal [1986].

Information on hardware solutions for process synchronization can be found in Patterson and Hennessy [1998].

The semaphore concept was suggested by Dijkstra [1965a]. Patil [1971] examined the question of whether semaphores can solve all possible synchronization problems. Parnas [1975] discussed some of the flaws in Patil's arguments. Kosaraju [1973] followed up on Patil's work to produce a problem that cannot be solved by *wait* and *signal* operations. Lipton [1974] discussed the limitation of various synchronization primitives.

The classic process-coordination problems that we have described are paradigms for a large class of concurrency-control problems. The bounded-buffer problem, the dining-philosophers problem, and the sleeping-barber problem (Exercise 7.10) were suggested by Dijkstra [1965a, 1971]. The cigarette-smokers problem (Exercise 7.11) was developed by Patil [1971]. The readers–writers problem was suggested by Courtois and colleagues [1971]. The matter of concurrent reading and writing was discussed by Lamport [1977], as was the problem of synchronization of independent processes [1976].

The monitor concept was developed by Brinch Hansen [1973]. A complete description of the monitor was given by Hoare [1974]. Kessels [1977] proposed an extension to the monitor to allow automatic signaling. A paper describing the classifications for monitors was published by Buhr and colleagues [1995]. General discussions concerning concurrent programming were offered by Ben-Ari [1990] and Burns and Davies [1993].

Details covering how Java synchronizes threads can be found in Oaks and Wong [1999], Lea [1997], and Gosling and colleagues [1996]. Hartley [1998] makes numerous references to multithreaded and concurrent programming in Java. Java Report [1998] is devoted to advanced multithreading and synchronization topics in Java.

Synchronization primitives for Windows NT are discussed by Solomon [1998] and Pham and Garg [1996]. Details of the locking mechanisms used in Solaris 2 are presented by Khanna and colleagues[1992], Powell and colleagues [1991], and especially Eykholt and colleagues [1992]. Other references for Solaris 2 synchronization include Vahalia [1996] and Graham [1995].

Chapter 8

DEADLOCKS

When several processes compete for a finite number of resources, a situation may arise where a process requests a resource and the resource is not available at that time, in which case the process enters a wait state. It may happen that waiting processes will never again change state, because the resources that they have requested are held by other waiting processes. This situation is called a **deadlock**. We have already discussed this issue briefly in Chapter 7, in connection with semaphores.

Perhaps the best illustration of a deadlock can be drawn from a law passed by the Kansas legislature early in this century. It said, in part: "When two trains approach each other at a crossing, both shall come to a full stop and neither shall start up again until the other has gone."

In this chapter, we illustrate deadlock at the operating-system level and in multithreaded Java applications. We also describe methods that operating systems and programmers can use to deal with the deadlock problem.

8.1 ■ System Model

A system consists of a finite number of resources to be distributed among competing processes. The resources are partitioned into several types, each of which consists of multiple identical instances. Memory space, CPU cycles, files, object locks, and I/O devices (such as printers and tape drives) are examples of resource types. If a system has two CPUs, then the resource type *CPU* has two instances. Similarly, the resource type *printer* may have five instances.

If a process requests an instance of a resource type, the allocation of *any* instance of the type will satisfy the request. If it will not, then the instances are not identical, and the resource type classes have not been defined properly. For example, a system may have two printers. These two printers may be defined to be in the same resource class if no one cares which printer prints which output. However, if one printer is on the ninth floor and the other is in the basement, then people on the ninth floor may not see both printers as equivalent, and separate resource classes may need to be defined for each printer.

A process must request a resource before using it, and must release the resource after using it. A process may request as many resources as it requires to carry out its designated task. Obviously, the number of resources requested cannot exceed the total number of resources available in the system. In other words, a process cannot request three printers if the system only has two. If such a request is made, it will be rejected by the system.

Under the normal mode of operation, a process may use a resource in only the following sequence:

1. *Request:* If the request cannot be granted immediately (for example, the resource is being used by another process), then the requesting process must wait until it can acquire the resource.

2. *Use:* The process can operate on the resource (for example, if the resource is a printer, the process can print on the printer).

3. *Release:* The process releases the resource.

The request and release of resources are system calls, as explained in Chapter 3. Examples are the `request` and `release device`, `open` and `close file`, and `allocate` and `free memory` system calls. Request and release of resources that are not managed by the operating system can be accomplished through the P and V operations on semaphores, or through acquisition and release of a lock for a Java object via the `synchronized` keyword. For each use of a kernel-managed resource by a process or thread, the operating system checks to make sure that the process has requested and has been allocated the resource. A system table records whether each resource is free or allocated, and, for each resource that is allocated, to which process. If a process requests a resource that is currently allocated to another process, it can be added to a queue of processes waiting for this resource.

A set of processes is in a deadlock state when every process in the set is waiting for an event that can be caused by only another process in the set. The events with which we are mainly concerned here are resource acquisition and release. The resources may be either physical resources (for example, printers, tape drives, memory space, and CPU cycles) or logical resources (for example, files, semaphores, object locks, and monitors). Other types of events also may result in deadlock. For example, in Section 7.8, we saw a type of deadlock where a thread entered a `synchronized` method and performed a busy-wait loop before releasing the lock.

To illustrate a deadlock state, we consider a system that has three tape drives. Suppose that there are three processes, each holding one of these tape drives. If each process now requests another tape drive, the three processes will be in a deadlock state. Each is waiting for the event *tape drive is released*, which can be caused by only one of the other waiting processes. This example illustrates a deadlock of processes that are competing for the same resource type.

Deadlocks can also involve different resource types. For example, consider a system that has one printer and one tape drive. Suppose that process P_i is holding the tape drive and process P_j is holding the printer. If P_i requests the printer and P_j requests the tape drive, a deadlock occurs.

A programmer who is developing multithreaded applications must pay particular attention to this problem: Multithreaded programs are good candidates for deadlock because there are multiple threads possibly competing for shared resources (such as object locks).

8.2 ■ Deadlock Characterization

Deadlocks are undesirable. In a deadlock, processes never finish executing and system resources are tied up, preventing other jobs from ever starting. Before we discuss the various methods for dealing with the deadlock problem, we describe features that characterize deadlocks.

8.2.1 Necessary Conditions

A deadlock situation can arise if the following four conditions hold simultaneously in a system:

1. *Mutual exclusion:* At least one resource must be held in a nonsharable mode; that is, only one process at a time can use the resource. If another process requests that resource, the requesting process must be delayed until the resource has been released.

2. *Hold-and-wait:* There must exist a process that is holding at least one resource and is waiting to acquire additional resources that are currently being held by other processes.

3. *No preemption:* Resources cannot be preempted; that is, a resource can be released only voluntarily by the process holding it, after that process has completed its task.

4. *Circular wait:* There must exist a set $\{P_0, P_1, \cdots, P_n\}$ of waiting processes, such that P_0 is waiting for a resource that is held by P_1, P_1 is waiting for a

resource that is held by $P_2, \cdots, P_{n-1}$ is waiting for a resource that is held by P_n, and P_n is waiting for a resource that is held by P_0.

We emphasize that all four conditions must hold for a deadlock to occur. The circular-wait condition implies the hold-and-wait condition, so the four conditions are not completely independent.

8.2.2 Resource-Allocation Graph

Deadlocks can be described more precisely in terms of a directed graph called a **system resource-allocation graph**. This graph consists of a set of vertices V and a set of edges E. The set of vertices V is partitioned into two different types of nodes, $P = \{P_1, P_2, \cdots, P_n\}$, the set consisting of all the active processes in the system, and $R = \{R_1, R_2, \cdots, R_m\}$, the set consisting of all resource types in the system.

A directed edge from process P_i to resource type R_j is denoted by $P_i \rightarrow R_j$; it signifies that process P_i requested an instance of resource type R_j and is currently waiting for that resource. A directed edge from resource type R_j to process P_i is denoted by $R_j \rightarrow P_i$; it signifies that an instance of resource type R_j has been allocated to process P_i. A directed edge $P_i \rightarrow R_j$ is called a **request edge**; a directed edge $R_j \rightarrow P_i$ is called an **assignment edge**.

Pictorially, we represent each process P_i as a circle, and each resource type R_j as a square. Since resource type R_j may have more than one instance, we represent each such instance as a dot within the square. Note that a request edge points to only the square R_j, whereas an assignment edge must also designate one of the dots in the square.

When process P_i requests an instance of resource type R_j, a request edge is inserted in the resource-allocation graph. When this request can be fulfilled, the request edge is *instantaneously* transformed to an assignment edge. When the process no longer needs access to the resource it releases the resource, and as a result the assignment edge is deleted.

The resource-allocation graph shown in Figure 8.1 depicts the following situation.

- The sets P, R, and E:
  - $P = \{P_1, P_2, P_3\}$
  - $R = \{R_1, R_2, R_3, R_4\}$
  - $E = \{P_1 \rightarrow R_1, P_2 \rightarrow R_3, R_1 \rightarrow P_2, R_2 \rightarrow P_2, R_2 \rightarrow P_1, R_3 \rightarrow P_3\}$
- Resource instances:
  - One instance of resource type R_1
  - Two instances of resource type R_2

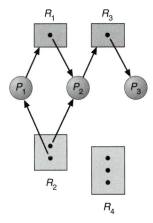

Figure 8.1 Resource-allocation graph.

- One instance of resource type R_3

- Three instances of resource type R_4

- Process states:

    - Process P_1 is holding an instance of resource type R_2, and is waiting for an instance of resource type R_1.

    - Process P_2 is holding an instance of R_1 and R_2, and is waiting for an instance of resource type R_3.

    - Process P_3 is holding an instance of R_3.

Given the definition of a resource-allocation graph, we can show that, if the graph contains no cycles, then no process in the system is deadlocked. If, on the other hand, the graph contains a cycle, then a deadlock may exist.

If each resource type has exactly one instance, then a cycle implies that a deadlock has occurred. If the cycle involves only a set of resource types, each of which has only a single instance, then a deadlock has occurred. Each process involved in the cycle is deadlocked. In this case, a cycle in the graph is both a necessary and a sufficient condition for the existence of deadlock.

If each resource type has several instances, then a cycle does not necessarily imply that a deadlock occurred. In this case, a cycle in the graph is a necessary but not a sufficient condition for the existence of deadlock.

To illustrate this concept, let us return to the resource-allocation graph depicted in Figure 8.1. Suppose that P_3 requests an instance of resource type R_2. Since no resource instance is currently available, a request edge $P_3 \rightarrow R_2$ is

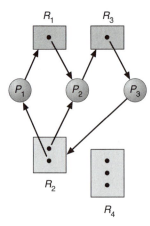

Figure 8.2   Resource-allocation graph with a deadlock.

added to the graph (Figure 8.2). At this point, two minimal cycles exist in the system:

$$P_1 \rightarrow R_1 \rightarrow P_2 \rightarrow R_3 \rightarrow P_3 \rightarrow R_2 \rightarrow P_1$$

$$P_2 \rightarrow R_3 \rightarrow P_3 \rightarrow R_2 \rightarrow P_2$$

Processes P_1, P_2, and P_3 are deadlocked. Process P_2 is waiting for the resource R_3, which is held by process P_3. Process P_3, on the other hand, is waiting for either process P_1 or process P_2 to release resource R_2. In addition, process P_1 is waiting for process P_2 to release resource R_1.

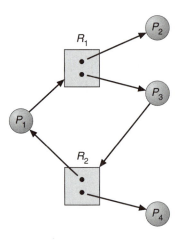

Figure 8.3   Resource-allocation graph with a cycle but no deadlock.

Now consider the resource-allocation graph in Figure 8.3. In this example, we also have a cycle

$$P_1 \rightarrow R_1 \rightarrow P_3 \rightarrow R_2 \rightarrow P_1$$

However, there is no deadlock. Observe that process P_4 may release its instance of resource type R_2. That resource can then be allocated to P_3, breaking the cycle.

In summary, if a resource-allocation graph does not have a cycle, then the system is *not* in a deadlock state. On the other hand, if there is a cycle, then the system may or may not be in a deadlock state. This observation is important when we deal with the deadlock problem.

Before we proceed with a discussion of handling deadlocks, let us see how deadlock can occur in a multithreaded Java program, as shown in Figure 8.4.

In that example, threadA attempts to acquire the objects' locks in the order of (1) mutexX, (2) mutexY and threadB attempts using the order of (1) mutexY, (2) mutexX. Deadlock is possible in the following scenario:

threadA $\rightarrow$ mutexY $\rightarrow$ threadB $\rightarrow$ mutexX $\rightarrow$ threadA

Note that, even though deadlock is possible, it would not have occurred if threadA was able to acquire and release the locks for mutexX and mutexY prior to threadB attempting to acquire the locks. This example illustrates the problem: It is difficult to identify and test for and an application may deadlock under only certain circumstances.

8.3 ▪ Methods for Handling Deadlocks

Principally, there are three different methods for dealing with the deadlock problem:

1. We can use a protocol to ensure that the system will *never* enter a deadlock state.

2. We can allow the system to enter a deadlock state and then recover.

3. We can ignore the problem, and pretend that deadlocks never occur in the system.

The third solution is the one used by most operating systems, including UNIX. The JVM also does nothing to manage deadlocks. It is up to the application developer to write programs that handle deadlocks. We elaborate briefly on each method. Then, in Sections 8.4 through 8.7, we present detailed algorithms.

To ensure that deadlocks never occur, the system can use either a deadlock-prevention or a deadlock-avoidance scheme. **Deadlock prevention** is a set of methods for ensuring that at least one of the necessary conditions (Section 8.2.1) cannot hold. These methods prevent deadlocks by constraining how requests for resources can be made. We discuss these methods in Section 8.4.

```
class Mutex { }

class A extends Thread
{
    public A(Mutex f, Mutex s) {
        first = f;
        second = s;
    }

    public void run() {
        synchronized (first) {
            // do something
            synchronized (second) {
                // do something else
            }
        }
    }
    private Mutex first, second;
}

class B extends Thread
{
    public B(Mutex f, Mutex s) {
        first = f;
        second = s;
    }

    public void run() {
        synchronized (second) {
            // do something
            synchronized (first) {
                // do something else
            }
        }
    }
    private Mutex first, second;
}

public class DeadlockExample
{
    // Figure 8.5
}
```

Figure 8.4   Deadlock example.

```
public static void main(String arg[]) {
    Mutex mutexX = new Mutex();
    Mutex mutexY = new Mutex();

    A threadA = new A(mutexX,mutexY);
    B threadB = new B(mutexX,mutexY);

    threadA.start();
    threadB.start();
}
```

Figure 8.5   Creating the threads.

Deadlock avoidance, on the other hand, requires that the operating system be given in advance additional information concerning which resources a process will request and use during that process's lifetime. With this additional knowledge, the operating system can decide for each request whether or not the process should wait. Each request requires that the system consider the resources currently available, the resources currently allocated to each process, and the future requests and releases of each process, to decide whether the current request can be satisfied or must be delayed. We discuss these schemes in Section 8.5.

If a system does not employ either a deadlock-prevention or a deadlock-avoidance algorithm, then a deadlock situation may occur. In this environment, the system can provide an algorithm that examines the state of the system to determine whether a deadlock has occurred, and an algorithm to recover from the deadlock (if a deadlock has indeed occurred). We discuss these matters in Sections 8.6 and 8.7.

If a system does not ensure that a deadlock will never occur, and also does not provide a mechanism for deadlock detection and recovery, then the system may reach a deadlock state yet have no way of recognizing what has happened. In this case, the undetected deadlock will result in the deterioration of the system performance, because resources are being held by processes that cannot run, and because more and more processes, as they make requests for resources, enter a deadlock state. Eventually, the system will stop functioning and will need to be restarted manually.

Although this method does not seem to be a viable way of handling the deadlock problem, it is nevertheless used in some operating systems. In many systems, deadlocks occur infrequently (say, once per year); thus, it is cheaper to use this method than to undertake the costly deadlock prevention, deadlock avoidance, or deadlock detection and recovery methods that must be used constantly. Also, there are circumstances in which the system is in a frozen state without it being in a deadlock state: Consider a real-time process that is running at the highest priority (or any process that is running on a nonpreemptive scheduler) and never returning control to the operating system. Thus, systems must have manual recovery methods for nondeadlock conditions, and may simply use those same techniques for deadlock recovery.

As noted earlier, the JVM does nothing to manage deadlocks, it is up to the application developer to write programs that are deadlock-free. In this section we will look at an example illustrating how deadlock is possible using selected methods of the core Java API and how the programmer can develop programs that appropriately handle deadlock.

In Chapter 5, we introduced Java threads and the API that allows users to create and manipulate threads. The suspend() and resume() methods were deprecated in Java 2 because they could lead to deadlock. The suspend() method suspends execution of the thread currently running. The resume() method resumes execution of a suspended thread. Once a thread has been suspended, the only way it can continue is if another thread resumes it. Furthermore, a suspended thread continues to hold all locks while it is blocked. Deadlock is possible if a suspended thread holds a lock on an object and the thread that may resume it requires ownership of this lock prior to resuming the suspended thread.

The resume() method cannot lead to a deadlock state, but because it is used in association with suspend(), it also has been deprecated. stop() has been deprecated as well, but not because it can lead to deadlock. Unlike when a thread has been suspended, when a thread has been stopped, it releases all the locks that it owns. However, locks are generally used in the following scenario: (1) acquire the lock, (2) access a shared data structure, and (3) release the lock. If a thread is in the middle of step 2 when it is stopped, it will release the lock, but it may leave the shared data structure in an inconsistent state. For this reason, stop() has been deprecated.

Chapter 5 provided a multithreaded applet that displayed the time of day. This program was written using the deprecated methods suspend(), resume(), and stop(). When this applet started, the applet created a second thread that output the time of day. We will call this second thread the *clock thread* for the purposes of this discussion. Rather than having the clock thread running if the applet was not being displayed in the browser's window, the stop() method for the applet would suspend the clock thread and resume it in the applet's start() method. (Recall that the stop() method of an applet is called when the browser leaves the page the applet is on. The start() method of an applet is called when the applet is first created or the browser returns to the applet's web page.)

This time of day applet can be rewritten so that it is Java 2 compliant, and thus doesn't use the suspend() and resume() methods. Rather it will use a boolean variable that indicates whether the clock thread can run or not. This variable will be set to true in the start() method of the applet indicating that the clock thread can run. The stop() method of the applet will set it to false. The clock thread will check the value of this boolean variable in its run()

method and will only proceed if it is true. Because the thread for the applet and the clock thread will be sharing this variable, access to it will be controlled using a synchronized block. This program is shown in Figure 8.6.

If the clock thread sees the boolean value is false, it suspends itself by calling the wait() method for the object mutex. When the applet wishes to resume the clock thread, it sets the boolean variable to true and calls notify() for the mutex object. This call to notify() awakens the clock thread where it checks the value of the boolean variable and, seeing that it is now true, proceeds in its run() method displaying the date and time.

Removing the deprecated stop() method will be accomplished using a similar tactic. The clock thread first gets a reference to itself by calling Thread.currentThread() at the beginning of its run() method. The while loop of the run() method will be true as long as the value of clockThread is the same as the reference to itself. When the destroy() method for the applet is called (thereby indicating that the applet is to be terminated), it sets clockThread = null. The clock thread stops execution by exiting the while loop and returning from run().

8.4 ■ Deadlock Prevention

As we noted in Section 8.2.1, for a deadlock to occur, each of the four necessary conditions must hold. By ensuring that at least one of these conditions cannot hold, we can *prevent* the occurrence of a deadlock. Let us elaborate this approach by examining each of the four necessary conditions separately.

8.4.1 Mutual Exclusion

The mutual-exclusion condition must hold for nonsharable resources. For example, a printer or synchronized method cannot be simultaneously shared by several processes. Sharable resources, on the other hand, do not require mutually exclusive access, and thus cannot be involved in a deadlock. Read-only files and non-synchronized methods are good examples of a sharable resource. If several processes attempt to open a read-only file at the same time, they can be granted simultaneous access to the file. A process never needs to wait for a sharable resource. In general, however, it is not possible to prevent deadlocks by denying the mutual-exclusion condition: Some resources are intrinsically nonsharable.

8.4.2 Hold-and-Wait

To ensure that the hold-and-wait condition never occurs in the system, we must guarantee that, whenever a process requests a resource, it does not hold any other resources. One protocol that can be used requires each process to request

```java
import java.applet.*;
import java.awt.*;

public class ClockApplet extends Applet implements Runnable
{
    public void run() {
        Thread me = Thread.currentThread();

        while (clockThread == me) {
            try {
                Thread.sleep(1000);
                repaint();
                synchronized (mutex) {
                    while (ok == false)
                        mutex.wait();
                }
            }
            catch (InterruptedException e) { }
        }
    }

    public void start() {
        // Figure 8.7
    }

    public void stop() {
        // Figure 8.7
    }

    public void destroy() {
        clockThread = null;
    }

    public void paint(Graphics g) {
        g.drawString( new java.util.Date().toString(), 10, 30);
    }

    private volatile Thread clockThread;
    private boolean ok = false;
    private Object mutex = new Object();
}
```

Figure 8.6   Applet that displays the date and time of day.

```
// this method is called when the applet is
// started or we return to the applet
public void start() {
    if (clockThread == null) {
        ok = true;
        clockThread = new Thread(this);
        clockThread.start();
    }
    else {
        synchronized(mutex) {
            ok = true;
            mutex.notify();
        }
    }
}

// this method is called when we
// leave the page the applet is on
public void stop() {
    if (clockThread != null) {
        synchronized(mutex) {
            ok = false;
        }
        clockThread = null;
    }
}
```

Figure 8.7   start() and stop() methods for the applet.

and be allocated all its resources before it begins execution. We can implement this provision by requiring that system calls requesting resources for a process precede all other system calls.

An alternative protocol allows a process to request resources only when the process has none. A process may request some resources and use them. Before it can request any additional resources, however, it must release all the resources that it is currently allocated.

To illustrate the difference between these two protocols, we consider a process that copies data from a tape drive to a disk file, sorts the disk file, and then prints the results to a printer. If all resources must be requested at the beginning of the process, then the process must initially request the tape drive, disk file, and the printer. It will hold the printer for its entire execution, even though it needs the printer only at the end.

The second method allows the process to request initially only the tape drive and disk file. It copies from the tape drive to the disk, then releases both the tape drive and the disk file. The process must then again request the disk file and the printer. After copying the disk file to the printer, it releases these two resources and terminates.

There are two main disadvantages to these protocols. First, *resource utilization* may be low, because many of the resources may be allocated but unused for a long period. In the example given, for instance, we can release the tape drive and disk file, and then again request the disk file and printer, only if we can be sure that our data will remain on the disk file. If we cannot be assured that they will, then we must request all resources at the beginning for both protocols.

Second, *starvation* is possible. A process that needs several popular resources may have to wait indefinitely, because at least one of the resources that it needs is always allocated to some other process.

This solution also is impractical in Java, because a process requests resources (locks) by entering either `synchronized` methods or blocks. Because lock resources are requested in this manner, it would be difficult to write an application that follows either of the protocols that we have given.

8.4.3 No Preemption

The third necessary condition is that there be no preemption of resources that have already been allocated. To ensure that this condition does not hold, we can use the following protocol. If a process that is holding some resources requests another resource that cannot be immediately allocated to it (that is, the process must wait), then all resources currently being held are preempted. That is, these resources are implicitly released. The preempted resources are added to the list of resources for which the process is waiting. The process will be restarted only when it can regain its old resources, as well as the new ones that it is requesting.

Alternatively, if a process requests some resources, we first check whether they are available. If they are, we allocate them. If they are not available, we check whether they are allocated to some other process that is waiting for additional resources. If so, we preempt the desired resources from the waiting process and allocate them to the requesting process. If the resources are not either available or held by a waiting process, the requesting process must wait. While it is waiting, some of its resources may be preempted, but only if another process requests them. A process can be restarted only when it is allocated the new resources that it is requesting and recovers any resources that were preempted while it was waiting.

This protocol is often applied to resources whose state can be easily saved and restored later, such as CPU registers and memory space. It cannot generally be applied to resources such as printers and tape drives. It also cannot be applied to objects, because the preempted process might leave the object in an undetermined state.

8.4.4 Circular Wait

One way to ensure that the circular-wait condition never holds is to impose a total ordering of all resource types, and to require that each process requests resources in an increasing order of enumeration.

Let $R = \{R_1, R_2, \cdots, R_m\}$ be the set of resource types. We assign to each resource type a unique integer number, which allows us to compare two resources and to determine whether one precedes another in our ordering. Formally, we define a one-to-one function $F: R \rightarrow N$, where N is the set of natural numbers. For example, if the set of resource types R includes tape drives, disk drives, and printers, then the function F might be defined as follows:

F(tape drive) = 1,
F(disk drive) = 5,
F(Printer) = 12.

We can now consider the following protocol to prevent deadlocks: Each process can request resources only in an increasing order of enumeration. That is, a process can initially request any number of instances of a resource type, say R_i. After that, the process can request instances of resource type R_j if and only if $F(R_j) > F(R_i)$. If several instances of the same resource type are needed, a *single* request for all of them must be issued. For example, using the function defined previously, a process that wants to use the tape drive and printer at the same time must first request the tape drive and then request the printer.

Alternatively, we can require that, whenever a process requests an instance of resource type R_j, it has released any resources R_i such that $F(R_i) \geq F(R_j)$.

We could accomplish this scheme in a Java application by developing an ordering among all objects in the system. All lock requests for objects must be made in increasing order. For example, if the lock ordering in the Java program shown in Figure 8.4 was

F(mutexX) = 1,
F(mutexY) = 5.

then `class B` could not request the locks out of order. Keep in mind that developing an ordering, or hierarchy, in itself does not prevent deadlock. It is up to the application developers to write programs that follow the ordering. Also note that the function F should be defined according to the normal order of usage of the resources in a system. For example, because the tape drive is usually needed before the printer, it would be reasonable to define F(tape drive) $< F$(printer).

8.5 ■ Deadlock Avoidance

Deadlock-prevention algorithms prevent deadlocks by restraining how requests can be made. The restraints ensure that at least one of the necessary conditions for deadlock cannot occur, and, hence, that deadlocks cannot hold. Possible side effects of preventing deadlocks by this method are low device utilization, reduced system throughput, and potential process starvation.

An alternative method for avoiding deadlocks is to require that a user (process) supply additional information about how resources are to be requested. For example, in a system with one tape drive and one printer, we might be told that process P will request first the tape drive, and later the printer, before releasing both resources. Process Q, on the other hand, will request first the printer, and then the tape drive. With this knowledge of the complete sequence of requests and releases for each process, we can decide for each request whether or not the process should wait. Each request requires that the system consider the resources currently available, the resources currently allocated to each process, and the future requests and releases of each process, to decide whether the current request can be satisfied or must wait to avoid a possible future deadlock.

The various algorithms differ in the amount and type of information required. The simplest and most useful model requires that each process declare the *maximum number* of resources of each type that it may need. Given a priori information about the maximum number of resources of each type that may be requested for each process, we can construct an algorithm that ensures that the system will never enter a deadlock state. This algorithm defines the *deadlock-avoidance* approach. A deadlock-avoidance algorithm dynamically examines the resource-allocation state to ensure that there can never be a circular-wait condition. The resource-allocation **state** is defined by the number of available and allocated resources, and the maximum demands of the processes.

In this text, we present a deadlock-avoidance algorithm for an environment where there is only one instance of each resource type. The Bibliographic Notes provide information about the more general case, in which the system has several instances of a resource type.

If we have a resource-allocation system with only one instance of each resource type, we can use a variant of the resource-allocation graph defined in Section 8.2.2 for deadlock avoidance.

In addition to the request and assignment edges, we introduce a new type of edge, called a **claim edge**. A claim edge $P_i \rightarrow R_j$ indicates that process P_i may request resource R_j at some time in the future. This edge resembles a request edge in direction, but is represented by a dashed line. When process P_i requests resource R_j, the claim edge $P_i \rightarrow R_j$ is converted to a request edge. Similarly, when a resource R_j is released by P_i, the assignment edge $R_j \rightarrow P_i$ is reconverted to a claim edge $P_i \rightarrow R_j$. We note that the resources must be claimed a priori in the system. That is, before process P_i starts executing, all its claim edges must already appear in the resource-allocation graph. We can relax this condition by allowing a claim edge $P_i \rightarrow R_j$ to be added to the graph only if all the edges associated with process P_i are claim edges.

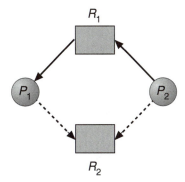

Figure 8.8 Resource-allocation graph for deadlock avoidance.

Suppose that process P_i requests resource R_j. The request can be granted only if converting the request edge $P_i \rightarrow R_j$ to an assignment edge $R_j \rightarrow P_i$ does not result in the formation of a cycle in the resource-allocation graph. Note that we check for safety by using a cycle-detection algorithm. An algorithm for detecting a cycle in this graph requires an order of n^2 operations, where n is the number of processes in the system.

If no cycle exists, then the allocation of the resource will leave the system in a safe state. If a cycle is found, then the allocation will put the system in an unsafe state. Therefore, process P_i will have to wait for its requests to be satisfied.

To illustrate this algorithm, we consider the resource-allocation graph of Figure 8.8. Suppose that P_2 requests R_2. Although R_2 is currently free, we cannot allocate it to P_2, since this action will create a cycle in the graph (Figure 8.9). A cycle indicates that the system is in an unsafe state. If P_1 requests R_2, and P_2 requests R_1, then a deadlock will occur.

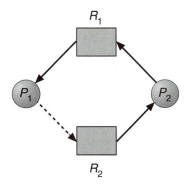

Figure 8.9 An unsafe state in a resource-allocation graph.

8.6 ■ Deadlock Detection

If a system does not employ either a deadlock-prevention or a deadlock-avoidance algorithm, then a deadlock situation may occur. In this environment, the system must provide one of these options:

- An algorithm that examines the state of the system to determine whether a deadlock has occurred

- An algorithm to recover from the deadlock

In the following discussion, we discuss these two requirements as they pertain to systems with only a single instance of each resource type. The Bibliographic Notes provide information about the more general case where the system has several instances of a resource type. At this point, however, let us note that a detection and recovery scheme requires overhead that includes not only the run-time costs of maintaining the necessary information and executing the detection algorithm, but also the potential losses inherent in recovering from a deadlock.

If all resources have only a single instance, then we can define a deadlock-detection algorithm that uses a variant of the resource-allocation graph, called a **wait-for graph**. We obtain this graph from the resource-allocation graph by removing the nodes of type resource and collapsing the appropriate edges.

More precisely, an edge from P_i to P_j in a wait-for graph implies that process P_i is waiting for process P_j to release a resource that P_i needs. An edge $P_i \rightarrow P_j$ exists in a wait-for graph if and only if the corresponding resource-allocation graph contains two edges $P_i \rightarrow R_q$ and $R_q \rightarrow P_j$ for some resource R_q. For example, in Figure 8.10, we present a resource-allocation graph and the corresponding wait-for graph.

As before, a deadlock exists in the system if and only if the wait-for graph contains a cycle. To detect deadlocks, the system needs to *maintain* the wait-for graph and periodically to *invoke an algorithm* that searches for a cycle in the graph.

An algorithm to detect a cycle in a graph requires an order of $O(n^2)$ operations, where n is the number of vertices in the graph.

We shift now our attention to the question of when should the detection algorithm be invoked? The answer depends on two factors:

1. How *often* is a deadlock likely to occur?

2. How *many* processes will be affected by deadlock when it happens?

If deadlocks occur frequently, then the detection algorithm should be invoked frequently. Resources allocated to deadlocked processes will be idle until the deadlock can be broken. In addition, the number of processes involved in the deadlock cycle may grow.

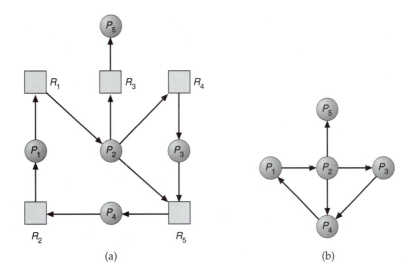

Figure 8.10   (a) Resource-allocation graph. (b) Corresponding wait-for graph.

Deadlocks can come into being only when some process makes a request that cannot be granted immediately. It is possible that this request is the final request that completes a chain of waiting processes. In the extreme, we could invoke the deadlock-detection algorithm every time a request for allocation cannot be granted immediately. In this case, we can identify not only the set of processes that is deadlocked, but also the specific process that "caused" the deadlock. (In reality, each of the deadlocked processes is a link in the cycle in the resource graph, so all of them, jointly, caused the deadlock.) If there are many different resource types, one request may cause many cycles in the resource graph, each cycle completed by the most recent request, and caused by the one identifiable process.

Of course, invoking the deadlock-detection algorithm for every request may incur a considerable overhead in computation time. A less expensive alternative is simply to invoke the algorithm at less frequent intervals—for example, once per hour, or whenever CPU utilization drops below 40 percent. (A deadlock eventually cripples system throughput and will cause CPU utilization to drop.) If the detection algorithm is invoked at arbitrary points in time, there may be many cycles in the resource graph. We would generally not be able to tell which of the many deadlocked processes caused the deadlock.

8.7 ■ Recovery from Deadlock

When a detection algorithm determines that a deadlock exists, several alternatives exist. One possibility is to inform the operator that a deadlock has occurred, and to let the operator deal with the deadlock manually. The other possibility is to let the system *recover* from the deadlock automatically. There are two options for breaking a deadlock. One solution is simply to abort one or more processes to break the circular wait. The second option is to preempt some resources from one or more of the deadlocked processes.

8.7.1 Process Termination

To eliminate deadlocks by aborting a process, we use one of two methods. In both methods, the system reclaims all resources allocated to the terminated processes.

- *Abort all deadlocked processes:* This method clearly will break the deadlock cycle, but at a great expense, since these processes may have computed for a long time, and the results of these partial computations must be discarded, and probably must be recomputed later.

- *Abort one process at a time until the deadlock cycle is eliminated:* This method incurs considerable overhead, since, after each process is aborted, a deadlock-detection algorithm must be invoked to determine whether any processes are still deadlocked.

Notice that aborting a process may not be easy. If the process was in the midst of updating a file, terminating it in the middle will leave that file in an incorrect state. Terminating a Java thread causes the thread to release any locks it was holding. This may result in leaving an object(s) in an arbitrary state.

If the partial termination method is used, then, given a set of deadlocked processes, we must determine which process (or processes) should be terminated in an attempt to break the deadlock. This determination is a policy decision, similar to CPU scheduling problems. The question is basically an economic one; we should abort those processes the termination of which will incur the minimum cost. Unfortunately, the term *minimum cost* is not a precise one. Many factors may determine which process is chosen, including:

1. What the priority of the process is

2. How long the process has computed, and how much longer the process will compute before completing its designated task

3. How many and what type of resources the process has used (for example, whether the resources are simple to preempt)

4. How many more resources the process needs in order to complete

5. How many processes will need to be terminated

6. Whether the process is interactive or batch

8.7.2 Resource Preemption

To eliminate deadlocks using resource preemption, we successively preempt some resources from processes and give these resources to other processes until the deadlock cycle is broken.

If preemption is required to deal with deadlocks, then three matters need to be addressed:

1. *Selection of a victim:* Which resources and which processes are to be preempted? As in process termination, we must determine the order of preemption to minimize cost. Cost factors may include such parameters as the number of resources a deadlock process is holding, and the amount of time a deadlocked process has thus far consumed during its execution.

2. *Rollback:* If we preempt a resource from a process, what should be done with that process? Clearly, it cannot continue with its normal execution; it is missing some needed resource. We must roll back the process to some safe state, and restart it from that state. Since, in general, it is difficult to determine what a safe state is, the simplest solution is a total rollback: Abort the process and then restart it. However, it is more effective to roll back the process only as far as necessary to break the deadlock. On the other hand, this method requires the system to keep more information about the state of all the running processes.

3. *Starvation:* How do we ensure that starvation will not occur? That is, how can we guarantee that resources will not always be preempted from the same process? In a system where victim selection is based primarily on cost factors, it may happen that the same process is always picked as a victim. As a result, this process never completes its designated task, a starvation situation that needs to be dealt with in any practical system. Clearly, we must ensure that a process can be picked as a victim only a (small) finite number of times. The most common solution is to include the number of rollbacks in the cost factor.

8.8 ■ Summary

A deadlock state occurs when two or more processes are waiting indefinitely for an event that can be caused only by one of the waiting processes. Principally, there are three methods for dealing with deadlocks:

1. Use some protocol to ensure that the system will never enter a deadlock state.

2. Allow the system to enter deadlock state and then recover.

3. Ignore the problem, and pretend that deadlocks never occur in the system.

The third solution is the one used by most operating systems, including UNIX and the JVM. A deadlock situation may occur if and only if four necessary conditions hold simultaneously in the system: mutual exclusion, hold-and-wait, no preemption, and circular wait. To prevent deadlocks, we ensure that at least one of the necessary conditions never holds.

Another method for avoiding deadlocks that is less stringent than the prevention algorithms is to have a priori information on how each process will be utilizing the resources. Using this information, we can define a deadlock-avoidance algorithm.

If a system does not employ a protocol to ensure that deadlocks will never occur, then a detection and recovery scheme must be employed. A deadlock-detection algorithm must be invoked to determine whether a deadlock has occurred. If a deadlock is detected, the system must recover either by terminating some of the deadlocked processes, or by preempting resources from some of the deadlocked processes.

In a system that selects victims for rollback primarily on the basis of cost factors, starvation may occur. As a result, the selected process never completes its designated task.

Finally, researchers have argued that none of these basic approaches alone are appropriate for the entire spectrum of resource-allocation problems in operating systems. The basic approaches can be combined, allowing the separate selection of an optimal one for each class of resources in a system.

■ Exercises

8.1 List three examples of deadlocks that are not related to a computer-system environment.

8.2 Is it possible to have a deadlock involving only one single process? Explain your answer.

8.3 Consider the traffic deadlock depicted in Figure 8.11.

    a. Show that the four necessary conditions for deadlock indeed hold in this example.

    b. State a simple rule that will avoid deadlocks in this system.

8.4 Suppose that a system is in an unsafe state. Show that it is possible for the processes to complete their execution without entering a deadlock state.

8.5 A possible solution for preventing deadlocks is to have a single, higher-order resource that must be requested before any other resource. For example, if multiple threads attempt to access the locks for five Java objects $A \cdots E$, deadlock is possible. We can prevent the deadlock by adding a sixth object F. Whenever a thread wants to acquire the lock for

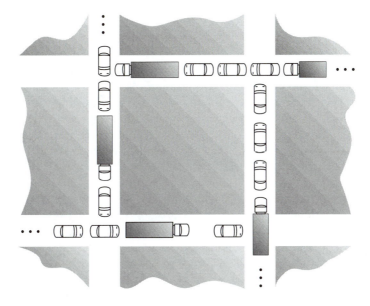

Figure 8.11   Traffic deadlock for Exercise 8.3.

any object $A \cdots E$, it must first acquire the lock for object F. This solution is known as **containment**: The locks for objects $A \cdots E$ are contained within the lock for object F. Compare this scheme with the circular-wait scheme of Section 8.4.4.

8.6 Write a Java program that illustrates deadlock by having `synchronized` methods calling other `synchronized` methods.

8.7 Write a Java program that illustrates deadlock by having separate threads attempting to perform operations on different semaphores.

8.8 Consider a system consisting of four resources of the same type that are shared by three processes, each of which needs at most two resources. Show that the system is deadlock free.

8.9 Consider a system consisting of m resources of the same type, being shared by n processes. Resources can be requested and released by processes only one at a time. Show that the system is deadlock free if the following two conditions hold:

    a. The maximum need of each process is between 1 and m resources

    b. The sum of all maximum needs is less than $m + n$

8.10 Can a system detect that some of its processes are starving? If you answer "yes," explain how it can. If you answer "no," explain how the system can deal with the starvation problem.

8.11 Consider the following resource-allocation policy. Requests and releases for resources are allowed at any time. If a request for resources cannot be satisfied because the resources are not available, then we check any processes that are blocked, waiting for resources. If they have the desired resources, then these resources are taken away from them and are given to the requesting process. The vector of resources for which the process is waiting is increased to include the resources that were taken away.

For example, consider a system with three resource types and the vector *Available* initialized to (4, 2, 2). If P_0 asks for (2, 2, 1), it gets them. If P_1 asks for (1, 0, 1), it gets them. Then, if P_0 asks for (0, 0, 1), it is blocked (resource not available). If P_2 now asks for (2, 0, 0), it gets the available one (1, 0, 0) and one that was allocated to P_0 (since P_0 is blocked). P_0's *Allocation* vector goes down to (1, 2, 1), and its *Need* vector goes up to (1, 0, 1).

  a. Can deadlock occur? If you answer "yes," give an example. If you answer "no," specify which necessary condition cannot occur.

  b. Can indefinite blocking occur? Explain your answer.

8.12 A railroad tunnel with a single set of tracks conects two Vermont villages. The railroad can become deadlocked if both a northbound and southbound train enter the tunnel at the same time (the trains are unable to back up). Write a Java program that prevents deadlock using either semaphores or Java synchronization. Initially, do not be concerned about northbound trains starving southbound trains from using the tunnel (or vice versa) (and do not be concerned about trains failing to stop and crashing into each other). Once your solution prevents deadlock, modify it such that it is starvation free.

Bibliographical Notes

Dijkstra [1965a] was one of the first and most influential contributors in the deadlock area. Holt [1972] was the first person to formalize the notion of deadlocks in terms of a graph-theoretical model similar to the one presented in this chapter. Starvation was covered by Holt [1972]. Hyman [1985] provided the deadlock example from the Kansas legislature.

The various prevention algorithms were suggested by Havender [1968], who has devised the resource-ordering scheme for the IBM OS/360 system.

A deadlock-avoidance algorithm (the banker's algorithm) for a single resource type was developed by Dijkstra [1965a], and was extended to multiple resource types by Habermann [1969]. Exercises 8.8 and 8.9 are from Holt [1971].

A deadlock-detection algorithm for multiple instances of a resource type was presented by Coffman and colleagues [1971].

Bach [1987] describes how many of the algorithms in the traditional UNIX kernel handle deadlock. The description of how Java 2 handles deadlocks is derived from Oaks and Wong [1999].

Part Three

STORAGE MANAGEMENT

The main purpose of a computer system is to execute programs. These programs, with the data that they access, must be (at least partially) in main memory during execution.

To improve both the utilization of its CPU and the speed of its response to its users, the computer must keep several processes in memory. The many different memory-management schemes reflect various approaches to memory management; the effectiveness of a given algorithm depends on the particular situation.

Since main memory is usually too small to accommodate all the data and programs permanently, the computer system must provide secondary storage to back it up. Most modern computer systems use disks as the primary on-line storage medium for information (both programs and data). The file system provides the mechanism for on-line storage of and access to both the disks.

The devices that attach to a computer vary in multiple dimensions. Devices transfer a character or a block of characters at a time. They can be accessed only sequentially or randomly. They transfer data synchronously or asynchronously. They are dedicated or shared. They can be read only or both read and write. They vary greatly in speed. In many ways, they are also the slowest major components of the computer. Because they vary so widely, the operating system must provide a wide range of functionality to allow applications to control all aspects of the devices.

Chapter 9

MEMORY MANAGEMENT

In Chapter 6, we showed how the CPU can be shared by a set of processes. As a result of CPU scheduling, we can improve both the utilization of the CPU and the speed of the computer's response to its users. To realize this increase in performance, however, we must keep several processes in memory; we must *share* memory.

In this chapter, we discuss various ways to manage memory. The memory-management algorithms vary from a primitive bare-machine approach to paging and segmentation strategies. Each approach has its own advantages and disadvantages. Selection of a memory-management method for a specific system depends on many factors, especially on the *hardware* design of the system. As we shall see, many algorithms require hardware support.

9.1 ■ Background

As we saw in Chapter 1, memory is central to the operation of a modern computer system. Memory consists of a large array of words or bytes, each with its own address. The CPU fetches instructions from memory according to the value of the program counter. These instructions may cause additional loading from and storing to specific memory addresses.

A typical instruction-execution cycle, for example, first fetches an instruction from memory. The instruction is then decoded and may cause operands to be fetched from memory. After the instruction has been executed on the operands, results may be stored back in memory. Notice that the memory unit sees only a stream of memory addresses; it does not know how they are generated (the instruction counter, indexing, indirection, literal addresses, and so on) or what they are for (instructions or data). Accordingly, we can ignore *how* a memory address is generated by a program. We are interested in only the sequence of memory addresses generated by the running program.

9.1.1 Address Binding

Usually, a program resides on a disk as a binary executable file. The program must be brought into memory and placed within a process for it to be executed. Depending on the memory management in use, the process may be moved between disk and memory during its execution. The collection of processes on the disk that is waiting to be brought into memory for execution forms the **input queue**.

The normal procedure is to select one of the processes in the input queue and to load that process into memory. As the process is executed, it accesses instructions and data from memory. Eventually, the process terminates, and its memory space is declared available.

Most systems allow a user process to reside in any part of the physical memory. Thus, although the address space of the computer starts at 00000, the first address of the user process does not need to be 00000. This arrangement affects the addresses that the user program can use. In most cases, a user program will go through several steps (some of which may be optional) before being executed (Figure 9.1). Addresses may be represented in different ways during these steps. Addresses in the source program are generally symbolic (such as count). A compiler will typically **bind** these symbolic addresses to relocatable addresses (such as "14 bytes from the beginning of this module"). The linkage editor or loader will in turn bind these relocatable addresses to absolute addresses (such as 74014). Each binding is a mapping from one address space to another.

Classically, the binding of instructions and data to memory addresses can be done at any step along the way:

- *Compile time:* If it is known at compile time where the process will reside in memory, then **absolute** code can be generated. For example, if it is known a priori that a user process resides starting at location R, then the generated compiler code will start at that location and extend up from there. If, at some later time, the starting location changes, then it will be necessary to recompile this code. The MS-DOS .COM-format programs are absolute code bound at compile time.

- *Load time:* If it is not known at compile time where the process will reside in memory, then the compiler must generate **relocatable** code. In this case, final binding is delayed until load time. If the starting address changes, we need only to reload the user code to incorporate this changed value.

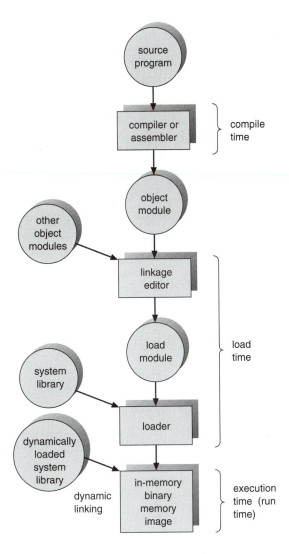

Figure 9.1   Multistep processing of a user program.

- *Execution time:* If the process can be moved during its execution from one memory segment to another, then binding must be delayed until run time. Special hardware must be available for this scheme to work, as will be discussed in Section 9.1.2. Most general-purpose operating systems use this method.

A major portion of this chapter is devoted to showing how these various bindings can be implemented effectively in a computer system, and discussing appropriate hardware support.

9.1.2 Logical Versus Physical Address Space

An address generated by the CPU is commonly referred to as a **logical address,** whereas an address seen by the memory unit—that is, the one loaded into the **memory address register** of the memory—is commonly referred to as a **physical address**.

The compile-time and load-time address-binding methods result in an environment where the logical and physical addresses are the same. However, the execution-time address-binding scheme results in an environment where the logical and physical addresses differ. In this case, we usually refer to the logical address as a **virtual address**. We use *logical address* and *virtual address* interchangeably in this text. The set of all logical addresses generated by a program is a **logical address space;** the set of all physical addresses corresponding to these logical addresses is a **physical address space**. Thus, in the execution-time address-binding scheme, the logical and physical address spaces differ.

The run-time mapping from virtual to physical addresses is done by the **memory-management unit** (**MMU**), which is a hardware device. There are many different methods for accomplishing such a mapping, as we discuss in Sections 9.3, 9.4, 9.5, and 9.6. For the time being, we illustrate this mapping with a simple MMU scheme, which is a generalization of the base-register scheme described in Section 2.5.3.

As illustrated in Figure 9.2, this method requires hardware support slightly different from the hardware configuration discussed in Section 2.4. The base register is now called a **relocation register**. The value in the relocation register

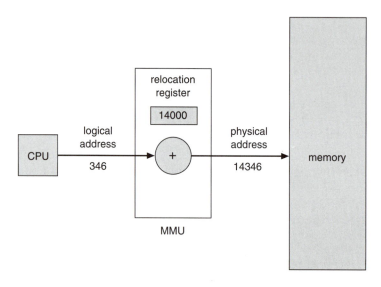

Figure 9.2   Dynamic relocation using a relocation register.

is *added* to every address generated by a user process at the time it is sent to memory. For example, if the base is at 14,000, then an attempt by the user to address location 0 is dynamically relocated to location 14,000; an access to location 346 is mapped to location 14,346. The MS-DOS operating system running on the Intel 80X86 family of processors uses four relocation registers when loading and running processes.

Notice that the user program never sees the *real* physical addresses. The program can create a pointer to location 346, store it in memory, manipulate it, compare it to other addresses—all as the number 346. Only when it is used as a memory address (in an indirect load or store, perhaps) is it relocated relative to the base register. The user program deals with *logical* addresses. The memory-mapping hardware converts logical addresses into physical addresses. This form of execution-time binding was discussed in Section 9.1.1. The final location of a referenced memory address is not determined until the reference is made.

Notice also that we now have two different types of addresses: logical addresses (in the range 0 to *max*) and physical addresses (in the range $R + 0$ to $R + max$ for a base value R). The user generates only logical addresses and thinks that the process runs in locations 0 to *max*. The user program supplies logical addresses; these logical addresses must be mapped to physical addresses before they are used.

The concept of a *logical address space* that is bound to a separate *physical address space* is central to proper memory management.

9.1.3 Dynamic Loading

In our discussion so far, the entire program and data of a process must be in physical memory for the process to execute. The size of a process is limited to the size of physical memory. To obtain better memory-space utilization, we can use **dynamic loading**. With dynamic loading, a routine is not loaded until it is called. All routines are kept on disk in a relocatable load format. The main program is loaded into memory and is executed. When a routine needs to call another routine, the calling routine first checks to see whether the other routine has been loaded. If it has not been, the relocatable linking loader is called to load the desired routine into memory and to update the program's address tables to reflect this change. Then, control is passed to the newly loaded routine.

The advantage of dynamic loading is that an unused routine is never loaded. This method is particularly useful when large amounts of code are needed to handle infrequently occurring cases, such as error routines. In this case, although the total program size may be large, the portion that is actually used (and hence actually loaded) may be much smaller.

Dynamic loading does not require special support from the operating system. It is the responsibility of the users to design their programs to take advantage of such a method. Operating systems may help the programmer, however, by providing library routines to implement dynamic loading.

9.1.4 Dynamic Linking and Shared Libraries

Notice that Figure 9.1 also shows **dynamically linked** libraries. Some operating systems support only **static linking,** in which system language libraries are treated like any other object module and are combined by the loader into the binary program image. The concept of dynamic linking is similar to that of dynamic loading. Rather than loading being postponed until execution time, linking is postponed. This feature is usually used with system libraries, such as language subroutine libraries. Without this facility, all programs on a system need to have a copy of their language library (or at least the routines referenced by the program) included in the executable image. This requirement wastes both disk space and main memory. With dynamic linking, a **stub** is included in the image for each library-routine reference. This stub is a small piece of code that indicates how to locate the appropriate memory-resident library routine, or how to load the library if the routine is not already present.

When this stub is executed, it checks to see whether the needed routine is already in memory. If the routine is not in memory, the program loads it into memory. Either way, the stub replaces itself with the address of the routine, and executes the routine. Thus, the next time that that code segment is reached, the library routine is executed directly, incurring no cost for dynamic linking. Under this scheme, all processes that use a language library execute only one copy of the library code.

This feature can be extended to library updates (such as bug fixes). A library may be replaced by a new version, and all programs that reference the library will automatically use the new version. Without dynamic linking, all such programs would need to be relinked to gain access to the new library. So that programs will not accidentally execute new, incompatible versions of libraries, version information is included in both the program and the library. More than one version of a library may be loaded into memory, and each program uses its version information to decide which copy of the library to use. Minor changes retain the same version number, whereas major changes increment the version number. Thus, only programs that are compiled with the new library version are affected by the incompatible changes incorporated in it. Other programs linked before the new library was installed will continue using the older library. This system is also known as **shared libraries**.

Unlike dynamic loading, dynamic linking generally requires help from the operating system. If the processes in memory are protected from one another (Section 9.3), then the operating system is the only entity that can check to see whether the needed routine is in another process's memory space, or that can allow multiple processes to access the same memory addresses. We elaborate on this concept when we discuss paging in Section 9.4.5.

9.1.5 Overlays

So that a process can be larger than the amount of memory allocated to it, we can use **overlays**. The idea of overlays is to keep in memory only those instructions and data that are needed at any given time. When other instructions are needed, they are loaded into space that was occupied previously by instructions that are no longer needed.

As an example, consider a two-pass assembler. During pass 1, it constructs a symbol table; then, during pass 2, it generates machine-language code. We may be able to partition such an assembler into pass 1 code, pass 2 code, the symbol table, and common support routines used by both pass 1 and pass 2. Assume that the sizes of these components are as follows (K stands for "kilobyte," which is 1,024 bytes):

Pass 1	70K
Pass 2	80K
Symbol table	20K
Common routines	30K

To load everything at once, we would require 200K of memory. If only 150K is available, we cannot run our process. However, notice that pass 1 and pass 2 do not need to be in memory at the same time. We thus define two overlays: Overlay A is the symbol table, common routines, and pass 1, and overlay B is the symbol table, common routines, and pass 2.

We add an overlay driver (10K) and start with overlay A in memory. When we finish pass 1, we jump to the overlay driver, which reads overlay B into memory, overwriting overlay A, and then transfers control to pass 2. Overlay A needs only 120K, whereas overlay B needs 130K (Figure 9.3). We can now run our assembler in the 150K of memory. It will load somewhat faster because fewer data need to be transferred before execution starts. However, it will run somewhat slower, due to the extra I/O to read the code for overlay B over the code for overlay A.

The code for overlay A and the code for overlay B are kept on disk as absolute memory images, and are read by the overlay driver as needed. Special relocation and linking algorithms are needed to construct the overlays.

As in dynamic loading, overlays do not require any special support from the operating system. They can be implemented completely by the user with simple file structures, reading from the files into memory and then jumping to that memory and executing the newly read instructions. The operating system notices only that there is more I/O than usual.

The programmer, on the other hand, must design and program the overlay structure properly. This task can be a major undertaking, requiring complete knowledge of the structure of the program, its code, and its data structures. Because the program is, by definition, large (small programs do not need to be overlayed), obtaining a sufficient understanding of the program may be

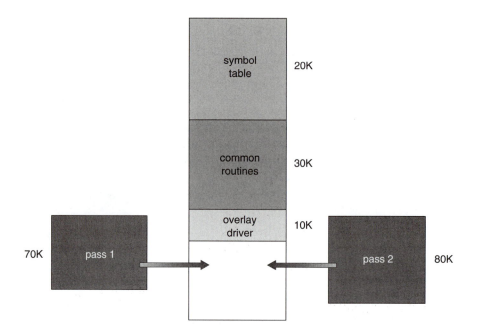

Figure 9.3   Overlays for a two-pass assembler.

difficult. For these reasons, the use of overlays is currently limited to micro-computer and other systems that have limited amounts of physical memory and that lack hardware support for more advanced techniques. Some micro-computer compilers provide to the programmer support of overlays to make the task easier. Automatic techniques to run large programs in limited amounts of physical memory are certainly preferable.

9.2 ▪ Swapping

A process needs to be in memory to be executed. A process, however, can be **swapped** temporarily out of memory to a **backing store,** and then brought back into memory for continued execution. For example, assume a multipro-gramming environment with a round-robin CPU-scheduling algorithm. When a quantum expires, the memory manager will start to swap out the process that just finished, and to swap in another process to the memory space that has been freed (Figure 9.4). In the meantime, the CPU scheduler will allocate a time slice to some other process in memory. When each process finishes its quantum, it will be swapped with another process. Ideally, the memory manager can swap processes fast enough that there are always processes in memory, ready to execute, when the CPU scheduler wants to reschedule the CPU. The quantum

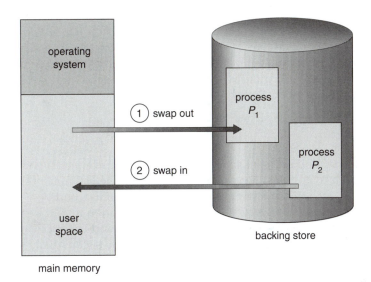

Figure 9.4 Swapping of two processes using a disk as a backing store.

must also be sufficiently large that reasonable amounts of computing are done between swaps.

A variant of this swapping policy is used for priority-based scheduling algorithms. If a higher-priority process arrives and wants service, the memory manager can swap out the lower-priority process so that it can load and execute the higher-priority process. When the higher-priority process finishes, the lower-priority process can be swapped back in and continued. This variant of swapping is sometimes called **roll out, roll in**.

Normally a process that is swapped out will be swapped back into the same memory space that it occupied previously. This restriction is dictated by the method of address binding. If binding is done at assembly or load time, then the process cannot be moved to different locations. If execution-time binding is being used, then it is possible to swap a process into a different memory space, because the physical addresses are computed during execution time.

Swapping requires a **backing store**. The backing store is commonly a fast disk. It must be large enough to accommodate copies of all memory images for all users, and must provide direct access to these memory images. The system maintains a **ready queue** consisting of all processes whose memory images are on the backing store or in memory and are ready to run. Whenever the CPU scheduler decides to execute a process, it calls the dispatcher. The dispatcher checks to see whether the next process in the queue is in memory. If the process is not, and there is no free memory region, the dispatcher swaps out a process currently in memory and swaps in the desired process. It then reloads registers as normal and transfers control to the selected process.

It should be clear that the context-switch time in such a swapping system is fairly high. To get an idea of the context-switch time, let us assume that the user process is of size 1 megabyte and the backing store is a standard hard disk with a transfer rate of 5 megabytes per second. The actual transfer of the 1MB process to or from memory takes

$$1000K/5000K \text{ per second} = 1/5 \text{ second}$$
$$= 200 \text{ milliseconds}$$

Assuming that no head seeks are necessary and an average latency of 8 milliseconds, the swap time takes 208 milliseconds. Since we must both swap out and swap in, the total swap time is then about 416 milliseconds.

For efficient CPU utilization, we want our execution time for each process to be long relative to the swap time. Thus, in a round-robin CPU-scheduling algorithm, for example, the time quantum should be substantially larger than 0.416 seconds.

Notice that the major part of the swap time is transfer time. The total transfer time is directly proportional to the *amount* of memory swapped. If we have a computer system with 128 megabytes of main memory and a resident operating system taking 5MB, the maximum size of the user process is 123MB. However, many user processes may be much smaller than this size—say, 1MB. A 1MB process could be swapped out in 208 milliseconds, compared to the 24.6 seconds for swapping 123MB. Therefore, it would be useful to know exactly how much memory a user process *is* using, not simply how much it *might be* using. Then, we would need to swap only what is actually used, reducing swap time. For this method to be effective, the user must keep the system informed of any changes in memory requirements. Thus, a process with dynamic memory requirements will need to issue system calls (`request memory` and `release memory`) to inform the operating system of its changing memory needs.

There are other constraints on swapping. If we want to swap a process, we must be sure that it is completely idle. Of particular concern is any pending I/O. A process may be waiting for an I/O operation when we want to swap that process to free up its memory. However, if the I/O is asynchronously accessing the user memory for I/O buffers, then the process cannot be swapped. Assume that the I/O operation was queued because the device was busy. Then, if we were to swap out process P_1 and swap in process P_2, the I/O operation might then attempt to use memory that now belongs to process P_2. The two main solutions to this problem are (1) never to swap a process with pending I/O, or (2) to execute I/O operations only into operating-system buffers. Transfers between operating-system and process memory then occur only when the process is swapped in.

The assumption that swapping requires few if any head seeks needs further explanation. We postpone discussing this issue until Chapter 13, where secondary-storage structure is covered. Generally, swap space is allocated as a chunk of disk, separate from the file system, so that its use is as fast as possible.

Currently, standard swapping is used in few systems. It requires too much swapping time and provides too little execution time to be a reasonable memory-management solution. Modified versions of swapping, however, are found on many systems.

A modification of swapping is used in many versions of UNIX. Swapping was normally disabled, but would start if many processes were running and were using a threshold amount of memory. Swapping would again be halted if the load on the system was reduced. Memory management in UNIX is described fully in Section 20.6.

Early PCs lacked sophisticated hardware (or operating systems that take advantage of the hardware) to implement more advanced memory-management methods, but they were used to run multiple, large processes by a modified version of swapping. A prime example is the Microsoft Windows 3.1 operating system, which supports concurrent execution of processes in memory. If a new process is loaded and there is insufficient main memory, an old process is swapped to disk. This operating system, however, does not provide full swapping, because the user, rather than the scheduler, decides when it is time to preempt one process for another. Any swapped-out process remains swapped out (and not executing) until the user selects that process to run. Follow-on Microsoft operating systems, such as Windows NT, take advantage of advanced MMU features now found even on PCs. In Section 9.6, we describe the memory-management hardware found on the Intel 386 family of processors used in many PCs. In that section, we also describe the memory management used on this CPU by another advanced operating system for PCs: IBM OS/2.

9.3 ■ Contiguous Memory Allocation

The main memory must accommodate both the operating system and the various user processes. The memory is usually divided into two partitions: one for the resident operating system, and one for the user processes. It is possible to place the operating system in either low memory or high memory. The major factor affecting this decision is the location of the interrupt vector. Since the interrupt vector is often in low memory, it is more common to place the operating system in low memory. Thus, in this text, we shall discuss only the situation where the operating system resides in low memory. The development of the other situation is similar.

Because it is desirable, in general, that there be several user processes residing in memory at the same time, we need to consider the problem of how to allocate available memory to the various processes that are in the input queue waiting to be brought into memory. Before doing so, we must discuss the issue of memory protection—protecting the operating system from user processes, and protecting user processes from one another. We can provide this

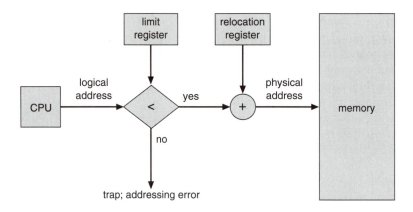

Figure 9.5   Hardware support for relocation and limit registers.

protection by using a relocation register, as discussed in Section 9.1.2, with a limit register, as discussed in Section 2.5.3. The relocation register contains the value of the smallest physical address; the limit register contains the range of logical addresses (for example, relocation = 100,040 and limit = 74,600). With relocation and limit registers, each logical address must be less than the limit register; the MMU maps the logical address *dynamically* by adding the value in the relocation register. This mapped address is sent to memory (Figure 9.5).

When the CPU scheduler selects a process for execution, the dispatcher loads the relocation and limit registers with the correct values as part of the context switch. Because every address generated by the CPU is checked against these registers, we can protect both the operating system and the other users' programs and data from being modified by this running process.

Note that the relocation-register scheme provides an effective way to allow the operating-system size to change dynamically. This flexibility is desirable in many situations. For example, the operating system contains code and buffer space for device drivers. If a device driver (or other operating-system service) is not commonly used, it is undesirable to keep the code and data in memory, as we might be able to use that space for other purposes. Such code is sometimes called **transient** operating-system code; it comes and goes as needed. Thus, using this code changes the size of the operating system during program execution.

One of the simplest methods for memory allocation is to divide memory into a number of fixed-sized **partitions**. Each partition may contain exactly one process. Thus, the degree of multiprogramming is bound by the number of partitions. When a partition is free, a process is selected from the input queue and is loaded into the free partition. When the process terminates, the partition becomes available for another process. This method was originally used by the IBM OS/360 operating system (called MFT); it is no longer in use. The method described next is a generalization of the fixed-partition scheme (called

MVT); it is used primarily in a batch environment. Note that many of the ideas presented here are also applicable to a time-sharing environment where pure segmentation is used for memory management (Section 9.5).

The operating system keeps a table indicating which parts of memory are available and which are occupied. Initially, all memory is available for user processes, and is considered as one large block of available memory, a **hole**. When a process arrives and needs memory, we search for a hole large enough for this process. If we find one, we allocate only as much memory as is needed, keeping the rest available to satisfy future requests.

As processes enter the system, they are put into an input queue. The operating system takes into account the memory requirements of each process and the amount of available memory space in determining which processes are allocated memory. When a process is allocated space, it is loaded into memory and it can then compete for the CPU. When a process terminates, it releases its memory, which the operating system may then fill with another process from the input queue.

At any given time, we have a list of available block sizes and the input queue. The operating system can order the input queue according to a scheduling algorithm. Memory is allocated to processes until, finally, the memory requirements of the next process cannot be satisfied; no available block of memory (hole) is large enough to hold that process. The operating system can then wait until a large enough block is available, or it can skip down the input queue to see whether the smaller memory requirements of some other process can be met.

In general, there is at any time a *set* of holes, of various sizes, scattered throughout memory. When a process arrives and needs memory, we search this set for a hole that is large enough for this process. If the hole is too large, it is split into two: One part is allocated to the arriving process; the other is returned to the set of holes. When a process terminates, it releases its block of memory, which is then placed back in the set of holes. If the new hole is adjacent to other holes, we merge these adjacent holes to form one larger hole. At this point, we may need to check whether there are processes waiting for memory and whether this newly freed and recombined memory could satisfy the demands of any of these waiting processes.

This procedure is a particular instance of the general **dynamic storage-allocation problem**, which is how to satisfy a request of size n from a list of free holes. There are many solutions to this problem. The set of holes is searched to determine which hole is best to allocate. The **first-fit, best-fit,** and **worst-fit** strategies are the most common ones used to select a free hole from the set of available holes.

- *First fit:* Allocate the *first* hole that is big enough. Searching can start either at the beginning of the set of holes or where the previous first-fit search ended. We can stop searching as soon as we find a free hole that is large enough.

- *Best fit:* Allocate the *smallest* hole that is big enough. We must search the entire list, unless the list is kept ordered by size. This strategy produces the smallest leftover hole.

- *Worst fit:* Allocate the *largest* hole. Again, we must search the entire list, unless it is sorted by size. This strategy produces the largest leftover hole, which may be more useful than the smaller leftover hole from a best-fit approach.

Simulations have shown that both first fit and best fit are better than worst fit in terms of decreasing both time and storage utilization. Neither first fit nor best fit is clearly better in terms of storage utilization, but first fit is generally faster.

The algorithms just described suffer from **external fragmentation**. As processes are loaded and removed from memory, the free memory space is broken into little pieces. External fragmentation exists when enough total memory space exists to satisfy a request, but it is not contiguous; storage is fragmented into a large number of small holes.

This fragmentation problem can be severe. In the worst case, we could have a block of free (wasted) memory between every two processes. If all this memory were in one big free block, we might be able to run several more processes. The selection of the first-fit versus best-fit strategies can affect the amount of fragmentation. (First fit is better for some systems, whereas best fit is better for others.) Another factor is which end of a free block is allocated. (Which is the leftover piece—the one on the top, or the one on the bottom?) No matter which algorithms are used, however, external fragmentation will be a problem.

Depending on the total amount of memory storage and the average process size, external fragmentation may be either a minor or a major problem. Statistical analysis of first fit, for instance, reveals that, even with some optimization, given N allocated blocks, another $0.5N$ blocks will be lost due to fragmentation. That is, one-third of memory may be unusable! This property is known as the **50-percent rule**.

There is another problem that arises with the multiple-partition allocation scheme. Consider a hole of 18,464 bytes. Suppose that the next process requests 18,462 bytes. If we allocate exactly the requested block, we are left with a hole of 2 bytes. The overhead to keep track of this hole will be substantially larger than the hole itself. The general approach is to break the physical memory into fixed-sized blocks, and allocate memory in unit of block sizes. With this approach, the allocated memory to a process may be slightly larger than the requested memory. The difference between these two numbers is **internal fragmentation** —memory that is internal to a partition, but is not being used.

One solution to the problem of external fragmentation is **compaction**. The goal is to shuffle the memory contents to place all free memory together in one large block. Compaction is not always possible. If relocation is static and is done at assembly or load time, compaction cannot be done; compaction is possible *only* if relocation is dynamic, and is done at execution time. If addresses are relocated dynamically, relocation requires only moving the program and data, and then changing the base register to reflect the new base address. When compaction is possible, we must determine its cost. The simplest compaction algorithm is simply to move all processes toward one end of memory; all holes move in the other direction, producing one large hole of available memory. This scheme can be expensive.

Another possible solution to the external-fragmentation problem is to permit the logical address space of a process to be noncontiguous, thus allowing a process to be allocated physical memory wherever the latter is available. There are two complementary techniques for achieving this solution: paging (Section 9.4) and segmentation (Section 9.5). These two techniques can also be combined (Section 9.6).

9.4 ■ Paging

Paging is a scheme that permits the physical address space of a process to be noncontiguous. Paging avoids the considerable problem of fitting the varying-sized memory chunks onto the backing store, from which most of the previous memory-management schemes suffered. When some code fragments or data residing in main memory need to be swapped out, space must be found on the backing store. The fragmentation problems discussed in connection with main memory are also prevalent with backing store, except that access is much slower, so compaction is impossible. Because of its advantages over the previous methods, paging in its various forms is commonly used in many operating systems.

9.4.1 Basic Method

Physical memory is broken into fixed-sized blocks called **frames**. Logical memory is also broken into blocks of the same size called **pages**. When a process is to be executed, its pages are loaded into any available memory frames from the backing store. The backing store is divided into fixed-sized blocks that are of the same size as the memory frames.

The hardware support for paging is illustrated in Figure 9.6. Every address generated by the CPU is divided into two parts: a **page number** (*p*) and a **page offset** (*d*). The page number is used as an index into a **page table**. The page table contains the base address of each page in physical memory. This base address is combined with the page offset to define the physical memory address that is sent to the memory unit. The paging model of memory is shown in Figure 9.7.

The page size (like the frame size) is defined by the hardware. The size of a page is typically a power of 2 varying between 512 bytes and 16 megabytes per page, depending on the computer architecture. The selection of a power of

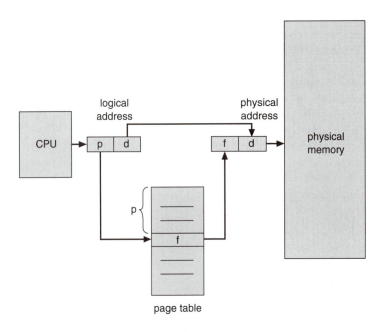

Figure 9.6 Paging hardware.

2 as a page size makes the translation of a logical address into a page number and page offset particularly easy. If the size of logical address space is 2^m, and a page size is 2^n addressing units (bytes or words), then the high-order $m - n$ bits of a logical address designate the page number, and the n low-order bits designate the page offset. Thus, the logical address is as follows:

page number	page offset
p	d
$m - n$	n

where p is an index into the page table and d is the displacement within the page.

As a concrete (although minuscule) example, consider the memory of Figure 9.8. Using a page size of 4 bytes and a physical memory of 32 bytes (8 pages), we show how the user's view of memory can be mapped into physical memory. Logical address 0 is page 0, offset 0. Indexing into the page table, we find that page 0 is in frame 5. Thus, logical address 0 maps to physical address 20 (= (5 × 4) + 0). Logical address 3 (page 0, offset 3) maps to physical address 23 (= (5 × 4) + 3). Logical address 4 is page 1, offset 0; according to the page table, page 1 is mapped to frame 6. Thus, logical address 4 maps to physical address 24 (= (6 × 4) + 0). Logical address 13 maps to physical address 9.

Notice that paging itself is a form of dynamic relocation. Every logical address is bound by the paging hardware to some physical address. The

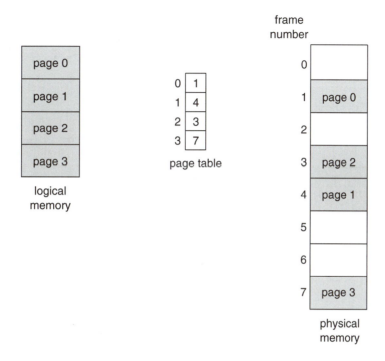

Figure 9.7 Paging model of logical and physical memory.

observant reader will have realized that using paging is similar to using a table of base (relocation) registers, one for each frame of memory.

When we use a paging scheme, we have no external fragmentation: *Any* free frame can be allocated to a process that needs it. However, we may have some internal fragmentation. Notice that frames are allocated as units. If the memory requirements of a process do not happen to fall on page boundaries, the *last* frame allocated may not be completely full. For example, if pages are 2048 bytes, a process of 72,766 bytes would need 35 pages plus 1086 bytes. It would be allocated 36 frames, resulting in an internal fragmentation of 2048 − 1086 = 962 bytes. In the worst case, a process would need n pages plus one byte. It would be allocated $n + 1$ frames, resulting in an internal fragmentation of almost an entire frame.

If process size is independent of page size, we expect internal fragmentation to average one-half page per process. This consideration suggests that small page sizes are desirable. However, there is overhead involved in each page-table entry, and this overhead is reduced as the size of the pages increases. Also, disk I/O is more efficient when the number of data being transferred is larger (Chapter 13). Generally, page sizes have grown over time as processes, data sets, and main memory have become larger. Today, pages typically are between 2 and 8 KB. Some CPUs and kernels even support multiple page sizes.

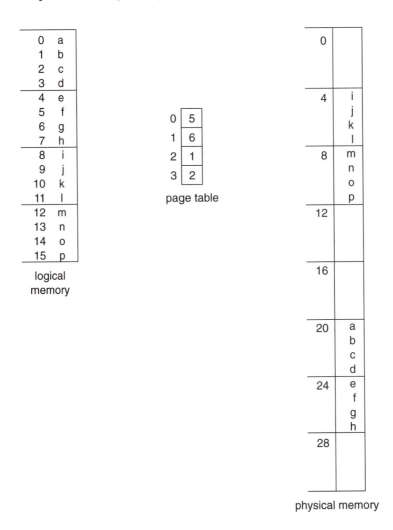

Figure 9.8   Paging example for a 32-byte memory with 4-byte pages.

For instance, Solaris uses 4K and 8K pages, depending on the data stored by the pages. Researchers are now developing variable on-the-fly page-size support.

Each page-table entry is usually 4 bytes long, but that size can vary as well. A 32-bit entry can point to one of 2^{32} physical page frames. If a frame is 4K, then a system with 4-byte entries can address 2^{36} bytes (or 64 GB) of physical memory.

When a process arrives in the system to be executed, its size, expressed in pages, is examined. Each page of the process needs one frame. Thus, if the process requires n pages, there must be at least n frames available in memory. If there are n frames available, they are allocated to this arriving process. The first page of the process is loaded into one of the allocated frames, and the frame number is put in the page table for this process. The next page is loaded into another frame, and its frame number is put into the page table, and so on (Figure 9.9).

An important aspect of paging is the clear separation between the user's view of memory and the actual physical memory. The user program views that memory as one single contiguous space, containing only this one program. In fact, the user program is scattered throughout physical memory, which also holds other programs. The difference between the user's view of memory and the actual physical memory is reconciled by the address-translation hardware. The logical addresses are translated into physical addresses. This mapping is hidden from the user and is controlled by the operating system. Notice that the user process by definition is unable to access memory it does not own. It has no way of addressing memory outside of its page table, and the table includes only those pages that the process owns.

Since the operating system is managing physical memory, it must be aware of the allocation details of physical memory: which frames are allocated, which frames are available, how many total frames there are, and so on. This information is generally kept in a data structure called a **frame table**. The frame table has one entry for each physical page frame, indicating whether the latter is free or allocated and, if it is allocated, to which page of which process or processes.

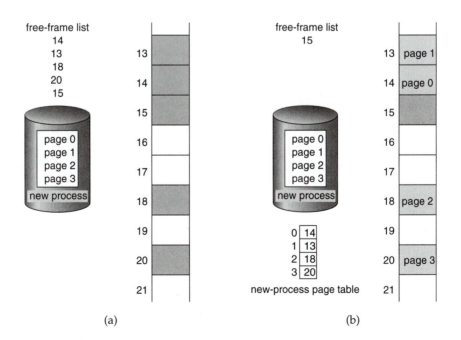

(a)   (b)

Figure 9.9 Free frames. (a) Before allocation. (b) After allocation.

In addition, the operating system must be aware that user processes operate in user space, and all logical addresses must be mapped to produce physical addresses. If a user makes a system call (to do I/O, for example) and provides an address as a parameter (a buffer, for instance), that address must be mapped to produce the correct physical address. The operating system maintains a copy of the page table for each process, just as it maintains a copy of the instruction counter and register contents. This copy is used to translate logical addresses to physical addresses whenever the operating system must map a logical address to a physical address manually. It is also used by the CPU dispatcher to define the hardware page table when a process is to be allocated the CPU. Paging therefore increases the context-switch time.

9.4.2 Structure of the Page Table

Each operating system has its own methods for storing page tables. Most allocate a page table for each process. A pointer to the page table is stored with the other register values (like the instruction counter) in the process control block. When the dispatcher is told to start a process, it must reload the user registers and define the correct hardware page-table values from the stored user page table.

9.4.2.1 Hardware Support

The hardware implementation of the page table can be done in a number of different ways. In the simplest case, the page table is implemented as a set of dedicated **registers**. These registers should be built with very high-speed logic to make the paging address translation efficient. Every access to memory must go through the paging map, so efficiency is a major consideration. The CPU dispatcher reloads these registers, just as it reloads the other registers. Instructions to load or modify the page-table registers are, of course, privileged, so that only the operating system can change the memory map. The DEC PDP-11 is an example of such an architecture. The address consists of 16 bits, and the page size is 8K. The page table thus consists of eight entries that are kept in fast registers.

The use of registers for the page table is satisfactory if the page table is reasonably small (for example, 256 entries). Most contemporary computers, however, allow the page table to be very large (for example, 1 million entries). For these machines, the use of fast registers to implement the page table is not feasible. Rather, the page table is kept in main memory, and a **page-table base register** (**PTBR**) points to the page table. Changing page tables requires changing only this one register, substantially reducing context-switch time.

The problem with this approach is the time required to access a user memory location. If we want to access location i, we must first index into the page table, using the value in the PTBR offset by the page number for i. This task requires a memory access. It provides us with the frame number, which is combined with the page offset to produce the actual address. We can then access the desired place in memory. With this scheme, *two* memory accesses are needed to access a byte (one for the page-table entry, one for the byte). Thus, memory access is slowed by a factor of 2. This delay would be intolerable under most circumstances. We might as well resort to swapping!

The standard solution to this problem is to use a special, small, fast-lookup hardware cache, variously called **associative registers** or **translation look-aside buffers** (TLBs). A set of associative registers is built of especially high-speed memory. Each register consists of two parts: a key and a value. When the associative registers are presented with an item, it is compared with all keys simultaneously. If the item is found, the corresponding value field is output. The search is fast; the hardware, however, is expensive. Typically, the number of entries in a TLB is between 8 and 2048.

Associative registers are used with page tables in the following way. The associative registers contain only a few of the page-table entries. When a logical address is generated by the CPU, its page number is presented to a set of associative registers that contain page numbers and their corresponding frame numbers. If the page number is found in the associative registers, its frame number is immediately available and is used to access memory. The whole task may take less than 10 percent longer than it would were an unmapped memory reference used.

If the page number is not in the associative registers, a memory reference to the page table must be made. When the frame number is obtained, we can use it to access memory (Figure 9.10). In addition, we add the page number and frame number to the associative registers, so that they will be found quickly on the next reference. If the TLB is already full of entries, the operating system must select one for replacement. Unfortunately, every time a new page table is selected (for instance, each context switch), the TLB must be **flushed** (erased) to ensure that the next executing process does not use the wrong translation information. Otherwise, there could be old entries in the TLB that contain valid virtual addresses but have incorrect or invalid physical addresses left over from the previous process.

The percentage of times that a page number is found in the associative registers is called the **hit ratio**. An 80-percent hit ratio means that we find the desired page number in the associative registers 80 percent of the time. If it takes 20 nanoseconds to search the associative registers, and 100 nanoseconds to access memory, then a mapped memory access takes 120 nanoseconds when the page number is in the associative registers. If we fail to find the page number in the associative registers (20 nanoseconds), then we must first access memory for the page table and frame number (100 nanoseconds), and then access the desired byte in memory (100 nanoseconds), for a total of 220 nanoseconds. To find the **effective memory-access time,** we must weigh each case by its probability:

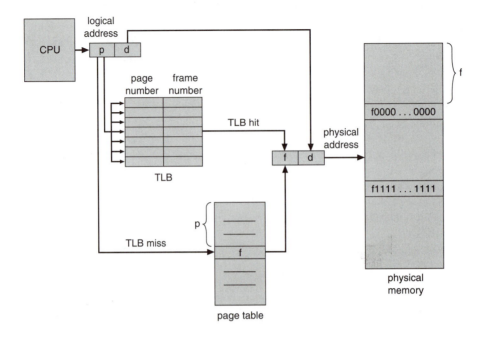

Figure 9.10   Paging hardware with TLB.

$$\text{effective access time} = 0.80 \times 120 + 0.20 \times 220$$
$$= 140 \text{ nanoseconds.}$$

In this example, we suffer a 40-percent slowdown in memory access time (from 100 to 140 nanoseconds).

For a 98-percent hit ratio, we have

$$\text{effective access time} = 0.98 \times 120 + 0.02 \times 220$$
$$= 122 \text{ nanoseconds.}$$

This increased hit rate produces only a 22-percent slowdown in access time.

The hit ratio is clearly related to the number of associative registers. With the number of associative registers ranging between 16 and 512, a hit ratio of 80 to 98 percent can be obtained. The Motorola 68030 processor (used in Apple Macintosh systems) has a 22-entry TLB. The Intel 80486 CPU (found in some PCs) has 32 registers, and claims a 98-percent hit ratio. The UltraSPARC I & II processors provide two separate TLBs, one for pages containing instructions and the other for pages containing data. Each is 64 entries long.

9.4.2.2 Protection

Memory protection in a paged environment is accomplished by protection bits that are associated with each frame. Normally, these bits are kept in the page table. One bit can define a page to be either read-write or read-only. Every reference to memory goes through the page table to find the correct frame number. At the same time that the physical address is being computed, the protection bits can be checked to verify that no writes are being made to a read-only page. An attempt to write to a read-only page causes a hardware trap to the operating system (memory-protection violation).

We can easily expand this approach to provide a finer level of protection. We can create hardware to provide read-only, read–write, or execute-only protection. Or, by providing separate protection bits for each kind of access, we can allow any combination of these accesses; illegal attempts will be trapped to the operating system.

One more bit is generally attached to each entry in the page table: a **valid–invalid** bit. When this bit is set to "valid," this value indicates that the associated page is in the process's logical address space, and is thus a legal (valid) page. If the bit is set to "invalid," this value indicates that the page is not in the process's logical address space. Illegal addresses are trapped by using the valid–invalid bit. The operating system sets this bit for each page to allow or disallow accesses to that page. For example, in a system with a 14-bit address space (0 to 16,383), we may have a program that should use only addresses 0 to 10,468. Given a page size of 2K, we get the situation shown in Figure 9.11. Addresses in pages

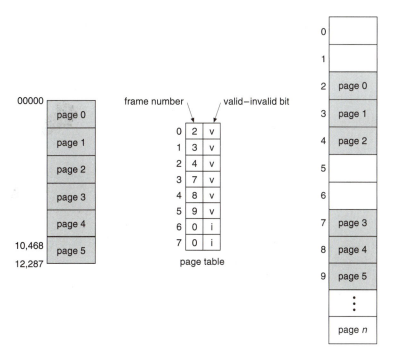

Figure 9.11 Valid (v) or invalid (i) bit in a page table.

0, 1, 2, 3, 4, and 5 are mapped normally through the page table. Any attempt to generate an address in pages 6 or 7, however, finds that the valid–invalid bit is set to invalid, and the computer will trap to the operating system (invalid page reference).

Notice that, because the program extends to only address 10,468, any reference beyond that address is illegal. However, references to page 5 are classified as valid, so accesses to addresses up to 12,287 are valid. Only the addresses from 12,288 to 16,383 are invalid. This problem is a result of the 2K page size and reflects the internal fragmentation of paging.

Rarely does a process use all its address range. In fact, many processes use only a small fraction of the address space available to them. It would be wasteful in these cases to create a page table with entries for every page in the address range. Most of this table would be unused, but would take up valuable memory space. Some systems provide hardware, in the form of a **page-table length register** (**PTLR**), to indicate the size of the page table. This value is checked against every logical address to verify that the address is in the valid

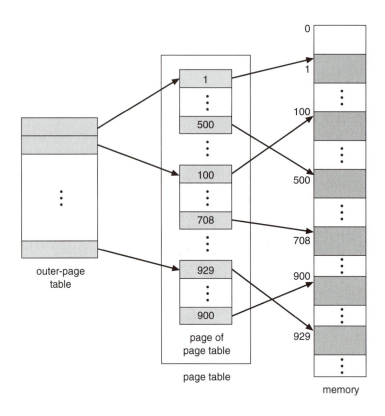

Figure 9.12   A two-level page-table scheme.

range for the process. Failure of this test causes an error trap to the operating system.

9.4.3 Multilevel Paging

Most modern computer systems support a large logical address space: (2^{32} to 2^{64}). In such an environment, the page table itself becomes excessively large. For example, consider a system with a 32-bit logical address space. If the page size in such a system is 4K bytes (2^{12}), then a page table may consist of up to 1 million entries ($2^{32}/2^{12}$). Assuming that each entry consists of 4 bytes, each process may need up to 4 megabytes of physical address space for the page table alone. Clearly, we would not want to allocate the page table contiguously in main memory. One simple solution to this problem is to divide the page table into smaller pieces. There are several ways to accomplish this division.

One way is to use a two-level paging algorithm, in which the page table itself is also paged (Figure 9.12). Remember our example to our 32-bit machine with a page size of 4K bytes. A logical address is divided into a page number consisting of 20 bits, and a page offset consisting of 12 bits. Because we page the page table, the page number is further divided into a 10-bit page number, and a 10-bit page offset. Thus, a logical address is as follows:

page number		page offset
p_1	p_2	d
10	10	12

where p_1 is an index into the outer page table, and p_2 is the displacement within the page of the outer page table. The address-translation method for this architecture is shown in Figure 9.13. The VAX architecture supports two-level paging. The VAX is a 32-bit machine with page size of 512 bytes. The logical address space of a process is divided into four equal sections, each of

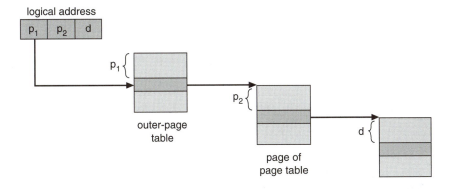

Figure 9.13 Address translation for a two-level 32-bit paging architecture.

which consists of 2^{30} bytes. Each section represents a different part of the logical address space of a process. The first 2 high-order bits of the logical address designate the appropriate section. The next 21 bits represent the logical page number of that section, and the final 9 bits represent an offset in the desired page. By partitioning the page table in this manner, the operating system can leave partitions unused until a process needs them. An address on the VAX architecture is as follows:

section	page	offset
s	p	d
2	21	9

where s designates the section number, p is an index into the page table, and d is the displacement within the page.

The size of a one-level page table for a VAX process using one section still is 2^{21} bits * 4 bytes per entry = 8 megabytes. So that main-memory use is reduced even further, the VAX pages the user-process page tables.

For a system with a 64-bit logical address space, a two-level paging scheme is no longer appropriate. To illustrate this point, let us suppose that the page size in such a system is 4K bytes (2^{12}). In this case, the page table will consist of up to 2^{52} entries. If we use a two-level paging scheme, then the inner page tables could conveniently be one page long, or contain 2^{10} 4-byte entries. The addresses would look like:

outer page	inner page	offset
$p1$	$p2$	d
42	10	12

The outer page table will consist of 2^{42} entries, or 2^{44} bytes. The obvious method to avoid such a large table is to divide the outer page table into smaller pieces. This approach is also used on some 32-bit processors for added flexibility and efficiency.

We can divide the outer page table in various ways. We can page the outer page table, giving us a three-level paging scheme. Suppose that the outer page table is made up of standard-size pages (2^{10} entries, or 2^{12} bytes); a 64-bit address space is still daunting:

2nd outer page	outer page	inner page	offset
$p1$	$p2$	$p3$	d
32	10	10	12

The outer page table is still 2^{34} bytes large.

The next step would be a four-level paging scheme, where the second-level outer page table itself is also paged. The SPARC architecture (with 32-bit addressing) supports a three-level paging scheme, whereas the 32-bit Motorola 68030 architecture supports a four-level paging scheme.

How does multilevel paging affect system performance? Given that each level is stored as a separate table in memory, converting a logical address to a physical one may take four memory accesses. We have now quintupled the amount of time needed for one memory access! Caching again pays dividends, however, and performance remains reasonable. Given a cache hit rate of 98 percent, we have

$$\text{effective access time} = 0.98 \times 120 + 0.02 \times 520$$
$$= 128 \text{ nanoseconds.}$$

Thus, even with the extra levels of table lookup, we have only a 28-percent slowdown in memory access time.

9.4.4 Inverted Page Table

Usually, each process has a page table associated with it. The page table has one entry for each page that the process is using (or one slot for each virtual address, regardless of the latter's validity). This table representation is a natural one, since processes reference pages through the pages' virtual addresses. The operating system must then translate this reference into a physical memory address. Since the table is sorted by virtual address, the operating system is able to calculate where in the table the associated physical-address entry is, and to use that value directly. One of the drawbacks of this method is that each page table may consist of millions of entries. These tables may consume large amounts of physical memory, which is required just to keep track of how the other physical memory is being used.

To solve this problem, we can use an **inverted page table**. An inverted page table has one entry for each real page (frame) of memory. Each entry consists of the virtual address of the page stored in that real memory location, with information about the process that owns that page. Thus, there is only one page table in the system, and it has only one entry for each page of physical memory. Figure 9.14 shows the operation of an inverted page table. Compare it to Figure 9.6, which depicts a standard page table in operation. Examples of systems using such an algorithm are the IBM System/38 computer, the IBM RISC System 6000, IBM RT, and Hewlett-Packard Spectrum workstations.

To illustrate this method, we describe a simplified version of the implementation of the inverted page table used in the IBM RT. Each virtual address in the system consists of a triple

<process-id, page-number, offset>.

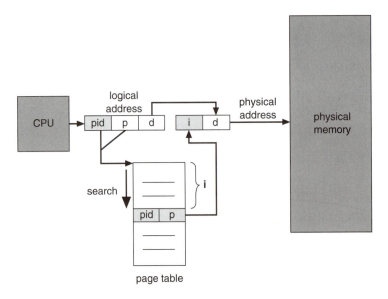

Figure 9.14 Inverted page table.

Each inverted page-table entry is a pair <process-id, page-number>. When a memory reference occurs, part of the virtual address, consisting of <process-id, page-number>, is presented to the memory subsystem. The inverted page table is then searched for a match. If a match is found—say, at entry i—then the physical address <i, offset> is generated. If no match is found, then an illegal address access has been attempted.

Although this scheme decreases the amount of memory needed to store each page table, it increases the amount of time needed to search the table when a page reference occurs. Because the inverted page table is sorted by a physical address, but lookups occur on virtual addresses, the whole table might need to be searched for a match. This search would take far too long. To alleviate this problem, we use a hash table to limit the search to one—or at most a few—page-table entries. Of course, each access to the hash table adds a memory reference to the procedure, so one virtual-memory reference requires at least two real-memory reads: one for the hash-table entry and one for the page table. To improve performance, we use associative memory registers to hold recently located entries. These registers are searched first, before the hash table is consulted.

9.4.5 Shared Pages

Another advantage of paging is the possibility of *sharing* common code. This consideration is particularly important in a time-sharing environment. Consider a system that supports 40 users, each of whom executes a text editor. If the text editor consists of 150K of code and 50K of data space, we would need 8000K to support the 40 users. If the code is **reentrant,** however, it can be shared, as shown in Figure 9.15. Here we see a three-page editor (each page of size 50K; the large page size is used to simplify the figure) being shared among three processes. Each process has its own data page.

Reentrant code (also called pure code) is non–self-modifying code. If the code is reentrant, then it never changes during execution. Thus, two or more processes can execute the same code at the same time. Each process has its own copy of registers and data storage to hold the data for the process's execution. The data for two different processes will, of course, vary for each process.

Only one copy of the editor needs to be kept in physical memory. Each user's page table maps onto the same physical copy of the editor, but data pages are mapped onto different frames. Thus, to support 40 users, we need only one copy of the editor (150K), plus 40 copies of the 50K of data space per user. The total space required is now 2150K, instead of 8000K—a significant savings.

Other heavily used programs also can be shared: compilers, window systems, database systems, and so on. To be sharable, the code must be reentrant. The read-only nature of shared code should not be left to the

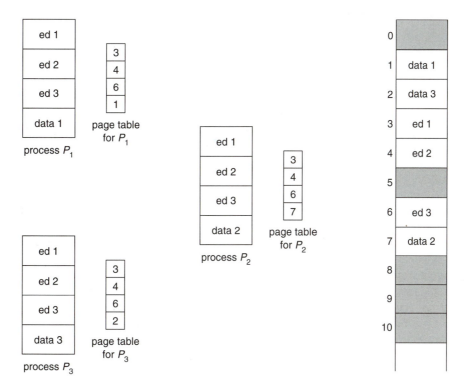

Figure 9.15 Sharing of code in a paging environment.

correctness of the code; the operating system should enforce this property. This sharing of memory among processes on a system is similar to the sharing of the address space of a task by threads, described in Chapter 4.

Systems that use inverted page tables have difficulty implementing shared memory. Shared memory is usually implemented as two virtual addresses that are mapped to one physical address. This standard method cannot be used, however, as there is only one virtual page entry for every physical page, so one physical page cannot have the two (or more) shared virtual addresses.

9.5 ■ Segmentation

An important aspect of memory management that became unavoidable with paging is the separation of the user's view of memory and the actual physical memory. The user's view of memory is not the same as the actual physical memory. The user's view is mapped onto physical memory. The mapping allows differentiation between logical memory and physical memory.

9.5.1 Basic Method

What is the user's view of memory? Does the user think of memory as a linear array of bytes, some containing instructions and others containing data, or is there some other preferred memory view? There is general agreement that the user or programmer of a system does not think of memory as a linear array of bytes. Rather, the user prefers to view memory as a collection of variable-sized segments, with no necessary ordering among segments (Figure 9.16).

Consider how you think of a program when you are writing it. You think of it as a main program with a set of subroutines, procedures, functions, or modules. There may also be various data structures: tables, arrays, stacks, variables, and so on. Each of these modules or data elements is referred to by name. You talk about "the symbol table," "function *Sqrt*," "the main program," without caring what addresses in memory these elements occupy. You are not concerned with whether the symbol table is stored before or after the *Sqrt* function. Each of these segments is of variable length; the length is intrinsically defined by the purpose of the segment in the program. Elements within a segment are identified by their offset from the beginning of the segment: the first statement of the program, the seventeenth entry in the symbol table, the fifth instruction of the *Sqrt* function, and so on.

Segmentation is a memory-management scheme that supports this user view of memory. A logical address space is a collection of segments. Each segment has a name and a length. The addresses specify both the segment name and the offset within the segment. The user therefore specifies each address by two quantities: a segment name and an offset. (Contrast this scheme with the paging scheme, where the user specified only a single address, which was

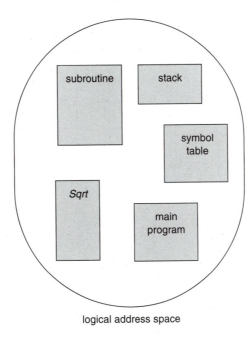

logical address space

Figure 9.16 User's view of a program.

partitioned by the hardware into a page number and an offset, all invisible to the programmer.)

For simplicity of implementation, segments are numbered and are referred to by a segment number, rather than by a segment name. Thus, a logical address consists of a two tuple:

$$<\text{segment-number, offset}>.$$

Normally, the user program is compiled, and the compiler automatically constructs segments reflecting the input program. A Pascal compiler might create separate segments for (1) the global variables; (2) the procedure call stack, to store parameters and return addresses; (3) the code portion of each procedure or function; and (4) the local variables of each procedure and function. A FORTRAN compiler might create a separate segment for each common block. Arrays might be assigned separate segments. The loader would take all these segments and assign them segment numbers.

9.5.2 Hardware

Although the user can now refer to objects in the program by a two-dimensional address, the actual physical memory is still, of course, a one-dimensional

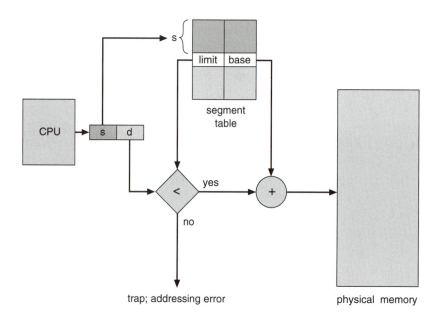

Figure 9.17   Segmentation hardware.

sequence of bytes. Thus, we must define an implementation to map two-dimensional user-defined addresses into one-dimensional physical addresses. This mapping is effected by a **segment table**. Each entry of the segment table has a segment **base** and a segment **limit**. The segment base contains the starting physical address where the segment resides in memory, whereas the segment limit specifies the length of the segment.

The use of a segment table is illustrated in Figure 9.17. A logical address consists of two parts: a segment number, s, and an offset into that segment, d. The segment number is used as an index into the segment table. The offset d of the logical address must be between 0 and the segment limit. If it is not, we trap to the operating system (logical addressing attempt beyond end of segment). If this offset is legal, it is added to the segment base to produce the address in physical memory of the desired byte. The segment table is thus essentially an array of base–limit register pairs.

As an example, consider the situation shown in Figure 9.18. We have five segments numbered from 0 through 4. The segments are stored in physical memory as shown. The segment table has a separate entry for each segment, giving the beginning address of the segment in physical memory (the base) and the length of that segment (the limit). For example, segment 2 is 400 bytes long, and begins at location 4300. Thus, a reference to byte 53 of segment 2 is mapped onto location 4300 + 53 = 4353. A reference to segment 3, byte 852, is mapped to 3200 (the base of segment 3) + 852 = 4052. A reference to byte 1222 of segment

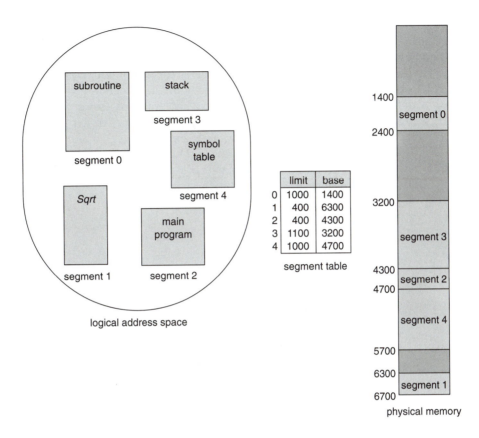

Figure 9.18   Example of segmentation.

0 would result in a trap to the operating system, as this segment is only 1000 bytes long.

9.5.3 Protection and Sharing

A particular advantage of segmentation is the association of protection with the segments. Because the segments represent a semantically defined portion of the program, it is likely that all entries in the segment will be used the same way. Hence, we have some segments that are instructions, whereas other segments are data. In a modern architecture, instructions are non–self-modifying, so instruction segments can be defined as read only or execute only. The memory-mapping hardware will check the protection bits associated with each segment-table entry to prevent illegal accesses to memory, such as attempts to write into a read-only segment, or to use an execute-only segment as data. By placing an array in its own segment, the memory-management hardware will automatically check that array indexes are legal and do not stray outside the array boundaries. Thus, many common program errors will be detected by the hardware before they can cause serious damage.

Another advantage of segmentation involves the *sharing* of code or data. Each process has a segment table associated with it, which the dispatcher uses to define the hardware segment table when this process is given the CPU. Segments are shared when entries in the segment tables of two different processes point to the same physical location (Figure 9.19).

The sharing occurs at the segment level. Thus, any information can be shared if it is defined to be a segment. Several segments can be shared, so a program composed of several segments can be shared.

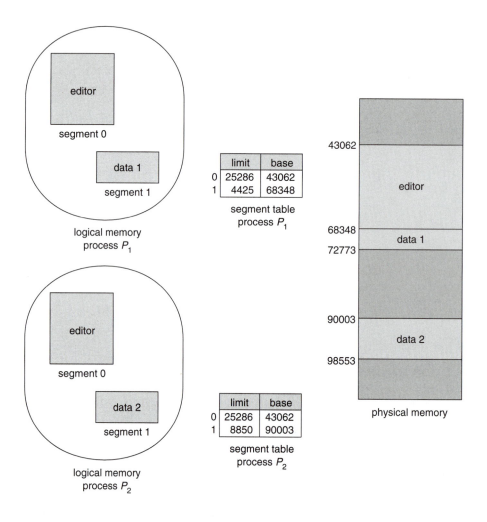

Figure 9.19   Sharing of segments in a segmented memory system.

For example, consider the use of a text editor in a time-sharing system. A complete editor might be quite large, composed of many segments. These segments can be shared among all users, limiting the physical memory needed to support editing tasks. Rather than n copies of the editor, we need only one copy. For each user, we still need separate, unique segments to store local variables. These segments, of course, would not be shared.

It is also possible to share only parts of programs. For example, common subroutine packages can be shared among many users if they are defined as sharable, read-only segments. Two FORTRAN programs, for instance, may use the same *Sqrt* subroutine, but only one physical copy of the *Sqrt* routine would be needed.

Although this sharing appears simple, there are subtle considerations. Code segments typically contain references to themselves. For example, a conditional jump normally has a transfer address. The transfer address is a segment number and offset. The segment number of the transfer address will be the segment number of the code segment. If we try to share this segment, all sharing processes must define the shared code segment to have the same segment number.

For instance, if we want to share the *Sqrt* routine, and one process wants to make it segment 4 and another wants to make it segment 17, how should the *Sqrt* routine refer to itself? Because there is only one physical copy of *Sqrt*, it must refer to itself in the same way for both users—it must have a unique segment number. As the number of users sharing the segment increases, so does the difficulty of finding an acceptable segment number.

Read-only data segments that contain no physical pointers may be shared as different segment numbers, as may code segments that refer to themselves not directly, but rather only indirectly. For example, conditional branches that specify the branch address as an offset from the current program counter or relative to a register containing the current segment number would allow code to avoid direct reference to the current segment number.

9.5.4 Fragmentation

The long-term scheduler must find and allocate memory for all the segments of a user program. This situation is similar to paging *except* that the segments are of *variable* length; pages are all the same size. Thus, as with the variable-sized partition scheme, memory allocation is a dynamic storage-allocation problem, usually solved with a best-fit or first-fit algorithm.

Segmentation may then cause external fragmentation, when all blocks of free memory are too small to accommodate a segment. In this case, the process may simply have to wait until more memory (or at least a larger hole) becomes available, or compaction may be used to create a larger hole. Because segmentation is by its nature a dynamic relocation algorithm, we can compact memory whenever we want. If the CPU scheduler must wait for one process, due to a memory-allocation problem, it may (or may not) skip through the CPU queue looking for a smaller, lower-priority process to run.

How serious a problem is external fragmentation for a segmentation scheme? Would long-term scheduling with compaction help? The answers to these questions depend mainly on the average segment size. At one extreme, we could define each process to be one segment. This approach reduces to the variable-sized partition scheme. At the other extreme, every byte could be put in its own segment and relocated separately. This arrangement eliminates external fragmentation altogether; however, every byte would need a base register for its relocation, doubling memory use! Of course, the next logical step —fixed-sized, small segments—is paging. Generally, if the average segment size is small, external fragmentation will also be small. (By analogy, consider putting suitcases in the trunk of a car; they never quite seem to fit. However, if you open the suitcases and put the individual items in the trunk, everything fits.) Because the individual segments are smaller than the overall process, they are more likely to fit in the available memory blocks.

9.6 ■ Segmentation with Paging

Both paging and segmentation have their advantages and disadvantages. In fact, of the two most popular microprocessors now being used, the Motorola 68000 line is designed based on a flat address space, whereas the Intel 80X86 and Pentium family are based on segmentation. Both are merging memory models toward a mixture of paging and segmentation. It is possible to combine these two methods to improve on each. This combination is best illustrated by the architecture of the Intel 386.

The IBM OS/2 32-bit version is an operating system running on top of the Intel 386 (and later) architecture. The 386 uses segmentation with paging for memory management. The maximum number of segments per process is 16K, and each segment can be as large as 4 gigabytes. The page size is 4K bytes. We shall not give a complete description of the memory-management structure of the 386 in this text. Rather, we shall present the major ideas.

The logical address space of a process is divided into two partitions. The first partition consists of up to 8K segments that are private to that process. The second partition consists of up to 8K segments that are shared among all the processes. Information about the first partition is kept in the **local descriptor table** (**LDT**), information about the second partition is kept in the **global descriptor table** (**GDT**). Each entry in the LDT and GDT table consists of 8 bytes, with detailed information about a particular segment including the base location and length of that segment.

The logical address is a pair (selector, offset), where the selector is a 16-bit number:

s	g	p
13	1	2

in which s designates the segment number, g indicates whether the segment is in the GDT or LDT, and p deals with protection. The offset is a 32-bit number specifying the location of the byte (word) within the segment in question.

The machine has six segment registers, allowing six segments to be addressed at any one time by a process. It has six 8-byte microprogram registers to hold the corresponding descriptors from either the LDT or GDT. This cache lets the 386 avoid having to read the descriptor from memory for every memory reference.

The physical address on the 386 is 32 bits long and is formed as follows. The segment register points to the appropriate entry in the LDT or GDT. The base and limit information about the segment in question are used to generate a **linear address**. First, the limit is used to check for address validity. If the address is not valid, a memory fault is generated, resulting in a trap to the operating system. If it is valid, then the value of the offset is added to the value of the base, resulting in a 32-bit linear address. This address is then translated into a physical address.

As pointed out previously, each segment is paged, and each page is 4K bytes. A page table may thus consist of up to 1 million entries. Because each entry consists of 4 bytes, each process may need up to 4 megabytes of physical address space for the page table alone. Clearly, we would not want to allocate the page table contiguously in main memory. The solution adopted in the 386 is to use a two-level paging scheme. The linear address is divided into a page number consisting of 20 bits, and a page offset consisting of 12 bits. Since we page the page table, the page number is further divided into a 10-bit page directory pointer and a 10-bit page table pointer. The logical address is as follows:

page number		page offset
p_1	p_2	d
10	10	12

The address-translation scheme for this architecture is similar to the scheme shown in Figure 9.13. The Intel address translation is shown in more detail in Figure 9.20. So that the efficiency of physical-memory use can be improved, Intel 386 page tables can be swapped to disk. In this case, an invalid bit is used in the page-directory entry to indicate whether the table to which the entry is pointing is in memory or on disk. If the table is on disk, the operating system can use the other 31 bits to specify the disk location of the table; the table then can be brought into memory on demand.

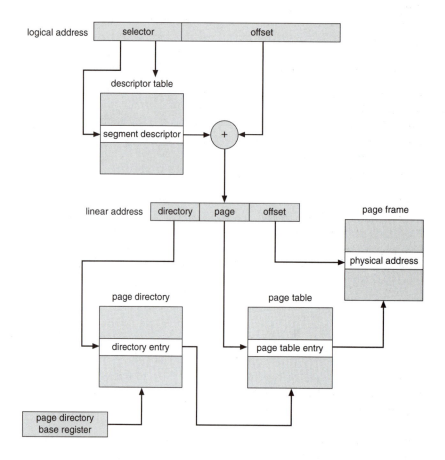

Figure 9.20   Intel 80386 address translation.

9.7 ■ Summary

Memory-management algorithms for multiprogrammed operating systems range from the simple single-user system approach to paged segmentation. The greatest determinant of the method used in a particular system is the hardware provided. Every memory address generated by the CPU must be checked for legality and possibly mapped to a physical address. The checking cannot be implemented (efficiently) in software. Hence, we are constrained by the hardware available.

The memory-management algorithms discussed (contiguous allocation, paging, segmentation, and combinations of paging and segmentation) differ in many aspects. Important considerations that you should use in comparing different memory-management strategies follow:

- *Hardware support:* A simple base register or a pair of base and limit registers is sufficient for the single and multiple partition schemes, whereas paging and segmentation need mapping tables to define the address map.

- *Performance:* As the memory-management algorithm becomes more complex, the time required to map a logical address to a physical address increases. For the simple systems, we need only to compare or add to the logical address—operations that are fast. Paging and segmentation can be as fast if the table is implemented in fast registers. If the table is in memory, however, user memory accesses can be degraded substantially. A set of associative registers can reduce the performance degradation to an acceptable level.

- *Fragmentation:* A multiprogrammed system will generally perform more efficiently if it has a higher level of multiprogramming. For a given set of processes, we can increase the multiprogramming level only by packing more processes into memory. To accomplish this task, we must reduce memory waste or fragmentation. Systems with fixed-sized allocation units, such as the single-partition scheme and paging, suffer from internal fragmentation. Systems with variable-sized allocation units, such as the multiple-partition scheme and segmentation, suffer from external fragmentation.

- *Relocation:* One solution to the external-fragmentation problem is compaction. Compaction involves shifting a program in memory without the program noticing the change. This consideration requires that logical addresses be relocated dynamically, at execution time. If addresses are relocated only at load time, we cannot compact storage.

- *Swapping:* Any algorithm can have swapping added to it. At intervals determined by the operating system, usually dictated by CPU-scheduling policies, processes are copied from main memory to a backing store, and later are copied back to main memory. This scheme allows more processes to be run than can be fit into memory at one time.

- *Sharing:* Another means of increasing the multiprogramming level is to share code and data among different users. Sharing generally requires that either paging or segmentation be used, to provide small packets of information (pages or segments) that can be shared. Sharing is a means of running many processes with a limited amount of memory, but shared programs and data must be designed carefully.

- *Protection:* If paging or segmentation is provided, different sections of a user program can be declared execute only, read only, or read–write. This restriction is necessary with shared code or data, and is generally useful in any case to provide simple run-time checks for common programming errors.

■ Exercises

9.1 Name two differences between logical and physical addresses.

9.2 Explain the difference between internal and external fragmentation.

9.3 Describe the following allocation algorithms:

   a. First fit

   b. Best fit

   c. Worst fit

9.4 When a process is rolled out of memory, it loses its ability to use the CPU (at least for a while). Describe another situation where a process loses its ability to use the CPU, but where the process does not get rolled out.

9.5 Given memory partitions of 100K, 500K, 200K, 300K, and 600K (in order), how would each of the first-fit, best-fit, and worst-fit algorithms place processes of 212K, 417K, 112K, and 426K (in order)? Which algorithm makes the most efficient use of memory?

9.6 Consider a system where a program can be separated into two parts: code and data. The CPU knows whether it wants an instruction (instruction fetch) or data (data fetch or store). Therefore, two base–limit register pairs are provided: one for instructions and one for data. The instruction base–limit register pair is automatically set to read only, so programs can be shared among different users. Discuss the advantages and disadvantages of this scheme.

9.7 Why are page sizes always powers of 2?

9.8 Consider a logical address space of eight pages of 1,024 words each, mapped onto a physical memory of 32 frames.

   a. How many bits are there in the logical address?

   b. How many bits are there in the physical address?

9.9 Why is it that, on a system with paging, a process cannot access memory that it does not own? How could the operating system allow access to other memory? Why should it or should it not?

9.10 Consider a paging system with the page table stored in memory.

   a. If a memory reference takes 200 nanoseconds, how long does a paged memory reference take?

   b. If we add associative registers, and 75 percent of all page-table references are found in the associative registers, what is the effective memory reference time? (Assume that finding a page-table entry in the associative registers takes zero time, if the entry is there.)

9.11 What is the effect of allowing two entries in a page table to point to the same page frame in memory? Explain how you could use this effect to decrease the amount of time needed to copy a large amount of memory from one place to another. What would the effect of updating some byte in the one page be on the other page?

9.12 Why are segmentation and paging sometimes combined into one scheme?

9.13 Describe a mechanism by which one segment could belong to the address space of two different processes.

9.14 Explain why it is easier to share a reentrant module using segmentation than it is to do so when pure paging is used.

9.15 Sharing segments among processes without requiring the same segment number is possible in a dynamically linked segmentation system.

a. Define a system that allows static linking and sharing of segments without requiring that the segment numbers be the same.

b. Describe a paging scheme that allows pages to be shared without requiring that the page numbers be the same.

9.16 Consider the following segment table:

Segment	Base	Length
0	219	600
1	2300	14
2	90	100
3	1327	580
4	1952	96

What are the physical addresses for the following logical addresses?

a. 0,430

b. 1,10

c. 2,500

d. 3,400

e. 4,112

9.17 Consider the Intel address-translation scheme shown in Figure 9.20.

a. Describe all the steps that are taken by the Intel 80386 in translating a logical address into a physical address.

b. What are the advantages to the operating system of hardware that provides such complicated memory-translation hardware?

c. Are there any disadvantages to this address-translation system? If so, what are they? If not, why is it not used by every manufacturer?

9.18 In the IBM/370, memory protection is provided through the use of *keys*. A key is a 4-bit quantity. Each 2K block of memory has a key (the storage key) associated with it. The CPU also has a key (the protection key) associated with it. A store operation is allowed only if both keys are equal, or if either is zero. Which of the following memory-management schemes could be used successfully with this hardware?

a. Bare machine

b. Single-user system

c. Multiprogramming with a fixed number of processes

d. Multiprogramming with a variable number of processes

e. Paging

f. Segmentation

Bibliographical Notes

Dynamic storage allocation was discussed by Knuth [1973, Section 2.5], who found through simulation results that first fit is generally superior to best fit. Knuth [1973] discussed the 50-percent rule.

The concept of paging can be credited to the designers of the Atlas system, which has been described by Kilburn and colleagues [1961] and by Howarth and colleagues [1961]. The concept of segmentation was first discussed by Dennis [1965]. Paged segmentation was first supported in the GE 645, on which MULTICS was originally implemented [Organick 1972].

Inverted page tables were discussed in an article about the IBM RT storage manager by Chang and Mergen [1988].

Cache memories, including associative memory, were described and analyzed by Smith [1982]. This paper also includes an extensive bibliography on the subject. Hennessy and Patterson [1996] discussed the hardware aspects of TLBs, caches, and MMUs.

The Motorola 68000 microprocessor family was described in Motorola [1989a]. Information on the paging hardware of 80386 can be found in Intel [1986]. Tanenbaum [1992] also discussed Intel 80386 paging. The Intel 80486 hardware also is described in an Intel publication [1989].

Memory management for several architectures—such as the Pentium II, PowerPC, and UltraSPARC—was described by Jacob and Mudge [1998b].

Chapter 10

VIRTUAL
MEMORY

In Chapter 9, we discussed various memory-management strategies that are used in computer systems. All these strategies have the same goal: to keep many processes in memory simultaneously to allow multiprogramming. However, they tend to require the entire process to be in memory before the process can execute.

Virtual memory is a technique that allows the execution of processes that may not be completely in memory. The main visible advantage of this scheme is that programs can be larger than physical memory. Further, it abstracts main memory into an extremely large, uniform array of storage, separating logical memory as viewed by the user from physical memory. This technique frees programmers from concern about memory storage limitations. Virtual memory is not easy to implement, however, and may substantially decrease performance if it is used carelessly. In this chapter, we discuss virtual memory in the form of demand paging, and examine its complexity and cost.

10.1 ■ Background

The memory-management algorithms outlined in Chapter 9 are necessary because of one basic requirement: The instructions being executed must be in physical memory. The first approach to meeting this requirement is to place the entire logical address space in physical memory. Overlays and dynamic loading can help to ease this restriction, but they generally require special precautions and extra work by the programmer. This restriction seems both necessary and reasonable, but it is also unfortunate, since it limits the size of a program to the size of physical memory.

In fact, an examination of real programs shows us that, in many cases, the entire program is not needed. For instance,

- Programs often have code to handle unusual error conditions. Since these errors seldom, if ever, occur in practice, this code is almost never executed.

- Arrays, lists, and tables are often allocated more memory than they actually need. An array may be declared 100 by 100 elements, even though it is seldom larger than 10 by 10 elements. An assembler symbol table may have room for 3000 symbols, although the average program has less than 200 symbols.

- Certain options and features of a program may be used rarely. For instance, the routines on U.S. government computers that balance the budget have only recently been used.

Even in those cases where the entire program is needed, it may not all be needed at the same time (such is the case with overlays, for example).

The ability to execute a program that is only partially in memory would confer many benefits:

- A program would no longer be constrained by the amount of physical memory that is available. Users would be able to write programs for an extremely large **virtual** address space, simplifying the programming task.

- Because each user program could take less physical memory, more programs could be run at the same time, with a corresponding increase in CPU utilization and throughput, but with no increase in response time or turnaround time.

- Less I/O would be needed to load or swap each user program into memory, so each user program would run faster.

Thus, running a program that is not entirely in memory would benefit both the system and the user.

Virtual memory is the separation of user logical memory from physical memory. This separation allows an extremely large virtual memory to be provided for programmers when only a smaller physical memory is available (Figure 10.1). Virtual memory makes the task of programming much easier, because the programmer no longer needs to worry about the amount of physical memory available, or about what code can be placed in overlays; she can concentrate instead on the problem to be programmed. On systems that support virtual memory, overlays have almost disappeared.

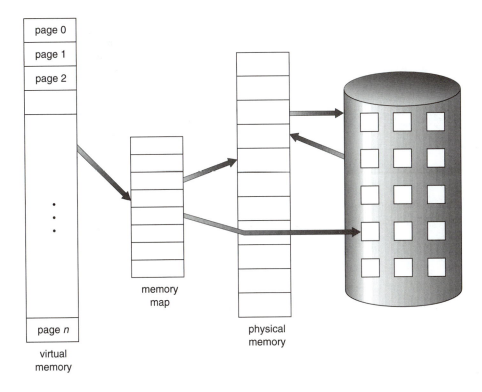

page 0
page 1
page 2

page *n*

virtual
memory

memory
map

physical
memory

Figure 10.1   Diagram showing virtual memory that is larger than physical memory.

Virtual memory is commonly implemented by **demand paging**. It can also be implemented in a segmentation system. Several systems provide a paged segmentation scheme, where segments are broken into pages. Thus, the user view is segmentation, but the operating system can implement this view with demand paging. **Demand segmentation** can also be used to provide virtual memory. Burroughs' computer systems have used demand segmentation. The IBM OS/2 operating system also uses demand segmentation. However, segment-replacement algorithms are more complex than are page-replacement algorithms because the segments have variable sizes. We do not cover demand segmentation in this text; refer to the Bibliographical Notes for relevant references.

10.2 ■ Demand Paging

A demand-paging system is similar to a paging system with swapping (Figure 10.2). Processes reside on secondary memory (which is usually a disk). When we want to execute a process, we swap it into memory. Rather than swapping

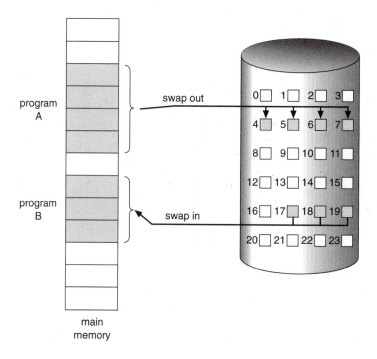

Figure 10.2   Transfer of a paged memory to contiguous disk space.

the entire process into memory, however, we use a **lazy swapper**. A lazy swapper never swaps a page into memory unless that page will be needed. Since we are now viewing a process as a sequence of pages, rather than as one large contiguous address space, use of *swap* is technically incorrect. A swapper manipulates entire processes, whereas a *pager* is concerned with the individual pages of a process. We thus use *pager*, rather than *swapper*, in connection with demand paging.

10.2.1 Basic Concepts

When a process is to be swapped in, the pager guesses which pages will be used before the process is swapped out again. Instead of swapping in a whole process, the pager brings only those necessary pages into memory. Thus, it avoids reading into memory pages that will not be used anyway, decreasing the swap time and the amount of physical memory needed.

With this scheme, we need some form of hardware support to distinguish between those pages that are in memory and those pages that are on the disk. The *valid–invalid* bit scheme described in Section 9.4.2 can be used for this purpose. This time, however, when this bit is set to "valid," this value indicates that the associated page is both legal and in memory. If the bit is set to "invalid," this value indicates that the page either is not valid (that is, not in the logical address space of the process), or is valid but is currently on the disk. The page-table entry for a page that is brought into memory is set as usual, but the page-table entry for a page that is not currently in memory is simply marked invalid, or contains the address of the page on disk. This situation is depicted in Figure 10.3.

Notice that marking a page invalid will have no effect if the process never attempts to access that page. Hence, if we guess right and page in all and only those pages that are actually needed, the process will run exactly as though we had brought in all pages. While the process executes and accesses pages that are **memory resident,** execution proceeds normally.

But what happens if the process tries to use a page that was not brought into memory? Access to a page marked invalid causes a **page-fault trap**. The paging hardware, in translating the address through the page table, will notice that the invalid bit is set, causing a trap to the operating system. This trap is the result

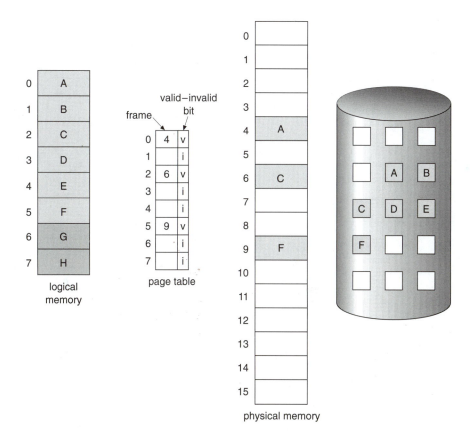

Figure 10.3 Page table when some pages are not in main memory.

of the operating system's failure to bring the desired page into memory (in an attempt to minimize disk-transfer overhead and memory requirements), rather than an invalid address error as a result of an attempt to use an illegal memory address (such as an incorrect array subscript). We must therefore correct this oversight. The procedure for handling this page fault is straightforward (Figure 10.4):

1. We check an internal table (usually kept with the process control block) for this process, to determine whether the reference was a valid or invalid memory access.

2. If the reference was invalid, we terminate the process. If it was valid, but we have not yet brought in that page, we now page it in.

3. We find a free frame (by taking one from the free-frame list, for example).

4. We schedule a disk operation to read the desired page into the newly allocated frame.

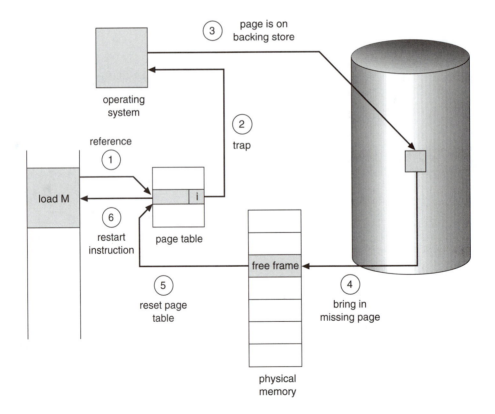

Figure 10.4   Steps in handling a page fault.

5. When the disk read is complete, we modify the internal table kept with the process and the page table to indicate that the page is now in memory.

6. We restart the instruction that was interrupted by the illegal address trap. The process can now access the page as though it had always been in memory.

It is important to realize that, because we save the state (registers, condition code, instruction counter) of the interrupted process when the page fault occurs, we can restart the process in *exactly* the same place and state, except that the desired page is now in memory and is accessible. In this way, we are able to execute a process, even though portions of it are not (yet) in memory. When the process tries to access locations that are not in memory, the hardware traps to the operating system (page fault). The operating system reads the desired page into memory and restarts the process as though the page had always been in memory.

In the extreme case, we could start executing a process with *no* pages in memory. When the operating system sets the instruction pointer to the first instruction of the process, which is on a non–memory-resident page, the process immediately faults for the page. After this page is brought into memory, the process continues to execute, faulting as necessary until every page that it needs is in memory. At that point, it can execute with no more faults. This scheme is **pure demand paging:** Never bring a page into memory until it is required.

Theoretically, some programs may access several new pages of memory with each instruction execution (one page for the instruction and many for data), possibly causing multiple page faults per instruction. This situation would result in unacceptable system performance. Fortunately, analysis of running processes shows that this behavior is exceedingly unlikely. Programs tend to have **locality of reference,** described in Section 10.5.1, which results in reasonable performance from demand paging.

The hardware to support demand paging is the same as the hardware for paging and swapping:

- *Page table:* This table has the ability to mark an entry invalid through a valid–invalid bit or special value of protection bits.

- *Secondary memory:* This memory holds those pages that are not present in main memory. The secondary memory is usually a high-speed disk. It is known as the swap device, and the section of disk used for this purpose is known as **swap space** or **backing store**. Swap-space allocation is discussed in Chapter 13.

In addition to this hardware support, considerable software is needed, as we shall see. Additional architectural constraints must be imposed. A crucial one is the need to be able to restart any instruction after a page fault. In most cases, this requirement is easy to meet. A page fault could occur at any memory reference. If the page fault occurs on the instruction fetch, we can restart by fetching the instruction again. If a page fault occurs while we are fetching an operand, we must fetch and decode the instruction again, and then fetch the operand.

As a worst-case example, consider a three-address instruction such as ADD the content of A to B placing the result in C. These are the steps to execute this instruction:

1. Fetch and decode the instruction (ADD).

2. Fetch A.

3. Fetch B.

4. Add A and B.

5. Store the sum in C.

If we faulted when we tried to store in C (because C is in a page not currently in memory), we would have to get the desired page, bring it in, correct the page table, and restart the instruction. The restart would require fetching the instruction again, decoding it again, fetching the two operands again, and then adding again. However, there is not much repeated work (less than one complete instruction), and the repetition is necessary only when a page fault occurs.

The major difficulty occurs when one instruction may modify several different locations. For example, consider the IBM System 360/370 MVC (move character) instruction, which can move up to 256 bytes from one location to another (possibly overlapping) location. If either block (source or destination) straddles a page boundary, a page fault might occur after the move is partially done. In addition, if the source and destination blocks overlap, the source block may have been modified, in which case we cannot simply restart the instruction.

This problem can be solved in two different ways. In one solution, the microcode computes and attempts to access both ends of both blocks. If a page fault is going to occur, it will happen at this step, before anything is modified. The move can then take place, as we know that no page fault can occur, since all the relevant pages are in memory. The other solution uses temporary registers to hold the values of overwritten locations. If there is a page fault, all the old values are written back into memory before the trap occurs. This action restores memory to its state before the instruction was started, so that the instruction can be repeated.

A similar architectural problem occurs in machines that use special addressing modes, including autodecrement and autoincrement modes (for example, the PDP-11). These addressing modes use a register as a pointer and automatically decrement or increment the register as indicated. Autodecrement automatically decrements the register *before* using its contents as the operand address; autoincrement automatically increments the register *after* using its contents as the operand address. Thus, the instruction

$$\text{MOV (R2)+,-(R3)}$$

copies the contents of the location pointed to by register 2 into the location pointed to by register 3. Register 2 is incremented (by 2 for a word, since the PDP-11 is a byte-addressable computer) after it is used as a pointer; register 3 is decremented (by 2) before it is used as a pointer. Now consider what will happen if we get a fault when trying to store into the location pointed to by register 3. To restart the instruction, we must reset the two registers to the values they had before we started the execution of the instruction. One solution is to create a new special status register to record the register number and amount modified for any register that is changed during the execution of an instruction. This status register allows the operating system to *undo* the effects of a partially executed instruction that causes a page fault.

These are by no means the only architectural problems resulting from adding paging to an existing architecture to allow demand paging, but they illustrate some of the difficulties. Paging is added between the CPU and the memory in a computer system. It should be entirely transparent to the user process. Thus, people often assume that paging could be added to any system. Although this assumption is true for a non–demand-paging environment, where a page fault represents a fatal error, it is not true where a page fault means only that an additional page must be brought into memory and the process restarted.

10.2.2 Performance of Demand Paging

Demand paging can have a significant effect on the performance of a computer system. To see why, let us compute the **effective access time** for a demand-paged memory. For most computer systems, the memory access time, denoted *ma*, now ranges from 10 to 200 nanoseconds. As long as we have no page faults, the effective access time is equal to the memory access time. If, however, a page fault occurs, we must first read the relevant page from disk, and then access the desired word.

Let p be the probability of a page fault ($0 \leq p \leq 1$). We would expect p to be close to zero; that is, there will be only a few page faults. The *effective* access time is then

$$\text{effective access time} = (1 - p) \times ma + p \times \text{page fault time.}$$

To compute the effective access time, we must know how much time is needed to service a page fault. A page fault causes the following sequence to occur:

1. Trap to the operating system.

2. Save the user registers and process state.

3. Determine that the interrupt was a page fault.

4. Check that the page reference was legal and determine the location of the page on the disk.

5. Issue a read from the disk to a free frame:

   a. Wait in a queue for this device until the read request is serviced.

   b. Wait for the device seek and/or latency time.

   c. Begin the transfer of the page to a free frame.

6. While waiting, allocate the CPU to some other user (CPU scheduling; optional).

7. Interrupt from the disk (I/O completed).

8. Save the registers and process state for the other user (if step 6 executed).

9. Determine that the interrupt was from the disk.

10. Correct the page table and other tables to show that the desired page is now in memory.

11. Wait for the CPU to be allocated to this process again.

12. Restore the user registers, process state, and new page table, then resume the interrupted instruction.

Not all these steps are necessary in every case. For example, we are assuming that, in step 6, the CPU is allocated to another process while the I/O occurs. This arrangement allows multiprogramming to maintain CPU utilization, but requires additional time to resume the page-fault service routine when the I/O transfer is complete.

In any case, we are faced with three major components of the page-fault service time:

1. Service the page-fault interrupt.

2. Read in the page.

3. Restart the process.

The first and third tasks may be reduced, with careful coding, to several hundred instructions. These tasks may take from 1 to 100 microseconds each. The page-switch time, on the other hand, will probably be close to 24 milliseconds. A typical hard disk has an average latency of 8 milliseconds, a seek of 15 milliseconds, and a transfer time of 1 millisecond. Thus, the total paging time would be close to 25 milliseconds, including hardware and software time. Remember also that we are looking at only the device-service time. If a queue of processes is waiting for the device (other processes that have caused page faults), we have to add device-queueing time as we wait for the paging device to be free to service our request, increasing even more the time to swap.

If we take an average page-fault service time of 25 milliseconds and a memory access time of 100 nanoseconds, then the effective access time in nanoseconds is

$$\text{effective access time} = (1 - p) \times (100) + p \, (25 \text{ milliseconds})$$
$$= (1 - p) \times 100 + p \times 25{,}000{,}000$$
$$= 100 + 24{,}999{,}900 \times p.$$

We see then that the effective access time is directly proportional to the page-fault rate. If one access out of 1000 causes a page fault, the effective access time is 25 microseconds. The computer would be slowed down by a factor of 250 because of demand paging! If we want less than 10-percent degradation, we need

$$110 > 100 + 25{,}000{,}000 \times p,$$
$$10 > 25{,}000{,}000 \times p,$$
$$p < 0.0000004.$$

That is, to keep the slowdown due to paging to a reasonable level, we can allow only less than 1 memory access out of 2,500,000 to page fault.

It is important to keep the page-fault rate low in a demand-paging system. Otherwise, the effective access time increases, slowing process execution dramatically.

One additional aspect of demand paging is the handling and overall use of swap space. Disk I/O to swap space is generally faster than that to the file system. It is faster because swap space is allocated in much larger blocks, and file lookups and indirect allocation methods are not used (see Chapter 13). It is therefore possible for the system to gain better paging throughput, by copying an entire file image into the swap space at process startup, and then to perform demand paging from the swap space. Systems with limited swap space can employ a different scheme when binary files are used. Demand pages for such files are brought directly from the file system. However, when page replacement is called for, these pages can simply be overwritten (because they are never modified) and read in from the file system again if needed. Yet another option is initially to demand pages from the file system, but to write the pages to swap space as they are replaced. This approach will ensure that only needed pages are ever read from the file system, but all subsequent paging is done from swap space. This method appears to be a good compromise; it is used in BSD UNIX.

10.3 ■ Page Replacement

In our presentation so far, the page-fault rate has not been not a serious problem, because each page is faulted for at most once, when it is first referenced. This representation is not strictly accurate. Consider that, if a process of 10 pages actually uses only one-half of them, then demand paging saves the I/O necessary to load the five pages that are never used. We could also increase our degree of multiprogramming by running twice as many processes. Thus, if we had 40 frames, we could run eight processes, rather than the four that could run if each required 10 frames (five of which were never used).

If we increase our degree of multiprogramming, we are **over-allocating** memory. If we run six processes, each of which is 10 pages in size, but actually uses only five pages, we have higher CPU utilization and throughput, with 10 frames to spare. It is possible, however, that each of these processes, for a particular data set, may suddenly try to use all 10 of its pages, resulting in a need for 60 frames, when only 40 are available. Although this situation may be unlikely, it becomes much more likely as we increase the multiprogramming level, so that the average memory usage is close to the available physical memory. (In our example, why stop at a multiprogramming level of six, when we can move to a level of seven or eight?)

Further, consider that system memory is not used only for holding program pages. Buffers for I/O also consume a significant amount of memory. This use can increase the strain on memory-placement algorithms. Deciding how much memory to allocate to I/O and how much to program pages is a significant challenge. Some systems allocate a fixed percentage of memory for I/O buffers, whereas others allow both user processes and the I/O subsystem to compete for all system memory.

Over-allocation manifests itself as follows. While a user process is executing, a page fault occurs. The hardware traps to the operating system, which checks its internal tables to see that this page fault is a genuine one rather than an illegal memory access. The operating system determines where the desired page is residing on the disk, but then finds that there are *no* free frames on the free-frame list: All memory is in use (Figure 10.5).

The operating system has several options at this point. It could terminate the user process. However, demand paging is the operating system's attempt to improve the computer system's utilization and throughput. Users should not be aware that their processes are running on a paged system—paging should be logically transparent to the user. So this option is not the best choice.

We could swap out a process, freeing all its frames, and reducing the level of multiprogramming. This option is a good one in certain circumstances;

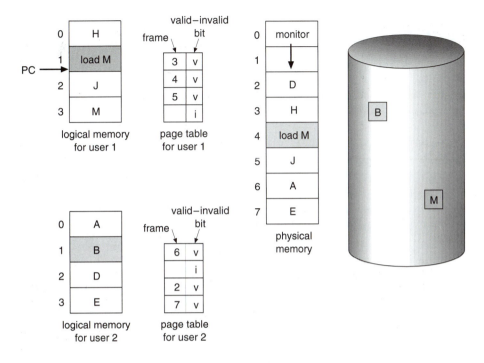

Figure 10.5   Need for page replacement.

we consider it further in Section 10.5. Here, we discuss a more intriguing possibility: **page replacement**.

10.3.1 Basic Scheme

Page replacement takes the following approach. If no frame is free, we find one that is not currently being used and free it. We can free a frame by writing its contents to swap space, and changing the page table (and all other tables) to indicate that the page is no longer in memory (Figure 10.6). We can now use the freed frame to hold the page for which the process faulted. We modify the page-fault service routine to include page replacement:

1. Find the location of the desired page on the disk.

2. Find a free frame:

    a. If there is a free frame, use it.

    b. If there is no free frame, use a page-replacement algorithm to select a **victim** frame.

c. Write the victim page to the disk; change the page and frame tables accordingly.

3. Read the desired page into the (newly) free frame; change the page and frame tables.

4. Restart the user process.

Notice that, if no frames are free, *two* page transfers (one out and one in) are required. This situation effectively doubles the page-fault service time and increases the effective access time accordingly.

We can reduce this overhead by using a **modify** (**dirty**) **bit**. Each page or frame may have a modify bit associated with it in the hardware. The modify bit for a page is set by the hardware whenever any word or byte in the page is written into, indicating that the page has been modified. When we select a page for replacement, we examine its modify bit. If the bit is set, we know that the page has been modified since it was read in from the disk. In this case, we must write that page to the disk. If the modify bit is not set, however, the page has *not* been modified since it was read into memory. Therefore, if the copy of the page on the disk has not been overwritten (by some other page, for example), then we can avoid writing the memory page to the disk; it is already there. This

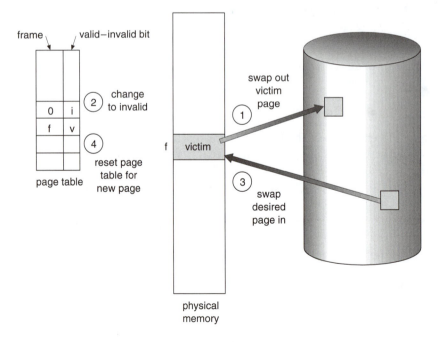

Figure 10.6   Page replacement.

technique also applies to read-only pages (for example, pages of binary code). Such pages cannot be modified; thus, they may be discarded when desired. This scheme can reduce significantly the time required to service a page fault, since it reduces I/O time by one-half *if* the page is not modified.

Page replacement is basic to demand paging. It completes the separation between logical memory and physical memory. With this mechanism, an enormous virtual memory can be provided for programmers on a smaller physical memory. With nondemand paging, user addresses are mapped into physical addresses, so the two sets of addresses can be different. All the pages of a process still must be in physical memory, however. With demand paging, the size of the logical address space is no longer constrained by physical memory. If we have a user process of 20 pages, we can execute it in 10 frames simply by using demand paging, and using a replacement algorithm to find a free frame whenever necessary. If a page that has been modified is to be replaced, its contents are copied to the disk. A later reference to that page will cause a page fault. At that time, the page will be brought back into memory, perhaps replacing some other page in the process.

We must solve two major problems to implement demand paging: We must develop a **frame-allocation algorithm** and a **page-replacement algorithm**. If we have multiple processes in memory, we must decide how many frames to allocate to each process. Further, when page replacement is required, we must select the frames that are to be replaced. Designing appropriate algorithms to solve these problems is an important task, because disk I/O is so expensive. Even slight improvements in demand-paging methods yield large gains in system performance.

There are many different page-replacement algorithms. Probably every operating system has its own unique replacement scheme. How do we select a particular replacement algorithm? In general, we want the one with the lowest **page-fault rate**.

We evaluate an algorithm by running it on a particular string of memory references and computing the number of page faults. The string of memory references is called a **reference string**. We can generate reference strings artificially (by a random-number generator, for example) or we can trace a given system and record the address of each memory reference. The latter choice produces a large number of data (on the order of 1 million addresses per second). To reduce the number of data, we use two facts.

First, for a given page size (and the page size is generally fixed by the hardware or system), we need to consider only the page number, rather than the entire address. Second, if we have a reference to a page *p*, then any *immediately* following references to page *p* will never cause a page fault. Page *p* will be in memory after the first reference; the immediately following references will not fault.

For example, if we trace a particular process, we might record the following address sequence:

0100, 0432, 0101, 0612, 0102, 0103, 0104, 0101, 0611, 0102, 0103,
0104, 0101, 0610, 0102, 0103, 0104, 0101, 0609, 0102, 0105,

which, at 100 bytes per page, is reduced to the following reference string

$$1, 4, 1, 6, 1, 6, 1, 6, 1, 6, 1.$$

To determine the number of page faults for a particular reference string and page-replacement algorithm, we also need to know the number of page frames available. Obviously, as the number of frames available increases, the number of page faults decreases. For the reference string considered previously, for example, if we had three or more frames, we would have only three faults, one fault for the first reference to each page. On the other hand, with only one frame available, we would have a replacement with every reference, resulting in 11 faults. In general, we expect a curve such as that in Figure 10.7. As the number of frames increases, the number of page faults drops to some minimal level. Of course, adding physical memory increases the number of frames.

To illustrate the page-replacement algorithms, we shall use the reference string

$$7, 0, 1, 2, 0, 3, 0, 4, 2, 3, 0, 3, 2, 1, 2, 0, 1, 7, 0, 1$$

for a memory with three frames.

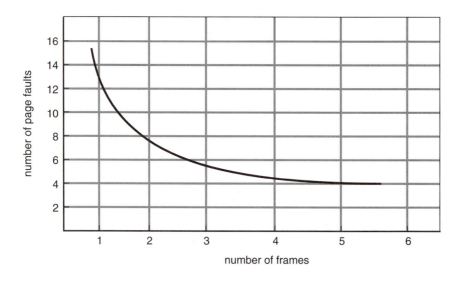

Figure 10.7   Graph of page faults versus the number of frames.

10.3.2 FIFO Page Replacement

The simplest page-replacement algorithm is a FIFO algorithm. A FIFO replacement algorithm associates with each page the time when that page was brought into memory. When a page must be replaced, the oldest page is chosen. Notice that it is not strictly necessary to record the time when a page is brought in. We can create a FIFO queue to hold all pages in memory. We replace the page at the head of the queue. When a page is brought into memory, we insert it at the tail of the queue.

For our example reference string, our three frames are initially empty. The first three references (7, 0, 1) cause page faults, and are brought into these empty frames. The next reference (2) replaces page 7, because page 7 was brought in first. Since 0 is the next reference and 0 is already in memory, we have no fault for this reference. The first reference to 3 results in page 0 being replaced, since it was the first of the three pages in memory (0, 1, and 2) to be brought in. Because of this replacement, the next reference, to 0, will fault. Page 1 is then replaced by page 0. This process continues as shown in Figure 10.8. Every time a fault occurs, we show which pages are in our three frames. There are 15 faults altogether.

The FIFO page-replacement algorithm is easy to understand and program. However, its performance is not always good. The page replaced may be an initialization module that was used a long time ago and is no longer needed. On the other hand, it could contain a heavily used variable that was initialized early and is in constant use.

Notice that, even if we select for replacement a page that is in active use, everything still works correctly. After we page out an active page to bring in a new one, a fault occurs almost immediately to retrieve the active page. Some other page will need to be replaced to bring the active page back into memory. Thus, a bad replacement choice increases the page-fault rate and slows process execution, but does not cause incorrect execution.

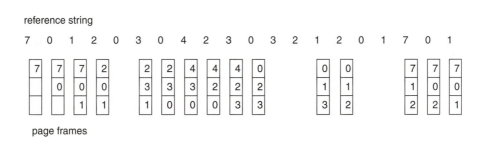

Figure 10.8 FIFO page-replacement algorithm.

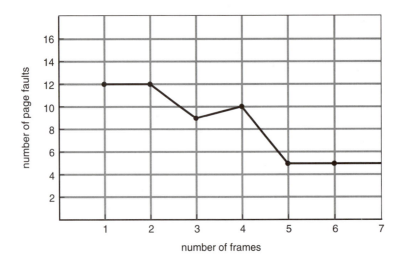

Figure 10.9 Page-fault curve for FIFO replacement on a reference string.

To illustrate the problems that are possible with a FIFO page-replacement algorithm, we consider the reference string

$$1, 2, 3, 4, 1, 2, 5, 1, 2, 3, 4, 5.$$

Figure 10.9 shows the curve of page faults versus the number of available frames. We notice that the number of faults for four frames (10) is *greater* than the number of faults for three frames (nine)! This most unexpected result is known as **Belady's anomaly:** For some page-replacement algorithms, the page-fault rate may *increase* as the number of allocated frames increases. We would expect that giving more memory to a process would improve its performance. In some early research, investigators noticed that this assumption was not always true. Belady's anomaly was discovered as a result.

10.3.3 Optimal Page Replacement

One result of the discovery of Belady's anomaly was the search for an **optimal** page-replacement algorithm. An optimal page-replacement algorithm has the lowest page-fault rate of all algorithms. An optimal algorithm will never suffer from Belady's anomaly. An optimal page-replacement algorithm exists, and has been called OPT or MIN. It is simply

> Replace the page that will not be used
> for the longest period of time.

Use of this page-replacement algorithm guarantees the lowest possible page-fault rate for a fixed number of frames.

reference string

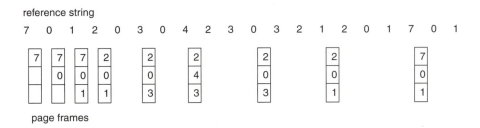

Figure 10.10   Optimal page-replacement algorithm.

For example, on our sample reference string, the optimal page-replacement algorithm would yield nine page faults, as shown in Figure 10.10. The first three references cause faults that fill the three empty frames. The reference to page 2 replaces page 7, because 7 will not be used until reference 18, whereas page 0 will be used at 5, and page 1 at 14. The reference to page 3 replaces page 1, as page 1 will be the last of the three pages in memory to be referenced again. With only nine page faults, optimal replacement is much better than a FIFO algorithm, which had 15 faults. (If we ignore the first three, which all algorithms must suffer, then optimal replacement is twice as good as FIFO replacement.) In fact, no replacement algorithm can process this reference string in three frames with less than nine faults.

Unfortunately, the optimal page-replacement algorithm is difficult to implement, because it requires future knowledge of the reference string. (We encountered a similar situation with the SJF CPU-scheduling algorithm in Section 6.3.2.) As a result, the optimal algorithm is used mainly for comparison studies. For instance, it may be useful to know that, although a new algorithm is not optimal, it is within 12.3 percent of optimal at worst and within 4.7 percent on average.

10.3.4 LRU Page Replacement

If the optimal algorithm is not feasible, perhaps an approximation to the optimal algorithm is possible.   The key distinction between the FIFO and OPT algorithms (other than looking backward or forward in time) is that the FIFO algorithm uses the time when a page was brought into memory; the OPT algorithm uses the time when a page is to be *used*. If we use the recent past as an approximation of the near future, then we will replace the page that *has not been used* for the longest period of time (Figure 10.11). This approach is the **least recently used (LRU)** algorithm.

LRU replacement associates with each page the time of that page's last use. When a page must be replaced, LRU chooses that page that has not been used for the longest period of time. This strategy is the optimal page-replacement algorithm looking backward in time, rather than forward. (Strangely, if we

reference string

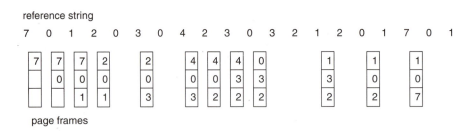

Figure 10.11   LRU page-replacement algorithm.

let S^R be the reverse of a reference string S, then the page-fault rate for the OPT algorithm on S is the same as the page-fault rate for the OPT algorithm on S^R. Similarly, the page-fault rate for the LRU algorithm on S is the same as the page-fault rate for the LRU algorithm on S^R.)

The result of applying LRU replacement to our example reference string is shown in Figure 10.11. The LRU algorithm produces 12 faults. Notice that the first five faults are the same as the optimal replacement. When the reference to page 4 occurs, however, LRU replacement sees that, of the three frames in memory, page 2 was used least recently. The most recently used page is page 0, and just before that page 3 was used. Thus, the LRU algorithm replaces page 2, not knowing that page 2 is about to be used. When it then faults for page 2, the LRU algorithm replaces page 3 since, of the three pages in memory {0, 3, 4}, page 3 is the least recently used. Despite these problems, LRU replacement with 12 faults is still much better than FIFO replacement with 15.

The LRU policy is often used as a page-replacement algorithm and is considered to be good. The major problem is *how* to implement LRU replacement. An LRU page-replacement algorithm may require substantial hardware assistance. The problem is to determine an order for the frames defined by the time of last use. Two implementations are feasible:

- *Counters:* In the simplest case, we associate with each page-table entry a time-of-use field, and add to the CPU a logical clock or counter. The clock is incremented for every memory reference. Whenever a reference to a page is made, the contents of the clock register are copied to the time-of-use field in the page-table entry for that page. In this way, we always have the "time" of the last reference to each page. We replace the page with the smallest time value. This scheme requires a search of the page table to find the LRU page, and a write to memory (to the time-of-use field in the page table) for each memory access. The times must also be maintained when page tables are changed (due to CPU scheduling). Overflow of the clock must be considered.

- *Stack:* Another approach to implementing LRU replacement is to keep a **stack** of page numbers. Whenever a page is referenced, it is removed from the stack and put on the top. In this way, the top of the stack is always the most recently used page and the bottom is the LRU page (Figure 10.12). Because entries must be removed from the middle of the stack, it is best implemented by a doubly linked list, with a head and tail pointer. Removing a page and putting it on the top of the stack then requires changing six pointers at worst. Each update is a little more expensive, but there is no search for a replacement; the tail pointer points to the bottom of the stack, which is the LRU page. This approach is particularly appropriate for software or microcode implementations of LRU replacement.

Neither optimal replacement nor LRU replacement suffers from Belady's anomaly. There is a class of page-replacement algorithms, called **stack algorithms,** that can never exhibit Belady's anomaly. A stack algorithm is an algorithm for which it can be shown that the set of pages in memory for n frames is always a *subset* of the set of pages that would be in memory with $n + 1$ frames. For LRU replacement, the set of pages in memory would be the n most recently referenced pages. If the number of frames is increased, these n pages will still be the most recently referenced and so will still be in memory.

Note that neither implementation of LRU would be conceivable without hardware assistance beyond the standard TLB registers. The updating of the clock fields or stack must be done for *every* memory reference. If we were to use an interrupt for every reference, to allow software to update such data structures, it would slow every memory reference by a factor of at least 10, hence slowing every user process by a factor of 10. Few systems could tolerate that level of overhead for memory management.

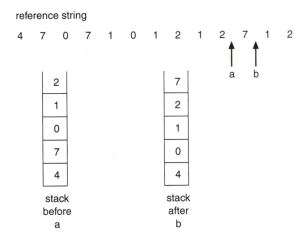

Figure 10.12   Use of a stack to record the most recent page references.

10.3.5 LRU Approximation Page Replacement

Few computer systems provide sufficient hardware support for true LRU page replacement. Some systems provide no hardware support, and other page-replacement algorithms (such as a FIFO algorithm) must be used. Many systems provide some help, however, in the form of a **reference bit**. The reference bit for a page is set, by the hardware, whenever that page is referenced (either a read or a write to any byte in the page). Reference bits are associated with each entry in the page table.

Initially, all bits are cleared (to 0) by the operating system. As a user process executes, the bit associated with each page referenced is set (to 1) by the hardware. After some time, we can determine which pages have been used and which have not been used by examining the reference bits. We do not know the *order* of use, but we know which pages were used and which were not used. This partial ordering information leads to many page-replacement algorithms that approximate LRU replacement.

10.3.5.1 Additional-Reference-Bits Algorithm

We can gain additional ordering information by recording the reference bits at regular intervals. We can keep an 8-bit byte for each page in a table in memory. At regular intervals (say, every 100 milliseconds), a timer interrupt transfers control to the operating system. The operating system shifts the reference bit for each page into the high-order bit of its 8-bit byte, shifting the other bits right 1 bit, discarding the low-order bit. These 8-bit shift registers contain the history of page use for the last eight time periods. If the shift register contains 00000000, then the page has not been used for eight time periods; a page that is used at least once each period would have a shift register value of 11111111.

A page with a history register value of 11000100 has been used more recently than has one with 01110111. If we interpret these 8-bit bytes as unsigned integers, the page with the lowest number is the LRU page, and it can be replaced. Notice that the numbers are not guaranteed to be unique, however. We can either replace (swap out) all pages with the smallest value, or use a FIFO selection among them.

The number of bits of history can be varied, of course, and would be selected (depending on the hardware available) to make the updating as fast as possible. In the extreme case, the number can be reduced to zero, leaving only the reference bit itself. This algorithm is called the **second-chance page-replacement algorithm**.

10.3.5.2 Second-Chance Algorithm

The basic algorithm of second-chance replacement is a FIFO replacement algorithm. When a page has been selected, however, we inspect its reference bit. If the value is 0, we proceed to replace this page. If the reference bit is 1, however, we give that page a second chance and move on to select the next FIFO page.

When a page gets a second chance, its reference bit is cleared and its arrival time is reset to the current time. Thus, a page that is given a second chance will not be replaced until all other pages are replaced (or given second chances). In addition, if a page is used often enough to keep its reference bit set, it will never be replaced.

One way to implement the second-chance (sometimes referred to as the clock) algorithm is as a circular queue. A pointer indicates which page is to be replaced next. When a frame is needed, the pointer advances until it finds a page with a 0 reference bit. As it advances, it clears the reference bits (Figure 10.13). Once a victim page is found, the page is replaced, and the new page is inserted in the circular queue in that position. Notice that, in the worst case, when all bits are set, the pointer cycles through the whole queue, giving each page a second chance. It clears all the reference bits before selecting the next page for replacement. Second-chance replacement degenerates to FIFO replacement if all bits are set.

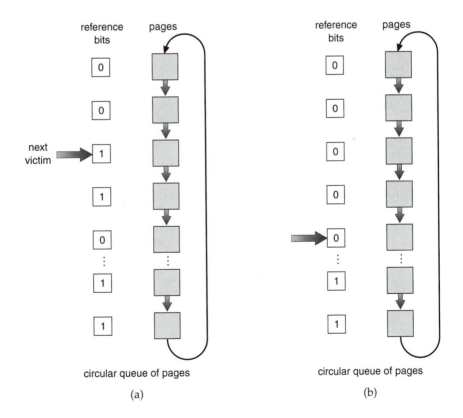

(a)   (b)

Figure 10.13   Second-chance (clock) page-replacement algorithm.

10.3.5.3 Enhanced Second-Chance Algorithm

We can enhance the second-chance algorithm by considering both the reference bit and the modify bit (Section 10.3) as an ordered pair. With these two bits, we have the following four possible classes:

1. (0, 0) neither recently used nor modified—best page to replace

2. (0, 1) not recently used but modified—not quite as good, because the page will need to be written out before replacement

3. (1, 0) recently used but clean—it probably will be used again soon

4. (1, 1) recently used and modified—it probably will be used again soon, and the page will be need to be written out to disk before it can be replaced

When page replacement is called for, each page is in one of these four classes. We use the same scheme as the clock algorithm, but instead of examining whether the page to which we are pointing has the reference bit set to 1, we examine the class to which that page belongs. We replace the first page encountered in the lowest nonempty class. Notice that we may have to scan the circular queue several times before we find a page to be replaced.

This algorithm is used in the Macintosh virtual-memory-management scheme. The major difference between this algorithm and the simpler clock algorithm is that here we give preference to those pages that have been modified to reduce the number of I/Os required.

10.3.6 Counting-Based Page Replacement

There are many other algorithms that can be used for page replacement. For example, we could keep a counter of the number of references that have been made to each page, and develop the following two schemes.

- The **least frequently used (LFU) page-replacement algorithm** requires that the page with the smallest count be replaced. The reason for this selection is that an actively used page should have a large reference count. This algorithm suffers from the situation in which a page is used heavily during the initial phase of a process, but then is never used again. Since it was used heavily, it has a large count and remains in memory even though it is no longer needed. One solution is to shift the counts right by 1 bit at regular intervals, forming an exponentially decaying average usage count.

- The **most frequently used (MFU) page-replacement algorithm** is based on the argument that the page with the smallest count was probably just brought in and has yet to be used.

As you might expect, neither MFU nor LFU replacement is common. The implementation of these algorithms is expensive, and they do not approximate OPT replacement well.

10.3.7 Page-Buffering Algorithm

Other procedures are often used in addition to a specific page-replacement algorithm. For example, systems commonly keep a **pool** of free frames. When a page fault occurs, a victim frame is chosen as before. However, the desired page is read into a free frame from the pool before the victim is written out. This procedure allows the process to restart as soon as possible, without waiting for the victim page to be written out. When the victim is later written out, its frame is added to the free-frame pool.

An expansion of this idea is to maintain a list of modified pages. Whenever the paging device is idle, a modified page is selected and is written to the disk. Its modify bit is then reset. This scheme increases the probability that a page will be clean when it is selected for replacement, and will not need to be written out.

Another modification is to keep a pool of free frames, but to remember which page was in each frame. Since the frame contents are not modified when a frame is written to the disk, the old page can be reused directly from the free-frame pool if it is needed before that frame is reused. No I/O is needed in this case. When a page fault occurs, we first check whether the desired page is in the free-frame pool. If it is not, we must select a free frame and read into it.

This technique is used in the VAX/VMS system, with a FIFO replacement algorithm. When the FIFO replacement algorithm mistakenly replaces a page that is still in active use, that page is quickly retrieved from the free-frame buffer, and no I/O is necessary. The free-frame buffer provides protection against the relatively poor, but simple, FIFO replacement algorithm. This method is necessary because the early versions of the VAX did not implement the reference bit correctly.

10.4 ■ Allocation of Frames

How do we allocate the fixed amount of free memory among the various processes? If we have 93 free frames and two processes, how many frames does each process get?

The simplest case of virtual memory is the single-user system. Consider a single-user system with 128K memory composed of pages of size 1K. Thus, there are 128 frames. The operating system may take 35K, leaving 93 frames for the user process. Under pure demand paging, all 93 frames would initially be put on the free-frame list. When a user process started execution, it would generate a sequence of page faults. The first 93 page faults would all get free frames from the free-frame list. When the free-frame list was exhausted, a page-replacement algorithm would be used to select one of the 93 in-memory pages to be replaced with the ninety-fourth, and so on. When the process terminated, the 93 frames would once again be placed on the free-frame list.

There are many variations on this simple strategy. We can require that the operating system allocate all its buffer and table space from the free-frame list. When this space is not in use by the operating system, it can be used to support user paging. We can try to keep three free frames reserved on the free-frame list at all times. Thus, when a page fault occurs, there is a free frame available to page into. While the page swap is taking place, a replacement can be selected, which is then written to the disk as the user process continues to execute.

Other variants are also possible, but the basic strategy is clear: The user process is allocated any free frame.

A different problem arises when demand paging is combined with multi-programming. Multiprogramming puts two (or more) processes in memory at the same time.

10.4.1 Minimum Number of Frames

There are, of course, various constraints on our strategies for the allocations of frames. We cannot allocate more than the total number of available frames (unless there is page sharing). There is also a minimum number of frames that can be allocated. Obviously, as the number of frames allocated to each process decreases, the page fault-rate increases, slowing process execution.

Besides the undesirable performance properties of allocating only a few frames, there is a minimum number of frames that must be allocated. This minimum number is defined by the instruction-set architecture. Remember that, when a page fault occurs before an executing instruction is complete, the instruction must be restarted. Consequently, we must have enough frames to hold all the different pages that any single instruction can reference.

For example, consider a machine in which all memory-reference instructions have only one memory address. Thus, we need at least one frame for the instruction and one frame for the memory reference. In addition, if one-level indirect addressing is allowed (for example, a load instruction on page 16 can refer to an address on page 0, which is an indirect reference to page 23), then paging requires at least three frames per process. Think about what might happen if a process had only two frames.

The minimum number of frames is defined by the computer architecture. For example, the move instruction for the PDP-11 is more than one word for some addressing modes, and thus the instruction itself may straddle two pages. In addition, each of its two operands may be indirect references, for a total of six frames. The worst case for the IBM 370 is probably the MVC instruction. Since the instruction is storage to storage, it takes 6 bytes and can straddle two pages. The block of characters to move and the area to be moved to can each also straddle two pages. This situation would require six frames. (Actually, the worst case occurs when the MVC instruction is the operand of an EXECUTE instruction that straddles a page boundary; in this case, we need eight frames.)

The worst-case scenario occurs in architectures that allow multiple levels of indirection (for example, each 16-bit word could contain a 15-bit address plus a 1-bit indirect indicator). Theoretically, a simple load instruction could reference an indirect address that could reference an indirect address (on another page) that could also reference an indirect address (on yet another page), and so on, until every page in virtual memory had been touched. Thus, in the worst case, the entire virtual memory must be in physical memory. To overcome this difficulty, we must place a limit on the levels of indirection (for example, limit an instruction to at most 16 levels of indirection). When the first indirection occurs, a counter is set to 16; the counter is then decremented for each successive indirection for this instruction. If the counter is decremented to 0, a trap occurs (excessive indirection). This limitation reduces the maximum number of memory references per instruction to 17, requiring the same number of frames.

The minimum number of frames per process is defined by the architecture, whereas the maximum number is defined by the amount of available physical memory. In between, we are still left with significant choice in frame allocation.

10.4.2 Allocation Algorithms

The easiest way to split m frames among n processes is to give everyone an equal share, m/n frames. For instance, if there are 93 frames and five processes, each process will get 18 frames. The leftover 3 frames could be used as a free-frame buffer pool. This scheme is called **equal allocation**.

An alternative is to recognize that various processes will need differing amounts of memory. Consider a system with a 1K frame size. If a small student process of 10K and an interactive database of 127K are the only two processes running in a system with 62 free frames, it does not make much sense to give each process 31 frames. The student process does not need more than 10 frames, so the other 21 are strictly wasted.

To solve this problem, we can use **proportional allocation**. We allocate available memory to each process according to its size. Let the size of the virtual memory for process p_i be s_i, and define

$$S = \sum s_i.$$

Then, if the total number of available frames is m, we allocate a_i frames to process p_i, where a_i is approximately

$$a_i = s_i/S \times m.$$

Of course, we must adjust each a_i to be an integer, which is greater than the minimum number of frames required by the instruction set, with a sum not exceeding m.

For proportional allocation, we would split 62 frames between two processes, one of 10 pages and one of 127 pages, by allocating 4 frames and 57 frames, respectively, since

$$10/137 \times 62 \approx 4,$$
$$127/137 \times 62 \approx 57.$$

In this way, both processes share the available frames according to their "needs," rather than equally.

In both equal and proportional allocation, of course, the allocation to each process may vary according to the multiprogramming level. If the multiprogramming level is increased, each process will lose some frames to provide the memory needed for the new process. On the other hand, if the multiprogramming level decreases, the frames that had been allocated to the departed process can now be spread over the remaining processes.

Notice that, with either equal or proportional allocation, a high-priority process is treated the same as a low-priority process. By its definition, however, we may want to give the high-priority process more memory to speed its execution, to the detriment of low-priority processes.

One approach is to use a proportional allocation scheme where the ratio of frames depends not on the relative sizes of processes, but rather on the processes' priorities, or on a combination of size and priority.

10.4.3 Global Versus Local Allocation

Another important factor in the way frames are allocated to the various processes is page replacement. With multiple processes competing for frames, we can classify page-replacement algorithms into two broad categories: **global replacement** and **local replacement**. Global replacement allows a process to select a replacement frame from the set of all frames, even if that frame is currently allocated to some other process; one process can take a frame from another. Local replacement requires that each process select from only its own set of allocated frames.

For example, consider an allocation scheme where we allow high-priority processes to select frames from low-priority processes for replacement. A process can select a replacement from among its own frames or the frames of any lower-priority process. This approach allows a high-priority process to increase its frame allocation at the expense of the low-priority process.

With a local replacement strategy, the number of frames allocated to a process does not change. With global replacement, a process may happen to select only frames allocated to other processes, thus increasing the number of frames allocated to it (assuming that other processes do not choose *its* frames for replacement).

One problem with a global replacement algorithm is that a process cannot control its own page-fault rate. The set of pages in memory for a process depends not only on the paging behavior of that process, but also on the paging behavior of other processes. Therefore, the same process may perform quite differently (taking 0.5 seconds for one execution and 10.3 seconds for the next execution) due to totally external circumstances. Such is not the case with a local replacement algorithm. Under local replacement, the set of pages in memory for a process is affected by the paging behavior of only that process. For its part, local replacement might hinder a process by not making available to it other, less used pages of memory. Thus, global replacement generally results in greater system throughput, and is therefore the more common method.

10.5 ■ Thrashing

If the number of frames allocated to a low-priority process falls below the minimum number required by the computer architecture, we must suspend that process' execution. We should then page out its remaining pages, freeing all its allocated frames. This provision introduces a swap-in, swap-out level of intermediate CPU scheduling.

In fact, look at any process that does not have "enough" frames. Although it is technically possible to reduce the number of allocated frames to the minimum, there is some (larger) number of pages in active use. If the process does not have this number of frames, it will quickly page fault. At this point, it must replace some page. However, since all its pages are in active use, it must replace a page that will be needed again right away. Consequently, it quickly faults again, and again, and again. The process continues to fault, replacing pages for which it then faults and brings back in right away.

This high paging activity is called **thrashing**. A process is thrashing if it is spending more time paging than executing.

10.5.1 Cause of Thrashing

Thrashing results in severe performance problems. Consider the following scenario, which is based on the actual behavior of early paging systems.

The operating system monitors CPU utilization. If CPU utilization is too low, we increase the degree of multiprogramming by introducing a new process to the system. A global page-replacement algorithm is used; it replaces pages with no regard to the process to which they belong. Now suppose that a process enters a new phase in its execution and needs more frames. It starts faulting and taking frames away from other processes. These processes need those pages, however, and so they also fault, taking frames from other processes. These faulting processes must use the paging device to swap pages in and out. As they queue up for the paging device, the ready queue empties. As processes wait for the paging device, CPU utilization decreases.

The CPU scheduler sees the decreasing CPU utilization, and *increases* the degree of multiprogramming as a result. The new process tries to get started by taking frames from running processes, causing more page faults, and a longer queue for the paging device. As a result, CPU utilization drops even further, and the CPU scheduler tries to increase the degree of multiprogramming even more. Thrashing has occurred and system throughput plunges. The page-fault rate increases tremendously. As a result, the effective memory access time increases. No work is getting done, because the processes are spending all their time paging.

This phenomenon is illustrated in Figure 10.14, in which CPU utilization is plotted against the degree of multiprogramming. As the degree of multi-programming increases, CPU utilization also increases, although more slowly, until a maximum is reached. If the degree of multiprogramming is increased even further, thrashing sets in and CPU utilization drops sharply. At this point, to increase CPU utilization and stop thrashing, we must *decrease* the degree of multiprogramming.

We can limit the effects of thrashing by using a **local** (or **priority**) **replacement algorithm**. With local replacement, if one process starts thrashing, it cannot steal frames from another process and cause the latter to thrash also. Pages are replaced with regard to the process of which they are a part. However, if processes are thrashing, they will be in the queue for the paging device most of the time. The average service time for a page fault will increase, due to the longer average queue for the paging device. Thus, the effective access time will increase even for a process that is not thrashing.

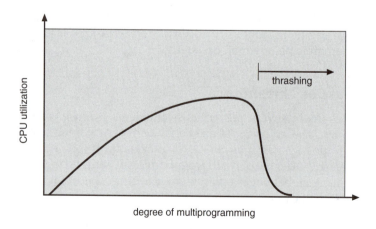

Figure 10.14   Thrashing.

To prevent thrashing, we must provide a process as many frames as it needs. But how do we know how many frames it "needs"? There are several techniques. The working-set strategy (discussed in Section 10.5.2) starts by looking at how many frames a process is actually using. This approach defines the **locality model** of process execution.

The locality model states that, as a process executes, it moves from locality to locality. A locality is a set of pages that are actively used together (Figure 10.15). A program is generally composed of several different localities, which may overlap.

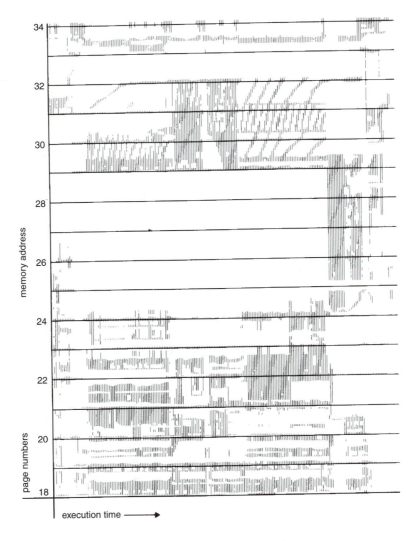

Figure 10.15 Locality in a memory-reference pattern.

For example, when a subroutine is called, it defines a new locality. In this locality, memory references are made to the instructions of the subroutine, its local variables, and a subset of the global variables. When the subroutine is exited, the process leaves this locality, since the local variables and instructions of the subroutine are no longer in active use. We may return to this locality later. Thus, we see that localities are defined by the program structure and its data structures. The locality model states that all programs will exhibit this basic memory reference structure. Note that the locality model is the unstated principle behind the caching discussions so far in this book. If accesses to any types of data were random rather than patterned, caching would be useless.

Suppose that we allocate enough frames to a process to accommodate its current locality. It will fault for the pages in its locality until all these pages are in memory; then, it will not fault again until it changes localities. If we allocate fewer frames than the size of the current locality, the process will thrash, since it cannot keep in memory all the pages that it is actively using.

10.5.2 Working-Set Model

The **working-set model** is based on the assumption of locality. This model uses a parameter, Δ, to define the **working-set window**. The idea is to examine the most recent Δ page references. The set of pages in the most recent Δ page references is the **working set** (Figure 10.16). If a page is in active use, it will be in the working set. If it is no longer being used, it will drop from the working set Δ time units after its last reference. Thus, the working set is an approximation of the program's locality.

For example, given the sequence of memory references shown in Figure 10.16, if $\Delta = 10$, then the working set at time t_1 is $\{1, 2, 5, 6, 7\}$. By time t_2, the working set has changed to $\{3, 4\}$.

The accuracy of the working set depends on the selection of Δ. If Δ is too small, it will not encompass the entire locality; if Δ is too large, it may overlap several localities. In the extreme, if Δ is infinite, the working set is the set of pages touched during the process execution.

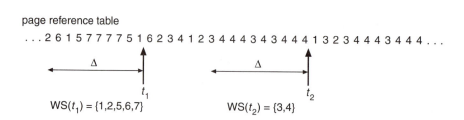

page reference table

. . . 2 6 1 5 7 7 7 7 5 1 6 2 3 4 1 2 3 4 4 4 3 4 3 4 4 4 1 3 2 3 4 4 4 3 4 4 4 . . .

Δ t_1 Δ t_2

$WS(t_1) = \{1, 2, 5, 6, 7\}$ $WS(t_2) = \{3, 4\}$

Figure 10.16   Working-set model.

The most important property of the working set is its size. If we compute the working-set size, WSS_i, for each process in the system, we can then consider

$$D = \sum WSS_i,$$

where D is the total demand for frames. Each process is actively using the pages in its working set. Thus, process i needs WSS_i frames. If the total demand is greater than the total number of available frames ($D > m$), thrashing will occur, because some processes will not have enough frames.

Use of the working-set model is then simple. The operating system monitors the working set of each process and allocates to that working set enough frames to provide it with its working-set size. If there are enough extra frames, another process can be initiated. If the sum of the working-set sizes increases, exceeding the total number of available frames, the operating system selects a process to suspend. The process' pages are written out and its frames are reallocated to other processes. The suspended process can be restarted later.

This working-set strategy prevents thrashing while keeping the degree of multiprogramming as high as possible. Thus, it optimizes CPU utilization.

The difficulty with the working-set model is keeping track of the working set. The working-set window is a moving window. At each memory reference, a new reference appears at one end and the oldest reference drops off the other end. A page is in the working set if it is referenced anywhere in the working-set window. We can approximate the working-set model with a fixed interval timer interrupt and a reference bit.

For example, assume Δ is 10,000 references and we can cause a timer interrupt every 5000 references. When we get a timer interrupt, we copy and clear the reference-bit values for each page. Thus, if a page fault occurs, we can examine the current reference bit and 2 in-memory bits to determine whether a page was used within the last 10,000 to 15,000 references. If it was used, at least 1 of these bits will be on. If it has not been used, these bits will be off. Those pages with at least 1 bit on will be considered to be in the working set. Note that this arrangement is not entirely accurate, because we cannot tell where, within an interval of 5000, a reference occurred. We can reduce the uncertainty by increasing the number of our history bits and the frequency of interrupts (for example, 10 bits and interrupts every 1000 references). However, the cost to service these more frequent interrupts will be correspondingly higher.

10.5.3 Page-Fault Frequency

The working-set model is successful, and knowledge of the working set can be useful for prepaging (Section 10.7.1), but it seems a clumsy way to control thrashing. A strategy that uses the **page-fault frequency** (PFF) takes a more direct approach.

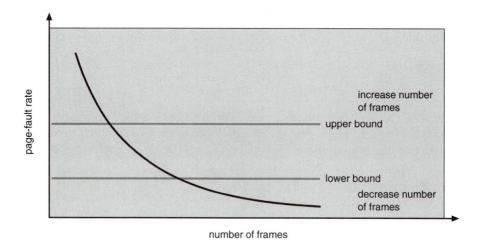

number of frames

Figure 10.17   Page-fault frequency.

The specific problem is how to prevent thrashing. Thrashing has a high page-fault rate. Thus, we want to control the page-fault rate. When it is too high, we know that the process needs more frames. Similarly, if the page-fault rate is too low, then the process may have too many frames. We can establish upper and lower bounds on the desired page-fault rate (Figure 10.17). If the actual page-fault rate exceeds the upper limit, we allocate that process another frame; if the page-fault rate falls below the lower limit, we remove a frame from that process. Thus, we can directly measure and control the page-fault rate to prevent thrashing.

As with the working-set strategy, we may have to suspend a process. If the page-fault rate increases and no free frames are available, we must select some process and suspend it. The freed frames are then distributed to processes with high page-fault rates.

10.6 ▪ Operating-System Examples

In this section we describe how Windows NT and Solaris 2 implement virtual memory.

10.6.1 Window NT

Windows NT implements virtual memory using demand paging with **clustering**. Clustering handles page faults by bringing in not only the faulting page, but also multiple pages surrounding the faulting page. When a process is first created, it is assigned a working-set minimum and maximum. The **working-set minimum** is the minimum number of pages the process is guaranteed to have in memory. If sufficient memory is available, a process may be assigned as many pages as its **working-set maximum**. The virtual-memory manager maintains a list of free page frames. Associated with this list is a threshold value that is used to indicate whether there is sufficient free memory available or not. If a page fault occurs for a process that is below its working-set maximum, the virtual-memory manager allocates a page from this list of free pages. If a process is at its working-set maximum and it incurs a page fault, it must select a page for replacement using a local, FIFO page-replacement policy. When the amount of free memory falls below the threshold, the virtual-memory manager uses a tactic known as **automatic working-set trimming** to restore the value above the threshold. Automatic working-set trimming works by evaluating the number of pages allocated to processes. If a process has been allocated more pages than its working-set minimum, the virtual-memory manager uses a FIFO algorithm to remove pages until the process reaches its working-set minimum. A process that is at its working-set minimum may be allocated pages from the free page frame list once sufficient free memory is available.

10.6.2 Solaris 2

When a process incurs a page fault, the kernel assigns a page to the faulting process from the list of free pages it maintains. Therefore, it is imperative that the kernel maintain a sufficient amount of free memory available. Associated with this list of free pages are two parameters—*minfree* and *lotsfree*—which are respectively low-water and high-water marks for available free memory. Four times per second, the kernel checks the amount of free memory. If that amount falls below *minfree*, a process known as **pageout** starts up. The pageout process is similar to the second-chance algorithm described in Section 10.3.5.2; it is also known as the **two-handed–clock algorithm**. It works as follows: The first hand of the clock scans all pages in memory setting the reference bit to 0. At a later point in time, the second hand of the clock examines the reference bit for the pages in memory, returning those pages whose bit is still set to 0 to the free list. The pageout process continues executing until the amount of free memory exceeds the *lotsfree* parameter. Furthermore, the pageout process is dynamic: It adjusts the speed of the hands of the clock if available memory gets too low. If the pageout process in unable to keep the amount of free memory at *lotsfree*, the kernel begins swapping processes, thereby freeing all pages allocated to the process.

10.7 ■ Other Considerations

The selections of a replacement algorithm and allocation policy are the major decisions that we make for a paging system. There are many other considerations as well.

10.7.1 Prepaging

An obvious property of a pure demand-paging system is the large number of page faults that occur when a process is started. This situation is a result of trying to get the initial locality into memory. The same situation may arise at other times. For instance, when a swapped-out process is restarted, all its pages are on the disk and each must be brought in by its own page fault. **Prepaging** is an attempt to prevent this high level of initial paging. The strategy is to bring into memory at one time all the pages that will be needed.

In a system using the working-set model, for example, we keep with each process a list of the pages in its working set. If we must suspend a process (due to an I/O wait or a lack of free frames), we remember the working set for that process. When the process is to be resumed (I/O completion or enough free frames), we automatically bring back into memory its entire working set before restarting the process.

Prepaging may be an advantage in some cases. The question is simply whether the cost of using prepaging is less than the cost of servicing the corresponding page faults. It may well be the case that many of the pages brought back into memory by prepaging are not used.

Assume that s pages are prepaged and a fraction α of these s pages are actually used ($0 \leq \alpha \leq 1$). The question is whether the cost of the $s * \alpha$ saved page faults is greater or less than the cost of prepaging $s * (1 - \alpha)$ unnecessary pages. If α is close to zero, prepaging loses; if α is close to one, prepaging wins.

10.7.2 Page Size

The designers of an operating system for an existing machine seldom have a choice concerning the page size. However, when new machines are being designed, a decision regarding the best page size must be made. As you might expect, there is no single best page size. Rather, there is a set of factors that support various sizes. Page sizes are invariably powers of 2, generally ranging from 4,096 (2^{12}) to 4,194,304 (2^{22}) bytes.

How do we select a page size? One concern is the size of the page table. For a given virtual-memory space, decreasing the page size increases the number of pages, and hence the size of the page table. For a virtual memory of 4 megabytes (2^{22}), there would be 4,096 pages of 1,024 bytes, but only 512 pages of 8,192 bytes. Because each active process must have its own copy of the page table, a large page size is desirable.

On the other hand, memory is better utilized with smaller pages. If a process is allocated memory starting at location 00000, continuing until it has as much as it needs, it probably will not end exactly on a page boundary. Thus, a part of the final page must be allocated (because pages are the units of allocation) but is unused (internal fragmentation). Assuming independence of process size and page size, we would expect that, on the average, one-half of the final page of each process will be wasted. This loss would be only 256 bytes for a page of 512 bytes, but would be 4,096 bytes for a page of 8,192 bytes. To minimize internal fragmentation, we need a small page size.

Another problem is the time required to read or write a page. I/O time is composed of seek, latency, and transfer times. Transfer time is proportional to the amount transferred (that is, the page size)— a fact that would seem to argue for a small page size. Remember from Chapter 2, however, that latency and seek time normally dwarf transfer time. At a transfer rate of 2 megabytes per second, it takes only 0.2 milliseconds to transfer 512 bytes. Latency, on the other hand, is perhaps 8 milliseconds and seek time 20 milliseconds. Of the total I/O time (28.2 milliseconds), therefore, 1 percent is attributable to the actual transfer. Doubling the page size increases I/O time to only 28.4 milliseconds. It takes 28.4 milliseconds to read a single page of 1,024 bytes, but 56.4 milliseconds to read the same amount as two pages of 512 bytes each. Thus, a desire to minimize I/O time argues for a larger page size.

With a smaller page size, however, total I/O should be reduced, since locality will be improved. A smaller page size allows each page to match program locality more accurately. For example, consider a process of size 200K, of which only one-half (100K) are actually used in an execution. If we have only one large page, we must bring in the entire page, a total of 200K transferred and allocated. If we had pages of only 1 byte, then we could bring in only the 100K that are actually used, resulting in only 100K being transferred and allocated. With a smaller page size, we have better **resolution,** allowing us to isolate only the memory that is actually needed. With a larger page size, we must allocate and transfer not only what is needed, but also anything else that happens to be in the page, whether it is needed or not. Thus, a smaller page size should result in less I/O and less total allocated memory.

On the other hand, did you notice that with a page size of 1 byte, we would have a page fault for *each* byte? A process of 200K, using only one-half of that memory, would generate only one page fault with a page size of 200K, but 102,400 page faults for a page size of 1 byte. Each page fault generates the large amount of overhead needed for processing the interrupt, saving registers, replacing a page, queueing for the paging device, and updating tables. To minimize the number of page faults, we need to have a large page size.

The historical trend is toward larger page sizes. Indeed, the first edition of the Operating Systems Concepts book (1983) used 4,096 bytes as the upper bound on page sizes, and this value was the most common page size in 1990. The Intel 80386 has a page size of 4K; the Pentium II allows page sizes to be either 4K or 4MB; the UltraSPARC allows either 8K, 64K, 512K, or 4MB page sizes. The evolution to larger page sizes is probably the result of CPU speeds and main memory capacity increasing faster than have disk speeds. Page faults are more costly today, in overall system performance, than previously. It is therefore advantageous to increase page sizes to reduce their frequency. Of course, there is more internal fragmentation as a result.

There are other factors to consider (such as the relationship between page size and sector size on the paging device). The problem has no best answer. Some factors (internal fragmentation, locality) argue for a small page size, whereas others (table size, I/O time) argue for a large page size.

10.7.3 Inverted Page Table

In Section 9.4.4, the concept of an inverted page table was introduced. The purpose of this form of page management was to reduce the amount of physical memory that is needed to track virtual-to-physical address translations. We accomplish this savings by creating a table that has one entry per physical memory page, indexed by the pair <process-id, page-number>.

Because they keep information about which virtual-memory page is stored in each physical frame, inverted page tables reduce the amount of physical memory needed to store this information. However, the inverted page table no longer contains complete information about the logical address space of a process, and that information is required if a referenced page is not currently in memory. Demand paging requires this information to process page faults. For this information to be available, an external page table (one per process) must be kept. Each such table looks like the traditional per-process page table, containing information on where each virtual page is located.

But do external page tables negate the utility of inverted page tables? Since these tables are referenced only when a page fault occurs, they do not need to be available quickly. Instead, they are themselves paged in and out of memory as necessary. Unfortunately, a page fault may now result in the virtual-memory manager causing another page fault as it pages in the external page table it needs to locate the virtual page on the backing store. This special case requires careful handling in the kernel and a delay in the page-lookup processing.

10.7.4 Program Structure

Demand paging is designed to be transparent to the user program. In many cases, the user is completely unaware of the paged nature of memory. In other cases, however, system performance can be improved if the user (or compiler) has an awareness of the underlying demand paging.

Let's look at a contrived but informative example. Assume that pages are 128 words in size. Consider a Java program whose function is to initialize to 0 each element of a 128 by 128 array. The following code is typical:

```
int A[][] = new int[128][128];

for (int j = 0; j < 128; j++)
    for (int i = 0; i < 128; i++)
        A[i][j] = 0;
```

Notice that the array is stored row major. That is, the array is stored A[0][0], A[0][1], $\cdots$, A[0][127], A[1][0], A[1][1], $\cdots$, A[127][127]. For pages of 128 words, each row takes one page. Thus, the preceding code zeros one word in each page, then another word in each page, and so on. If the operating system allocates less than 128 frames to the entire program, then its execution will result in $128 \times 128 = 16{,}384$ page faults. Changing the code to

```
int A[][] = new int[128][128];

for (int i = 0; i < 128; i++)
    for (int j = 0; j < 128; j++)
        A[i][j] = 0;
```

on the other hand, zeros all the words on one page before starting the next page, reducing the number of page faults to 128.

Careful selection of data structures and programming structures can increase locality and hence lower the page-fault rate and the number of pages in the working set. A stack has good locality, since access is always made to the top. A hash table, on the other hand, is designed to scatter references, producing bad locality. Of course, locality of reference is just one measure of the efficiency of the use of a data structure. Other heavily weighed factors include search speed, total number of memory references, and total number of pages touched.

At a later stage, the compiler and loader can have a significant effect on paging. Separating code and data and generating reentrant code means that code pages can be read only and hence will never be modified. Clean pages do not have to be paged out to be replaced. The loader can avoid placing routines across page boundaries, keeping each routine completely in one page. Routines that call each other many times can be packed into the same page. This packaging is a variant of the bin-packing problem of operations research: Try to pack the variable-sized load segments into the fixed-sized pages so that interpage references are minimized. Such an approach is particularly useful for large page sizes.

The choice of programming language can affect paging as well. For example, C and C++ use pointers frequently, and pointers tend to randomize access to memory. Contrast these langauges with Java, which does not provide pointers. Java programs will have better locality of reference than C or C++ programs on a virtual memory system.

10.7.5 I/O Interlock

When demand paging is used, we sometimes need to allow some of the pages to be **locked** in memory. One such situation occurs when I/O is done to or from user (virtual) memory. I/O is often implemented by a separate I/O processor. For example, a magnetic-tape controller is generally given the number of bytes to transfer and a memory address for the buffer (Figure 10.18). When the transfer is complete, the CPU is interrupted.

We must be sure the following sequence of events does not occur: A process issues an I/O request, and is put in a queue for that I/O device. Meanwhile, the CPU is given to other processes. These processes cause page faults, and, using a global replacement algorithm, one of them replaces the page containing the memory buffer for the waiting process. The pages are paged out. Some time later, when the I/O request advances to the head of the device queue, the I/O occurs to the specified address. However, this frame is now being used for a different page belonging to another process.

There are two common solutions to this problem. One solution is never to execute I/O to user memory. Instead, data are always copied between system memory and user memory. I/O takes place only between system memory and the I/O device. To write a block on tape, we first copy the block to system memory, and then write it to tape.

This extra copying may result in unacceptably high overhead. Another solution is to allow pages to be **locked** into memory. A lock bit is associated with every frame. If the frame is locked, it cannot be selected for replacement. Under this approach, to write a block on tape, we lock into memory the pages containing the block. The system can then continue as usual. Locked pages cannot be replaced. When the I/O is complete, the pages are unlocked.

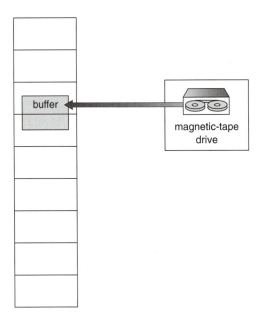

Figure 10.18   The reason why frames used for I/O must be in memory.

Frequently, some or all of the operating-system kernel is locked into memory. Most operating systems cannot tolerate a page fault caused by the kernel. Consider the result of the page-replacement routine causing a page fault.

Another use for a lock bit involves normal page replacement. Consider the following sequence of events. A low-priority process faults. Selecting a replacement frame, the paging system reads the necessary page into memory. Ready to continue, the low-priority process enters the ready queue and waits for the CPU. Since it is a low-priority process, it may not be selected by the CPU scheduler for a while. While the low-priority process waits, a high-priority process faults. Looking for a replacement, the paging system sees a page that is in memory but has not been referenced or modified: It is the page that the low-priority process just brought in. This page looks like a perfect replacement: It is clean and will not need to be written out, and it apparently has not been used for a long time.

Whether the high-priority process should be able to replace the low-priority process is a policy decision. After all, we are simply delaying the low-priority process for the benefit of the high-priority process. On the other hand, we are wasting the effort spent to bring in the page of the low-priority process. If we decide to prevent replacing a newly brought-in page until it can be used at least once, then we can use the lock bit to implement this mechanism. When a page is selected for replacement, its lock bit is turned on; it remains on until the faulting process is again dispatched.

Using a lock bit can be dangerous, however: The lock bit may get turned on but never turned off. Should this situation occur (due to a bug in the operating system, for example), the locked frame becomes unusable. The Macintosh Operating System provides a page-locking mechanism because it is a single-user system, and the overuse of locking would hurt only the user doing the locking. Multiuser systems must be less trusting of users. For instance, Solaris allows locking "hints," but it is free to disregard these hints if the free-frame pool becomes too small or if an individual process requests that too many pages be locked in memory.

10.7.6   Real-Time Processing

The discussions in this chapter have concentrated on providing the best overall utilization of a computer system by optimizing the use of memory. By using memory for active data, and moving inactive data to disk, we increase overall system throughput. However, individual processes may suffer as a result, because they now may take additional page faults during their execution.

Consider a real-time process or thread, as described in Chapter 4. Such a process expects to gain control of the CPU, and to run to completion with a minimum of delays. Virtual memory is the antithesis of real-time computing, because it can introduce unexpected, long-term delays in the execution of a process while pages are brought into memory. Therefore, real-time systems almost never have virtual memory.

In the case of Solaris 2, the developers at Sun Microsystems wanted to allow both time-sharing and real-time computing within a system. To solve the page-fault problem, they had Solaris 2 allow a process to tell it which pages are important to that process. In addition to allowing the hints on page use, the operating system allows privileged users to require pages to be locked into memory. If abused, this mechanism could lock all other processes out of the system. It is necessary to allow real-time processes to have bounded and low-dispatch latency.

10.8 ■ Summary

It is desirable to be able to execute a process whose logical address space is larger than the available physical address space. The programmer can make such a process executable by restructuring it using overlays, but doing so is generally a difficult programming task. Virtual memory is a technique to allow a large logical address space to be mapped onto a smaller physical memory. Virtual memory allows extremely large processes to be run, and also allows the degree of multiprogramming to be raised, increasing CPU utilization. Further, it frees application programmers from worrying about memory availability.

Pure demand paging never brings in a page until that page is referenced. The first reference causes a page fault to the operating-system resident monitor. The operating system consults an internal table to determine where the page is located on the backing store. It then finds a free frame and reads the page in from the backing store. The page table is updated to reflect this change, and the instruction that caused the page fault is restarted. This approach allows a process to run even though its entire memory image is not in main memory at once. As long as the page-fault rate is reasonably low, performance is acceptable.

We can use demand paging to reduce the number of frames allocated to a process. This arrangement can raise the degree of multiprogramming (allowing more processes to be available for execution at one time) and—in theory, at least—the CPU utilization of the system. It also allows processes to be run even though their memory requirements exceed the total available physical memory. Such processes run in virtual memory.

If total memory requirements exceed the physical memory, then it may be necessary to replace pages from memory to free frames for new pages. Various page-replacement algorithms are used. FIFO page replacement is easy to program, but suffers from Belady's anomaly. Optimal page replacement requires future knowledge. LRU replacement is an approximation of optimal, but even it may be difficult to implement. Most page-replacement algorithms, such as the second-chance algorithm, are approximations of LRU replacement.

In addition to a page-replacement algorithm, a frame-allocation policy is needed. Allocation can be fixed, suggesting local page replacement, or dynamic, suggesting global replacement. The working-set model assumes that processes execute in localities. The working set is the set of pages in the current locality. Accordingly, each process should be allocated enough frames for its current working set.

If a process does not have enough memory for its working set, it will thrash. Providing enough frames to each process to avoid thrashing may require process swapping and scheduling.

In addition to requiring that we solve the major problems of page replacement and frame allocation, the proper design of a paging system requires that we consider page size, I/O, locking, prepaging, program structure, and other topics. Virtual memory can be thought of as one level of a hierarchy of storage levels in a computer system. Each level has its own access time, size, and cost parameters. A full example of a hybrid, functional virtual-memory system is presented in the Mach chapter, which is available on our web site (http://www.bell-labs.com/topic/books/os-book).

■ Exercises

10.1 Under what circumstances do page faults occur? Describe the actions taken by the operating system when a page fault occurs.

10.2 Assume that you have a page-reference string for a process with m frames (initially all empty). The page-reference string has length p; n distinct page numbers occur in it. Answer these questions for any page-replacement algorithms:

   a. What is a lower bound on the number of page faults?

   b. What is an upper bound on the number of page faults?

10.3 A certain computer provides its users with a virtual-memory space of 2^{32} bytes. The computer has 2^{18} bytes of physical memory. The virtual memory is implemented by paging, and the page size is 4,096 bytes. A user process generates the virtual address 11123456. Explain how the system establishes the corresponding physical location. Distinguish between software and hardware operations.

10.4 Which of the following programming techniques and structures are "good" for a demand-paged environment? Which are "bad"? Explain your answers.

   a. Stack

   b. Hashed symbol table

    c. Sequential search

    d. Binary search

    e. Pure code

    f. Vector operations

    g. Indirection

10.5 Assume that we have a demand-paged memory. The page table is held in registers. It takes 8 milliseconds to service a page fault if an empty frame is available or if the replaced page is not modified, and 20 milliseconds if the replaced page is modified. Memory-access time is 100 nanoseconds.

    Assume that the page to be replaced is modified 70 percent of the time. What is the maximum acceptable page-fault rate for an effective access time of no more than 200 nanoseconds?

10.6 Consider the following page-replacement algorithms. Rank these algorithms on a five-point scale from "bad" to "perfect" according to their page-fault rate. Separate those algorithms that suffer from Belady's anomaly from those that do not.

    a. LRU replacement

    b. FIFO replacement

    c. Optimal replacement

    d. Second-chance replacement

10.7 When virtual memory is implemented in a computing system, it carries certain costs and certain benefits. List those costs and the benefits. It is possible for the costs to exceed the benefits. Explain what measures you can take to ensure that this imbalance does not occur.

10.8 An operating system supports a paged virtual memory, using a central processor with a cycle time of 1 microsecond. It costs an additional 1 microsecond to access a page other than the current one. Pages have 1000 words, and the paging device is a drum that rotates at 3000 revolutions per minute, and transfers 1 million words per second. The following statistical measurements were obtained from the system:

- 1 percent of all instructions executed accessed a page other than the current page.

- Of the instructions that accessed another page, 80 percent accessed a page already in memory.

- When a new page was required, the replaced page was modified 50 percent of the time.

Calculate the effective instruction time on this system, assuming that the system is running one process only, and that the processor is idle during drum transfers.

10.9 Consider a demand-paging system with the following time-measured utilizations:

CPU utilization	20%
Paging disk	97.7%
Other I/O devices	5%

For each of the following, say whether it will (or is likely to) improve CPU utilization. Explain your answers.

a. Install a faster CPU.

b. Install a bigger paging disk.

c. Increase the degree of multiprogramming.

d. Decrease the degree of multiprogramming.

e. Install more main memory.

f. Install a faster hard disk, or multiple controllers with multiple hard disks.

g. Add prepaging to the page-fetch algorithms.

h. Increase the page size.

10.10 Consider the two-dimensional array A:

```
int A[][] = new int[100][100];
```

where A[0][0] is at location 200, in a paged system with pages of size 200. A small process is in page 0 (locations 0 to 199) for manipulating the matrix; thus, every instruction fetch will be from page 0.

For three page frames, how many page faults are generated by the following array-initialization loops, using LRU replacement, and assuming page frame 1 has the process in it, and the other two are initially empty:

```
a. for (int j = 0; j < 100; j++)
     for (int i = 0; i < 100; i++)
        A[i][j] = 0;
```

```
b. for (int i = 0; i < 100; i++)
      for (int j = 0; j < 100; j++)
        A[i][j] = 0;
```

10.11 Consider the following page-reference string:

$$1, 2, 3, 4, 2, 1, 5, 6, 2, 1, 2, 3, 7, 6, 3, 2, 1, 2, 3, 6.$$

How many page faults would occur for the following replacement algorithms, assuming one, two, three, four, five, six, or seven frames? Remember that all frames are initially empty, so your first unique pages will all cost one fault each.

- LRU replacement
- FIFO replacement
- Optimal replacement

10.12 Suppose that you want to use a paging algorithm that requires a reference bit (such as second-chance replacement or working-set model), but the hardware does not provide one. Sketch how you could simulate a reference bit even if one were not provided by the hardware, or explain why it is not possible to do so. If it is possible, calculate what the cost would be.

10.13 You have devised a new page-replacement algorithm that you think may be optimal. In some contorted test cases, Belady's anomaly occurs. Is the new algorithm optimal? Explain your answer.

10.14 Suppose that your replacement policy (in a paged system) is to examine each page regularly and to discard that page if it has not been used since the last examination. What would you gain and what would you lose by using this policy rather than LRU or second-chance replacement?

10.15 Segmentation is similar to paging, but uses variable-sized "pages." Define two segment-replacement algorithms based on FIFO and LRU page-replacement schemes. Remember that, since segments are not the same size, the segment that is chosen to be replaced may not be big enough to leave enough consecutive locations for the needed segment. Consider strategies for systems where segments cannot be relocated, and those for systems where they can.

10.16 A page-replacement algorithm should minimize the number of page faults. We can do this minimization by distributing heavily used pages evenly over all of memory, rather than having them compete for a small number of page frames. We can associate with each page frame a counter of the number of pages that are associated with that frame. Then, to replace a page, we search for the page frame with the smallest counter.

    a. Define a page-replacement algorithm using this basic idea. Specifically address the problems of (1) what the initial value of the counters is, (2) when counters are increased, (3) when counters are decreased, and (4) how the page to be replaced is selected.

b. How many page faults occur for your algorithm for the following reference string, for four page frames?

$$1, 2, 3, 4, 5, 3, 4, 1, 6, 7, 8, 7, 8, 9, 7, 8, 9, 5, 4, 5, 4, 2.$$

c. What is the minimum number of page faults for an optimal page-replacement strategy for the reference string in part b with four page frames?

10.17 Consider a demand-paging system with a paging disk that has an average access and transfer time of 20 milliseconds. Addresses are translated through a page table in main memory, with an access time of 1 microsecond per memory access. Thus, each memory reference through the page table takes two accesses. To improve this time, we have added an associative memory that reduces access time to one memory reference, if the page-table entry is in the associative memory.

Assume that 80 percent of the accesses are in the associative memory, and that, of the remaining, 10 percent (or 2 percent of the total) cause page faults. What is the effective memory access time?

10.18 Consider a demand-paged computer system where the degree of multiprogramming is currently fixed at four. The system was recently measured to determine utilization of CPU and the paging disk. The results are one of the following alternatives. For each case, what is happening? Can you increase the degree of multiprogramming to increase the CPU utilization? Is the paging helping in improving performance?

a. CPU utilization, 13 percent; disk utilization, 97 percent

b. CPU utilization, 87 percent; disk utilization, 3 percent

c. CPU utilization, 13 percent; disk utilization, 3 percent

10.19 We have an operating system for a machine that uses base and limit registers, but we have modified the machine to provide a page table. Can we set up the page tables to simulate base and limit registers? How can we do so, or why can we not do so?

10.20 What is the cause of thrashing? How does the system detect thrashing? Once it detects thrashing, what can the system do to eliminate this problem?

10.21 Write a Java program that implements the FIFO and LRU page-replacement algorithms presented in this chapter.   First, generate a random page-reference string where page numbers range from 0 to 9. Apply the random page-reference string to each algorithm and record the number of page faults incurred by each algorithm. Implement the replacement algorithms such that the number of page frames can vary from 1 to 7. Assume that demand paging is used.

Bibliographical Notes

Demand paging was first used in the Atlas system, implemented on the Manchester University MUSE computer around 1960 [Kilburn et al. 1961]. Another early demand-paging system was MULTICS, implemented on the GE 645 system [Organick 1972].

Belady and colleagues [1969] were the first researchers to observe that the FIFO replacement strategy may have the anomaly that bears Belady's name. Mattson and colleagues [1970] demonstrated that stack algorithms are not subject to Belady's anomaly.

The optimal replacement algorithm was presented by Belady [1966]. It was proved to be optimal by Mattson and colleagues [1970]. Belady's optimal algorithm is for a fixed allocation; Prieve and Fabry [1976] have an optimal algorithm for situations where the allocation can vary.

The enhanced clock algorithm was discussed by Carr and Hennessy [1981]; it is used in the Macintosh virtual memory-management scheme, and was described by Goldman [1989].

The working-set model was developed by Denning [1968]. Discussions concerning the working-set model were presented by Denning [1980].

The scheme for monitoring the page-fault rate was developed by Wulf [1969], who successfully applied this technique to the Burroughs B5500 computer system. Gupta and Franklin [1978] provided a performance comparison between the working-set scheme and the page-fault-frequency replacement scheme.

Solomon [1998] describes how Windows NT implements virtual memory. Graham [1995] and Vahalia [1996] discuss virtual memory on Solaris. Details of OS/2 were described by Iacobucci [1988].

Good discussions are available for the Intel 80386 paging hardware [Intel 1986] and the Motorola 68030 hardware [Motorola 1989b]. Virtual-memory management in the VAX/VMS operating system was discussed by Levy and Lipman [1982]. Discussions concerning workstation operating systems and virtual memory were presented by Hagmann [1989]. A comparison of an implementation of virtual memory in the MIPS, PowerPC, and Pentium architectures can be found in Jacob and Mudge [1998a]. A companion article (Jacob and Mudge [1998b]) describes the hardware support necessary for implementation of virtual memory in six different architectures, including the UltraSPARC.

Chapter 11

FILE SYSTEMS

For most users, the file system is the most visible aspect of an operating system. It provides the mechanism for on-line storage of and access to both data and programs that belong to the operating system and to all the users of the computer system. The file system consists of two distinct parts: a collection of **files,** each storing related data, and a **directory structure,** which organizes and provides information about all the files in the system. In this chapter, we consider the various aspects of files, and the variety of directory structures. We also discuss ways to handle **file protection,** which is necessary in an environment where multiple users have access to files, and where it is usually desirable to control by whom and in what ways files may be accessed. We also discuss file storage and access on the most common secondary-storage medium, the disk. We explore ways to allocate disk space, to recover freed space, to track the locations of data, and to interface other parts of the operating system to secondary storage.

11.1 ■ File Concept

Computers can store information on several different storage media, such as magnetic disks, magnetic tapes, and optical disks. So that the computer system will be convenient to use, the operating system provides a uniform logical view of information storage. The operating system abstracts from the physical properties of its storage devices to define a logical storage unit, the *file*. Files are mapped, by the operating system, onto physical devices. These storage devices are usually *nonvolatile*, so the contents are persistent through power failures and system reboots.

A file is a named collection of related information that is recorded on secondary storage. From a user's perspective, a file is the smallest allotment of logical secondary storage; that is, data cannot be written to secondary storage unless they are within a file. Commonly, files represent programs (both source and object forms) and data. Data files may be numeric, alphabetic, alphanumeric, or binary. Files may be free-form, such as text files, or may be formatted rigidly. In general, a file is a sequence of bits, bytes, lines, or records whose meaning is defined by the file's creator and user. The concept of a file is thus extremely general.

The information in a file is defined by its creator. Many different types of information may be stored in a file: source programs, object programs, executable programs, numeric data, text, payroll records, graphic images, sound recordings, and so on. A file has a certain defined **structure** according to its type. A **text file** is a sequence of characters organized into lines (and possibly pages); a **source file** is a sequence of subroutines and functions, each of which is further organized as declarations followed by executable statements; an **object file** is a sequence of bytes organized into blocks understandable by the system's linker; an **executable file** is a series of code sections that the loader can bring into memory and execute. The internal structure of files is discussed in Section 11.1.5.

11.1.1 File Attributes

A file is named, for the convenience of its human users, and is referred to by its name. A name is usually a string of characters, such as "example.c". Some systems differentiate between upper- and lower-case characters in names, whereas other systems consider the two cases to be equivalent. When a file is named, it becomes independent of the process, of the user, and even of the system that created it. For instance, one user might create file "example.c", whereas another user might edit that file by specifying its name. The file's owner might write the file to a floppy disk or magnetic tape, and might read it off onto another system, where it could still be called "example.c".

A file has certain other attributes, which vary from one operating system to another, but typically consist of these:

- *Name*: The symbolic file name is the only information kept in human-readable form.

- *Type*: This information is needed for those systems that support different types.

- *Location*: This information is a pointer to a device and to the location of the file on that device.

- *Size*: The current size of the file (in bytes, words, or blocks), and possibly the maximum allowed size are included in this attribute.

- *Protection*: Access-control information controls who can do reading, writing, executing, and so on.

- *Time, date,* and *user identification*: This information may be kept for (1) creation, (2) last modification, and (3) last use. These data can be useful for protection, security, and usage monitoring.

The information about all files is kept in the directory structure that also resides on secondary storage. It may take from 16 to over 1000 bytes to record this information for each file. In a system with many files, the size of the directory itself may be megabytes. Because directories, like files, must be nonvolatile, they must be stored on the device and brought into memory piecemeal, as needed. We discuss the directory-structure organization in Section 11.3.

11.1.2 File Operations

A file is an **abstract data type**. To define files properly, we need to consider the operations that can be performed on them. The operating system provides system calls to create, write, read, reposition, delete, and truncate files. Let us consider what the operating system must do for each of the six basic file operations. It should then be easy to see how to implement similar operations, such as renaming a file.

- *Creating a file*: Two steps create a file. First, space in the file system must be found for the file. We discuss how to allocate space for the file in Chapter 11. Second, an entry for the new file must be made in the directory. The directory entry records the name of the file and the location in the file system.

- *Writing a file*: To write a file, we make a system call specifying both the name of the file and the information to be written to the file. Given the name of the file, the system searches the directory to find the location of the file. The system must keep a **write pointer** to the location in the file where the next write is to take place. The write pointer must be updated whenever a write occurs.

- *Reading a file*: To read from a file, we use a system call that specifies the name of the file and where (in memory) the next block of the file should be put. Again, the directory is searched for the associated directory entry, and the system keeps a **read pointer** to the location in the file where the next read is to take place. Once the read has taken place, the read pointer is updated. Since, in general, a file is either being read or written, most systems keep only one **current-file-position pointer**. Both the read and write operations use this same pointer, saving space and reducing the system complexity.

- *Repositioning within a file*: The directory is searched for the appropriate entry, and the current file position is set to a given value. Repositioning within a file does not need to involve any actual I/O. This file operation is also known as a **file seek**.

- *Deleting a file*: To delete a file, we search the directory for the named file. Having found the associated directory entry, we release all file space (so that it can be reused by other files) and erase the directory entry.

- *Truncating a file*: There are occasions when the user wants the attributes of a file to remain the same, but wants to erase the contents of the file. Rather than forcing the user to delete the file and then to recreate it, this function allows all attributes to remain unchanged (except for file length), but for the file to be reset to length zero.

These six basic operations certainly comprise the minimal set of required file operations. Other common operations include **appending** new information to the end of an existing file, and **renaming** an existing file. These primitive operations may then be combined to perform other file operations. For instance, we can create a **copy** of a file, or copy the file to another I/O device, such as a printer or a display, by creating a new file, then reading from the old and writing to the new. We also want to have operations that allow a user to get and set the various attributes of a file. For example, we may want to have an operation that allows a user to determine the status of a file, such as the file's length, and have an operation that allows a user to set file attributes, such as the file's owner.

Most of the file operations mentioned involve searching the directory for the entry associated with the named file. To avoid this constant searching, many systems will **open** a file when that file first is used actively. The operating system keeps a small table containing information about all open files: the **open-file table**. When a file operation is requested, an index into this table is used, so no searching is required. When the file is no longer actively used, it is **closed** by the process, and the operating system removes its entry in the open-file table.

Some systems implicitly open a file when the first reference is made to it. The file is automatically closed when the job or program that opened the file terminates. Most systems, however, require that a file be opened explicitly by the programmer with a system call (open) before that file can be used. The open operation takes a file name and searches the directory, copying the directory entry into the open-file table, assuming the file protections allow such access. The open system call will typically return a pointer to the entry in the open-file table. This pointer, rather than the actual file name, is used in all I/O operations, avoiding any further searching, and simplifying the system-call interface.

The implementation of the `open` and `close` operations in a multiuser environment, such as UNIX, is more complicated. In such a system, several users may open the file at the same time. Typically, the operating system uses two levels of internal tables. There is a per-process table of all the files that each process has open. Stored in this table is information regarding the use of the file by the process. For instance, the current file pointer for each file is found here, indicating the location in the file which the next `read` or `write` call will affect.

Each entry in the per-process table in turn points to a systemwide open-file table. The systemwide table contains information that is process independent, such as the location of the file on disk, access dates, and file size. Once a file is opened by one process, another process executing an `open` call simply results in a new entry being added to the process' open file table with a new current file pointer, and a pointer to the appropriate entry in the systemwide table. Typically, the open-file table also has an **open count** associated with each file, indicating the number of processes which have the file open. Each `close` decreases this count, and when the count reaches zero, the file is no longer in use, and the file's entry is removed from the open file table.

In summary, there are several pieces of information associated with an open file.

- *File pointer*: On systems that do not include a file offset as part of the `read` and `write` system calls, the system must track the last read/write location as a current-file-position pointer. This pointer is unique to each process operating on the file, and therefore must be kept separate from the on-disk file attributes.

- *File open count*: As files are closed, the operating system must reuse its open-file table entries, or it could run out of space in the table. Because multiple processes may open a file, the system must wait for the last file to close before removing the open-file table entry. This counter tracks the number of opens and closes, and reaches zero on the last close. The system can then remove the entry.

- *Disk location of the file*: Most file operations require the system to modify data within the file. The information needed to locate the file on disk is kept in memory to avoid having to read it from disk for each operation.

Some operating systems provide facilities for locking sections of an open file for multiprocess access, to share sections of a file among several processes, and even to map sections of a file into memory on virtual-memory systems. This last function is called **memory mapping** a file; it allows a part of the virtual address space to be logically associated with a section of a file. Reads and writes to that memory region are then treated as reads and writes to the file, greatly simplifying file use. Closing the file results in all the memory-mapped data being written back to disk and removed from the virtual memory of the

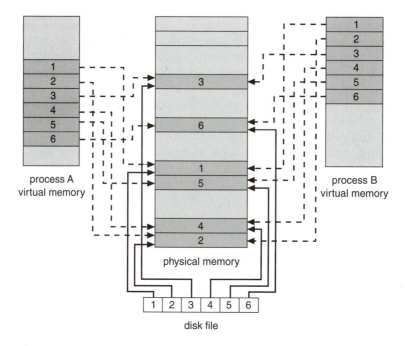

Figure 11.1   Memory-mapped files.

process. Multiple processes may be allowed to map the same file into the virtual memory of each, to allow sharing of data. Writes by any of the processes modify the data in virtual memory and can be seen by all other processes that map the same section of the file. Given our knowledge of virtual memory from Chapter 10, it should be clear how the sharing of memory-mapped sections of memory is implemented: Each sharing process' virtual-memory map points to the same page of physical memory—the page that holds a copy of the disk block. This memory sharing is illustrated in Figure 11.1. So that access to the shared data is coordinated, the processes involved may use one of the mechanisms for achieving mutual exclusion described in Chapter 7.

11.1.3 File Types

One major consideration in designing a file system, and the entire operating system, is whether the operating system should recognize and support file types. If an operating system recognizes the type of a file, it can then operate on the file in reasonable ways. For example, a common mistake occurs when a user tries to print the binary-object form of a program. This attempt normally produces garbage, but the printing of such a file can be prevented *if* the operating system has been told that the file is a binary-object program.

A common technique for implementing file types is to include the type as part of the file name. The name is split into two parts—a name and an **extension,** usually separated by a period character (Figure 11.2). In this way, the user and the operating system can tell from the name alone what the type of a file is. For example, in MS-DOS, a name can consist of up to eight characters followed by a period and terminated by an up-to-three-character extension. The system uses the extension to indicate the type of the file and the type of operations that can be done on that file. For instance, only a file with a ".com", ".exe", or ".bat" extension can be executed. The ".com" and ".exe" files are two forms of binary executable files, whereas a ".bat" file is a **batch** file containing, in ASCII format, commands to the operating system. MS-DOS recognizes only a few extensions, but application programs also use them to indicate file types in which they are interested. For example, a word processor might create files with a ".doc" extension. The operating system could then respond to the selection of that file (an open call, for instance) by invoking the word processor and giving it the file as its input. These extensions can be overridden if the operating system permits, but they can save typing and help users to understand the type of each file. Some operating systems include extension support, whereas others leave it to the applications to change their behavior based on the extension. In the latter

file type	usual extension	function
executable	exe, com, bin or none	ready-to-run machine-language program
object	obj, o	compiled, machine language, not linked
source code	c, cc, pas, java, asm, a	source code in various languages
batch	bat, sh	commands to the command interpreter
text	txt, doc	textual data, documents
word processor	wpd, tex, doc, etc	various word-processor formats
library	lib, a, DLL	libraries of routines for programmers
print or view	ps, dvi, gif	ASCII or binary file in a format for printing or viewing
archive	arc, zip, tar	related files grouped into one file, sometimes compressed, for archiving or storage

Figure 11.2   Common file types.

case, extensions can be considered as hints to the applications that operate on them.

Another example of the utility of file types comes from the TOPS-20 operating system. If the user tries to execute an object program whose source file has been modified (edited) since the object file was produced, the source file will be recompiled automatically. This function ensures that the user always runs an up-to-date object file. Otherwise, the user could waste significant time executing the old object file. Notice that, for this function to be possible, the operating system must be able to discriminate the source file from the object file, to check the time that each file was last modified or created, and to determine the language of the source program (so that it can use the correct compiler).

Consider the Apple Macintosh operating system. In this system, each file has a type, such as "text" or "pict". Each file also has a creator attribute containing the name of the program that created it. This attribute is set by the operating system during the create call, so its use is enforced and supported by the system. For instance, a file produced by a word processor has the word processor's name as its creator. When the user opens that file, by double-clicking the mouse on the icon representing the file, the word processor is invoked automatically, and the file is loaded, ready to be edited.

The UNIX system is unable to provide such a feature because it uses a crude **magic number** stored at the beginning of some files to indicate roughly the type of the file: executable program, batch file (known as a *shell script*), Postscript file, and so on. Not all files have magic numbers, so system features cannot be based solely on this type of information. UNIX does not record the name of the creating program, either. UNIX also allows hints about file-name extensions, but these extensions are not enforced or depended on by the operating system; they are mostly used to aid users in determining the type of contents of the file.

11.1.4 File Structure

We can also use file types to indicate the internal structure of the file. As mentioned in Section 11.1.3, source and object files have structures that match the expectations of the programs that read them. Further, certain files must conform to a required structure that is understood by the operating system. For example, the operating system may require that an executable file have a specific structure so that it can determine where in memory to load the file and what the location of the first instruction is. Some operating systems extend this idea into a set of system-supported file structures, with sets of special operations for manipulating files with those structures. For instance, DEC's popular VMS operating system has a file system that does support multiple file structures. It defines three file structures.

Our discussion points to one of the disadvantages of having the operating system support multiple file structures: The resulting size of the operating system is cumbersome. If the operating system defines five different file structures, it needs to contain the code to support these file structures. In addition, every file may need to be definable as one of the file types supported by the operating system. Severe problems may result from new applications that require information structured in ways not supported by the operating system.

For example, assume that a system supports two types of files: text files (composed of ASCII characters separated by a carriage return and line feed) and executable binary files. Now, if we (as users) want to define an encrypted file to protect our files from being read by unauthorized people, we may find that neither file type is appropriate. The encrypted file is not ASCII text lines, but rather is (apparently) random bits. Although it may appear to be a binary file, it is not executable. As a result, we may have to circumvent or misuse the operating system's file-types mechanism, or to modify or abandon our encryption scheme.

Some operating systems impose (and support) a minimal number of file structures. This approach has been adopted in UNIX, MS-DOS, and others. UNIX considers each file to be a sequence of 8-bit bytes; no interpretation of these bits is made by the operating system. This scheme provides maximum flexibility, but little support. Each application program must include its own code to interpret an input file into the appropriate structure. However, all operating systems must support at least one structure—that of an executable file—so that the system is able to load and run programs.

Another example of an operating system that supports a minimal number of file structures is the Macintosh Operating System, which expects files to contain two parts: a **resource fork** and a **data fork**. The resource fork contains information of interest to the user. For instance, it holds the labels of any buttons displayed by the program. A foreign user may want to relabel these buttons in his own language, and the Macintosh Operating System provides tools to allow modification of the data in the resource fork. The data fork contains program code or data: the traditional file contents. To accomplish the same task on a UNIX or MS-DOS system, the programmer would need to change and recompile the source code, unless she created her own user-changeable data file. The moral of this example is that it is useful for an operating system to support structures that will be used frequently, and that will save the programmer substantial work. Too few structures make programming inconvenient, whereas too many cause operating-system bloat and programmer confusion.

11.1.5 Internal File Structure

Internally, locating an offset within a file can be complicated for the operating system. Recall from Chapter 2 that disk systems typically have a well-defined block size determined by the size of a sector. All disk I/O is performed in units of one block (physical record), and all blocks are the same size. It is unlikely that the physical record size will exactly match the length of the desired logical record. Logical records may even vary in length. **Packing** a number of logical records into physical blocks is a common solution to this problem.

For example, the UNIX operating system defines all files to be simply a stream of bytes. Each byte is individually addressable by its offset from the beginning (or end) of the file. In this case, the logical record is 1 byte. The file system automatically packs and unpacks bytes into physical disk blocks (say, 512 bytes per block) as necessary.

The logical record size, physical block size, and packing technique determine how many logical records are in each physical block. The packing can be done either by the user's application program or by the operating system.

In either case, the file may be considered to be a sequence of blocks. All the basic I/O functions operate in terms of blocks. The conversion from logical records to physical blocks is a relatively simple software problem.

Notice that disk space being always allocated in blocks has the result that, in general, some portion of the last block of each file may be wasted. If each block is 512 bytes, then a file of 1,949 bytes would be allocated four blocks (2,048 bytes); the final 99 bytes would be wasted. The wasted bytes allocated to keep everything in units of blocks (instead of bytes) is **internal fragmentation**. All file systems suffer from internal fragmentation; the larger the block size, the greater the internal fragmentation.

11.1.6 Consistency Semantics

Consistency semantics is an important criterion for evaluation of any file system that supports sharing of files. It is a characterization of the system that specifies the semantics of multiple users accessing a shared file simultaneously. In particular, these semantics should specify when modifications of data by one user are observable by other users. There are various different consistency semantics. We describe the one used in UNIX.

The UNIX file system (see Chapter 17) uses the following consistency semantics:

- Writes to an open file by a user are visible immediately to other users that have this file open at the same time.

- There is a mode of sharing where users share the pointer of current location into the file. Thus, the advancing of the pointer by one user affects all sharing users. Here, a file has a single image that interleaves all accesses, regardless of their origin.

These semantics lend themselves to an implementation where a file is associated with a single physical image that is accessed as an exclusive resource. Contention for this single image results in user processes being delayed.

11.2 ■ Access Methods

Files store information. When it is used, this information must be accessed and read into computer memory. There are several ways that the information in the file can be accessed. Some systems provide only one access method for files. On other systems, such as those of IBM, many different access methods are supported, and choosing the right one for a particular application is a major design problem.

11.2.1 Sequential Access

The simplest access method is **sequential access**. Information in the file is processed in order, one record after the other. This mode of access is by far the most common; for example, editors and compilers usually access files in this fashion.

The bulk of the operations on a file are reads and writes. A read operation reads the next portion of the file and automatically advances a file pointer, which tracks the I/O location. Similarly, a write appends to the end of the file and advances to the end of the newly written material (the new end of file). Such a file can be reset to the beginning, and, on some systems, a program may be able to skip forward or backward n records, for some integer n (perhaps only for $n = 1$). Sequential access is depicted in Figure 11.3. Sequential access is based on a tape model of a file, and works as well on sequential-access devices as it does on random-access ones.

11.2.2 Direct Access

Another method is **direct access** (or **relative access**). A file is made up of fixed-length **logical records** that allow programs to read and write records rapidly in no particular order. The direct-access method is based on a disk model of a file; disks allow random access to any file block. For direct access, the file is viewed as a numbered sequence of blocks or records. A direct-access file allows arbitrary blocks to be read or written. Thus, we can read block 14, then read block 53, and then write block 7. There are no restrictions on the order of reading or writing for a direct-access file.

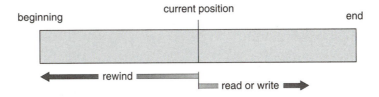

Figure 11.3   Sequential-access file.

Direct-access files are useful for immediate access to large amounts of information. Databases often have this need. When a query concerning a particular subject arrives, we identify (compute) the block that contains the answer, and then read that block directly to provide the desired information.

For example, on an airline-reservation system, we might store all the information about a particular flight (for example, flight 713) in the block identified by the flight number. Thus, the number of available seats for flight 713 is stored in block 713 of the reservation file. To store information about a larger set, such as people, we might compute a hash function on the people's names, or search a small in-memory index to determine a block to read and search.

The file operations must be modified to include the block number as a parameter. Thus, we have read n, where n is the block number, rather than read next, and write n, rather than write next. An alternative approach is to retain read next and write next, as we do with sequential access, and to add an operation, position file to n, where n is the block number. Then, to effect a read n, we position file to n and then read next.

The block number provided by the user to the operating system is normally a **relative block number,** which is an index relative to the beginning of the file. Thus, the first relative block of the file is 0, the next is 1, and so on, even though the actual absolute disk address of the block may be 14703 for the first block, and 3192 for the second. The use of relative block numbers allows the operating system to decide where the file should be placed (called the allocation problem, as discussed in Chapter 11), and helps to prevent the user from accessing portions of the file system that may not be part of his file. Some systems start their relative block numbers at 0; others start at 1.

Given a logical record length L, a request for record N is turned into an I/O request for L bytes starting at location $L * (N - 1)$ within the file (assuming first record is $N = 1$). Since logical records are of a fixed size, it is also easy to read, write, or delete a record.

Not all operating systems support both sequential and direct access for files. Some systems allow only sequential file access; others allow only direct access. Some systems require that a file be defined as sequential or direct when it is created; such a file can be accessed only in a manner consistent with its declaration. Notice, on the one hand, that it is easy to simulate sequential access on a direct-access file. If we simply keep a variable cp, which defines our current position, then we can simulate sequential file operations, as shown in Figure 11.4. On the other hand, it is extremely inefficient and clumsy to simulate a direct-access file on a sequential-access file.

11.2.3 Other Access Methods

Other access methods can be built on top of a direct-access method. These additional methods generally involve the construction of an **index** for the file. The index, like an index in the back of a book, contains pointers to the various

sequential access	implementation for direct access
reset	$cp = 0;$
read next	read cp; $cp = cp + 1;$
write next	write cp; $cp = cp + 1;$

Figure 11.4 Simulation of sequential access on a direct-access file.

blocks. To find a record in the file, we first search the index, and then use the pointer to access the file directly and to find the desired record.

For example, a retail-price file might list the universal product codes (UPCs) for items, with the associated prices. Each record consists of a 10-digit UPC and a 6-digit price, for a 16-byte record. If our disk has 1,024 bytes per block, we can store 64 records per block. A file of 120,000 records would occupy about 2000 blocks (2 million bytes). By keeping the file sorted by UPC, we can define an index consisting of the first UPC in each block. This index would have 2000 entries of 10 digits each, or 20,000 bytes, and thus could be kept in memory. To find the price of a particular item, we can (binary) search the index. From this search, we know exactly which block contains the desired record and access that block. This structure allows us to search a large file doing little I/O.

With large files, the index file itself may become too large to be kept in memory. One solution is to create an index for the index file. The primary index file then contains pointers to secondary index files, which point to the actual data items.

For example, IBM's indexed sequential access method (ISAM) uses a small master index that points to disk blocks of a secondary index. The secondary index blocks point to the actual file blocks. The file is kept sorted on a defined key. To find a particular item, we first make a binary search of the master index, which provides the block number of the secondary index. This block is read in, and again a binary search is used to find the block containing the desired record. Finally, this block is searched sequentially. In this way, any record can be located from its key by at most two direct-access reads. Figure 11.5 shows a similar situation as implemented by VMS index and relative files.

11.3 ■ Directory Structure

The file systems of computers can be extensive. Some systems store thousands of files on hundreds of gigabytes of disk. To manage all these data, we need to organize them. This organization is usually done in two parts. First, the file system is broken into **partitions,** also known as **minidisks** in the IBM world or **volumes** in the PC and Macintosh arenas. Typically, each disk on a system contains at least one partition, which is a low-level structure in which files

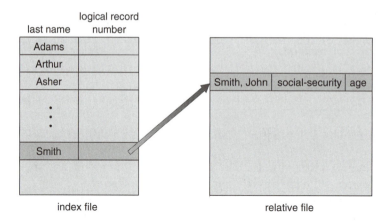

Figure 11.5   Example of index and relative files.

and directories reside. Some systems use partitions to provide several separate areas within one disk, treating each as a separate storage device, whereas other systems allow partitions to be larger than a disk so that they can group disks into one logical structure. Then the user needs to be concerned with only the logical directory and file structure; she can ignore completely the problems of physically allocating space for files. For this reason, partitions can be thought of as virtual disks.

Second, each partition contains information about files within it. This information is kept in entries in a **device directory** or **volume table of contents**. The device directory (more commonly known simply as a *directory*) records information—such as name, location, size, and type—for all files on that partition. Figure 11.6 shows the typical file-system organization.

The directory can be viewed as a symbol table that translates file names into their directory entries. If we take such a view, then it becomes apparent that the directory itself can be organized in many ways. We want to be able to insert entries, to delete entries, to search for a named entry, and to list all the entries in the directory. In Section 11.8, we discuss the appropriate data structures that we can use in the implementation of the directory structure. In this section, we examine several schemes for defining the logical structure of the directory system. When considering a particular directory structure, we need to keep in mind the operations that are to be performed on a directory:

- *Search for a file*: We need to be able to search a directory structure to find the entry for a particular file. Since files have symbolic names and similar names may indicate a relationship between files, we may want to be able to find all files whose names match a particular pattern.

- *Create a file*: We need to be able to create new files and to add them to the directory.

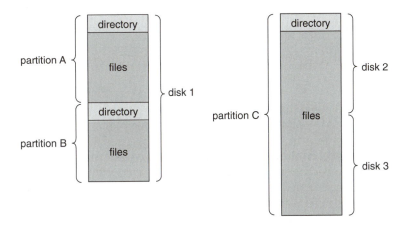

Figure 11.6   A typical file-system organization.

- *Delete a file*: When a file is no longer needed, we need to be able to remove it from the directory.

- *List a directory*: We need to be able to list the files in a directory, and the contents of the directory entry for each file in the list.

- *Rename a file*: Because the name of a file represents its contents to its users, we need to be able to change the name when the contents or use of the file changes. Renaming a file may also allow its position within the directory structure to be changed.

- *Traverse the file system*: It is useful to be able to access every directory, and every file within a directory structure. For reliability, it is a good idea to save the contents and structure of the entire file system at regular intervals. This savings often consists of copying all files to magnetic tape. This technique provides a backup copy in case of system failure or if the file is simply no longer in use. In this case, the file can be copied to tape, and the disk space of that file released for reuse by another file.

In Sections 11.3.1 through 11.3.5, we describe the most common schemes for defining the logical structure of a directory.

11.3.1 Single-Level Directory

The simplest directory structure is the single-level directory. All files are contained in the same directory, which is easy to support and understand (Figure 11.7).

A single-level directory has significant limitations, however, when the number of files increases or when there is more than one user. Since all files are in the same directory, they must have unique names. If we have two

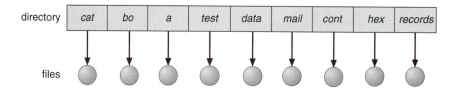

Figure 11.7   Single-level directory.

users who call their data file *test*, then the unique-name rule is violated. (For example, in one programming class, 23 students called the program for their second assignment *prog2*; another 11 called it *assign2*.) Although file names are generally selected to reflect the content of the file, they are often limited in length. The MS-DOS operating system allows only 11-character file names; UNIX allows 255 characters.

Even with a single user, as the number of files increases, it becomes difficult to remember the names of all the files, so as to create only files with unique names. It is not uncommon for a user to have hundreds of files on one computer system and an equal number of additional files on another system. In such an environment, keeping track of so many files is a daunting task.

11.3.2   Two-Level Directory

The major disadvantage to a single-level directory is the confusion of file names created by different users. The standard solution is to create a *separate* directory for each user.

In the two-level directory structure, each user has her own **user file directory** (**UFD**). Each UFD has a similar structure, but lists only the files of a single user. When a user job starts or a user logs in, the system's **master file directory** (**MFD**) is searched. The MFD is indexed by user name or account number, and each entry points to the UFD for that user (Figure 11.8).

When a user refers to a particular file, only his own UFD is searched. Thus, different users may have files with the same name, as long as all the file names within each UFD are unique.

To create a file for a user, the operating system searches only that user's UFD to ascertain whether another file of that name exists. To delete a file, the operating system confines its search to the local UFD; thus, it cannot accidentally delete another user's file that has the same name.

The user directories themselves must be created and deleted as necessary. A special system program is run with the appropriate user name and account information. The program creates a new user file directory and adds an entry for it to the master file directory. The execution of this program might be restricted to system administrators. The allocation of disk space for user directories can be handled with the techniques discussed in Section 11.6 for files themselves.

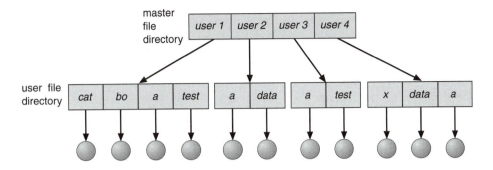

Figure 11.8   Two-level directory structure.

The two-level directory structure solves the name-collision problem, but it still has problems. This structure effectively isolates one user from another. This isolation is an advantage when the users are completely independent, but is a disadvantage when the users *want* to cooperate on some task and to access one another's files. Some systems simply do not allow local user files to be accessed by other users.

If access is to be permitted, one user must have the ability to name a file in another user's directory. To name a particular file uniquely in a two-level directory, we must give both the user name and the file name. A two-level directory can be thought of as a tree—or an inverted tree—of height 2. The root of the tree is the master file directory. Its direct descendants are the UFDs. The descendants of the user file directories are the files themselves. The files are the leaves of the tree. Specifying a user name and a file name defines a path in the tree from the root (the master file directory) to a leaf (the specified file). Thus, a user name and a file name define a **path name**. Every file in the system has a path name. To name a file uniquely, a user must know the path name of the file desired.

For example, if user A wishes to access her own test file named *test*, she can simply refer to *test*. To access the test file of user B (with directory-entry name *userb*), however, she might have to refer to */userb/test*. Every system has its own syntax for naming files in directories other than the user's own.

There is additional syntax to specify the partition of a file. For instance, in MS-DOS a partition is specified by a letter followed by a colon. Thus, a file specification might be "C:\userb\test". Some systems go even further and separate the partition, directory-name, and file-name parts of the specification. For instance, in VMS, the file "login.com" might be specified as: "u:[sst.jdeck]login.com;1", where "u" is the name of the partition, "sst" is the name of the directory, "jdeck" is the name of subdirectory, and "1" is the version number. Other systems simply treat the partition name as part of the directory name. The first name given is that of the partition, and the rest is the directory and file. For instance, "/u/pbg/test" might specify partition "u", directory "pbg", and file "test".

A special case of this situation occurs in regard to the system files. Those programs provided as a part of the system (loaders, assemblers, compilers, utility routines, libraries, and so on) are generally defined as files. When the appropriate commands are given to the operating system, these files are read by the loader and are executed. Many command interpreters act by simply treating the command as the name of a file to load and execute. As the directory system is defined presently, this file name would be searched for in the current user file directory. One solution would be to copy the system files into each user file directory. However, copying all the system files would be enormously wasteful of space. (If the system files require 5 megabytes, then supporting 12 users would require $5 \times 12 = 60$ megabytes just for copies of the system files.)

The standard solution is to complicate the search procedure slightly. A special user directory is defined to contain the system files (for example, user 0). Whenever a file name is given to be loaded, the operating system first searches the local user file directory. If the file is found, it is used. If it is not found, the system automatically searches the special user directory that contains the system files. The sequence of directories searched when a file is named is called the **search path**. This idea can be extended, such that the search path contains an unlimited list of directories to search when a command name is given. This method is the one used most often in UNIX and MS-DOS.

11.3.3 Tree-Structured Directories

Once we have seen how to view a two-level directory as a two-level tree, the natural generalization is to extend the directory structure to a tree of arbitrary height (Figure 11.9). This generalization allows users to create their own subdirectories and to organize their files accordingly. The MS-DOS system, for instance, is structured as a tree. In fact, a tree is the most common directory structure. The tree has a root directory. Every file in the system has a unique path name.

A **directory** (or subdirectory) contains a set of files or subdirectories. A directory is simply another file, but it is treated in a special way. All directories have the same internal format. One bit in each directory entry defines the entry as a file (0) or as a subdirectory (1). Special system calls create and delete directories.

In normal use, each user has a **current directory**. The current directory should contain most of the files that are of current interest to the user. When reference is made to a file, the current directory is searched. If a file is needed that is not in the current directory, then the user must either specify a path name or change the current directory to be the directory holding that file. So that the user can change the current directory to a different directory, a system call is provided that takes a directory name as a parameter and uses that parameter to

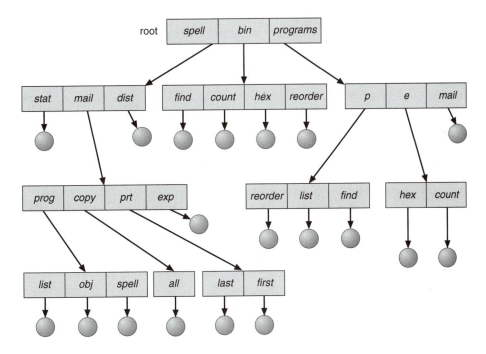

Figure 11.9 Tree-structured directory.

redefine the current directory. From one `change directory` system call to the next, all `open` system calls search the current directory for the specified file.

The initial current directory of a user is designated when the user job starts or the user logs in. The operating system searches the accounting file (or some other predefined location) to find an entry for this user (for accounting purposes). In the accounting file is a pointer to (or the name of) the user's initial directory. This pointer is copied to a local variable for this user, which specifies the user's initial current directory.

Path names can be of two types: absolute or relative. An **absolute path name** begins at the root and follows a path down to the specified file, giving the directory names on the path. A **relative path name** defines a path from the current directory. For example, in the tree-structured file system of Figure 11.9, if the current directory is *root/spell/mail*, then the relative path name *prt/first* refers to the same file as does the absolute path name *root/spell/mail/prt/first*.

Allowing the user to define his own subdirectories permits him to impose a structure on his files. This structure might result in separate directories for files associated with different topics (for example, we created a subdirectory to hold the text of this book) or different forms of information (for example, the directory *programs* may contain source programs; the directory *bin* may store all the binaries).

An interesting policy decision in a tree-structured directory structure is how to handle the deletion of a directory. If a directory is empty, its entry in its containing directory can simply be deleted. However, suppose the directory to be deleted is not empty, but instead contains several files, or possibly subdirectories. One of two approaches can be taken. Some systems, such as MS-DOS, will not delete a directory unless it is empty. Thus, to delete a directory, the user must first delete (or move out) all the files in that directory. If there are any subdirectories, she must apply this procedure recursively to them, deleting them as well, which may be a substantial amount of work.

An alternative approach—taken by the UNIX rm command—is to provide the option that, when a request is made to delete a directory, all that directory's files and subdirectories are also to be deleted. Note that either approach is easy to implement; the choice is one of policy. The latter policy is more convenient, but more dangerous, because an entire directory structure may be removed with one command. If that command was issued in error, a large number of files and directories would need to be restored from backup tapes (assuming that a backup exists).

With a tree-structured directory system, users can access, in addition to their files, the files of other users. For example, user B can access files of user A by specifying their path names. User B can specify either an absolute or a relative path name. Alternatively, user B could change her current directory to be user A's directory, and access the files by their file names. Some systems also allow a user to define his own search paths. In this case, user B could define her search path to be (1) her local directory, (2) the system file directory, and (3) user A's directory, in that order. As long as the name of a file of user A did not conflict with the name of a local file or system file, it could be referred to simply by its name.

Note that a path to a file in a tree-structured directory can be longer than that in a two-level directory. To allow users to access programs without having to remember these long paths, the Macintosh system automates the search for executable programs. It maintains a file, called the "Desktop File," which contains the name and location of all the executable programs that it has seen. When a new hard disk or floppy disk is added to the system, or the network is accessed, the operating system traverses the directory structure, searching for executable programs on the device and recording the pertinent information. This mechanism supports the double-click execution functionality described previously. A double-click on a file causes its creator attribute to be read, and the "Desktop File" to be searched for a match. Once the match is found, the appropriate executable program is started with the clicked-on file as its input.

11.3.4 Acyclic-Graph Directories

Consider two programmers who are working on a joint project. The files associated with that project can be stored in a subdirectory, separating them from other projects and from the files of the two programmers. But since both programmers are equally responsible for the project, both want the subdirectory to be in their own directories. The common subdirectory should be *shared*. A shared directory or file will exist in the file system in two (or more) places at once. Notice that a shared file (or directory) is not the same as two copies of the file. With two copies, each programmer can view the copy rather than the original, but if one programmer changes the file, the changes will not appear in the other's copy. With a shared file, there is only *one* actual file, so any changes made by one person would be immediately visible to the other. This form of sharing is particularly important for shared subdirectories; a new file created by one person will automatically appear in all the shared subdirectories.

A tree structure prohibits the sharing of files or directories. An **acyclic graph,** which is a graph with no cycles, allows directories to have shared subdirectories and files (Figure 11.10). The *same* file or subdirectory may be in two different directories. An acyclic graph is a natural generalization of the tree-structured directory scheme. When several people are working as a team, all the files to be shared can be put together into one directory. The user file directories of all the team members each contain this directory of shared files as a subdirectory. Even when there is a single user, his file organization may require that some files be put into several different subdirectories. For example, a program written for a particular project should be both in the directory of all programs and in the directory for that project.

Shared files and subdirectories can be implemented in several ways. A common way, exemplified by many of the UNIX systems, is to create a new

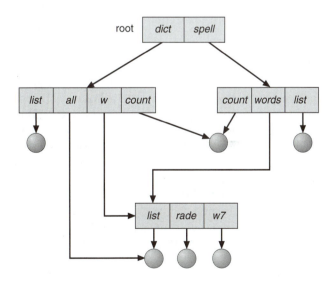

Figure 11.10   Acyclic-graph directory structure.

directory entry called a **link**. A link is effectively a pointer to another file or subdirectory. For example, a link may be implemented as an absolute or relative path name—called a **symbolic link**. When a reference to a file is made, we search the directory. If the directory entry is marked as a link, then the name of the real file (or directory) is given. We **resolve** the link by using the path name to locate the real file. Links are easily identified by their format in the directory entry (or by their having a special type on systems that support types); they serve as named indirect pointers. The operating system ignores these links when traversing directory trees to preserve the acyclic structure of the system.

The other approach to implementing shared files is simply to duplicate all information about them in both sharing directories. Thus, both entries are identical and equal. A link is clearly different from the original directory entry; thus, the two are not equal. Duplicate directory entries, however, make the original and the copy indistinguishable. A major problem with duplicate directory entries is maintaining consistency if the file is modified.

An acyclic-graph directory structure is more flexible than is a simple tree structure, but is also more complex. Several problems must be considered carefully. Notice that a file may now have multiple absolute path names. Consequently, distinct file names may refer to the same file. This situation is similar to the aliasing problem for programming languages. If we are trying to traverse the entire file system (to find a file, to accumulate statistics on all files, or to copy all files to backup storage), this problem becomes significant, since we do not want to traverse shared structures more than once.

Another problem involves deletion. When can the space allocated to a shared file be deallocated and reused? One possibility is to remove the file whenever anyone deletes it, but this action may leave dangling pointers to the now-nonexistent file. Worse, if the remaining file pointers contain actual disk addresses, and the space is subsequently reused for other files, these dangling pointers may point into the middle of other files.

In a system where sharing is implemented by symbolic links, this situation is somewhat easier to handle. The deletion of a link does not need to affect the original file; only the link is removed. If the file entry itself is deleted, the space for the file is deallocated, leaving the links dangling. We can search for these links and remove them also, but unless a list of the associated links is kept with each file, this search can be expensive. Alternatively, we can leave the links until an attempt is made to use them. At that time, we can determine that the file of the name given by the link does not exist, and can fail to resolve the link name; the access is treated just like any other illegal file name. (In this case, the system designer should consider carefully what to do when a file is deleted and another file of the same name is created, before a symbolic link to the original file is used.) In the case of UNIX, symbolic links are left when a file is deleted, and it is up to the user to realize that the original file is gone or has been replaced.

Another approach to deletion is to preserve the file until all references to it are deleted. To implement this approach, we must have some mechanism for determining that the last reference to the file has been deleted. We could keep a list of all references to a file (directory entries or symbolic links). When a link or a copy of the directory entry is established, a new entry is added to the file-reference list. When a link or directory entry is deleted, we remove its entry on the list. The file is deleted when its file-reference list is empty.

The trouble with this approach is the variable and potentially large size of the file-reference list. However, we do not need to keep the entire list—we need to keep only a count of the *number* of references. A new link or directory entry increments the reference count; deleting a link or entry decrements the count. When the count is 0, the file can be deleted; there are no remaining references to it. The UNIX operating system uses this approach for nonsymbolic links, or **hard links,** keeping a reference count in the file information block (or inode, see Section 20.7.2). By effectively prohibiting multiple references to directories, we maintain an acyclic-graph structure.

So that its users avoid these problems, some systems do not allow shared directories or links. For example, in MS-DOS, the directory structure is a tree structure, rather than an acyclic graph, thereby avoiding the problems associated with file deletion in an acyclic-graph directory structure.

11.3.5 General Graph Directory

One serious problem with using an acyclic-graph structure is that it is difficult to ensure that there are no cycles. If we start with a two-level directory and allow users to create subdirectories, a tree-structured directory results. It should be fairly easy to see that simply adding new files and subdirectories to an existing tree-structured directory preserves the tree-structured nature. However, when we add links to an existing tree-structured directory, the tree structure is destroyed, resulting in a simple graph structure (Figure 11.11).

The primary advantage of an acyclic graph is the relative simplicity of the algorithms to traverse the graph and to determine when there are no more references to a file. We want to avoid traversing shared sections of a graph twice, mainly for performance reasons. If we have just searched a major shared subdirectory for a particular file, without finding that file, we want to avoid searching that subdirectory again; the second search would be a waste of time.

If cycles are allowed to exist in the directory, we likewise want to avoid searching any component twice, for reasons of correctness as well as performance. A poorly designed algorithm might result in an infinite loop continually searching through the cycle and never terminating. One solution is to limit arbitrarily the number of directories that can be accessed during a search.

We face a similar problem when we try to determine when a file can be deleted. As is true in acyclic-graph directory structures, a value of 0 in the reference count means that there are no more references to the file or directory,

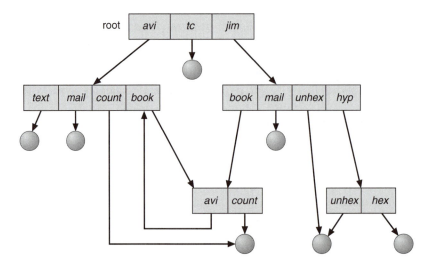

Figure 11.11   General graph directory.

and thus that the file can be deleted. However, it is also possible, when cycles exist, that the reference count may be nonzero, even when it is no longer possible to refer to a directory or file. This anomaly results from the possibility of self-referencing (a cycle) in the directory structure. In this case, it is generally necessary to use a **garbage-collection** scheme to determine when the final reference has been deleted and the disk space can be reallocated. Garbage collection involves traversing the entire file system, marking everything that can be accessed. Then, a second pass collects everything that is not marked onto a list of free space. (A similar marking procedure can be used to ensure that a traversal or search will cover everything in the file system once and only once.) Garbage collection for a disk-based file system, however, is extremely time consuming and is thus seldom attempted.

Garbage collection is necessary only because of possible cycles in the graph. Thus, working with an acyclic-graph structure is much easier. The difficulty is to avoid cycles as new links are added to the structure. How do we know when a new link will complete a cycle? There are algorithms to detect cycles in graphs; however, they are computationally expensive, especially when the graph is on disk storage. Generally, for these reasons, tree directory structures are more common than are acyclic-graph structures.

11.4 ■ Protection

When information is kept in a computer system, one major concern is **reliability,** or guarding against physical damage. Another is **protection,** or guarding against improper access.

Reliability is generally provided by duplicate copies of files. Many computers have systems programs that automatically (or through computer-operator intervention) copy disk files to tape at regular intervals (once per day or week or month) to maintain a copy in case a file system is destroyed accidentally or maliciously. File systems can be damaged by hardware problems (such as errors in reading or writing), power surges or failures, head crashes, dirt, temperature extremes, or vandalism. Files may be deleted accidentally. Bugs in the file-system software can also cause file contents to be lost. Reliability is covered in Chapter 13.

Protection can be provided in many ways. For a small, single-user system, we might physically remove the floppy disks and lock them in a desk drawer or file cabinet. In a multiuser system, other mechanisms are needed.

11.4.1 Types of Access

The need for protecting files is a direct result of the ability to access files. On systems that do not permit access to the files of other users, protection is not needed. Thus, one extreme would be to provide complete protection by prohibiting access. The other extreme is to provide free access with no protection. Both approaches are too extreme for general use. What is needed is **controlled access**.

Protection mechanisms provide controlled access by limiting the types of file access that can be made. Access is permitted or denied depending on several factors, one of which is the type of access requested. Several different types of operations may be controlled:

- *Read*: Read from the file.

- *Write*: Write or rewrite the file.

- *Execute*: Load the file into memory and execute it.

- *Append*: Write new information at the end of the file.

- *Delete*: Delete the file and free its space for possible reuse.

- *List*: List the name and attributes of the file.

Other operations—such as renaming, copying, or editing the file—also may be controlled. For many systems, however, these higher-level functions (such as copying) may be implemented by a system program that makes lower-level system calls. Protection is provided at only the lower level. For instance, copying a file may be implemented simply by a sequence of read requests. In this case, a user with read access can also cause the file to be copied, printed, and so on.

Many different protection mechanisms have been proposed. Each scheme has its advantages and disadvantages, so you must select the one appropriate for its intended application. A small computer system that is used by only a few members of a research group may not need the same types of protection as a large corporate computer that is used for research, finance, and personnel operations. In this section, we discuss protection as it relates to the file system. In Chapter 18, we provide a complete treatment of the protection problem.

11.4.2 Access Lists and Groups

The most common approach to the protection problem is to make access dependent on the identity of the user. Various users may need different types of access to a file or directory. The most general scheme to implement identity-dependent access is to associate with each file and directory an **access list,** specifying for each listed user name and the types of access allowed. When a user requests access to a particular file, the operating system checks the access list associated with that file. If that user is listed for the requested access, the access is allowed. Otherwise, a protection violation occurs, and the user job is denied access to the file.

The main problem with access lists is their length. If we want to allow everyone to read a file, we must list all users and give them read access. This technique has two undesirable consequences:

1. Constructing such a list may be a tedious and unrewarding task, especially if we do not know in advance the list of users in the system.

2. The directory entry that previously was of fixed size needs now to be of variable size, resulting in more complicated space management.

We can resolve these problems by using a condensed version of the access list.

To condense the length of the access list, many systems recognize three classifications of users in connection with each file:

- **Owner**: The user who created the file is the owner.

- **Group**: A set of users who are sharing the file and need similar access is a group, or work group.

- **Universe**: All other users in the system constitute the universe.

As an example, consider a person, Sara, who is writing a new book. She has hired three graduate students (Jim, Dawn, and Jill) to help her with the project. The text of the book is kept in a file named *book*. The protection associated with this file is as follows:

- Sara should be able to invoke all operations on the file.

- Jim, Dawn, and Jill should be able only to read and write the file; they should not be allowed to delete the file.

- All other users should be able to read the file, but not to write to or delete it. (Sara is interested in letting as many people as possible read the text so that she can obtain appropriate feedback.)

To achieve such a protection, we must create a new group, say *text*, with members Jim, Dawn, and Jill. The name of the group *text* must be then associated with the file *book*, and the access right must be set in accordance with the policy we have outlined.

Note that, for this scheme to work properly, group membership must be controlled tightly. This control can be accomplished in various ways. For example, in the UNIX system, groups can be created and modified by only the manager of the facility (or by any superuser). Thus, this control is achieved through human interaction. The VMS system uses access lists.

With this more limited protection classification, we need only three fields to define protection. Each field is often a collection of bits, each of which either allows or prevents the access associated with it. For example, the UNIX system defines three fields of 3 bits each: **rwx,** where **r** controls read access, **w** controls write access, and **x** controls execution. A separate field is kept for the file owner, for the file's group, and for all other users. In this scheme, 9 bits per file are needed to record protection information. Thus, for our example, the protection fields for the file *book* are as follows: For the owner Sara, all 3 bits are set; for the group *text*, the **r** and **w** bits are set; and for the universe, only the **r** bit is set.

Notice, however, that this scheme is not as general as is the access-list scheme. To illustrate our point, let us return to the book example. Suppose that Sara has a massive argument with Jason and now wants to exclude him from the list of people who can read the text. She cannot do so under the basic protection scheme outlined.

11.4.3 Other Protection Approaches

There are other approaches to the protection problem. One is to associate a password with each file. Just as access to the computer system itself is often controlled by a password, access to each file can be controlled by a password. If the passwords are chosen randomly and changed often, this scheme may be effective in limiting access to a file to only those users who know the password. There are, however, several disadvantages to this scheme. First, if we associate a separate password with each file, the number of passwords that a user must remember may become large, making the scheme impractical. If only one password is used for all the files, then, once it is discovered, all files are accessible. Some systems (for example, TOPS-20) allow a user to associate a password with a subdirectory, rather than with an individual file, to deal with this problem. The IBM VM/CMS operating system allows three passwords for a minidisk: one each for read, write, and multiwrite access. Second, commonly, only one password is associated with each file. Thus, protection is on an all-

or-nothing basis. To provide protection on a more detailed level, we must use multiple passwords.

Limited file protection is also currently available on single-user systems, such as MS-DOS and the Macintosh operating system. These operating systems, when originally designed, essentially ignored the protection problem. Now, however, they are being placed on networks where file sharing and communication are necessary, so protection mechanisms are being retrofitted for them. It is almost always easier to include a feature in the original design of an operating system than it is to add a feature to an existing system. Such updates usually are less than perfectly effective and are not seamless.

In a multilevel directory structure, we need not only to protect individual files, but also to protect collections of files contained in a subdirectory; that is, we need to provide a mechanism for directory protection. The directory operations that must be protected are somewhat different from the file operations. We want to control the creation and deletion of files in a directory. In addition, we probably want to control whether a user can determine the existence of a file in a directory. Sometimes, knowledge of the existence and name of a file may be significant in itself. Thus, listing the contents of a directory must be a protected operation. Therefore, if a path name refers to a file in a directory, the user must be allowed access to both the directory and the file. In systems where files may have numerous path names (such as acyclic or general graphs), users may have different access rights to a file, depending on the path names that they use.

11.4.4 An Example: UNIX

In the UNIX system, directory protection is handled like file protection. That is, associated with each subdirectory are three fields—owner, group, and universe —each consisting of the 3 bits **rwx**. Thus, a user can list the content of a subdirectory only if the **r** bit is set in the appropriate field. Similarly, a user can change his current directory to another current directory (say *foo*) only if the **x** bit associated with the *foo* subdirectory is set in the appropriate field.

A sample directory listing from a UNIX environment is shown in Figure 11.12. The first field describes the file or directory's protection. A **d** as the first character indicates a subdirectory. Also shown are the number of links to the file, the owner's name, the group's name, the size of the file in units of bytes, the creation date, and finally the file's name (with optional extension).

11.5 ■ File-System Structure

Disks provide the bulk of secondary storage on which a file system is maintained. To improve I/O efficiency, we perform transfers between memory and disk in units of **blocks**. Each block is one or more sectors. Sectors on different disk drives vary from 32 bytes to 4,096 bytes; usually, they are 512 bytes. Disks

-rw-rw-r–	1 pbg	staff	31200	Sep 3 08:30	intro.ps
drwx——	5 pbg	staff	512	Jul 8 09:33	private/
drwxrwxr-x	2 pbg	staff	512	Jul 8 09:35	doc/
drwxrwx—	2 pbg	student	512	Aug 3 14:13	student-proj/
-rw-r–r–	1 pbg	staff	9423	Feb 24 1998	program.c
-rwxr-xr-x	1 pbg	staff	20471	Feb 24 1998	program
drwx–x–x	4 pbg	faculty	512	Jul 31 10:31	lib/
drwx——	3 pbg	staff	1024	Aug 29 06:52	mail/
drwxrwxrwx	3 pbg	staff	512	Jul 8 09:35	test/

Figure 11.12   A sample directory listing.

have two important characteristics that make them a convenient medium for storing multiple files:

1. They can be rewritten in place; it is possible to read a block from the disk, to modify the block, and to write it back into the same place.

2. We can access directly any given block of information on the disk. Thus, it is simple to access any file either sequentially or randomly, and switching from one file to another requires only moving the read–write heads and waiting for the disk to rotate.

We discuss disk structure in Chapter 13.

11.5.1 File-System Organization

To provide an efficient and convenient access to the disk, the operating system imposes a **file system** to allow the data to be stored, located, and retrieved easily. Developing a file system poses two different design problems. The first problem is defining how the file system should look to the user. This task involves the definition of a file and its attributes, operations allowed on a file, and the directory structure for organizing the files. Next, algorithms and data structures must be created that map the logical file system onto the physical secondary-storage devices.

The file system itself is generally composed of many different levels. The structure shown in Figure 11.13 is an example of a layered design. Each level in the design uses the features of lower levels to create new features for use by higher levels.

The lowest level, the **I/O control,** consists of **device drivers** and interrupt handlers to transfer information between the memory and the disk system. A device driver can be thought of as a translator. Its input consists of high-level commands, such as "retrieve block 123." Its output consists of low-level, hardware-specific instructions, which are used by the hardware controller, which interfaces the I/O device to the rest of the system. The device driver

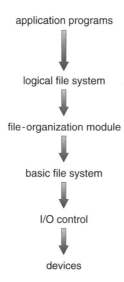

Figure 11.13   Layered file system.

usually writes specific bit patterns to special locations in the I/O controller's memory to tell the controller on which device location to act and what actions to take. Device drivers and the I/O infrastructure are covered in Chapter 12.

The **basic file system** needs only to issue generic commands to the appropriate device driver to read and write physical blocks on the disk. Each physical block is identified by its numeric disk address (for example, drive 1, cylinder 73, track 2, sector 10).

The **file-organization module** knows about files and their logical blocks, as well as physical blocks. By knowing the type of file allocation used and the location of the file, the file-organization module can translate logical block addresses to physical block addresses for the basic file system to transfer. Each file's logical blocks are numbered from 0 (or 1) through N, whereas the physical blocks containing the data usually do not match the logical numbers, so a translation is needed to locate each block. The file-organization module also includes the free-space manager, which tracks unallocated blocks and provides these blocks to the file-organization module when requested.

Finally, the **logical file system** uses the directory structure to provide the file-organization module with the information the latter needs, given a symbolic file name. The logical file system is also responsible for protection and security, as we discussed in Section 11.4 and will discuss further in Chapter 18.

To create a new file, an application program calls the logical file system. The logical file system knows the format of the directory structures. To create a new file, it reads the appropriate directory into memory, updates it with the new entry, and writes it back to the disk. Some operating systems, including

UNIX, treat a directory exactly as a file—one with a type field indicating that it is a directory. Other operating systems, including Windows NT, implement separate system calls for files and directories and treat directories as entities separate from files. When a directory is treated as a special file, the logical file system can call the file-organization module to map the directory I/O into disk-block numbers, which are passed on to the basic file system and I/O control system.

Now that a file has been created, it can be used for I/O. For each I/O operation, the directory structure could be searched to find the file, its parameters checked, its data blocks located, and finally the operation on those data blocks performed. Each operation would entail high overhead. Rather, before the file can be used for I/O procedures, it must be **opened**. When a file is opened, the directory structure is searched for the desired file entry. Parts of the directory structure are usually cached in memory to speed directory operations. Once the file is found, the associated information—such as size, owner, access permissions, and data-block locations—are generally copied into a table in memory. This **open-file** table contains information about all the currently opened files (Figure 11.14).

The first reference to a file (normally an open) causes the directory structure to be searched and the directory entry for this file to be copied into the table of opened files. The index into this table is returned to the user program, and all further references are made through the index rather than with a symbolic name. The name given to the index varies. UNIX systems refer to it as a **file descriptor,** Windows NT as a **file handle,** and other systems as a **file control block**. Consequently, as long as the file is not closed, all file operations are done on the open-file table. When the file is closed by all users that have opened it, the updated file information is copied back to the disk-based directory structure.

Some systems complicate this scheme even further by using multiple levels of in-memory tables. For example, in the BSD UNIX file system, each process has an open-file table that holds a list of pointers, indexed by descriptor. The

index	file name	permissions	access dates	pointer to disk block
0	TEST.C	rw rw rw	. . .	$\longrightarrow$
1	MAIL.TXT	rw		$\longrightarrow$
2				
.				
.				
.				
n				

Figure 11.14   A typical open-file table.

pointers lead to a systemwide open-file table. This table contains information about the underlying entity that is open. For files, it points to a table of active inodes. For other entities, such as network connections and devices, it points to similar access information. The **active-inodes table** is an in-memory cache of inodes currently in use, and includes the inode index fields that point to the on-disk data blocks. Once a file is opened, all but the actual data blocks are in memory for rapid access by any process accessing the file. In reality, the open first searches the open-file table to see whether the file is already in use by another process. If the file is in use, a per-process open-file table entry is created that points to the systemwide open-file table. If the file is not in use, the inode is copied into the active-inodes table, and both a new systemwide entry and a new per-process entry are created.

The BSD UNIX system is typical in its use of caches wherever disk I/O can be saved. Its average cache hit rate of 85 percent shows that these techniques are well worth implementing. The BSD UNIX system is described in Chapter 20. The open-file table is detailed in Section 11.1.2.

11.5.2 File-System Mounting

Just as a file must be opened before it is used, a file system must be **mounted** before it can be available to processes on the system. The mount procedure is straightforward. The operating system is given the name of the device, and the location within the file structure at which to attach the file system (called the **mount point**). For instance, on a UNIX system, a file system containing the user's home directories might be mounted as */home*; then, to access the directory structure within that file system, we precede the directory names with */home*, as in */home/jane*. Mounting that file system under */users* would allow a user to use the path name */users/jane* to reach the same directory.

Next, the operating system verifies that the device contains a valid file system. It does so by asking the device driver to read the device directory and verifying that the directory has the expected format. Finally, the operating system notes in its directory structure that a file system is mounted at the specified mount point. This scheme enables the operating system to traverse its directory structure, switching among file systems as appropriate.

Consider the actions of the Macintosh Operating System. Whenever the system encounters a disk for the first time (hard disks are found at boot time, floppy disks are seen when they are inserted into the drive), the Macintosh Operating System searches for a file system on the device. If it finds one, it automatically mounts the file system at the root level, adding a folder icon on the screen labeled with the name of the file system (as stored in the device directory). The user is then able to click on the icon and thus to display the newly mounted file system.

File-system mounting is discussed further in Sections 17.6 and 20.7.5.

11.6 ■ Allocation Methods

The direct-access nature of disks allows us flexibility in the implementation of files. In almost every case, many files will be stored on the same disk. The main problem is how to allocate space to these files so that disk space is utilized effectively and files can be accessed quickly. Three major methods of allocating disk space are in wide use: *contiguous*, *linked*, and *indexed*. Each method has its advantages and disadvantages. Accordingly, some systems (such as Data General's RDOS for its Nova line of computers) support all three. More commonly, a system will use one particular method for all files.

11.6.1 Contiguous Allocation

The **contiguous** allocation method requires each file to occupy a set of contiguous blocks on the disk. Disk addresses define a linear ordering on the disk. Notice that, with this ordering, assuming that only one job is accessing the disk, an access to block $b + 1$ after block b normally requires no head movement. When head movement is needed (from the last sector of one cylinder to the first sector of the next cylinder), it is only one track. Thus, the number of disk seeks required for accessing contiguously allocated files is minimal, as is seek time when a seek is finally needed. The IBM VM/CMS operating system uses contiguous allocation because the approach provides such good performance.

Contiguous allocation of a file is defined by the disk address (first block) and length (in block units). If the file starts at location b and is n blocks long, then it occupies blocks $b, b + 1, b + 2, \cdots, b + n - 1$. The directory entry for each file indicates the address of the starting block and the length of the area allocated for this file (Figure 11.15).

Accessing a file that has been allocated contiguously is easy. For sequential access, the file system remembers the disk address of the last block referenced and, when necessary, reads the next block. For direct access to block i of a file that starts at block b, we can immediately access block $b + i$. Thus, both sequential and direct access can be supported by contiguous allocation.

One difficulty with contiguous allocation is finding space for a new file. The implementation of the free-space management system, discussed in Section 11.7, determines how this task is accomplished. Any management system can be used, but some are slower than others.

The contiguous disk-space-allocation problem can be seen to be a particular application of the general **dynamic storage-allocation problem** discussed in Section 9.3, which is how to satisfy a request of size n from a list of free holes. *First fit* and *best fit* are the most common strategies that we can use to select a free hole from the set of available holes. Simulations have shown that both first fit and best fit are more efficient than worst fit in terms of both time and storage utilization. Neither first fit nor best fit is clearly best in terms of storage utilization, but first fit is generally faster.

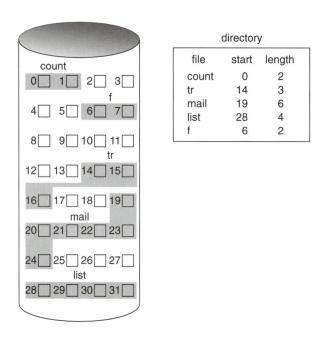

Figure 11.15   Contiguous allocation of disk space.

These algorithms suffer from the problem of **external fragmentation**. As files are allocated and deleted, the free disk space is broken into little pieces. External fragmentation exists whenever free space is broken into chunks. It becomes a problem when the largest contiguous chunk is insufficient for a request; storage is fragmented into a number of holes, no one of which is large enough to store the data. Depending on the total amount of disk storage and the average file size, external fragmentation may be either a minor or a major problem.

Some older microcomputer systems used contiguous allocation on floppy disks. To prevent loss of significant amounts of disk space to external fragmentation, the user had to run a repacking routine that copied the entire file system onto another floppy disk or onto a tape. The original floppy disk was then freed completely, creating one large contiguous free space. The routine then copied the files back onto the floppy disk by allocating contiguous space from this one large hole. This scheme effectively **compacts** all free space into one contiguous space, solving the fragmentation problem. The cost of this compaction is time. The time cost is particularly severe for large hard disks that use contiguous allocation, where compacting all the space may take hours and may be necessary on a weekly basis. During this **down time,** normal system operation generally cannot be permitted, so such compaction is avoided at all costs on production machines.

There are other problems with contiguous allocation. A major problem is determining how much space is needed for a file. When the file is created, the total amount of space it will need must be found and allocated. How does the creator (program or person) know the size of the file to be created? In some cases, this determination may be fairly simple (copying an existing file, for example); in general, however, the size of an output file may be difficult to estimate.

If we allocate too little space to a file, we may find that that file cannot be extended. Especially with a best-fit allocation strategy, the space on both sides of the file may be in use. Hence, we cannot make the file larger in place. Two possibilities then exist. First, the user program can be terminated, with an appropriate error message. The user must then allocate more space and run the program again. These repeated runs may be costly. To prevent them, the user will normally overestimate the amount of space needed, resulting in considerable wasted space.

The other possibility is to find a larger hole, to copy the contents of the file to the new space, and to release the previous space. This series of actions may be repeated as long as space exists, although it can also be time consuming. Notice, however, that in this case, the user never needs to be informed explicitly about what is happening; the system continues despite the problem, although more and more slowly.

Even if the total amount of space needed for a file is known in advance, preallocation may be inefficient. A file that grows slowly over a long period (months or years) must be allocated enough space for its final size, even though much of that space may be unused for a long time. The file, therefore, has a large amount of *internal fragmentation*.

To avoid several of these drawbacks, some operating systems use a modified contiguous allocation scheme, in which a contiguous chunk of space is allocated initially, and then, when that amount is not large enough, another chunk of contiguous space, an **extent,** is added to the initial allocation. The location of a file's blocks is then recorded as a location and a block count, plus a link to the first block of the next extent. On some systems, the owner of the file can set the extent size, but this setting results in inefficiencies if the owner is incorrect. Internal fragmentation can still be a problem if the extents are too large, and external fragmentation can be a problem as extents of varying sizes are allocated and deallocated.

11.6.2 Linked Allocation

Linked allocation solves all problems of contiguous allocation. With linked allocation, each file is a linked list of disk blocks; the disk blocks may be scattered anywhere on the disk. The directory contains a pointer to the first and last blocks of the file. For example, a file of five blocks might start at block 9, continue at block 16, then block 1, block 10, and finally block 25 (Figure 11.16).

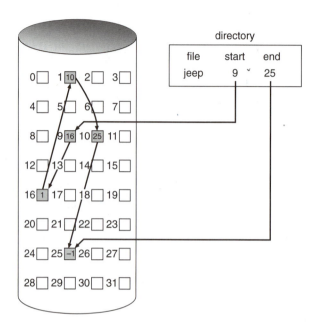

Figure 11.16   Linked allocation of disk space.

Each block contains a pointer to the next block. These pointers are not made available to the user. Thus, if each block is 512 bytes, and a disk address (the pointer) requires 4 bytes, then the user sees blocks of 508 bytes.

To create a new file, we simply create a new entry in the directory. With linked allocation, each directory entry has a pointer to the first disk block of the file. This pointer is initialized to *nil* (the end-of-list pointer value) to signify an empty file. The size field is also set to 0. A write to the file causes a free block to be found via the free-space management system, and this new block is then written to, and is linked to the end of the file. To read a file, we simply read blocks by following the pointers from block to block.

There is no external fragmentation with linked allocation, and we can use any free block on the free-space list to satisfy a request. Notice also that there is no need to declare the size of a file when that file is created. A file can continue to grow as long as there are free blocks. Consequently, it is never necessary to compact disk space.

Linked allocation does have disadvantages, however. The major problem is that it can be used effectively for only sequential-access files. To find the *i*th block of a file, we must start at the beginning of that file, and follow the pointers until we get to the *i*th block. Each access to a pointer requires a disk read, and sometimes a disk seek. Consequently, it is inefficient to support a direct-access capability for linked allocation files.

Another disadvantage to linked allocation is the space required for the pointers. If a pointer requires 4 bytes out of a 512-byte block, then 0.78 percent of the disk is being used for pointers, rather than for information. Each file requires slightly more space than it otherwise would.

The usual solution to this problem is to collect blocks into multiples, called **clusters,** and to allocate the clusters rather than blocks. For instance, the file system may define a cluster as 4 blocks, and operate on the disk in only cluster units. Pointers then use a much smaller percentage of the file's disk space. This method allows the logical-to-physical block mapping to remain simple, but improves disk throughput (fewer disk head seeks) and decreases the space needed for block allocation and free-list management. The cost of this approach is an increase in internal fragmentation, because more space is wasted if a cluster is partially full than when a block is partially full. Clusters can improve the disk access time for many other algorithms, so they are used in most operating systems.

Yet another problem is reliability. Since the files are linked together by pointers scattered all over the disk, consider what would happen if a pointer were lost or damaged. A bug in the operating-system software or a disk hardware failure might result in the wrong pointer being picked up. This error could result in linking into the free-space list or into another file. Partial solutions are to use doubly linked lists or to store the file name and relative block number in each block; however, these schemes require even more overhead for each file.

An important variation on the linked allocation method is the use of a **file-allocation table (FAT)**. This simple but efficient method of disk-space allocation is used by the MS-DOS and OS/2 operating systems. A section of disk at the beginning of each partition is set aside to contain the table. The table has one entry for each disk block, and is indexed by block number. The FAT is used much as is a linked list. The directory entry contains the block number of the first block of the file. The table entry indexed by that block number then contains the block number of the next block in the file. This chain continues until the last block, which has a special end-of-file value as the table entry. Unused blocks are indicated by a 0 table value. Allocating a new block to a file is a simple matter of finding the first 0-valued table entry, and replacing the previous end-of-file value with the address of the new block. The 0 is then replaced with the end-of-file value. An illustrative example is the FAT structure of Figure 11.17 for a file consisting of disk blocks 217, 618, and 339.

Note that the FAT allocation scheme can result in a significant number of disk head seeks, unless the FAT is cached. The disk head must move to the start of the partition to read the FAT and find the location of the block in question, then move to the location of the block itself. In the worst case, both moves occur for each of the blocks. A benefit is that random access time is improved, because the disk head can find the location of any block by reading the information in the FAT.

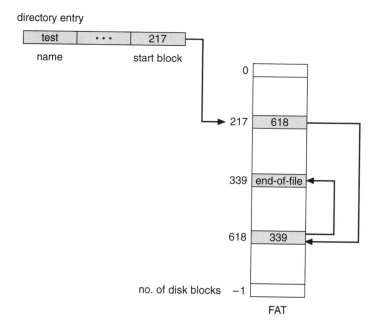

Figure 11.17   File-allocation table.

11.6.3 Indexed Allocation

Linked allocation solves the external-fragmentation and size-declaration problems of contiguous allocation. However, in the absence of a FAT, linked allocation cannot support efficient direct access, since the pointers to the blocks are scattered with the blocks themselves all over the disk and need to be retrieved in order. **Indexed allocation** solves this problem by bringing all the pointers together into one location: the **index block**.

Each file has its own index block, which is an array of disk-block addresses. The ith entry in the index block points to the ith block of the file. The directory contains the address of the index block (Figure 11.18). To read the ith block, we use the pointer in the ith index-block entry to find and read the desired block. This scheme is similar to the paging scheme described in Chapter 9.

When the file is created, all pointers in the index block are set to *nil*. When the ith block is first written, a block is obtained from the free-space manager, and its address is put in the ith index-block entry.

Indexed allocation supports direct access, without suffering from external fragmentation, because any free block on the disk may satisfy a request for more space.

Indexed allocation does suffer from wasted space. The pointer overhead of the index block is generally greater than the pointer overhead of linked allocation. Consider a common case in which we have a file of only one or two

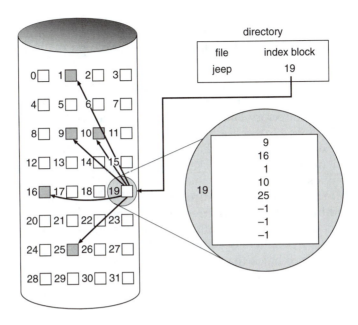

Figure 11.18 Indexed allocation of disk space.

blocks. With linked allocation, we lose the space of only one pointer per block (one or two pointers). With indexed allocation, an entire index block must be allocated, even if only one or two pointers will be non-*nil*.

This point raises the question of how large the index block should be. Every file must have an index block, so we want the index block to be as small as possible. If the index block is too small, however, it will not be able to hold enough pointers for a large file, and a mechanism will have to be available to deal with this issue:

- *Linked scheme*: An index block is normally one disk block. Thus, it can be read and written directly by itself. To allow for large files, we may link together several index blocks. For example, an index block might contain a small header giving the name of the file, and a set of the first 100 disk-block addresses. The next address (the last word in the index block) is *nil* (for a small file) or is a pointer to another index block (for a large file).

- *Multilevel index*: A variant of the linked representation is to use a first-level index block to point to a set of second-level index blocks, which in turn point to the file blocks. To access a block, the operating system uses the first-level index to find a second-level index block, and that block to find the desired data block. This approach could be continued to a third or fourth level, depending on the desired maximum file size. With 4,096-byte blocks, we could store 1,024 4-byte pointers in an index block. Two levels of indexes allow 1,048,576 data blocks, which allows a file of up to 4 gigabytes.

- *Combined scheme*: Another alternative, used in the BSD UNIX system, is to keep the first, say, 15 pointers of the index block in the file's index block (or inode). (The directory entry points to the inode, as discussed in Section 20.7.) The first 12 of these pointers point to **direct blocks;** that is, they contain addresses of blocks that contain data of the file. Thus, the data for small (no more than 12 blocks) files do not need a separate index block. If the block size is 4K, then up to 48K of data may be accessed directly. The next three pointers point to **indirect blocks**. The first indirect block pointer is the address of a **single indirect block**. The single indirect block is an index block, containing not data, but rather the addresses of blocks that do contain data. Then there is a **double indirect block** pointer, which contains the address of a block that contains the addresses of blocks that contain pointers to the actual data blocks. The last pointer would contain the address of a **triple indirect block**. Under this method, the number of blocks that can be allocated to a file exceeds the amount of space addressable by the 4-byte file pointers used by many operating systems. A 32-bit file pointer reaches only 2^{32} bytes, or 4 gigabytes. An inode is shown in Figure 11.19.

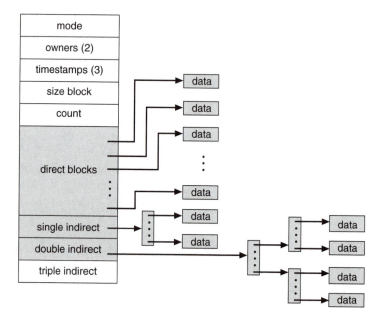

Figure 11.19   The UNIX inode.

Note that indexed allocation suffers from some of the same performance problems as does linked allocation. Specifically, the index blocks can be cached in memory, but the data blocks may be spread all over a partition.

11.6.4 Performance

The allocation methods that we have discussed vary in their storage efficiency and data-block access times. Both are important criteria in selecting the proper method or methods for an operating system to implement.

One difficulty in comparing the performance of the various systems is determining how the systems will be used. A system with mostly sequential access should use a method different from that for a system with mostly random access. For any type of access, contiguous allocation requires only one access to get a disk block. Since we can easily keep the initial address of the file in memory, we can calculate immediately the disk address of the ith block (or the next block) and read it directly.

For linked allocation, we can also keep the address of the next block in memory and read it directly. This method is fine for sequential access; for direct access, however, an access to the ith block might require i disk reads. This problem indicates why linked allocation should not be used for an application requiring direct access.

As a result, some systems support direct-access files by using contiguous allocation and sequential access by linked allocation. For these systems, the type of access to be made must be declared when the file is created. A file created for sequential access will be linked and cannot be used for direct access. A file created for direct access will be contiguous and can support both direct access and sequential access, but its maximum length must be declared when it is created. Notice that, in this case, the operating system must have appropriate data structures and algorithms to support *both* allocation methods. Files can be converted from one type to another by the creation of a new file of the desired type, into which the contents of the old file are copied. The old file may then be deleted, and the new file renamed.

Indexed allocation is more complex. If the index block is already in memory, then the access can be made directly. However, keeping the index block in memory requires considerable space. If this memory space is not available, then we may have to read first the index block and then the desired data block. For a two-level index, two index-block reads might be necessary. For an extremely large file, accessing a block near the end of the file would require reading in all the index blocks to follow the pointer chain before the data block finally could be read. Thus, the performance of indexed allocation depends on the index structure, on the size of the file, and on the position of the block desired.

Some systems combine contiguous allocation with indexed allocation by using contiguous allocation for small files (up to three or four blocks), and automatically switching to an indexed allocation if the file grows large. Since most files are small, and contiguous allocation is efficient for small files, average performance can be good.

For instance, in 1991 Sun Microsystems changed its version of the UNIX operating system to improve performance in the file-system allocation algorithm. The performance measurements indicated that the maximum disk throughput on a typical workstation (12-MIPS Sparcstation1) took 50 percent of the CPU and produced a disk bandwidth of only 1.5 megabytes per second. To improve performance, Sun made changes to allocate space in clusters of size 56K whenever possible. This allocation reduced external fragmentation, and thus seek and latency times. In addition, the disk-reading routines were optimized to read in these large clusters. The inode structure was left unchanged. These changes, plus the use of read-ahead and free-behind (discussed in Section 11.9.2), resulted in 25 percent less CPU being used for substantially improved throughput.

Many other optimizations are in use. Given the disparity between CPU and disk speed, it is not unreasonable to add thousands of extra instructions to the operating system to save just a few disk head movements. Furthermore, this disparity is increasing over time, to the point where hundreds of thousands of instructions reasonably could be used to optimize head movements.

11.7 ■ Free-Space Management

Since there is only a limited amount of disk space, it is necessary to reuse the space from deleted files for new files, if possible. (Write-once optical disks only allow one write to any given sector, and thus such reuse is not physically possible.) To keep track of free disk space, the system maintains a **free-space list**. The free-space list records all disk blocks that are **free**—those not allocated to some file or directory. To create a file, we search the free-space list for the required amount of space, and allocate that space to the new file. This space is then removed from the free-space list. When a file is deleted, its disk space is added to the free-space list. The free-space list, despite its name, might not be implemented as a list, as we shall discuss.

11.7.1 Bit Vector

Frequently, the free-space list is implemented as a **bit map** or **bit vector**. Each block is represented by 1 bit. If the block is free, the bit is 1; if the block is allocated, the bit is 0.

For example, consider a disk where blocks 2, 3, 4, 5, 8, 9, 10, 11, 12, 13, 17, 18, 25, 26, and 27 are free, and the rest of the blocks are allocated. The free-space bit map would be

001111001111110001100000011100000 · · ·

The main advantage of this approach is that it is relatively simple and efficient to find the first free block, or n consecutive free blocks on the disk. Indeed, many computers supply bit-manipulation instructions that can be used effectively for that purpose. For example, the Intel family starting with the 80386 and the Motorola family starting with the 68020 (processors that have powered PCs and Macintosh systems, respectively) have instructions that return the offset in a word of the first bit with the value 1. In fact, the Apple Macintosh Operating System uses the bit-vector method to allocate disk space. To find the first free block, the Macintosh Operating System checks sequentially each word in the bit map to see whether that value is not 0, since a 0-valued word has all 0 bits and represents a set of allocated blocks. The first non-0 word is scanned for the first 1 bit, which is the location of the first free block. The calculation of the block number is

(number of bits per word) × (number of 0-value words) + offset of first 1 bit

Again, we see hardware features driving software functionality. Unfortunately, bit vectors are inefficient unless the entire vector is kept in main memory (and is written to disk occasionally for recovery needs). Keeping it in main memory is possible for smaller disks, such as on microcomputers, but not for larger ones. A 1.3-gigabyte disk with 512-byte blocks would need a bit map of over 332K to track its free blocks. Clustering the blocks in groups of four reduces this number to 83K per disk.

11.7.2 Linked List

Another approach is to link together all the free disk blocks, keeping a pointer to the first free block in a special location on the disk and caching it in memory. This first block contains a pointer to the next free disk block, and so on. In our example (Section 11.7.1), we would keep a pointer to block 2, as the first free block. Block 2 would contain a pointer to block 3, which would point to block 4, which would point to block 5, which would point to block 8, and so on (Figure 11.20). However, this scheme is not efficient; to traverse the list, we must read each block, which requires substantial I/O time. Fortunately, traversing the free list is not a frequent action. Usually, the operating system simply needs a free block so that it can allocate that block to a file, so the first block in the free list is used. Note that the FAT method incorporates free-block accounting into the allocation data structure. No separate method is needed.

11.7.3 Grouping

A modification of the free-list approach is to store the addresses of n free blocks in the first free block. The first $n - 1$ of these blocks are actually free. The final block contains the addresses of another n free blocks, and so on. The importance

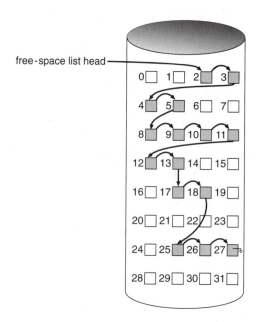

free-space list head

Figure 11.20   Linked free-space list on disk.

of this implementation is that the addresses of a large number of free blocks can be found quickly, unlike in the standard linked-list approach.

11.7.4 Counting

Another approach is to take advantage of the fact that, generally, several contiguous blocks may be allocated or freed simultaneously, particularly when space is allocated with the contiguous allocation algorithm or through clustering. Thus, rather than keeping a list of n free disk addresses, we can keep the address of the first free block and the number n of free contiguous blocks that follow the first block. Each entry in the free-space list then consists of a disk address and a count. Although each entry requires more space than would a simple disk address, the overall list will be shorter, as long as the count is generally greater than 1.

11.8 ■ Directory Implementation

The selection of directory-allocation and directory-management algorithms has a large effect on the efficiency, performance, and reliability of the file system. Therefore, it is important to understand the tradeoffs involved in these algorithms.

11.8.1 Linear List

The simplest method of implementing a directory is to use a linear list of file names with pointers to the data blocks. A linear list of directory entries requires a linear search to find a particular entry. This method is simple to program but is time consuming to execute. To create a new file, we must first search the directory to be sure that no existing file has the same name. Then, we add a new entry at the end of the directory. To delete a file, we search the directory for the named file, then release the space allocated to it. To reuse the directory entry, we can do one of several things. We can mark the entry as unused (by assigning it a special name, such as an all-blank name, or with a used–unused bit in each entry), or we can attach it to a list of free directory entries. A third alternative is to copy into the freed location the final entry in the directory, and to decrease the length of the directory. We can also use a linked list to decrease the time to delete a file.

The real disadvantage of a linear list of directory entries is the linear search to find a file. Directory information is used frequently, and a slow implementation of access to it would be noticed by users. In fact, many operating systems implement a software cache to store the most recently used directory information. A cache hit avoids constantly rereading the information from disk. A sorted list allows a binary search and decreases the average search time. However, the requirement that the list be kept sorted may complicate creating and deleting files, since we may have to move substantial amounts of directory information to maintain a sorted directory. A more sophisticated tree data structure, such as a B-tree, might help here. An advantage of the sorted list is that a sorted directory listing can be produced without a separate sort step.

11.8.2 Hash Table

Another data structure that has been used for a file directory is a **hash table**. In this method, a linear list stores the directory entries, but a hash data structure is also used. The hash table takes a value computed from the file name and returns a pointer to the file name in the linear list. Therefore, it can greatly decrease the directory search time. Insertion and deletion are also fairly straightforward, although some provision must be made for **collisions**—situations where two file names hash to the same location. The major difficulties with a hash table are the generally fixed size of the hash table and the dependence of the hash function on the size of the hash table.

For example, assume that we make a linear-probing hash table that holds 64 entries. The hash function converts file names into integers from 0 to 63, for instance, by using the remainder of a division by 64. If we later try to create a sixty-fifth file, we must enlarge the directory hash table—say, to 128 entries. As a result, we need a new hash function, which must map file names to the range 0 to 127, and we must reorganize the existing directory entries to reflect their new hash-function values. Alternately, a **chained-overflow hash table** can be used. Each hash entry can be a linked list instead of an individual value, and we can resolve collisions by adding the new entry to the linked list. Lookups may be slowed, because searching for a name might require stepping through a linked list of colliding table entries, but this operation is likely to be much faster than a linear search through the entire directory.

11.9 ■ Efficiency and Performance

Now that we have discussed the block-allocation and directory-management options, we can further consider their effect on performance and efficient disk use. Disks tend to be a major bottleneck in system performance, since they are the slowest main computer component. In this section, we discuss techniques that improve the efficiency and performance of secondary storage.

11.9.1 Efficiency

The efficient use of disk space is heavily dependent on the disk allocation and directory algorithms in use. For instance, UNIX inodes are preallocated on a partition. Even an "empty" disk has a percentage of its space lost to inodes. However, by preallocating the inodes and spreading them across the partition, we improve the file system's performance. This improved performance is a result of the UNIX allocation and free-space algorithms, which try to keep a file's data blocks near that file's inode block to reduce seek time.

As another example, let us reconsider the clustering scheme discussed in Section 11.6, which aids in file-seek and file-transfer performance at the cost of internal fragmentation. To reduce this fragmentation, BSD UNIX varies the cluster size as a file grows. Large clusters are used where they can be filled, and small clusters are used for small files and the last cluster of a file. This system is described in Chapter 20.

Also requiring consideration are the types of data normally kept in a file's directory (or inode) entry. Commonly, a "last write date" is recorded to supply information to the user and to determine whether the file needs to be backed up. Some systems also keep a "last access date," so that a user can determine when the file was last read. The result of keeping this information is that, whenever the file is read, a field in the directory structure needs to be written to. This change requires the block to be read into memory, a section changed, and the block written back out to disk, because operations on disks occur only in block (or cluster) chunks. So, any time a file is opened for reading, its directory entry must be read and written as well. This requirement causes inefficient operation for frequently accessed files, so we must weigh its benefit against its performance cost when designing a file system. Generally, *every* data item associated with a file needs to be considered for its affect on efficiency and performance.

As an example, consider how efficiency is affected by the size of the pointers used to access data. Most systems use either 16- or 32-bit pointers throughout the operating system. These pointer sizes limit the length of a file to either 2^{16} (64K), or 2^{32} bytes (4 gigabytes). Some systems implement 64-bit pointers to increase this limit to 2^{64} bytes, which is a very large number indeed. However, 64-bit pointers take more space to store, and in turn make the allocation and free-space management methods (linked lists, indexes, and so on) use more disk space.

One of the difficulties in choosing a pointer size, or indeed any fixed allocation size within an operating system, is planning for the effects of changing technology. Consider that the IBM PC XT had a 10-megabyte hard drive, and an MS-DOS file system that could support only 32 megabytes. (Each FAT entry was 12 bits, pointing to an 8K cluster.) As disk capacities increased, larger disks had to be split into 32-megabyte partitions, because the file system could not track blocks beyond 32 megabytes. As hard disks of over 100-megabyte capacities became common, the disk data structures and algorithms in MS-DOS had to be modified to allow larger file systems. (Each FAT entry was expanded to 16 bits, and later to 32 bits.) The initial file-system decisions were made for efficiency reasons; however, with the advent of MS-DOS, Version 4, millions of computer users were inconvenienced when they had to switch to the new, larger file system.

As another example, consider the evolution of Sun's Solaris operating system. Originally, many data structures were of fixed lengths, allocated at system startup. These structures included the process table and the open-file table. When the process table became full, no more processes could be created. When the file table became full, no more files could be opened. The system would fail to provide services to the users. These table sizes could be increased only by recompiling the kernel and rebooting the system. Since the release of Solaris 2, almost all kernel structures are allocated dynamically, eliminating these artificial limits on system performance. Of course, the algorithms that manipulate these tables are more complicated, and the operating system is a little slower because it must dynamically allocate and deallocate table entries, but that price is the usual one for more functional generality.

11.9.2 Performance

Once the basic disk methods are selected, there are still several ways to improve performance. As noted in Chapter 2, most disk controllers include local memory to form an on-board **cache** that is sufficiently large to store entire tracks at a time. Once a seek is performed, the track is read into the disk cache starting at the sector under the disk head (alleviating latency time). The disk controller then transfers any sector requests to the operating system. Once blocks make it from the disk controller into main memory, the operating system may cache the blocks there. Some systems maintain a separate section of main memory for a **disk cache,** where blocks are kept under the assumption that they will be used again shortly. LRU is a reasonable general-purpose algorithm for block replacement. Other systems (such as Sun's version of UNIX) treat all unused physical memory as a buffer pool that is shared by the paging system and the disk-block caching system. A system performing many I/O operations will use most of its memory as a block cache, whereas a system executing many programs will use more memory as paging space.

Some systems optimize their disk cache by using different replacement algorithms, depending on the access type of the file. A file being read or written sequentially should not have its blocks replaced in LRU order, because the most recently used block will be used last, or perhaps never again. Instead, sequential access may be optimized by techniques known as free-behind and read-ahead. **Free-behind** removes a block from the buffer as soon as the next block is requested. The previous blocks are not likely to be used again and waste buffer space. With **read-ahead,** a requested block and several subsequent blocks are read and cached. It is likely that these blocks will be requested after the current block is processed. Retrieving these blocks from the disk in one transfer and caching them saves considerable time. A track cache on the controller does not eliminate the need for read-ahead on a multiprogrammed system, because of the high latency and overhead of many small transfers from track cache to main memory.

Another method of using main memory to improve performance is common on personal computers. A section of memory is set aside and treated as a **virtual disk,** or **RAM disk**. In this case, a RAM disk device driver accepts all the standard disk operations, but performs those operations on the memory section, instead of on a disk. All disk operations can then be executed on this RAM disk and, except for the lightning-fast speed, users will not notice a difference. Unfortunately, RAM disks are useful only for temporary storage, since a power failure or a reboot of the system will usually erase them. Commonly, temporary files such as intermediate compiler files are stored there.

The difference between a RAM disk and a disk cache is that the contents of the RAM disk are totally user controlled, whereas those of the disk cache are under the control of the operating system. For instance, a RAM disk will stay empty until the user (or programs, at a user's direction) creates files there. Figure 11.21 shows the possible caching locations in a system.

11.10 ■ Recovery

Since files and directories are kept both in main memory and on disk, we must take care to ensure that system failure does not result in loss of data or in data inconsistency.

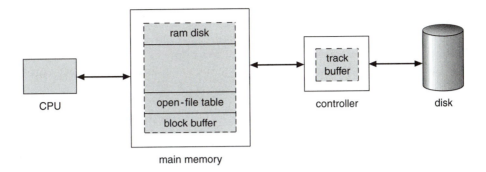

Figure 11.21   Various disk-caching locations.

11.10.1 Consistency Checking

As we discussed in Section 11.8, part of the directory information is kept in main memory (in the cache) to speed up access. The directory information in main memory is generally more up to date than is the corresponding information on the disk, because the write of cached directory information to disk does not necessarily occur as soon as the update takes place.

Consider the possible effect of a computer crash. The table of opened files is generally lost, and with it any changes in the directories of opened files. This event can leave the file system in an inconsistent state: The actual state of some files is not as described in the directory structure. Frequently, a special program is run at reboot time to check for and correct disk inconsistencies.

The **consistency checker** compares the data in the directory structure with the data blocks on disk, and tries to fix any inconsistencies it finds. The allocation and free-space management algorithms dictate what types of problems the checker can find, and how successful it will be in fixing those problems. For instance, if linked allocation is used and there is a link from any block to its next block, then the entire file can be reconstructed from the data blocks, and the directory structure can be recreated. The loss of a directory entry on an indexed allocation system could be disastrous, because the data blocks have no knowledge of one another. For this reason, UNIX caches directory entries for reads, but any data write that results in space allocation generally causes the inode block to be written to disk before the corresponding data blocks are.

11.10.2 Backup and Restore

Because magnetic disks sometimes fail, we must ensure that the data are not lost forever. To this end, we can use system programs to **back up** data from disk to another storage device, such as a floppy disk, magnetic tape, or optical disk. Recovery from the loss of an individual file, or of an entire disk, may then be a matter of **restoring** the data from backup.

To minimize the copying needed, we can use information from each file's directory entry. For instance, if the backup program knows when the last backup of a file was done, and the file's last write date in the directory indicates that the file has not changed since then, then the file does not need to be copied again. A typical backup schedule follows:

- *Day* 1: Copy to a backup medium all files from the disk—called a **full backup**.

- *Day* 2: Copy to another medium all files changed since day 1—an **incremental backup**.

- *Day* 3: Copy to another medium all files changed since day 2.

.

.

.

- *Day* N: Copy to another medium all files changed since day N − 1. Then, go back to day 1.

The new cycle can have its backup written over the previous set, or onto a new set of backup media. In this manner, we can restore an entire disk by starting restores with the full backup, and continuing through each of the incremental backups. Of course, the larger N is, the more tapes or disks need to be read for a complete restore. An added advantage of this backup cycle is that we can restore any file accidently deleted during the cycle by retrieving the deleted file from the backup of the previous day. The length of the cycle is a compromise between the amount of backup medium needed and the number of days back from which a restore can be done.

It can happen that a user notices that a particular file is missing or corrupted long after the damage was done. To protect against this situation, it is usual to take a full backup from time to time that will be saved "forever," rather than its backup medium being reused. It is also a good idea to store these permanent backups in a location far away from the regular backups, to protect against hazards such as a fire that destroys the computer content and all the backups too.

If the backup cycle reuses media, we must be careful not to reuse the media too many times—if the media wear out, it may not be possible to restore data.

11.11 ■ Summary

A file is an abstract data type defined and implemented by the operating system. It is a sequence of logical records. A logical record may be a byte, a line (fixed or variable length), or a more complex data item. The operating system may specifically support various record types or may leave that support to the application program.

The major task for the operating system is to map the logical file concept onto physical storage devices such as magnetic tape or disk. Since the physical record size of the device may not be the same as the logical record size, it may be necessary to block logical records into physical records. Again, this task may be supported by the operating system or left for the application program.

Tape-based file systems are constrained; most file systems are disk-based. Tapes are commonly used for data transport between machines, or for backup or archival storage.

Each device in a file system keeps a volume table of contents or device directory listing the location of the files on the device. In addition, it is useful to create directories to allow files to be organized. A single-level directory in a multiuser system causes naming problems, since each file must have a unique name. A two-level directory solves this problem by creating a separate directory for each user. Each user has her own directory, which contains her own files.

The directory lists the files by name, and includes such information as the file's location on the disk, length, type, owner, time of creation, time of last use, and so on.

The natural generalization of a two-level directory is a tree-structured directory. A tree-structured directory allows a user to create subdirectories to organize his files. Acyclic-graph directory structures allow subdirectories and files to be shared, but complicate searching and deletion. A general graph structure allows complete flexibility in the sharing of files and directories, but sometimes requires garbage collection to recover unused disk space.

Since files are the main information-storage mechanism in most computer systems, file protection is needed. Access to files can be controlled separately for each type of access: read, write, execute, append, list directory, and so on. File protection can be provided by passwords, by access lists, or by special ad hoc techniques.

The file system resides permanently on *secondary storage*, which has the main requirement that it must be able to hold a large amount of data, permanently. The most common secondary-storage medium is the disk.

File systems are often implemented in a layered or modular structure. The lower levels deal with the physical properties of storage devices. Upper levels deal with symbolic file names and logical properties of files. Intermediate levels map the logical file concepts into physical device properties.

The various files can be allocated space on the disk in three ways: through contiguous, linked, or indexed allocation. Contiguous allocation can suffer from external fragmentation. Direct-access is very inefficient with linked allocation. Indexed allocation may require substantial overhead for its index block. There are many ways in which these algorithms can be optimized. Contiguous space may be enlarged through extents to increase flexibility and to decrease external fragmentation. Indexed allocation can be done in clusters of multiple blocks to increase throughput and to reduce the number of index entries needed. Indexing in large clusters is similar to contiguous allocation with extents.

Free-space allocation methods also influence the efficiency of use of disk space, the performance of the file system, and the reliability of secondary storage. The methods used include bit vectors and linked lists. Optimizations include grouping, counting, and the FAT, which places the linked list in one contiguous area.

The directory-management routines must consider efficiency, performance, and reliability. A hash table is the most frequently used method; it is fast and efficient. Unfortunately, damage to the table or a system crash could result in the directory information not corresponding to the disk's contents. A *consistency checker*—a systems program such as fsck in UNIX, or chkdsk in MS-DOS—can be used to repair the damage.

■ Exercises

11.1 Consider a file system where a file can be deleted and its disk space reclaimed while links to that file still exist. What problems may occur if a new file is created in the same storage area or with the same absolute path name? How can these problems be avoided?

11.2 Some systems automatically delete all user files when a user logs off or a job terminates, unless the user explicitly requests that the files be kept; other systems keep all files unless the user explicitly deletes files. Discuss the relative merits of each approach.

11.3 Why do some systems keep track of the type of a file, whereas others leave it to the user or simply do not implement multiple file types? Which system is "better"? Justify your answer.

11.4 Similarly, some systems support many types of structures for a file's data, whereas other systems simply support a stream of bytes. What are the advantages and disadvantages of each?

11.5 What are the advantages and the disadvantages of recording the name of the creating program with the file's attributes (as is done in the Macintosh operating system)?

11.6 Could you simulate a multilevel directory structure with a single-level directory structure in which arbitrarily long names can be used? If your answer is yes, explain how you can do so, and contrast this scheme with the multilevel directory scheme. If your answer is no, explain what prevents your simulation's success. Would your answer change if file names were limited to seven characters? Explain your answer.

11.7 Explain the purpose of the open and close operations.

11.8 Some systems automatically open a file when it is referenced for the first time, and close the file when the job terminates. Discuss the advantages and the disadvantages of this scheme. Compare it to the more traditional one, where the user has to open and close the file explicitly.

11.9 Give an example of an application in which data in a file should be accessed in the following order:

   a. Sequentially

   b. Randomly

11.10 Some systems provide file sharing by maintaining a single copy of a file; other systems maintain several copies, one for each of the users sharing the file. Discuss the relative merits of each approach.

11.11 In some systems, a subdirectory can be read and written by an authorized user, just as ordinary files can be.

   a. Describe two protection problems that could arise.

   b. Suggest a scheme for dealing with each of the protection problems that you named in part a.

11.12 Consider a system that supports 5,000 users. Suppose that you want to allow 4,990 of these users to be able to access one file.

   a. How would you specify this protection scheme in UNIX?

   b. Suggest a protection scheme that is more effective than the scheme provided by UNIX.

11.13 Researchers have suggested that, instead of having an access list associated with each file (specifying which users can access the file, and how), we should have a *user control list* associated with each user (specifying which files a user can access, and how). Discuss the relative merits of these two schemes.

11.14 Consider a file currently consisting of 100 blocks. Assume that the file control block (and the index block, in the case of indexed allocation) is already in memory. Calculate how many disk I/O operations are required for contiguous, linked, and indexed (single-level) allocation strategies, if, for one block, the following conditions hold. In the contiguous-allocation case, assume that there is no room to grow in the beginning, but there is room to grow in the end. Assume that the block information to be added is stored in memory.

   a. The block is added at the beginning.

   b. The block is added in the middle.

   c. The block is added at the end.

   d. The block is removed from the beginning.

   e. The block is removed from the middle.

   f. The block is removed from the end.

11.15 Consider a system where free space is kept in a free-space list.

   a. Suppose that the pointer to the free-space list is lost. Can the system reconstruct the free-space list? Explain your answer.

   b. Suggest a scheme to ensure that the pointer is never lost as a result of memory failure.

11.16 What problems could occur if a system allowed a file system to be mounted simultaneously at more than one location?

11.17 Why must the bit map for file allocation be kept on mass storage, rather than in main memory?

11.18 Consider a system that supports the strategies of contiguous, linked, and indexed allocation. What criteria should you use in deciding which strategy is best utilized for a particular file?

11.19 Consider a file system on a disk that has both logical and physical block sizes of 512 bytes. Assume that the information about each file is already in memory. For each of the three allocation strategies (contiguous, linked, and indexed), answer these questions:

   a. How is the logical-to-physical address mapping accomplished in this system? (For the indexed allocation, assume that a file is always less than 512 blocks long.)

   b. If we are currently at logical block 10 (the last block accessed was block 10) and want to access logical block 4, how many physical blocks must be read from the disk?

11.20 One problem with contiguous allocation is that the user must preallocate enough space for each file. If the file grows to be larger than the space allocated for it, special actions must be taken. One solution to this problem is to define a file structure consisting of an initial contiguous area (of a specified size). If this area is filled, the operating system automatically defines an overflow area that is linked to the initial contiguous area. If the overflow area is filled, another overflow area is allocated. Compare this implementation of a file with the standard contiguous and linked implementations.

11.21 Fragmentation on a storage device could be eliminated by recompaction of the information. Typical disk devices do not have relocation or base registers (such as are used when memory is to be compacted), so how can we relocate files? Give three reasons why recompaction and relocation of files often are avoided.

11.22 How do caches help improve performance? Why do systems not use more or larger caches?

11.23 In what situations would using memory as a RAM disk be more useful than using it as a disk cache?

11.24 Why is it advantageous for the user for an operating system to allocate its internal tables dynamically? What are the penalties to the operating system for doing so?

11.25 Consider the following backup scheme:

- Day 1: Copy to a backup medium all files from the disk.
- Day 2: Copy to another medium all files changed since day 1.
- Day 3: Copy to another medium all files changed since day 1.

This schedule differs from the one in Section 11.10.2 in that all subsequent backups copy all files modified since the first full backup. What are the benefits of this system over the one in Section 11.10.2? What are the drawbacks? Are restore operations made easier or more difficult? Explain your answer.

Bibliographical Notes

General discussions concerning file systems were offered by Grosshans [1986]. Database systems and their file structures were described in full in Silberschatz and colleagues [1997].

A multilevel directory structure was first implemented on the MULTICS system [Organick 1972]. Most operating systems now implement multilevel directory structures. These include UNIX, the Apple Macintosh operating system [Apple 1991], and MS-DOS.

The Network File System (NFS) was designed by Sun Microsystems, and allows directory structures to be spread across networked computer systems.

Discussions concerning NFS were presented in Sandberg and colleagues [1985], Sandberg [1987], and Sun Microsystems' publication [1990].

Apple publication [1991] describes the Apple Macintosh disk-space management scheme. The MS-DOS FAT system was explained in Norton and Wilton [1988]; the OS/2 description is found in Iacobucci [1988]. IBM allocation methods were described by Deitel [1990]. The internals of the BSD UNIX system were covered in full by Leffler and colleagues [1989]. McVoy and Kleiman [1991] presented optimizations to these methods made in SunOS.

Chapter 12

I/O SYSTEMS

The two main jobs of a computer are I/O and processing. In many cases, the main job is I/O, and the processing is merely incidental. For instance, when we browse a web page or edit a file, our immediate interest is to read or type in information; it is not to compute an answer.

The role of the operating system in computer I/O is to manage and control I/O operations and I/O devices. Although related topics appear in other chapters, here we bring together the pieces to paint a complete picture. First, we describe the basics of I/O hardware, because the nature of the hardware interface places requirements on the internal facilities of the operating system. Next, we discuss the I/O services that the operating system provides, and the embodiment of these services in the application I/O interface. Then, we explain how the operating system bridges the gap between the hardware interface and the application interface. Finally, we discuss the performance aspects of I/O, and the principles of operating-system design that improve the I/O performance.

12.1 ■ Overview

The control of devices connected to the computer is a major concern of operating-system designers. Because I/O devices vary so widely in their function and speed (consider a mouse, a hard disk, and a CD-ROM jukebox), a variety of methods are needed to control them. These methods form the **I/O**

subsystem of the kernel, which separates the rest of the kernel from the complexity of managing I/O devices.

I/O-device technology exhibits two conflicting trends. On the one hand, we see increasing standardization of software and hardware interfaces. This trend helps us to incorporate improved device generations into existing computers and operating systems. On the other hand, we see an increasingly broad variety of I/O devices. Some new devices are so unlike previous devices that it is a challenge to incorporate them into our computers and operating systems. This challenge is met by a combination of hardware and software techniques. The basic I/O hardware elements—such as ports, buses, and device controllers—accommodate a wide variety of I/O devices. To encapsulate the details and oddities of different devices, we structure the kernel of an operating system to use **device-driver modules**. The device drivers present a uniform device-access interface to the I/O subsystem, much as system calls provide a standard interface between the application and the operating system.

In this chapter, we describe the basic hardware mechanisms that perform I/O, and the way that the operating system organizes the I/O devices into categories to form a general application-I/O interface. We discuss the kernel mechanisms that bridge the gap between I/O hardware and application software, and we describe the structure, services, and performance of the I/O subsystem.

12.2 ■ I/O Hardware

Computers operate a great many kinds of devices. General types include storage devices (disks, tapes), transmission devices (network cards, modems), and human-interface devices (screen, keyboard, mouse). Other devices are more specialized. Consider the steering of a military fighter jet or of a space shuttle. In these aircraft, a human gives input to the flight computer via a joystick, and the computer sends output commands that cause motors to move rudders, flaps, and thrusters.

Despite the incredible variety of I/O devices that can be used with a computer, we need only a few concepts to understand how the devices are attached, and how the software can control the hardware.

A device communicates with a computer system by sending signals over a cable or even through the air. The device communicates with the machine via a connection point termed a **port** (for example, a serial port). If one or more devices use a common set of wires, the connection is called a **bus**. In slightly more formal terms, a bus is a set of wires and a rigidly defined protocol that specifies a set of messages that can be sent on the wires. In terms of the electronics, the messages are conveyed by patterns of electrical voltages that are applied to the wires with defined timings. When device A has a cable that plugs into device B, and device B has a cable that plugs into device C, and device C

plugs into a port on the computer, this arrangement is called a **daisy chain**. It usually operates as a bus.

Buses are used widely in computer architecture. Figure 12.1 shows a typical PC bus structure. This figure shows a PCI bus (the common PC system bus) that connects the processor–memory subsystem to the fast devices, and an expansion bus that connects relatively slow devices, such as the keyboard and serial and parallel ports. In the upper-right portion of the figure, four disks are connected together on a SCSI bus that is plugged into a SCSI controller.

A **controller** is a collection of electronics that can operate a port, a bus, or a device. A serial-port controller is an example of a simple device controller. It is a single chip in the computer that controls the signals on the wires of a serial port. By contrast, a SCSI bus controller is not simple. Because the SCSI protocol is complex, the SCSI bus controller is often implemented as a separate circuit board (a **host adapter**) that plugs into the computer. It typically contains a processor, microcode, and some private memory to enable it to process the SCSI protocol messages. Some devices have their own built-in controllers. If you look at a disk drive, you will see a circuit board attached to one side. This board is the disk controller. It implements the disk side of the protocol for some kind

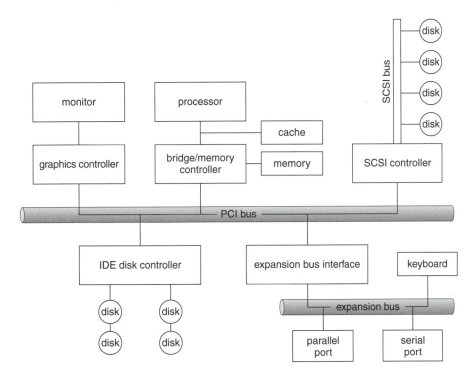

Figure 12.1 A typical PC bus structure.

of connection (SCSI or IDE, for instance). It has microcode and a processor to do many tasks, such as bad-sector mapping, prefetching, buffering, and caching.

How can the processor give commands and data to a controller to accomplish an I/O transfer? The short answer is that the controller has one or more registers for data and control signals. The processor communicates with the controller by reading and writing bit patterns in these registers. One way that this communication can occur is through the use of special I/O instructions that specify the transfer of a byte or word to an I/O port address. The I/O instruction triggers bus lines to select the proper device and to move bits into or out of a device register. Alternately, the device controller can support memory-mapped I/O. In this case, the device-control registers are mapped into the address space of the processor. The CPU executes I/O requests using the standard data-transfer instructions to read and write the device-control registers.

Several systems use both techniques. For instance, PC compatibles use I/O instructions to control some devices, and use memory-mapped I/O to control others. Figure 12.2 shows the usual PC I/O port addresses. The graphics controller has I/O ports for basic control operations, but the controller has a large memory-mapped region to hold screen contents. The processor sends output to the screen by writing data into the memory-mapped region. The controller generates the screen image based on the contents of this memory. This technique is simple to use. Moreover, writing millions of bytes to the graphics memory is faster than issuing millions of I/O instructions. But the ease of writing to a memory-mapped I/O controller is offset by a disadvantage: Because a common type of software fault is a write through an incorrect pointer to an unintended region of memory, a memory-mapped device register is

I/O address range (hexadecimal)	device
000-00F	DMA controller
020-021	interrupt controller
040-043	timer
200-20F	game controller
2F8-2FF	serial port (secondary)
320-32F	hard disk controller
378-37F	parallel port
3D0-3DF	graphics controller
3F0-3F7	diskette drive controller
3F8-3FF	serial port (primary)

Figure 12.2   Device I/O port locations on PC-compatible computers.

vulnerable to accidental modification. Of course, protected memory reduces this risk.

An I/O port typically consists of four registers, called the status, control, data-in, and data-out registers. The status register contains bits that can be read by the host. These bits indicate states such as whether the current command has completed, whether a byte is available to be read from the data-in register, and whether there has been a device error. The control register can be written by the host to start a command or to change the mode of a device. For instance, a certain bit in the control register of a serial port chooses between full-duplex and half-duplex communication, another enables parity checking, a third bit sets the word length to 7 or 8 bits, and other bits select one of the speeds supported by the serial port. The data-in register is read by the host to get input, and the data-out register is written by the host to send output. The data registers are typically 1 to 4 bytes. Some controllers have FIFO chips that can hold several bytes of input or output data to expand the capacity of the controller beyond the size of the data register. A FIFO chip can hold a small burst of data until the device or host is able to receive those data.

12.2.1 Polling

The complete protocol for interaction between the host and a controller can be intricate, but the basic **handshaking** notion is simple. We explain handshaking by an example. We assume that 2 bits are used to coordinate the producer–consumer relationship between the controller and the host. The controller indicates its state through the busy bit in the status register. (Recall that to **set** a bit means to write a 1 into the bit, and to **clear** a bit means to write a 0 into it.) The controller sets the busy bit when it is busy working, and clears the busy bit when it is ready to accept the next command. The host signals its wishes via the command-ready bit in the command register. The host sets the command-ready bit when a command is available for the controller to execute. For this example, the host writes output through a port, coordinating with the controller by handshaking as follows.

1. The host repeatedly reads the busy bit until that bit becomes clear.

2. The host sets the write bit in the command register and writes a byte into the data-out register.

3. The host sets the command-ready bit.

4. When the controller notices that the command-ready bit is set, it sets the busy bit.

5. The controller reads the command register and sees the write command. It reads the data-out register to get the byte, and does the I/O to the device.

6. The controller clears the `command-ready` bit, clears the `error` bit in the status register to indicate that the device I/O succeeded, and clears the `busy` bit to indicate that it is finished.

This loop is repeated for each byte.

In step 1, the host is **busy-waiting** or **polling**: It is in a loop, reading the `status` register over and over until the busy bit becomes clear. If the controller and device are fast, this method is a reasonable one. But if the wait may be long, the host should probably switch to another task. But then how does the host know when the controller has become idle? For some devices, the host must service the device quickly, or data will be lost. For instance, when data are streaming in on a serial port or from a keyboard, the small buffer on the controller will overflow and data will be lost if the host waits too long before returning to read the bytes.

In many computer architectures, three CPU-instruction cycles are sufficient to poll a device: `read` a device register, `logical--and` to extract a status bit, and `branch` if not zero. Clearly, the basic polling operation is efficient. But polling becomes inefficient when it is attempted repeatedly, yet rarely finds a device to be ready for service, while other useful CPU processing remains undone. In such instances, it may be more efficient to arrange for the hardware controller to notify the CPU when the device becomes ready for service, rather than to require the CPU to poll repeatedly for an I/O completion. The hardware mechanism that enables a device to notify the CPU is called an interrupt.

12.2.2 Interrupts

The basic **interrupt** mechanism works as follows. The CPU hardware has a wire called the **interrupt request line** that the CPU senses after executing every instruction. When the CPU detects that a controller has asserted a signal on the interrupt request line, the CPU saves a small amount of state, such as the current value of the instruction pointer, and jumps to the **interrupt-handler** routine at a fixed address in memory. The interrupt handler determines the cause of the interrupt, performs the necessary processing, and executes a `return from interrupt` instruction to return the CPU to the execution state prior to the interrupt. We say that the device controller **raises** an interrupt by asserting a signal on the interrupt request line, the CPU **catches** the interrupt and **dispatches** to the interrupt handler, and the handler **clears** the interrupt by servicing the device. Figure 12.3 summarizes the interrupt-driven I/O cycle.

This basic interrupt mechanism enables the CPU to respond to an asynchronous event, such as a device controller becoming ready for service. In a modern operating system, we need more sophisticated interrupt-handling features. First, we need the ability to defer interrupt handling during critical processing. Second, we need an efficient way to dispatch to the proper interrupt handler for a device, without first polling all the devices to see which one raised

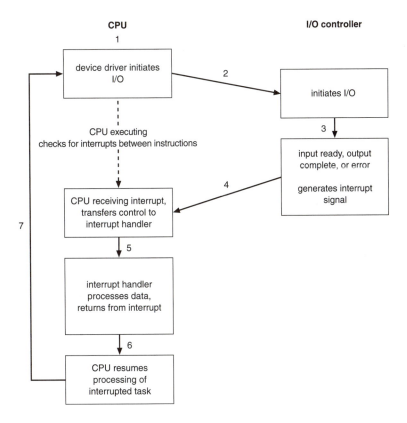

Figure 12.3   Interrupt-driven I/O cycle.

the interrupt. Third, we need multilevel interrupts, so that the operating system can distinguish between high- and low-priority interrupts, and can respond with the appropriate degree of urgency. In modern computer hardware, these three features are provided by the CPU and by the **interrupt-controller** hardware.

Most CPUs have two interrupt request lines. One is the **nonmaskable interrupt,** which is reserved for events such as unrecoverable memory errors. The second interrupt line is **maskable**: It can be turned off by the CPU before the execution of critical instruction sequences that must not be interrupted. The maskable interrupt is used by device controllers to request service.

The interrupt mechanism accepts an address—a number that selects a specific interrupt-handling routine from a small set. In most architectures, this address is an offset in a table called the **interrupt vector**. This vector contains the memory addresses of specialized interrupt handlers. The purpose of a vectored interrupt mechanism is to reduce the need for a single interrupt handler to search all possible sources of interrupts to determine which one needs service. In practice, however, computers have more devices (and hence, interrupt handlers) than they have address elements in the interrupt vector. A common way to solve this problem is to use the technique of **interrupt chaining,** in which each element in the interrupt vector points to the head of a list of interrupt handlers. When an interrupt is raised, the handlers on the corresponding list are called one by one, until one is found that can service the request. This structure is a compromise between the overhead of a huge interrupt table and the inefficiency of a dispatching to a single interrupt handler.

Figure 12.4 illustrates the design of the interrupt vector for the Intel Pentium Processor. We use the first 32 events, which are nonmaskable, to signal various error conditions. We use the events from 32 to 255, which are maskable, for purposes such as device-generated interrupts.

The interrupt mechanism also implements a system of **interrupt priority levels**. This mechanism enables the CPU to defer the handling of low-priority interrupts without masking off all interrupts, and makes it possible for a high-priority interrupt to preempt the execution of a low-priority interrupt.

A modern operating system interacts with the interrupt mechanism in several ways. At boot time, the operating system probes the hardware buses to determine what devices are present, and installs the corresponding interrupt handlers into the interrupt vector. During I/O, interrupts are raised by the various device controllers when they are ready for service. These interrupts signify that output has completed, or that input data are available, or that a

vector number	description
0	divide error
1	debug exception
2	null interrupt
3	breakpoint
4	INTO-detected overflow
5	bound range exception
6	invalid opcode
7	device not available
8	double fault
9	coprocessor segment overrun (reserved)
10	invalid task state segment
11	segment not present
12	stack fault
13	general protection
14	page fault
15	(Intel reserved, do not use)
16	floating-point error
17	alignment check
18	machine check
19–31	(Intel reserved, do not use)
32–255	maskable interrupts

Figure 12.4   Intel Pentium processor event-vector table.

failure has been detected. The interrupt mechanism also handles a wide variety of **exceptions,** such as dividing by zero, accessing a protected or nonexistent memory address, or attempting to execute a privileged instruction from user mode. The events that trigger interrupts have a common property: They are occurrences that induce the CPU to execute an urgent, self-contained routine.

An operating system has other good uses for an efficient hardware mechanism that saves a small amount of processor state, and then calls a privileged routine in the kernel. For example, many operating systems use the interrupt mechanism for virtual-memory paging. A page fault is an exception that raises an interrupt. The interrupt suspends the current process and jumps to the page-fault handler in the kernel. This handler saves the state of the process, moves the process to the wait queue, performs page-cache management, schedules an I/O operation to fetch the page, schedules another process to resume execution, and then returns from the interrupt.

Another example is found in the implementation of system calls. A **system call** is a function that is called by an application to invoke a kernel service. The system call checks the arguments given by the application, builds a data structure to convey the arguments to the kernel, and then executes a special instruction called a **software interrupt,** or a **trap**. This instruction has an operand that identifies the desired kernel service. When the system call executes the trap instruction, the interrupt hardware saves the state of the user code, switches to supervisor mode, and dispatches to the kernel routine that implements the requested service. The trap is given a relatively low interrupt priority compared to those assigned to device interrupts—executing a system call on behalf of an application is less urgent than is servicing a device controller before the latter's FIFO queue overflows and loses data.

We can also use interrupts to manage the flow of control within the kernel. For example, consider the processing required to complete a disk read. One step is to copy data from the kernel space to the user buffer. This copying is time consuming, but it is not urgent—it should not block other high-priority interrupt handling. Another step is to start the next pending I/O for that disk drive. This step has higher priority: If the disks are to be used efficiently, we need to start the next I/O as soon as the previous one completes. Consequently, the kernel code that completes a disk read is implemented by a pair of interrupt handlers. The high-priority handler records the I/O status, clears the device interrupt, starts the next pending I/O, and raises a low-priority interrupt to complete the work. Later, when the CPU is not occupied with high-priority work, the low-priority interrupt will be dispatched. The corresponding handler completes the user-level I/O by copying data from kernel buffers to the application space, and then by calling the scheduler to place the application on the ready queue.

A threaded kernel architecture is well-suited to implement multiple interrupt priorities and to enforce the precedence of interrupt handling over background processing in kernel and application routines. We illustrate this point with the Solaris kernel. In Solaris, interrupt handlers are executed as kernel threads. A range of high priorities is reserved for these threads. These priorities give interrupt handlers precedence over application code and kernel housekeeping, and implement the priority relationships among interrupt handlers. The priorities cause the Solaris thread scheduler to preempt low-priority interrupt handlers in favor of higher-priority ones, and the threaded implementation enables multiprocessor hardware to run several interrupt handlers concurrently. We describe the interrupt architecture of UNIX and Windows NT in Chapters 20 and 22, respectively.

In summary, interrupts are used throughout modern operating systems to handle asynchronous events and to trap to supervisor-mode routines in the kernel. To enable the most urgent work to be done first, modern computers use a system of interrupt priorities. Device controllers, hardware faults, and system calls all raise interrupts to trigger kernel routines. Because interrupts are used so heavily for time-sensitive processing, efficient interrupt handling is required for good system performance.

12.2.3 Direct Memory Access

For a device that does large transfers, such as a disk drive, it seems wasteful to use an expensive general-purpose processor to watch status bits and to feed data into a controller register 1 byte at a time—a process termed **programmed I/O (PIO)**. Many computers avoid burdening the main CPU with PIO by offloading some of this work to a special-purpose processor called a direct-memory-access (DMA) controller. To initiate a DMA transfer, the host writes a DMA command block into memory. This block contains a pointer to the source of a transfer, a pointer to the destination of the transfer, and a count of the number of bytes to be transferred. The CPU writes the address of this command block to the DMA controller, then goes on with other work. The DMA controller then proceeds to operate the memory bus directly, placing addresses on the bus to perform transfers without the help of the main CPU. A simple DMA controller is a standard component in PCs, and **bus-mastering** I/O boards for the PC usually contain their own high-speed DMA hardware.

Handshaking between the DMA controller and the device controller is performed via a pair of wires called DMA-request and DMA-acknowledge. The device controller places a signal on the DMA-request wire when a word of data is available for transfer. This signal causes the DMA controller to seize the memory bus, to place the desired address on the memory-address wires, and to place a signal on the DMA-acknowledge wire. When the device controller receives the DMA-acknowledge signal, it transfers the word of data to memory, and removes the DMA-request signal. When the entire transfer is finished, the DMA controller interrupts the CPU. This process is depicted in Figure 12.5. Note that, when the DMA controller seizes the memory bus, the CPU is momentarily prevented from accessing main memory, although it can still access data

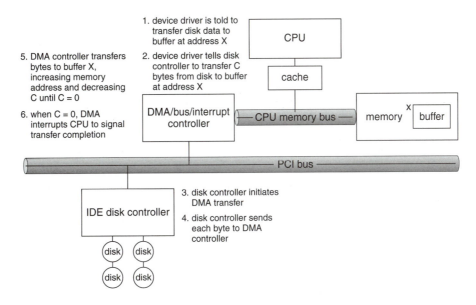

Figure 12.5 Steps in a DMA transfer.

items in its primary and secondary cache. Although this **cycle stealing** can slow down the CPU computation, offloading the data-transfer work to a DMA controller generally improves the total system performance. Some computer architectures use physical memory addresses for DMA, but others perform **direct virtual-memory access** (**DVMA**), using virtual addresses that undergo virtual- to physical-memory address translation. DVMA can perform a transfer between two memory-mapped devices without the intervention of the CPU or the use of main memory.

On protected-mode kernels, the operating system generally prevents processes from issuing device commands directly. This discipline protects data from access-control violations, and also protects the system from erroneous use of device controllers that could cause a system crash. Instead, the operating system exports functions that a sufficiently privileged process can use to access low-level operations on the underlying hardware. On kernels without memory protection, processes can access device controllers directly. We can use this direct access to obtain high performance, since with it we can avoid kernel communication, context switches, and layers of kernel software. Unfortunately, direct access interferes with system security and stability. The trend in general-purpose operating systems is to protect memory and devices, so that the system can try to guard against erroneous or malicious applications.

Although the hardware aspects of I/O are complex when considered at the level of detail of electronics-hardware designers, the concepts that we have just described are sufficient to understand many I/O aspects of operating systems. Let's review the main concepts:

- A bus

- A controller

- An I/O port and its registers

- The handshaking relationship between the host and a device controller

- The execution of this handshaking in a polling loop or via interrupts

- The offloading of this work to a DMA controller for large transfers

A previous example illustrated the handshaking between a device controller and the host. In reality, the wide variety of available devices poses a problem for operating-system implementors. Each kind of device has its own set of capabilities, control-bit definitions, and protocol for interacting with the host—and they are all different. How can the operating system be designed such that new devices can be attached to the computer without the operating system being rewritten? Also, when the devices vary so widely, how can the operating system give a convenient, uniform I/O interface to applications?

12.3 ■ Application I/O Interface

In this section, we discuss structuring techniques and interfaces for the operating system that enable I/O devices to be treated in a standard, uniform way. We explain, for instance, how an application can open a file on a disk without knowing what kind of disk it is, and how new disks and other devices can be added to a computer without the operating system being disrupted.

Like other complex software-engineering problems, the approach here involves abstraction, encapsulation, and software layering. Specifically, we can abstract away the detailed differences in I/O devices by identifying a few general kinds. Each of these general kinds is accessed through a standardized set of functions—an **interface**. The actual differences are encapsulated in kernel modules called **device drivers** that internally are custom tailored to each device, but that export one of the standard interfaces. Figure 12.6 illustrates how the I/O-related portions of the kernel are structured in software layers.

The purpose of the device-driver layer is to hide the differences among device controllers from the I/O subsystem of the kernel, much as the I/O system calls encapsulate the behavior of devices in a few generic classes that hide hardware differences from applications. Making the I/O subsystem independent of the hardware simplifies the job of the operating-system developer. It also benefits the hardware manufacturers. They either design new devices to be compatible with an existing host controller interface (such as SCSI-2), or they write device drivers to interface the new hardware to popular operating systems. Thus, new peripherals can be attached to a computer without waiting

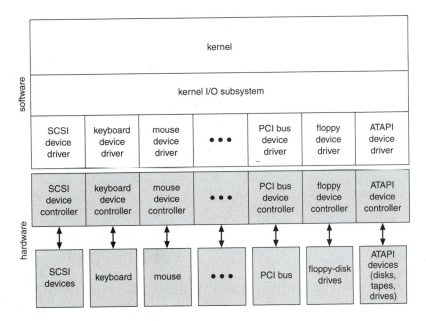

Figure 12.6   A kernel I/O structure.

for the operating-system vendor to develop support code. Unfortunately for device-hardware manufacturers, each type of operating system has its own standards for the device-driver interface. A given device may ship with multiple device drivers—for instance, drivers for MS-DOS, Windows 95, Windows NT, and Solaris.

Devices vary in many dimensions, as illustrated in Figure 12.7.

- *Character stream or block*: A **character-stream device** transfers bytes one by one, whereas a **block device** transfers a block of bytes as a unit.

- *Sequential or random-access*: A **sequential device** transfers data in a fixed order that is determined by the device, whereas the user of a **random-access device** can instruct the device to seek to any of the available data storage locations.

- *Synchronous or asynchronous*: A **synchronous device** is one that performs data transfers with predictable response times. An **asynchronous device** exhibits irregular or unpredictable response times.

- *Sharable or dedicated*: A **sharable device** can be used concurrently by several processes or threads; a **dedicated device** cannot be.

- *Speed of operation*: Device speeds range from a few bytes per second to a few gigabytes per second.

aspect	variation	example
data-transfer mode	character block	terminal disk
access method	sequential random	modem CD-ROM
transfer schedule	synchronous asynchronous	tape keyboard
sharing	dedicated sharable	tape keyboard
device speed	latency seek time transfer rate delay between operations	
I/O direction	read only write only read–write	CD-ROM graphics controller disk

Figure 12.7   Characteristics of I/O devices.

- *Read–write, read only, or write only*: Some devices perform both input and output, whereas others support only one data direction.

For the purpose of application access, many of these differences are hidden by the operating system, and the devices are grouped into a few conventional types. The resulting styles of device access have been found to be useful and broadly applicable. Although the exact system calls may differ across operating systems, the device categories are standard. The major access conventions include block I/O, character-stream I/O, memory-mapped file access, and network sockets. Operating systems also provide special system calls to access a few additional devices, such as a time-of-day clock and a timer. Some operating systems provide a set of system calls for graphical display, video, and audio devices.

Most operating systems also have an **escape** or **back-door** system call that transparently passes arbitrary commands from an application to a device driver. In UNIX, this system call is ioctl (for I/O control). The ioctl system call enables an application to access any functionality that can be implemented by any device driver, without the need to invent a new system call. The ioctl system call has three arguments. One is a file descriptor that connects the application to the driver by referring to a hardware device managed by that driver. The second argument to ioctl is an integer that selects one of the commands implemented in the driver. The third argument is a pointer. It can point to an arbitrary data structure in memory, thus enabling the application and driver to communicate any necessary control information or data.

12.3.1 Block and Character Devices

The **block-device** interface captures all the aspects necessary for accessing disk drives and other block-oriented devices. The expectation is that the device understands commands such as read and write, and, if it is a random-access device, it has a seek command to specify which block to transfer next. Applications normally access such a device through a file-system interface. The operating system itself, and special applications such as database-management systems, may prefer to access a block device as a simple linear array of blocks. This mode of access is sometimes called **raw I/O**. We can see that read, write, and seek capture the essential behaviors of block storage devices, so that applications are insulated from the low-level differences among those devices.

Memory-mapped file access can be layered on top of block-device drivers. Rather than offering read and write operations, a memory-mapped interface provides access to disk storage via an array of bytes in main memory. The system call that maps a file into memory returns the virtual-memory address of an array of characters that contains a copy of the file. The actual data transfers are performed only when needed to satisfy access to the memory image. Because the transfers are handled by the same mechanism as that used for demand-paged virtual-memory access, memory-mapped I/O is efficient. Memory mapping is also convenient for programmers—access to a memory-mapped file is as simple as reading and writing to memory. It is common for operating systems that offer virtual memory to use the mapping interface for kernel services. For instance, to execute a program, the operating system maps the executable into memory, and then transfers control to the entry address of the executable. The mapping interface is also commonly used for kernel access to swap space on disk.

A keyboard is an example of a device that is accessed through a **character-stream** interface. The basic system calls in this interface enable an application to get or put one character. On top of this interface, libraries can be built that offer line-at-a-time access, with buffering and editing services (for example, when a user types a backspace, the preceding character is removed from the input stream). This style of access is convenient for input devices such as keyboards, mice, and modems, which produce data for input "spontaneously"—that is, at times that cannot necessarily be predicted by the application. This access style is also good for output devices such as printers or audio boards, which naturally fit the concept of a linear stream of bytes.

12.3.2 Network Devices

Because the performance and addressing characteristics of network I/O differ significantly from those of disk I/O, most operating systems provide a network I/O interface that is different from the read--write--seek interface used for disks. One interface that is available in many operating systems, including UNIX and Windows NT, is the network **socket** interface.

Think of a wall socket for electricity: Any electrical appliance can be plugged in. By analogy, the system calls in the socket interface enable an application to create a socket, to connect a local socket to a remote address (which plugs this application into a socket created by another application), to listen for any remote application to plug into the local socket, and to send and receive packets over the connection. To support the implementation of servers, the socket interface also provides a function called select that manages a set of sockets. A call to select returns information about which sockets have a packet waiting to be received, and which sockets have room to accept a packet to be sent. The use of select eliminates the polling and busy waiting that would otherwise be necessary for network I/O. These functions encapsulate the essential behaviors of networks, greatly facilitating the creation of distributed applications that can use any underlying network hardware and protocol stack.

Many other approaches to interprocess communication and network communication have been implemented. For instance, Windows NT provides one interface to the network interface card, and a second interface to the network protocols (Section 22.7). In UNIX, which has a long history as a proving ground for network technology, we find half-duplex pipes, full-duplex FIFOs, full-duplex streams, message queues, and sockets. Information on UNIX networking is given in Section 20.9.

12.3.3 Clocks and Timers

Most computers have hardware clocks and timers that provide three basic functions:

- Give the current time

- Give the elapsed time

- Set a timer to trigger operation X at time T

These functions are used heavily by the operating system, and also by time-sensitive applications. Unfortunately, the system calls that implement these functions are not standardized across operating systems.

The hardware to measure elapsed time and to trigger operations is called a **programmable interval timer**. It can be set to wait a certain amount of time and then to generate an interrupt. It can be set to do this operation once, or to repeat the process, to generate periodic interrupts. This mechanism is used by the scheduler to generate an interrupt that will preempt a process at the end of its time slice. It is used by the disk I/O subsystem to invoke the flushing of dirty cache buffers to disk periodically, and by the network subsystem to cancel operations that are proceeding too slowly because of network congestion or failures. The operating system may also provide an interface for user processes to use timers. The operating system can support more timer requests than the number of timer hardware channels by simulating virtual clocks. Under this scheme, the kernel (or the timer device driver) maintains a list of interrupts wanted by its own routines and by user requests, sorted in earliest-time-first order. It sets the timer for the earliest time. When the timer interrupts, the kernel signals the requester and reloads the timer with the next earliest time.

On many computers, the interrupt rate is generated by the ticking of the hardware clock at between 18 and 60 ticks per second. This resolution is coarse —a modern computer can execute hundreds of millions of instructions per second. The precision of triggers is limited by the coarse resolution of the timer, as well as by the overhead of maintaining virtual clocks. Also, if the timer ticks are used to maintain the system time-of-day clock, the system clock can drift. In most computers, the hardware clock is constructed from a high-frequency counter. In some of them, the value of this counter can be read from a device register, in which case the counter can be considered to be a high-resolution clock. Although this clock does not generate interrupts, it offers accurate measurements of time intervals.

12.3.4 Blocking and Nonblocking I/O

One remaining aspect of the system-call interface relates to the choice between blocking I/O and nonblocking (asynchronous) I/O. When an application issues a **blocking** system call, the execution of the application is suspended. The application is moved from the operating system's run queue to a wait queue. After the system call completes, the application is moved back to the run queue, where it is eligible to resume execution, at which time it will receive the values returned by the system call. The physical actions performed by I/O devices are generally asynchronous—they take a varying or unpredictable amount of time. Nevertheless, most operating systems use blocking system calls for the application interface, because blocking application code is easier to understand than nonblocking application code.

Some user-level processes need **nonblocking I/O**. One example is a user interface that receives keyboard and·mouse input while processing and displaying data on the screen. Another example is a video application that reads frames from a file on disk while simultaneously decompressing and displaying the output on the display.

One way that an application writer can overlap execution with I/O is to write a multithreaded application. Some threads can perform blocking system calls, while others continue executing. The Solaris developers used this technique to implement a user-level library for asynchronous I/O, freeing the application writer from that task. Some operating systems provide nonblocking I/O system calls. A nonblocking call does not halt the execution of the application for an extended time. Instead, it returns quickly, with a return value that indicates how many bytes were transferred.

An alternative to a nonblocking system call is an asynchronous system call. An asynchronous call returns immediately, without waiting for the I/O to complete. The application continues to execute its code, and the completion of the I/O at some future time is communicated to the application, either through the setting of some variable in the address space of the application, or through the triggering of a signal or software interrupt or a call-back routine that is executed outside the linear control flow of the application. Note the difference between nonblocking and asynchronous system calls. A nonblocking read returns immediately with whatever data are available—the full number of bytes requested, fewer, or none at all. An asynchronous read call requests a transfer that will be performed in its entirety, but that will complete at some future time.

A good example of nonblocking behavior is the select system call for network sockets. This system call takes an argument that specifies a maximum waiting time. By setting it to 0, an application can poll for network activity without blocking. But using select introduces extra overhead, because the select call only checks whether I/O is possible. For a data transfer, select must be followed by some kind of read or write command. A variation of this approach, found in Mach, is a blocking multiple-read call. It specifies desired reads for several devices in one system call, and returns as soon as any one of them completes.

12.4 ■ Kernel I/O Subsystem

Kernels provide many services related to I/O. In this section, we describe several services that are provided by the kernel's I/O subsystem, and we discuss the way that they build on the hardware and device-driver infrastructure.

The services that we describe are I/O scheduling, buffering, caching, spooling, device reservation, and error handling.

12.4.1 I/O Scheduling

To schedule a set of I/O requests, we determine a good order in which to execute the requests. The order in which applications issue system calls rarely is the best choice. Scheduling can improve overall system performance, can share device access fairly among processes, and can reduce the average waiting time for I/O to complete. Here is a simple example to illustrate the opportunity. Suppose that a disk arm is near the beginning of a disk, and that three applications issue blocking read calls to that disk. Application 1 requests a block near the end of the disk, application 2 requests one near the beginning, and application 3's request is in the middle of the disk. It is clear that the operating system can reduce the distance that the disk arm travels by serving the applications in order 2, 3, 1. Rearranging the order of service in this way is the essence of I/O scheduling. Operating-system developers implement scheduling by maintaining a queue of requests for each device. When an application issues a blocking I/O system call, the request is placed on the queue for that device. The I/O scheduler rearranges the order of the queue to improve the overall system efficiency and the average response time experienced by applications. The operating system may also try to be fair, such that no one application receives especially poor service, or it may give priority service for delay-sensitive requests. For instance, requests from the virtual-memory subsystem may take priority over application requests. Several scheduling algorithms for disk I/O are detailed in Section 13.2.

One way that the I/O subsystem improves the efficiency of the computer is by scheduling I/O operations. Another way is by using storage space in main memory or on disk, via techniques called buffering, caching, and spooling.

12.4.2 Buffering

A **buffer** is a memory area that stores data while they are transferred between two devices or between a device and an application. Buffering is done for three reasons. One reason is to cope with a speed mismatch between the producer and consumer of a data stream. Suppose, for example, that a file is being received via modem for storage on the hard disk. The modem is about a thousand times slower than the hard disk. So a buffer is created in main memory to accumulate bytes that are received from the modem. When an entire buffer of data has arrived, the buffer can be written to disk in a single operation. Since the disk write is not instantaneous and the modem still needs a place to store additional incoming data, two buffers are used. After the modem fills the first buffer, the disk write is requested. The modem then starts to fill the second buffer while the first buffer is written to disk. By the time that the modem has filled the second buffer, the disk write from the first one should have completed, so the modem can switch back to the first buffer while the disk writes the second one. This **double buffering** decouples the producer of data from the consumer, thus relaxing timing requirements between them. The need for this decoupling is illustrated in Figure 12.8, which lists the enormous differences in device speeds for typical computer hardware.

A second use of buffering is to adapt between devices that have different data-transfer sizes. Such disparities are especially common in computer networking, where buffers are used widely for fragmentation and reassembly of messages. At the sending side, a large message is fragmented into small network packets. The packets are sent over the network, the receiving side places them in a reassembly buffer to form an image of the source data.

A third use of buffering is to support **copy semantics** for application I/O. An example will clarify the meaning of *copy semantics*. Suppose that an application has a buffer of data that it wishes to write to disk. It calls the `write` system call, providing a pointer to the buffer, and an integer specifying the number of bytes to write. After the system call returns, what happens if

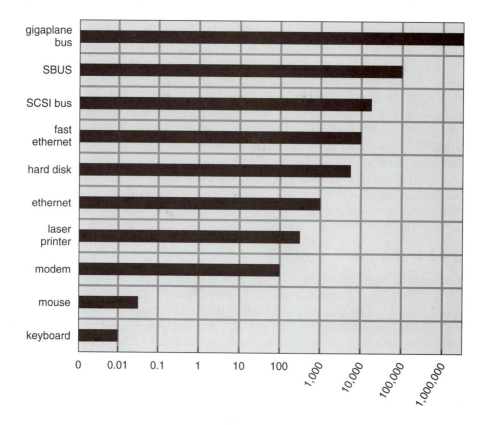

Figure 12.8   Sun Enterprise 6000 device-transfer rates (logarithmic).

the application changes the contents of the buffer? With copy semantics, the version of the data written to disk is guaranteed to be the version at the time of the application system call, independent of any subsequent changes in the application's buffer. A simple way that the operating system can guarantee copy semantics is for the `write` system call to copy the application data into a kernel buffer before returning control to the application. The disk write is performed from the kernel buffer, so that subsequent changes to the application buffer have no effect. Copying of data between kernel buffers and application data space is common in operating systems, despite the overhead that this operation introduces, because of the clean semantics. We can obtain the same effect more efficiently by clever use of virtual-memory mapping and copy-on-write page protection.

12.4.3 Caching

A **cache** is region of fast memory that holds copies of data. Access to the cached copy is more efficient than is access to the original. For instance, the instructions of the currently running process are stored on disk, cached in physical memory, and copied again in the CPU's secondary and primary caches. The difference between a buffer and a cache is that a buffer may hold the only existing copy of a data item, whereas a cache, by definition, just holds on faster storage a copy of an item that resides elsewhere.

Caching and buffering are two distinct functions, but sometimes a region of memory can be used for both purposes. For instance, to preserve copy semantics and to enable efficient scheduling of disk I/O, the operating system uses buffers in main memory to hold disk data. These buffers are also used as a cache, to improve the I/O efficiency for files that are shared by applications, or that are being written and reread rapidly. When the kernel receives a file I/O request, the kernel first accesses the buffer cache to see whether that region of the file is already available in main memory. If so, a physical disk I/O can be avoided or deferred. Also, disk writes are accumulated in the buffer cache for several seconds, so that large transfers are gathered to allow efficient write schedules. This strategy of delaying writes to improve I/O efficiency is discussed, in the context of remote file access, in Section 17.3.

12.4.4 Spooling and Device Reservation

A **spool** is a buffer that holds output for a device, such as a printer, that cannot accept interleaved data streams. Although a printer can serve only one job at a time, several applications may wish to print their output concurrently, without having their output mixed together. The operating system solves this problem by intercepting all output to the printer. Each application's output is spooled to a separate disk file. When an application finishes printing, the spooling system queues the corresponding spool file for output to the printer. The spooling system copies the queued spool files to the printer one at a time. In some operating systems, spooling is managed by a system daemon process. In other operating systems, it is handled by an in-kernel thread. In either case, the operating system provides a control interface that enables users and system administrators to display the queue, to remove unwanted jobs before those jobs print, to suspend printing while the printer is serviced, and so on.

Some devices, such as tape drives and printers, cannot usefully multiplex the I/O requests of multiple concurrent applications. Spooling is one way that operating systems can coordinate concurrent output. Another way to deal with concurrent device access is to provide explicit facilities for coordination. Some operating systems (including VMS) provide support for exclusive device access, by enabling a process to allocate an idle device, and to deallocate that device when it is no longer needed. Other operating systems enforce a limit of one open file handle to such a device. Many operating systems provide functions that enable processes to coordinate exclusive access among themselves. For instance, Windows NT provides system calls to wait until a device object becomes available. It also has a parameter to the open system call that declares the types of access to be permitted to other concurrent threads. On these systems, it is up to the applications to avoid deadlock.

12.4.5 Error Handling

An operating system that uses protected memory can guard against many kinds of hardware and application errors, so that a complete system failure is not the usual result of each minor mechanical glitch. Devices and I/O transfers can fail in many ways, either for transient reasons, such as a network becoming overloaded, or for "permanent" reasons, such as a disk controller becoming defective. Operating systems often can compensate effectively for transient failures. For instance, a disk read failure results in a read retry, and a network send error results in a resend, if the protocol so specifies. Unfortunately, if an important component experiences a permanent failure, the operating system is unlikely to recover.

As a general rule, an I/O system call will return 1 bit of information about the status of the call, signifying either success or failure. The UNIX operating system uses an additional integer variable named errno to return an error code —one of about 100 values—indicating the general nature of the failure (for example, argument out of range, bad pointer, or file not open). By contrast, some hardware can provide highly detailed error information, although many current operating systems are not designed to convey this information to the application. For instance, a failure of a SCSI device is reported by the SCSI protocol in terms of a **sense key** that identifies the general nature of the failure, such as hardware error or illegal request; an **additional sense code** that states the category of failure, such as a bad command parameter or a self-test failure; and an **additional sense-code qualifier** that gives even more detail, such as which command parameter was in error, or which hardware subsystem failed its self-test. Further, many SCSI devices maintain internal pages of error-log information that can be requested by the host, but that seldom are.

12.4.6 Kernel Data Structures

The kernel needs to keep state information about the use of I/O components. It does so through a variety of in-kernel data structures, such as the open-file table structure from Section 11.5. The kernel uses many similar structures to track network connections, character-device communications, and other I/O activities.

UNIX provides file-system access to a variety of entities, such as user files, raw devices, and the address spaces of processes. Although each of these entities supports a read operation, the semantics differ. For instance, to read a user file, the kernel needs to probe the buffer cache before deciding whether to perform a disk I/O. To read a raw disk, the kernel needs to ensure that the request size is a multiple of the disk sector size, and is aligned on a sector

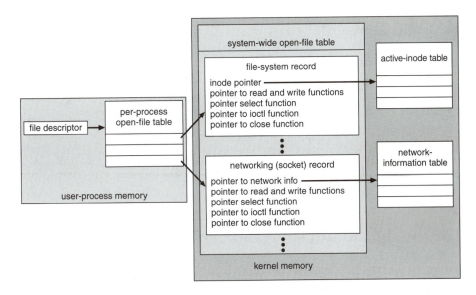

Figure 12.9   UNIX I/O kernel structure.

boundary. To read a process image, it is merely necessary to copy data from memory. UNIX encapsulates these differences within a uniform structure by using an object-oriented technique. The open-file record, shown in Figure 12.9, contains a dispatch table that holds pointers to the appropriate routines, depending on the type of file.

Some operating systems use object-oriented methods even more extensively. For instance, Windows NT uses a message-passing implementation for I/O. An I/O request is converted into a message that is sent through the kernel to the I/O manager and then to the device driver, each of which may change the message contents. For output, the message contains the data to be written. For input, the message contains a buffer to receive the data. The message-passing approach can add overhead, by comparison with procedural techniques that use shared data structures, but it simplifies the structure and design of the I/O system, and adds flexibility.

In summary, the I/O subsystem coordinates an extensive collection of services, which are available to applications and to other parts of the kernel. The I/O subsystem supervises

- Management of the name space for files and devices

- Access control to files and devices

- Operation control (for example, a modem cannot seek)

- File system space allocation

- Device allocation

- Buffering, caching, and spooling

- I/O scheduling

- Device status monitoring, error handling, and failure recovery

- Device driver configuration and initialization

The upper levels of the I/O subsystem access devices via the uniform interface provided by the device drivers.

12.5 ■ I/O Requests Handling

Earlier, in Section 12.2, we described the handshaking between a device driver and a device controller, but we did not explain how the operating system connects an application request to a set of network wires or to a specific disk sector. Let us consider the example of reading a file from disk.

The application refers to the data by a file name. Within a disk, it is the job of the file system to map from the file name through the file-system directories to obtain the space allocation of the file. For instance, in MS-DOS, the name maps to a number that indicates an entry in the file-access table, and that table entry tells which disk blocks are allocated to the file. In UNIX, the name maps to an inode number, and the corresponding inode contains the space-allocation information.

How is the connection made from the file name to the disk controller (the hardware port address or the memory-mapped controller registers)?

First, we consider MS-DOS, a relatively simple operating system. The first part of an MS-DOS file name, preceding the colon, is a string that identifies a specific hardware device. For example, c: is the first part of every file name on the primary hard disk. The fact that c: represents the primary hard disk is built into the operating system; c: is mapped to a specific port address through a device table. Because of the colon separator, the device name space is separate from the file-system name space within each device. This separation makes it easy for the operating system to associate extra functionality with each device. For instance, it is easy to invoke spooling on any files written to the printer.

If, instead, the device name space is incorporated in the regular file-system name space, as it is in UNIX, the normal file-system name services are provided automatically. If the file system provides ownership and access control to all file names, then devices have owners and access control. Since files are stored on devices, such an interface provides access to the I/O system at two levels. We can use names to access the devices themselves, or to access the files that are stored on the devices.

UNIX represents device names in the regular file-system name space. Unlike an MS-DOS file name, which has the colon separator, a UNIX path name has no clear separation of the device portion. In fact, no part of the path name is the name of a device. UNIX has a **mount table** that associates prefixes of path names with specific device names. To resolve a path name, UNIX looks up the name in the mount table to find the longest matching prefix; the corresponding entry in the mount table gives the device name. This device name also has the form of a name in the file-system name space. When UNIX looks up this name in the file-system directory structures, instead of finding an inode number, UNIX finds a *<major, minor>* device number. The major device number identifies a device driver that should be called to handle I/O to this device. The minor device number is passed to the device driver to index into a device table. The corresponding device-table entry gives the port address or the memory-mapped address of the device controller.

Modern operating systems obtain significant flexibility from the multiple stages of lookup tables in the path between a request and a physical device controller. The mechanisms that pass requests between applications and drivers are general. Thus, we can introduce new devices and drivers into a computer without recompiling the kernel. In fact, some operating systems have the ability to load device drivers on demand. At boot time, the system first probes the hardware buses to determine what devices are present, and then the system loads in the necessary drivers; either immediately, or when first required by an I/O request.

UNIX System V has an interesting mechanism, called streams, that enables an application to assemble pipelines of driver code dynamically. A **stream** is a full-duplex connection between a device driver and a user-level process. It consists of a **stream head** that interfaces with the user process, a **driver end** that controls the device, and zero or more **stream modules** between them. Modules can be pushed onto a stream to add functionality in a layered fashion. For instance, a process can open a serial-port device via a stream, and can push on a module to handle input editing. Streams can be used for interprocess and network communication. In fact, in System V, the socket mechanism is implemented by streams.

Now we describe the typical lifecycle of a blocking read request, as depicted in Figure 12.10. The figure suggests that an I/O operation requires a great many steps, which together consume a tremendous number of CPU cycles.

1. A process issues a blocking `read` system call to a file descriptor of a file that has been opened previously.

2. The system-call code in the kernel checks the parameters for correctness. In the case of input, if the data are already available in the buffer cache, the data are returned to the process and the I/O request is completed.

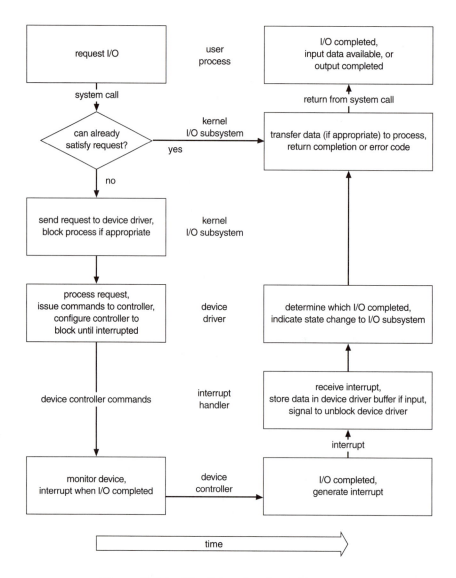

Figure 12.10   The lifecycle of an I/O request.

3. If the data are not in the buffer cache, a physical I/O needs to be performed, so the process is removed from the run queue and is placed on the wait queue for the device, and the I/O request is scheduled. Eventually, the I/O subsystem sends the request to the device driver. Depending on the operating system, the request is sent via a subroutine call or via an in-kernel message.

4. The device driver allocates kernel buffer space to receive the data, and schedules the I/O. Eventually, the driver sends commands to the device controller by writing into the device control registers.

5. The device controller operates the device hardware to perform the data transfer.

6. The driver may poll for status and data, or it may have set up a DMA transfer into kernel memory. We assume that the transfer is managed by a DMA controller, which generates an interrupt when the transfer completes.

7. The appropriate interrupt handler receives the interrupt via the interrupt-vector table, stores any necessary data, signals the device driver, and returns from the interrupt.

8. The device driver receives the signal, determines which I/O request completed, determines the request's status, and signals the kernel I/O subsystem that the request has been completed.

9. The kernel transfers data or return codes to the address space of the requesting process, and moves the process from the wait queue back to the ready queue.

10. The process is unblocked when it is moved to the ready queue. When the scheduler assigns the process to the CPU, the process resumes execution at the completion of the system call.

12.6 ■ Performance

I/O is a major factor in system performance. It places heavy demands on the CPU to execute device-driver code and to schedule processes fairly and efficiently as they block and unblock. The resulting context switches stress the CPU and its hardware caches. I/O also exposes any inefficiencies in the interrupt-handling mechanisms in the kernel, and I/O loads down the memory bus during data copy between controllers and physical memory, and again during copies between kernel buffers and application data space. Coping gracefully with all these demands is one of the major concerns of a computer architect.

Although modern computers can handle hundreds of interrupts per second, interrupt handling is a relatively expensive task: Each interrupt causes the system to perform a state change, to execute the interrupt handler, and then to restore state. Programmed I/O can be more efficient than interrupt-driven I/O, if the number of cycles spent busy-waiting is not excessive. An I/O completion typically unblocks a process, leading to the full overhead of a context switch.

Network traffic can also cause a high context-switch rate. Consider, for instance, a remote login from one machine to another. Each character that is typed on the local machine must be transported to the remote machine. On the local machine, the character is typed; a keyboard interrupt is generated; and the character is passed through the interrupt handler to the device driver, to the kernel, and then to the user process. The user process issues a network I/O system call to send the character to the remote machine. The character then flows into the local kernel, through the network layers that construct a network packet, and into the network device driver. The network device driver transfers the packet to the network controller, which sends the character, and generates an interrupt. The interrupt is passed back up through the kernel to cause the network I/O system call to complete.

Now, the remote system's network hardware receives the packet, and an interrupt is generated. The character is unpacked from the network protocols and is given to the appropriate network daemon. The network daemon identifies which remote login session is involved, and passes the packet to the appropriate subdaemon for that session. Throughout this flow there are context switches and state switches (Figure 12.11). Usually, the receiver echoes the character back to the sender; that approach doubles the work.

The Solaris developers reimplemented the **telnet daemon** using in-kernel threads to eliminate the context switches involved in moving each character between daemons and the kernel. Sun estimates that this improvement increased the maximum number of network logins from a few hundred to a few thousand on a large server.

Other systems use separate **front-end processors** for terminal I/O, to reduce the interrupt burden on the main CPU. For instance, a **terminal concentrator** can multiplex the traffic from hundreds of remote terminals into one port on a large computer. An **I/O channel** is a dedicated, special-purpose CPU found in mainframes and in other high-end systems. The job of a channel is to offload I/O work from the main CPU. The idea is that the channels keep the data flowing smoothly, while the main CPU remains free to process the data. By comparison with the device controllers and DMA controllers found in smaller computers, a channel can process more general and sophisticated programs, so channels can be tuned for particular workloads.

We can employ several principles to improve the efficiency of I/O:

- Reduce the number of context switches.

- Reduce the number of times that data must be copied in memory while they are being passed between device and application.

- Reduce the frequency of interrupts by using large transfers, smart controllers, and polling (if busy-waiting can be minimized).

- Increase concurrency by using DMA-knowledgeable controllers or channels to offload simple data copying from the CPU.

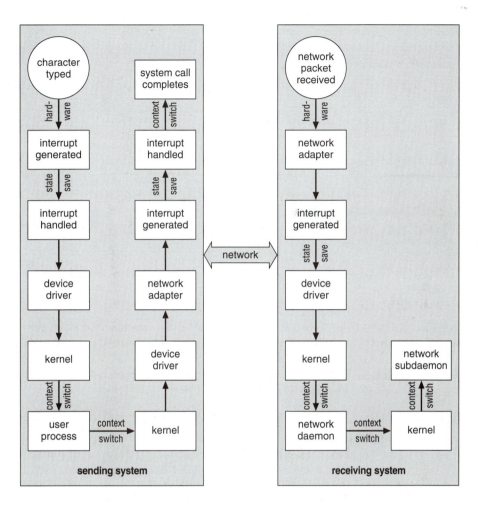

Figure 12.11 Intercomputer communications.

- Move processing primitives into hardware, to allow their operation in device controllers concurrent with the CPU and bus operation.

- Balance CPU, memory subsystem, bus, and I/O performance, because an overload in any one area will cause idleness in others.

Devices vary greatly in complexity. For instance, a mouse is simple. The mouse movements and button clicks are converted into numeric values, which are passed from hardware, through the mouse device driver, to the application. By contrast, the functionality provided by the NT disk device driver is complex. Not only does it manage individual disks, but also it implements RAID arrays (see Section 13.5). To do these tasks, it converts an application's read or write request into a coordinated set of disk I/O operations. Moreover, it implements

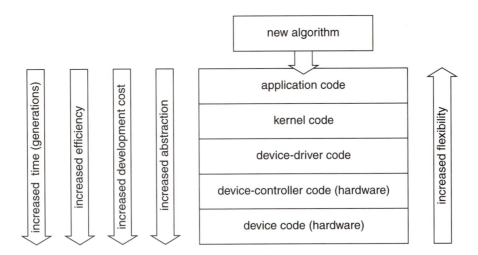

Figure 12.12 Device-functionality progression.

sophisticated error-handling and data-recovery algorithms, and takes many steps to optimize disk performance, because of the importance of secondary-storage performance to the overall performance of the system.

Where should the I/O functionality be implemented—in the device hardware, in the device driver, or in application software? Sometimes, we observe the progression depicted in Figure 12.12.

- Initially, we implement experimental I/O algorithms at application level, because application code is flexible, and application bugs are unlikely to cause system crashes. Furthermore, by developing code at the application level, we avoid the need to reboot or reload device drivers after every change to the code. An application-level implementation can be inefficient, however, because of the overhead of context switches, and because the application cannot take advantage of internal kernel data structures and kernel functionality (such as efficient in-kernel messaging, threading, and locking).

- When an application-level algorithm has demonstrated its worth, we may reimplement it in the kernel. This step can improve the performance, but the development work is more challenging, because an operating-system kernel is a large, complex software system. Moreover, we must debug thoroughly an in-kernel implementation to avoid data corruption and system crashes.

- We may obtain the highest performance by using a specialized implementation in hardware, either in the device or in the controller. The disadvantages of a hardware implementation include the difficulty and expense of making further improvements or of fixing bugs, the increased development time (months rather than days), and the decreased flexibility. For instance, a hardware RAID controller may not provide any means for the kernel to influence the order or location of individual block reads and writes, even if the kernel has special information about the workload that would enable the kernel to improve the I/O performance.

12.7 ■ Summary

The basic hardware elements involved in I/O are buses, device controllers, and the devices themselves. The work of moving data between devices and main memory is performed by the CPU as programmed I/O, or is offloaded to a DMA controller. The kernel module that controls a device is a device driver. The system-call interface provided to applications is designed to handle several basic categories of hardware, including block devices, character devices, memory-mapped files, network sockets, and programmed interval timers. The system calls usually block the process that issues them, but nonblocking and asynchronous calls are used by the kernel itself, and by applications that must not sleep while waiting for an I/O operation to complete.

The kernel's I/O subsystem provides numerous services. Among these are I/O scheduling, buffering, spooling, error handling, and device reservation. Another service is name translation, to make the connection between hardware devices and the symbolic file names used by applications. It involves several levels of mapping that translate from a character string name to a specific device driver and device address, and then to physical addresses of I/O ports or bus controllers. This mapping may occur within the file-system name space, as it does in UNIX, or in a separate device name space, as it does in MS-DOS.

I/O system calls are costly in terms of CPU consumption, because of the numerous layers of software between a physical device and the application. These layers imply the overheads of context switching to cross the kernel's protection boundary, of signal and interrupt handling to service the I/O devices, and of the load on the CPU and memory system to copy data between kernel buffers and application space.

■ Exercises

12.1 State three advantages of placing functionality in a device controller, rather than in the kernel. State three disadvantages.

12.2 Consider the following I/O scenarios on a single-user PC.

   a. A mouse used with a graphical user interface

   b. A tape drive on a multitasking operating system (assume no device preallocation is available)

    c. A disk drive containing user files

    d. A graphics card with direct bus connection, accessible through memory-mapped I/O

For each of these I/O scenarios, would you design the operating system to use buffering, spooling, caching, or a combination? Would you use polled I/O, or interrupt-driven I/O? Give reasons for your choices.

12.3 The example of handshaking in Section 12.2 used 2 bits: a busy bit and a `command-ready` bit. Is it possible to implement this handshaking with only 1 bit? If it is, describe the protocol. If it is not, explain why 1 bit is insufficient.

12.4 Describe three circumstances under which blocking I/O should be used. Describe three circumstances under which nonblocking I/O should be used. Why not just implement nonblocking I/O and have processes busy-wait until their device is ready?

12.5 Why might a system use interrupt-driven I/O to manage a single serial port, but polling I/O to manage a front-end processor, such as a terminal concentrator?

12.6 Polling for an I/O completion can waste a large number of CPU cycles if the processor iterates a busy-waiting loop many times before the I/O completes. But if the I/O device is ready for service, polling can be much more efficient than is catching and dispatching an interrupt. Describe a hybrid strategy that combines polling, sleeping, and interrupts for I/O device service. For each of these three strategies (pure polling, pure interrupts, hybrid), describe a computing environment in which that strategy is more efficient than is either of the others.

12.7 UNIX coordinates the activities of the kernel I/O components by manipulating shared in-kernel data structures, whereas Windows NT uses object-oriented message passing between kernel I/O components. Discuss three pros and three cons of each approach.

12.8 How does DMA increase system concurrency? How does it complicate the hardware design?

12.9 Write (in pseudocode) an implementation of virtual clocks, including the queuing and management of timer requests for the kernel and applications. Assume that the hardware provides three timer channels.

12.10 Why is it important to scale up system bus and device speeds as the CPU speed increases?

Bibliographical Notes

Vahalia [1996] provides a good overview of I/O and networking in UNIX. McKusick and colleagues [1996] detail the I/O structures and methods employed in BSD UNIX. The I/O implementation in the sample MINIX OS is described in Tanenbaum and Woodhull [1997]. Solomon [1998] includes detailed information on the NT message-passing implementation of I/O.

For details of hardware-level I/O handling and memory-mapping functionality, processor reference manuals [Motorola 1993, Intel 1993] are among the best sources. Hennessy and Patterson [1996] describe multiprocessor systems and cache-consistency issues. Tanenbaum [1990] describes hardware I/O design at a low level, and Sargent and Shoemaker [1995] provide a programmer's guide to low-level PC hardware and software. The IBM PC-compatible device I/O address map is given in IBM [1983]. An issue of *IEEE Computer* [1994] was devoted to advanced I/O hardware and software.

Chapter 13

MASS- STORAGE STRUCTURE

The file system can be viewed logically as consisting of three parts. In Chapter 11, we saw the user and programmer interface to the file system. We have also described the internal data structures and algorithms used by the operating system to implement this interface. In this chapter, we discuss the lowest level of the file system: the secondary and tertiary storage structures. We first describe disk-scheduling algorithms that schedule the order of disk I/Os to improve performance. Next, we discuss disk formatting, and management of boot blocks, damaged blocks, and swap space. We examine secondary storage structure, covering disk reliability and stable-storage implementation. We conclude with a brief description of the types of storage devices used for tertiary storage, and the problems that arise when an operating system uses tertiary storage.

13.1 ■ Disk Structure

Disks provide the bulk of secondary storage for modern computer systems. Magnetic tape was used as an early secondary-storage medium, but the access time is much slower than for disks. Thus, tapes are currently used mainly for backup, for storage of infrequently used information, as a medium for transferring information from one system to another, and for storing quantities of data that are impractically large for disk systems. Tape storage is described in Section 13.7.

Modern disk drives are addressed as large one-dimensional arrays of **logical blocks,** where the logical block is the smallest unit of transfer. The size of a logical block is usually 512 bytes, although some disks can be **low-level formatted** to choose a different logical block size, such as 1,024 bytes. This option is described in Section 13.3.1.

The one-dimensional array of logical blocks is mapped onto the sectors of the disk sequentially. Sector 0 is the first sector of the first track on the outermost cylinder. The mapping then proceeds in order through that track, then through the rest of the tracks in that cylinder, and then through the rest of the cylinders from outermost to innermost.

By using this mapping, we can—at least in theory—convert a logical block number into an old-style disk address that consists of a cylinder number, a track number within that cylinder, and a sector number within that track. In practice, it is difficult to perform this translation, for two reasons. First, most disks have some defective sectors, but the mapping hides this by substituting spare sectors from elsewhere on the disk. Second, the number of sectors per track is not a constant. The farther a track is from the center of the disk, the greater its length, so the more sectors it can hold. Thus, modern disks are organized into zones of cylinders. The number of sectors per track is constant within a zone. But as we move from inner zones to outer zones, the number of sectors per track increases. Tracks in the outermost zone typically hold 40 percent more sectors than do tracks in the innermost zone.

The number of sectors per track has been increasing as disk technology improves, and it is common to have more than 100 sectors per track in the outer zone of a disk. Similarly, the number of cylinders per disk has been increasing, and several thousand cylinders is not unusual.

13.2 ▪ Disk Scheduling

One of the responsibilities of the operating system is to use the hardware efficiently. For the disk drives, meeting this responsibility entails having a fast access time and disk bandwidth. The access time has two major components (also see Section 2.3.2). The **seek time** is the time for the disk arm to move the heads to the cylinder containing the desired sector. The **rotational latency** is the additional time waiting for the disk to rotate the desired sector to the disk head. The disk **bandwidth** is the total number of bytes transferred, divided by the total time between the first request for service and the completion of the last transfer. We can improve both the access time and the bandwidth by scheduling the servicing of disk I/O requests in a good order.

As we discussed in Chapter 2, whenever a process needs I/O to or from the disk, it issues a system call to the operating system. The request specifies several pieces of information:

- Whether this operation is input or output

- What the disk address for the transfer is

- What the memory address for the transfer is

- What the number of bytes to be transferred is

If the desired disk drive and controller are available, the request can be serviced immediately. If the drive or controller is busy, any new requests for service will need to be placed on the queue of pending requests for that drive. For a multiprogramming system with many processes, the disk queue may often have several pending requests. Thus, when one request is completed, the operating system has an opportunity to choose which pending request to service next.

13.2.1 FCFS Scheduling

The simplest form of disk scheduling is, of course, **first-come, first-served (FCFS)**. This algorithm is intrinsically fair, but it generally does not provide the fastest service. Consider, for example, a disk queue with requests for I/O to blocks on cylinders

$$98, 183, 37, 122, 14, 124, 65, 67,$$

in that order. If the disk head is initially at cylinder 53, it will first move from 53 to 98, then to 183, 37, 122, 14, 124, 65, and finally to 67, for a total head movement of 640 cylinders. This schedule is diagrammed in Figure 13.1.

The problem with this schedule is illustrated by the wild swing from 122 to 14 and then back to 124. If the requests for cylinders 37 and 14 could be serviced

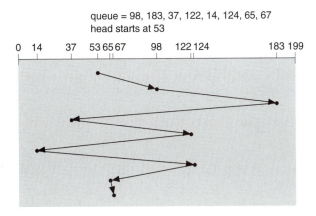

Figure 13.1   FCFS disk scheduling.

together, before or after the requests at 122 and 124, the total head movement could be decreased substantially, and performance could be thereby improved.

13.2.2 SSTF Scheduling

It seems reasonable to service all the requests close to the current head position, before moving the head far away to service other requests. This assumption is the basis for the **shortest-seek-time-first** (SSTF) algorithm. The SSTF algorithm selects the request with the minimum seek time from the current head position. Since seek time increases with the number of cylinders traversed by the head, SSTF chooses the pending request closest to the current head position.

For our example request queue, the closest request to the initial head position (53) is at cylinder 65. Once we are at cylinder 65, the next closest request is at cylinder 67. From there, the request at cylinder 37 is closer than 98, so 37 is served next. Continuing, we service the request at cylinder 14, then 98, 122, 124, and finally at 183 (Figure 13.2). This scheduling method results in a total head movement of only 236 cylinders—little more than one-third of the distance needed for FCFS scheduling. This algorithm gives a substantial improvement in performance.

SSTF scheduling is essentially a form of shortest-job-first (SJF) scheduling, and, like SJF scheduling, it may cause **starvation** of some requests. Remember that requests may arrive at any time. Suppose that we have two requests in the queue, for cylinders 14 and 186, and while servicing the request from 14, a new request near 14 arrives. This new request will be serviced next, making the request at 186 wait. While this request is being serviced, another request close to 14 could arrive. In theory, a continual stream of requests near one another could arrive, causing the request for cylinder 186 to wait indefinitely. This scenario becomes increasingly likely if the pending-request queue grows long.

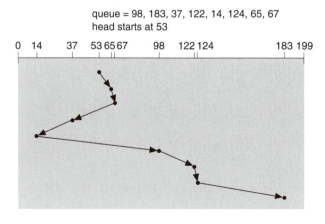

Figure 13.2   SSTF disk scheduling.

Although the SSTF algorithm is a substantial improvement over the FCFS algorithm, it is not optimal. In the example, we can do better by moving the head from 53 to 37, even though the latter is not closest, and then to 14, before turning around to service 65, 67, 98, 122, 124, and 183. This strategy reduces the total head movement to 208 cylinders.

13.2.3 SCAN Scheduling

In the **SCAN** algorithm, the disk arm starts at one end of the disk, and moves toward the other end, servicing requests as it reaches each cylinder, until it gets to the other end of the disk. At the other end, the direction of head movement is reversed, and servicing continues. The head continuously scans back and forth across the disk. We again use our example.

Before applying SCAN to schedule the requests on cylinders 98, 183, 37, 122, 14, 124, 65, and 67, we need to know the direction of head movement, in addition to the head's current position (53). If the disk arm is moving toward 0, the head will service 37 and then 14. At cylinder 0, the arm will reverse and will move toward the other end of the disk, servicing the requests at 65, 67, 98, 122, 124, and 183 (Figure 13.3). If a request arrives in the queue just in front of the head, it will be serviced almost immediately; a request arriving just behind the head will have to wait until the arm moves to the end of the disk, reverses direction, and comes back.

The SCAN algorithm is sometimes called the **elevator algorithm,** since the disk arm behaves just like an elevator in a building, first servicing all the requests going up, and then reversing to service requests the other way.

Assuming a uniform distribution of requests for cylinders, consider the density of requests when the head reaches one end and reverses direction. At

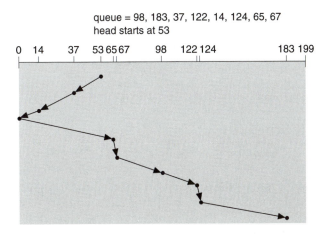

Figure 13.3   SCAN disk scheduling.

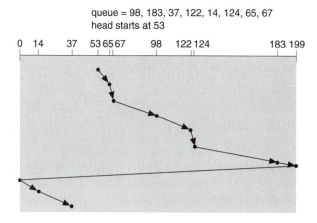

queue = 98, 183, 37, 122, 14, 124, 65, 67
head starts at 53

Figure 13.4   C-SCAN disk scheduling.

this point, there are relatively few requests immediately in front of the head, since these cylinders have recently been serviced. The heaviest density of requests is at the other end of the disk. These requests have also waited the longest, so why not go there first? That is the idea of the next algorithm.

13.2.4 C-SCAN Scheduling

Circular SCAN (C-SCAN) is a variant of SCAN that is designed to provide a more uniform wait time. Like SCAN, C-SCAN moves the head from one end of the disk to the other, servicing requests along the way. When the head reaches the other end, however, it immediately returns to the beginning of the disk, without servicing any requests on the return trip (Figure 13.4). The C-SCAN scheduling algorithm essentially treats the cylinders as a circular list that wraps around from the final cylinder to the first one.

13.2.5 LOOK Scheduling

Notice that, as we described them, both SCAN and C-SCAN move the disk arm across the full width of the disk. In practice, neither algorithm is implemented this way. More commonly, the arm goes only as far as the final request in each direction. Then, it reverses direction immediately, without first going all the way to the end of the disk. These versions of SCAN and C-SCAN are called LOOK and C-LOOK, because they look for a request before continuing to move in a given direction (Figure 13.5).

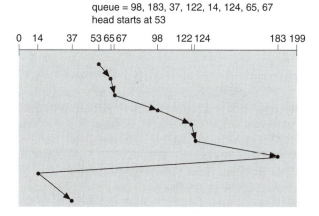

Figure 13.5 C-LOOK disk scheduling.

13.2.6 Selection of a Disk-Scheduling Algorithm

Given so many disk-scheduling algorithms, how do we choose the best one? SSTF is common and has a natural appeal. SCAN and C-SCAN perform better for systems that place a heavy load on the disk, because they are less likely to have the starvation problem described earlier. For any particular list of requests, it is possible to define an optimal order of retrieval, but the computation needed to find an optimal schedule may not justify the savings over SSTF or SCAN.

With any scheduling algorithm, however, performance depends heavily on the number and types of requests. For instance, suppose that the queue usually has just one outstanding request. Then, all scheduling algorithms are forced to behave the same, because they have only one choice for where to move the disk head: They all behave like FCFS scheduling.

Notice also that the requests for disk service can be greatly influenced by the file-allocation method. A program reading a contiguously allocated file will generate several requests that are close together on the disk, resulting in limited head movement. A linked or indexed file, on the other hand, may include blocks that are widely scattered on the disk, resulting in greater head movement.

The location of directories and index blocks also is important. Since every file must be opened to be used, and opening a file requires searching the directory structure, the directories will be accessed frequently. Suppose that a directory entry is on the first cylinder and a file's data are on the final cylinder. In this case, the disk head has to move the entire width of the disk. If the directory entry were on the middle cylinder, the head has to move at most one-half the width. Caching the directories and index blocks in main memory can also help to reduce the disk-arm movement, particularly for read requests.

Because of these complexities, the disk-scheduling algorithm should be written as a separate module of the operating system, so that it can be replaced with a different algorithm if necessary. Either SSTF or LOOK is a reasonable choice for the default algorithm.

Note that the scheduling algorithms described here consider only the seek distances. For modern disks, the rotational latency can be nearly as large as the average seek time. But it is difficult for the operating system to schedule for improved rotational latency because modern disks do not disclose the physical location of logical blocks. Disk manufacturers have been alleviating this problem by implementing disk-scheduling algorithms in the controller hardware built into the disk drive. If the operating system sends a batch of requests to the controller, the controller can queue them and then schedule them to improve both the seek time and the rotational latency. If I/O performance were the only consideration, the operating system would gladly turn over the responsibility of disk scheduling to the disk hardware. In practice, however, the operating system may have other constraints on the service order for requests. For instance, demand paging may take priority over application I/O, and writes are more urgent than reads if the cache is running out of free pages. Also, it may be desirable to guarantee the order of a set of disk writes to make the file system robust in the face of system crashes; consider what could happen if the operating system allocated a disk page to a file, and the application wrote data into that page before the operating system had a chance to flush the modified inode and free-space list back to disk. To accommodate such requirements, an operating system may choose to do its own disk scheduling, and to spoon-feed the requests to the disk controller, one by one.

13.3 ■ Disk Management

The operating system is responsible for several other aspects of disk management, too. Here we discuss disk initialization, booting from disk, and bad-block recovery.

13.3.1 Disk Formatting

A new magnetic disk is a blank slate: It is just platters of a magnetic recording material. Before a disk can store data, it must be divided into sectors that the disk controller can read and write. This process is called **low-level formatting,** or **physical formatting**. Low-level formatting fills the disk with a special data structure for each sector. The data structure for a sector typically consists of a header, a data area (usually 512 bytes in size), and a trailer. The header and trailer contain information used by the disk controller, such as a sector number and an **error-correcting code** (ECC). When the controller writes a sector of data during normal I/O, the ECC is updated with a value calculated from all the bytes in the data area. When the sector is read, the ECC is recalculated and is compared with the stored value. If the stored and calculated numbers are different, this mismatch indicates that the data area of the sector has become corrupted and that the disk sector may be bad (see Section 13.3.3). The ECC is an error-**correcting** code because it contains enough information that, if only 1 or 2 bits of data have been corrupted, the controller can identify which bits have changed, and can calculate what their correct values should be. The ECC processing is done automatically by the controller whenever a sector is read or written.

Most hard disks are low-level formatted at the factory as a part of the manufacturing process. This formatting enables the manufacturer to test the disk, and to initialize the mapping from logical block numbers to defect-free sectors on the disk. For many hard disks, when the disk controller is instructed to low-level format the disk, it can also be told how many bytes of data space to leave between the header and trailer of all sectors. It is usually possible to choose among a few sizes, such as 256, 512, and 1,024 bytes. Formatting a disk with a larger sector size means that fewer sectors can fit on each track, but that also means fewer headers and trailers are written on each track, and thus increases the space available for user data. Some operating systems can handle only a sector size of 512 bytes.

To use a disk to hold files, the operating system still needs to record its own data structures on the disk. It does so in two steps. The first step is to **partition** the disk into one or more groups of cylinders. The operating system can treat each partition as though the latter were a separate disk. For instance, one partition can hold a copy of the operating system's executable code, while another holds user files. After partitioning, the second step is **logical formatting,** or "making a file system." In this step, the operating system stores the initial file-system data structures onto the disk. These data structures may include maps of free and allocated space (a FAT or inodes) and an initial empty directory.

Some systems give special programs the ability to use a disk partition as a large sequential array of logical blocks, without any file-system data structures. This array is sometimes called **raw I/O**. For example, some database systems prefer raw I/O because it enables them to control the exact disk location where each database record is stored. Raw I/O bypasses all the file-system services, such as the buffer cache, prefetching, space allocation, file names, and directories. We can make certain applications more efficient by implementing their own special-purpose storage services on a raw partition, but most applications perform better when they use the regular file-system services.

13.3.2 Boot Block

For a computer to start running—for instance, when it is powered up or rebooted—it needs to have an initial program to run. This initial **bootstrap** program tends to be simple. It initializes all aspects of the system, from CPU registers to device controllers and the contents of main memory, and then starts the operating system. To do its job, the bootstrap program finds the operating-system kernel on disk, loads that kernel into memory, and jumps to an initial address to begin the operating-system execution.

For most computers, the bootstrap is stored in **read-only memory (ROM)**. This location is convenient, because ROM needs no initialization, and is at a fixed location that the processor can start executing when powered up or reset. And, since ROM is read only, it cannot be infected by a computer virus. The problem is that changing this bootstrap code requires changing the ROM hardware chips. For this reason, most systems store a tiny **bootstrap loader** program in the boot ROM, whose only job is to bring in a full bootstrap program from disk. The full bootstrap program can be changed easily: A new version is simply written onto the disk. The full bootstrap program is stored in a partition called the **boot blocks,** at a fixed location on the disk. A disk that has a boot partition is called a **boot disk** or **system disk**.

The code in the boot ROM instructs the disk controller to read the boot blocks into memory (no device drivers are loaded at this point), and then starts executing that code. The full bootstrap program is more sophisticated than the bootstrap loader in the boot ROM, and is able to load the entire operating system from a nonfixed location on disk, and to start the operating system running. Even so, the full bootstrap code may be small. For example, MS-DOS uses one 512-byte block for its boot program (Figure 13.6).

13.3.3 Bad Blocks

Because disks have moving parts and small tolerances (recall that the disk head flies just above the disk surface), they are prone to failure. Sometimes, the failure is complete, and the disk needs to be replaced, and its contents restored from backup media to the new disk. More frequently, one or more sectors become defective. Most disks even come from the factory with **bad blocks**.

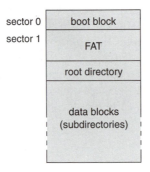

Figure 13.6   MS-DOS disk layout.

Depending on the disk and controller in use, these blocks are handled in a variety of ways.

On simple disks, such as some disks with IDE controllers, bad blocks are handled manually. For instance, the MS-DOS `format` command does a logical format, and, as a part of the process, scans the disk to find bad blocks. If `format` finds a bad block, it writes a special value into the corresponding FAT entry to tell the allocation routines not to use that block. If blocks go bad during normal operation, a special program (such as `chkdsk`) must be run manually to search for the bad blocks and to lock them away as before. Data that resided on the bad blocks usually are lost.

More sophisticated disks, such as the SCSI disks used in high-end PCs and most workstations, are smarter about bad-block recovery. The controller maintains a list of bad blocks on the disk. The list is initialized during the low-level format at the factory, and is updated over the life of the disk. Low-level formatting also sets aside spare sectors not visible to the operating system. The controller can be told to replace each bad sector logically with one of the spare sectors. This scheme is known as **sector sparing** or **forwarding**.

A typical bad-sector transaction might be as follows:

- The operating system tries to read logical block 87.

- The controller calculates the ECC and finds that the sector is bad. It reports this finding to the operating system.

- The next time that the system is rebooted, a special command is run to tell the SCSI controller to replace the bad sector with a spare.

- After that, whenever the system requests logical block 87, the request is translated into the replacement sector's address by the controller.

Note that such a redirection by the controller could invalidate any optimization by the operating system's disk-scheduling algorithm! For this reason, most disks are formatted to provide a few spare sectors in each cylinder, and a spare cylinder as well. When a bad block is remapped, the controller uses a spare sector from the same cylinder, if possible.

As an alternative to sector sparing, some controllers can be instructed to replace a bad block by **sector slipping**. Here is an example. Suppose that logical block 17 becomes defective, and the first available spare follows sector 202. Then, sector slipping would remap all the sectors from 17 to 202, moving them all down one spot. That is, sector 202 would be copied into the spare, then sector 201 into 202, and then 200 into 201, and so on, until sector 18 is copied into sector 19. Slipping the sectors in this way frees up the space of sector 18, so sector 17 can be mapped to it.

The replacement of a bad block generally is not a totally automatic process, because the data in the bad block usually are lost. Thus, whatever file was using that block must be repaired (for instance, by restoration from a backup tape), and that requires manual intervention.

13.4 ■ Swap-Space Management

Swap-space management is another low-level task of the operating system. Virtual memory uses disk space as an extension of main memory. Since disk access is much slower than memory access, using swap space significantly decreases system performance. The main goal for the design and implementation of swap space is to provide the best throughput for the virtual-memory system. In this section, we discuss how swap space is used, where swap space is located on disk, and how swap space is managed.

13.4.1 Swap-Space Use

Swap space is used in various ways by different operating systems, depending on the implemented memory-management algorithms. For instance, systems that implement swapping may use swap space to hold the entire process image, including the code and data segments. Paging systems may simply store pages that have been pushed out of main memory. The amount of swap space needed on a system can therefore vary depending on the amount of physical memory, the amount of virtual memory it is backing, and the way in which the virtual memory is used. It can range from a few megabytes of disk space to hundreds of megabytes or more.

Some operating systems, such as UNIX, allow the use of multiple swap spaces. These swap spaces are usually put on separate disks, so the load placed on the I/O system by paging and swapping can be spread over the system's I/O devices.

Note that it is safer to overestimate than to underestimate swap space, because if a system runs out of swap space it may be forced to abort processes or may crash entirely. Overestimation results in wasted disk space that could otherwise be used for files, but does no other harm.

13.4.2 Swap-Space Location

There are two places that a swap space can reside: Swap space can be carved out of the normal file system, or it can be in a separate disk partition. If the swap space is simply a large file within the file system, normal file-system routines can be used to create it, to name it, and to allocate its space. This approach is therefore easy to implement. Unfortunately, it is also inefficient. Navigating the directory structure and the disk-allocation data structures takes time, and (potentially) extra disk accesses. External fragmentation can greatly increase swapping times by forcing multiple seeks during reading or writing of a process image. We can improve performance by caching the block location information in physical memory, and by using special tools to allocate physically contiguous blocks for the swap file, but the cost of traversing the file-system data structures still remains.

More commonly, swap space is created in a separate disk partition. No file system or directory structure is placed on this space. Rather, a separate swap-space storage manager is used to allocate and deallocate the blocks. This manager uses algorithms that are optimized for speed, rather than for storage efficiency. Internal fragmentation may increase, but this tradeoff is acceptable because data in the swap space generally live for much shorter amounts of time than do files in the file system, and the swap area may be accessed much more frequently. This approach creates a fixed amount of swap space during disk partitioning. Adding more swap space can be done only via repartitioning of the disk (which involves moving or destroying and restoring the other file-system partitions from backup), or via adding another swap space elsewhere.

Some operating systems are flexible and can swap both in raw partitions and in file-system space. Solaris 2 is an example. The policy and implementation are separate, allowing the machine's administrator to decide which type to use. The tradeoff is between the convenience of allocation and management in the file system, and the performance of swapping in raw partitions.

13.4.3 Swap-Space Management

To illustrate the methods used to manage swap space, we now follow the evolution of swapping and paging in UNIX. As discussed fully in Chapter 20, UNIX started with an implementation of swapping that copied entire processes between contiguous disk regions and memory. UNIX evolved to a combination of swapping and paging as paging hardware became available.

In 4.3BSD, swap space is allocated to a process when the process is started. Enough space is set aside to hold the program, known as the **text pages** or the **text segment,** and the **data segment** of the process. Preallocating all the needed space in this way generally prevents a process from running out of swap space while it executes. When a process starts, its text is paged in from the file system. These pages are written out to swap when necessary, and are read back in from there, so the file system is consulted only once for each text page. Pages from the data segment are read in from the file system, or are created (if they are uninitialized), and are written to swap space and paged back in as needed. One optimization (for instance, when two users run the same editor) is that processes with identical text pages share these pages, both in physical memory and in swap space.

Two per-process **swap maps** are used by the kernel to track swap-space use. The text segment is a fixed size, so its swap space is allocated in 512K chunks, except for the final chunk, which holds the remainder of the pages, in 1K increments (Figure 13.7).

The data-segment swap map is more complicated, because the data segment can grow over time. The map is of fixed size, but contains swap addresses for blocks of varying size. Given index i, a block pointed to by swap-map entry i is of size $2^i \times 16K$, to a maximum of 2 megabytes. This data structure is shown

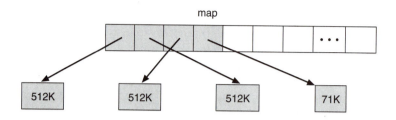

Figure 13.7   4.3BSD text-segment swap map.

in Figure 13.8. (The block size minimum and maximum are variable, and can be changed at system reboot.) When a process tries to grow its data segment beyond the final allocated block in its swap area, the operating system allocates another block, twice as large as the previous one. This scheme results in small processes using only small blocks. It also minimizes fragmentation. The blocks of large processes can be found quickly, and the swap map remains small.

In Solaris 1 (SunOS 4), the designers made changes to standard UNIX methods to improve efficiency and to reflect technological changes. When a process executes, text-segment pages are brought in from the file system, are accessed in main memory, and are thrown away if selected for pageout. It is more efficient to reread a page from the file system than to write it to swap space and then to reread it from there.

More changes were made in Solaris 2. The biggest change is that Solaris 2 allocates swap space only when a page is forced out of physical memory, rather than when the virtual-memory page is first created. This change gives better performance on modern computers, which have more physical memory than older systems, and tend to page less.

13.5 ■ Disk Reliability

Disks used to be the least reliable component of a system. They still have relatively high failure rates, and their failure causes a loss of data and significant downtime while the disk is replaced and the data restored. Recovering from a

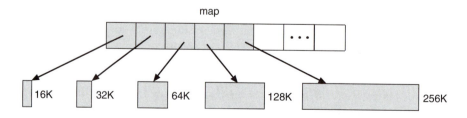

Figure 13.8   4.3BSD data-segment swap map.

disk crash may take hours, as backup copies of the lost data are found on tape and restored to the replacement disk. Under normal circumstances, the restored disk is not a precise image of the disk that crashed, because any changes to the data since the last backup are lost. Therefore, improving the reliability of disk systems is an important research topic.

Several improvements in disk-use techniques have been proposed. These methods involve the use of multiple disks working cooperatively. To improve speed, **disk striping** (or interleaving) uses a group of disks as one storage unit. Each data block is broken into several subblocks, with one subblock stored on each disk. The time required to transfer a block into memory improves dramatically, because all the disks transfer their subblocks in parallel. If the disks have their rotations **synchronized,** the performance improves further, because all the disks become ready to transfer their subblocks at the same time, rather than waiting for the slowest rotational latency. The larger the number of disks that are striped together, the larger the total transfer rate of the system.

This organization is usually called a **redundant array of independent disks (RAID)**. In addition to improving performance, various RAID schemes also improve the reliability of the storage system by storing redundant data. Redundancy can be organized in various ways, with differing performances and costs.

The simplest RAID organization, called **mirroring** or **shadowing,** just keeps a duplicate copy of each disk. This solution is costly, because twice as many disks are used to store the same quantity of data. But it is about twice as fast when reading, because one-half of the read requests can be sent to each disk. Another RAID organization, called **block interleaved parity,** uses much less redundancy. A small fraction of the disk space is used to hold parity blocks. For instance, suppose that there are nine disks in the array. Then, for every eight data blocks stored in the array, one parity block would also be stored. Each bit position in this parity block would contain the parity for the corresponding bit positions in each of the eight data blocks, just like computing a ninth parity bit in main memory for each 8-bit byte. If one disk block becomes bad, all its data bits are essentially erased—an **erasure error**—but they can be recomputed from the other data blocks plus the parity block. Thus, a single disk crash no longer causes a loss of data.

A parity RAID system has the combined speed of multiple disks and controllers. But the performance is a concern during writing, because updating any single data subblock forces the corresponding parity subblock to be recomputed and rewritten. By distributing the parity subblocks over all the disks, rather than setting aside one disk exclusively for parity, we can spread the workload evenly. Because the combined speed, cost, and reliability of a parity RAID can be attractive, many vendors are producing RAID hardware and software. If a system has many hundreds of disks, failures might cause data loss several times per year. This figure improves to once every few decades when the redundant data in RAID are used for recovery from disk failures.

13.6 ▪ Stable-Storage Implementation

There are many applications that require the availability of stable storage. By definition, information residing in stable storage is *never* lost. To implement such storage, we need to replicate the needed information on multiple storage devices (usually disks) with independent failure modes. We need to coordinate the writing of updates in a way that guarantees that a failure during an update does not leave all the copies in a damaged state, and that, when we are recovering from a failure, we can force all copies to a consistent and correct value, even if there is another failure during the recovery. In the remainder of this section, we discuss how to meet our needs.

A disk write results in one of three outcomes:

1. *Successful completion:* The data were written correctly on disk.

2. *Partial failure:* A failure occurred in the midst of transfer, so only some of the sectors were written with the new data, and the sector being written during the failure may have been corrupted.

3. *Total failure:* The failure occurred before the disk write started, so the previous data values on the disk remain intact.

We require that, whenever a failure occurs during writing of a block, the system detects it and invokes a recovery procedure to restore the block to a consistent state. To do that, the system must maintain two physical blocks for each logical block. An output operation is executed as follows:

1. Write the information onto the first physical block.

2. When the first write completes successfully, write the same information onto the second physical block.

3. Declare the operation complete only after the second write completes successfully.

During recovery from a failure, each pair of physical blocks is examined. If both are the same and no detectable error exists, then no further action is necessary. If one block contains a detectable error, then we replace its contents with the value of the other block. If both blocks contain no detectable error, but they differ in content, then we replace the content of the first block with the value of the second. This recovery procedure ensures that a write to stable storage either succeeds completely or results in no change.

We can extend this procedure easily to allow the use of an arbitrarily large number of copies of each block of stable storage. Although a large number of copies further reduces the probability of a failure, it is usually reasonable to simulate stable storage with only two copies. The data in stable storage are guaranteed to be safe unless a failure destroys all the copies.

13.7 ■ Tertiary-Storage Structure

Would you buy a VCR that had inside it only one tape that you could not take out or replace? Or an audio cassette player or CD player that had one album sealed inside? Of course not. You expect to use a VCR or CD player with many relatively inexpensive tapes or disks. On a computer as well, using many inexpensive cartridges with one drive lowers the overall cost.

13.7.1 Tertiary-Storage Devices

Low cost is the defining characteristic of tertiary storage. So, in practice, tertiary storage is built with **removable media**. The most common examples of removable media are floppy disks and CD-ROMs; many other kinds of tertiary-storage devices are available as well.

13.7.1.1 Removable Disks

Removable disks are one kind of tertiary storage. Floppy disks are an example of removable **magnetic disks**. They are made from a thin flexible disk coated with magnetic material, enclosed in a protective plastic case. Although common floppy disks can hold only about 1 megabyte, similar technology is used for removable magnetic disks that hold more than 1 gigabyte. Removable magnetic disks can be nearly as fast as hard disks, although the recording surface is at greater risk of damage from scratches.

A magneto-optic disk is another kind of removable disk. It records data on a rigid platter coated with magnetic material, but the recording technology is quite different from that for a magnetic disk. The magneto-optic head flies much farther from the disk surface than a magnetic disk head does, and the magnetic material is covered with a thick protective layer of plastic or glass. This arrangement makes the disk much more resistant to head crashes.

The drive has a coil that produces a magnetic field; at room temperature, the field is too large and too weak to magnetize a bit on the disk. To write a bit, the disk head flashes a laser beam at the disk surface. The laser is aimed at a tiny spot where a bit is to be written. The laser heats this spot, which makes the spot susceptible to the magnetic field. So the large, weak magnetic field can record a tiny bit.

The magneto-optic head is too far from the disk surface to read the data by detecting the tiny magnetic fields in the way that the head of a hard disk does. Instead, the drive reads a bit using a property of laser light called the **Kerr effect**. When a laser beam is bounced off of a magnetic spot, the polarization of the laser beam is rotated clockwise or counter-clockwise, depending on the orientation of the magnetic field. This rotation is what the head detects to read a bit.

Another category of removable disk is the **optical disk**. These disks do not use magnetism at all. They use special materials that can be altered by laser light to have spots that are relatively dark or bright. Each spot stores a bit. Two examples of optical-disk technology are phase-change disks and dye-polymer disks.

The **phase-change disk** is coated with a material that can freeze into either a crystalline or an amorphous state. The two states reflect laser light with different strength. The drive uses laser light at different powers to melt and refreeze spots on the disk, changing the spots between the crystalline and amorphous states.

The **dye-polymer disk** uses a different physical property: It records data by making bumps. The disk is coated with a plastic containing a dye that absorbs laser light. The laser can heat a small spot, causing the spot to swell and thus to form a bump; the laser can also warm a bump, causing the spot to soften and thus to contract back to being flat.

The phase-change and dye-polymer technologies are not as popular as the magneto-optic method because of their high cost and low performance, but they illustrate the search for new and better recording methods.

The kinds of disks described here have the property that they can be used over and over. They are called **read–write disks**. In contrast, **write-once, read-many-times (WORM) disks** form another category. One way to make a WORM disk is to manufacture a thin aluminum film sandwiched between two glass or plastic platters. To write a bit, the drive uses a laser light to burn a small hole through the aluminum. Because this hole cannot be reversed, any sector on the disk can be written only once. Although it is possible to destroy the information on a WORM disk by burning holes everywhere, it is virtually impossible to alter data on the disk, because holes can only be added, and the ECC code associated with each sector is likely to detect such additions. WORM disks are considered to be durable and reliable because the metal layer is safely encapsulated between the protective glass or plastic platters, and magnetic fields cannot damage the recording.

Read-only disks, such as CD-ROM and DVD, come from the factory with the data prerecorded. They use technology similar to that of WORM disks, and they too are durable.

13.7.1.2 Tapes

Magnetic tape is another type of removable medium. As a general rule, a tape is less expensive than an optical or magnetic disk, and the tape holds more data. Tape drives and disk drives have similar transfer rates. But random access to tape is much slower than a disk seek, because it requires a fast-forward or rewind operation that takes tens of seconds, or even minutes.

Although a typical tape drive is more expensive than a typical disk drive, the cost of a tape cartridge is much lower than the cost of the equivalent capacity of magnetic disks. So tape is an economical medium for purposes that do not require fast random access. Tapes are commonly used to hold backup copies of disk data. They are also used in large supercomputer centers to hold the enormous volumes of data used in scientific research and by large commercial enterprises.

Some tapes can hold much more data than can a disk drive; the surface area of a tape is usually much larger than the surface area of a disk. The storage capacity of tapes could improve even further, because at present the **areal density** (bits per square inch) of tape technology is about 100 times less than that for magnetic disks.

Large tape installations typically use robotic tape changers that move tapes between tape drives and storage slots in a tape library. These mechanisms give the computer automated access to a large number of relatively inexpensive tape cartridges. A library that holds a few tapes is a **tape stacker**; a library that holds thousands of tapes is a **tape silo**.

A robotic tape library lowers the overall cost of data storage. A disk-resident file that will not be needed for a while can be **archived** to tape, where the cost per megabyte is substantially lower; if the file is needed in the future, the computer can **stage** it back into disk storage for active use. A robotic tape library is sometimes called **near-line** storage, since it is between the high performance of **on-line** magnetic disks and the low cost of **off-line** tapes sitting on shelves in a storage room.

13.7.1.3 Future Technology

In the future, other storage technologies may become important. For instance, laser light can be used to record holographic photographs on special media. We can think of a black-and-white photograph as a two-dimensional array of pixels. Each pixel represents 1 bit; 0 for black, or 1 for white. A sharp photograph can hold millions of bits of data. And all the pixels in a hologram are transferred in one flash of laser light, so the data rate is extremely high. Holographic storage is prohibitively expensive today, but with continued development it may become commercially viable.

Whether the storage medium is a magneto-optic disk, a CD-ROM, or a magnetic tape, the operating system needs to provide several capabilities to use removable media for data storage. These capabilities are discussed in Section 13.7.2.

13.7.2 Operating-System Jobs

Two major jobs of an operating system are to manage physical devices and to present a virtual-machine abstraction to applications. In this chapter, we saw that, for hard disks, the operating system provides two abstractions. One is the raw device, which is just an array of data blocks. The other is a file system. For a file system on a magnetic disk, the operating system queues and schedules the interleaved requests from several applications. Now, we shall see how the operating system does its job when the storage media are removable.

13.7.2.1 Application Interface

Most operating systems handle removable disks almost exactly as they do fixed disks. When a new cartridge is inserted into the drive ("mounted"), the cartridge must be formatted, and then an empty file system is generated on the disk. This file system is used just like a file system on a hard disk.

Tapes are often handled differently. The operating system usually presents a tape as a raw storage medium. An application does not open a file on the tape; it opens the whole tape drive as a raw device. Usually, the tape drive then is reserved for the exclusive use of that application until the application exits or closes the tape device. This exclusivity makes sense, because random access on a tape can take tens of seconds, or even a few minutes, so interleaving random accesses to tapes from more than one application would be likely to cause thrashing.

When the tape drive is presented as a raw device, the operating system does not provide file-system services. The application must decide how to use the array of blocks. For instance, a program that backs up a hard disk to tape might store a list of file names and sizes at the beginning of the tape, and then copy the data of the files to the tape in that order.

It is easy to see the problems that can arise from this way of using tape. Since every application makes up its own rules for how to organize a tape, a tape full of data can generally be used by only the program that created it. For instance, even if we know that a backup tape contains a list of file names and file sizes followed by the file data in that order, we still would find it difficult to use the tape. How exactly are the file names stored? Are the file sizes in binary or in ASCII? Are the files written one per block, or are they all concatenated together in one tremendously long string of bytes? We do not even know the block size on the tape, because this variable is generally one that can be chosen separately for each block that is written.

For a disk drive, the basic operations are read, write, and seek. Tape drives, on the other hand, have a different set of basic operations. Instead of seek, a tape drive uses the locate operation. The tape seek operation is more precise than the disk seek operation, because it positions the tape to a specific logical block, rather than an entire track. Locating to block 0 is the same as rewinding the tape.

For most kinds of tape drives, it is possible to locate to any block that has been written on a tape; in a partly filled tape, however, it is not possible to locate into the empty space beyond the written area. It is impossible because most tape drives manage their physical space differently from disk drives. For a disk drive, the sectors have a fixed size, and the formatting process must be used to place empty sectors in their final positions before any data can be written. Most tape drives have a variable block size, and the size of each block is determined on the fly, when that block is written. If an area of defective tape is encountered during writing, the bad area is skipped and the block is written again. This operation explains why it is not possible to locate into the empty space beyond the written area—the positions and numbers of the logical blocks have not yet been determined.

Most tape drives have a `read position` operation that returns the logical block number where the tape head is. Many tape drives also support a `space` operation for relative motion. So, for example, the operation `space -2` would locate backward over two logical blocks.

For most kinds of tape drives, writing a block has the side effect of logically erasing everything beyond the position of the write. In practice, this side effect means that most tape drives are append-only devices, because updating a block in the middle of the tape also effectively erases everything beyond that block. The tape drive implements this appending by placing an end-of-tape (EOT) mark after a block that is written. The drive refuses to locate past the EOT mark, but it is possible to locate to the EOT and then to start writing. Doing so overwrites the old EOT mark, and places a new one at the end of the new blocks just written.

In principle, it is possible to implement a file system on a tape. But many of the file-system data structures and algorithms would be different from those used for disks, because of the append-only property of tape.

13.7.2.2 File Naming

Another question that the operating system needs to handle is how to name files on removable media. For a fixed disk, naming is not difficult. On a PC, the file name consists of a drive letter followed by a path name. In UNIX, the file name does not contain a drive letter, but the mount table enables the operating system to discover on what drive the file is located. But if the disk is removable, knowing a drive that contained the cartridge at some time in the past does not mean knowing how to find the file. If every removable cartridge in the world had a different serial number, the name of a file on a removable device could be prefixed with the serial number, but to ensure that no two serial numbers are the same would require each one to be about 12 digits in length. Who could remember the names of her files if she had to memorize a 12-digit serial number for each one?

The problem becomes even more difficult when we want to write data on a removable cartridge on one computer, and then use the cartridge in another computer. If both machines are of the same type and have the same kind of removable drive, the only difficulty is knowing the contents and data layout on the cartridge. But if the machines or drives are different, many additional problems can arise. Even if the drives are compatible, different computers may store bytes in different orders, and may use different encodings for binary numbers and even for letters (such as ASCII on PCs versus EBCDIC on mainframes).

Today's operating systems generally leave the name-space problem unsolved for removable media, and depend on applications and users to figure out how to access and interpret the data. Fortunately, a few kinds of removable media are so well standardized that all computers use them the same way. One example is the CD. Music CDs use a universal format that is understood by any CD drive. Data CDs are available in only a few different formats, so it is usual for a CD drive and the operating-system device driver to be programmed to handle all the common formats.

13.7.2.3 Hierarchical Storage Management

A **robotic jukebox** enables the computer to change the removable cartridge that is in a tape or disk drive without human assistance. Two major uses of this technology are for backups and for hierarchical storage systems. The use of a jukebox for backups is simple—when one cartridge becomes full, the computer instructs the jukebox to switch to the next cartridge.

A hierarchical storage system extends the storage hierarchy beyond primary memory and secondary storage (that is, magnetic disk) to incorporate tertiary storage. Tertiary storage is usually implemented as a jukebox of tapes or removable disks. This level of the storage hierarchy is larger and cheaper, and probably slower.

Although the virtual-memory system can be extended in a straightforward manner to tertiary storage, this extension is rarely carried out in practice. The reason is that a retrieval from a jukebox can take tens of seconds or even minutes, and such a long delay is intolerable for demand paging and for other forms of virtual-memory use.

The usual way to incorporate tertiary storage is to extend the file system. Small and frequently used files remain on magnetic disk, while large old files that are not actively used are archived to the jukebox. In some file-archiving systems, the directory entry for the file continues to exist, but the contents of the file no longer occupy space in secondary storage. If an application tries to open the file, the open system call is suspended until the file contents can be staged in from tertiary storage. When the contents are again available from magnetic disk, the open operation returns control to the application, which proceeds to use the disk-resident copy of the data. Hierarchical storage management (HSM) has been implemented in ordinary time-sharing systems such as TOPS-20, which ran on minicomputers from Digital Equipment Corporation in the late 1970s. Today, HSM is usually found in supercomputing centers and other large installations that have enormous volumes of data.

13.8 ■ Summary

Disk drives are the major secondary-storage I/O device on most computers. Requests for disk I/O are generated by the file system and by the virtual-memory system. Each request specifies the address on the disk to be referenced, in the form of a logical block number.

Disk-scheduling algorithms can improve the effective bandwidth, the average response time, and the variance in response time. Algorithms such as SSTF, SCAN, C-SCAN, LOOK, and C-LOOK are designed to make such improvements by reordering the disk queue to decrease the total seek time.

Performance can be harmed by external fragmentation. One way to reorganize a disk to reduce fragmentation is to back up and restore the entire disk or partition. The blocks are read from their scattered locations, and the restore writes them back contiguously. Some systems have utilities that scan the file system to identify fragmented files; they then move blocks around to decrease the fragmentation. Defragmenting a badly fragmented file system can significantly improve the performance, but the system is generally unusable while the defragmentation is in progress. Sophisticated file systems, such as the UNIX Fast File System, incorporate many strategies to control fragmentation during space allocation, so that disk reorganization is unnecessary.

The operating system manages the disk blocks. First, a disk must be low-level formatted to create the sectors on the raw hardware. Then, the disk can be partitioned and file systems created, and boot blocks can be allocated to store the system's bootstrap program. Finally, when a block is corrupted, the system must have a way to lock out that block, or to replace it logically with a spare.

Because an efficient swap space is a key to good performance, systems usually bypass the file system and use a raw disk partition to store memory pages that do not fit within physical memory. Some systems use a file within the file system instead, but there can be a performance penalty. Other systems allow the user or system administrator to make the decision by providing both options.

The write-ahead log scheme requires the availability of stable storage. To implement such storage, we need to replicate the needed information on multiple nonvolatile storage devices (usually disks) with independent failure modes. We also need to update the information in a controlled manner to ensure that we can recover the stable data after any failure during data transfer or recovery.

Tertiary storage is built from disk and tape drives that use removable media. Many different technologies are suitable, including magnetic tape, removable magnetic and magneto-optic disks, and optical disks.

For removable disks, the operating system generally provides the full services of a file-system interface, including space management and request-queue scheduling. For many operating systems, the name of a file on a removable cartridge is a combination of a drive name and a file name within that drive. This convention is simpler but potentially more confusing than is using a name that identifies a specific cartridge.

For tapes, the operating system generally just provides a raw interface. Many operating systems have no built-in support for jukeboxes. Jukebox support can be provided by a device driver or by a privileged application designed for backups or for HSM.

▪ Exercises

13.1 None of the disk-scheduling disciplines, except FCFS, are truly fair (starvation may occur).

    a. Explain why this assertion is true.

    b. Describe a way to modify algorithms such as SCAN to ensure fairness.

    c. Explain why fairness is an important goal in a time-sharing system.

    d. Give three or more examples of circumstances in which it is important that the operating system be *un*fair in serving I/O requests.

13.2 Suppose that a disk drive has 5000 cylinders, numbered 0 to 4999. The drive is currently serving a request at cylinder 143, and the previous request was at cylinder 125. The queue of pending requests, in FIFO order, is

$$86, 1470, 913, 1774, 948, 1509, 1022, 1750, 130.$$

Starting from the current head position, what is the total distance (in cylinders) that the disk arm moves to satisfy all the pending requests, for each of the following disk-scheduling algorithms?

    a. FCFS

    b. SSTF

    c. SCAN

    d. LOOK

    e. C-SCAN

13.3 From elementary physics, we know that, when an object is subjected to a constant acceleration a, the relationship between distance d and time t is given by $d = \frac{1}{2}at^2$. Suppose that, during a seek, the disk in Exercise 13.2 accelerates the disk arm at a constant rate for the first half of the seek, then decelerates the disk arm at the same rate for the second half of the seek. Assume that the disk can perform a seek to an adjacent cylinder in 1 millisecond, and a full-stroke seek over all 5000 cylinders in 18 milliseconds.

    a. The distance of a seek is the number of cylinders that the head moves. Explain why the seek time is proportional to the square root of the seek distance.

b. Write an equation for the seek time as a function of the seek distance. This equation should be of the form $t = x + y\sqrt{L}$, where t is the time in milliseconds, and L is the seek distance in cylinders.

c. Calculate the total seek time for each of the schedules in Exercise 13.2. Determine which schedule is the fastest (has the smallest total seek time).

d. The *percentage speedup* is the time saved divided by the original time. What is the percentage speedup of the fastest schedule over FCFS?

13.4 Suppose that the disk in Exercise 13.3 rotates at 7200 RPM.

a. What is the average rotational latency of this disk drive?

b. What seek distance can be covered in the time that you found for part a?

13.5 The accelerating seek described in Exercise 13.3 is typical of hard-disk drives. By contrast, floppy disks (and many hard disks manufactured before the mid-1980s) typically seek at a fixed rate. Suppose that the disk in Exercise 13.3 has a constant-rate seek, rather than a constant-acceleration seek, so the seek time is of the form $t = x + yL$, where t is the time in milliseconds, and L is the seek distance. Suppose that the time to seek to an adjacent cylinder is 1 millisecond, as before, and is 0.5 milliseconds for each additional cylinder.

a. Write an equation for this seek time as a function of the seek distance.

b. Using the seek-time function from part a, calculate the total seek time for each of the schedules in Exercise 13.2. Is your answer the same as it was for Exercise 13.3(c)? Explain why it is the same or why it is different.

c. What is the percentage speedup of the fastest schedule over FCFS in this case?

13.6 Write a Java program for disk scheduling using the SCAN and C-SCAN disk-scheduling algorithms.

13.7 Compare the performance of C-SCAN and SCAN scheduling, assuming a uniform distribution of requests. Consider the average response time (the time between the arrival of a request and the completion of that request's service), the variation in response time, and the effective bandwidth. How does performance depend on the relative sizes of seek time and rotational latency?

13.8 Is disk scheduling, other than FCFS scheduling, useful in a single-user environment? Explain your answer.

13.9 Explain why SSTF scheduling tends to favor middle cylinders over the innermost and outermost cylinders.

13.10 Requests are not usually uniformly distributed. For example, a cylinder containing the file system FAT or inodes can be expected to be accessed more frequently than a cylinder that only contains files. Suppose that you know that 50 percent of the requests are for a small, fixed number of cylinders.

    a. Would any of the scheduling algorithms discussed in this chapter be particularly good for this case? Explain your answer.

    b. Propose a disk-scheduling algorithm that gives even better performance by taking advantage of this "hot spot" on the disk.

    c. File systems typically find data blocks via an indirection table, such as a FAT in DOS or inodes in UNIX. Describe one or more ways to take advantage of this indirection to improve the disk performance.

13.11 Why is rotational latency usually not considered in disk scheduling? How would you modify SSTF, SCAN, and C-SCAN to include latency optimization?

13.12 How would the use of a RAM disk affect your selection of a disk-scheduling algorithm? What factors would you need to consider? Do the same considerations apply to hard-disk scheduling, given that the file system stores recently used blocks in a buffer cache in main memory?

13.13 Why is it important to balance file system I/O among the disks and controllers on a system in a multitasking environment?

13.14 What are the tradeoffs involved in rereading code pages from the file system, versus using swap space to store them?

13.15 Is there any way to implement truly stable storage? Explain your answer.

13.16 The reliability of a hard-disk drive is typically described in terms of a quantity called *mean time between failures* (MTBF). Although this quantity is called a "time," the MTBF actually is measured in drive-hours per failure.

    a. If a system contains 1,000 disk drives, each of which has a 750,000 hour MTBF, which of the following best describes how often a drive failure will occur in that disk farm: once per thousand years, once per century, once per decade, once per year, once per month, once per week, once per day, once per hour, once per minute, or once per second?

b. Mortality statistics indicate that, on the average, a U.S. resident has about 1:1,000 chance of dying between ages 20 and 21 years. Deduce the MTBF hours for 20 year olds. Convert this figure from hours to years. What does this MTBF tell you about the expected lifetime of a 20 year old?

c. The manufacturer guarantees a 1-million hour MTBF for a certain model of disk drive. What can you conclude about the number of years for which one of these drives is under warrantee?

13.17 The term *fast wide SCSI-II* denotes a SCSI bus that operates at a data rate of 20 megabytes per second when it moves a packet of bytes between the host and a device. Suppose that a fast wide SCSI-II disk drive spins at 7,200 RPM, has a sector size of 512 bytes, and holds 160 sectors per track.

a. Estimate the sustained transfer rate of this drive in megabytes per second.

b. Suppose that the drive has 7000 cylinders, 20 tracks per cylinder, a head switch time (from one platter to another) of 0.5 milliseconds, and an adjacent cylinder seek time of 2 milliseconds. Use this additional information to give an accurate estimate of the sustained transfer rate for a huge transfer.

c. Suppose that the average seek time for the drive is 8 milliseconds. Estimate the I/Os per second and the effective transfer rate for a random-access workload that reads individual sectors that are scattered across the disk.

d. Calculate the random-access I/Os per second and transfer rate for I/O sizes of 4 kilobytes, 8 kilobytes, and 64 kilobytes.

e. If multiple requests are in the queue, a scheduling algorithm such as SCAN should be able to reduce the average seek distance. Suppose that a random-access workload is reading 8-kilobytes pages, the average queue length is 10, and the scheduling algorithm reduces the average seek time to 3 milliseconds. Calculate the I/Os per second and the effective transfer rate of the drive.

13.18 More than one disk drive can be attached to a SCSI bus. In particular, a fast wide SCSI-II bus (see Exercise 13.17) can be connected to at most 15 disk drives. Recall that this bus has a bandwidth of 20 megabytes per second. At any time, only one packet can be transferred on the bus between some disk's internal cache and the host. However, a disk can be moving its disk arm while some other disk is transferring a packet on the bus. Also, a disk can be transferring data between its magnetic platters and its internal cache while some other disk is transferring a packet on the bus. Considering the transfer rates that you calculated for the various workloads in Exercise 13.17, discuss how many disks can be used effectively by one fast wide SCSI-II bus.

13.19 Remapping of bad blocks by sector sparing or sector slipping could influence performance. Suppose that the drive in Exercise 13.17 has a total of 100 bad sectors at random locations, and that each bad sector is mapped to a spare that is located on a different track, but within the same cylinder. Estimate the number of I/Os per second and the effective transfer rate for a random-access workload consisting of 8-kilobyte reads, with a queue length of 1 (that is, the choice of scheduling algorithm is not a factor). What is the effect of a bad sector on performance?

13.20 Discuss the relative advantages and disadvantages of sector sparing and sector slipping.

13.21 The operating system generally treats removable disks as shared file systems, but assigns a tape drive to only one application at a time. Give three reasons that could explain this difference in treatment of disks and tapes. Describe the additional features that an operating system would need to support shared file-system access to a tape jukebox. Would the applications sharing the tape jukebox need any special properties, or could they use the files as though the files were disk-resident? Explain your answer.

13.22 In a disk jukebox, what would be the effect if the number of open files was greater than the number of drives in the jukebox?

13.23 What would be the effects on cost and performance if tape storage had the same areal density as disk storage?

13.24 If magnetic hard disks eventually have the same cost per gigabyte as do tapes, will tapes become obsolete, or will they still be needed? Explain your answer.

13.25 You can use simple estimates to compare the cost and performance of a terabyte storage system made entirely from disks with one that incorporates tertiary storage. Suppose that magnetic disks each hold 10 gigabytes, cost $1,000, transfer 5 megabytes per second, and have an average access latency of 15 milliseconds. Suppose that a tape library costs $10 per gigabyte, transfers 10 megabytes per second, and has an average access latency of 20 seconds. Compute the total cost, the maximum total data rate, and the average waiting time for a pure disk system. If you make any assumptions about the workload, describe and justify them. Now, suppose that 5 percent of the data are frequently used, so they must reside on disk, but the other 95 percent are archived in the tape library. Further suppose that 95 percent of the requests are handled by the disk system, and the other 5 percent are handled by the library.

What are the total cost, the maximum total data rate, and the average waiting time for this hierarchical storage system?

13.26 Imagine that a holographic storage drive has been invented. Suppose that a holographic drive costs \$10,000 and has an average access time of 40 milliseconds. Suppose that it uses a \$100 cartridge the size of a CD. This cartridge holds 40,000 images, and each image is a square black-and-white picture with resolution 6000 × 6000 pixels (each pixel stores 1 bit). Suppose that the drive can read or write 1 picture in 1 millisecond. Answer the following questions.

   a. What would be some good uses for this device?

   b. How would this device affect the I/O performance of a computing system?

   c. Which other kinds of storage devices, if any, would become obsolete as a result of this device being invented?

13.27 Suppose that a one-sided 5.25-inch optical-disk cartridge has an areal density of 1 gigabit per square inch. Suppose that a magnetic tape has an areal density of 20 megabits per square inch, and is 1/2 inch wide and 1,800 feet long. Calculate an estimate of the storage capacities of these two kinds of storage cartridges. Suppose that an optical tape exists that has the same physical size as the tape, but the same storage density as the optical disk. What volume of data could the optical tape hold? What would be a marketable price for the optical tape if the magnetic tape cost \$25?

13.28 Suppose that we agree that 1 kilobyte is 1,024 bytes, 1 megabyte is $1,024^2$ bytes, and 1 gigabyte is $1,024^3$ bytes. This progression continues through terabytes, petabytes, and exabytes ($1,024^6$). There are currently several new proposed scientific projects that plan to record and store a few exabytes of data during the next decade. To answer the following questions, you will need to make a few reasonable assumptions; state the assumptions that you make.

   a. How many disk drives would be required to hold 4 exabytes of data?

   b. How many magnetic tapes would be required to hold 4 exabytes of data?

   c. How many optical tapes would be required to hold 4 exabytes of data (see Exercise 13.27)?

   d. How many holographic storage cartridges would be required to hold 4 exabytes of data (see Exercise 13.26)?

e. How many cubic feet of storage space would each option require?

13.29 Discuss how an operating system could maintain a free-space list for a tape-resident file system. Assume that the tape technology is append-only, and that it uses the EOT mark and `locate`, `space`, and `read position` commands as described in Section 13.7.2.1.

Bibliographical Notes

Discussions of redundant arrays of independent disks (RAID) are presented by Patterson and colleagues [1988] and in the detailed survey of Chen and colleagues [1994]. Disk-system architectures for high-performance computing are discussed by Katz and associates [1989].

Teorey and Pinkerton [1972] present an early comparative analysis of disk-scheduling algorithms. They use simulations that model a disk for which seek time is linear in the number of cylinders crossed. For this disk, LOOK is a good choice for queue lengths below 140, and C-LOOK is good for queue lengths above 100. King [1990] describes ways to improve the seek time by moving the disk arm when the disk is otherwise idle. Worthington and colleagues [1994] describe disk-scheduling algorithms that consider rotational latency in addition to seek time, and discuss the performance effects of defect management. The placement of hot data to improve seek times has been considered by Ruemmler and Wilkes [1991], and Akyurek and Salem [1993].

Ruemmler and Wilkes [1994] describe an accurate performance model for a modern disk drive. Worthington and colleagues [1995] tell how to determine low-level disk properties such as the zone structure.

The I/O size and randomness of the workload has a considerable influence on disk performance. Ousterhout and colleagues [1985], and Ruemmler and Wilkes [1993], report numerous interesting workload characteristics, including that most files are small, most newly created files are deleted soon thereafter, most files that are opened for reading are read sequentially in their entirety, and most seeks are short. McKusick and colleagues [1984] describe the Berkeley Fast File System, which uses many sophisticated techniques to obtain good performance for a wide variety of workloads. McVoy and Kleiman [1991] discuss further improvements to the basic FFS.

Quinlan [1991] describes how to implement a file system on WORM storage with a magnetic disk cache; Richards [1990] discusses a file-system approach to tertiary storage. Maher and colleagues [1994] give an overview of the integration of distributed file systems and tertiary storage.

The concept of a storage hierarchy has been studied for more than one-quarter of a century. For instance, a 1970 paper by Mattson and associates [1970] describes a mathematical approach to predict the performance of a storage hierarchy. Alt [1993] describes the accommodation of removable storage in a commercial operating system, and Miller and Katz [1993] describe the characteristics of tertiary-storage access in a supercomputing environment. Benjamin [1990] gives an overview of the massive storage requirements for the EOSDIS project at NASA.

Holographic-storage technology is the subject of an article by Psaltis and Mok [1995]; a collection of holographic-storage papers dating from 1963 has been assembled by Sincerbox [1994]. Asthana and Finkelstein [1995] describe several emerging storage technologies, including holographic storage, optical tape, and electron trapping.

Part Four

DISTRIBUTED SYSTEMS

A *distributed system* is a collection of processors that do not share memory or a clock. Instead, each processor has its own local memory, and the processors communicate with each other through various communication lines. The processors in a distributed system vary in size and function. They may include small microprocessors, workstations, minicomputers, and large general-purpose computer systems.

A distributed system gives its users access to the various resources that it maintains. Access to a shared resource allows computation speedup, as well as improved data availability and reliability.

A distributed file system is a file-service system whose users, servers, and storage devices are dispersed among the various sites of a distributed system. Accordingly, service activity has to be carried out across the network; instead of a single centralized data repository, there are multiple and independent storage devices.

A distributed system must provide mechanisms for synchronizing processes, for managing interprocess communication, for dealing with the deadlock problem, and for handling various failures that are not encountered in a centralized system.

Chapter 14

NETWORK STRUCTURES

A *distributed system* is a collection of processors that do not share memory or a clock. Instead, each processor has its own local memory. The processors communicate with one another through various communication networks, such as high-speed buses or telephone lines. In this chapter, we discuss the general structure of distributed systems and the networks that interconnect them. Detailed discussions are given in Chapters 15 through 17.

14.1 ■ Background

A **distributed system** is a collection of loosely coupled processors interconnected by a communication network. From the point of view of a specific processor in a distributed system, the rest of the processors and their respective resources are **remote**, whereas its own resources are **local**.

The processors in a distributed system may vary in size and function. They may include small microprocessors, workstations, minicomputers, and large general-purpose computer systems. These processors are referred to by a number of different names, such as *sites, nodes, computers, machines, hosts,* and so on, depending on the context in which they are mentioned. We mainly use *site* to indicate the location of a machine, and *host* to refer to a specific system at a site. Generally, one host at one site, the *server,* has a resource that another host at another site, the *client* (or *user*), would like to use. The purpose of the

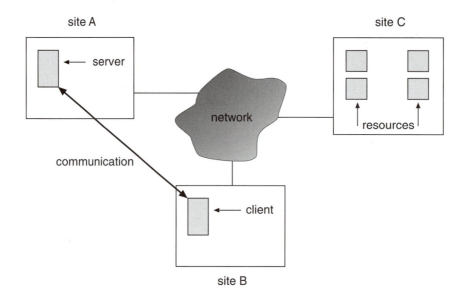

Figure 14.1   A distributed system.

distributed system is to provide an efficient and convenient environment for this type of sharing of resources. A distributed system is shown in Figure 14.1.

14.1.1 Advantages of Distributed Systems

There are four major reasons for building distributed systems: *resource sharing*, *computation speedup*, *reliability*, and *communication*. In this section, we briefly elaborate on each of them.

14.1.1.1 Resource Sharing

If a number of different sites (with different capabilities) are connected to one another, then a user at one site may be able to use the resources available at another. For example, a user at site A may be using a laser printer available at only site B. Meanwhile, a user at B may access a file that resides at A. In general, **resource sharing** in a distributed system provides mechanisms for sharing files at remote sites, processing information in a distributed database, printing files at remote sites, using remote specialized hardware devices (such as a high-speed array processor), and performing other operations.

14.1.1.2 Computation Speedup

If a particular computation can be partitioned into a number of subcomputations that can run concurrently, then the availability of a distributed system may allow us to distribute the computation among the various sites, to run the computation concurrently and thus to provide **computation speedup**. In addition, if a particular site is currently overloaded with jobs, some of them may be moved to other, lightly loaded, sites. This movement of jobs is called **load sharing**. Automated load sharing, in which the distributed operating system automatically moves jobs, is not yet common in commercial systems.

14.1.1.3 Reliability

If one site fails in a distributed system, the remaining sites can potentially continue operating, giving the sytem better **reliability**. If the system is composed of multiple large autonomous installations (that is, general-purpose computers), the failure of one of them should not affect the rest. If, on the other hand, the system is composed of small machines, each of which is responsible for some crucial system function (such as terminal character I/O or the file system), then a single failure may halt the operation of the whole system. In general, with enough redundancy (in both hardware and data), the system can continue operation, even if some of its sites have failed.

The failure of a site must be detected by the system, and appropriate action may be needed to recover from the failure. The system must no longer use the services of that site. In addition, if the function of the failed site can be taken over by another site, the system must ensure that the transfer of function occurs correctly. Finally, when the failed site recovers or is repaired, mechanisms must be available to integrate it back into the system smoothly. As we shall see in Chapters 15 through 17, these actions present difficult problems that have many possible solutions.

14.1.1.4 Communication

When several sites are connected to one another by a **communication** network, the users at different sites have the opportunity to exchange information. At a low level, **messages** are passed between systems in a manner similar to the single-computer message system discussed in Section 4.5. Given message passing, all the higher-level functionality found in standalone systems can be expanded to encompass the distributed system. Such functions include file transfer, login, mail, World Wide Web browsing, and remote procedure calls (RPCs).

The advantage of a distributed system is that these functions can be carried out over great distances. A project can be performed by two people at geographically disparate sites. By transferring the files of the project, logging in to each other's remote systems to run programs, and exchanging mail to coordinate the work, users minimize the limitations inherent in long-distance work. That is how we wrote this book.

The advantages of distributed systems have resulted in an industry-wide trend toward **downsizing**. Many companies are replacing their mainframes with networks of workstations or personal computers. Companies get a bigger bang for the buck (better functionality for the cost), more flexibility in locating resources and expanding facilities, better user interfaces, and easier maintenance.

Obviously, an operating system that was designed as a collection of processes that communicate through a message system can be extended more easily to a distributed system than can a non–message-passing system. For instance, MS-DOS is not easily integrated into a network because its kernel is interrupt based and lacks any support for message passing.

14.1.2 Types of Distributed Operating Systems

In this section, we describe the two general categories of network-oriented operating systems. Network operating systems are simpler to implement but generally more difficult for users to access and utilize than are distributed operating systems, which provide more features.

14.1.2.1 Network Operating Systems

A **network operating system** provides an environment in which users, who are aware of the multiplicity of machines, can access remote resources by either logging into the appropriate remote machine or transferring data from the remote machine to their own machines.

Remote Login

An important function of a network operating system is to allow users to log in remotely on another computer. The Internet provides the **telnet** facility for this purpose. To illustrate this facility, let us suppose that a user at Brown University wishes to compute on "cs.utexas.edu," a computer that is located at the University of Texas. To do so, the user must have a valid account on that machine. To log in remotely, the user issues the command

telnet cs.utexas.edu

This command results in a connection being formed between the local machine at Brown University and the "cs.utexas.edu" computer. After this connection has been established, the networking software creates a transparent, bidirectional link such that all characters entered by the user are sent to a process on "cs.utexas.edu," and all the output from that process is sent back to the user. The process on the remote machine asks the user for a login name and a password. Once the correct information has been received, the process acts as a proxy for the user, who can compute on the remote machine just as any local user can.

Remote File Transfer

Another major function of a network operating system is to provide a mechanism for **remote file transfer** from one machine to another. In such an environment, each computer maintains its own local file system. If a user at one site (say, "cs.brown.edu") wants to access a file located on another computer (say, "cs.utexas.edu"), then the file must be copied explicitly from the computer at Texas to the computer at Brown.

The Internet provides a mechanism for such a transfer with the File Transfer Protocol (FTP) program. Suppose that a user on cs.brown.edu wants to copy a file *paper.tex* that resides on cs.utexas.edu into a local file *my-paper.tex*. The user must first invoke the FTP program, by executing

ftp cs.utexas.edu

The program then asks the user for the login name and a password. Once the correct information has been received, the user must connect to the subdirectory where the file *paper.tex* resides, and then copy the file by executing

get *paper.tex my-paper.tex*

In this scheme, the file location is not transparent to the user; users must know exactly where each file is. Moreover, there is no real file sharing, because a user can only *copy* a file from one site to another. Thus, several copies of the same file may exist, resulting in a waste of space. In addition, if these copies are modified, the various copies will be inconsistent.

Notice that, in our example, the user at Brown University must have login permission on "cs.utexas.edu." FTP also provides a way to allow a user who does not have an account on the Texas computer to copy files remotely. This remote copying is accomplished through the "anonymous ftp" method, which works as follows. The file to be copied (that is, *paper.tex*) must be placed in a special subdirectory (say, *ftp*) with the protection set to allow the public to read the file. A user who wishes to copy the file uses the ftp command as before. When the user is asked for the login name, the user supplies the name "anonymous," and an arbitrary password.

Once anonymous login is accomplished, care must be taken by the system to ensure that this partially authorized user does not access inappropriate files. Generally, the user is allowed to access only those files that are in the directory tree of user "anonymous." Any files placed here are accessible to any anonymous users, subject to the usual file-protection scheme used on that machine. Anonymous users, however, cannot access files outside of this directory tree.

The FTP mechanism is implemented in a manner similar to telnet. There is a daemon on the remote site that watches for connection requests to the system's FTP port. Login authentication is accomplished, and the user is allowed to execute commands remotely. Unlike the telnet daemon, which executes any command for the user, the FTP daemon responds only to a predefined set of file-related commands. These include

- get: Transfer a file from the remote machine to the local machine.

- put: Transfer from the local machine to the remote machine.

- ls or dir: List files in the current directory on the remote machine.

- cd: Change the current directory on the remote machine.

There are also various commands to change transfer modes (for binary or ASCII files) and to determine connection status.

An important point about telnet and FTP is that they require the user to change paradigms. FTP requires the user to know a command set entirely different from the normal operating-system commands. Telnet requires a smaller shift: The user must know appropriate commands on the remote system. For instance, a user on a UNIX machine who telnets to a VMS machine must switch to VMS commands for the duration of the telnet session. Facilities are more convenient for users if they do not require the use of a different set of commands. Distributed operating systems are designed to ameliorate this problem.

14.1.2.2 Distributed Operating Systems

In a distributed operating system, the users access remote resources in the same manner as they do local resources. Data and process migration from one site to another are under the control of the distributed operating system.

Data Migration

Suppose that a user on site A wants to access data (such as a file) that reside at site B. There are two basic methods for the system to transfer the data. One approach to **data migration** is to transfer the entire file to site A. From that point on, all access to the file is local. When the user no longer needs access to the file, a copy of the file (if it has been modified) is sent back to site B. Even if only a modest change has been made to a large file, all the data must be transferred. This mechanism can be thought of as an automated FTP system. This approach was used in the Andrew file system, as we discuss in Chapter 17, but it was found to be too inefficient.

The other approach is to transfer to site A only those portions of the file that are actually *necessary* for the immediate task. If another portion is required later, another transfer will take place. When the user no longer wants to access the file, any part of it that has been modified must be sent back to site B. (Note the similarity to demand paging.) The Sun Microsystems' Network File System (NFS) protocol uses this method (see Chapter 17), as do newer versions of Andrew. The Microsoft SMB protocol (running on top of either TCP/IP or the Microsoft NETBUI protocol) also allows file sharing over a network. SMB is described in Section 22.7.1.

Clearly, if only a small part of a large file is being accessed, the latter approach is preferable. If significant portions of the file are being accessed, it is more efficient to copy the entire file.

Note that it is not sufficient merely to transfer data from one site to another. The system must also perform various data translations if the two sites involved are not directly compatible (for instance, if they use different character-code representations or represent integers with a different number or order of bits).

Computation Migration

In some circumstances, it may be more efficient to transfer the computation, rather than the data, across the system; this approach is called **computation migration**. For example, consider a job that needs to access various large files that reside at different sites, to obtain a summary of those files. It would be more efficient to access the files at the sites where they reside and then to return the desired results to the site that initiated the computation. Generally, if the time to transfer the data is longer than the time to execute the remote command, the remote command should be used.

Such a computation can be carried out in different ways. Suppose that process P wants to access a file at site A. Access to the file is carried out at site A, and could be initiated by a **remote procedure call** (**RPC**). An RPC uses a datagram protocol (UDP on the Internet) to execute a routine on a remote system (Section 15.2). Process P invokes a predefined procedure at site A. The procedure executes appropriately, and then returns the results to P.

Alternatively, process P can send a *message* to site A. The operating system at site A would then create a new process Q whose function is to carry out the designated task. When process Q completes its execution, it sends the needed result back to P via the message system. Note that, in this scheme, process P may execute concurrently with process Q, and, in fact, may have several processes running concurrently on several sites.

Both methods could be used to access several files residing at various sites. One remote procedure call might result in the invocation of another remote procedure call, or even in the transfer of messages to another site. Similarly, process Q could, during the course of its execution, send a message to another site, which in turn would create another process. This process might either send a message back to Q or repeat the cycle.

Process Migration

A logical extension to computation migration is **process migration**. When a process is submitted for execution, it is not always executed at the site in which it is initiated. It may be advantageous to execute the entire process, or parts of it, at different sites. This scheme may be used for several reasons:

- *Load balancing:* The processes (or subprocesses) may be distributed across the network to even the workload.

- *Computation speedup:* If a single process can be divided into a number of subprocesses that may run concurrently on different sites, then the total process turnaround time can be reduced.

- *Hardware preference:* The process may have characteristics that make it more suitable for execution on some specialized processor (such as matrix inversion on an array processor, rather than on a microprocessor).

- *Software preference:* The process may require software that is available at only a particular site, and either the software cannot be moved, or it is less expensive to move the process.

- *Data access:* Just as in computation migration, if the data being used in the computation are numerous, it may be more efficient to have a process run remotely, rather than to transfer all the data locally.

We use basically two complementary techniques to move processes in a computer network. In the first, the system can attempt to hide the fact that the process has migrated from the client. This scheme has the advantage that the user does not need to code her program explicitly to accomplish the migration. This method is usually employed for achieving load balancing and computation speedup among homogeneous systems, as they do not need user input to help them execute programs remotely.

The other approach is to allow (or require) the user to specify explicitly how the process should migrate. This method is usually employed in a situation when the process must be moved to satisfy a hardware or software preference.

You have probably realized that the Web has many aspects of a distributed-computing environment. Certainly it provides data migration (between a web server and a web client). It also provides computation migration. For instance, a web client could trigger a database operation on a web server. Finally, with Java, it provides a form of process migration: Java applets are sent from the server to the client where they are executed. A network operating system provides most of these features, but a distributed operating system makes them seamless, and easily accessible. The result is a powerful and easy to use facility—one of the reasons for the huge growth of the World Wide Web.

14.1.3 Putting It All Together

Now that we understand the motivation for building distributed systems and the types of distributed operating systems, we can examine the pieces that are necessary to implement such systems. In the remainder of this chapter, we explore the lowest level: the underlying computer network. In Chapter 15, we discuss how computers can communicate over the network. Following that, Chapter 16 describes the methods necessary for distributed operating systems to coordinate their actions. The final chapter in this Part, Chapter 17, explores inter-computer data sharing using distributed coordination, communication, and the underlying networking.

14.2 ■ Network Types

There are basically two types of networks: local-area networks and wide-area networks. The main difference between the two is the way in which they are geographically distributed. **Local-area networks** (**LANs**) comprise processors distributed over small geographical areas, such as a single building or a number of adjacent buildings. **Wide-area networks** (**WANs**), on the other hand, comprise autonomous processors distributed over a large geographical area (such as the United States). These differences imply major variations in the speed and reliability of the communications network, and are reflected in the design of the distributed operating system.

14.2.1 Local-Area Networks

LANs emerged in the early 1970s as a substitute for large mainframe computer systems. For many enterprises, it is more economical to have many small computers, each with its own self-contained applications, than to have a single large system. Because each small computer is likely to need a full complement of peripheral devices (such as disks and printers), and because some form of data sharing is likely to occur in a single enterprise, it is a natural step to connect these small systems into a network.

LANs are usually designed to cover a small geographical area (such as a single building, or a few adjacent buildings) and are generally used in an office environment. All the sites in such systems are close to one another, so the communication links tend to have a higher speed and lower error rate than do their counterparts in WANs. So that this higher speed and reliability can be attained, high-quality (expensive) cables are needed. It is also possible to use the cable exclusively for data network traffic. Over longer distances, the cost of using high-quality cable is enormous, and the exclusive use of the cable tends to be prohibitive.

The most common links in a LAN are twisted pair and fiber optics cabling. The most common configurations are multiaccess bus, ring, and star networks. Communication speeds range from 1 megabit per second, for networks such as AppleTalk and infra-red, to 1 gigabit per second for gigabit-ethernet. Ten megabits per second is most common, and is the speed of *10BaseT Ethernet*. *100BaseT Ethernet* requires a higher-quality cable but runs at 100 megabits per second, and is becoming common. Optical-fiber–based FDDI networking has been increasing its market share. Such networks are token based and run at over 100 megabits per second.

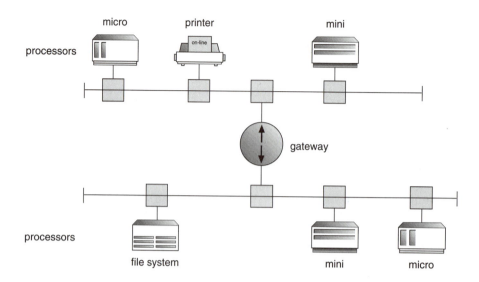

Figure 14.2   Local-area network.

A typical LAN may consist of a number of different computers, from mainframes to laptops or PDAs, various shared peripheral devices (such as laser printers or magnetic-tape units), and one or more gateways (specialized processors) that provide access to other networks (Figure 14.2). An Ethernet scheme is commonly used to construct LANs. There is no central controller in an Ethernet network, because it is a multiaccess bus, so new hosts can be added easily to the network.

14.2.2 Wide-Area Networks

WANs emerged in the late 1960s, mainly as an academic research project to provide efficient communication between sites, allowing hardware and software to be shared conveniently and economically by a wide community of users. The first WAN to be designed and developed was the **Arpanet**. Work on the Arpanet began in 1968. The Arpanet has grown from a four-site experimental network to a worldwide network of networks, the Internet, comprising millions of computer systems. There are also several international, private, commercial networks which carry communications between fixed communication points, such as company branch offices. These networks provide their customers with the ability to access a wide range of hardware and software computing resources.

Because the sites in a WAN are physically distributed over a large geographical area, the communication links are by default relatively slow and unreliable. Typical links are telephone lines, microwave links, and satellite channels. These communication links are controlled by special **communication processors** (Figure 14.3), which are responsible for defining the interface through which the sites communicate over the network, as well as for transferring information among the various sites.

As an example, let us consider the Internet WAN. The system provides an ability for hosts at geographically separated sites to communicate with one another. The host computers typically differ from one another in type, speed, word length, operating system, and so on. Hosts are generally on LANs, which are in turn connected to the Internet via regional networks. The regional networks, such as NSFnet in the Northeast United States, are interlinked with **routers** (described in Section 14.3.2) to form the worldwide network. Connections between networks frequently use a telephone-system service called T1, which provides a transfer rate of 1.544 megabits per second over a leased line. For sites requiring faster Internet access, T1s are collected into multiple-T1 units that work in parallel to provide more throughput. For instance, a T3 is composed of 28 T1 connections and has a transfer rate of 45 megabits per second. The routers control the path each message takes through the net. This routing may be either dynamic, to increase communications

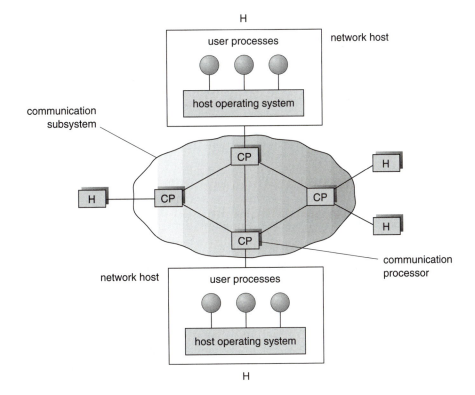

Figure 14.3 Communication processors in a wide-area network.

efficiency, or static, to reduce security risks or to allow communications charges to be computed.

Other WANs in operation use standard telephone lines as their primary means of communication. **Modems** are the devices that accept digital data from the computer side and convert it to the analog signals that the telephone system uses. A modem at the destination site converts the analog signal back to digital and the destination receives the data. The UNIX news network, UUCP, allows systems to communicate with each other at predetermined times, via modems, to exchange messages. The messages are then routed to other nearby systems and in this way either are propagated to all hosts on the network (public messages) or are transferred to their destination (private messages). WANs are generally slower than LANs; their transmission rates range from 1200 bits per second to over 1 megabit per second.

UUCP is rapidly being superceded by the Point-to-Point Protocol (PPP). PPP is a version of IP that functions over modem connections, allowing home computers to be fully connected to the Internet.

14.3 ■ Communication

Now that we have discussed the physical aspects of networking, we turn to the internal workings. The designer of a **communication** network must address five basic issues:

- *Naming and name resolution:* How do two processes locate each other to communicate?

- *Routing strategies:* How are messages sent through the network?

- *Packet strategies:* Are packets sent individually or as a sequence?

- *Connection strategies:* How do two processes send a sequence of messages?

- *Contention:* How do we resolve conflicting demands for its use, given that the network is a shared resource?

In Sections 14.3.1 through 14.3.5, we elaborate each of these issues.

14.3.1 Naming and Name Resolution

The first component of network communication is the naming of the systems in the network. For a process at site A to exchange information with a process at site B, they must be able to specify each other. Within a computer system, each process has a process-id, and messages may be addressed with the process-id. Because networked systems share no memory, they initially have no knowledge of the host of their target process, or even if the other process exists.

To solve this problem, processes on remote systems are generally identified by the pair <host name, identifier>, where "host name" is a name unique within the network, and "identifier" may be a process-id or other unique number within that host. A *host name* is usually an alphanumeric identifier, rather than a number, to make it easier for users to specify. For instance, site A might have hosts named "homer," "marge," "bart," and "lisa." "Bart" is certainly easier to remember than is "12814831100."

Names are convenient for humans to use, but computers prefer numbers for speed and simplicity. For this reason, there must be a mechanism to **resolve** the host name into a host-id that describes the destination system to the networking hardware. This resolve mechanism is similar to the name-to-address binding which occurs during program compilation, linking, loading, and execution (Chapter 9). In the case of host names, there are two possibilities. First, every host may have a data file containing the names and addresses of all the other hosts reachable on the network (similar to binding at compile time). The problem with this model is that adding or removing a host from the network requires updating the data files on all the hosts. The alternative is to distribute the information among systems on the network. The network must then use a protocol to distribute and retrieve the information. This scheme is like execution-time binding. The first method was the original method used on the Internet; as the Internet grew, however, it became untenable, so the second method, the **domain name service** (**DNS**) is now in use.

DNS specifies the naming structure of the hosts, as well as name to address resolution. Hosts on the Internet are logically addressed with a multipart name. Names progress from the most specific to the most general part of the address, with periods separating the fields. For instance, "bob.cs.brown.edu" refers to host "bob" in the Department of Computer Science at Brown University. Generally, the system resolves addresses by examining the host name components in reverse order. Each component has a **name server** (simply a process on a system) that accepts a name and returns the address of the name server responsible for that name. As the final step, the name server for the host in question is contacted and a host-id is returned. For our example system, "bob.cs.brown.edu", the following steps would be taken as result of a request made by a process on system A to communicate with "bob.cs.brown.edu":

1. The kernel of system A issues a request to the name server for the "edu" domain, asking for the address of the name server for "brown.edu". The name server for the "edu" domain must be at a known address, so that it can be queried. (Other top-level domains include "com" for commercial sites, "org" for organizations, and one for each country connected to the network (for systems specified by their country rather than organization type)).

2. The "edu" name server returns the address of the host on which the "brown.edu" name server resides.

3. The kernel on system A then queries the name server at this address and asks about "cs.brown.edu".

4. An address is returned and a request to that address for "bob.cs.brown.edu" now, finally, returns an **Internet address** host-id for that host (for example, 128.148.31.100).

This protocol may seem inefficient, but local caches are usually kept at each name server to speed the process. For example, the "edu" name server would have "brown.edu" in its cache, and would inform system A that it can resolve two portions of the name, returning a pointer to the "cs.brown.edu" name server. Of course, the contents of these caches must be refreshed over time in case the name server is moved or its address changes. In fact, this service is such an important one that there are many optimizations in the protocol, and many safeguards. Consider what would happen if the primary "edu" name server crashed. It is possible that no "edu" hosts would be able to have their addresses resolved, making them all unreachable! The solution is to use secondary, back-up name servers that duplicate the contents of the primary servers.

Before the domain name service was introduced, all hosts on the Internet needed to have copies of a file that contained the names and addresses of each host on the network. All changes to this file had to be registered at one site (host SRI-NIC), and periodically all hosts had to copy the updated file from SRI-NIC to be able to contact new systems or find hosts whose addresses changed. Under the domain name service, each name server site is responsible for updating the host information for that domain. For instance, any host changes at Brown University are the responsibility of the name server for "brown.edu", and do not have to be reported anywhere else. DNS lookups will automatically retrieve the updated information because "brown.edu" is contacted directly. Within domains, there can be autonomous subdomains to distribute further the responsibility for host-name and host-id changes.

Generally, it is the responsibility of the operating system to accept from its processes a message destined for <host name, identifier>, and to transfer that message to the appropriate host. The kernel on the destination host is then responsible for transferring the message to the process named by the identifier. This exchange is by no means trivial; it is described in Section 14.3.4.

14.3.2 Routing Strategies

When a process at site A wants to communicate with a process at site B, how is the message sent? If there is only one physical path from A to B (such as in a star or hierarchical network), the message must be sent through that path. However, if there are multiple physical paths from A to B, then several routing options exist. Each site has a **routing table,** indicating the alternative paths that can be used to send a message to other sites. The table may include information about the speed and cost of the various communication paths, and it may be updated as necessary, either manually or via programs that exchange routing information. The three most common routing schemes are **fixed routing, virtual routing,** and **dynamic routing:**

- *Fixed routing:* A path from A to B is specified in advance and does not change unless a hardware failure disables this path. Usually, the shortest path is chosen, so that communication costs are minimized.

- *Virtual routing:* A path from A to B is fixed for the duration of one **session**. Different sessions involving messages from A to B may have different paths. A session could be as short as a file transfer or as long as a remote-login period.

- *Dynamic routing:* The path used to send a message from site A to site B is chosen only when a message is sent. Because the decision is made dynamically, separate messages may be assigned different paths. Site A will make a decision to send the message to site C; C, in turn, will decide to send it to site D, and so on. Eventually, a site will deliver the message to B. Usually, a site sends a message to another site on that link that is the one least used at that particular time.

There are tradeoffs among these three schemes. Fixed routing cannot adapt to link failures or load changes. In other words, if a path has been established between A and B, the messages must be sent along this path, even if the path is down or is used heavily while another possible path is used lightly. We can partially remedy this problem by using virtual routing, and can avoid it completely by using dynamic routing. Fixed routing and virtual routing ensure that messages from A to B will be delivered in the order in which they were sent. In dynamic routing, messages may arrive out of order. We can remedy this problem by appending a sequence number to each message.

Note that dynamic routing is the most complicated to set up and run. It is the best way to manage routing in complicated environments, however. UNIX provides both static routing for use on hosts within simple networks, and dynamic routing for complicated network environments. It is also possible to mix the two. Within a site, the hosts may just need to know how to reach the system that connects the local network to other networks (such as companywide networks or the Internet). Such a node is known as a **gateway**. These individual hosts have a static route to the gateway. The gateway itself uses dynamic routing to reach any host on the rest of the network.

A **router** is the entity within the computer network responsible for routing messages. A router can be a host computer with routing software, or a special-purpose device. Either way, a router must have at least two network connections, or else it would have nowhere to route messages. A router decides whether any given message needs to be passed from the network on which it is received to any other network connected to the router. It makes this determination by examining the destination Internet address of the message. The router examines its tables to determine the location of the destination host, or at least of the network to which to send the message toward the destination host. In the case of static routing, this table is changed only by manual update (a new file is loaded onto the router). With dynamic routing, a **routing protocol** is used between routers to inform them of network changes and to allow them to update their routing tables automatically. Note that gateways and routers typically are dedicated hardware devices. They run code out of firmware, rather than a general-purpose operating system running network applications.

14.3.3 Packet Strategies

Messages are generally of variable length. To simplify the system design, we commonly implement communication with fixed-length messages called **packets, frames,** or **datagrams**. A communication implemented in one packet can be sent to its destination in a **connectionless message**. A connectionless message can be **unreliable,** in which case the sender has no guarantee that, and cannot tell whether, the packet reached its destination. Alternatively, the packet can be **reliable,** in which case usually a packet is returned from the destination indicating that the packet arrived. (Of course, the return packet could be lost along the way.) If a message is too long to fit within one packet, or if the packets need to flow back and forth between the two communicators, a connection is established to allow the reliable exchange of multiple packets.

14.3.4 Connection Strategies

Once messages are able to reach their destinations, processes may institute **communications sessions** to exchange information. There are a number of different ways to connect pairs of processes that want to communicate over the network. The three most common schemes are **circuit switching, message switching,** and **packet switching:**

- *Circuit switching:* If two processes want to communicate, a permanent physical link is established between them. This link is allocated for the duration of the communication session, and no other process can use that link during this period (even if the two processes are not actively communicating for a while). This scheme is similar to that used in the telephone system. Once a communication line has been opened between two parties (that is, party A calls party B), no one else can use this circuit, until the communication is terminated explicitly (for example, when one of the parties hangs up).

- *Message switching:* If two processes want to communicate, a **temporary** link is established for the duration of one message transfer. Physical links are allocated dynamically among correspondents as needed, and are allocated for only short periods. Each message is a block of data, with system information (such as the source, the destination, and error-correction codes) that allows the communication network to deliver the message to the destination correctly. This scheme is similar to the post-office mailing system. Each letter is considered a message that contains both the destination address and source (return) address. Note that many messages (from different users) can be shipped over the same link.

- *Packet switching:* One logical message may have to be divided into a number of packets. Each packet may be sent to its destination separately, and therefore must include a source and destination address with its data. Each packet may take a different path through the network. The packets must be reassembled into messages as they arrive.

There are obvious tradeoffs among these schemes. Circuit switching requires substantial set-up time, but incurs less overhead for shipping each message, and may waste network bandwidth. Message and packet switching, on the other hand, require less set-up time, but incur more overhead per message. Also, in packet switching, each message must be divided into packets and later reassembled. Packet switching is the most common method used on data networks because it makes the best use of network bandwidth, and it is not harmful for data to be broken into packets, possibly routed separately, and reassembled at the destination. Breaking up an audio signal (say, a telephone communication), on the other hand, could cause great confusion if it was not done carefully.

14.3.5 Contention

Depending on the network topology, a link may connect more than two sites in the computer network, so it is possible that several sites will want to transmit information over a link simultaneously. This situation occurs mainly in a ring or multiaccess bus network. In this case, the transmitted information may become scrambled and must be discarded. The sites must be notified about the problem, so that they can retransmit the information. If no special provisions are made, this situation may be repeated, resulting in degraded performance. Several techniques have been developed to avoid repeated collisions, including **collision detection CD, token passing,** and **message slots.**

- *CSMA/CD:* Before transmitting a message over a link, a site must listen to determine whether another message is currently being transmitted over that link; this technique is called **carrier sense with multiple access (CSMA)**. If the link is free, the site can start transmitting. Otherwise, it must wait (and continue to listen) until the link is free. If two or more sites begin transmitting at exactly the same time (each thinking that no other site is using the link), then they will register a **collision detection** (**CD**) and will stop transmitting. Each site will try again after some random time interval. Note that, when site A starts transmitting over a link, it must listen continuously to detect collisions with messages from other sites. The main problem with this approach is that, when the system is very busy, many collisions may occur, and thus performance may be degraded. Nevertheless, CSMA/CD has been used successfully in the Ethernet system, the most common network system. (The Ethernet protocol is defined by the IEEE 802.3 standard.) To limit the number of collisions, we limit the number of hosts per Ethernet network. Adding more hosts to a congested network could result in poor network throughput. As systems get faster, they are able to send more packets per time segment. As a result, the number of systems per Ethernet segment generally is decreasing, to keep networking performance reasonable.

- *Token passing:* A unique message type, known as a **token,** continuously circulates in the system (usually a ring structure). A site that wants to transmit information must wait until the token arrives. It removes the token from the ring and begins to transmit its messages. When the site completes its round of message passing, it retransmits the token. This action, in turn, allows another site to receive and remove the token, and to start its message transmission. If the token gets lost, then the systems must detect the loss and generate a new token. They usually do that by declaring an **election,** to elect a unique site where a new token will be generated. Later, in Section 16.4, we present one election algorithm. A token-passing scheme has been adopted by the IBM and HP/Apollo systems. The benefit of a token-passing network is that performance is constant. Adding new systems to a network may lengthen the time a system waits for the token, but it will not cause a large performance decrease as may happen on Ethernet. On lightly loaded networks, however, Ethernet is more efficient, because systems may send messages at any time.

- *Message slots:* A number of fixed-length message slots continuously circulate in the system (usually a ring structure). Each slot can hold a fixed-sized message and control information (such as what the source and destination are, and whether the slot is empty or full). A site that is ready to transmit must wait until an empty slot arrives. It then inserts its message into the slot, setting the appropriate control information. The slot with its message then continues in the network. When it arrives at a site, that site inspects the control information to determine whether the slot contains a message for this site. If not, that site recirculates the slot and message. Otherwise, it removes the message, resetting the control information to indicate that the slot is empty. The site can then either use the slot to send its own message or release the slot. Because a slot can contain only fixed-sized messages, a single logical message may have to be broken down into several smaller packets, each of which is sent in a separate slot. This scheme has been adopted in the experimental Cambridge Digital Communication Ring.

14.4   ■   Communication Protocols

When we are designing a communication network, we must deal with the inherent complexity of coordinating asynchronous operations communicating in a potentially slow and error-prone environment. It is also essential that the systems on the network agree on a protocol or a set of protocols for determining host names, locating hosts on the network, establishing connections, and so on. We can simplify the design problem (and related implementation) by partitioning the problem into multiple layers. Each layer on one system communicates with the equivalent layer on other systems. Each layer may have its own protocols, or may be a logical segmentation. The protocols may be implemented in hardware or software. For instance, Figure 14.4 shows the logical communications between two computers, with the three lowest-level layers implemented in hardware. Following the International Standards Organization (ISO), we refer to the layers with the following descriptions:

1. **Physical layer:** The physical layer is responsible for the handling both the mechanical and the electrical details of the physical transmission of a bit stream. At the physical layer, the communicating systems must agree on the electrical representation of a binary 0 and 1, so that when data are sent

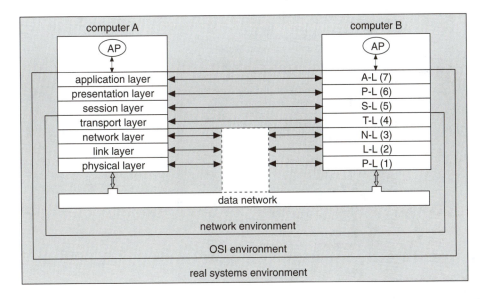

Figure 14.4   Two computers communicating via the ISO network model.

as a stream of electrical signals, the receiver is able to interpret the data properly as binary data. This layer is implemented in the hardware of the networking device.

2. **Data-link layer:** The data-link layer is responsible for handling the *frames,* or fixed-length parts of packets, including any error detection and recovery that occurred in the physical layer.

3. **Network layer:** The network layer is responsible for providing connections and for routing packets in the communication network, including handling

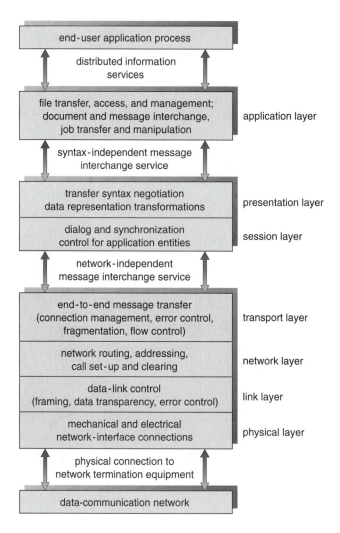

Figure 14.5   The ISO protocol layer.

the address of outgoing packets, decoding the address of incoming packets, and maintaining routing information for proper response to changing load levels. Routers work at this layer.

4. **Transport layer:** The transport layer is responsible for low-level access to the network and for transfer of messages between the clients, including partitioning messages into packets, maintaining packet order, controlling flow, and generating physical addresses.

5. **Session layer:** The session layer is responsible for implementing sessions, or process-to-process communications protocols. Typically, these protocols are the actual communications for remote logins, and for file and mail transfers.

6. **Presentation layer:** The presentation layer is responsible for resolving the differences in formats among the various sites in the network, including character conversions, and half duplex–full duplex modes (character echoing).

7. **Application layer:** The application layer is responsible for interacting directly with the users. This layer deals with file transfer, remote-login protocols, and electronic mail, as well as with schemas for distributed databases.

Figure 14.5 summarizes the ISO **protocol stack** (a set of cooperating protocols), showing the physical flow of data. As mentioned, logically each layer of a protocol stack communicates with the equivalent layer on other systems. But physically, a message starts at or above the application layer, and is passed through each lower level in turn. Each of these layers may modify the message and include message header data for the equivalent layer on the receiving side. Finally, the message makes it to the data-network layer and is transferred as one or more packets (Figure 14.6). These data are received by the data-link layer of the target system, and the message is moved up through the protocol stack; it is analyzed, modified, and stripped of headers as it progresses. It finally reaches the application layer for use by the receiving process.

The ISO model formalizes some of the earlier work done in network protocols, but was developed in late 1970s and is not in widespread use. Part of the basis for ISO is the more timeworn and widely used protocol stack developed under UNIX for use in the Arpanet (which became the Internet).

Most Internet sites still communicate via the *Internet Protocol*, commonly known as *IP*. Services are implemented on top of IP via the connectionless **User Datagram Protocol (UDP)**, and the connection-oriented **Transmission Control Protocol/Internet Protocol (TCP/IP)**. The TCP/IP protocol stack has fewer layers than does the ISO model. Theoretically, because it combines several functions in each layer, it is more difficult to implement but more efficient than ISO

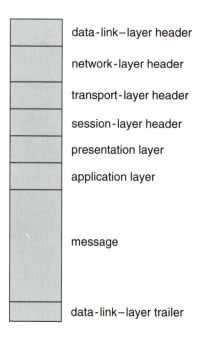

data-link–layer header

network-layer header

transport-layer header

session-layer header

presentation layer

application layer

message

data-link–layer trailer

Figure 14.6   An ISO network message.

networking. The TCP/IP stack (with its ISO correspondence) is shown in Figure 14.7. The IP protocol is responsible for transmitting IP **datagrams,** the basic unit of information, across a TCP/IP Internet.   TCP uses IP to transport a reliable stream of information between two processes. UDP/IP is an unreliable, connectionless transport protocol.   It uses IP to transfer the packets, but adds error correction and a protocol **port address** to specify the process on the remote system for which the packet is destined.

14.5 ■ Robustness

A distributed system may suffer from various types of hardware failure. The failure of a link, the failure of a site, and the loss of a message are the most common failures. To ensure that the system is robust, we must **detect** any of these failures, **reconfigure** the system such that computation may continue, and **recover** when a site or a link is repaired.

14.5.1 Failure Detection

In an environment with no shared memory, it is generally not possible to differentiate among link failure, site failure, and message loss. We can usually detect that one of these failures has occurred, but we may not be able to identify

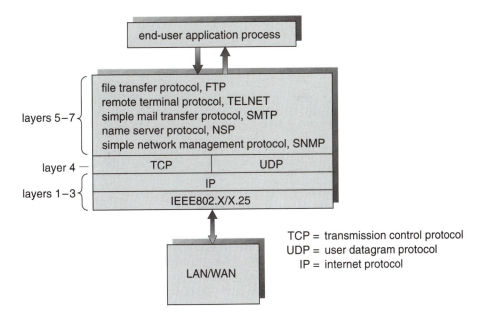

Figure 14.7   The TCP/IP protocol layers.

what kind of failure it is. Once a failure has been detected, appropriate action must be taken, depending on the particular application.

To detect link and site failure, we use a **handshaking** procedure. Suppose that sites A and B have a direct physical link between them. At fixed intervals, both sites send each other an *I-am-up* message. If site A does not receive this message within a predetermined time period, it can assume that site B has failed, that the link between A and B has failed, or that the message from B has been lost. At this point, site A has two choices. It can wait for another time period to receive an *I-am-up* message from B, or it can send an *Are-you-up?* message to B.

If site A does not receive an *I-am-up* message or a reply to its inquiry, the procedure can be repeated. The only conclusion that site A can draw safely is that some type of failure has occurred.

Site A can try to differentiate between link failure and site failure by sending an *Are-you-up?* message to B by another route (if one exists). If and when B receives this message, it immediately replies positively. This positive reply tells A that B is up, and that the failure is in the direct link between them. Since we do not know in advance how long it will take the message to travel from A to B and back, we must use a **time-out scheme**. At the time A sends the *Are-you-up?* message, it specifies a time interval during which it is willing to wait for the reply from B. If A receives the reply message within that time interval, then it can safely conclude that B is up. If, however, it does not receive the reply message within the time interval (that is, if a time-out occurs), then A may conclude only that one or more of the following situations has occurred:

- Site B is down.

- The direct link (if one exists) from A to B is down.

- The alternative path from A to B is down.

- The message has been lost.

Site A cannot, however, determine which of these events has indeed occurred.

14.5.2 Reconfiguration

Suppose that site A has discovered, through the mechanism described in the previous section, that a failure has occurred. It must then initiate a procedure that will allow the system to reconfigure and to continue its normal mode of operation.

- If a direct link from A to B has failed, this information must be broadcast to every site in the system, so that the various routing tables can be updated accordingly.

- If the system believes that a site has failed (because that site can be reached no longer), then every site in the system must be so notified, so that they will no longer attempt to use the services of the failed site. The failure of a site that serves as a central coordinator for some activity (such as deadlock detection) requires the election of a new coordinator. Similarly, if the failed site is part of a logical ring, then a new logical ring must be constructed. Note that, if the site has not failed (that is, if it is up but cannot be reached), then we may have the undesirable situation where two sites serve as the coordinator. When the network is partitioned, the two coordinators (each for its own partition) may initiate conflicting actions. For example, if the coordinators are responsible for implementing mutual exclusion, we may have a situation where two processes may be executing simultaneously in their critical sections.

14.5.3 Recovery from Failure

When a failed link or site is repaired, it must be integrated into the system gracefully and smoothly.

- Suppose that a link between A and B has failed. When it is repaired, both A and B must be notified. We can accomplish this notification by continuously repeating the handshaking procedure, described in Section 14.5.1.

- Suppose that site B has failed. When it recovers, it must notify all other sites that it is up again. Site B then may have to receive from the other sites various information to update its local tables; for example, it may need routing table information, a list of sites that are down, or undelivered messages and mail. Note that, if the site has not failed, but simply could not be reached, then this information is still required.

14.6 ■ Design Issues

It has been the challenge of many designers to make the multiplicity of processors and storage devices **transparent** to the users. Ideally, a distributed system should look to its users like a conventional, centralized system. The user interface of a transparent distributed system should not distinguish between local and remote resources. That is, users should be able to access remote distributed systems as though the latter were local, and it should be the responsibility of the distributed system to locate the resources and to arrange for the appropriate interaction.

Another aspect of transparency is **user mobility**. It would be convenient to allow users to log in to any machine in the system, and not to force them to use a specific machine. A transparent distributed system facilitates user mobility by bringing over the user's environment (for example, home directory) to wherever she logs in. Both the Andrew file system from CMU and Project Athena from MIT provide this functionality on a large scale. NFS can provide this transparency on a smaller scale.

We use the term *fault tolerance* in a broad sense. Communication faults, machine failures (of type fail-stop), storage-device crashes, and decays of storage media are all considered to be faults that should be tolerated to some extent. A **fault-tolerant system** should continue to function, perhaps in a degraded form, when faced with these failures. The degradation can be in performance, in functionality, or in both. It should be, however, proportional, in some sense, to the failures that cause it. A system that grinds to a halt when only a few of its components fail is certainly not fault tolerant. Unfortunately, fault tolerance is difficult to implement. Most commercial systems provide only limited fault tolerance. For instance, the DEC VAXcluster allows multiple computers to share a set of disks. If a system crashes, users may still access their information from another system. Of course, if a disk fails, all the systems will lose access. But in this case, RAID can ensure continued access to the data even in the event of a failure (Section 13.5).

The capability of a system to adapt to increased service load is its **scalability**. Systems have bounded resources and can become completely saturated under increased load. For example, regarding a file system, saturation occurs either when a server's CPU runs at a high utilization rate, or when disks are almost full. Scalability is a relative property, but it can be measured accurately.

A scalable system reacts more gracefully to increased load than does a nonscalable one. First, its performance degrades more moderately than that of a nonscalable system. Second, its resources reach a saturated state later, compared to those of a nonscalable system. Even perfect design cannot accommodate an ever growing load. Adding new resources might solve the problem, but it might generate additional indirect load on other resources (for example, adding machines to a distributed system can clog the network and increase service loads). Even worse, expanding the system can incur expensive design modifications. A scalable system should have the potential to grow without these problems. In a distributed system, the ability to scale up gracefully is of special importance, since expanding the network by adding new machines or interconnecting two networks is commonplace. In short, a scalable design should withstand high service load, accommodate growth of the user community, and enable simple integration of added resources.

Fault tolerance and scalability are related to each other. A heavily loaded component can become paralyzed and behave like a faulty component. Also, shifting the load from a faulty component to that component's backup can saturate the latter. Generally, having spare resources is essential for ensuring reliability as well as for handling peak loads gracefully. An inherent advantage that a distributed system has is a potential for fault tolerance and scalability because of the multiplicity of resources. However, inappropriate design can obscure this potential. Fault-tolerance and scalability considerations call for a design demonstrating distribution of control and data.

Very large-scale distributed systems, to a great extent, are still only theoretical. There are no magic guidelines to ensure the scalability of a system. It is easier to point out why current designs are *not* scalable. We shall discuss several designs that pose problems, and shall propose possible solutions, all in the context of scalability.

One principle for designing very large-scale systems is that the service demand from any component of the system should be bounded by a constant that is independent of the number of nodes in the system. Any service mechanism whose load demand is proportional to the size of the system is destined to become clogged once the system grows beyond a certain size. Adding more resources would not alleviate such a problem. The capacity of this mechanism simply limits the growth of the system.

Central control schemes and central resources should not be used to build scalable (and fault-tolerant) systems. Examples of centralized entities are central authentication servers, central naming servers, and central file servers. Centralization is a form of functional asymmetry among machines constituting the system. The ideal alternative is a configuration that is functionally symmetric; that is, all the component machines have an equal role in the operation of the system, and hence each machine has some degree of autonomy. Practically, it is virtually impossible to comply with such a principle. For instance, incorporating diskless machines violates functional symmetry, since the workstations depend on a central disk. However, autonomy and symmetry are important goals to which we should aspire.

The practical approximation to symmetric and autonomous configuration is **clustering,** in which the system is partitioned into a collection of semi-autonomous clusters. A **cluster** consists of a set of machines and a dedicated cluster server. So that cross-cluster resource references are relatively infrequent, each machine's requests should be satisfied by its own cluster server most of the time. Of course, this scheme depends on the ability to localize resource references and to place the component units appropriately. If the cluster is well balanced — that is, if the server in charge suffices to satisfy all the cluster demands — it can be used as a modular building block to scale up the system.

A major problem in the design of any service is the decision on the process structure of the server. Servers are supposed to operate efficiently in peak periods, when hundreds of active clients need to be served simultaneously. A single-process server is certainly not a good choice, since whenever a request necessitates disk I/O, the whole service will be blocked. Assigning a process for each client is a better choice; however, the expense of frequent context switches between the processes must be considered. A related problem occurs because all the server processes need to share information.

It appears that one of the best solutions for the server architecture is the use of lightweight processes or threads, which we discussed in Chapter 5. The abstraction presented by a group of lightweight processes is that of multiple threads of control associated with some shared resources. Usually, a lightweight process is not bound to a particular client. Instead, it serves single requests of different clients. Scheduling of threads can be preemptive or nonpreemptive. If threads are allowed to run to completion (nonpreemptive), then their shared data do not need to be protected explicitly. Otherwise, some explicit locking mechanism must be used. It is clear that some form of lightweight-processes scheme is essential if servers are to be scalable.

14.7 ■ Networking Example

We now return to the name-resolution issue raised in Section 14.3.1, and examine its operation with respect to the TCP/IP protocol stack on the Internet. We consider the processing needed to transfer a packet between hosts on different Ethernet networks.

In a TCP/IP network, every host has a name and an associated 32-bit Internet number (host-id). Both of these strings must be unique, and, so that the name space can be managed, they are segmented. The name is hierarchical (as explained in Section 14.3.1), describing the host name and then the organizations with which the host is associated. The host-id is split into a network number and a host number. The proportion of the split varies, depending on the size of the network. Once a network number is assigned by the Internet administrators, the site with that number is free to assign host-ids.

The sending system checks its routing tables to locate a router to send the packet on its way. The routers use the network part of the host-id to transfer the packet from its source network to the destination network. The destination system then receives the packet. The packet may be a complete message, or it may just be a component of a message, with more packets needed before the message is reassembled and passed to the TCP/UDP layer for transmission to the destination process.

Now we know how a packet moves from its source network to its destination. Within a network, how does a packet move from sender (host or router) to receiver? Every Ethernet device has a unique byte number, called the **Medium Access Control** (**MAC**) **address**, assigned to it for addressing. Two devices on a local area network communicate with each other only with this number. If a system needs to send data to another system, the kernel generates an **Address Resolution Protocol** (**ARP**) packet containing the IP address of the destination system. This packet is **broadcast** to all other systems on that Ethernet network. A broadcast uses a special network address (usually, the maximum address) to signal that all hosts should receive and process the packet. The broadcast is not resent by gateways, so only systems on the local network receive them. Only the system whose IP address matches the IP address of the ARP request responds and sends back its MAC address to the system that did the query. For efficiency, the host caches the IP-MAC address pair in an internal table. The cache entries are **aged,** so that they eventually get removed from the cache if an access to that system is not required in the given time. In this way hosts that are removed from a network are eventually "forgotten." For added performance, ARP entries for heavily used hosts may be hardwired in the ARP cache.

Once an Ethernet device has announced its host-id and address, communication can begin. A process may specify the name of a host with which to communicate. The kernel takes that name and determines the Internet number of the target, using a DNS lookup. The message is passed from the application layer, through the software layers, and to the hardware layer. At the hardware layer, the packet (or packets) has the Ethernet address at its start, and a trailer at the end to indicate the end of the packet and containing a **checksum** for detection of packet damage (Figure 14.8). The packet is placed on the network by the Ethernet device. Note that the data section of the packet may contain some or all of the data of the original message, but may also contain some of the upper-level headers that compose the message. In other words, all parts of the original message must be sent from source to destination, and all headers above the 802.3 layer (data-link layer) are included as data in the Ethernet packets.

If the destination is on the same local network as the source, the system can look in its ARP cache, can find the Ethernet address of the host, and can place the packet on the wire. The destination Ethernet device then sees its address in the packet and reads in the packet, passing it up the protocol stack.

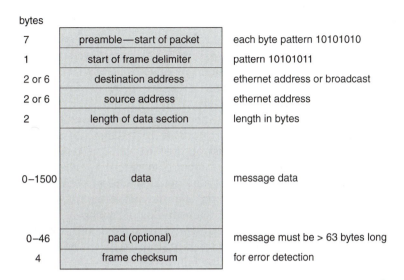

Figure 14.8   An Ethernet packet.

If the destination system is on a network different from that of the source, the source system finds an appropriate router on its network and sends the packet there. Routers then pass the packet along the WAN until it reaches its destination network. The router that connects the destination network checks its ARP cache, finds the Ethernet number of the destination, and sends the packet to that host. Through all of these transfers, the data-link–layer header may change as the Ethernet address of the next router in the chain is used, but the other headers of the packet remain the same until the packet is received and they are processed by the protocol stack, and finally the packet is passed to the receiving process by the kernel.

14.8 ■ Summary

A distributed system is a collection of processors that do not share memory or a clock. Instead, each processor has its own local memory, and the processors communicate with one another through various communication lines, such as high-speed buses or telephone lines. The processors in a distributed system vary in size and function. They may include small microprocessors, workstations, minicomputers, and large general-purpose computer systems.

The processors in the system are connected through a communication network, which can be configured in a number of different ways. The network may be fully or partially connected. It may be a tree, a star, a ring, or a multiaccess bus. The communication-network design must include routing and connection strategies, and must solve the problems of contention and security.

Principally, there are two types of distributed systems: LANs and WANs. The main difference between the two is in the way they are distributed geographically. LANs are composed of processors that are distributed over small geographical areas, such as a single building or a few adjacent buildings. WANs are composed of autonomous processors that are distributed over a large geographical area (such as the United States).

Protocol stacks, as specified by network layering models, massage the message, adding information to it to ensure that it reaches its destination. A naming system such as DNS must be used to translate from a host name to network address, and another protocol (such as ARP) may be needed to translate the network number to a network device address (an Ethernet address, for instance). If systems are located on separate networks, routers are needed to pass packets from source network to destination network.

A distributed system may suffer from various types of hardware failure. For a distributed system to be fault tolerant, it must detect hardware failures and reconfigure the system. When the failure is repaired, the system must be reconfigured again.

■ Exercises

14.1 What are two main differences between a WAN and a LAN?

14.2 Even though the ISO model of networking specifies seven layers of functionality, most computer systems use fewer layers to implement a network. Why do they use fewer layers? What problems could the use of fewer layers cause?

14.3 Explain why a doubling of the speed of the systems on an Ethernet segment may result in decreased network performance. What changes could ameliorate the problem?

14.4 Under what circumstances is a token-ring network more effective than an Ethernet network?

14.5 Why would it be a bad idea for gateways to pass broadcast packets between networks? What would be the advantages of doing so?

14.6 What are the advantages of using dedicated hardware devices for routers and gateways? What are the disadvantages over using general-purpose computers?

14.7 In what ways is using a name server better than using static host tables? What are the problems or complications associated with name servers? What methods could you use to decrease the amount of traffic name servers generate to satisfy translation requests?

14.8 The original *HTTP* protocol uses TCP/IP as the underlying network protocol. For each page, graphic, or applet, a separate TCP session was contructed, used, and torn down. Because of the overhead of building and destroying TCP/IP connections, there were performance problems with this implementation method. Would using UDP rather than TCP be a good alternative? What other changes could you make to improve HTTP performance?

14.9 Of what use is an address-resolution protocol? Why is it better to use such a protocol than to make each host read each packet to determine to whom that packet is destined? Does a token-ring network need such a protocol? Explain your answer.

14.10 What are the advantages and the disadvantages of making the computer network transparent to the user?

14.11 What are two formidable problems that designers must solve to implement a network-transparent system?

14.12 Process migration within a heterogeneous network is usually impossible, given the differences in architectures and operating systems. Describe a method for process migration across different architectures running:

    a. The same operating system

    b. Different operating systems

14.13 To build a robust distributed system, you must know what kinds of failures can occur.

    a. List three possible types of failure in a distributed system.

    b. Specify which of the entries in your list also are applicable to a centralized system.

14.14 Is it always crucial to know that the message you have sent has arrived at its destination safely? If your answer is "yes," explain why. If your answer is "no," give appropriate examples.

14.15 Present an algorithm for reconstructing a logical ring after a process in the ring fails.

14.16 Consider a distributed system with two sites, A and B. Consider whether site A can distinguish among the following:

    a. B goes down.

    b. The link between A and B goes down.

    c. B is extremely overloaded and its response time is 100 times longer than normal.

What implications does your answer have for recovery in distributed systems?

Bibliographical Notes

Tanenbaum [1996] and Halsall [1992] provided general overviews of computer networks. Fortier [1989] presented a detailed discussion of networking hardware and software.

The Internet and several other networks were discussed in Quarterman and Hoskins [1986]. The Internet and its protocols were described in Comer [1991] and Comer and Stevens [1991, 1993]. UNIX network programming was described thoroughly in Stevens [1990]. The general state of networks has been given in Quarterman [1990].

Discussions concerning distributed operating-system structures have been offered by Popek and Walker [1985] (the Locus system), Cheriton and Zwaenepoel [1983] (the V kernel), Ousterhout and colleagues [1988] (the Sprite network operating system), Balkovich and colleagues [1985] (Project Athena), and both Tanenbaum and colleagues [1990] and Mullender and colleagues [1990] (the Amoeba distributed operating system). A comparison of Amoeba and Sprite is offered by Douglis and colleagues [1991]. Mullender [1993] provides thorough coverage of many distributed computing topics.

Discussions concerning load balancing and load sharing were presented by Chow and Abraham [1982], Eager and colleagues[1986], and Ferguson and colleagues [1988]. Discussions concerning process migration were presented by Eager and colleagues[1986], Zayas [1987], Smith [1988], Jul and colleagues [1988], Artsy [1989], and Douglis and Ousterhout [1987, 1989b].

Schemes for sharing idle workstations in a distributed shared computing environment are presented by Nichols [1987], Mutka and Livny [1987], and Litzkow and colleagues [1988].

Chapter 15

DISTRIBUTED COMMUNICATION

In this chapter, we discuss several different strategies that allow distributed applications to communicate. As examples, we present Java solutions using two different communication strategies. The first is sockets, a TCP/IP scheme that allows distributed processes to communicate over a network. The second is a Java-based communication protocol that allows a thread in one Java program to invoke a remote method in another Java program.

15.1 ▪ Sockets

A **socket** is defined as an endpoint for communication. A pair of processes (or threads) communicating over a network employs a pair of sockets—one for each process. A socket is made up of an IP address concatenated with a port number. In general, sockets use a client–server architecture. The server waits for incoming client requests by listening to a specified port. Once a request is received, the server accepts a connection from the client socket to complete the connection.

Servers implementing specific services (such as telnet, ftp, mail, and http), listen to well-known ports (a telnet server listens to port 23, an ftp server listens to port 21, and a web server (http) listens to port 80). All ports below 1024 are considered well known; we can use them to implement such standard services.

When a client thread initiates a request for a connection, it is assigned a port by the host computer. This port is an arbitrary number > 1024. For example, if a client on host X with IP address 146.86.5.20 wishes to establish

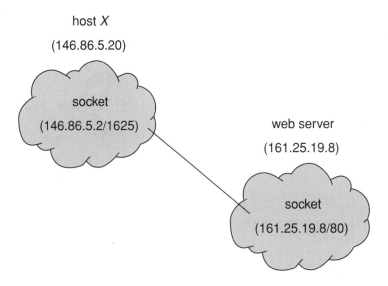

Figure 15.1   Communication using sockets.

a connection with a web server (which is listening on port 80) at address 161.25.19.8, host X may be assigned port 1625. The connection will consist of a pair of sockets: (146.86.5.20:1625) on host X, and (161.25.19.8:80) on the web server. This situation is illustrated in Figure 15.1. The packets traveling between the hosts are delivered to the appropriate threads, based on the destination port number.

All connections must be unique. Therefore, if another process also on host X wished to establish another connection with the same web server, it would be assigned a port number > 1024 and $\neq$ 1625. This ensures that all connections consist of a unique pair of sockets.

15.1.1 Servers and Threads

Typically, servers may have several concurrent requests. The amount of time a client may have to wait to be serviced by a single-threaded server may be unacceptable. To remedy this situation, a server may handle concurrent requests by assigning a separate thread to service each incoming request. For example, a busy web server may assign a separate thread to service each request for a web page.

15.1.2 Java Sockets

Java provides three different types of sockets. **Connection-oriented (TCP) sockets** are implemented with the Socket class. **Connectionless (UDP) sockets** use the DatagramSocket class. A third type is the MulticastSocket class,

```java
import java.net.*;

public class Server
{
    public Server() {
        // create the socket
        try {
            s = new ServerSocket(5155);
        }
        catch (java.io.IOException e) {
            System.out.println(e);
            System.exit(1);
        }

        // OK, now listen for connections
        System.out.println("Server is listening.");

        try {
            while (true) {
                client = s.accept();

                // create a separate thread
                // to service the request
                c = new Connection(client);
                c.start();
            }
        }
        catch (java.io.IOException e) {
            System.out.println(e);
        }
    }

    public static void main(String args[]) {
        Server timeOfDayServer = new Server();
    }

    private ServerSocket s;
    private Socket client;
    private Connection c;
}
```

Figure 15.2 Time-of-day server.

and it is a subclass of the DatagramSocket class. A multicast socket allows data to be sent to multiple recipients.

15.1.3 Time-of Day-Server

As an example of Java-based sockets, we now present several Java classes to implement a multithreaded time-of-day server. The operation allows clients to request the time of day from the server. The server listens to port 5155, although the port could be any arbitrary number > 1024. When a connection is received, the server creates a new thread to serve the request. This new thread returns to the client the current time of day.

15.1.3.1 The Server

The time-of-day server server is shown in Figure 15.2. The server creates a ServerSocket that specifies that it will listen to port 5155. It then begins listening to the port with the accept() method. The server blocks on the accept() method waiting for a client to request a connection. When a connection request is received, accept() returns a socket that the server can use to communicate with the client. The server creates a new thread to service the request and passes the socket to this thread. The server then resumes listening for more requests.

The details illustrating how the server communicates with the socket are specified in the Connection class, which is shown in Figure 15.3. Each Connection thread is passed the socket for the client to which it will provide the time of day. The thread first establishes a PrintWriter object that it will use to communicate with the client. A PrintWriter object allows the thread to write to the socket using the normal print() and println() methods for output. The thread sends the time of day to the client calling the method println(). Once it has written the time of day to the socket, it closes the socket and the thread terminates.

To start the server, the statement

```
java Server
```

is entered on the command line. The server remains running while it listens for connections to port 5155. Whenever it receives a connection request from a client, the server creates a separate Connection thread to service the request, then resumes listening to port 5155.

15.1.3.2 The Client

A client communicates with the server by creating a socket and connecting to the port the server is listening on. It can simply establish a telnet connection to port 5155. For example, the command

```
telnet 127.0.0.1 5155
```

```
import java.net.*;
import java.io.*;

public class Connection extends Thread
{
    public Connection(Socket s) {
        outputLine = s;
    }

    public void run() {
        try {
            // create a PrintWriter object
            // with automatic flushing.
            // This allows ordinary file
            // IO over the socket.

            PrintWriter pout = new PrintWriter
                (outputLine.getOutputStream(), true);

            // now send a message to the client
            pout.println("The Date and Time is" +
                new java.util.Date().toString());

            // now close the socket
            outputLine.close();
        }
        catch (java.io.IOException e) {
            System.out.println(e);
        }
    }

    private Socket outputLine;
}
```

Figure 15.3   Thread to service time-of-day requests.

opens a socket and requests a connection with the server at address 127.0.0.1 on port 5155. The server responds with the time of day. The IP address 127.0.0.1 is a special address known as the **local host**. When a computer refers to address 127.0.0.1, it is referring to itself. This mechanism allows a client and server on the same host to communicate using the TCP/IP protocol even if the computer is not connected to a network.

We can implement this scheme with the Java program shown in Figure 15.4. The client creates a Socket and requests a connection with the server on port

```
import java.net.*;
import java.io.*;

public class Client
{
    public Client() {
        try {
            Socket s = new Socket("127.0.0.1",5155);

            InputStream in = s.getInputStream();
            BufferedReader bin = new BufferedReader
                (new InputStreamReader(in));

            System.out.println(bin.readLine());
            s.close();
        }
        catch (java.io.IOException e) {
            System.out.println(e);
            System.exit(1);
        }
    }

    public static void main(String args[]) {
        Client client = new Client();
    }
}
```

Figure 15.4   The client.

5155. Once the connection is made, the client can read from the socket using normal file I/O statements. After it has received the time of day from the server, the client closes the socket and exits.

To run the client program, the statement

```
java Client
```

is entered on the command line.

15.2 ■ Remote Procedure Calls

Communication using sockets—although common and efficient—is considered a low-level form of communication between distributed processes or threads. One reason is that sockets allow only an unstructured stream of bytes to be exchanged between the communicating threads. It is the responsibility of the client or server application to impose a structure on the data. Let's look at two alternative, higher-level methods of communication.

The first approach is a **remote procedure call** (**RPC**). An RPC system allows a thread to call a procedure or function in another process. This other process may be in a separate address space on the same computer, or it may be running on a different computer that is connected by a network. The semantics of RPCs allow the calling thread to invoke the remote procedure just as it would a local procedure.

The advantage of RPCs over sockets is that the RPC system manages the communication channel, so application programs can be written such that the location of a procedure—whether it is local or remote—is transparent.

15.3 ■ Remote Method Invocation

The second approach that we explore is **remote method invocation** (**RMI**), a Java feature similar to RPCs. RMI allows a thread to invoke a method on a remote object. Objects are considered remote if they reside in a different **Java Virtual Machine** (**JVM**). Therefore, the remote object may be in a different JVM on the same computer or on a remote host connected by a network. This situation is illustrated in Figure 15.5. There are two fundamental differences between RMI and RPCs. First, RPCs support only procedural programming whereby only remote procedures or functions may be called. RMI is object-based: It supports invocation of methods on remote objects. Second, the parameters to remote procedures are ordinary data structures in RPC; with RMI it is possible to pass objects as parameters to remote methods. By allowing a Java program to invoke methods on remote objects, RMI makes it possible for users to develop Java applications that are distributed across a network.

To make remote methods transparent to both the client and the server, RMI implements the remote object using stubs and skeletons. A **stub** is a proxy for the remote object; it resides with the client. When a client invokes a remote method, it is this stub for the remote object that is called. This client-

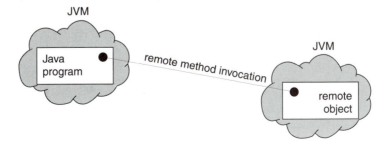

Figure 15.5   Remote method invocation.

side stub is responsible for creating a **parcel** consisting of the name of the method to be invoked on the server and that method's parameters, a process known as **marshalling** the parameters. The stub then sends this parcel to the server, where it is received by the skeleton for the remote object. The **skeleton** is responsible for **unmarshalling** the parameters and invoking the desired method on the server. The skeleton then marshals the return value (or exception, if any) into a parcel and returns this parcel to the client. The stub unmarshals the return value and passes it to the client.

Let us demonstrate how this process works. Assume that a client wishes to invoke a method on a remote object `Server` with the signature `someMethod(Object, Object)` that returns a `boolean` value. The client executes the statement

```
boolean val = Server.someMethod(A, B);
```

The call to `someMethod()` with the parameters `A` and `B` invokes the stub for the remote object. The stub marshals into a parcel the parameters `A` and `B` and the name of the method that is to be invoked on the server, then sends this parcel to the server. The skeleton on the server unmarshalls the parameters and invokes the method `someMethod()`. The actual implementation of `someMethod()` resides on the server. Once the method is completed, the skeleton marshals the `boolean` value returned from `someMethod()` and sends this value back to the client. The stub unmarshals this return value and passes it to the client. The process is shown in Figure 15.6.

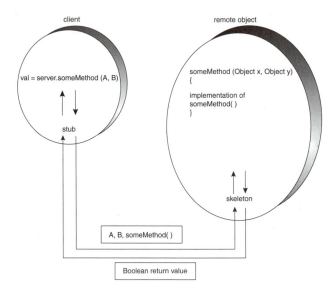

Figure 15.6   Marshalling parameters.

Fortunately, the level of abstraction that RMI provides makes the stubs and skeletons transparent, allowing the Java developer to write programs that invoke distributed methods just as they would invoke local methods. It is crucial, however, that you understand a few rules about the behavior of parameter passing.

- If the marshalled parameters are local (nonremote) objects, they are passed by copy using a technique known as **object serialization**. However, if the parameters are also remote objects, they are passed by reference. In our example, if A is a local object and B a remote object, A is serialized and passed by copy, and B is passed by reference. This would in turn allow the server to invoke methods on B remotely. Passing remote objects as parameters is an important RMI technique.

- If local objects are to be passed as parameters to remote objects, they must implement the interface java.io.Serializable. Many objects in the core Java API implement Serializable, allowing them to be used with RMI. Object serialization allows the state of an object to be written to a byte stream.

Next, we build a distributed message-passing solution to the producer–consumer problem that uses RMI. This distributed solution will consist of a remote object for messages that will be passed by reference, allowing the producer and consumer threads to invoke the send() and receive() methods remotely.

15.3.1 Remote Objects

We define remote objects by first declaring an interface that specifies the methods that may be invoked remotely. In the example of the message-passing solution to the producer–consumer problem, they are the send() and receive()

```
import java.util.*;
import java.rmi.*;

public interface MessageQueue
        extends java.rmi.Remote
{
    public void send(Object item) throws
        java.rmi.RemoteException;

    public Object receive() throws
        java.rmi.RemoteException;
}
```

Figure 15.7   The MessageQueue interface.

methods. This interface must extend the java.rmi.Remote interface, which identifies the object as being remote. Further, each method declared in the interface must throw the exception java.rmi.RemoteException. This situation is shown in Figure 15.7.

```java
import java.util.*;
import java.rmi.*;

public class MessageQueueImpl
      extends java.rmi.server.UnicastRemoteObject
      implements MessageQueue {
    public MessageQueueImpl()
         throws RemoteException {
       queue = new Vector();
    }

    public synchronized void send(Object item)
         throws RemoteException {
       // Figure 15.9
    }

    public synchronized Object receive()
         throws RemoteException {
       // Figure 15.9
    }

    public static void main(String args[]) {
       System.setSecurityManager
          (new RMISecurityManager());

       try {
          MessageQueue server = new MessageQueueImpl();
          Naming.rebind("MessageServer", server);
          System.out.println("Server Bound");
       }
       catch(Exception e) {
          System.err.println(e);
       }
    }

    private Vector queue;
}
```

Figure 15.8   Implementation of the MessageQueue interface.

The class that defines the remote object must implement the `MessageQueue` interface (Figure 15.8). In addition to defining the methods of the interface, the class must also extend `java.rmi.server.UnicastRemoteObject`. Extending `UnicastRemoteObject` allows the creation of a single remote object that listens for network requests using RMI's default scheme of sockets for network communication. This object also includes a `main()` method. The `main()` method installs a special security manager, `RMISecurityManager`. The role of the `RMISecurityManager` is to enforce security restrictions on misbehaving or malicious classes that may be loaded from the network. If a security manager is not installed, RMI will allow classes to be loaded from only the local file system and not from the network. (Java security managers are covered in Chapter 19). Next, an instance of the object is created and is registered with the RMI registry running on the server with the `rebind()` method. In this case, the

```java
// This implements a non-blocking send
public synchronized void send(Object item)
      throws RemoteException {
    queue.addElement(item);

    System.out.println("Producer entered " + item +
       " size = " + queue.size());
}

// This implements a non-blocking receive
public synchronized Object receive()
      throws RemoteException {
    Object item;

    if (queue.size() == 0)
       return null;
    else {
        item = queue.firstElement();
        queue.removeElementAt(0);

        System.out.println("Consumer removed " + item +
           " size = " + queue.size());

        return item;
    }
}
```

Figure 15.9 `send()` and `receive()` methods.

```java
import java.util.*;
import java.rmi.*;

public class Factory
{
    public Factory() {
        // remote object
        MessageQueue mailBox;

        System.setSecurityManager(new RMISecurityManager());

        try {
            mailBox = (MessageQueue)Naming.lookup
                ("rmi://127.0.0.1/MessageServer");

            Producer producerThread = new Producer(mailBox);
            Consumer consumerThread = new Consumer(mailBox);

            producerThread.start();
            consumerThread.start();
        }
        catch (Exception e) {
            System.err.println(e);
        }
    }

    // producer and consumer will call this to nap
    public static void napping() {
        int sleepTime = (int)(NAP_TIME * Math.random());
        try { Thread.sleep(sleepTime*1000); }
        catch(InterruptedException e) { }
    }

    public static void main(String args[]) {
        Factory client = new Factory();
    }

    private static final int NAP_TIME = 5;

}
```

Figure 15.10   The client.

object instance registers itself with the name `MessageServer`. Also note that the constructor for the `MessageQueueImpl` class must throw a `RemoteException` if a communication or network failure prevents RMI from exporting the remote object.

Note that the implementations of the `send()` and `receive()` methods are declared as `synchronized`. We can also use Java thread synchronization, described in Chapter 7, to prevent concurrent access to remote objects.

15.3.2 Access to the Remote Object

Once an object is registered on the server, a client (as shown in Figure 15.10) can get a reference to this remote object from the RMI registry running on the server by using the `Naming.lookup()` method. RMI provides a URL-based lookup scheme using the form `rmi://host/objectName`, where `host` is the IP name of the server on which the remote object `objectName` resides. `objectName` is the name of the remote object specified by the server in the `rebind()` method (in this case, `MessageServer`.) The client must also install an `RMISecurityManager` to ensure security from the remote stubs it may load from the network. Once the client has a reference to the remote object, it creates separate producer and consumer threads, passing to each thread a reference to the remote object. The source-code fragments for the producer and consumer threads are shown in Figures 15.11 and 15.12. Note that the producer and consumer threads invoke the remote methods `send()` and `receive()` as normal method invocations.

15.3.3 Running of the Programs

We now demonstrate the steps necessary to run the example programs. For simplicity, we are assuming that all programs are running on the local host. However, communication is still considered remote, because the client and server programs are each running in their own JVM.

1. *Compile all source files.*

2. *Generate the stub and skeleton.* The tool RMIc is used to generate the stub and skeleton class files, which is done by the user entering

   ```
   rmic MessageQueueImpl
   ```

   on the command line; this create the files `MessageQueueImpl_Skel.class` and `MessageQueueImpl_Stub.class`. (If you are running this example on two different computers, make sure that all the class files—including the stub classes—are available on each computer. It is possible to load classes dynamically using RMI, a topic beyond the scope of this text but covered in texts mentioned in the Bibliographical Notes.)

```
import java.util.*;

class Producer extends Thread
{
    public Producer(MessageQueue m) {
        mbox = m;
    }

    public void run() {
        Date message;

        while (true) {
            Factory.napping();

            message = new Date();

            try {
                mbox.send(message);
            }
            catch (Exception e) {
                System.err.println(e);
            }
        }
    }

    private MessageQueue mbox;
}
```

Figure 15.11   Producer thread.

3. *Start the registry and create the remote object.* To start the registry on UNIX platforms, the user may type

   `rmiregistry &`

   For Windows, the user may type

   `start rmiregistry`

   This command starts the registry with which the remote object will register. Next, create an instance of the remote object with

   `java MessageQueueImpl`

   This remote object will register using the name `MessageServer`.

4. *Reference the remote object.* The statement

   `java Factory`

```
import java.util.*;

class Consumer extends Thread
{
    public Consumer(MessageQueue m) {
       mbox = m;
    }

    public void run() {
       Date message;

       while (true) {
          Factory.napping();

          try {
             message = (Date)mbox.receive();
             if (message != null) {
                // Consume the item
                     ;
             }
          }
          catch (Exception e) {
             System.err.println(e);
          }
       }
    }

    private MessageQueue mbox;
}
```

Figure 15.12   Consumer thread.

is entered on the command line to start the client program. This program will get a reference to the remote object `MessageServer`, and will create the producer and consumer threads, passing to each thread the reference to the remote object. The producer and consumer threads can now invoke the methods `send()` and `receive()` on the remote object.

15.4 ■ CORBA

RMI is a technology that allows threads to invoke methods on distributed objects. RMI is native Java technology, however, so it requires all distributed applications to be written in Java. Many existing systems that we might also want to be distributed are written in C, C++, COBOL, or Ada. No communication protocol discussed so far provides a convenient mechanism for these disparite applications to communicate.

The **Common Object Request Broker Architecture (CORBA)** is **middleware**—an intermediate software layer—that allows heterogeneous client and server applications to communicate. For example, a C++ program could use CORBA to access a database service written in COBOL. CORBA allows applications written in different languages to communicate using an **interface-definition language (IDL)** and an **Object Request Broker (ORB)**. An IDL allows a distributed object—such as a database—to describe an interface to the services that it provides. The IDL is a generic programming language; it allows a service to describe itself independently of any specific language. To communicate with a server, a client needs to communicate with only the interface specified with the IDL. The server object implements the interface specified by the IDL. The ORB forms the backbone of CORBA, allowing clients to invoke methods on distributed objects and accept return values. There is an ORB on both the client and the server side, and a protocol, the **Internet InterORB Protocol (IIOP)**, that specifies how the ORBs can communicate.

When a client application requests a reference for a remote object, it is the responsibility of the client ORB to find the remote object in the distributed system. The client ORB is also responsible for routing the remote method calls to the appropriate server, and for accepting results from the server. The server ORB allows the server to register new CORBA objects and is also responsible for accepting requests from client ORBs for invoking methods on the server. The server ORB also passes return values back to the client.

A CORBA system works as follows. Once a client has a reference for a remote object, any method invocations for this object are made through the client-side stub. This stub uses the client's ORB to communicate with the server. When the server ORB receives a client request for invoking a method, it calls the appropriate skeleton, which in turn invokes the implementation of the remote method on the server. Return values are passed back along the same path. This situation is shown in Figure 15.13.

In many ways, the ORB behaves much like RMI. However RMI is Java-to-Java technology. CORBA provides interoperability between heterogeneous clients and servers, allowing applications that are written in different languages to communicate.

15.5 ■ Object Registration

Both RMI and CORBA are **distributed object systems:** Objects are distributed across a network and applications can communicate with the distributed objects. An important feature of such systems is an **object-registration service,** with which an object registers itself. Applications that wish to use a distributed object obtain a reference to the object through this service. The **rmiregistry**

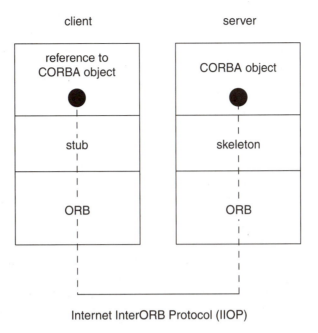

client   server

Internet InterORB Protocol (IIOP)

Figure 15.13 CORBA model.

acts as the registration service for RMI. Once the registry is started, a remote object registers itself with a unique name using the Naming.rebind() method. Clients use this name when they request a reference to the remote object from the registration server. Using RMI, a client obtains a reference to a remote object using the Naming.lookup() method. In a CORBA system, the ORB on the server side is responsible for providing the registration service.

15.6 ■ Summary

In this chapter, we presented several methods that allow distributed applications to communicate. The first, a socket, is defined as an endpoint for communication. A connection between a pair of applications consists of a pair of sockets, one at each end of the communication channel. RPCs are another form of distributed communication. An RPC occurs when a process or thread calls a procedure on a remote application. RMI is the Java version of an RPC. RMI allows a thread to invoke a method on a remote object just as it would invoke a method on a local object. The primary distinction between RPCs and RMIs is that the data being passed to a remote procedure in the latter case are in the form of an ordinary data structure. RMI allows objects to be passed in remote method calls. We also discussed CORBA, a technology that allows communication among distributed applications written in different languages.

RMI and CORBA are both distributed object systems. An important feature of these systems is an object-registration service that registers distributed objects. Clients contact the registration service when they wish to locate a distributed object.

▪ Exercises

15.1 Write a socket-based *Fortune Teller* server. Your program should create a server that listens to a specified port. When a connection is received by a client, the server should respond with a random fortune chosen from its database of fortunes.

15.2 Two problems may arise when we multithread a server. The first is that we may pay a high overhead for thread creation if a server creates a separate thread whenever it receives a request. The second problem is that too many threads may be created if there are several concurrent requests to the server. (This problem is especially severe for thread architectures that use the one-to-one model.) One way of addressing these problems is with a *thread pool:* a collection (pool) of threads waiting to be assigned a task. Rather than creating a thread when a request is made, the server creates several threads up front and adds them to the pool. When the server receives a request, it removes a thread from this pool and assigns to that thread the task of handling the request. When the request has been serviced, the server puts the thread back in the pool.

Implement the time-of-day server using a thread pool.

15.3 Implement Algorithm 3 from Chapter 7 using RMI.

15.4 This chapter provided a distributed solution to the bounded-buffer problem that used message passing. Another solution to the bounded-buffer problem used Java synchronization; it was shown in Chapter 7. Modify this second solution using RMI, so that the solution works in a distributed environment.

15.5 We solved the readers–writers problem by using Java synchronization in Chapter 7. Modify that solution so that it works in a distributed environment using RMI.

15.6 Implement a distributed solution to the dining-philosophers problem using RMI.

15.7 Explain the differences and similarities between RMI and CORBA.

Bibliographical Notes

Tanenbaum [1996] describes sockets and RPCs. Waldo [1998] discusses RPCs and RMI. Farley [1998] provides a wealth of information on distributed computing with Java. Farley focuses on using RMI, and also contains a section describing how to use CORBA with Java. Niemeyer and Peck [1997] and Horstmann and Cornell [1998a] give good introductions to using RMI. The RMI homepage at [http://www.javasoft.com/products/jdk/rmi] lists up-to-date resources. The OMG homepage [http://www.omg.org] is a good starting point on the Web for information regarding CORBA.

Chapter 16

DISTRIBUTED COORDINATION

In Chapter 7, we described various mechanisms that allow processes to synchronize their actions. In Chapter 8, we described various methods that an operating system can use to deal with the deadlock problem. In this chapter, we examine how the centralized synchronization mechanisms can be extended to a distributed environment. We also discuss various methods for handling deadlocks in a distributed system.

16.1 ■ Event Ordering

In a centralized system, it is always possible to determine the order in which two events have occurred, since there is a single common memory and clock. In many applications, it is of utmost importance to be able to determine order. For example, in a resource-allocation scheme, we specify that a resource can be used only *after* the resource has been granted. In a distributed system, however, there is no common memory and no common clock. Therefore, it is sometimes impossible to say which of two events occurred first. The **happened-before relation** is only a partial ordering of the events in distributed systems. Since the ability to define a total ordering is crucial in many applications, we present a distributed algorithm for extending the *happened-before* relation to a consistent total ordering of all the events in the system.

16.1.1 The Happened-Before Relation

Since we are considering only sequential processes, all events executed in a single process are totally ordered. Also, by the law of causality, a message can be received only after it has been sent. Therefore, we can define the *happened-before* relation (denoted by $\rightarrow$) on a set of events as follows (assuming that sending and receiving a message constitutes an event):

1. If A and B are events in the same process, and A was executed before B, then $A \rightarrow B$.

2. If A is the event of sending a message by one process and B is the event of receiving that message by another process, then $A \rightarrow B$.

3. If $A \rightarrow B$ and $B \rightarrow C$, then $A \rightarrow C$.

Since an event cannot happen before itself, the $\rightarrow$ relation is an irreflexive partial ordering.

If two events, A and B, are not related by the $\rightarrow$ relation (that is, A did not happen before B, and B did not happen before A), then we say that these two events were executed **concurrently**. In this case, neither event can causally affect the other. If, however, $A \rightarrow B$, then it is possible for event A to affect event B causally.

The definitions of concurrency and of *happened-before* can best be illustrated by a space–time diagram, such as that in Figure 16.1. The horizontal direction represents space (that is, different processes), and the vertical direction represents time. The labeled vertical lines denote processes (or processors). The labeled dots denote events. A wavy line denotes a message sent from one process to another. From this diagram, it is clear that events A and B are concurrent if and only if no path exists either from A to B or from B to A.

For example, consider Figure 16.1. Some of the events related by the *happened-before* relation are

$$p_1 \rightarrow q_2,$$
$$r_0 \rightarrow q_4,$$
$$q_3 \rightarrow r_4,$$
$$p_1 \rightarrow q_4 \text{ (since } p_1 \rightarrow q_2 \text{ and } q_2 \rightarrow q_4).$$

Some of the concurrent events in the system are

$$q_0 \text{ and } p_2,$$
$$r_0 \text{ and } q_3,$$
$$r_0 \text{ and } p_3,$$
$$q_3 \text{ and } p_3.$$

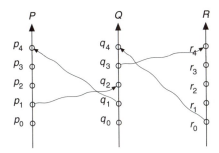

Figure 16.1   Relative time for three concurrent processes.

We cannot know which of two concurrent events, such as q_0 and p_2, happened first. However, since neither event can affect the other (there is no way for one of them to know whether the other has occurred yet), it is not important which of them happened first. It is important only that any processes that care about the order of two concurrent events agree on some order.

16.1.2 Implementation

To determine that an event A happened before an event B, we need either a common clock or a set of perfectly synchronized clocks. Since, in a distributed system, neither of these timekeepers is available, we must define the *happened-before* relation without the use of physical clocks.

We associate with each system event a **timestamp**. We can then define the **global-ordering requirement**: For every pair of events A and B, if A $\rightarrow$ B, then the timestamp of A is less than the timestamp of B. We shall see that the converse does not need to be true.

How do we enforce the global-ordering requirement in a distributed environment? We define within *each* process P_i a **logical clock**, LC_i. The logical clock can be implemented as a simple counter that is incremented between any two successive events executed within a process. Since the logical clock has a monotonically increasing value, it assigns a unique number to every event, and if an event A occurs before event B in process P_i, then $LC_i(A) < LC_i(B)$. The timestamp for an event is the value of the logical clock for that event. Clearly, this scheme ensures that, for any two events in the same process, the global-ordering requirement is met.

Unfortunately, this scheme does not ensure that the global-ordering requirement is met across processes. To illustrate the problem, we consider two processes P_1 and P_2 that communicate with each other. Suppose that P_1 sends a message to P_2 (event A) with $LC_1(A) = 200$, and P_2 receives the message (event B) with $LC_2(B) = 195$ (because the processor for P_2 is slower than the processor for P_1 and so its logical clock ticks slower). This situation violates our requirement, since A → B, but the timestamp of A is greater than the timestamp of B.

To resolve this difficulty, we require a process to advance its logical clock when it receives a message whose timestamp is greater than the current value of its logical clock. In particular, if process P_i receives a message (event B) with timestamp t and $LC_i(B) \leq t$, then it should advance its clock such that $LC_i(B) = t + 1$. Thus, in our example, when P_2 receives the message from P_1, it will advance its logical clock such that $LC_2(B) = 201$.

Finally, to realize a total ordering, we need only to observe that, with our timestamp-ordering scheme, if the timestamps of two events A and B are the same, then the events are concurrent. In this case, we may use process identity numbers to break ties and to create a total ordering. The use of timestamps is discussed later in this chapter.

16.2 ■ Mutual Exclusion

In this section, we present different algorithms for implementing mutual exclusion in a distributed environment. We assume that the system consists of n processes, each of which resides at a different processor. To simplify our discussion, we assume that processes are numbered uniquely from 1 to n, and that there is a one-to-one mapping between processes and processors (that is, each process has its own processor).

16.2.1 Centralized Approach

In a **centralized** approach to providing mutual exclusion, one of the processes in the system is chosen to coordinate the entry to the critical section. Each process that wants to invoke mutual exclusion sends a *request* message to the coordinator. When the process receives a *reply* message from the coordinator, it can proceed to enter its critical section. After exiting its critical section, the process sends a *release* message to the coordinator and proceeds with its execution.

On receiving a *request* message, the coordinator checks to see whether some other process is in its critical section. If no process is in its critical section, the coordinator immediately sends back a *reply* message. Otherwise, the request is queued. When the coordinator receives a *release* message, it removes one of the request messages from the queue (in accordance with some scheduling algorithm) and sends a *reply* message to the requesting process.

This algorithm ensures mutual exclusion. In addition, if the scheduling policy within the coordinator is fair (such as first-come, first-served scheduling), no starvation can occur. This scheme requires three messages per critical-section entry: a *request*, a *reply*, and a *release*.

If the coordinator process fails, then a new process must take its place. In Section 16.4, we describe various algorithms for electing a unique new coordinator. Once a new coordinator has been elected, it must poll all the processes in the system, to reconstruct its *request* queue. Once the queue has been constructed, the computation may resume.

16.2.2 Fully Distributed Approach

If we want to **distribute** the decision making across the entire system, then the solution is far more complicated. We present an algorithm that is based on the event-ordering scheme described in Section 16.1.

When a process P_i wants to enter its critical section, it generates a new timestamp, TS, and sends the message *request*(P_i, TS) to all other processes in the system (including itself). On receiving a *request* message, a process may reply immediately (that is, send a *reply* message back to P_i), or it may defer sending a reply back (because it is already in its critical section, for example). A process that has received a *reply* message from all other processes in the system can enter its critical section, queueing incoming requests and deferring them. After exiting its critical section, the process sends *reply* messages to all its deferred requests.

The decision whether process P_i replies immediately to a *request*(P_j, TS) message or defers its reply is based on three factors:

1. If process P_i is in its critical section, then it defers its reply to P_j.

2. If process P_i does *not* want to enter its critical section, then it sends a reply immediately to P_j.

3. If process P_i wants to enter its critical section but has not yet entered it, then it compares its own *request* timestamp with the timestamp TS of the incoming request made by process P_j. If its own *request* timestamp is greater than TS, then it sends a reply immediately to P_j (P_j asked first). Otherwise, the reply is deferred.

This algorithm exhibits the following desirable behavior:

- Mutual exclusion is obtained.

- Freedom from deadlock is ensured.

- Freedom from starvation is ensured, since entry to the critical section is scheduled according to the timestamp ordering. The timestamp ordering ensures that processes are served in a first-come, first-served order.

- The number of messages per critical-section entry is $2 \times$ number of required messages per critical-section entry when processes act independently and concurrently.

To illustrate how the algorithm functions, we consider a system consisting of processes P_1, P_2, and P_3. Suppose that processes P_1 and P_3 want to enter their critical sections. Process P_1 then sends a message *request* (P_1, timestamp = 10) to processes P_2 and P_3, while process P_3 sends a message *request* (P_3, timestamp = 4) to processes P_1 and P_2. The timestamps 4 and 10 were obtained from the logical clocks described in Section 16.1. When process P_2 receives these *request* messages, it replies immediately. When process P_1 receives the *request* from process P_3 it replies immediately, since the timestamp (10) on its own *request* message is greater than the timestamp (4) for process P_3. When process P_3 receives the *request* from process P_1, it defers its reply, since the timestamp (4) on its *request* message is less than the timestamp (10) for the message of process P_1. On receiving replies from both process P_1 and process P_2, process P_3 can enter its critical section. After exiting its critical section, process P_3 sends a reply to process P_1, which can then enter its critical section.

Note that this scheme requires the participation of all the processes in the system. This approach has three undesirable consequences:

1. The processes need to know the identities of all other processes in the system. When a new process joins the group of processes participating in the mutual-exclusion algorithm, the following actions need to be taken:

   a. The process must receive the names of all the other processes in the group.

   b. The name of the new process must be distributed to all the other processes in the group.

   These tasks are not as trivial as they may seem, since some *request* and *reply* messages may be circulating in the system when the new process joins the group. See the Bibliographical Notes for more details.

2. If one of the processes fails, then the entire scheme collapses. We can resolve this difficulty by continuously monitoring the state of all the processes in the system. If one process fails, then all other processes are notified, so that they will no longer send *request* messages to the failed process. When a process recovers, it must initiate the procedure that allows it to rejoin the group.

3. Processes that have not entered their critical section must pause frequently to assure other processes that they intend to enter the critical section. This protocol is therefore suited for small, stable sets of cooperating processes.

16.2.3 Token-Passing Approach

Another method of providing mutual exclusion is **token passing**, in which a token circulates among the processes in the system. A **token** is a special type of message that is passed around the system. Possession of the token entitles the holder to enter the critical section. Since there is only a single token in the system, only one process can be in its critical section at a time.

We assume that the processes in the system are *logically* organized in a ring structure. The *physical* communication network does not need to be a ring. As long as the processes are connected to one another, it is possible to implement a logical ring. To implement mutual exclusion, we pass the token around the ring. When a process receives the token, it may enter its critical section, keeping the token. After the process exits its critical section, the token is passed around again. If the process receiving the token does not want to enter its critical section, it passes the token to its neighbor. This scheme is similar to Algorithm 1 in Chapter 7, but a token is substituted for a shared variable.

Since there is only a single token, only one process at a time can be in its critical section. In addition, if the ring is unidirectional, freedom from starvation is ensured. The number of messages required to implement mutual exclusion may vary from one message per entry, in the case of high contention (that is, every process wants to enter its critical section), to an infinite number of messages, in the case of low contention (that is, no process wants to enter its critical section).

Two types of failure must be considered. First, if the token is lost, an election must be called to generate a new token. Second, if a process fails, a new logical ring must be established. There are several different algorithms for election and for reconstructing a logical ring. In Section 16.4, we present an election algorithm. The development of an algorithm for reconstructing the ring is left to you in Exercise 16.5.

16.3 ■ Deadlock Handling

The deadlock-prevention, deadlock-avoidance, and deadlock-detection algorithms presented in Chapter 8 can be extended so that they can also be used in a distributed system. In the following, we describe several of these distributed algorithms.

16.3.1 Deadlock Prevention

The deadlock-prevention and deadlock-avoidance algorithms presented in Chapter 8 can also be used in a distributed system, provided that appropriate modifications are made. For example, we can use the resource-ordering deadlock-prevention technique by simply defining a *global* ordering among the system resources. That is, all resources in the entire system are assigned unique numbers, and a process may request a resource (at any processor) with unique number i only if it is not holding a resource with a unique number greater than i. Similarly, we can use the deadlock-avoidance algorithm (described in Section 8.5) in a distributed system by designating one of the processes in the system as the process that maintains the resource-allocation graph. Every resource request must be channeled through this process.

These two schemes can be used in dealing with the deadlock problem in a distributed environment. The first scheme is simple to implement and requires little overhead. The second scheme can also be implemented easily, but it may require too much overhead. The process maintaining the resource-allocation graph may become a bottleneck. Thus, this scheme does not seem to be of practical use in a distributed system.

In this section, we present a new deadlock-prevention scheme that is based on a timestamp-ordering approach with resource preemption. For simplicity, we consider only the case of a single instance of each resource type.

To control the preemption, we assign a **unique priority number** to each process. We use these numbers to decide whether a process P_i should wait for a process P_j. For example, we can let P_i wait for P_j if P_i has a priority higher than that of P_j; otherwise, P_i is rolled back. This scheme prevents deadlocks because, for every edge $P_i \rightarrow P_j$ in the wait-for graph, P_i has a higher priority than P_j. Thus, a cycle cannot exist.

One difficulty with this scheme is the possibility of starvation. Some processes with extremely low priority may always be rolled back. This difficulty can be avoided through the use of timestamps. Each process in the system is assigned a unique timestamp when it is created. Two complementary deadlock-prevention schemes using timestamps have been proposed:

- **The wait–die scheme:** This approach is based on a nonpreemptive technique. When process P_i requests a resource currently held by P_j, P_i is allowed to wait only if it has a smaller timestamp than does P_j (that is, P_i is older than P_j). Otherwise, P_i is rolled back (dies). For example, suppose that processes P_1, P_2, and P_3 have timestamps 5, 10, and 15, respectively. If P_1 requests a resource held by P_2, P_1 will wait. If P_3 requests a resource held by P_2, P_3 will be rolled back.

- **The wound–wait scheme:** This approach is based on a preemptive technique and is a counterpart to the wait–die system. When process P_i requests a resource currently held by P_j, P_i is allowed to wait only if it has a larger timestamp than does P_j (that is, P_i is younger than P_j). Otherwise, P_j is rolled back (P_j is *wounded* by P_i). Returning to our previous example, with processes P_1, P_2, and P_3, if P_1 requests a resource held by P_2, then the resource will be preempted from P_2 and P_2 will be rolled back. If P_3 requests a resource held by P_2, then P_3 will wait.

Both schemes can avoid starvation, provided that, when a process is rolled back, it is *not* assigned a new timestamp. Since timestamps always increase, a process that is rolled back will eventually have the smallest timestamp. Thus, it will not be rolled back again. There are, however, significant differences in the way the two schemes operate.

- In the wait–die scheme, an older process must wait for a younger one to release its resource. Thus, the older the process gets, the more it tends to wait. By contrast, in the wound–wait scheme, an older process never waits for a younger process.

- In the wait–die scheme, if a process P_i dies and is rolled back because it requested a resource held by process P_j, then P_i may reissue the same sequence of requests when it is restarted. If the resource is still held by P_j, then P_i will die again. Thus, P_i may die several times before acquiring the needed resource. Contrast this series of events with what happens in the wound–wait scheme. Process P_i is wounded and rolled back because P_j requested a resource it holds. When P_i is restarted and requests the resource now being held by P_j, P_i waits. Thus, there are fewer rollbacks in the wound–wait scheme.

The major problem with both schemes is that unnecessary rollbacks may occur.

16.3.2 Deadlock Detection

The deadlock-prevention algorithm may preempt resources even if no deadlock has occurred. To prevent unnecessary preemptions, we can use a deadlock-detection algorithm. We construct a wait-for graph describing the resource-allocation state. Since we are assuming only a single resource of each type, a cycle in the wait-for graph represents a deadlock.

The main problem in a distributed system is deciding how to maintain the wait-for graph. We elaborate this problem by describing several common techniques to deal with this issue. These schemes require that each site keep a **local wait-for graph**. The nodes of the graph correspond to all the processes (local as well as nonlocal) that are currently either holding or requesting any of the resources local to that site. For example, in Figure 16.2 we have a system consisting of two sites, each maintaining its local wait-for graph. Note that processes P_2 and P_3 appear in both graphs, indicating that the processes have requested resources at both sites.

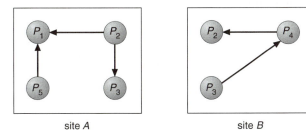

site A   site B

Figure 16.2   Two local wait-for graphs.

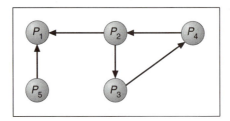

Figure 16.3 Global wait-for graph for Figure 16.2.

These local wait-for graphs are constructed in the usual manner for local processes and resources. When a process P_i in site A needs a resource held by process P_j in site B, a request message is sent by P_i to site B. The edge $P_i \rightarrow P_j$ is then inserted in the local wait-for graph of site B.

Clearly, if any local wait-for graph has a cycle, deadlock has occurred. On the other hand, the fact that there are no cycles in any of the local wait-for graphs does not mean that there are no deadlocks. To illustrate this problem, we consider the system depicted in Figure 16.2. Each wait-for graph is acyclic; nevertheless, a deadlock exists in the system. To prove that a deadlock has not occurred, we must show that the *union* of all local graphs is acyclic. The graph (shown in Figure 16.3) that we obtain by taking the union of the two wait-for graphs of Figure 16.2 does indeed contain a cycle, implying that the system is in a deadlock state.

There are a number of different methods for organizing the wait-for graph in a distributed system. We shall describe several common schemes.

16.3.2.1 Centralized Approach

In the centralized approach, a **global wait-for graph** is constructed as the union of all the local wait-for graphs. It is maintained in a *single* process: the **deadlock-detection coordinator**. Since there is communication delay in the system, we must distinguish between two types of wait-for graphs. The **real wait-for graph** describes the real but unknown state of the system at any instance in time, as would be seen by an omniscient observer. The **constructed wait-for graph** is an approximation generated by the coordinator during the execution of its algorithm. Obviously, the constructed graph must be generated such that, whenever the detection algorithm is invoked, the reported results are correct in a sense that, if a deadlock exists, then it is reported properly, and if a deadlock is reported, then the system is indeed in a deadlock state. As we shall show, it is not easy to construct such correct algorithms.

There are three different points in time when the wait-for graph may be constructed:

1. Whenever a new edge is inserted or removed in one of the local wait-for graphs

2. Periodically, when a number of changes have occurred in a wait-for graph

3. Whenever the coordinator needs to invoke the cycle-detection algorithm

Let us consider option 1. Whenever an edge is either inserted or removed in a local graph, the local site must also send a message to the coordinator to notify it of this modification. On receiving such a message, the coordinator updates its global graph. Alternatively, a site can send a number of such changes in a single message periodically. Returning to our previous example, the coordinator process will maintain the global wait-for graph as depicted in Figure 16.3. When site B inserts the edge $P_3 \rightarrow P_4$ in its local wait-for graph, it also sends a message to the coordinator. Similarly, when site A deletes the edge $P_5 \rightarrow P_1$, because P_1 has released a resource that was requested by P_5, an appropriate message is sent to the coordinator.

When the deadlock-detection algorithm is invoked, the coordinator searches its global graph. If a cycle is found, a victim is selected to be rolled back. The coordinator must notify all the sites that a particular process has been selected as victim. The sites, in turn, roll back the victim process.

Note that, in this scheme (option 1), unnecessary rollbacks may occur, as a result of two situations:

- **False cycles** may exist in the global wait-for graph. To illustrate this point, we consider a snapshot of the system as depicted in Figure 16.4. Suppose that P_2 releases the resource it is holding in site A, resulting in the deletion of the edge $P_1 \rightarrow P_2$ in A. Process P_2 then requests a resource held by P_3 at site B, resulting in the addition of the edge $P_2 \rightarrow P_3$ in B. If the *insert* $P_2 \rightarrow P_3$ message from B arrives before the *delete* $P_1 \rightarrow P_2$ message from A, the coordinator may discover the false cycle $P_1 \rightarrow P_2 \rightarrow P_3 \rightarrow P_1$ after the *insert* (but before the *delete*). Deadlock recovery may be initiated, although no deadlock has occurred.

- Unnecessary rollbacks may also result when a deadlock has indeed occurred and a victim has been picked, but at the same time one of the processes was aborted for reasons unrelated to the deadlock (such as the

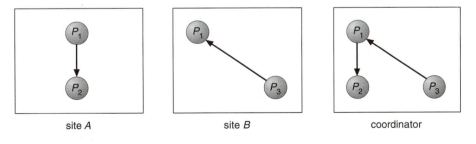

site A site B coordinator

Figure 16.4   Local and global wait-for graphs.

process exceeding its allocated time). For example, suppose that site A in Figure 16.2 decides to abort P_2. At the same time, the coordinator has discovered a cycle and picked P_3 as a victim. Both P_2 and P_3 are now rolled back, although only P_2 needed to be rolled back.

Note that the same problems are inherited in solutions employing the other two options (that is, options 2 and 3).

We now present a **centralized deadlock-detection algorithm,** using option 3, which detects all deadlocks that actually occur, and does not detect false deadlocks. To avoid the report of false deadlocks, we require that requests from different sites be appended with unique identifiers (timestamps). When process P_i, at site A, requests a resource from P_j, at site B, a request message with timestamp TS is sent. The edge $P_i \rightarrow P_j$ with the label TS is inserted in the local wait-for graph of A. This edge is inserted in the local wait-for graph of B only if B has received the request message and cannot grant the requested resource immediately. A request from P_i to P_j in the same site is handled in the usual manner; no timestamps are associated with the edge $P_i \rightarrow P_j$. The detection algorithm is then as follows:

1. The coordinator sends an initiating message to each site in the system.

2. On receiving this message, a site sends its local wait-for graph to the coordinator. Note that each of these wait-for graphs contains all the local information that the site has about the state of the real graph. The graph reflects an instantaneous state of the site, but it is not synchronized with respect to any other site.

3. When the coordinator has received a reply from each site, it constructs a graph as follows:

   a. The constructed graph contains a vertex for every process in the system.

   b. The graph has an edge $P_i \rightarrow P_j$ if and only if (1) there is an edge $P_i \rightarrow P_j$ in one of the wait-for graphs, or (2) an edge $P_i \rightarrow P_j$ with some label TS appears in more than one wait-for graph.

We assert that, if there is a cycle in the constructed graph, then the system is in a deadlock state. If there is no cycle in the constructed graph, then the system was not in a deadlock state when the detection algorithm was invoked as result of the initiating messages sent by the coordinator (in step 1).

16.3.2.2 Fully Distributed Approach

In the **fully distributed deadlock-detection algorithm,** all controllers share equally the responsibility for detecting deadlock. In this scheme, every site constructs a wait-for graph that represents a part of the total graph, depending on the dynamic behavior of the system. The idea is that, if a deadlock exists, a cycle will appear in (at least) one of the partial graphs. We present one such algorithm, which involves construction of partial graphs in every site.

Each site maintains its own local wait-for graph. A local wait-for graph in this scheme differs from the one described earlier in that we add one additional node P_{ex} to the graph. An arc $P_i \rightarrow P_{ex}$ exists in the graph if P_i is waiting for a data item in another site being held by *any* process. Similarly, an arc $P_{ex} \rightarrow P_j$ exists in the graph if there exists a process at another site that is waiting to acquire a resource currently being held by P_j in this local site.

To illustrate this situation, we consider the two local wait-for graphs of Figure 16.2. The addition of the node P_{ex} in both graphs results in the local wait-for graphs shown in Figure 16.5.

If a local wait-for graph contains a cycle that does not involve node P_{ex}, then the system is in a deadlock state. If, however, there exists a cycle involving P_{ex}, then there is a *possibility* of a deadlock. To ascertain whether a deadlock does exist, we must invoke a distributed deadlock-detection algorithm.

Suppose that, at site S_i, the local wait-for graph contains a cycle involving node P_{ex}. This cycle must be of the form

$$P_{ex} \rightarrow P_{k_1} \rightarrow P_{k_2} \rightarrow \cdots \rightarrow P_{k_n} \rightarrow P_{ex},$$

which indicates that process P_{k_n} in site S_i is waiting to acquire a data item located in some other site—say, S_j. On discovering this cycle, site S_i sends to site S_j a deadlock-detection message containing information about that cycle.

When site S_j receives this deadlock-detection message, it updates its local wait-for graph with the new information. Then, it searches the newly constructed wait-for graph for a cycle not involving P_{ex}. If one exists, a deadlock is found and an appropriate recovery scheme is invoked. If a cycle involving P_{ex} is discovered, then S_j transmits a deadlock-detection message to the appropriate site—say, S_k. Site S_k, in return, repeats the procedure. Thus, after a finite number of rounds, either a deadlock is discovered, or the deadlock-detection computation halts.

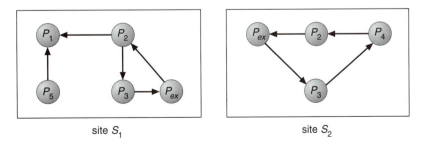

site S_1 site S_2

Figure 16.5   Augmented local wait-for graphs of Figure 16.2.

To illustrate this procedure, we consider the local wait-for graphs of Figure 16.5. Suppose that site S_1 discovers the cycle

$$P_{ex} \rightarrow P_2 \rightarrow P_3 \rightarrow P_{ex}.$$

Since P_3 is waiting to acquire a data item in site S_2, a deadlock-detection message describing that cycle is transmitted from site S_1 to site S_2. When site S_2 receives this message, it updates its local wait-for graph, obtaining the wait-for graph of Figure 16.6. This graph contains the cycle

$$P_2 \rightarrow P_3 \rightarrow P_4 \rightarrow P_2,$$

which does not include node P_{ex}. Therefore, the system is in a deadlock state and an appropriate recovery scheme must be invoked.

Note that the outcome would be the same if site S_2 discovered the cycle first in its local wait-for graph and sent the deadlock-detection message to site S_1. In the worst case, both sites discover the cycle at about the same time, and two deadlock-detection messages are sent: one by S_1 to S_2 and another by S_2 to S_1. This situation results in unnecessary message transfer and overhead in updating the two local wait-for graphs and searching for cycles in both graphs.

To reduce message traffic, we assign to each process P_i a unique identifier, which we denote by $ID(P_i)$. When site S_k discovers that its local wait-for graph contains a cycle involving node P_{ex} of the form

$$P_{ex} \rightarrow P_{K_1} \rightarrow P_{K_2} \rightarrow \cdots \rightarrow P_{K_n} \rightarrow P_{ex},$$

it sends a deadlock-detection message to another site only if

$$ID(P_{K_n}) < ID(P_{K_1}).$$

Otherwise, site S_k continues its normal execution, leaving the burden of initiating the deadlock-detection algorithm to some other site.

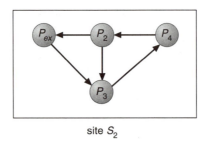

site S_2

Figure 16.6   Augmented local wait-for graph in site S_2 of Figure 16.5.

To illustrate this scheme, we consider again the wait-for graphs maintained at sites S_1 and S_2 of Figure 16.5. Suppose that

$$ID(P_1) \; < \; ID(P_2) \; < \; ID(P_3) \; < \; ID(P_4).$$

Let both sites discover these local cycles at about the same time. The cycle in site S_1 is of the form

$$P_{ex} \; \rightarrow \; P_2 \; \rightarrow \; P_3 \; \rightarrow \; P_{ex}.$$

Since $ID(P_3) \; > \; ID(P_2)$, site S_1 does not send a deadlock-detection message to site S_2.

The cycle in site S_2 is of the form

$$P_{ex} \; \rightarrow \; P_3 \; \rightarrow \; P_4 \; \rightarrow \; P_2 \; \rightarrow \; P_{ex}.$$

Since $ID(P_2) \; < \; ID(P_3)$, site S_2 does send a deadlock-detection message to site S_1, which, on receiving the message, updates its local wait-for graph. Site S_1 then searches for a cycle in the graph and discovers that the system is in a deadlock state.

16.4 ■ Election Algorithms

As we pointed out in Section 14.3, many distributed algorithms employ a coordinator process that performs functions needed by the other processes in the system. These functions include enforcing mutual exclusion, maintaining a global wait-for graph for deadlock detection, replacing a lost token, or controlling an input or output device in the system. If the coordinator process fails due to the failure of the site at which it resides, the system can continue execution only by restarting a new copy of the coordinator on some other site. The algorithms that determine where a new copy of the coordinator should be restarted are called **election algorithms**.

Election algorithms assume that a unique priority number is associated with each active process in the system. For ease of notation, we assume that the priority number of process P_i is i. To simplify our discussion, we assume a one-to-one correspondence between processes and sites, and thus refer to both as processes. The coordinator is always the process with the largest priority number. Hence, when a coordinator fails, the algorithm must elect that active process with the largest priority number. This number must be sent to each active process in the system. In addition, the algorithm must provide a mechanism for a recovered process to identify the current coordinator.

In this section, we present two interesting examples of election algorithms for two different configurations of distributed systems. The first algorithm is applicable to systems where every process can send a message to every other process in the system. The second algorithm is applicable to systems organized as a ring (logically or physically). Both algorithms require n^2 messages for an election, where n is the number of processes in the system. We assume that a process that has failed knows on recovery that it indeed has failed and thus takes appropriate actions to rejoin the set of active processes.

16.4.1 The Bully Algorithm

Suppose that process P_i sends a request that is not answered by the coordinator within a time interval T. In this situation, it is assumed that the coordinator has failed, and P_i tries to elect itself as the new coordinator. This task is completed through the following algorithm.

Process P_i sends an election message to every process with a higher priority number. Process P_i then waits for a time interval T for an answer from any one of these processes.

If no response is received within time T, P_i assumes that all processes with numbers greater than i have failed, and elects itself the new coordinator. Process P_i restarts a new copy of the coordinator and sends a message to inform all active processes with priority numbers less than i that P_i is the new coordinator.

However, if an answer is received, P_i begins a time interval T', waiting to receive a message informing it that a process with a higher priority number has been elected. (Some other process is electing itself coordinator, and should report the results within time T'.) If no message is sent within T', then the process with a higher number is assumed to have failed, and process P_i restarts the algorithm.

If P_i is not the coordinator, then, at any time during execution, P_i may receive one of the following two messages from process P_j:

1. P_j is the new coordinator ($j > i$). Process P_i, in turn, records this information.

2. P_j started an election ($j < i$). Process P_i sends a response to P_j and begins its own election algorithm, provided that P_i has not already initiated such an election.

The process that completes its algorithm has the highest number and is elected as the coordinator. It has sent its number to all active processes with smaller numbers. After a failed process recovers, it immediately begins execution of the same algorithm. If there are no active processes with higher numbers, the recovered process forces all processes with lower numbers to let it become the coordinator process, even if there is a currently active coordinator with a lower number. For this reason, the algorithm is termed the **bully algorithm**.

Let us demonstrate the operation of the algorithm with a simple example of a system consisting of processes P_1 through P_4. The operations are as follows:

1. All processes are active; P_4 is the coordinator process.

2. P_1 and P_4 fail. P_2 determines P_4 has failed by sending a request that is not answered within time T. P_2 then begins its election algorithm by sending a request to P_3.

3. P_3 receives the request, responds to P_2, and begins its own algorithm by sending an election request to P_4.

4. P_2 receives P_3's response, and begins waiting for an interval T'.

5. P_4 does not respond within an interval T, so P_3 elects itself the new coordinator, and sends the number 3 to P_2 and P_1 (which P_1 does not receive, since it has failed).

6. Later, when P_1 recovers, it sends an election request to P_2, P_3, and P_4.

7. P_2 and P_3 respond to P_1 and begin their own election algorithms. P_3 will again be elected, using the same events as before.

8. Finally, P_4 recovers and notifies P_1, P_2, and P_3 that it is the current coordinator. (P_4 sends no election requests, since it is the process with the highest number in the system.)

16.4.2 Ring Algorithm

The **ring algorithm** assumes that the links are unidirectional, and that processes send their messages to their right neighbors. The main data structure used by the algorithm is the **active list,** a list that contains the priority numbers of all active processes in the system when the algorithm ends; each process maintains its own active list. The algorithm works as follows:

1. If process P_i detects a coordinator failure, it creates a new active list that is initially empty. It then sends a message *elect (i)* to its right neighbor, and adds the number i to its active list.

2. If P_i receives a message *elect (j)* from the process on the left, it must respond in one of three ways:

    a. If this is the first *elect* message it has seen or sent, P_i creates a new active list with the numbers i and j. It then sends the message *elect (i)*, followed by the message *elect (j)*.

    b. If $i \neq j$ (that is, the message received does not contain P_i's number), then P_i adds j to its active list and forwards the message to its right neighbor.

    c. If $i = j$ (that is, P_i receives the message *elect (i)*), then the active list for P_i now contains the numbers of all the active processes in the system. Process P_i can now determine the largest number in the active list to identify the new coordinator process.

This algorithm does not specify how a recovering process determines the number of the current coordinator process. One solution is to require a recovering process to send an inquiry message. This message is forwarded around the ring to the current coordinator, which in turn sends a reply containing its number.

16.5 ▪ Summary

In a distributed system with no common memory and no common clock, it is sometimes impossible to determine the exact order in which two events occur. The *happened-before* relation is only a partial ordering of the events in distributed systems. We can use timestamps to provide a consistent event ordering in a distributed system.

Mutual exclusion in a distributed environment can be implemented in a variety of ways. In a centralized approach, one of the processes in the system is chosen to coordinate the entry to the critical section. In the fully distributed approach, the decision making is distributed across the entire system. A distributed algorithm, which is applicable to ring-structured networks, is the token-passing approach.

The primary method for dealing with deadlocks in a distributed environment is deadlock detection. The main problem is deciding how to maintain the wait-for graph. Different methods for organizing the wait-for graph include a centralized approach and a fully distributed approach.

Some of the distributed algorithms require the use of a coordinator. If the coordinator fails owing to the failure of the site at which it resides, the system can continue execution only by restarting a new copy of the coordinator on some other site. It does so by maintaining a backup coordinator that is ready to assume responsibility if the coordinator fails. Another approach is to choose the new coordinator after the coordinator has failed. The algorithms that determine where a new copy of the coordinator should be restarted are called *election* algorithms. We can use either of two algorithms—the bully algorithm or a ring algorithm—to elect a new coordinator in case of failures.

▪ Exercises

16.1 Your company is building a computer network, and you have been asked to write an algorithm for achieving distributed mutual exclusion. Which scheme will you use? Explain your choice.

16.2 Why is deadlock detection much more expensive in a distributed environment than it is in a centralized environment?

16.3 Your company is building a computer network, and you are asked to develop a scheme for dealing with the deadlock problem.

   a. Would you use a deadlock-detection scheme, or a deadlock-prevention scheme?

   b. If you were to use a deadlock-prevention scheme, which one would you use? Explain your choice.

   c. If you were to use a deadlock-detection scheme, which one would you use? Explain your choice.

16.4 Consider the following *hierarchical* deadlock-detection algorithm, in which the global wait-for graph is distributed over a number of different *controllers*, which are organized in a tree. Each nonleaf controller maintains a wait-for graph that contains relevant information from the graphs of the controllers in the subtree below it. In particular, let S_A, S_B, and S_C be controllers such that S_C is the lowest common ancestor of S_A and S_B (S_C must be unique, since we are dealing with a tree). Suppose that node T_i appears in the local wait-for graph of controllers S_A and S_B. Then, T_i must also appear in the local wait-for graph of

   - Controller S_C

   - Every controller in the path from S_C to S_A

   - Every controller in the path from S_C to S_B

In addition, if T_i and T_j appear in the wait-for graph of controller S_D and there exists a path from T_i to T_j in the wait-for graph of one of the children of S_D, then an edge $T_i \rightarrow T_j$ must be in the wait-for graph of S_D.

Show that, if a cycle exists in any of the wait-for graphs, then the system is deadlocked.

16.5 Derive an election algorithm for bidirectional rings that is more efficient than the one presented in this chapter. How many messages are needed for n processes?

Bibliographical Notes

The distributed algorithm for extending the *happened-before* relation to a consistent total ordering of all the events in the system (Section 16.1) was developed by Lamport [1978a].

The first general algorithm for implementing mutual exclusion in a distributed environment also was developed by Lamport [1978a]. Lamport's scheme requires $3 \times (n - 1)$ messages per critical-section entry. Subsequently, Ricart and Agrawala [1981] proposed a distributed algorithm that requires only

$2 \times (n-1)$ messages. Their algorithm was presented in Section 16.2.2. A square root algorithm for distributed mutual exclusion was presented by Maekawa [1985]. The token-passing algorithm for ring-structured systems presented in Section 16.2.3 was developed by Le Lann [1977]. Discussions concerning mutual exclusion in computer networks were presented by Carvalho and Roucairol [1983]. An efficient and fault-tolerant solution of distributed mutual exclusion was presented by Agrawal and El Abbadi [1991].

Distributed synchronization was discussed by Reed and Kanodia [1979] (shared-memory environment), Lamport [1978a, 1978b], and Schneider [1982] (totally disjoint processes). A distributed solution to the dining-philosophers problem was presented by Chang [1980].

Rosenkrantz and colleagues [1978] reported the timestamp distributed deadlock-prevention algorithm. The fully distributed deadlock-detection scheme presented in Section 16.3.2 was developed by Obermarck [1982]. The hierarchical deadlock-detection scheme of Exercise 16.2 appeared in Menasce and Muntz [1979].

The bully algorithm was presented by Garcia-Molina [1982]. The election algorithm for a ring-structured system was written by Le Lann [1977].

Chapter 17

DISTRIBUTED FILE SYSTEMS

In the previous chapter, we discussed network construction and the low-level protocols needed for messages to be transferred between systems. Now we discuss one use of this infrastructure. A **distributed file system** (DFS) is a distributed implementation of the classical time-sharing model of a file system, where multiple users share files and storage resources (Chapter 11). The purpose of a DFS is to support the same kind of sharing when the files are physically dispersed among the various sites of a distributed system.

In this chapter, we discuss the various ways a DFS can be designed and implemented. First, we discuss common concepts on which DFSs are based. Then, we illustrate our concepts by examining one influential distributed file system—NFS.

17.1 ■ Background

A distributed system is a collection of loosely coupled machines interconnected by a communication network. We use the term **machine** to denote either a mainframe or a workstation. From the point of view of a specific machine in a distributed system, the rest of the machines and their respective resources are **remote,** whereas the machine's own resources are **local**.

To explain the structure of a DFS, we need to define the terms *service, server,* and *client*. A **service** is a software entity running on one or more machines and providing a particular type of function to a priori unknown clients. A **server** is the service software running on a single machine. A **client** is a process that can invoke a service using a set of operations that forms its **client interface**. Sometimes, a lower-level interface is defined for the actual cross-machine interaction; it is the **intermachine interface**.

Using this terminology, we say that a file system provides file services to clients. A client interface for a file service is formed by a set of primitive **file operations,** such as create a file, delete a file, read from a file, and write to a file. The primary hardware component that a file server controls is a set of local secondary-storage devices (usually, magnetic disks), on which files are stored, and from which they are retrieved according to the client requests.

A DFS is a file system whose clients, servers, and storage devices are dispersed among the machines of a distributed system. Accordingly, service activity has to be carried out across the network, and instead of a single centralized data repository, there are multiple and independent storage devices. As will become evident, the concrete configuration and implementation of a DFS may vary. There are configurations where servers run on dedicated machines, as well as configurations where a machine can be both a server and a client. A DFS can be implemented as part of a distributed operating system, or alternatively by a software layer whose task is to manage the communication between conventional operating systems and file systems. The distinctive features of a DFS are the multiplicity and autonomy of clients and servers in the system.

Ideally, a DFS should appear to its clients to be a conventional, centralized file system. The multiplicity and dispersion of its servers and storage devices should be made transparent. That is, the client interface of a DFS should not distinguish between local and remote files. It is up to the DFS to locate the files and to arrange for the transport of the data. A transparent DFS facilitates user mobility by bringing the user's environment (that is, home directory) to wherever a user logs in.

The most important *performance* measurement of a DFS is the amount of time needed to satisfy various service requests. In conventional systems, this time consists of disk access time and a small amount of CPU processing time. In a DFS, however, a remote access has the additional overhead attributed to the distributed structure. This overhead includes the time needed to deliver the request to a server, as well as the time for getting the response across the network back to the client. For each direction, in addition to the actual transfer of the information, there is the CPU overhead of running the communication protocol software. The performance of a DFS can be viewed as another dimension of the DFS's transparency. That is, the performance of an ideal DFS would be comparable to that of a conventional file system.

The fact that a DFS manages a set of dispersed storage devices is the DFS's key distinguishing feature. The overall storage space managed by a DFS is composed of different, and remotely located, smaller storage spaces. Usually, there is correspondence between these constituent storage spaces and sets of files. We use the term **component unit** to denote the smallest set of files that can be stored on a single machine, independently from other units. All files belonging to the same component unit must reside in the same location.

17.2 ■ Naming and Transparency

Naming is a mapping between logical and physical objects. For instance, users deal with logical data objects represented by file names, whereas the system manipulates physical blocks of data, stored on disk tracks. Usually, a user refers to a file by a textual name. The latter is mapped to a lower-level numerical identifier that in turn is mapped to disk blocks. This multilevel mapping provides users with an abstraction of a file that hides the details of how and where on the disk the file is actually stored.

In a **transparent DFS,** a new dimension is added to the abstraction: that of hiding where in the network the file is located. In a conventional file system, the range of the naming mapping is an address within a disk. In a DFS, this range is augmented to include the specific machine on whose disk the file is stored. Going one step farther with the concept of treating files as abstractions leads to the possibility of **file replication**. Given a file name, the mapping returns a set of the locations of this file's replicas. In this abstraction, both the existence of multiple copies and their location are hidden.

17.2.1 Naming Structures

There are two related notions regarding name mappings in a DFS that need to be differentiated:

- **Location transparency:** The name of a file does not reveal any hint of the file's physical storage location.

- **Location independence:** The name of a file does not need to be changed when the file's physical storage location changes.

Both definitions are relative to the level of naming discussed previously, since files have different names at different levels (that is, user-level textual names, and system-level numerical identifiers). A location-independent naming scheme is a dynamic mapping, since it can map the same file name to different locations at two different times. Therefore, location independence is a stronger property than is location transparency.

In practice, most of the current DFSs provide a static, location-transparent mapping for user-level names. These systems, however, do not support **file migration;** that is, changing the location of a file automatically is impossible. Hence, the notion of location independence is irrelevant for these systems. Files are associated permanently with a specific set of disk blocks. Files and disks can be moved between machines manually, but file migration implies an automatic, operating-system initiated action. Only Andrew and a few experimental file systems support location independence and file mobility. Andrew supports file mobility mainly for administrative purposes. A protocol provides migration of Andrew's component units to satisfy high-level user requests, without changing either the user-level names, or the low-level names of the corresponding files.

There are a few aspects that can further differentiate location independence and static location transparency:

- Divorce of data from location, as exhibited by location independence, provides better abstraction for files. A file name should denote the file's most significant attributes, which are its contents, rather than its location. Location-independent files can be viewed as logical data containers that are not attached to a specific storage location. If only static location transparency is supported, the file name still denotes a specific, although hidden, set of physical disk blocks.

- Static location transparency provides users with a convenient way to share data. Users can share remote files by simply naming the files in a location-transparent manner, as though the files were local. Nevertheless, sharing the storage space is cumbersome, because logical names are still statically attached to physical storage devices. Location independence promotes sharing the storage space itself, as well as the data objects. When files can be mobilized, the overall, systemwide storage space looks like a single, virtual resource. A possible benefit of such a view is the ability to balance the utilization of disks across the system.

- Location independence separates the naming hierarchy from the storage-devices hierarchy and from the intercomputer structure. By contrast, if static location transparency is used (although names are transparent), we can easily expose the correspondence between component units and machines. The machines are configured in a pattern similar to the naming structure. This configuration may restrict the architecture of the system unnecessarily and conflict with other considerations. A server in charge of a root directory is an example of a structure that is dictated by the naming hierarchy and contradicts decentralization guidelines.

Once the separation of name and location has been completed, files residing on remote server systems may be accessed by various clients. In fact, these clients may be **diskless** and rely on servers to provide all files, including the operating-system kernel. Special protocols are needed for the boot sequence, however. Consider the problem of getting the kernel to a diskless workstation. The diskless workstation has no kernel, so it cannot use the DFS code to retrieve the kernel. Instead, a special boot protocol, stored in read-only memory (ROM) on the client, is invoked. It enables networking and retrieves only one special file (the kernel or boot code) from a fixed location. Once the kernel is copied over the network and loaded, its DFS makes all the other operating-system files available. The advantages of diskless clients are many, including lower cost (because no disk is needed on each machine) and greater convenience (when an operating-system upgrade occurs, only the server copy needs to be modified, rather than all the clients as well). The disadvantages are the added complexity of the boot protocols and the performance loss resulting from the use of a network rather than of a local disk.

The current trend is to use clients with local disks. Disk drives are rapidly increasing in capacity and decreasing in cost, with new generations appearing every year or so. The same cannot be said for networks, which evolve every 5 to 10 years. Overall, systems are growing more quickly than are networks, so extra work is needed to limit network access to improve system throughput.

17.2.2   Naming Schemes

There are three main approaches to naming schemes in a DFS. In the simplest approach, files are named by some combination of their host name and local name, which guarantees a unique systemwide name. In Ibis, for instance, a file is identified uniquely by the name `host:local-name`, where `local-name` is a UNIX-like path. This naming scheme is neither location transparent nor location independent. Nevertheless, the same file operations can be used for both local and remote files. The DFS is structured as a collection of isolated component units that are entire conventional file systems. In this first approach, component units remained isolated, although means are provided to refer to a remote file. We do not consider this scheme any further in this text.

The second approach was popularized by Sun's Network File System (NFS). NFS is the file-system component of ONC+, a networking package that is supported by many UNIX vendors. NFS provides means to attach remote directories to local directories, thus giving the appearance of a coherent directory tree. Early NFS versions allowed only previously mounted remote directories to be accessed transparently. With the advent of the **automount** feature, mounts are done on demand, based on a table of mount points and file-structure names. Components are integrated to support transparent sharing, although this integration is limited and is not uniform, because each machine may attach different remote directories to its tree. The resulting structure is versatile. Usually, it is a forest of UNIX trees with shared subtrees.

We can achieve total integration of the component file systems by using the third approach. A single global name structure spans all the files in the system. Ideally, the composed file-system structure is isomorphic to the structure of a conventional file system. In practice, however, the many special files (for example, UNIX device files and machine-specific binary directories) make this goal difficult to attain.

An important criterion for evaluation of the naming structures is their **administrative complexity**. The most complex and most difficult-to-maintain structure is the NFS structure. Because any remote directory can be attached anywhere onto the local directory tree, the resulting hierarchy can be highly unstructured. The effect of a server becoming unavailable is that some arbitrary set of directories on different machines becomes unavailable. In addition, a separate accreditation mechanism controls which machine is allowed to attach which directory to its tree. This mechanism can lead to the situation in which a user can access a remote directory tree on one client, whereas access is denied to that user on another client.

17.2.3 Implementation Techniques

Implementation of transparent naming requires a provision for the mapping of a file name to the associated location. Keeping this mapping manageable calls for aggregating sets of files into component units, and providing the mapping on a component unit basis rather than on a single-file basis. This aggregation serves administrative purposes as well. UNIX-like systems use the hierarchical directory tree to provide name-to-location mapping, and to aggregate files recursively into directories.

To enhance the availability of the crucial mapping information, we can use methods such as replication, local caching, or both. As we noted, location independence means that the mapping changes over time; hence, replicating the mapping renders a simple yet consistent update of this information impossible. A technique to overcome this obstacle is to introduce low-level, **location-independent file identifiers**. Textual file names are mapped to lower-level file identifiers that indicate to which component unit the file belongs. These identifiers are still location independent. They can be replicated and cached freely without being invalidated by migration of component units. A second level of mapping, which maps component units to locations and needs a simple yet consistent update mechanism, is the inevitable price. Implementing UNIX-like directory trees using these low-level, location-independent identifiers makes the whole hierarchy invariant under component-unit migration. The only aspect that does change is the component-unit–location mapping.

A common way to implement these low-level identifiers is to use structured names. These names are bit strings that usually have two parts. The first part identifies the component unit to which the file belongs; the second part identifies the particular file within the unit. Variants with more parts are possible. The invariant of structured names, however, is that individual parts of the name are unique at all times only within the context of the rest of the parts. We can obtain uniqueness at all times by taking care not to reuse a name that is still used, by adding sufficiently more bits (this method is used in Andrew), or by using a timestamp as one of the parts of the name (as done in Apollo Domain). Another way to view this process is that we are taking a location-transparent system, such as Ibis, and adding another level of abstraction to produce a location-independent naming scheme.

The use of the techniques of aggregation of files into component units, and of lower-level location-independent file identifiers, is exemplified in Andrew and Locus.

17.3 ■ Remote File Access

Consider a user who requests access to a remote file. Assuming that the server storing the file was located by the naming scheme, the actual data transfer to satisfy the user request for the remote access must take place.

One way to achieve this transfer is through a **remote-service mechanism,** whereby requests for accesses are delivered to the server, the server machine performs the accesses, and their results are forwarded back to the user. One of the most common ways of implementing remote service is the **remote procedure call (RPC)** paradigm, which we discussed in Section 15.2. There is a direct analogy between disk-access methods in conventional file systems and the remote-service method in a DFS: Using the remote-service method is analogous to performing a disk access for each access request.

To ensure reasonable performance of a remote-service mechanism, we can use a form of **caching**. In conventional file systems, the rationale for caching is to reduce disk I/O (thereby increasing performance), whereas in DFSs, the goal is to reduce both network traffic and disk I/O. In the following, we discuss the implementation of caching in a DFS, and contrast it with the basic remote-service paradigm.

17.3.1 Basic Caching Scheme

The concept of caching is simple. If the data needed to satisfy the access request are not already cached, then a copy of those data is brought from the server to the client system. Accesses are performed on the cached copy. The idea is to retain recently accessed disk blocks in the cache, so that repeated accesses to the same information can be handled locally, without additional network traffic. A replacement policy (for example, least recently used) keeps the cache size bounded. There is no direct correspondence between accesses and traffic to the server. Files are still identified with one master copy residing at the server machine, but copies of (parts of) the file are scattered in different caches. When a cached copy is modified, the changes need to be reflected on the master copy to preserve the relevant consistency semantics. The problem of keeping the cached copies consistent with the master file is the **cache-consistency problem,** which we discuss in Section 17.3.4. DFS caching could just as easily be called **network virtual memory:** It acts similarly to demand-paged virtual memory, except that the backing store is not a local disk, but rather is a remote server.

The granularity of the cached data can vary from blocks of a file to an entire file. Usually, more data are cached than are needed to satisfy a single access, so that many accesses can be served by the cached data. This procedure is much like disk read-ahead (Section 11.9.2). The Andrew system caches files in large chunks (64K). The other systems discussed in this chapter support caching of individual blocks driven by clients' demands. Increasing the caching unit increases the hit ratio, but also increases the miss penalty because each miss requires more data to be transferred. It also increases the potential for consistency problems. Selecting the unit of caching involves considering parameters such as the network transfer unit and the RPC protocol service unit (in case an RPC protocol is used). The network transfer unit (for Ethernet, a packet) is about 1.5K, so larger units of cached data need to be disassembled for delivery and reassembled on reception.

Block size and the total cache size are obviously of importance for block-caching schemes. In UNIX-like systems, common block sizes are 4K or 8K. For large caches (over 1 megabyte), large block sizes (over 8K) are beneficial. For smaller caches, large block sizes are less beneficial because they result in fewer blocks in the cache, and a lower hit ratio.

17.3.2 Cache Location

Where should the cached data be stored? Disk caches have one clear advantage over main-memory cache: They are reliable. Modifications to cached data are lost in a crash if the cache is kept in volatile memory. Moreover, if the cached data are kept on disk, they are still there during recovery and there is no need to fetch them again. On the other hand, main-memory caches have several advantages of their own:

- Main-memory caches permit workstations to be diskless.

- Data can be accessed more quickly from a cache in main memory than from one on a disk.

- The current technology trend is toward bigger and less expensive memories. The achieved performance speedup is predicted to outweigh the advantages of disk caches.

- The server caches (the ones used to speed up disk I/O) will be in main memory regardless of where user caches are located; if we use main-memory caches on the user machine too, we can build a single caching mechanism for use by both servers and users (as is done in Sprite).

Many remote-access implementations can be thought of as a hybrid of caching and remote service. In NFS, for instance, the implementation is based on remote service but is augmented with caching for performance. On the other hand, Sprite's implementation is based on caching, but under certain circumstances a remote-service method is adopted. Thus, to evaluate the two methods, we evaluate to what degree either method is emphasized.

17.3.3 Cache-Update Policy

The policy used to write modified data blocks back to the server's master copy has a critical effect on the system's performance and reliability. The simplest policy is to write data through to disk as soon as they are placed on any cache. The advantage of such a **write-through policy** is reliability: Little information is lost when a client system crashes. However, this policy requires each write access to wait until the information is sent to the server, so it causes poor write performance. Caching with write-through is equivalent to using remote service for write accesses and exploiting caching for only read accesses.

An alternative is the **delayed-write policy,** where we delay updates to the master copy. Modifications are written to the cache, then are written through to the server at a later time. This policy has two advantages over write-through. First, because writes are to the cache, write accesses complete much more quickly. Second, data may be overwritten before they are written back, in which case all but the last update never needs to be written at all. Unfortunately, delayed write schemes introduce reliability problems, since unwritten data are lost whenever a user machine crashes.

There are several variations of the delayed-write policy that differ in when modified data blocks are flushed to the server. One alternative is to flush a block when it is about to be ejected from the client's cache. This option can result in good performance, but some blocks can reside in the client's cache a long time before they are written back to the server. A compromise between this alternative and the write-through policy is to scan the cache at regular intervals and to flush blocks that have been modified since the most recent scan, just as UNIX scans its local cache. Sprite uses this policy with a 30-second interval. NFS uses this policy as well for file data, but once a write is issued to the server during a cache flush, the write must reach the server's disk before it is considered to be complete. NFS treats metadata (directory data and file-attribute data) differently. Any metadata changes are issued synchronously to the server. Thus, file loss and directory-structure corruption are avoided on client or server crash.

Yet another variation on delayed-write is to write data back to the server when the file is closed. This **write-on-close policy** is used in the Andrew system. In the case of files that are open for short periods or are modified rarely, this policy does not significantly reduce network traffic. In addition, the write-on-close policy requires the closing process to delay while the file is written through, which reduces the performance advantages of delayed-writes. The performance advantages of this policy over delayed-write with more frequent flushing are apparent for files that are open for long periods and are modified frequently.

17.3.4 Consistency

A client machine is faced with the problem of deciding whether or not a locally cached copy of the data is consistent with the master copy (and hence can be used). If the client machine determines that its cached data are out of date, accesses can no longer be served by those cached data. An up-to-date copy of the data needs to be cached. There are two approaches to verify the validity of cached data:

- **Client-initiated approach:** The client initiates a validity check in which it contacts the server and checks whether the local data are consistent with the master copy. The frequency of the validity check is the crux of this approach and determines the resulting consistency semantics. It can range from a check before every access, to a check on only first access to a file (on file open, basically). Every access that is coupled with a validity check is delayed, compared with an access served immediately by the cache. Alternatively, a check can be initiated every fixed interval of time. Depending on its frequency, the validity check can load both the network and the server.

- **Server-initiated approach:** The server records, for each client, the (parts of) files that it caches. When the server detects a potential inconsistency, it must react. A potential for inconsistency occurs when a file is cached by two different clients in conflicting modes. If UNIX semantics (Section 11.1.6), is implemented, we can resolve the potential inconsistency by having the server play an active role. The server must be notified whenever a file is opened, and the intended mode (read or write mode) must be indicated for every open. Assuming such notification, the server can act when it detects a file that is opened simultaneously in conflicting modes by disabling caching for that particular file. Actually, disabling caching results in switching to a remote-service mode of operation.

17.3.5 A Comparison of Caching and Remote Services

Essentially, the choice between caching and remote service trades off a potentially increased performance with decreased simplicity. We evaluate this trade-off by listing the advantages and disadvantages of the two methods:

- A substantial number of the remote accesses can be handled efficiently by the local cache when caching is used. Capitalizing on locality in file-access patterns makes caching even more attractive. Thus, most of the remote accesses will be served as fast as will local ones. Moreover, servers are contacted only occasionally, rather than for each access. Consequently, server load and network traffic are reduced, and the potential for scalability is enhanced. By contrast, every remote access is handled across the network when the remote-service method is used. The penalty in network traffic, server load, and performance is obvious.

- Total network overhead in transmitting big chunks of data (as is done in caching) is lower than when series of responses to specific requests are transmitted (as in the remote-service method).

- Disk-access routines on the server may be better optimized if it is known that requests are always for large, contiguous segments of data, rather than for random disk blocks.

- The cache-consistency problem is the major drawback of caching. In access patterns that exhibit infrequent writes, caching is superior. However, when writes are frequent, the mechanisms employed to overcome the consistency problem incur substantial overhead in terms of performance, network traffic, and server load.

- So that caching will confer a benefit, execution should be carried out on machines that have either local disks or large main memories. Remote access on diskless, small-memory-capacity machines should be done through the remote-service method.

- In caching, since data are transferred en masse between the server and client, rather than in response to the specific needs of a file operation, the lower intermachine interface is different from the upper-user interface. The remote-service paradigm, on the other hand, is just an extension of the local file-system interface across the network. Thus, the intermachine interface mirrors the local user-file-system interface.

17.4 ■ Stateful Versus Stateless Service

There are two approaches to server-side information: Either the server tracks each file being accessed by each client, or it simply provides blocks as they are requested by the client without knowledge of those blocks' usage.

The typical scenario of a **stateful file service** is as follows. A client must perform an open on a file before accessing that file. The server fetches information about the file from its disk, stores it in its memory, and gives the client a connection identifier that is unique to the client and the open file. (In UNIX terms, the server fetches the inode and gives the client a file descriptor, which serves as an index to an in-core table of inodes.) This identifier is used for subsequent accesses until the session ends. A stateful service is characterized as a connection between the client and the server during a session. Either on closing the file, or by a garbage-collection mechanism, the server must reclaim the main-memory space used by clients who are no longer active.

The advantage of stateful service is increased performance. File information is cached in main memory and can be accessed easily via the connection identifier, thereby saving disk accesses. In addition, a stateful server would know whether a file were open for sequential access and could therefore read ahead the next blocks. Stateless servers cannot do so, since they have no knowledge of the purpose of the client's requests. The key point regarding fault tolerance in a stateful service approach is that main-memory information is kept by the server about its clients.

A **stateless file server** avoids this state information by making each request self-contained. That is, each request identifies the file and the position in the file (for read and write accesses) in full. The server does not need to keep a table of open files in main memory, although it usually does so for efficiency reasons. Moreover, there is no need to establish and terminate a connection by open and close operations. They are totally redundant, since each file operation stands on its own and is not considered as part of a session. A client process would open a file, and that open would not result in a remote message being sent. Reads and writes would, of course, take place as remote messages (or cache lookups). The final close by the client would again result in only a local operation.

The distinction between stateful and stateless service becomes evident when we consider the effects of a crash occurring during a service activity. A stateful server loses all its volatile state in a crash. Ensuring the graceful recovery of such a server involves restoring this state—usually by a recovery protocol based on a dialog with clients. Less graceful recovery requires that the operations that were underway when the crash occurred be aborted. A different problem is caused by client failures. The server needs to become aware of such failures, so that it can reclaim space allocated to record the state of crashed client processes. This phenomenon is sometimes referred to as **orphan detection and elimination**.

A stateless server avoids these problems, since a newly reincarnated server can respond to a self-contained request without any difficulty. Therefore, the effects of server failures and recovery are almost unnoticeable. There is no difference between a slow server and a recovering server from a client's point of view. The client keeps retransmitting its request if it receives no response.

The penalty for using the robust stateless service is longer request messages, and slower processing of requests, since there is no in-core information to speed the processing. In addition, stateless service imposes additional constraints on the design of the DFS. First, since each request identifies the target file, a uniform, systemwide, low-level naming scheme should be used. Translating remote to local names for each request would cause even slower processing of the requests. Second, since clients retransmit requests for file operations, these operations must be **idempotent;** that is, each operation must have the same effect and return the same output if executed several times consecutively. Self-contained read and write accesses are idempotent, as long as they use an absolute byte count to indicate the position within the file they access and do not rely on an incremental offset (as done in UNIX read and write system calls). However, we must be careful when implementing destructive operations (such as deleting a file) to make them idempotent too.

In some environments, a stateful service is a necessity. If the server employs the server-initiated method for cache validation, it cannot provide stateless service, since it maintains a record of which files are cached by which clients.

The way UNIX uses file descriptors and implicit offsets is inherently stateful. Servers must maintain tables to map the file descriptors to inodes, and must store the current offset within a file. This requirement is why NFS, which employs a stateless service, does not use file descriptors, and does include an explicit offset in every access.

17.5 ■ File Replication

Replication of files on different machines is a useful redundancy for improving availability. Multimachine replication can benefit performance too: Selecting a nearby replica to serve an access request results in shorter service time.

The basic requirement of a replication scheme is that different replicas of the same file reside on failure-independent machines. That is, the availability of one replica is not affected by the availability of the rest of the replicas. This obvious requirement implies that replication management is inherently a location-opaque activity. Provisions for placing a replica on a particular machine must be available.

It is desirable to hide the details of replication from users. It is the task of the naming scheme to map a replicated file name to a particular replica. The existence of replicas should be invisible to higher levels. At lower levels, however, the replicas must be distinguished from one another by different lower-level names. Another transparency requirement is providing replication control at higher levels. Replication control includes determination of the degree of replication and of the placement of replicas. Under certain circumstances, it is desirable to expose these details to users. Locus, for instance, provides users and system administrators with mechanisms to control the replication scheme.

The main problem associated with replicas is their update. From a user's point of view, replicas of a file denote the same logical entity, and thus an update to any replica must be reflected on all other replicas. More precisely, the relevant consistency semantics must be preserved when accesses to replicas are viewed as virtual accesses to the replicas' logical files. If consistency is not of primary importance, it can be sacrificed for availability and performance. In this fundamental tradeoff in the area of fault tolerance, the choice is between preserving consistency at all costs, thereby creating a potential for indefinite blocking, and sacrificing consistency under some (we hope rare) circumstance of catastrophic failures for the sake of guaranteed progress. Locus, for example, employs replication extensively and sacrifices consistency in the case of network partition, for the sake of availability of files for read and write accesses.

Ibis uses a variation of the primary-copy approach. The domain of the name mapping is a pair <primary-replica-identifier, local-replica-identifier>. If there is no local replica, a special value is used. Thus, the mapping is relative to a machine. If the local replica is the primary one, the pair contains two identical identifiers. Ibis supports demand replication, an automatic replication-control policy similar to whole-file caching. Under demand replication, reading of a nonlocal replica causes it to be cached locally, thereby generating a new nonprimary replica. Updates are performed on only the primary copy and cause all other replicas to be invalidated by sending appropriate messages. Atomic and serialized invalidation of all nonprimary replicas is not guaranteed. Hence, a stale replica may be considered valid. To satisfy remote write accesses, we migrate the primary copy to the requesting machine.

17.6 ■ Example System: NFS

The Network File System (NFS) is both an implementation and a specification of a software system for accessing remote files across LANs (or even WANs). NFS is part of ONC+, which most UNIX vendors and some PC operating systems are supporting. The implementation is part of the Solaris operating system, which is a modified version of UNIX SVR4, running on Sun workstations and other hardware. It uses either the TCP/IP or UDP/IP protocols (depending on the interconnecting network). The specification and the implementation are intertwined in our description of NFS. Whenever detail is needed, we refer to the Sun implementation; whenever the description is general, it applies to the specification also.

17.6.1 Overview

NFS views a set of interconnected workstations as a set of independent machines with independent file systems. The goal is to allow some degree of sharing among these file systems (on explicit request) in a transparent manner. Sharing is based on a client–server relationship. A machine may be, and often is, both a client and a server. Sharing is allowed between any pair of machines, rather than with only dedicated server machines. To ensure machine independence, sharing of a remote file system affects only the client machine and no other machine.

So that a remote directory will be accessible in a transparent manner from a particular machine—say, from *M1*—a client of that machine has to carry out a mount operation first. The semantics of the operation are that a remote

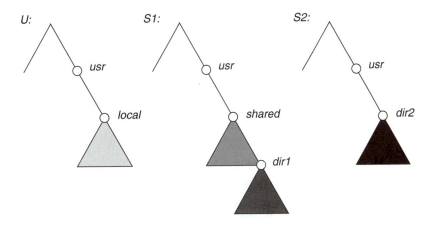

Figure 17.1   Three independent file systems.

directory is mounted over a directory of a local file system. Once the mount operation is completed, the mounted directory looks like an integral subtree of the local file system, replacing the subtree descending from the local directory. The local directory becomes the name of the root of the newly mounted directory. Specification of the remote directory as an argument for the mount operation is done in a nontransparent manner; the location (that is, host name) of the remote directory has to be provided. However, from then on, users on machine *M1* can access files in the remote directory in a totally transparent manner.

To illustrate file mounting, we consider the file system depicted in Figure 17.1, where the triangles represent subtrees of directories that are of interest. In this figure, three independent file systems of machines named *U, S1,* and *S2* are shown. At this point, at each machine, only the local files can be accessed. In Figure 17.2(a), the effects of the mounting of *S1:/usr/shared* over *U:/usr/local* are shown. This figure depicts the view users on *U* have of their file system. Observe that they can access any file within the *dir1* directory, for instance, using the prefix */usr/local/dir1* on *U* after the mount is complete. The original directory */usr/local* on that machine is no longer visible.

Subject to access-rights accreditation, potentially any file system, or any directory within a file system, can be mounted remotely on top of any local directory. Diskless workstations can even mount their own roots from servers.

Cascading mounts are also permitted in some NFS implementations. That is, a file system can be mounted over another file system that is not a local one, but rather is a remotely mounted one. However, a machine is affected by only those mounts that it has itself invoked.

By mounting a remote file system, the client does not gain access to other file systems that were, by chance, mounted over the former file system. Thus, the mount mechanism does not exhibit a transitivity property. In Figure 17.2(b),

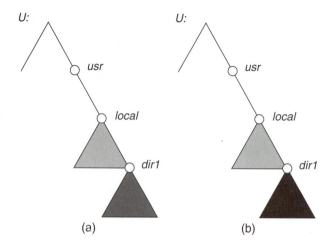

Figure 17.2   Mounting in NFS. (a) Mounts. (b) Cascading mounts.

we illustrate cascading mounts by continuing our previous example. The figure shows the result of mounting *S2:/usr/dir2* over *U:/usr/local/dir1*, which is already remotely mounted from *S1*. Users can access files within *dir2* on *U* using the prefix */usr/local/dir1*. If a shared file system is mounted over a user's home directories on all machines in a network, a user can log in to any workstation and get his home environment. This property permits **user mobility**.

One of the design goals of NFS was to operate in a heterogeneous environment of different machines, operating systems, and network architectures. The NFS specification is independent of these media and thus encourages other implementations. This independence is achieved through the use of RPC primitives built on top of an External Data Representation (XDR) protocol used between two implementation-independent interfaces. Hence, if the system consists of heterogeneous machines and file systems that are properly interfaced to NFS, file systems of different types can be mounted both locally and remotely.

The NFS specification distinguishes between the services provided by a mount mechanism and the actual remote-file-access services. Accordingly, two separate protocols are specified for these services; a **mount protocol**, and a protocol for remote file accesses, the **NFS protocol**. The protocols are specified as sets of RPCs. These RPCs are the building blocks used to implement transparent remote file access.

17.6.2 The Mount Protocol

The mount protocol establishes the initial logical connection between a server and a client. In Sun's implementation, each machine has a server process, outside the kernel, performing the protocol functions.

A mount operation includes the name of the remote directory to be mounted and the name of the server machine storing it. The mount request is mapped to the corresponding RPC and is forwarded to the mount server running on the specific server machine. The server maintains an **export list** (the */etc/dfs/dfstab* in Solaris, which can be edited by only a superuser), which specifies local file systems that it exports for mounting, along with names of machines that are permitted to mount them. Unfortunately, this list has a maximum length, so NFS is limited in scalability. Recall that any directory within an exported file system can be mounted remotely by an accredited machine. Hence, a component unit is such a directory. When the server receives a mount request that conforms to its export list, it returns to the client a **file handle** that serves as the key for further accesses to files within the mounted file system. The file handle contains all the information that the server needs to distinguish an individual file it stores. In UNIX terms, the file handle consists of a file-system identifier, and an inode number to identify the exact mounted directory within the exported file system.

The server also maintains a list of the client machines and the corresponding currently mounted directories. This list is used mainly for administrative purposes—for instance, for notifying all clients that the server is going down. Addition and deletion of entries in this list are the only ways that the server state can be affected by the mount protocol.

Usually, a system has a static mounting preconfiguration that is established at boot time (*/etc/vfstab* in Solaris); however, this layout can be modified. In addition to the actual mount procedure, the mount protocol includes several other procedures, such as unmount and return export list.

17.6.3 The NFS Protocol

The NFS protocol provides a set of RPCs for remote file operations. The procedures support the following operations:

- Searching for a file within a directory
- Reading a set of directory entries
- Manipulating links and directories
- Accessing file attributes
- Reading and writing files

These procedures can be invoked only after a file handle for the remotely mounted directory has been established.

The omission of open and close operations is intentional. A prominent feature of NFS servers is that they are *stateless*. Servers do not maintain information about their clients from one access to another access. There are no parallels to UNIX's open-files table or file structures on the server side. Consequently, each request has to provide a full set of arguments, including a unique file identifier and an absolute offset inside the file for the appropriate operations. The resulting design is robust; no special measures need to be taken to recover a server after a crash. File operations need to be idempotent for this purpose.

Maintaining the list of clients that we mentioned seems to violate the statelessness of the server. However, this list is not essential for the correct operation of the client or the server, and hence it does not need to be restored after a server crash. Consequently, it might include inconsistent data and is treated as only a hint.

A further implication of the stateless-server philosophy and a result of the synchrony of an RPC is that modified data (including indirection and status blocks) must be committed to the server's disk before results are returned to the client. That is, a client can cache write blocks, but when it flushes them to the server, it assumes that they have reached the server's disks. Thus, a server crash and recovery will be invisible to a client; all blocks that the server is managing for the client will be intact. The consequent performance penalty can be large, because the advantages of caching are lost. In fact, there are several products now on the market that specifically address this NFS problem by providing fast stable storage (usually memory with battery backup) in which to store blocks written by NFS. These blocks remain intact even after system crash, and are written from this stable storage to disk periodically.

A single NFS write procedure call is guaranteed to be atomic, and also is not intermixed with other write calls to the same file. The NFS protocol, however, does not provide concurrency-control mechanisms. A write system call may be broken down into several RPC writes, because each NFS write or read call can contain up to 8K of data and UDP packets are limited to 1500 bytes. As a result, two users writing to the same remote file may get their data intermixed. The claim is that, because lock management is inherently stateful, a service outside the NFS should provide locking (and Solaris does). Users are advised to coordinate access to shared files using mechanisms outside the scope of NFS.

17.6.4 The NFS Architecture

The NFS architecture consists of three major layers; it is depicted schematically in Figure 17.3. The first layer is the UNIX file-system interface, based on the open, read, write, and close calls, and file descriptors.

The second layer is called the **Virtual File System** (**VFS**) layer; it serves two important functions:

1. It separates file-system generic operations from their implementation by defining a clean VFS interface. Several implementations for the VFS interface may coexist on the same machine, allowing transparent access to different types of file systems mounted locally.

2. The VFS is based on a file-representation structure called a **vnode** that contains a numerical designator for a file that is networkwide unique. (Recall that UNIX inodes are unique within only a single file system.) The kernel maintains one vnode structure for each active node (file or directory).

Thus, the VFS distinguishes local files from remote ones, and local files are further distinguished according to their file-system types.

Like the standard UNIX kernel, the kernel maintains a table (*/etc/mtab* in UNIX) recording the details of the mounts in which it took part as a client. Further, the vnodes for each directory that is mounted over are kept in memory at all times and are marked, so that requests concerning such directories will be redirected to the corresponding mounted file systems via the mount table. Essentially, the vnode structures, complemented by the mount table, provide a pointer for every file to its parent file system, as well as to the file system over which it is mounted.

The VFS activates file-system–specific operations to handle local requests according to their file-system types, and calls the NFS protocol procedures for remote requests. File handles are constructed from the relevant vnodes and are passed as arguments to these procedures. The layer implementing the NFS protocol is the bottom layer of the architecture and is called the NFS service layer.

As an illustration of the architecture, let us trace how an operation on an already-open remote file is handled (follow the example on Figure 17.3). The client initiates the operation by a regular system call. The operating-system

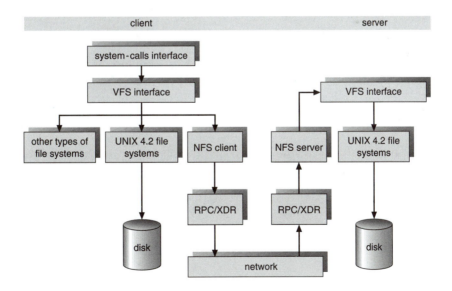

Figure 17.3 Schematic view of the NFS architecture.

layer maps this call to a VFS operation on the appropriate vnode. The VFS layer identifies the file as a remote one and invokes the appropriate NFS procedure. An RPC call is made to the NFS service layer at the remote server. This call is reinjected to the VFS layer on the remote system, which finds that it is local and invokes the appropriate file-system operation. This path is retraced to return the result. An advantage of this architecture is that the client and the server are identical; thus, a machine may be a client, or a server, or both.

The actual service on each server is performed by several kernel processes that provide a temporary substitute to a lightweight process (threads) facility.

17.6.5 Path-Name Translation

Path-name translation is done by breaking the path into component names and performing a separate NFS lookup call for every pair of component name and directory vnode. Once a mount point is crossed, every component lookup causes a separate RPC to the server (see Figure 17.4). This expensive path-name–traversal scheme is needed, since each client has a unique layout of its logical name space, dictated by the mounts it performed. It would have been much more efficient to hand a server a path name and to receive a target vnode once a mount point was encountered. At any point, however, there can be another mount point for the particular client of which the stateless server is unaware.

So that lookup is fast, a directory name lookup cache on the client's side holds the vnodes for remote directory names. This cache speeds up references to files with the same initial path name. The directory cache is discarded when attributes returned from the server do not match the attributes of the cached vnode.

Recall that mounting a remote file system on top of another already-mounted remote file system (cascading mount) is allowed in some implementations of NFS. However, a server cannot act as an intermediary between a client and another server. Instead, a client must establish a direct client–server

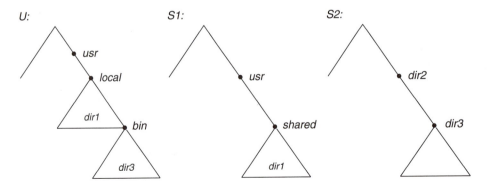

Figure 17.4   Path-name translation.

connection with the second server by directly mounting the desired directory. When a client has a cascading mount, more than one server can be involved in a path-name traversal. However, each component lookup is performed between the original client and some server. Therefore, when a client does a lookup on a directory on which the server has mounted a file system, the client sees the underlying directory, instead of the mounted directory.

17.6.6 Remote Operations

With the exception of opening and closing files, there is almost a one-to-one correspondence between the regular UNIX system calls for file operations and the NFS protocol RPCs. Thus, a remote file operation can be translated directly to the corresponding RPC. Conceptually, NFS adheres to the remote-service paradigm, but in practice buffering and caching techniques are employed for the sake of performance. There is no direct correspondence between a remote operation and an RPC. Instead, file blocks and file attributes are fetched by the RPCs and are cached locally. Future remote operations use the cached data, subject to consistency constraints.

There are two caches: file-attribute (inode-information) cache and file-blocks cache. On a file open, the kernel checks with the remote server whether to fetch or revalidate the cached attributes. The cached file blocks are used only if the corresponding cached attributes are up to date. The attribute cache is updated whenever new attributes arrive from the server. Cached attributes are (by default) discarded after 60 seconds. Both read-ahead and delayed-write techniques are used between the server and the client. Clients do not free delayed-write blocks until the server confirms that the data have been written to disk. In contrast to the system used in Sprite, delayed-write is retained even when a file is opened concurrently, in conflicting modes. Hence, UNIX semantics are not preserved.

Tuning the system for performance makes it difficult to characterize the consistency semantics of NFS. New files created on a machine may not be visible elsewhere for 30 seconds. It is indeterminate whether writes to a file at one site are visible to other sites that have this file open for reading. New opens of that file observe only the changes that have already been flushed to the server. Thus, NFS provides neither strict emulation of UNIX semantics, nor the session semantics of Andrew. In spite of these drawbacks, the utility and high performance of the mechanism makes it the most widely used multivendor distributed system in operation.

17.7 ■ Summary

A DFS is a file-service system whose clients, servers, and storage devices are dispersed among the various sites of a distributed system. Accordingly, service activity has to be carried out across the network; instead of a single centralized data repository, there are multiple and independent storage devices.

Ideally, a DFS should look to its clients like a conventional, centralized file system. The multiplicity and dispersion of its servers and storage devices should be made transparent. That is, the client interface of a DFS should not distinguish between local and remote files. It is up to the DFS to locate the files and to arrange for the transport of the data. A transparent DFS facilitates client mobility by bringing over the client's environment to the site where the client logs in.

There are several approaches to naming schemes in a DFS. In the simplest approach, files are named by some combination of their host name and local name, which guarantees a unique systemwide name. Another approach, popularized by NFS, provides a means to attach remote directories to local directories, thus giving the appearance of a coherent directory tree.

Requests to access a remote file are usually handled by two complementary methods. With remote service, requests for accesses are delivered to the server. The server machine performs the accesses, and their results are forwarded back to the client. With caching, if the data needed to satisfy the access request are not already cached, then a copy of those data is brought from the server to the client. Accesses are performed on the cached copy. The idea is to retain recently accessed disk blocks in the cache, so that repeated accesses to the same information can be handled locally, without additional network traffic. A replacement policy is used to keep the cache size bounded. The problem of keeping the cached copies consistent with the master file is the cache-consistency problem.

There are two approaches to server-side information. Either the server tracks each file being accessed by each client, or it simply provides blocks as they are requested by the client without knowledge of their use. These approaches are the stateful versus stateless service paradigms.

Replication of files on different machines is a useful redundancy for improving availability. Multimachine replication can benefit performance too, since selecting a nearby replica to serve an access request results in shorter service time.

■ Exercises

17.1 What are the benefits of a DFS when compared to a file system in a centralized system?

17.2 Which of the example DFSs discussed in this chapter would handle a large, multiclient database application most efficiently? Explain your answer.

17.3 Under which circumstances would a client prefer a location-transparent DFS? Under which would she prefer a location-independent DFS? Discuss the reasons for these preferences.

17.4 What aspects of a distributed system would you select for a system running on a totally reliable network?

17.5 Compare and contrast the techniques of caching disk blocks locally, on a client system, and remotely, on a server.

17.6 What are the benefits of mapping objects into virtual memory, as Apollo Domain does? What are the detriments?

Bibliographical Notes

Discussions concerning consistency and recovery control for replicated files were offered by Davcev and Burkhard [1985]. Management of replicated files in a UNIX environment was covered by Brereton [1986] and by Purdin and associates [1987]. Wah [1984] discussed the issue of file placement on distributed computer systems. A detailed survey of mainly centralized file servers was given in Svobodova [1984].

Sun's Network File System (NFS) was presented by Sandberg and colleagues [1985], Sandberg [1987], and Sun Microsystems [1990]

There are many different and interesting DFSs that were not covered in this text, including UNIX United, Andrew, Sprite, and Locus. UNIX United was described by Brownbridge and associates [1982]. The Locus system was discussed by Popek and Walker [1985]. The Sprite system was described by Ousterhout and colleagues [1988], and by Nelson and colleagues [1988]. The Andrew system was discussed by Morris and colleagues [1986], Howard and colleagues [1988], and Satyanarayanan [1990].

Part Five

PROTECTION AND SECURITY

Protection mechanisms provide controlled access by limiting the types of file access that can be made by the various users. Protection must also be available to ensure that, in addition to files, memory segments, the CPU, and other resources can be operated on by only those processes that have gained proper authorization from the operating system.

Protection is provided by a mechanism that controls the access of programs, processes, or users to the resources defined by a computer system. This mechanism must provide a means for specification of the controls to be imposed, and a means of enforcement.

The *security system* prevents unauthorized access to a system, and ensuing malicious destruction or alteration of data. Security ensures the authentication of users of the system to protect the integrity of the information stored in the system (both data and code), as well as of the physical resources of the computer system.

Chapter 18

PROTECTION

The various processes in an operating system must be protected from one another's activities. Various mechanisms ensure that the files, memory segments, CPU, and other resources can be operated on by only those processes that have gained proper authorization from the operating system.

Protection is any mechanism for controlling the access of programs, processes, or users to the resources defined by a computer system. This mechanism must provide a means for specification of the controls to be imposed, and a means of enforcement. We distinguish between protection and **security,** which is a measure of confidence that the integrity of a system and its data will be preserved. Security assurance is a much broader topic than is protection; we address it in Chapter 19.

In this chapter, we examine the problem of protection, and develop a unifying model for implementing protection.

18.1 ■ Goals of Protection

As computer systems have become more sophisticated and pervasive in their applications, the need to protect their integrity has also grown. Protection was originally conceived as an adjunct to multiprogramming operating systems, so that untrustworthy users might safely share a common logical name space, such as a directory of files, or share a common physical name space, such as memory. Modern protection concepts have evolved to increase the reliability of any complex system that makes use of shared resources.

There are several reasons for providing protection. Most obvious is the need to prevent mischievous, intentional violation of an access restriction by a user. Of more general importance, however, is the need to ensure that each program component active in a system uses system resources only in ways consistent with the stated policies for the uses of these resources. This requirement is an absolute one for a reliable system.

Protection can improve reliability by detecting latent errors at the interfaces between component subsystems. Early detection of interface errors can often prevent contamination of a healthy subsystem by a subsystem that is malfunctioning. An unprotected resource cannot defend against use (or misuse) by an unauthorized or incompetent user. A protection-oriented system provides means to distinguish between authorized and unauthorized usage.

For instance, Windows 3.1 had no memory protection, so a failing process frequently would crash the entire system. Windows 95 and NT, being more modern and designed to run on more modern hardware, provide memory protection for applications and the kernel. Thus, a failing process is less likely to cause an entire system crash.

The role of protection in a computer system is to provide a **mechanism** for the enforcement of the **policies** governing resource use. These policies can be established in a variety of ways. Some are fixed in the design of the system, whereas others are formulated by the management of a system. Still others are defined by the individual users to protect their own files and programs. A protection system must have the flexibility to enforce a variety of policies that can be declared to it.

Policies for resource use may vary, depending on the application, and they may be subject to change over time. For these reasons, protection can no longer be considered solely as a matter of concern to the designer of an operating system. It should also be available as a tool for the applications programmer, so that resources created and supported by an applications subsystem can be guarded against misuse. In this chapter, we describe the protection mechanisms the operating system should provide, so that an application designer can use them in designing her own protection software.

One important principle is the separation of *policy* from *mechanism*. Mechanisms determine *how* something will be done. In contrast, policies decide *what* will be done. For example, UNIX provides the protection mechanism to set, for each file, the `read`, `write`, and `execute` bits for the owner, the group, and the universe. The policy of how these bits are to be set is left to the individual users (or system administrator). The separation of policy and mechanism is important for flexibility. Policies are likely to change from place to place or time to time. (For example, in UNIX a user may decide to change the protection policy for one of her file.) In the worst case, every change in policy requires a change in the underlying mechanism. General mechanisms are more desirable, because with them a change in a policy requires the modification of only system parameters or tables.

18.2 ▪ Domain of Protection

A computer system is a collection of processes and objects. By **objects,** we mean both hardware objects (such as the CPU, memory segments, printers, disks, and tape drives), and software objects (such as files, programs, and semaphores). Each object has a unique name that differentiates it from all other objects in the system, and each can be accessed only through well-defined and meaningful operations. Objects are essentially **abstract data types**.

The operations that are possible may depend on the object. For example, a CPU can only be executed on. Memory segments can be read and written, whereas a card reader can only be read. Tape drives can be read, written, and rewound. Data files can be created, opened, read, written, closed, and deleted; program files can be read, written, executed, and deleted.

Obviously, a process should be allowed to access only those resources that it has been authorized to access. Furthermore, at any time, it should be able to access only those resources that it currently requires to complete its task. This requirement, commonly referred to as the **need-to-know principle,** is useful for limiting the amount of damage a faulty process can cause in the system. For example, when process p invokes procedure A, the procedure should be allowed to access only its own variables and the formal parameters passed to it; it should not be able to access all the variables of process p. Similarly, consider the case where process p invokes a compiler to compile a particular file. The compiler should not be able to access any arbitrary files, but only a well-defined subset of files (such as the source file, listing file, and so on) related to the file to be compiled. Conversely, the compiler may have private files used for accounting or optimization purposes, which process p should not be able to access.

18.2.1 Domain Structure

To facilitate understanding of various protection methods, we introduce the concept of a **protection domain**. A process operates within a protection domain, which specifies the resources that the process may access. Each domain defines a set of objects and the types of operations that may be invoked on each object. The ability to execute an operation on an object is an **access right**. A **domain** is a collection of access rights, each of which is an ordered pair <**object-name, rights-set**>. For example, if domain D has the access right <file F, {read,write}>, then a process executing in domain D can both read and write file F; it cannot, however, perform any other operation on that object.

Domains do not need to be disjoint; they may share access rights. For example, in Figure 18.1, we have three domains: D_1, D_2, and D_3. The access right <O_4, {print}> is shared by both D_2 and D_3, implying that a process executing in either one of these two domains can print object O_4. Note that

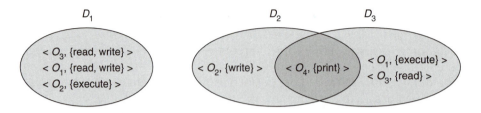

Figure 18.1   System with three protection domains.

a process must be executing in domain D_1 to read and write object O_1. On the other hand, only processes in domain D_3 may execute object O_1.

The association between a process and a domain may be either static (if the set of resources available to a process is fixed throughout the latter's lifetime) or dynamic. As might be expected, the problems inherent in establishing dynamic protection domains require more careful solution than do the simpler problems of the static case.

If the association between processes and domains is fixed, and we want to adhere to the need-to-know principle, then a mechanism must be available to change the content of a domain. A process may execute in two different phases. For example, it may need read access in one phase and write access in another. If a domain is static, we must define the domain to include both read and write access. However, this arrangement provides more rights than are needed in each of the two phases, since we have read access in the phase where we need only write access, and vice versa. Thus, the need-to-know principle is violated. We must allow the contents of a domain to be modified, so that it always reflects the minimum necessary access rights.

If the association is dynamic, a mechanism is available to allow a process to switch from one domain to another. We may also want to allow the content of a domain to be changed. If we cannot change the content of a domain, we can provide the same effect by creating a new domain with the changed content, and switching to that new domain when we want to change the domain content.

We note that a domain can be realized in a variety of ways:

- Each *user* may be a domain. In this case, the set of objects that can be accessed depends on the identity of the user. Domain switching occurs when the user is changed—generally when one user logs out and another user logs in.

- Each *process* may be a domain. In this case, the set of objects that can be accessed depends on the identity of the process. Domain switching corresponds to one process sending a message to another process, and then waiting for a response.

- Each *procedure* may be a domain. In this case, the set of objects that can be accessed corresponds to the local variables defined within the procedure. Domain switching occurs when a procedure call is made.

We shall discuss domain switching in Section 18.2.2.

18.2.2 Examples

Consider the standard dual-mode (monitor-user mode) model of operating-system execution. When a process executes in monitor mode, it can execute privileged instructions and thus gain complete control of the computer system. On the other hand, if the process executes in user mode, it can invoke only nonprivileged instructions. Consequently, it must ask the kernel for all domain changes (access to files, network functions, shared memory, kernel threads, and so on). These two modes protect the operating system (executing in monitor domain) from the user processes (executing in user domain). In a multiprogrammed operating system, two protection domains are insufficient, since users also want to be protected from one another. Therefore, a more elaborate scheme is needed. We illustrate this scheme by examining two influential operating systems—UNIX and MULTICS—to see how these concepts have been implemented in them.

18.2.2.1 Protection in UNIX

In the UNIX operating system, a domain is associated with the user. Switching the domain corresponds to changing the user identification temporarily. This change is accomplished through the file system as follows. An owner identification and a domain bit (known as the **setuid bit**) are associated with each file. When a user (with user-id = A) starts executing a file owned by B, whose associated domain bit is *off*, the user-id of the process is set to A. When the setuid bit is *on*, the user-id is set to that of the owner of the file: B. When the process exits, this temporary user-id change ends.

There are other common methods used to change domains in operating systems in which user-ids are used for domain definition, because almost all systems need to provide such a mechanism. This mechanism is used when an otherwise privileged facility needs to be made available to the general user population. For instance, it might be desirable to allow users to access a network without letting them write their own networking programs. In such a case, on a UNIX system, the setuid bit on a networking program would be set, causing the user-id to change when the program is run. The user-id would change to that of a user with network access privilege (such as *root*, the most powerful user-id).

This method can follow the need-to-know principle if the setuid programs are written to provide only one function. One problem with this method is that, if a user manages to create a file with user-id *root*, and with its setuid bit on, that user can become *root* and do anything and everything on the system. The setuid mechanism is discussed in Chapter 20.

There are many other methods used on operating systems. One variation is to place privileged programs in a special directory. The operating system would be designed to change the user-id of any program run from this directory, either to the equivalent of *root* or to the user-id of the owner of the directory. This eliminates the setuid problem of secret setuid programs, because all these programs are in one location. This method is less flexible than that used in UNIX, however.

Even more restrictive, and thus more protective, are systems that simply do not allow a change of user-id. In these instances, special techniques must be used to allow users access to privileged facilities. For instance, a **daemon** process may be started at boot time and run as a special user-id. Users then run a separate program, which sends requests to this process whenever they need to use the facility. This method is used by the TOPS-20 operating system.

In any of these systems, great care must be taken in writing privileged programs. Any oversight or carelessness can result in a total lack of protection on the system. Generally, these programs are the first to be attacked by people trying to break into a system; unfortunately, the attackers are frequently successful. For instance, there are many instances where security has been breached on UNIX systems because of the setuid feature. We discuss security in Chapter 19.

18.2.2.2 Protection in MULTICS

In the MULTICS system, the protection domains are organized hierarchically into a ring structure. Each ring corresponds to a single domain (Figure 18.2).

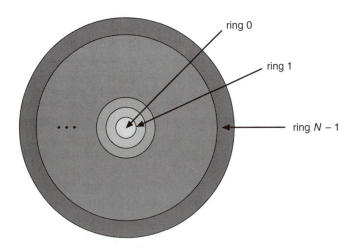

Figure 18.2   MULTICS ring structure.

The rings are numbered from 0 to 7. Let D_i and D_j be any two domain rings. If $j < i$, then D_i is a subset of D_j. That is, a process executing in domain D_j has more privileges than does a process executing in domain D_i. A process executing in domain D_0 has the most privileges. If there are only two rings, this scheme is equivalent to the monitor–user mode of execution, where monitor mode corresponds to D_0 and user mode corresponds to D_1.

MULTICS has a segmented address space; each segment is a file. Each segment is associated with one of the rings. A segment description includes an entry that identifies the ring number. In addition, it includes three access bits to control reading, writing, and execution. The association between segments and rings is a policy decision with which we are not concerned in this book. With each process, a **current-ring-number** counter is associated, identifying the ring in which the process is executing currently. When a process is executing in ring i, it cannot access a segment associated with ring j, $j < i$. It can, however, access a segment associated with ring k, $k \geq i$. The type of access, however, is restricted, according to the access bits associated with that segment.

Domain switching in MULTICS occurs when a process crosses from one ring to another by calling a procedure in a different ring. Obviously, this switch must be done in a controlled manner; otherwise, a process can start executing in ring 0, and no protection will be provided. To allow controlled domain switching, we modify the ring field of the segment descriptor to include the following:

- **Access bracket:** A pair of integers, $b1$ and $b2$, such that $b1 \leq b2$.

- **Limit:** An integer $b3$, such that $b3 > b2$.

- **List of gates:** Identifies the entry points (gates) at which the segments may be called.

If a process executing in ring i calls a procedure (segment) with access bracket $(b1, b2)$, then the call is allowed if $b1 \leq i \leq b2$, and the current ring number of the process remains i. Otherwise, a trap to the operating system occurs, and the situation is handled as follows:

- If $i < b1$, then the call is allowed to occur, because we have a transfer to a ring (domain) with fewer privileges. However, if parameters are passed that refer to segments in a lower ring (that is, segments that are not accessible to the called procedure), then these segments must be copied into an area that can be accessed by the called procedure.

- If $i > b2$, then the call is allowed to occur only if $b3$ is less than or equal to i, and the call has been directed to one of the designated entry points in the list of gates. This scheme allows processes with limited access rights to call procedures in lower rings that have more access rights, but only in a carefully controlled manner.

The main disadvantage of the ring (hierarchical) structure is that it does not allow us to enforce the need-to-know principle. In particular, if an object must be accessible in domain D_j but not accessible in domain D_i, then we must have $j < i$. But this requirement means that every segment accessible in D_i is also accessible in D_j.

The MULTICS protection system is generally more complex and less efficient than are those used in current operating systems. If protection interferes with the ease of use of the system, or significantly decreases system performance, then its use must be weighed carefully against the purpose of the system. For instance, it would be reasonable to have a complex protection system on a computer used by a university to process students' grades, and also used by students for class work. A similar protection system would not be suited to a computer being used for number crunching in which performance is of utmost importance. It would therefore be of benefit to separate the mechanism from the protection policy, allowing the same system to have complex or simple protection depending on the needs of its users. To separate mechanism from policy, we require more general models of protection.

18.3 ■ Access Matrix

Our model of protection can be viewed abstractly as a matrix, called an **access matrix**. The rows of the access matrix represent domains, and the columns represent objects. Each entry in the matrix consists of a set of access rights. Because objects are defined explicitly by the column, we can omit the object name from the access right. The entry access (i, j) defines the set of operations that a process, executing in domain D_i, can invoke on object O_j.

To illustrate these concepts, we consider the access matrix shown in Figure 18.3. There are four domains and four objects: three files (F_1, F_2, F_3), and one

object domain	F_1	F_2	F_3	printer
D_1	read		read	
D_2				print
D_3		read	execute	
D_4	read write		read write	

Figure 18.3   Access matrix.

laser printer. When a process executes in domain D_1, it can read files F_1 and F_3. A process executing in domain D_4 has the same privileges as it does in domain D_1, but in addition, it can also write onto files F_1 and F_3. Note that the laser printer can be accessed only by a process executing in domain D_2.

The access-matrix scheme provides us with the mechanism for specifying a variety of policies. The mechanism consists of implementing the access matrix and ensuring that the semantic properties we have outlined indeed hold. More specifically, we must ensure that a process executing in domain D_i can access only those objects specified in row i, and then only as allowed by the access-matrix entries.

Policy decisions concerning protection can be implemented by the access matrix. The policy decisions involve which rights should be included in the (i, j)th entry. We must also decide the domain in which each process executes. This last policy is usually decided by the operating system.

The users normally decide the contents of the access-matrix entries. When a user creates a new object O_j, the column O_j is added to the access matrix with the appropriate initialization entries, as dictated by the creator. The user may decide to enter some rights in some entries in column j and other rights in other entries, as needed.

The access matrix provides an appropriate mechanism for defining and implementing strict control for both the static and dynamic association between processes and domains. When we switch a process from one domain to another, we are executing an operation (switch) on an object (the domain). We can control domain switching by including domains among the objects of the access matrix. Similarly, when we change the content of the access matrix, we are performing an operation on an object: the access matrix. Again, we can control these changes by including the access matrix itself as an object. Actually, since each entry in the access matrix may be modified individually, we must consider each entry in the access matrix as an object to be protected.

object domain	F_1	F_2	F_3	laser printer	D_1	D_2	D_3	D_4
D_1	read		read			switch		
D_2				print			switch	switch
D_3		read	execute					
D_4	read write		read write		switch			

Figure 18.4 Access matrix of Figure 18.3 with domains as objects.

Now, we need to consider only the operations that are possible on these new objects (domains and the access matrix), and decide how we want processes to be able to execute these operations.

Processes should be able to switch from one domain to another. Domain switching from domain D_i to domain D_j is allowed to occur if and only if the access right **switch** $\in$ access(i, j). Thus, in Figure 18.4, a process executing in domain D_2 can switch to domain D_3 or to domain D_4. A process in domain D_4 can switch to D_1, and one in domain D_1 can switch to domain D_2.

Allowing controlled change to the contents of the access-matrix entries requires three additional operations: copy, owner, and control.

The ability to copy an access right from one domain (row) of the access matrix to another is denoted by an asterisk (*) appended to the access right. The copy right allows the copying of the access right only within the column (that is, for the object) for which the right is defined. For example, in Figure 18.5(a), a process executing in domain D_2 can copy the read operation into any entry associated with file F_2. Hence, the access matrix of Figure 18.5(a) can be modified to the access matrix shown in Figure 18.5(b).

There are two variants to this scheme:

1. A right is copied from access(i, j) to access(k, j); it is then removed from access(i, j); this action is a transfer of a right, rather than a copy.

object \\ domain	F_1	F_2	F_3
D_1	execute		write*
D_2	execute	read*	execute
D_3	execute		

(a)

object \\ domain	F_1	F_2	F_3
D_1	execute		write*
D_2	execute	read*	execute
D_3	execute	read	

(b)

Figure 18.5   Access matrix with copy rights.

2. Propagation of the copy right may be limited. That is, when the right R^* is copied from $access(i, j)$ to $access(k, j)$, only the right R (not R^*) is created. A process executing in domain D_k cannot further copy the right R.

A system may select only one of these three copy rights, or it may provide all three by identifying them as separate rights: copy, transfer, and limited copy.

The copy right allows a process to copy some rights from an entry in one column to another entry in the same column. We also need a mechanism to allow addition of new rights and removal of some rights. The owner right controls these operations. If $access(i, j)$ includes the owner right, then a process executing in domain D_i can add and remove any right in any entry in column j. For example, in Figure 18.6(a), domain D_1 is the owner of F_1, and thus can add and delete any valid right in column F_1. Similarly, domain D_2 is the owner of F_2 and F_3, and thus can add and remove any valid right within these two columns. Thus, the access matrix of Figure 18.6(a) can be modified to the access matrix shown in Figure 18.6(b).

The copy and owner rights allow a process to change the entries in a column. A mechanism is also needed to change the entries in a row. The

object domain	F_1	F_2	F_3
D_1	owner execute		write
D_2		read* owner	read* owner write*
D_3	execute		

(a)

object domain	F_1	F_2	F_3
D_1	owner execute		
D_2		owner read* write*	read* owner write*
D_3		write	write

(b)

Figure 18.6 Access matrix with owner rights.

object domain	F_1	F_2	F_3	laser printer	D_1	D_2	D_3	D_4
D_1	read		read			switch		
D_2				print			switch	switch control
D_3		read	execute					
D_4	write		write		switch			

Figure 18.7   Modified access matrix of Figure 18.4.

control right is applicable to only domain objects. If access(*i*, *j*) includes the control right, then a process executing in domain D_i can remove any access right from row *j*. For example, suppose that, in Figure 18.4, we include the control right in access(D_2, D_4). Then, a process executing in domain D_2 could modify domain D_4, as shown in Figure 18.7.

Although the copy and owner rights provide us with a mechanism to limit the propagation of access rights, they do not, however, provide us with the appropriate tools for preventing the propagation of information (that is, disclosure of information). The problem of guaranteeing that no information initially held in an object can migrate outside of its execution environment is called the **confinement problem**. This problem is in general unsolvable (see the Bibliographical Notes for references).

These operations on the domains and the access matrix are not in themselves particularly important. What is more important is that they illustrate the ability of the access-matrix model to allow the implementation and control of dynamic protection requirements. New objects and new domains can be created dynamically and included in the access-matrix model. However, we have shown only that the basic mechanism is here; the policy decisions concerning which domains are to have access to which objects in which ways must be made by the system designers and users.

18.4 ■ Implementation of Access Matrix

How can the access matrix be implemented effectively? In general, the matrix will be sparse; that is, most of the entries will be empty. Although there are data-structure techniques available for representing sparse matrices, they are not particularly useful for this application, because of the way in which the protection facility is used.

18.4.1 Global Table

The simplest implementation of the access matrix is a **global table** consisting of a set of ordered triples <domain, object, rights-set>. Whenever an operation M is executed on an object O_j within domain D_i, the global table is searched for a triple $<D_i, O_j, R_k>$, with $M \in R_k$. If this triple is found, the operation is allowed to continue; otherwise, an exception (error) condition is raised. This implementation suffers from several drawbacks. The table is usually large and thus cannot be kept in main memory, so additional I/O is needed. Virtual-memory techniques are often used for managing this table. In addition, it is difficult to take advantage of special groupings of objects or domains. For example, if a particular object can be read by everyone, it must have a separate entry in every domain.

18.4.2 Access Lists for Objects

Each column in the access matrix can be implemented as an **access list** for one object, as described in Section 11.4.2. Obviously, the empty entries can be discarded. The resulting list for each object consists of ordered pairs <domain, rights-set>, which define all domains with a nonempty set of access rights for that object.

This approach can be extended easily to define a list plus a **default** set of access rights. When an operation M on an object O_j is attempted in domain D_i, we search the access list for object O_j, looking for an entry $<D_i, R_k>$ with $M \in R_k$. If the entry is found, we allow the operation; if it is not found, we check the default set. If M is in the default set, we allow the access. Otherwise, access is denied and an exception condition occurs. Note that, for efficiency, we may check the default set first, and then search the access list.

18.4.3 Capability Lists for Domains

Rather than associating the columns of the access matrix with the objects as access lists, we can associate each row with its domain. A **capability list** for a domain is a list of objects together with the operations allowed on those objects. An object is often represented by its physical name or address, called a **capability**. To execute operation M on object O_j, the process executes the operation M, specifying the capability (pointer) for object O_j as a parameter. Simple **possession** of the capability means that access is allowed.

The capability list is associated with a domain, but is never directly accessible to a process executing in that domain. Rather, the capability list is itself a protected object, maintained by the operating system and accessed by the user only indirectly. Capability-based protection relies on the fact that the capabilities are never allowed to migrate into any address space directly accessible by a user process (where they could be modified). If all capabilities are secure, the object they protect is also secure against unauthorized access.

Capabilities were originally proposed as a kind of secure pointer, to meet the need for resource protection that was foreseen as multiprogrammed computer systems came of age. The idea of an inherently protected pointer (from the point of view of a user of a system) provides a foundation for protection that can be extended up to the applications level.

To provide inherent protection, we must distinguish capabilities from other kinds of objects, and must interpret them by an abstract machine on which higher-level programs run. Capabilities are usually distinguished from other data in one of two ways:

1. Each object has a **tag** to denote its type as either a capability or as accessible data. The tags themselves must not be directly accessible by an applications program. Hardware or firmware support may be used to enforce this restriction. Although only 1 bit is necessary to distinguish between capabilities and other objects, more bits are often used. This extension allows all objects to be tagged with their types by the hardware. Thus, the hardware can distinguish integers, floating-point numbers, pointers, Booleans, characters, instructions, capabilities, and uninitialized values by their tags.

2. The address space associated with a program can be **split** into two parts. One part is accessible to the program and contains the program's normal data and instructions. The other part, containing the capability list, is accessible by only the operating system. A segmented memory space (Section 9.5) is a useful way to support this approach.

Several capability-based protection systems have been developed. Hydra and CAP are important research platforms for capability-based developments, as described in the following paragraphs. The Mach operating system also uses a version of capability-based protection; it is described in the Appendix on our website (http://www.bell-labs.com/topic/books/os-book/Mach.ps).

Hydra is a capability-based protection system that provides considerable flexibility. The system provides a fixed set of possible access rights that are known to and interpreted by the system. These rights include such basic forms of access as the right to read, write, or execute a memory segment. In addition, the system provides the means for a user (of the protection system) to declare additional rights. The interpretation of user-defined rights is performed solely by the user's program, but the system provides access protection for the use of these rights, as well as for the use of system-defined rights.

A different approach to capability-based protection has been taken in the design of the Cambridge CAP system. CAP's capability system is simpler and superficially less powerful than that of Hydra. However, closer examination shows that it too can provide secure protection of user-defined objects. In CAP, there are two kinds of capabilities. The ordinary kind is a **data capability**. It provides access to objects, but the only rights provided are the standard read, write, or execute of the individual storage segments associated with the object. Data capabilities are interpreted by microcode in the CAP machine.

A **software capability** is protected by—but not interpreted by—the CAP microcode. It is interpreted by a **protected procedure** (that is, a privileged procedure), which can be written by an applications programmer as part of a subsystem. A particular kind of rights amplification is associated with a protected procedure. When executing the code body of such a procedure, a process temporarily acquires the rights to read or write the contents of a software capability itself. This specific kind of rights amplification corresponds to an implementation of the seal and unseal primitives on capabilities (see the Bibliographical Notes for references). Of course, this privilege is still subject to type verification to ensure that only software capabilities for a specified abstract type are allowed to be passed to any such procedure. Universal trust is not placed in any code other than the CAP machine's microcode.

18.4.4 A Lock–Key Mechanism

The **lock–key scheme** is a compromise between access lists and capability lists. Each object has a list of unique bit patterns, called **locks**. Similarly, each domain has a list of unique bit patterns, called **keys**. A process executing in a domain can access an object only if that domain has a key that matches one of the locks of the object.

Like a capability list, the list of keys for a domain must be managed by the operating system on behalf of the domain. Users are not allowed to examine or modify the list of keys (or locks) directly.

18.4.5 Comparison

Access lists correspond directly to the needs of the users. When a user creates an object, she can specify which domains can access the object, as well as the operations allowed. However, because access-rights information for a particular domain is not localized, determining the set of access rights for each domain is difficult. In addition, every access to the object must be checked, requiring a search of the access list. In a large system with long access lists, this search can be time consuming.

Capability lists do not correspond directly to the needs of the users; they are useful, however, for localizing information for a particular process. The process attempting access must present a capability for that access. Then, the protection system needs only to verify that the capability is valid. Revocation of capabilities, however, may be inefficient (Section 18.5).

The lock–key mechanism is a compromise between these two schemes. The mechanism can be both effective and flexible, depending on the length of the keys. The keys can be passed freely from domain to domain. In addition, access privileges may be effectively revoked by the simple technique of changing some of the locks associated with the object (Section 18.5).

Most systems use a combination of access lists and capabilities. When a process first tries to access an object, the access list is searched. If access is denied, an exception condition occurs. Otherwise, a capability is created and is attached to the process. Additional references use the capability to demonstrate swiftly that access is allowed. After the final access, the capability is destroyed. This strategy is used in the MULTICS system and in the CAL system; these systems use both access lists and capability lists.

As an example, consider a file system. Each file has an associated access list. When a process opens a file, the directory structure is searched to find the file, access permission is checked, and buffers are allocated. All this information is recorded in a new entry in a file table associated with the process. The operation returns an index into this table for the newly opened file. All operations on the file are made by specification of the index into the file table. The entry in the file table then points to the file and its buffers. When the file is closed, the file-table entry is deleted. Since the file table is maintained by the operating system, it cannot be corrupted by the user. Thus, the only files that the user can access are those that have been opened. Since access is checked when the file is opened, protection is ensured. This strategy is used in the UNIX system.

Note that the right to access *must* still be checked on each access, and the file-table entry has a capability only for the allowed operations. If a file is opened for reading, then a capability for read access is placed in the file-table entry. If an attempt is made to write onto the file, the system determines this protection violation by comparing the requested operation with the capability in the file-table entry.

18.5 ■ Revocation of Access Rights

In a dynamic protection system, it may sometimes be necessary to revoke access rights to objects that are shared by different users. Various questions about revocation may arise:

- *Immediate versus delayed:* Does revocation occur immediately, or is it delayed? If revocation is delayed, can we find out when it will take place?

- *Selective versus general:* When an access right to an object is revoked, does it affect *all* the users who have access rights to that object, or can we specify a select group of users whose access rights should be revoked?

- *Partial versus total:* Can a subset of the rights associated with an object be revoked, or must we revoke all access rights for this object?

- *Temporary versus permanent:* Can access be revoked permanently (that is, the revoked access right will never again be available), or can access be revoked and later be obtained again?

With an access-list scheme, revocation is easy. The access list is searched for the access right(s) to be revoked, and they are deleted from the list. Revocation is immediate, and can be general or selective, total or partial, and permanent or temporary.

Capabilities, however, present a much more difficult revocation problem. Since the capabilities are distributed throughout the system, we must find them before we can revoke them. There are several different schemes for implementing revocation for capabilities, including the following:

- *Reacquisition:* Periodically, capabilities are deleted from each domain. If a process wants to use a capability, it may find that that capability has been deleted. The process may then try to reacquire the capability. If access has been revoked, the process will not be able to reacquire the capability.

- *Back-pointers:* A list of pointers is maintained with each object, pointing to all capabilities associated with that object. When revocation is required, we can follow these pointers, changing the capabilities as necessary. This scheme has been adopted in the MULTICS system. It is quite general, although it is a costly implementation.

- *Indirection:* The capabilities do not point to the objects directly, but instead point indirectly. Each capability points to a unique entry in a global table, which in turn points to the object. We implement revocation by searching the global table for the desired entry and deleting it. When an access is attempted, the capability is found to point to an illegal table entry. Table entries can be reused for other capabilities without difficulty, since both the capability and the table entry contain the unique name of the object. The object for a capability and its table entry must match. This scheme was adopted in the CAL system. It does not allow selective revocation.

- *Keys:* A key is a unique bit pattern that can be associated with each capability. This key is defined when the capability is created, and it can be neither modified nor inspected by the process owning that capability. A **master key** associated with each object can be defined or replaced with the set-key operation. When a capability is created, the current value of the master key is associated with the capability. When the capability is exercised, its key is compared to the master key. If the keys match, the operation is allowed to continue; otherwise, an exception condition is raised. Revocation replaces the master key with a new value by the set-key operation, invalidating all previous capabilities for this object.

  Note that this scheme does not allow selective revocation, since only one master key is associated with each object. If we associate a list of keys with each object, then selective revocation can be implemented. Finally, we can group all keys into one global table of keys. A capability is valid only if its key matches some key in the global table. We implement revocation by removing the matching key from the table. With this scheme, a key can be associated with several objects, and several keys can be associated with each object, providing maximum flexibility.

In key-based schemes, the operations of defining keys, inserting them into lists, and deleting them from lists should not be available to all users. In particular, it would be reasonable to allow only the owner of an object to set the keys for that object. This choice, however, is a policy decision that the protection system can implement, but should not define.

18.6 ■ Language-Based Protection

To the degree that protection is provided in existing computer systems, it usually is achieved through the device of an operating-system kernel, which acts as a security agent to inspect and validate each attempt to access a protected resource. Since comprehensive access validation is potentially a source of considerable overhead, either we must give it hardware support to reduce the cost of each validation, or we must accept that the system designer may be inclined to compromise the goals of protection. It is difficult to satisfy all these goals if the flexibility to implement various protection policies is restricted by the support mechanisms provided or if protection environments are made larger than necessary to secure greater operational efficiency.

As operating systems have become more complex, and particularly as they have attempted to provide higher-level user interfaces, the goals of protection have become much more refined. In this refinement, we find that the designers of protection systems have drawn heavily on ideas that originated in programming languages and especially on the concepts of abstract data types and objects. Protection systems are now concerned not only with the identity of a resource to which access is attempted, but also with the functional nature of that access. In the newest protection systems, concern for the function to be invoked extends beyond a set of system-defined functions, such as standard file access methods, to include functions that may be user-defined as well.

Policies for resource use may also vary, depending on the application, and they may be subject to change over time. For these reasons, protection can no longer be considered as a matter of concern to only the designer of an operating system. It should also be available as a tool for use by the applications designer, so that resources of an applications subsystem can be guarded against tampering or the influence of an error.

At this point, programming languages enter the picture. Specifying the desired control of access to a shared resource in a system is making a declarative statement about the resource. This kind of statement can be integrated into a language by an extension of the latter's typing facility. When protection is declared along with data typing, the designer of each subsystem can specify its requirements for protection, as well as its need for use of other resources in a system. Such a specification should be given directly as a program is composed, and in the language in which the program itself is stated. There are several significant advantages to this approach:

1. Protection needs are simply declared, rather than programmed as a sequence of calls on procedures of an operating system.

2. Protection requirements may be stated independently of the facilities provided by a particular operating system.

3. The means for enforcement do not need to be provided by the designer of a subsystem.

4. A declarative notation is natural, because access privileges are closely related to the linguistic concept of data type.

There is a variety of techniques that can be provided by a programming language implementation to enforce protection, but any of these must depend on some degree of support from an underlying machine and its operating system. For example, suppose a language were used to generate code to run on the Cambridge CAP system. On this system, every storage reference made on the underlying hardware occurs indirectly through a capability. This restriction prevents any process from accessing a resource outside of its protection environment at any time. However, a program may impose arbitrary restrictions on how a resource may be used during execution of a particular code segment by any process. We can implement such restrictions most readily by using the software capabilities provided by CAP. A language implementation might provide standard, protected procedures to interpret software capabilities that would realize the protection policies that could be specified in the language. This scheme puts policy specification at the disposal of the programmers, while freeing them from the details of implementing its enforcement.

Even if a system does not provide a protection kernel as powerful as those of Hydra or CAP, there are still mechanisms available for implementing protection specifications given in a programming language. A compiler can separate references for which it can certify that no protection violation could occur from those for which a violation might be possible, and can treat them differently. The protection provided by this form of scheme rests on the assumption that the code generated by the compiler will not be modified prior to or during that code's execution.

What, then, are the relative merits of enforcement based solely on a kernel, as opposed to enforcement provided largely by a compiler?

- *Security:* Enforcement by a kernel provides a greater degree of security of the protection system itself than does the generation of protection-checking code by a compiler. In a compiler-supported scheme, security rests on correctness of the translator, on some underlying mechanism of storage management that protects the segments from which compiled code is executed, and, ultimately, on the security of files from which a program is loaded. Some of these same considerations also apply to a software-supported protection kernel, but to a lesser degree, since the kernel may reside in fixed physical storage segments and may be loaded from only a designated file. With a tagged capability system, in which all address computation is performed either by hardware or by a fixed microprogram, even greater security is possible. Hardware-supported protection is also relatively immune to protection violations that might occur as a result of either hardware or system software malfunction.

- *Flexibility:* There are limits to the flexibility of a protection kernel in implementing a user-defined policy, although it may supply adequate facilities for the system to provide enforcement for its own policies. With a programming language, protection policy can be declared and enforcement provided as needed by an implementation. If a language does not provide sufficient flexibility, it can be extended or replaced, with less perturbation of a system in service than would be caused by the modification of an operating-system kernel.

- *Efficiency:* The greatest efficiency is obtained when enforcement of protection is supported directly by hardware (or microcode). Insofar as software support is required, language-based enforcement has the advantage that static access enforcement can be verified off-line at compile time. Also, since the enforcement mechanism can be tailored by an intelligent compiler to meet the specified need, the fixed overhead of kernel calls can often be avoided.

In summary, the specification of protection in a programming language allows the high-level description of policies for the allocation and use of resources. A language implementation can provide software for protection enforcement when automatic hardware-supported checking is unavailable. In addition, it can interpret protection specifications to generate calls on whatever protection system is provided by the hardware and the operating system.

One way of making protection available to the application program is through the use of **software capability** that could be used as an object of computation. Inherent in this concept is the idea that certain program components might have the privilege of creating or examining these software capabilities. A capability-creating program would be able to execute a primitive operation that would seal a data structure, rendering the latter's contents inaccessible to any program components that did not hold either the seal or the unseal privileges. They might copy the data structure, or pass its address to other program components, but they could not gain access to its contents. The reason for introducing such software capabilities is to bring a protection mechanism into the programming language. The only problem with the concept as proposed is that the use of the seal and unseal operations takes a procedural approach to specifying protection. A nonprocedural or declarative notation seems a preferable way to make protection available to the applications programmer.

What is needed is a safe, dynamic access-control mechanism for distributing capabilities to system resources among user processes. If it is to contribute to the overall reliability of a system, the access-control mechanism should be safe to use. If it is to be useful in practice, it should also be reasonably efficient. This requirement has led to the development of a number of language constructs that allow the programmer to declare various restrictions on the use of a specific managed resource (see the Bibliographical Notes for appropriate references). These constructs provide mechanisms for three functions:

1. Distributing capabilities safely and efficiently among customer processes: In particular, mechanisms ensure that a user process will use the managed resource only if it was granted a capability to that resource.

2. Specifying the type of operations that a particular process may invoke on an allocated resource (for example, a reader of a file should be allowed only to read the file, whereas a writer should be able both to read and to write): It should not be necessary to grant the same set of rights to every user process, and it should be impossible for a process to enlarge its set of access rights, except with the authorization of the access control mechanism.

3. Specifying the order in which a particular process may invoke the various operations of a resource (for example, a file must be opened before it can be read): It should be possible to give two processes different restrictions on the order in which they can invoke the operations of the allocated resource.

The incorporation of protection concepts into programming languages, as a practical tool for system design, is at present in its infancy. It is likely that protection will become a matter of greater concern to the designers of new systems with distributed architectures and increasingly stringent requirements on data security. Then, the importance of suitable language notations in which to express protection requirements will be recognized more widely. Language-based protection is perhaps best exemplified by the Java JVM. Because the JVM protection features are widely known, they are described in Section 19.9.

18.7 ■ Summary

Computer systems contain many objects. These objects need to be protected from misuse. Objects may be hardware (such as memory, CPU time, or I/O devices) or software (such as files, programs, and abstract data types). An access right is permission to perform an operation on an object. A domain is a set of access rights. Processes execute in domains and may use any of the access rights in the domain to access and manipulate objects.

The access matrix is a general model of protection. The access matrix provides a mechanism for protection without imposing a particular protection policy on the system or its users. The separation of policy and mechanism is an important design property.

The access matrix is sparse. It is normally implemented either as access lists associated with each object, or as capability lists associated with each domain. We can include dynamic protection in the access-matrix model by considering domains and the access matrix itself as objects.

Real systems are much more limited, and tend to provide protection for only files. UNIX is representative, providing read, write, and execution protection separately for the owner, group, and general public for each file. MULTICS uses a ring structure in addition to file access. Hydra, the Cambridge CAP system, and Mach are capability systems that extend protection to user-defined software objects.

■ Exercises

18.1 What are the main differences between capability lists and access lists?

18.2 A Burroughs B7000/B6000 MCP file can be tagged as sensitive data. When such a file is deleted, its storage area is overwritten by some random bits. For what purpose would such a scheme be useful?

18.3 In a ring-protection system, level 0 has the greatest access to objects and level n (greater than zero) has fewer access rights. The access rights of a program at a particular level in the ring structure are considered as a set of capabilities. What is the relationship between the capabilities of a domain at level j and a domain at level i to an object (for $j > i$)?

18.4 Consider a computer system in which "computer games" can be played by students only between 10 P.M. and 6 A.M., by faculty members between 5 P.M. and 8 A.M., and by the computer center staff at all times. Suggest a scheme for implementing this policy efficiently.

18.5 The RC 4000 system (and other systems) have defined a tree of processes (called a process tree) such that all the descendants of a process are given resources (objects) and access rights by their ancestors only. Thus, a descendant can never have the ability to do anything that its ancestors cannot do. The root of the tree is the operating system, which has the ability to do anything. Assume the set of access rights was represented by an access matrix, A. $A(x, y)$ defines the access rights of process x to object y. If x is a descendant of z, what is the relationship between $A(x,y)$ and $A(z,y)$ for an arbitrary object y?

18.6 What hardware features must a computer system have for efficient capability manipulation? Can these features be used for memory protection?

18.7 Consider a computing environment where a unique number is associated with each process and with each object in the system. Suppose that we allow a process with number n to access an object with number m only if $n > m$. What type of protection structure do we have?

18.8 What protection problems may arise if a shared stack is used for parameter passing?

18.9 Consider a computing environment where a process is given the privilege of accessing an object only n times. Suggest a scheme for implementing this policy.

18.10 If all the access rights to an object are deleted, the object can no longer be accessed. At this point, the object should also be deleted, and the space it occupies should be returned to the system. Suggest an efficient implementation of this scheme.

18.11 What is the need-to-know principle? Why is it important for a protection system to adhere to this principle?

18.12 Why is it difficult to protect a system in which users are allowed to do their own I/O?

18.13 Capability lists are usually kept within the address space of the user. How does the system ensure that the user cannot modify the contents of the list?

Bibliographical Notes

The access-matrix model of protection between domains and objects was developed by Lampson [1969, 1971]. Harrison and colleagues [1976] used a formal version of this model to prove mathematically the properties of a protection system.

The concept of a capability evolved from Iliffe's and Jodeit's *codewords*, which were implemented in the Rice University computer [Iliffe and Jodeit 1962]. The term *capability* was introduced by Dennis and Van Horn [1966].

The Hydra system was described by Wulf and colleagues [1981]. The CAP system was described by Needham and Walker [1977]. Organick [1972] discussed the MULTICS ring-protection system.

The principle of separation of policy and mechanism was advocated by the designer of Hydra [Levin et al. 1975]. The confinement problem was first discussed by Lampson [1973], and was further examined by Lipner [1975].

The use of higher-level languages for specifying access control was suggested first by Morris [1973], who proposed the use of the `seal` and `unseal` operation discussed in Section 18.6. Kieburtz and Silberschatz [1978, 1983], and McGraw and Andrews [1979] proposed various language constructs for dealing with general dynamic resource-management schemes. Jones and Liskov [1978] considered the problem of how a static access-control scheme can be incorporated in a programming language that supports abstract data types.

Chapter 19

SECURITY

Protection, as we discussed it in Chapter 18, is strictly an *internal* problem: How do we provide controlled access to programs and data stored in a computer system? **Security,** on the other hand, requires not only an adequate protection system, but also consideration of the *external* environment within which the system operates. Internal protection is not useful if the operator's console is exposed to unauthorized personnel, or if files (stored, for example, on tapes and disks) can simply be removed from the computer system and taken to a system that has no protection. These security problems are essentially management, rather than operating-system, problems.

Both the information stored in the system (both data and code) and the physical resources of the computer system need to be protected from unauthorized access, malicious destruction or alteration, and accidental introduction of inconsistency. In this chapter, we examine the ways in which information may be misused or intentionally made inconsistent. We then present mechanisms to guard against such occurrences.

19.1 ■ The Security Problem

In Chapter 18, we discussed various mechanisms that the operating system can provide (with appropriate aid from the hardware) that allow users to protect their resources (usually programs and data). These mechanisms work well as long as the users do not try to circumvent the intended use of and access to these resources. Unfortunately, this situation is seldom realized. When it is not, security comes into play. We say that a system is *secure* if its resources are used and accessed as intended under all circumstances. Unfortunately, it is not generally possible to achieve total security. Nonetheless, mechanisms must be available to make security breaches a rare occurrence, rather than the norm.

Security violations (misuse) of the system can be categorized as being either **malicious** (intentional) or **accidental**. It is easier to protect against accidental misuse than to protect against malicious misuse. Among the forms of malicious access are the following:

- Unauthorized reading of data (theft of information)

- Unauthorized modification of data

- Unauthorized destruction of data

Absolute protection of the system from malicious abuse is not possible, but the cost to the perpetrator can be made sufficiently high to deter most, if not all, attempts to access, without proper authority, the information residing in the system.

To protect the system, we must take security measures at two levels:

- **Physical level:** The site or sites containing the computer systems must be physically secured against armed or surreptitious entry by intruders.

- **Human level:** Users must be screened carefully so that the chance of authorizing a user who then gives access to an intruder (in exchange for a bribe, for example) is reduced.

Security at both levels must be maintained if operating-system security is to be ensured. A weakness at a high level of security (physical or human) allows circumvention of strict low-level (operating-system) security measures.

It is worthwhile, in many applications, to devote considerable effort to the security of the computer system. Large commercial systems containing payroll or other financial data are inviting targets to thieves. Systems that contain data pertaining to corporate operations may be of interest to unscrupulous competitors. The advent of the Internet is exacerbating the security problem by allowing outsiders to access facilities within a company. Loss of certain data, whether via accident or fraud, can seriously impair the ability of the corporation to function.

On the other hand, the system hardware must provide protection (as discussed in Chapter 18) to allow for the implementation of security features. For instance, MS-DOS and Macintosh OS provide little security because the hardware for which they were originally designed for did not provide memory or I/O protection. Now that the hardware has become sufficiently sophisticated to provide protection, the designers of these operating systems are struggling to add security. Unfortunately, adding a feature to a functional system is a much more difficult and challenging task than is designing and implementing the feature before the system is built. Later operating systems, such as Windows NT, have been designed to provide security features from the beginning.

In the remainder of this chapter, we address security at the operating-system level. Security at the physical and human levels, although important, is beyond the scope of this text. Security within the operating system is implemented at several levels, ranging from passwords for access to the system to the isolation of concurrent processes running within the system. The file system also provides a degree of protection.

19.2 ■ Authentication

A major security problem for operating systems is **authentication**. The protection system depends on an ability to identify the programs and processes that are executing. This ability, in turn, eventually rests on our power to identify each user of the system. A user normally identifies himself. How do we determine whether a user's identity is authentic? Generally, authentication is based on one or more of three items: user possession (a key or card), user knowledge (a user identifier and password), or a user attribute (fingerprint, retina pattern, or signature).

19.2.1 Passwords

The most common authentication of a user's identity is via a user **password**. When the user identifies herself by user ID or account name, she is asked for a password. If the user-supplied password matches the password stored in the system, the system assumes that the user is legitimate.

Passwords often protect objects in the computer system, in the absence of more complete protection schemes. They can be considered a special case of either keys or capabilities. For instance, a password could be associated with each resource (such as a file). Whenever a user requests use of the resource, she must supply the password. If the password is correct, access is granted. Different passwords may be associated with different access rights, such as reading, appending, and updating a file.

19.2.2 Password Vulnerabilities

Although there are problems associated with their use, passwords are nevertheless extremely common, because they are easy to understand and use. The problems with passwords are related to the difficulty of keeping a password secret. Passwords can be compromised by being guessed, accidentally exposed, or illegally transferred from an authorized user to an unauthorized one, as we show next.

There are two common ways to guess a password. One is for the intruder (either human or program) to know the user or to have information about the user. All too frequently, people use obvious information (such as the names of their cats or spouses) as their passwords. The other way is to use brute force; we can try all possible combinations of letters, numbers, and punctuation until we find the password. Short passwords have too few possible permutations to prevent their being guessed by repeated trials. For example, a four-decimal password provides only 10,000 variations. On the average, guessing 5000 times would produce a correct hit. If a program could be written that would try a password every 1 millisecond, it would then take only about 5 seconds to guess a four-digit numerical password. Longer passwords are less susceptible to being guessed by enumeration, and systems that differentiate between uppercase and lowercase letters, and that allow use of numbers and all punctuation characters in passwords, make the task of guessing the password much more difficult. Of course, users must take advantage of the large password space and must not, for example, use only lowercase letters.

The failure of password security due to exposure can result from visual or electronic monitoring. An intruder looking over the shoulder of a user, or **shoulder surfing,** when the user is logging in, can learn the user's password easily by simply watching the keyboard. Alternatively, anyone with access to the network on which a computer resides can seamlessly add a network monitor; such **sniffing** allows her to see all data being transferred on the network, including user IDs and passwords. Exposure is a particularly severe problem if the password is written down where it can be read or lost. As we shall see, some systems force the user to select hard-to-remember or long passwords. Taken to an extreme, this requirement can cause a user to record the password, providing much lower security than is afforded by short, easy-to-remember passwords!

The final method of password compromise is the result of human nature. Most computer installations have the rule that users are not allowed to share accounts. This rule is sometimes implemented for accounting reasons, but often it is used to aid in security. For instance, if one user ID is shared by several users, and that user ID is associated with a security breach, then it is impossible to know which person was using that user ID at the time, or even whether the person was an authorized user. With one user per user ID, any user can be questioned directly about use of his account. Sometimes, users break account-sharing rules to help friends or to circumvent accounting; the result is access to the system by unauthorized, and possibly harmful, users.

Passwords can be either generated by the system or selected by a user. System-generated passwords may be difficult to remember, so users may write them down. User-selected passwords, however, are often easy to guess. At some sites, administrators occasionally check user passwords and notify the user if his password is too short or otherwise is easy to guess. Some systems also **age** passwords, forcing users to change their passwords at regular intervals (every three months, for instance). This method is not foolproof either, because users can easily toggle between two passwords. The solution to this problem, as implemented on some systems, is to record a password history for each user. For instance, the system could record the most recent n passwords and not allow them to be reused.

Several variants on these simple password schemes can be used. The system can limit the user's password to be only words that are not included in on-line dictionaries. Passwords can be changed frequently. In the extreme, a new password is selected (either by the system or by the user) at the end of *each* session, and that password must be used for the next session. Note that, even if a password is misused, it can be used only once, and its use prevents the legitimate user from using it later. Consequently, the legitimate user discovers the security violation at the next session, when he tries to use a now-invalid password. Administrators can then take steps to repair the breach of security.

19.2.3 Encrypted Passwords

One problem with all these approaches is the difficulty of keeping the password secret. The UNIX system uses encryption to avoid the necessity of keeping its password list secret. Each user has a password. The system contains a function that is extremely difficult (the designers hope impossible) to invert, but is simple to compute. That is, given a value x, it is easy to compute the function value $f(x)$. Given a function value $f(x)$, however, it is impossible to compute x. This function encodes all passwords. Only the encoded passwords are stored. When a user presents a password, that password is encoded and then is compared against the stored encoded password. Even if the stored encoded password is seen, it cannot be decoded, so the password cannot be determined. Thus, the password file does not need to be kept secret. The function $f(x)$ is typically an *encryption* algorithm that has been designed and tested rigorously, as discussed in Section 19.6.

The flaw in this method is that the system no longer has control over the passwords. Although the passwords are encrypted, anyone with a copy of the password file can run fast encryption routines against it, encrypting each word in a dictionary, for instance, and comparing the results against the passwords. If the user has selected a password that is also a word in the dictionary, the password is cracked. On sufficiently fast computers, or even on clusters of slow computers, such a comparison may take only a few hours. Because UNIX systems use a well-known encryption algorithm, a hacker might keep a cache of password–cipher pairs to find quickly passwords that have been cracked previously. For this reason, new versions of UNIX hide the password entries.

Another weakness in the UNIX password methods is that many UNIX systems treat only the first eight characters of the password as significant, so it is extremely important for users to take advantage of the available password space. To avoid the dictionary encryption method, some systems disallow the use of dictionary words as passwords. A good technique is to generate a password by using the first letter of each word of an easily remembered phrase, using both upper and lower characters with a number or punctuation mark thrown in for good measure. For example, the phrase "My mother's maiden name is Katherine!" might yield the password "MmmnisK!"—hard to crack, but easy for the user to remember.

19.2.4 One-Time Passwords

To avoid the problems of password sniffing and shoulder surfing, a system can use a set of *paired passwords*. When a session begins, the system randomly selects and presents one part of a password pair; the user must supply the other part. In this system, the system issues a *challenge* to which the user must *respond* with the correct answer.

This approach can be generalized to the use of an algorithm as a password. The algorithm might be an integer function, for example. The system selects and presents to the user a random integer. The user applies the function and replies with the correct result. The system also applies the function. If the two results match, access is allowed.

There is another password method that is not susceptible to exposure: A user types in a password, but any entity that intercepts and tries to reuse that password fails. Such a system uses algorithmic passwords. In this variation, system and the user share a secret. The secret is never transmitted over a medium that allows exposure. Rather, the secret is used as input to the function, along with a shared seed. A *seed* is a random number or alphanumeric sequence. The seed is the authentication challenge from the computer. The secret and the seed are used as input to the function $f(secret, seed)$. The result of this function is transmitted as the password to the computer. Because the computer also knows the secret and the seed, it can perform the same computation. If the results match, the user is authenticated. The next time that the user needs to be authenticated, another seed is generated and the same steps ensue. This time, the password is different. Since the password is different in each instance, anyone capturing the password from one session and trying to reuse it in another session will fail.

One-time passwords prevent improper authentication due to password exposure. There are many one-time password systems. Commercial implementations such as SecurID use hardware calculators. Most of these calculators are like a credit card with a keypad and display. Some systems use the current time as the random seed. The user enters via the keypad the shared secret also known as a *personal identification number* (PIN). The display shows the one-time password.

Another variation on one-time passwords is the use of a **code book**, or **one-time pad:** a list of single-use passwords. Each password on the list is used, in order, once, and then is crossed out or erased. The commonly used S/Key system uses either a software calculator or a code book based on these calculations as a source of one-time passwords.

19.3 ■ Program Threats

In an environment where a program written by one user may be used by another user, there is an opportunity for misuse, which may result in unexpected behavior. In Sections 19.3.1 and 19.3.2, we describe two common methods by which such behavior may occur: Trojan horses and trap doors.

19.3.1 Trojan Horse

Many systems have mechanisms for allowing programs written by users to be executed by other users. If these programs are executed in a domain that provides the access rights of the executing user, they may misuse these rights. Inside a text-editor program, for example, there may be code to search the file to be edited for certain keywords. If any are found, the entire file may be copied to a special area accessible to the creator of the text editor. A code segment that misuses its environment is called a **Trojan horse**. The Trojan-horse problem is exacerbated by long search paths (such as are common on UNIX systems). The search path lists the set of directories to search when an ambiguous program name is given. The path is searched for a file of that name and the file is executed. All the directories in the search path must be secure, or a Trojan horse could be slipped into the user's path and executed accidentally.

For instance, consider the use of the "." character in a search path. The "." tells the shell to include the current directory in the search. Thus, if a user has "." in her search path, has set her current directory to a friend's directory, and enters the name of a normal system command, the command may be executed from the friend's directory instead. The program would run within the user's domain, allowing the program to do anything that the user is allowed to do, including deleting the user's files, for instance.

A variation of the Trojan horse is a program that emulates a login program. An unsuspecting user starts to log in at a terminal, and notices that he has apparently mistyped his password. He tries again, and is successful. What has happened is that his authentication key and password have been stolen by the login emulator that was left running on the terminal by the thief. The emulator stored away the password, printed out a login error message, and exited; the user was then provided with a genuine login prompt. This type of attack can be defeated by the operating system printing a usage message at the end of an interactive session or by a nontrappable key sequence, such as the control-alt-delete combination that Windows NT uses.

19.3.2 Trap Door

The designer of a program or system might leave a hole, or **trap door,** in the software that only she is capable of using. This type of security breach was shown in the movie "War Games." For instance, the code might check for a specific user identifier or password, and might circumvent normal security procedures. There have been cases of programmers being arrested for embezzling from banks by including rounding errors in their code, and having the occasional half-cent credited to their accounts. This account crediting can add up to a large amount of money, considering the number of transactions that a large bank executes!

A clever trap door can be included in a compiler. The compiler generates standard object code as well as a trap door, regardless of the source code being compiled. This activity is particularly nefarious, because a search of the source code of the program will not reveal any problems. Only the source code of the compiler contains the information. Trap doors pose a difficult problem because, to detect them, we have to analyze all the source code for all components of a system. Given that software systems may consist of millions of lines of code, this analysis is not done frequently.

19.4 ■ System Threats

Most operating systems provide a means for processes to spawn other processes. In such an environment, it is possible to create a situation where operating-system resources and user files are misused. The two most common methods for achieving this misuse are worms and viruses.

19.4.1 Worms

A **worm** is a process that uses the **spawn** mechanism to clobber system performance. The worm spawns copies of itself, using up system resources and perhaps locking out system use by all other processes. On computer networks, worms are particularly potent: They may reproduce themselves among systems and thus shut down the entire network. Such an event occurred in 1988 to UNIX systems on the Internet, causing millions of dollars of lost system and programmer time.

The Internet links thousands of government, academic, research, and industrial computers internationally, and serves as the infrastructure for electronic exchange of scientific information. At the close of the workday on November 2, 1988, Robert Tappan Morris, Jr., a first-year Cornell graduate student, unleashed a worm program on one or more hosts connected to the Internet. Targeting Sun Microsystems' Sun 3 workstations and VAX computers running variants of Version 4 BSD UNIX, the worm quickly spread over great distances; within a few hours of its release, it had consumed system resources to the point of bringing down the infected machines.

Although Robert Morris designed the self-replicating program for rapid reproduction and distribution, some of the features of the UNIX networking environment provided the means to propagate the worm throughout the system. It is likely that Morris chose for initial infection an Internet host left open for and accessible to outside users. From there, the worm program exploited flaws in the UNIX operating system's security routines and took advantage of UNIX utilities that simplify resource sharing in local-area networks to gain unauthorized access to thousands of other connected sites. Morris' methods of attack are outlined next.

The worm was made up of two programs, a **grappling hook** (also called **bootstrap** or **vector**) program and the main program. Named *l1.c*, the grappling hook consisted of 99 lines of C code compiled and run on each machine it accessed. Once established on the system under attack, the grappling hook connected to the machine where it originated and uploaded a copy of the main worm onto the "hooked" system (Figure 19.1). The main program proceeded to search for other machines to which the newly infected system could connect easily. In these actions, Morris exploited the UNIX networking utility, rsh, for easy remote task execution. By setting up special files that list the host–login name pairs, the users can omit entering a password each time they access a remote account on the paired list. The worm searched these special files for site names that would allow remote execution without a password. Where remote shells were established, the worm program was uploaded and began executing anew.

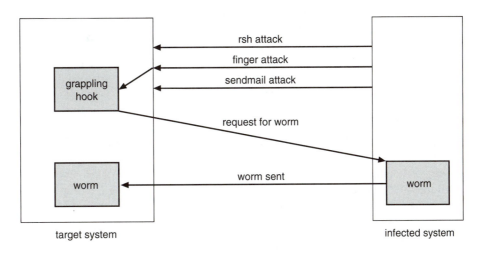

Figure 19.1   The Morris Internet worm.

The attack via remote access was one of three infection methods built into the worm. The other two methods involved operating-system bugs in the UNIX finger and sendmail programs. The finger utility functions as an electronic telephone directory; the command

```
finger username@hostname
```

returns a person's real and login names, along with other information that the user may have provided, such as office and home address and telephone number, research plan, or clever quotation. Finger runs as a background process (daemon) at each BSD site and responds to queries throughout the Internet. The point vulnerable to malicious entry involved reading input without checking bounds for overflow. Morris' program queried finger with a 536-byte string crafted to exceed the buffer allocated for input and to overwrite the stack frame. Instead of returning to the *main* routine in which it was before the Morris worm's call, the finger daemon was routed to a procedure within the invading 536-byte string that was now residing on the stack. The new procedure executed */bin/sh*, which, if successful, provided the worm a remote shell on the machine under attack.

The bug exploited in sendmail also involved using a daemon process for malicious entry. The sendmail program routes electronic mail in a network environment. Debugging code in the utility permits testers to verify and display the state of the mail system. The debugging option is useful to system administrators and is often left on as a background process. Morris included in his attack arsenal a call to **debug**, which, instead of specifying a user address, as would be normal in testing, issued a set of commands that mailed and executed a copy of the grappling-hook program.

Once in place, the main worm undertook systematic attempts to discover user passwords. It began by trying simple cases of no password or of passwords constructed of account–user-name combinations, then used comparisons with an internal dictionary of 432 favorite password choices, then went to the final stage of trying each word in the standard UNIX on-line dictionary as a possible password. This elaborate and efficient three-stage password-cracking algorithm enabled the worm to gain further access to other user accounts on the infected system. The worm then searched for *rsh* data files in these newly broken accounts. Any *rsh* entries were tried, and, as described previously, the worm could then gain access to user accounts on remote systems.

With each new access, the worm program searched for already-active copies of itself. If it found one, the new copy exited, except for every seventh instance. Had the worm exited on all duplicate sightings, it might have remained undetected. Allowing every seventh duplicate to proceed (possibly to confound efforts to stop its spread by baiting with "fake" worms) created a wholesale infestation of Sun and VAX systems on the Internet.

The very features of the UNIX network environment that assisted the worm's propagation also helped to stop its advance. Ease of electronic communication, mechanisms to copy source and binary files to remote machines, and access to both source code and human expertise allowed cooperative efforts to develop solutions to proceed apace. By the evening of the next day, November 3, methods of halting the invading program were circulated to system administrators via the Internet. Within days, specific software patches for the exploited security flaws were available.

One natural response is to question Morris' motives in unleashing the worm. The action has been characterized as both a harmless prank gone awry and a serious criminal offense. Based on the complexity of starting the attack, it is unlikely that the worm's release or the scope of its spread was unintentional. The worm program took elaborate steps to cover its tracks and to repel efforts to stop its spread. Yet the program contained no code aimed at damaging or destroying the systems on which it ran. The author clearly had the expertise to include such commands; in fact, data structures were present in the bootstrap code that could have been used to transfer Trojan-horse or virus programs (see Section 19.4.2). The actual behavior of the program may lead to interesting observations, but does not provide a sound basis for inferring motive. What is not open to speculation, however, is the legal outcome: A federal court convicted Morris and handed down a sentence of three years probation, 400 hours of community service, and a $10,000 fine. Morris' legal costs probably were in excess of $100,000.

19.4.2 Viruses

Another form of computer attack is a **virus**. Like worms, viruses are designed to spread into other programs and can wreak havoc in a system, including modifying or destroying files and causing system crashes and program malfunctions. Whereas a worm is structured as a complete, standalone program, a virus is a fragment of code embedded in a legitimate program. Viruses are a major problem for computer users, especially users of microcomputer systems. Multiuser computers, generally, are not prone to viruses because the executable programs are protected from writing by the operating system. Even if a virus does infect a program, its powers are limited because other aspects of the system are protected. Single-user systems have no such protections and, as a result, a virus has free run.

Viruses are usually spread by users downloading viral programs from public bulletin boards or exchanging floppy disks containing an infection. A case from February 1992 involving two Cornell University students provides an illustration. The students had developed three Macintosh game programs with an embedded virus that they distributed to worldwide software archives via the Internet. The virus was discovered when a mathematics professor in Wales downloaded the games, and antivirus programs on his system alerted him to an infection. Some 200 other users had also downloaded the games. Although the virus was not designed to destroy data, it could spread to application files and cause such problems as long delays and program malfunctions. The authors were easy to trace, since the games had been mailed electronically from a Cornell account. New York state authorities arrested the students on misdemeanor charges of computer tampering and may have since filed additional charges.

In another incident, a programmer in California being divorced by his wife gave her a disk to load on a disputed computer. The disk contained a virus and erased all the files on the system. The husband was arrested and charged with destruction of property. On occasion, upcoming viral infections are announced in high-profile media events. Such was the case with the Michelangelo virus, which was scheduled to erase infected hard-disk files on March 6, 1992, the Renaissance artist's five-hundred and seventeenth birthday. Because of the extensive publicity surrounding the virus, most U.S. sites had located and destroyed the virus before it was activated, so it caused little or no damage. Such cases both alert the general public to and alarm it about the virus problem. Antivirus programs are currently excellent sellers. Most commercial packages are effective against only particular, known viruses. They work by searching all the programs on a system for the specific pattern of instructions known to make up the virus. When they find a known pattern, they remove the instructions, "disinfecting" the program. These commercial packages have catalogs of hundreds of viruses for which they search. As each virus is cataloged, other viruses appear using varying techniques. For instance, in 1999 the "Melissa" virus spread extensively and clogged many e-mail servers. It used a Microsoft Outlook macro facility, and was disguised as an "important" message. When the user opened the message, the macro was triggered, and sent an e-mail message to the first 50 people in the user's address book.

The best protection against computer viruses is prevention, or the practice of **safe computing**. Purchasing only unopened software from vendors and avoiding free or pirated copies from public sources or floppy-disk exchange is the safest route to preventing infection. However, even new copies of legitimate software applications are not immune to virus infection: There have been cases where disgruntled employees of a software company have infected the master copies of software programs to do economic harm to the company selling the software.

Another safeguard, although it does not prevent infection, does permit early detection. A user must begin by completely reformatting the hard disk, especially the boot sector, which is often targeted for viral attack. Only secure software is uploaded, and a checksum for each file is calculated. The checksum list must be then be kept free from unauthorized access. Following any system reboot, a program can recompute the checksums and compare them to the original list; any differences serve as a warning of possible infection.

Because they usually work among systems, worms and viruses are generally considered to pose security, rather than protection, problems.

19.5 ■ Threat Monitoring

The security of a system can be improved by two management techniques. One is **threat monitoring:** The system can check for suspicious patterns of activity in an attempt to detect a security violation. A common example of this scheme is a time-sharing system that counts the number of incorrect passwords given when a user is trying to log in. More than a few incorrect attempts may signal an attempt to guess a password.

Another common technique is an **audit log**. An audit log simply records the time, user, and type of all accesses to an object. After security has been violated, administrators can use the audit log to determine how and when the problem occurred and perhaps what amount of damage was done. This information can be useful, both for recovery from the violation and, possibly, for development of tighter security measures to prevent future problems. Unfortunately, logs can become large, and logging uses system resources that are then unavailable to the users.

Rather than log system activities, we can scan the system periodically for security holes. These scans can be done when the computer has relatively little traffic, so they will have less effect than logging. Such a scan can check a variety of aspects of the system:

- Short or easy-to-guess passwords

- Unauthorized setuid programs, if the system supports this mechanism

- Unauthorized programs in system directories

- Unexpected long-running processes

- Improper directory protections, on both user and system directories

- Improper protections on system data files, such as the password file, device drivers, or even the operating-system kernel itself

- Dangerous entries in the program search path (for example, Trojan horses, as discussed in Section 19.3.1)

- Changes to system programs detected with checksum values

Any problems found by a security scan can either be fixed automatically or be reported to the managers of the system.

Networked computers are much more susceptible to security attacks than are standalone systems. Rather than attacks from a known set of access points, such as directly connected terminals, they face attacks from an unknown and large set of access points—a potentially severe security problem. To a lesser extent, systems connected to telephone lines via modems are also more exposed.

In fact, the U.S. federal government considers systems to be only as secure as is the system's most far-reaching connection. For instance, a top-secret system can be accessed only from within a building also considered top secret. The system loses its top-secret rating if any form of communication can occur outside that environment. Certain government facilities take extreme security precautions. For example, the connectors into which a terminal plugs to communicate with the secure computer can be locked in a safe in the office when the terminal is not being used. A person must know a physical lock combination, as well as authentication information for the computer itself, to gain access to the computer.

Unfortunately for systems administrators and computer-security professionals, it is frequently impossible to lock a machine in a room and to disallow all remote access. For instance, the Internet currently connects millions of computers, and it has become a mission-critical, indispensable resource for many companies and individuals. As there are in any club with millions of members, there are many good members and several bad members. The bad members have many tools they they can use across the Internet to attempt to gain access to the interconnected computers, just as did the Morris Internet worm.

The problem is, how can trusted computers be connected safely to an untrustworthy network? One solution is the use of a *firewall* to separate trusted and untrusted systems. A firewall is a computer or router that sits between the trusted and the untrusted. It limits network access between the two *security domains*, and monitors and logs all connections. For instance, *web servers* use

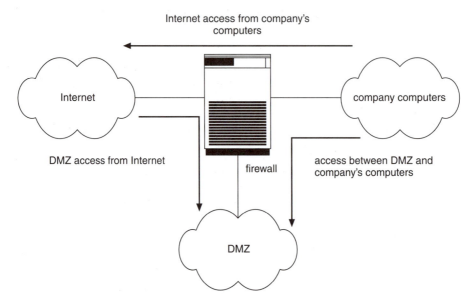

Figure 19.2   Network security through domain separation via firewall.

the `http` protocol to communicate with web browsers. A firewall therefore may need to allow http to pass. The Morris Internet worm used the `finger` protocol to break into computers, so `finger` would not be allowed to pass. In fact, a firewall can separate a network into multiple domains. A common implementation has the Internet as the untrusted domain; a semitrusted and semisecure network, called the *demilitarized zone (DMZ)*, as another domain; and a company's computers as a third domain (see Figure 19.2). Connections are allowed from the Internet to the DMZ computers, and from the company computers to the Internet, but are not allowed from the Internet or DMZ computers to the company computers. Optionally, controlled communications may be allowed between the DMZ and one or more company computers. For instance, a web server on the DMZ may need to query a database server on the corporate network. In this manner, all access is contained, and any DMZ systems that are broken into based on the protocols allowed through the firewall still are unable to access the company computers.

19.6 ■ Encryption

The various provisions that an operating system may make for authorization may not offer sufficient protection for highly sensitive data. Moreover, as computer networks gain popularity, more sensitive (classified) information is being transmitted over channels where eavesdropping and message interception are possible. To keep such sensitive information secure, we need mechanisms to allow a user to protect data that are transferred over the network.

Encryption is one common method of protecting information that is transmitted over unreliable links. The basic mechanism works as follows:

1. The information (text) is **encrypted** (encoded) from its initial readable form, called **clear text,** to an internal form, called **cipher text**. This latter internal text form, although readable, does not make any sense.

2. The cipher text can be stored in a readable file, or transmitted over unprotected channels.

3. To make sense of the cipher text, the receiver must **decrypt** (decode) it back into clear text.

Even if the encrypted information is accessed by an unauthorized person or program, it will be useless unless it can be decoded. The main challenge in using this approach is the development of encryption schemes that are impossible (or at least exceedingly difficult) to break.

Various methods meet this challenge. The most common ones provide a general encryption algorithm, E, a general decryption algorithm, D, and a secret key (or keys) to be supplied for each application. Let E_k and D_k denote the encryption and decryption algorithms, respectively, for a particular application with a key k. Then, the encryption algorithm must satisfy the following properties for any message m:

1. $D_k(E_k(m)) = m$.

2. Both E_k and D_k can be computed efficiently.

3. The security of the system depends on only the secrecy of the key, and does not depend on the secrecy of the algorithms E and D.

One such scheme, called the **data-encryption standard,** was adopted by the United States National Bureau of Standards. This scheme suffers from the **key-distribution problem:** Before communication can take place, the secret keys must be sent securely to both the sender and the receiver. This task cannot be carried out effectively in a communication-network environment. A solution to this problem is to use **public key encryption**. Each user has both a public and a private key, and two users can communicate knowing only each other's public key.

This algorithm is believed to be almost unbreakable. The basic concept is as follows. The public encryption key is a pair (e, n); the private key is a pair (d, n), where e, d, and n are positive integers. Each message is represented as an integer between 0 and $n - 1$. (A long message is broken into a series of smaller messages, each of which can be represented as such an integer.) The functions E and D are defined as

$$E(m) = m^e \bmod n = C,$$
$$D(C) = C^d \bmod n.$$

The main problem is choosing the encryption and decryption keys. The integer n is computed as the product of two large (100 or more digits) randomly chosen prime numbers p and q with

$$n = p \times q.$$

The value of d is chosen to be a large, randomly chosen integer relatively prime to $(p - 1) \times (q - 1)$. That is, d satisfies

$$\text{greatest common divisor } [d, (p - 1) \times (q - 1)] = 1.$$

Finally, the integer e is computed from p, q, and d to be the **multiplicative inverse** of d modulo $(p - 1) \times (q - 1)$. That is, e satisfies

$$e \times d \bmod (p - 1) \times (q - 1) = 1.$$

Note that, although n is publicly known, p and q are not. This condition is allowed because, as is well known, it is difficult to factor n. Consequently, the integers d and e cannot be guessed easily.

Let us illustrate this scheme with an example. Let $p = 5$ and $q = 7$. Then, $n = 35$ and $(p - 1) \times (q - 1) = 24$. Since 11 is relatively prime to 24, we can choose $d = 11$; and since $11 \times 11 \bmod 24 = 121 \bmod 24 = 1$, $e = 11$. Suppose now that $m = 3$. Then,

$$C = m^e \bmod n = 3^{11} \bmod 35 = 12,$$

and

$$C^d \bmod n = 12^{11} \bmod 35 = 3 = m.$$

Thus, if we encode m using e, we can decode m using d.

19.7 ■ Computer-Security Classifications

The U.S. Department of Defense's *Trusted Computer System Evaluation Criteria* specifies four divisions of security in systems: A, B, C, and D. The lowest-level classification is division D, or minimal protection. Division D comprises only one class, and is used for systems that were evaluated, but that failed to meet the requirements of any one of the other security classes. For instance, MS-DOS and Windows 3.1 are in division D.

Division C, the next level of security, provides discretionary protection and accountability of users and their actions through the use of audit capabilities. Division C has two levels: C1 and C2. A C1 class system incorporates some form of controls that allow users to protect private information and to keep other users from accidentally reading or destroying their data. A C1 environment is one in which cooperating users access data at the same levels of sensitivity. Most versions of UNIX are C1 class.

The sum total of all protection systems within a computer system (hardware, software, firmware) that correctly enforce a security policy is known as a **trusted computer base (TCB)**. The TCB of a C1 system controls access between users and files by allowing the user to specify and control sharing of objects by named individuals or defined groups. In addition, the TCB requires that the user identify himself before he starts any activities that the TCB is expected to mediate. This identification is accomplished via a protected mechanism or password; the TCB protects the authentication data such that they are inaccessible to unauthorized users.

A C2 class system adds to the requirements of a C1 system via an individual-level access control. For example, access rights of a file can be specified to the level of a single individual. In addition, the system administrator is capable of auditing selectively the actions of any one or more users based on individual identity. The TCB also protects itself from modification of its code or data structures. In addition, no information produced by a prior user is available to another user that accesses a storage object that has been released back to the system. Some special, secure versions of UNIX have been certified at the C2 level.

Division B mandatory-protection systems have all the properties of a class C2 system, plus they attach sensitivity labels to each object. The B1 class TCB maintains the security label of each object in the system; the label is used for decisions pertaining to mandatory access control. For example, a user at confidential level could not access a file at the more sensitive secret level. The TCB also denotes the sensitivity level at the top and bottom of each page of any human-readable output. In addition to the normal username–password authentication information, the TCB also maintains the clearance and authorizations of individual users and will support at least two levels of security. These levels are hierarchical, such that a user may access any objects that carry sensitivity labels equal to or lower than his security clearance. For example, a secret-level user could access a file at the confidential level in the absence of other access controls. Processes are also isolated through the use of distinct address spaces.

A B2 class system extends the sensitivity labels to each system resource such as storage objects. Physical devices are assigned minimum- and maximum-security levels which the system uses to enforce constraints imposed by the physical environments in which the devices are located. In addition, a B2 system supports covert channels and the auditing of events that may lead to the exploitation of a covert channel.

A B3 class system allows the creation of access-control lists that denote users or groups that are not granted access to a given named object. The TCB also contains a mechanism to monitor events that may indicate a violation of security policy. The mechanism notifies the security administrator and, if necessary, terminates the event in the least disruptive manner.

The highest-level classification is division A. A class A1 system is functionally equivalent to a B3 system architecturally, but uses formal design specifications and verification techniques, granting a high degree of assurance that the TCB has been implemented correctly. A system beyond class A1 might be designed and developed in a trusted facility by trusted personnel.

Note that the use of a TCB merely ensures that the system can enforce aspects of a security policy; the TCB does not specify what the policy should be. Typically, a given computing environment develops a security policy for **certification** and has the plan **accredited** by a security agency, such as by the National Computer Security Center. Certain computing environments may require other certification, such as by TEMPEST, which guards against electronic eavesdropping. For example, a TEMPEST-certified system has terminals that are shielded to prevent electromagnetic fields from escaping. This shielding ensures that equipment outside the room or building where the terminal is housed cannot detect what information is being displayed by the terminal.

19.8 ■ An Example Security Model: Windows NT

Microsoft Windows NT was designed to support a variety of security features and levels that range from minimal security to a U.S. government level C2 security classification. The default security level that NT uses could be described as minimal, but it can be readily configured by the system administrator to the desired level. A utility program, C2config.exe is provided to help the administrator choose the desired security settings. In this section, we examine features that Windows NT uses to perform security functions. For more information and background on Windows NT, see Chapter 22.

The NT security model is based on the common notion of *user accounts*. NT allows the creation of any number of user accounts, which can be grouped in any manner. Access to system objects can then be permitted or denied as desired. Users are identified to the system by a *unique* security ID. When a user logs on, NT creates a *security access token* that includes the security ID for the users, security IDs for any groups in which the user is a member, and a list of any special privileges that the user has. Examples of special privileges include backing up files and directories, shutting down the computer, logging on interactively, and changing the system clock. Every process that NT runs on behalf of a user gets a copy of the access token. The system uses the security IDs in the access token to permit or deny access to system objects whenever the user, or a process on behalf of the user, attempts to access the object. Authentication of a user account is typically accomplished via a username and password, although the modular design of NT allows the development of custom authentication packages. For example, a retinal (eye) scanner might be used to verify that the user is who she says she is.

Windows NT uses the idea of a subject to ensure that those programs that a user runs do not get greater access to the system than the user is authorized to have. A **subject** tracks and manages permissions for each program that a user runs; it is composed of the user's access token and the program acting on behalf of the user. Since NT operates with a client–server model, two classes of subjects are used to control access. An example of a **simple subject** is the typical application program that a user executes after he logs on. The simple subject is assigned a **security context** based on the security access token of the user. A **server subject** is a process implemented as a protected server that uses the security context of the client when acting on the client's behalf. The technique that allows one process to take on the security attributes of another is called **impersonation**.

As mentioned in Section 19.5, auditing is a useful security technique. NT has auditing built in, and allows many common security threats to be monitored. Examples of auditing that are useful to track threats are failure auditing for logon and logoff events to detect random password breakins, success auditing for logon and logoff events to detect logon activity at strange hours, success and failure write-access auditing for executable files to track a virus outbreak, and success and failure file-access auditing to detect access to sensitive files.

Security attributes of an object in NT are described by a **security descriptor**. The security descriptor contains the security ID of the owner of the object (who can change the access permissions), a group security ID used only by the POSIX subsystem, a discretionary access-control list that identifies which users or groups are allowed or are not allowed access, and a system access-control list that controls which auditing messages the system generates. For example, the security descriptor of the file *foo.bar* might have owner avi, and this discretionary access-control list:

- avi—all access

- group cs—read–write access

- user cliff—no access

In addition, it might have a system access-control list of audit writes by everyone. An **access-control list** is composed of access-control entries that contain the security ID of the individual, and an access mask that defines all possible actions on the object, with a value of AccessAllowed or AccessDenied for each action. Files in NT may have the following access types: ReadData, WriteData, AppendData, Execute, ReadExtendedAttribute, WriteExtendedAttribute, ReadAttributes, and WriteAttributes. We can see how these distinctions allow a high degree of control over access to objects.

NT classifies objects as either **container objects** or **noncontainer objects**. Container objects, such as directories, can logically contain other objects. By default, when an object is created within a container object, the new object inherits permissions from the parent object. It does so as well if the user copies a file from one directory to a new directory—the file will inherit the permissions of the destination directory. However, if the permission is changed on a directory, the new permissions do not apply automatically to existing files and subdirectories; the user may apply them explicitly if she wishes. Also, if the user moves a file into a new directory, the current permissions of the file move with it.

In addition, the system administrator can prohibit printing to a printer on the system for all or part of a day, and can use the NT Performance Monitor to help her spot approaching problems. In general, NT does a good job of providing features to help ensure a secure computing environment. Many of these features are not enabled by default, however, to provide an environment closer to the one to which the typical personal-computer user is accustomed. For a real multiuser environment, the system administrator should formulate a security plan and implement it, using the features that NT provides.

19.9 ■ Java Security

Security is an important feature of Java, because programs are capable of operating in a distributed environment. The best known example of such programs is the use of applets. An applet is a Java program that is downloaded from a web server and runs within a web page. If the JVM within a browser does not provide sufficient security features, an applet could perform malicious acts on the computer, such as changing or deleting important files, erasing entire file systems, or installing a virus that could attack the computer system at a later date. Therefore, security is an integral feature of Java technology. The basic concepts of the Java security model are discussed here.

The Java security model is designed to be flexible and configurable; it can be applied both to applications loaded from the local file system and to applets loaded from a network. When a Java program is loaded, its classes are mapped to a protection mechanism that ranges from access to all system features such as the file system and network to access to virtually no system features.

The **Java security model** consists of three separate components: (1) class loader, (2) class verifier, and (3) security manager (Figure 19.3). First, we look at the features of the Java language that also provide security.

The Java language has features that make it inherently secure and reliable. These features deal mostly with memory management. Languages such as

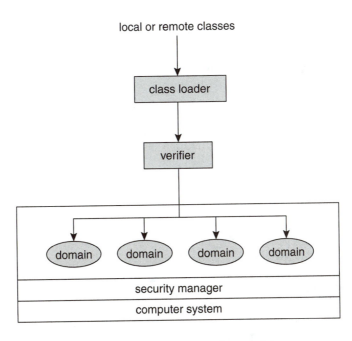

Figure 19.3   Java security model.

C and C++ allow the programmer to use pointers to virtually any memory location. Although this feature is a powerful one, it is also a major source of security violations and of random program crashes. Java does not allow pointers, so a program cannot directly access memory locations or perform pointer arithmetic. Java also prevents arrays and strings from going beyond their boundaries. By protecting memory, the Java compiler can control a program's access to system resources.

19.9.1 Class Loader

The **class loader** is responsible for reading the bytecode class files into the JVM. The class loader is important because it is the first line of defense in the security model. There are two types of class loaders: (1) the primordial, or internal, class loader, and (2) instances of java.lang.ClassLoader objects.

Each JVM has only one **primordial class loader**. The role of the primordial loader is to load all classes that are part of the Java API. The JVM considers all classes that are loaded by the primordial class loader to be trusted and grants them access to all system resources. Prior to Java 1.2, all classes specified in the CLASSPATH were loaded by the primordial loader. The CLASSPATH lists the path in the local file system where the class loader may locate classes that belong to a Java application. With Java 1.2, a URLClassLoader loads classes from the CLASSPATH.

The other type of class loaders are objects that are instances of types that extend the ClassLoader class. The URLClassLoader is an example of a **class loader object** that extends ClassLoader. Another example is the applet class loader that a browser creates to load the classes of an applet over a network. A Java application may also define its own class loaders by extending the ClassLoader class.

The primary security function of class loaders is to prevent classes that are loaded from untrusted sources from being confused with trusted classes. Each class loader takes responsibility for the classes that it loads by maintaining its own **namespace,** which contains a list of all classes that it has loaded. Classes loaded by different class loaders are in different namespaces and cannot interfere with one another. This approach also allows two different class loaders each to load a class with the same name. For example, a web page may reference two applets that each have a class called VisualGraphics. Java allows this by loading the classes for each applet with its own class loader. Thus, the two classes are in their own namespace. When the JVM needs access to a class, it asks the appropriate class loader.

The value of maintaining separate namespaces is integral to the security model. In Java, classes that belong to a package can access data from other classes in the same package. Such data are **package-friendly data;** they are data declared without the public, private, or protected modifiers. Without the namespace separation, a class called java.lang.somethingBad could be loaded, and the JVM would consider it as belonging to the package java.lang from the core API. This class would now have access to package-friendly data fields of the java.lang package. A potentially more compromising situation would arise if a class called java.lang.String were loaded. Without separation of namespaces, a mischievious class could fool the JVM into thinking that it was the String class for the core API. Namespace separation ensures that all classes that belong to the core API (such as those in the java.lang package) are loaded in the namespace for the primordial class loader.

19.9.2 Verifier

Once a class is loaded, the JVM does not create an object instance until the bytecodes for the class pass a **verification** procedure to ensure that the class is well-behaved Java code. The verifier checks that the class file is a valid Java bytecode and does not overflow or underflow the stack. It also ensures that the bytecode does not perform pointer arithmetic, which could potentially provide illegal memory access. Although the code produced by a compiler that implemented the language specification should pass verification, the JVM does not know whether the bytecode was written by a hacker intent on cracking the computer.

19.9.3 Security Manager and Protection Domains

Java security works by mapping a Java program to a certain protection mechanism, or to a security policy. A **security policy** defines a set of permissions that a Java program is granted. Examples of permissions include access to a specific file or directory, and access to the network. Security policies are divided into **protection domains,** each of which is a set of classes that are granted the same set of permissions. Protection domains range from having access to all system resources to having access to no system resources. Each class that is loaded belongs to one and only one protection domain. The primary role of the security manager is to ensure that a Java program runs within the confines on the protection domain to which it has been mapped (Figure 19.3). After a class has been loaded and verified, it is mapped to a protection domain. Whenever program code for this class attempts to access a resource in the computer system, the security manager checks that its protection domain allows such access.

An example of using protection domains follows. One policy is that classes loaded from the local file system are given access to all system resources. Therefore, all classes loaded locally are mapped to the protection domain that grants full access to all resources. Another policy is that applets loaded from a network be given access to few system resources (this policy is the default for applets loaded from a network.) Therefore, classes that belong to an applet loaded from a network are mapped to a protection domain that grants minimal access. Figure 19.4 highlights restrictions that are typically placed on an applet that is loaded from a network.

We may want to grant an applet specific permissions. For example, if an organizaion delivers a suite of applications—such as a word processor and spreadsheet—as a Java applet, we want this application suite to access the local file system, and that requires operations that otherwise would be unavailable to applets loaded over a network. In this instance, classes belonging to this applet are mapped to a protection domain that grants access to the local file system. (It is possible to grant access to *particular* directories or files, rather than to the entire file system.)

The role of a security manager is to enforce the rules of the security policy. Whenever a class tries to perform specific functions, the JVM first asks the security manager. For example, if an applet attempts to perform a restricted operation—such as opening a socket connection over the network—the security manager throws a security exception.

There may be only one security manager on a JVM (to enforce a single security policy); once it is started, it cannot be removed or replaced. By default, a security manager is only loaded for applets and not for Java applications. Therefore, the default behavior for applications is that no security policy is in place and classes belonging to an application are mapped to a protection domain that provides access to all system resources. However, a security manager can be installed and applications can be mapped to a more restrictive protection domain, thus allowing a security policy to be in effect for applications. Applets are treated differently, however. Most web browsers typically have a security policy that maps applets to a protection domain that restricts the activity of an applet as described in Figure 19.4. However, it is possible to implement a security policy that grants an applet certain privileges by mapping it to a less restrictive protection domain.

1. Cannot read or write to the local file system; includes reading, writing, and deleting files; creating, listing, or deleting directories

2. Cannot create a network connection on any other computer except the computer from which the applet was loaded; applets also cannot listen or accept network connections on any port numbered <= 1024

3. Cannot access certain AWT features; all windows created by an applet will display a message that they are "insecure"; applets also may not start print jobs or access the system clipboard

4. May not access system properties, such as determining a user's account name or home directory

Figure 19.4 Restrictions typically placed on an applet.

19.10 ▪ Summary

Protection is an internal problem. Security must consider both the computer system and the environment (people, buildings, businesses, valuable objects, and threats) within which the system is used.

The data stored in the computer system must be protected from unauthorized access, malicious destruction or alteration, and accidental introduction of inconsistency. It is easier to protect against accidental loss of data consistency than to protect against malicious access to the data. Absolute protection of the information stored in a computer system from malicious abuse is not possible, but the cost to the perpetrator can be made sufficiently high to deter most, if not all, attempts to access that information without proper authority.

The various authorization provisions in a computer system may not confer sufficient protection for highly sensitive data. In such cases, data may be encrypted. It is not possible for encrypted data to be read unless the reader knows how to decrypt the encrypted data.

The Java language and the JVM have features that are more properly categorized as providing protection than security. They include limited access to memory (no pointers), code checking, and checksum verification. Combined with the JVM's access-control mechanisms, they limit the access an applet has to the system on which it runs.

▪ Exercises

19.1 A password may become known to other users in a variety of ways. Is there a simple method for detecting that such an event has occurred? Explain your answer.

19.2 The list of all passwords is kept within the operating system. Thus, if a user manages to read this list, password protection is no longer provided. Suggest a scheme that avoids this problem. (Hint: Use different internal and external representations.)

19.3 An experimental addition to UNIX allows a user to connect a *watchdog* program to a file, such that the watchdog is invoked whenever a program requests access to the file. The watchdog then either grants or denies access to the file. Discuss two pros and two cons of using watchdogs for security.

19.4 The UNIX program COPS scans a given system for possible security holes, and alerts the user to possible problems. What are two potential hazards of using such a system for security? How can these problems be limited or eliminated?

19.5 Discuss a means by which managers of systems connected to the Internet could have designed their systems to limit or eliminate the damage done by the Morris worm. What are the drawbacks of making the change that you suggest?

19.6 Argue for or against the judicial sentence handed down against Robert Morris, Jr., for his creation and execution of an Internet worm.

19.7 Make a list of six security concerns for a computer system for a bank. For each concern, state whether it relates to physical security, human security, or operating-system security.

19.8 What are two advantages of encrypting data that are stored in the computer system?

Bibliographical Notes

Morris and Thompson [1979] discuss password security. Morshedian [1986] presents methods to fight password pirates. The issue of password cracking is discussed by Seely [1989]. Computer breakins are discussed by Lehmann [1987] and by Reid [1987].

Discussions concerning UNIX security are offered by Grampp and Morris [1984] and by Garfinkel and Spafford [1996]. The COPS security-scanning package (Exercise 19.4) for UNIX was written by Farmer at Purdue University. It is available to users on the Internet via the *ftp* program from host ftp.uu.net in directory /pub/security/cops.

Spafford [1989] presents a detailed technical discussion of the Internet worm. The Spafford article appears with three others in a special section on the Internet worm in *Communications of the ACM* (Volume 32, Number 6, June 1989).

Diffie and Hellman [1976, 1979] were the first authors to propose the use of public key cryptosystems and digital signatures. The most widely used digital-signature algorithms today are RSA [Rivest et al. 1978] (presented in Section 19.6) and the Digital Signature Algorithm, which has been established as a digital-signature standard by the U.S. government [DSS 1994]. RSA can also be used as a public-key-encryption system. Menezes and colleagues [1997] have written a useful resource on public-key algorithms, digital signatures, and other topics in cryptography.

Governments are, of course, concerned about security, and there have been many criteria published by various governments for the evaluation of security in computer systems. The *Trusted Computer System Evaluation Criteria (TCSEC)* [1985], known also as the *Orange Book*, was published by the U.S. Department of Defense. It describes a set of security levels, and the features that an operating system must have to qualify for each security rating. The *Information Technology*

Security Evaluation Criteria (ITSEC) [1991] is a set of criteria established for use by all European Union member nations to evaluate computer-system security. It differs from the *Orange Book* in several ways, including generalizing from the *Orange Book*'s focus on confidentiality of information. The *Common Criteria* [1998], a worldwide set of criteria for evaluating secure computer systems, resulted from the combined work of the *ITSEC* editorial board, and the U.S. and Canadian governments.

The *Microsoft Windows NT Workstation Resource Kit* [1996] describes what the security model of NT is and how to use that model.

Details concerning Java security are discussed by Gong and colleagues [1997] and by Oaks [1998].

Part Six

CASE STUDIES

We integrate the various concepts that we have discussed thus far describing three real operating systems: UNIX Berkeley 4.3BSD, Linux, and Microsoft Windows NT. We chose Berkeley 4.3BSD and Linux because UNIX at one time was almost small enough to understand, and yet was not a toy operating system. Most of its internal algorithms were selected for *simplicity*, rather than for speed or sophistication. Both Berkeley 4.3BSD and Linux are readily available to computer-science departments, so many students have access to these systems.

Windows NT is a relatively new operating system from Microsoft that is gaining popularity, not only for the standalone-machine market, but also in the workgroup-server market. Windows NT is a modern operating system whose design and implementation are drastically different from those of UNIX.

In addition, we briefly discuss several other highly influential operating systems. The order of presentation highlights the similarities and differences among the systems; it is neither chronological nor indicative of relative importance.

The Mach operating system is a modern operating system that provides compatibility with 4.3BSD; we provide a discussion of it on our website (URL:http://www.bell-labs.com/topic/books/os-book/Mach.ps).

Chapter 20

THE UNIX SYSTEM

Although operating-system concepts can be considered in purely theoretical terms, it is often useful to see how they are implemented in practice. This chapter presents an in-depth examination of the 4.3BSD operating system, a version of UNIX, as an example of the various concepts presented in this book. By examining a complete, real system, we can see how the various concepts discussed in this book relate both to one another and to practice. We consider first a brief history of UNIX, and present the system's user and programmer interfaces. Then, we discuss the internal data structures and algorithms used by the UNIX kernel to support the user–programmer interface.

20.1 ■ History

The first version of UNIX was developed in 1969 by Ken Thompson of the Research Group at Bell Laboratories to use an otherwise idle PDP-7. He was soon joined by Dennis Ritchie. Thompson, Ritchie, and other members of the Research Group produced the early versions of UNIX.

Ritchie had previously worked on the MULTICS project, and MULTICS had a strong influence on the newer operating system. Even the name UNIX is merely a pun on MULTICS. The basic organization of the file system, the idea of the command interpreter (the shell) as a user process, the use of a separate process for each command, the original line-editing characters (# to erase the most recently typed character and @ to erase the entire line), and numerous other features came directly from MULTICS. Ideas from various other operating systems, such as MIT's CTSS and the XDS-940 system, were also used.

Ritchie and Thompson worked quietly on UNIX for many years. Their work on the first version allowed them to move it to a PDP-11/20, for a second version. A third version resulted from their rewriting most of the operating system in the systems-programming language C, instead of the previously used assembly language. C was developed at Bell Laboratories to support UNIX. UNIX was also moved to larger PDP-11 models, such as the 11/45 and 11/70. Multiprogramming and other enhancements were added when it was rewritten in C and moved to systems (such as the 11/45) that had hardware support for multiprogramming.

As UNIX developed, it became widely used within Bell Laboratories and gradually spread to a few universities. The first version widely available outside Bell Laboratories was Version 6, released in 1976. (The version number for early UNIX systems corresponds to the edition number of the *UNIX Programmer's Manual* that was current when the distribution was made; the code and the manuals were revised independently.)

The small size, modularity, and clean design of early UNIX systems led to UNIX-based work at numerous other computer-science organizations, such as Rand, BBN, the University of Illinois, Harvard, Purdue, and even DEC. The most influential of the non–Bell Laboratories and non–AT&T UNIX development groups has been the University of California at Berkeley.

The first Berkeley VAX UNIX work began in 1978 with Bill Joy and Ozalp Babaoglu. This work was soon supported by the Defense Advanced Research Projects Agency (DARPA) for government use. The final Berkeley release, 4.4BSD, was completed in June 1993. It includes new X.25 networking support, and POSIX standard compliance. It also has a radically new file-system organization, with a new virtual-file-system interface and support for **stackable** file systems, allowing file systems to be layered on top of one another for easy inclusion of new features. An implementation of NFS is also included in the release (Chapter 17), as is a new log-based file system (see Chapter 13). The 4.4BSD virtual-memory system is derived from Mach (described in the Appendix). Several other changes, such as enhanced security and improved kernel structure, are also included. With the release of Version 4.4, Berkeley halted its research.

The current set of UNIX operating systems is not limited to those by Bell Laboratories (which is currently owned by Lucent Technology) and by Berkeley, however. Sun Microsystems helped to popularize the BSD flavor of UNIX by shipping it on its workstations. As UNIX has grown in popularity, it has been moved to many different computers and computer systems, and a wide variety of UNIX, and UNIX-like, operating systems has been created.

The wide popularity of UNIX with computer vendors has made UNIX the most portable of operating systems, and has led users to expect a UNIX environment independent of any specific computer manufacturer. The large number of implementations of the system, however, has led to remarkable variation in the programming and user interfaces distributed by the vendors. For true vendor independence, application-program developers need consistent interfaces. Such interfaces would allow all "UNIX" applications to run on all UNIX systems—and that certainly is not the current situation. This matter has become important as UNIX has become the preferred program-development platform for applications ranging from databases to graphics and networking; it has led to a strong market demand for UNIX standards. Figure 20.1 summarizes the relationships among the various versions of UNIX.

The UNIX system has grown from a personal project of two Bell Laboratories employees to an operating system being defined by multinational standardization bodies. Yet this system is still of interest to academia. We believe that UNIX has become and will remain an important part of operating-system theory and practice. UNIX is an excellent vehicle for academic study. For example, the Tunis operating system, the Xinu operating system, and the Minix operating system are based on the concepts of UNIX, but were developed explicitly for classroom study. There is a plethora of ongoing UNIX-related research systems, including Mach, Chorus, Comandos, and Roisin. The original developers, Ritchie and Thompson, were honored in 1983 by the Association for Computing Machinery Turing award for their work on UNIX.

The specific UNIX version used in this chapter is the VAX version of 4.3BSD. We chose this system because it implements many interesting operating-system concepts, such as demand paging with clustering, and networking. It has also been influential in other UNIX systems, in standards, and in networking developments. We used the VAX implementation because 4.3BSD was developed on the VAX and that machine still is a convenient point of reference, despite the recent proliferation of implementations on other hardware (such as the Motorola 68040 and 88000, the Intel Pentiums, the Sun SPARCs, DEC Alpha, HP Precision, and the MIPS CPUs).

20.2 ■ Design Principles

UNIX was designed to be a time-sharing system. The standard user interface (the shell) is simple and can be replaced by another, if desired. The file system is a multilevel tree, which allows users to create their own subdirectories. Each user data file is simply a sequence of bytes.

Disk files and I/O devices are treated as similarly as possible. Thus, device dependencies and peculiarities are kept in the kernel as much as possible; even in the kernel, most of them are confined to the device drivers.

UNIX supports multiple processes. A process can easily create new processes. CPU scheduling is a simple priority algorithm. 4.3BSD uses demand paging as a mechanism to support memory-management and CPU-scheduling decisions. Swapping is used if a system is suffering from excess paging.

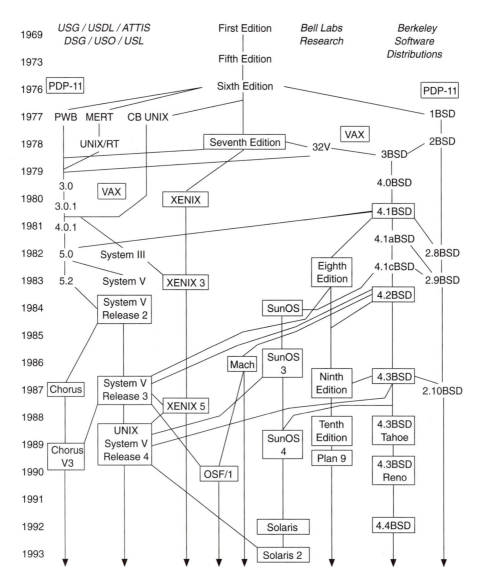

Figure 20.1   History of UNIX versions.

Because UNIX was originated first by one programmer, Ken Thompson, and then by another, Dennis Ritchie, as a system for their own convenience, it was small enough to understand. Most of the algorithms were selected for *simplicity,* rather than for speed or sophistication. The intent was to have the kernel and libraries provide a small set of facilities that was sufficiently powerful to allow a person to build a more complex system if one were needed. UNIX's clean design has resulted in many imitations and modifications.

Although the designers of UNIX had a significant amount of knowledge about other operating systems, UNIX had no elaborate design spelled out before its implementation. This flexibility appears to have been one of the key factors in the development of the system. Several design principles were used, however, even though they were not made explicit at the outset.

The UNIX system was designed by programmers for programmers. Thus, it has always been interactive, and facilities for program development have always been a high priority. Such facilities include the program make (which can check which of a collection of source files for a program need to be compiled and then do the compiling), and the **Source Code Control System** (**SCCS**) (which keeps successive versions of files available without the entire contents of each step being stored).

The operating system is written mostly in C, which was developed to support UNIX, since neither Thompson nor Ritchie enjoyed programming in assembly language. The avoidance of assembly language was also necessary because of the uncertainty about the machine or machines on which UNIX would be run. It has greatly simplified the problems of moving UNIX from one hardware system to another.

From the beginning, UNIX development systems have had all the UNIX sources available on-line, and the developers have used the systems under development as their primary systems. This pattern of development has greatly facilitated the discovery of deficiencies and their fixes, as well as of new possibilities and their implementations. It has also encouraged the plethora of UNIX variants existing today. The benefits have outweighed the disadvantages: If something is broken, it can be fixed at a local site; there is no need to wait for the next release of the system. Such fixes, as well as new facilities, may be incorporated into later distributions.

The size constraints of the PDP-11 (and earlier computers used for UNIX) forced a certain elegance. Where other systems have elaborate algorithms for dealing with pathological conditions, UNIX just does a controlled crash, called a **panic**. Instead of attempting to cure such conditions, UNIX tries to prevent them. Where other systems would use brute force or macro-expansion, UNIX mostly has had to develop more subtle—or at least simpler—approaches.

These early strengths of UNIX produced much of its popularity, which in turn produced new demands that challenged those strengths. UNIX was used for tasks such as networking, graphics, and real-time operation, which did not always fit into its original text-oriented model. Thus, changes were made to certain internal facilities and new programming interfaces were added. These new facilities, and others—particularly window interfaces—required large amounts of code to support them, radically increasing the size of the system. For instance, networking and windowing both doubled the size of the system. This pattern in turn pointed out the continued strength of UNIX—whenever a new development occurred in the industry, UNIX could usually absorb it, but still remain UNIX.

20.3 ■ Programmer Interface

As do most operating systems, UNIX consists of two separable parts: the kernel and the systems programs. We can view the UNIX operating system as being layered, as shown in Figure 20.2. Everything below the system-call interface and above the physical hardware is the **kernel**. The kernel provides the file system, CPU scheduling, memory management, and other operating-system functions through system calls. Systems programs use the kernel-supported system calls to provide useful functions, such as compilation and file manipulation.

System calls define the **programmer interface** to UNIX; the set of systems programs commonly available defines the **user interface**. The programmer and user interface define the context that the kernel must support.

System calls in VAX 4.3BSD are made by a trap to location 40 of the VAX interrupt vectors. Parameters are passed to the kernel on the hardware stack; the kernel returns values in registers R0 and R1. Register R0 may also return an error code. The carry bit distinguishes a normal return from an error return.

This level of detail is seldom seen by a UNIX programmer, fortunately. Most systems programs are written in C, and the *UNIX Programmer's Manual* presents all system calls as C functions. A system program written in C for 4.3BSD on the VAX can generally be moved to another 4.3BSD system and simply recompiled, even though the two systems may be quite different. The details of system calls are known only to the compiler. This feature is a major reason for the portability of UNIX programs.

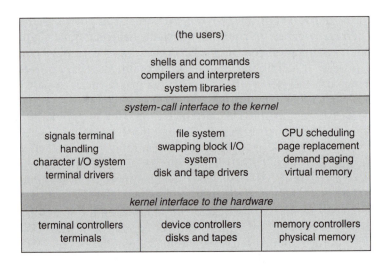

Figure 20.2   4.3BSD layer structure.

System calls for UNIX can be grouped into three rough categories: file manipulation, process control, and information manipulation. In Chapter 3, we listed a fourth category, device manipulation, but since devices in UNIX are treated as (special) files, the same system calls support both files and devices (although there is an extra system call for setting device parameters).

20.3.1 File Manipulation

A **file** in UNIX is a sequence of bytes. Different programs expect various levels of structure, but the kernel does not impose a structure on files. For instance, the convention for text files is lines of ASCII characters separated by a single newline character (which is the linefeed character in ASCII), but the kernel knows nothing of this convention.

Files are organized in tree-structured **directories**. Directories are themselves files that contain information on how to find other files. A **path name** to a file is a text string that identifies a file by specifying a path through the directory structure to the file. Syntactically, it consists of individual file-name elements separated by the slash character. For example, in */usr/local/font*, the first slash indicates the root of the directory tree, called the *root* directory. The next element, *usr,* is a subdirectory of the root, *local* is a subdirectory of *usr,* and *font* is a file or directory in the directory *local*. Whether *font* is an ordinary file or a directory cannot be determined from the path-name syntax.

The UNIX file system has both **absolute path names** and **relative path names**. Absolute path names start at the root of the file system and are distinguished by a slash at the beginning of the path name; */usr/local/font* is an absolute path name. Relative path names start at the **current directory,** which is an attribute of the process accessing the path name. Thus, *local/font* indicates a file or directory named *font* in the directory *local* in the current directory, which might or might not be */usr*.

A file may be known by more than one name in one or more directories. Such multiple names are known as **links,** and all links are treated equally by the operating system. 4.3BSD also supports **symbolic links,** which are files containing the path name of another file. The two kinds of links are also known as **hard links** and **soft links**. Soft (symbolic) links, unlike hard links, may point to directories and may cross file-system boundaries.

The file name "." in a directory is a hard link to the directory itself. The file name ".." is a hard link to the parent directory. Thus, if the current directory is */user/jlp/programs*, then *../bin/wdf* refers to */user/jlp/bin/wdf*.

Hardware devices have names in the file system. These **device special files** or **special files** are known to the kernel as device interfaces, but are nonetheless accessed by the user by much the same system calls as are other files.

Figure 20.3 shows a typical UNIX file system. The root (/) normally contains a small number of directories as well as */vmunix*, the binary boot image of the operating system; */dev* contains the device special files, such as */dev/console*,

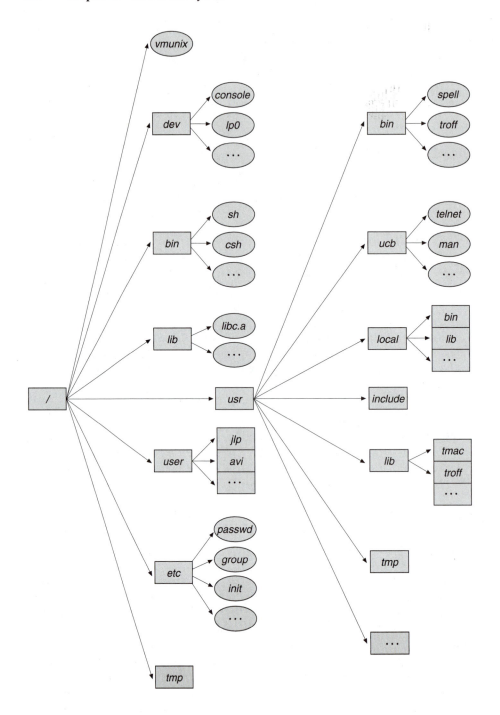

Figure 20.3   Typical UNIX directory structure.

/dev/lp0, /dev/mt0, and so on; */bin* contains the binaries of the essential UNIX systems programs. Other binaries may be in */usr/bin* (for applications systems programs, such as text formatters), */usr/ucb* (for systems programs written by Berkeley rather than by AT&T), or */usr/local/bin* (for systems programs written at the local site). Library files—such as the C, Pascal, and FORTRAN subroutine libraries—are kept in */lib* (or */usr/lib* or */usr/local/lib*).

The files of users themselves are stored in a separate directory for each user, typically in */user*. Thus, the user directory for "carol" would normally be in */user/carol*. For a large system, these directories may be further grouped to ease administration, creating a file structure with */user/prof/avi* and */user/staff/carol*. Administrative files and programs, such as the password file, are kept in */etc*. Temporary files can be put in */tmp*, which is normally erased during system boot, or in */usr/tmp*.

Each of these directories may have considerably more structure. For example, the font-description tables for the troff formatter for the Merganthaler 202 typesetter are kept in */usr/lib/troff/dev202*. All the conventions concerning the location of specific files and directories have been defined by programmers and their programs; the operating-system kernel needs only */etc/init*, which is used to initialize terminal processes, to be operable.

System calls for basic file manipulation are `creat`, `open`, `read`, `write`, `close`, `unlink`, and `trunc`. The `creat` system call, given a path name, creates an (empty) file (or truncates an existing one). An existing file is opened by the `open` system call, which takes a path name and a mode (such as read, write, or read–write) and returns a small integer, called a **file descriptor**. A file descriptor may then be passed to a `read` or `write` system call (along with a buffer address and the number of bytes to transfer) to perform data transfers to or from the file. A file is closed when its file descriptor is passed to the `close` system call. The `trunc` call reduces the length of a file to 0.

A file descriptor is an index into a small table of open files for this process. Descriptors start at 0 and seldom get higher than 6 or 7 for typical programs, depending on the maximum number of simultaneously open files.

Each `read` or `write` updates the current offset into the file, which is associated with the file-table entry and is used to determine the position in the file for the next `read` or `write`. The `lseek` system call allows the position to be reset explicitly. It also allows the creation of sparse files (files with "holes" in them). We can use the dup and dup2 system calls to produce a new file descriptor that is a copy of an existing one. The `fcntl` system call can also do that, and in addition can examine or set various parameters of an open file. For example, it can make each succeeding `write` to an open file append to the end of that file. There is an additional system call, `ioctl`, for manipulating device parameters. It can set the baud rate of a serial port, or rewind a tape, for instance.

Information about the file (such as its size, protection modes, owner, and so on) can be obtained by the `stat` system call. Several system calls allow some of this information to be changed: `rename` (change file name), chmod (change the protection mode), and chown (change the owner and group). Many of these system calls have variants that apply to file descriptors instead of file names. The link system call makes a hard link for an existing file, creating a new name for an existing file. A link is removed by the unlink system call; if it is the last link, the file is deleted. The symlink system call makes a symbolic link.

Directories are made by the mkdir system call and are deleted by rmdir. The current directory is changed by cd.

Although it is possible to use the standard file calls on directories, it is inadvisable to do so, since directories have an internal structure that must be preserved. Instead, another set of system calls is provided to open a directory, to step through each file entry within the directory, to close the directory, and to perform other functions; these are opendir, readdir, closedir, and others.

20.3.2 Process Control

A **process** is a program in execution. Processes are identified by their **process identifier,** which is an integer. A new process is created by the fork system call. The new process consists of a copy of the address space of the original process (the same program and the same variables with the same values). Both processes (the parent and the child) continue execution at the instruction after the fork with one difference: The return code for the fork is zero for the new (child) process, whereas the (nonzero) process identifier of the child is returned to the parent.

Typically, the execve system call is used after a fork by one of the two processes to replace that process' virtual-memory space with a new program. The execve system call loads a binary file into memory (destroying the memory image of the program containing the execve system call) and starts its execution.

A process may terminate by using the exit system call, and its parent process may wait for that event by using the wait system call. If the child process crashes, the system simulates the exit call. The wait system call provides the process id of a terminated child so that the parent can tell which of possibly many children terminated. A second system call, wait3, is similar to wait but also allows the parent to collect performance statistics about the child. Between the time the child exits, and the time the parent completes one of the wait system calls, the child is **defunct**. A defunct process can do nothing, but exists merely so that the parent can collect its status information. If the parent process of a defunct process exits before a child, the defunct process is inherited by the **init** process (which in turn waits on it) and becomes a **zombie** process. A typical use of these facilities is shown in Figure 20.4.

The simplest form of communication between processes is by **pipes,** which may be created before the fork, and whose endpoints are then set up between the fork and the execve. A pipe is essentially a queue of bytes between

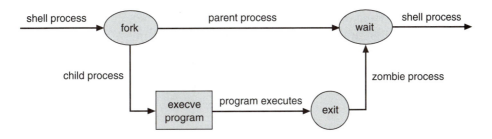

Figure 20.4 A shell forks a subprocess to execute a program.

two processes. The pipe is accessed by a file descriptor, like an ordinary file. One process writes into the pipe, and the other reads from the pipe. The size of the original pipe system was fixed by the system. With 4.3BSD, pipes are implemented on top of the socket system, which has variable-sized buffers. Reading from an empty pipe or writing into a full pipe causes the process to be blocked until the state of the pipe changes. Special arrangements are needed for a pipe to be placed between a parent and child (so that only one is reading and one is writing).

All user processes are descendants of one original process, called **init**. Each terminal port available for interactive use has a **getty** process forked for it by **init**. The **getty** process initializes terminal line parameters and waits for a user's **login name,** which it passes through an execve as an argument to a **login** process. The **login** process collects the user's password, encrypts the password, and compares the result to an encrypted string taken from the file /etc/passwd. If the comparison is successful, the user is allowed to log in. The **login** process executes a **shell,** or command interpreter, after setting the numeric **user identifier** of the process to that of the user logging in. (The shell and the user identifier are found in /etc/passwd by the user's login name.) It is with this shell that the user ordinarily communicates for the rest of the login session; the shell itself forks subprocesses for the commands the user tells it to execute.

The user identifier is used by the kernel to determine the user's permissions for certain system calls, especially those involving file accesses. There is also a **group identifier,** which is used to provide similar privileges to a collection of users. In 4.3BSD a process may be in several groups simultaneously. The **login** process puts the shell in all the groups permitted to the user by the files /etc/passwd and /etc/group.

There are actually two user identifiers used by the kernel: The **effective user identifier** is the identifier used to determine file access permissions. If the file of a program being loaded by an execve has the **setuid** bit set in its inode, the effective user identifier of the process is set to the user identifier of the owner of the file, whereas the **real user identifier** is left as it was. This scheme allows certain processes to have more than ordinary privileges while still being executable by ordinary users. The **setuid** idea was patented by Dennis Ritchie (U.S. Patent 4,135,240) and is one of the distinctive features of UNIX. There is a similar **setgid** bit for groups. A process may determine its real and effective user identifier with the **getuid** and **geteuid** calls, respectively. The **getgid** and **getegid** calls determine the process identifier and group identifier, respectively. The rest of a process' groups may be found with the **getgroups** system call.

20.3.3 Signals

Signals are a facility for handling exceptional conditions similar to software interrupts. There are 20 different signals, each of which corresponds to a distinct condition. A signal may be generated by a keyboard interrupt, by an error in a process (such as a bad memory reference), or by a number of asynchronous events (such as timers or job-control signals from the shell). Almost any signal may also be generated by the `kill` system call.

The **interrupt** signal, SIGINT, is used to stop a command before that command completes. It is usually produced by the ^C character (ASCII 3). As of 4.3BSD, the important keyboard characters are defined by a table for each terminal and can be redefined easily. The **quit** signal, SIGQUIT, is usually produced by the ^bs character (ASCII 28). The **quit** signal both stops the currently executing program and dumps its current memory image to a file named **core** in the current directory. The core file can be used by debuggers. SIGILL is produced by an illegal instruction and SIGSEGV by an attempt to address memory outside of the legal virtual-memory space of a process.

Arrangements can be made either for most signals to be ignored (to have no effect), or for a routine in the user process (a signal handler) to be called. A signal handler may safely do one of two things before returning from catching a signal: call the `exit` system call, or modify a global variable. There is one signal (the **kill** signal, number 9, SIGKILL) that cannot be ignored or caught by a signal handler. SIGKILL is used, for example, to kill a runaway process that is ignoring other signals such as SIGINT or SIGQUIT.

Signals can be lost: If another signal of the same kind is sent before a previous signal has been accepted by the process to which it is directed, the first signal will be overwritten and only the last signal will be seen by the process. In other words, a call to the signal handler tells a process that there has been at least one occurrence of the signal. Also, there is no relative priority among UNIX signals. If two different signals are sent to the same process at the same time, it is indeterminate which one the process will receive first.

Signals were originally intended to deal with exceptional events. As is true of the use of most other features in UNIX, however, signal use has expanded steadily. 4.1BSD introduced job control, which uses signals to start and stop subprocesses on demand. This facility allows one shell to control multiple processes: starting, stopping, and backgrounding them as the user wishes. 4.3BSD added the SIGWINCH signal, invented by Sun Microsystems, for informing a process that the window in which output is being displayed has changed size. Signals are also used to deliver urgent data from network connections.

Users also wanted more reliable signals, and a bug fix in an inherent race condition in the old signals implementation. Thus, 4.3BSD also brought with it a race-free, reliable, separately implemented signal capability. It allows individual signals to be blocked during critical sections, and has a new system call to let a process sleep until interrupted. It is similar to hardware-interrupt functionality. This capability is now part of the POSIX standard.

20.3.4 Process Groups

Groups of related processes frequently cooperate to accomplish a common task. For instance, processes may create, and communicate over, pipes. Such a set of processes is termed a **process group,** or a **job**. Signals may be sent to all processes in a group. A process usually inherits its process group from its parent, but the **setpgrp** system call allows a process to change its group.

Process groups are used by the C shell to control the operation of multiple jobs. Only one process group may use a terminal device for I/O at any time. This **foreground** job has the attention of the user on that terminal while all other nonattached jobs (**background** jobs) perform their function without user interaction. Access to the terminal is controlled by process group signals. Each job has a **controlling terminal** (again, inherited from its parent). If the process group of the controlling terminal matches the group of a process, that process is in the foreground, and is allowed to perform I/O. If a nonmatching (background) process attempts the same, a SIGTTIN or SIGTTOU signal is sent to its process group. This signal usually results in the process group freezing until it is foregrounded by the user, at which point it receives a SIGCONT signal, indicating that the process can perform the I/O. Similarly, a SIGSTOP may be sent to the foreground process group to freeze it.

20.3.5 Information Manipulation

System calls exist to set and return both an interval timer (getitimer/ setitimer) and the current time (gettimeofday/settimeofday) in microseconds. In addition, processes can ask for their process identifier (getpid), their group identifier (getgid), the name of the machine on which they are executing (gethostname), and many other values.

20.3.6 Library Routines

The system-call interface to UNIX is supported and augmented by a large collection of library routines and header files. The header files provide the definition of complex data structures used in system calls. In addition, a large library of functions provides additional program support.

For example, the UNIX I/O system calls provide for the reading and writing of blocks of bytes. Some applications may want to read and write only 1 byte at a time. Although it would be possible to read and write 1 byte at a time, that would require a system call for each byte—an extremely high overhead. Instead, a set of standard library routines (the standard I/O package accessed through the header file *<Stdio.h>*) provides another interface, which reads and writes several thousand bytes at a time using local buffers, and transfers between these buffers (in user memory) when I/O is desired. Formatted I/O is also supported by the standard I/O package.

Additional library support is provided for mathematical functions, network access, data conversion, and so on. The 4.3BSD kernel supports over 150 system calls; the C program library has over 300 library functions. Although the library functions eventually result in system calls where necessary (for example, the getchar library routine will result in a read system call if the file buffer is empty), it is generally unnecessary for the programmer to distinguish between the basic set of kernel system calls and the additional functions provided by library functions.

20.4 ■ User Interface

Both the programmer and the user of a UNIX system deal mainly with the set of systems programs that have been written and are available for execution. These programs make the necessary system calls to support their function, but the system calls themselves are contained within the program and do not need to be obvious to the user.

The common systems programs can be grouped into several categories; most of them are file or directory oriented. For example, the systems programs to manipulate directories are mkdir to create a new directory, rmdir to remove a directory, cd to change the current directory to another, and pwd to print the absolute path name of the current (working) directory.

The ls program lists the names of the files in the current directory. Any of 18 options can ask that properties of the files be displayed also. For example, the -l option asks for a long listing, showing the file name, owner, protection, date and time of creation, and size. The cp program creates a new file that is a copy of an existing file. The mv program moves a file from one place to another in the directory tree. In most cases, this move simply requires a renaming of the file; if necessary, however, the file is copied to the new location and the old copy is deleted. A file is deleted by the rm program (which makes an unlink system call).

To display a file on the terminal, a user can run cat. The cat program takes a list of files and concatenates them, copying the result to the standard output, commonly the terminal. On a high-speed cathode-ray tube (CRT) display, of course, the file may speed by too fast to be read. The more program displays the file one screen at a time, pausing until the user types a character to continue to the next screen. The head program displays just the first few lines of a file; tail shows the final few lines.

Those are the basic systems programs widely used in UNIX. In addition, there are a number of editors (ed, sed, emacs, vi, and so on), compilers (C, Pascal, FORTRAN, and so on), and text formatters (troff, TEX, scribe, and so on). There are also programs for sorting (sort) and comparing files (cmp, diff), looking for patterns (grep, awk), sending mail to other users (mail), and many other activities.

20.4.1 Shells and Commands

Both user-written and systems programs are normally executed by a command interpreter. The command interpreter in UNIX is a user process like any other. It is called a **shell** because it surrounds the kernel of the operating system. Users can write their own shell, and there are several shells in general use. The **Bourne shell,** written by Steve Bourne, is probably the most widely used—or, at least, it is the most widely available. The **C shell,** mostly the work of Bill Joy, a founder of Sun Microsystems, is the most popular on BSD systems. The Korn shell, by Dave Korn, has become popular because it combines the features of the Bourne shell and the C shell.

The common shells share much of their command-language syntax. UNIX is normally an interactive system. The shell indicates its readiness to accept another command by typing a prompt, and the user types a command on a single line. For instance, in the line

```
% ls -l
```

the percent sign is the usual C shell prompt, and the ls -l (typed by the user) is the (long) list-directory command. Commands can take arguments, which the user types after the command name on the same line, separated by white space (spaces or tabs).

Although there are a few commands built into the shells (such as cd), a typical command is an executable binary object file. A list of several directories, the **search path,** is kept by the shell. For each command, each of the directories in the search path is searched, in order, for a file of the same name. If a file is found, it is loaded and executed. The search path can be set by the user. The directories /bin and /usr/bin are almost always in the search path, and a typical search path on a BSD system might be

(. /home/prof/avi/bin /usr/local/bin /usr/ucb /bin /usr/bin)

The ls command's object file is /bin/ls, and the shell itself is /bin/sh (the Bourne shell) or /bin/csh (the C shell).

Execution of a command is done by a `fork` system call followed by an `execve` of the object file. The shell usually then does a `wait` to suspend its own execution until the command completes (Figure 20.4). There is a simple syntax (an ampersand [&] at the end of the command line) to indicate that the shell should *not* wait for the completion of the command. A command left running in this manner while the shell continues to interpret further commands is said to be a background command, or to be running in the background. Processes for which the shell *does* wait are said to run in the foreground.

The C shell in 4.3BSD systems provides a facility called **job control** (partially implemented in the kernel), as mentioned previously. Job control allows processes to be moved between the foreground and the background. The processes can be stopped and restarted on various conditions, such as a background job wanting input from the user's terminal. This scheme allows most of the control of processes provided by windowing or layering interfaces, but requires no special hardware. Job control is also useful in window systems, such as the X Window System developed at MIT. Each window is treated as a terminal, allowing multiple processes to be in the foreground (one per window) at any one time. Of course, background processes may exist on any of the windows. The Korn shell also supports job control, and it is likely that job control (and process groups) will be standard in future versions of UNIX.

20.4.2 Standard I/O

Processes can open files as they like, but most processes expect three file descriptors (numbers 0, 1, and 2) to be open when they start. These file descriptors are inherited across the `fork` (and possibly the `execve`) that created the process. They are known as **standard input** (0), **standard output** (1), and **standard error** (2). All three are frequently open to the user's terminal. Thus, the program can read what the user types by reading standard input, and the program can send output to the user's screen by writing to standard output. The standard-error file descriptor is also open for writing and is used for error output; standard output is used for ordinary output. Most programs can also accept a file (rather than a terminal) for standard input and standard output. The program does not care from where its input is coming from or to where its output is going. That is one of the elegant design features of UNIX.

The common shells have a simple syntax for changing what files are open for the standard I/O streams of a process. Changing a standard file is called **I/O redirection**. The syntax for I/O redirection is shown in Figure 20.5. In this example, the `ls` command produces a listing of the names of files in the current directory, the `pr` command formats that list into pages suitable for a printer, and the `lpr` command spools the formatted output to a printer, such as */dev/lp0*. The subsequent command forces all output and all error messages to be redirected to a file. Without the ampersand, error messages appear on the terminal.

Command	Meaning of command
% ls > filea	direct output of ls to file filea
% pr < filea > fileb	input from filea and output to fileb
% lpr < fileb	input from fileb
% % make program >& errs	save both standard output and standard error in a file

Figure 20.5   Standard I/O redirection.

20.4.3 Pipelines, Filters, and Shell Scripts

The first three commands of Figure 20.5 could have been coalesced into the one command

$$\% \text{ ls } | \text{ pr } | \text{ lpr}$$

Each vertical bar tells the shell to arrange for the output of the preceding command to be passed as input to the following command. A pipe carries the data from one process to the other: One process writes into one end of the pipe, and another process reads from the other end. In the example, the write end of one pipe would be set up by the shell to be the standard output of ls, and the read end of the pipe would be the standard input of pr; there would be another pipe between pr and lpr.

A command such as pr that passes its standard input to its standard output, performing some processing on it, is called a **filter**. Many UNIX commands can be used as filters. Complicated functions can be pieced together as pipelines of common commands. Also, common functions, such as output formatting, do not need to be built into numerous commands, because the output of almost any program can be piped through pr (or some other appropriate filter).

Both of the common UNIX shells are also programming languages, with shell variables and the usual higher-level programming-language control constructs (loops, conditionals). The execution of a command is analogous to a subroutine call. A file of shell commands, a **shell script,** can be executed like any other command, with the appropriate shell being invoked automatically to read it. **Shell programming** thus can be used to combine ordinary programs conveniently for sophisticated applications without the necessity of any programming in conventional languages.

This external user view is commonly thought of as the definition of UNIX, yet it is the most easily changed definition. Writing a new shell with a quite different syntax and semantics would greatly change the user view while not changing the kernel or even the programmer interface. Several menu-driven and iconic interfaces for UNIX now exist, and the X Window System is rapidly becoming a standard. The heart of UNIX is, of course, the kernel. This kernel is much more difficult to change than is the user interface, because all programs depend on the system calls that it provides to remain consistent. Of course, we can add new system calls to increase functionality, but then we must modify the programs to use the new calls.

20.5 ■ Process Management

A major design problem for operating systems is the representation of processes. One substantial difference between UNIX and many other systems is the ease with which multiple processes can be created and manipulated. These processes are represented in UNIX by various control blocks. There are no system control blocks accessible in the virtual address space of a user process; control blocks associated with a process are stored in the kernel. The information in these control blocks is used by the kernel for process control and CPU scheduling.

20.5.1 Process Control Blocks

The most basic data structure associated with processes is the **process structure**. A process structure contains everything that the system needs to know about a process when the process is swapped out, such as its unique process identifier, scheduling information (such as the priority of the process), and pointers to other control blocks. There is an array of process structures whose length is defined at system linking time. The process structures of ready processes are kept linked together by the scheduler in a doubly linked list (the ready queue), and there are pointers from each process structure to the process' parent, to its youngest living child, and to various other relatives of interest, such as a list of processes sharing the same program code (text).

The **virtual address space** of a user process is divided into text (program code), data, and stack segments. The data and stack segments are always in the same address space, but may grow separately, and usually in opposite directions: Most frequently, the stack grows down as the data grow up toward it. The text segment is sometimes (as on an Intel 8086 with separate instruction and data space) in an address space different from the data and stack, and is usually read-only. The debugger puts a text segment in read–write mode to allow insertion of breakpoints.

Every process with sharable text (almost all, under 4.3BSD) has a pointer from its process structure to a **text structure**. The text structure records how many processes are using the text segment, including a pointer into a list of their process structures, and where the page table for the text segment can be found on disk when it is swapped. The text structure itself is always resident in main memory: An array of such structures is allocated at system link time. The text, data, and stack segments for the processes may be swapped. When the segments are swapped in, they are paged.

The **page tables** record information on the mapping from the process' virtual memory to physical memory. The process structure contains pointers to the page table, for use when the process is resident in main memory, or the address of the process on the swap device, when the process is swapped. There is no special separate page table for a shared text segment; every process sharing the text segment has entries for its pages in the process' page table.

Information about the process that is needed only when the process is resident (that is, not swapped out) is kept in the **user structure** (or **u structure**), rather than in the process structure. The u structure is mapped read-only into user virtual address space, so user processes can read its contents. It is writable by the kernel. On the VAX, a copy of the VAX PCB is kept here for saving the process' general registers, stack pointer, program counter, and page-table base registers when the process is not running. There is space to keep system-call parameters and return values. All user and group identifiers associated with the process (rather than just the effective user identifier kept in the process structure) are kept here. Signals, timers, and quotas have data structures here. Of more obvious relevance to the ordinary user, the current directory and the table of open files are maintained in the user structure.

Every process has both a user and a system phase. Most ordinary work is done in **user mode,** but, when a system call is made, it is performed in **system mode**. The system and user phases of a process never execute simultaneously. When a process is executing in system mode, a **kernel stack** for that process is used, rather than the user stack belonging to that process. The kernel stack for the process immediately follows the user structure: The kernel stack and the user structure together compose the **system data segment** for the process. The kernel has its own stack for use when it is not doing work on behalf of a process (for instance, for interrupt handling).

Figure 20.6 illustrates how the system uses the process structure to find the various parts of a process.

The `fork` system call allocates a new process structure (with a new process identifier) for the child process, and copies the user structure. There is ordinarily no need for a new text structure, as the processes share their text; the appropriate counters and lists are merely updated. A new page table is constructed, and new main memory is allocated for the data and stack segments of the child process. The copying of the user structure preserves open file descriptors, user and group identifiers, signal handling, and most similar properties of a process.

The `vfork` system call does *not* copy the data and stack to the new process; rather, the new process simply shares the page table of the old one. A new user structure and a new process structure are still created. A common use of this system call is by a shell to execute a command and to wait for its completion. The parent process uses `vfork` to produce the child process. Because the child process wishes to use an `execve` immediately to change its virtual address space completely, there is no need for a complete copy of the parent process.

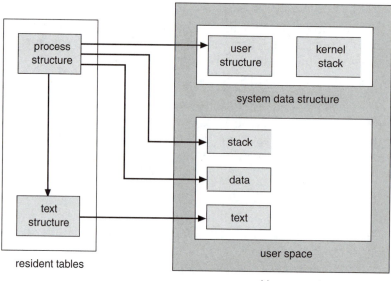

Figure 20.6   The way parts of a process are found with the process structure.

Such data structures as are necessary for manipulating pipes may be kept in registers between the vfork and the execve. Files may be closed in one process without affecting the other process, since the kernel data structures involved depend on the user structure, which is not shared. The parent is suspended when it calls vfork until the child either calls execve or terminates, so that the parent will not change memory that the child needs.

When the parent process is large, vfork can produce substantial savings in system CPU time. However, it is a fairly dangerous system call, since any memory change occurs in both processes until the execve occurs. An alternative is to share all pages by duplicating the page table, but to mark the entries of both page tables as **copy-on-write**. The hardware protection bits are set to trap any attempt to write in these shared pages. If such a trap occurs, a new frame is allocated and the shared page is copied to the new frame. The page tables are adjusted to show that this page is no longer shared (and therefore no longer needs to be write-protected), and execution can resume.

An execve system call creates no new process or user structure; rather, the text and data of the process are replaced. Open files are preserved (although there is a way to specify that certain file descriptors are to be closed on an execve). Most signal-handling properties are preserved, but arrangements to call a specific user routine on a signal are canceled, for obvious reasons. The process identifier and most other properties of the process are unchanged.

20.5.2 CPU Scheduling

CPU scheduling in UNIX is designed to benefit interactive processes. Processes are given small CPU time slices by a priority algorithm that reduces to round-robin scheduling for CPU-bound jobs.

Every process has a **scheduling priority** associated with it; larger numbers indicate lower priority. Processes doing disk I/O or other important tasks have priorities less than "pzero" and cannot be killed by signals. Ordinary user processes have positive priorities and thus are all less likely to be run than are any system processes, although user processes can set precedence over one another through the **nice** command.

The more CPU time a process accumulates, the lower (more positive) its priority becomes, and vice versa, so there is negative feedback in CPU scheduling and it is difficult for a single process to take all the CPU time. Process aging is employed to prevent starvation.

Older UNIX operating systems used a 1-second quantum for the round-robin scheduling. 4.3BSD reschedules processes every 0.1 second and recomputes priorities every second. The round-robin scheduling is accomplished by the timeout mechanism, which tells the clock interrupt driver to call a kernel subroutine after a specified interval; the subroutine to be called in this case causes the rescheduling and then resubmits a timeout to call itself again. The priority recomputation is also timed by a subroutine that resubmits a timeout for itself.

There is no preemption of one process by another in the kernel. A process may relinquish the CPU because it is waiting on I/O or because its time slice has expired. When a process chooses to relinquish the CPU, it goes to sleep on an **event**. The kernel primitive used for this purpose is called sleep (not to be confused with the user-level library routine of the same name). It takes an argument, which is by convention the address of a kernel data structure related to an **event** that the process wants to occur before that process is awakened. When the event occurs, the system process that knows about it calls wakeup with the address corresponding to the event, and all processes that had done a sleep on the same address are put in the ready queue to be run.

For example, a process waiting for disk I/O to complete will sleep on the address of the buffer header corresponding to the data being transferred. When the interrupt routine for the disk driver notes that the transfer is complete, it calls wakeup on the buffer header. The interrupt uses the kernel stack for whatever process happened to be running at the time, and the wakeup is done from that system process.

The process that actually does run is chosen by the scheduler. Sleep takes a second argument, which is the scheduling priority to be used for this purpose. This priority argument, if less than "pzero," also prevents the process from being awakened prematurely by some exceptional event, such as a **signal**.

When a signal is generated, it is left pending until the system half of the affected process next runs. This event usually happens soon, since the signal normally causes the process to be awakened if the process has been waiting for some other condition.

There is no memory associated with events, and the caller of the routine that does a `sleep` on an event must be prepared to deal with a premature return, including the possibility that the reason for waiting has vanished.

There are **race conditions** involved in the event mechanism. If a process decides (because of checking a flag in memory, for instance) to sleep on an event, and the event occurs before the process can execute the primitive that does the actual sleep on the event, the process sleeping may then sleep forever. We prevent this situation by raising the hardware processor priority during the critical section so that no interrupts can occur, and thus only the process desiring the event can run until it is sleeping. Hardware processor priority is used in this manner to protect critical regions throughout the kernel, and is the greatest obstacle to porting UNIX to multiple processor machines. However, this problem has not prevented such ports from being done repeatedly.

Many processes such as text editors are I/O bound and usually will be scheduled mainly on the basis of waiting for I/O. Experience suggests that the UNIX scheduler performs best with I/O-bound jobs, as can be observed when there are several CPU-bound jobs, such as text formatters or language interpreters, running.

What we have called CPU scheduling in this discussion corresponds closely to the short-term scheduling that we described in Chapter 4, although the negative-feedback property of the priority scheme provides a degree of long-term scheduling in that it largely determines the long-term job mix. Medium-term scheduling is done by the swapping mechanism described in Section 20.6.

20.6 ■ Memory Management

Much of UNIX's early development was done on a PDP-11. The PDP-11 has only eight segments in its virtual address space, and each of these are at most 8192 bytes. The larger machines, such as the PDP-11/70, allow separate instruction and address spaces, which effectively double the address space and number of segments, but this address space is still relatively small. In addition, the kernel was even more severely constrained due to dedication of one data segment to interrupt vectors, another to point at the per-process system data segment, and yet another for the UNIBUS (system I/O bus) registers. Further, on the smaller PDP-11s, total physical memory was limited to 256K. The total memory resources were insufficient to justify or support complex memory-management algorithms. Thus, UNIX swapped entire process memory images.

20.6.1 Swapping

Pre-3BSD UNIX systems use swapping exclusively to handle memory contention among processes: If there is too much contention, processes are swapped out until enough memory is available. Also, a few large processes can force many small processes out of memory, and a process larger than nonkernel main memory cannot be run at all. The system data segment (the u structure and kernel stack) and the user data segment (text [if nonsharable], data, and stack) are kept in contiguous main memory for swap-transfer efficiency, so external fragmentation of memory can be a serious problem.

Allocation of both main memory and swap space is done first fit. When the size of a process' memory image increases (due to either stack expansion or data expansion), a new piece of memory big enough for the whole image is allocated. The memory image is copied, the old memory is freed, and the appropriate tables are updated. (An attempt is made in some systems to find memory contiguous to the end of the current piece, to avoid some copying.) If no single piece of main memory is large enough, the process is swapped out such that it will be swapped back in with the new size.

There is no need to swap out a sharable text segment, because it is read-only, and there is no need to read in a sharable text segment for a process when another instance is already in core. That is one of the main reasons for keeping track of sharable text segments: less swap traffic. The other reason is the reduced amount of main memory required for multiple processes using the same text segment.

Decisions regarding which processes to swap in or out are made by the **scheduler process,** also known as the **swapper**. The scheduler wakes up at least once every 4 seconds to check for processes to be swapped in or out. A process is more likely to be swapped out if it is idle, has been in main memory a long time, or is large; if no obvious candidates are found, other processes are picked by age. A process is more likely to be swapped in if it has been swapped out a long time, or is small. There are checks to prevent thrashing, basically by not letting a process be swapped out if it has not been in memory for a certain amount of time.

If jobs do not need to be swapped out, the process table is searched for a process deserving to be brought in (determined by how small the process is and how long it has been swapped out). If there is not enough memory available, processes are swapped out until there is.

In 4.3BSD, swap space is allocated in pieces that are multiples of a power of 2 and a minimum size (for example, 32 pages), up to a maximum that is determined by the size of the swap-space partition on the disk. If several logical disk partitions may be used for swapping, they should be the same size, for this reason. The several logical disk partitions should also be on separate disk arms to minimize disk seeks.

Many UNIX systems still use the swapping scheme just described. All Berkeley UNIX systems, on the other hand, depend primarily on paging for memory-contention management, and depend only secondarily on swapping. They use a scheme similar in outline to the traditional one to determine which processes get swapped, in or out, but the details differ and the influence of swapping is less.

20.6.2 Paging

Berkeley introduced paging to UNIX with 3BSD. VAX 4.3BSD is a demand-paged virtual-memory system. External fragmentation of memory is eliminated by paging. (There is, of course, internal fragmentation, but it is negligible with a reasonably small page size.) Swapping can be kept to a minimum because more jobs can be kept in main memory, because paging allows execution with only parts of each process in memory.

Demand paging is done in a straightforward manner. When a process needs a page and the page is not there, a page fault to the kernel occurs, a frame of main memory is allocated, and the proper disk page is read into the frame.

There are a few optimizations. If the page needed is still in the page table for the process, but has been marked invalid by the page-replacement process, it can be marked valid and used without any I/O transfer. Pages can similarly be retrieved from the list of free frames. When most processes are started, many of their pages are prepaged and are put on the free list for recovery by this mechanism. Arrangements may also be made for a process to have no prepaging on startup, but that is seldom done, as it results in more page-fault overhead, being closer to pure demand paging.

If the page has to be fetched from disk, it must be locked in memory for the duration of the transfer. This locking ensures that the page will not be selected for page replacement. Once the page is fetched and mapped properly, it must remain locked if raw physical I/O is being done on it.

The page-replacement algorithm is more interesting. The VAX architecture has no hardware memory page-reference bit. This lack of hardware support makes many memory-management algorithms, such as page-fault frequency, unusable. 4.3BSD uses a modification of the second chance (clock) algorithm described in Section 10.3.5. The map of all nonkernel main memory (the **core map** or **cmap**) is swept linearly and repeatedly by a software **clock hand**. When the clock hand reaches a given frame, if the frame is marked as in use by some software condition (for example, physical I/O is in progress using it), or the frame is already free, the frame is left untouched, and the clock hand sweeps to the next frame. Otherwise, the corresponding text or process page-table entry for this frame is located. If the entry is already invalid, the frame is added to the free list; otherwise, the page-table entry is made invalid but reclaimable (that is, if it does not get paged out by the next time it is wanted, it can just be made valid again).

4.3BSD Tahoe added support for systems that do implement the reference bit. On such systems, one pass of the clock hand turns the reference bit off, and a second pass places those pages whose reference bits remain off onto the free list for replacement. Of course, if the page is dirty (the VAX *does* have a dirty bit), it must first be written to disk before being added to the free list. Pageouts are done in clusters to improve performance.

There are checks to make sure that the number of valid data pages for a process does not fall too low, and to keep the paging device from being flooded with requests. There is also a mechanism by which a process may limit the amount of main memory it uses.

The LRU clock-hand scheme is implemented in the *pagedaemon*, which is process 2 (remember that the *scheduler* is process 0, and *init* is process 1). This process spends most of its time sleeping, but a check is done several times per second (scheduled by a `timeout`) to see whether action is necessary; if it is, process 2 is awakened. Whenever the number of free frames falls below a threshold, *lotsfree*, the *pagedaemon* is awakened; thus, if there is always a large amount of free memory, the *pagedaemon* imposes no load on the system, because it never runs.

The sweep of the clock hand each time the *pagedaemon* process is awakened (that is, the number of frames scanned, which is usually more than the number paged out), is determined both by the number of frames lacking to reach *lotsfree* and by the number of frames that the *scheduler* has determined are needed for various reasons (the more frames needed, the longer the sweep). If the number of free frames rises to *lotsfree* before the expected sweep is completed, the hand stops and the *pagedaemon* process sleeps. The parameters that determine the range of the clock-hand sweep are determined at system startup according to the amount of main memory, such that *pagedaemon* does not use more than 10 percent of all CPU time.

If the *scheduler* decides that the paging system is overloaded, processes will be swapped out whole until the overload is relieved. This swapping usually happens only if several conditions are met: load average is high; free memory has fallen below a low limit, *minfree*; and the average memory available over recent time is less than a desirable amount, *desfree*, where *lotsfree* > *desfree* > *minfree*. In other words, only a chronic shortage of memory with several processes trying to run will cause swapping, and even then free memory has to be extremely low at the moment. (An excessive paging rate or a need for memory by the kernel itself may also enter into the calculations, in rare cases.) Processes may be swapped by the *scheduler*, of course, for other reasons (such as simply for not running for a long time).

The value of the parameter *lotsfree* is usually one-quarter of the memory in the map that the clock hand sweeps; *desfree* and *minfree* are usually the same across different systems, but are limited to fractions of available memory.

Every process' text segment is by default shared and read-only. This scheme is practical with paging, because there is no external fragmentation, and the swap space gained by sharing more than offsets the negligible amount of overhead involved, as the kernel virtual space is large.

CPU scheduling, memory swapping, and paging interact: The lower the priority of a process, the more likely that its pages will be paged out and the more likely that it will be swapped in its entirety. The age preferences in choosing processes to swap guard against thrashing, but paging does so more effectively. Ideally, processes will not be swapped out unless they are idle, because each process will need only a small working set of pages in main memory at any one time, and the *pagedaemon* will reclaim unused pages for use by other processes.

The amount of memory the process will need is some fraction of that process' total virtual size—up to one-half if that process has been swapped out for a long time.

The VAX 512-byte hardware pages are too small for I/O efficiency, so they are clustered in groups of two so that all paging I/O is actually done in 1024-byte chunks. In other words, the effective page size is not necessarily identical to the hardware page size of the machine, although it must be a multiple of the hardware page size.

20.7 ■ File System

The UNIX file system supports two main objects: files and directories. Directories are just files with a special format, so the representation of a file is the basic UNIX concept.

20.7.1 Blocks and Fragments

Most of the file system is taken up by **data blocks,** which contain whatever the users have put in their files. Let us consider how these data blocks are stored on the disk.

The hardware disk sector is usually 512 bytes. A block size larger than 512 bytes is desirable for speed. However, because UNIX file systems usually contain an enormous number of small files, much larger blocks would cause excessive internal fragmentation. That is why the earlier 4.1BSD file system was limited to a 1024-byte (1K) block.

The 4.3BSD solution is to use *two* block sizes for files that have no indirect blocks: All the blocks of a file are of a large block size (such as 8K), except the last. The final block is an appropriate multiple of a smaller fragment size (for example, 1024) to fill out the file. Thus, a file of size 18,000 bytes would have two 8K blocks and one 2K fragment (which would not be filled completely).

The block and fragment sizes are set during file-system creation according to the intended use of the file system: If many small files are expected, the fragment size should be small; if repeated transfers of large files are expected, the basic block size should be large. Implementation details force a maximum block-to-fragment ratio of $8:1$, and a minimum block size of 4K, so typical choices are $4,096:512$ for the former case and $8,192:1,024$ for the latter.

Suppose that data are written to a file in transfer sizes of 1K bytes, and the block and fragment sizes of the file system are 4K and 512 bytes. The file system will allocate a 1K fragment to contain the data from the first transfer. The next transfer will cause a new 2K fragment to be allocated. The data from the original fragment must be copied into this new fragment, followed by the second 1K transfer. The allocation routines do attempt to find the required space on the disk immediately following the existing fragment so that no copying is necessary, but, if they cannot do so, up to seven copies may be required before the fragment becomes a block. Provisions have been made for programs to discover the block size for a file so that transfers of that size can be made, to avoid fragment recopying.

20.7.2 Inodes

A file is represented by an inode (Figure 11.7). An **inode** is a record that stores most of the information about a specific file on the disk. The name *inode* (pronounced *EYE node*) is derived from "index node" and was originally spelled "i-node"; the hyphen fell out of use over the years. The term is also sometimes spelled "I node."

The inode contains the user and group identifiers of the file, the times of the last file modification and access, a count of the number of hard links (directory entries) to the file, and the type of the file (plain file, directory, symbolic link, character device, block device, or socket). In addition, the inode contains 15 pointers to the disk blocks containing the data contents of the file. The first 12 of these pointers point to **direct blocks;** that is, they contain addresses of blocks that contain data of the file. Thus, the data for small files (no more than 12 blocks) can be referenced immediately, because a copy of the inode is kept in main memory while a file is open. If the block size is 4K, then up to 48K of data may be accessed directly from the inode.

The next three pointers in the inode point to **indirect blocks**. If the file is large enough to use indirect blocks, the indirect blocks are each of the major block size; the fragment size applies to only data blocks. The first indirect block pointer is the address of a **single indirect block**. The single indirect block is an index block, containing not data, but rather the addresses of blocks that do contain data. Then, there is a **double-indirect-block pointer,** the address of a block that contains the addresses of blocks that contain pointers to the actual data blocks. The final pointer would contain the address of a **triple indirect block;** however, there is no need for it. The minimum block size for a file system in 4.3BSD is 4K, so files with as many as 2^{32} bytes will use only double, rather than triple, indirection. That is, as each block pointer takes 4 bytes, we have 49,152 bytes accessible in direct blocks, 4,194,304 bytes accessible by a single indirection, and 4,294,967,296 bytes reachable through double indirection, for a total of 4,299,210,752 bytes, which is larger than 2^{32} bytes. The number 2^{32} is significant because the file offset in the file structure in main memory is kept in a 32-bit word. Files therefore cannot be larger than 2^{32} bytes. Since file pointers are signed integers (for seeking backward and forward in a file), the actual maximum file size is 2^{32-1} bytes. Two gigabytes is large enough for most purposes.

20.7.3 Directories

There is no distinction between plain files and directories at this level of implementation; directory contents are kept in data blocks, and directories are represented by an inode in the same way as plain files. Only the inode type field distinguishes between plain files and directories. Plain files are not assumed to have a structure, however, whereas directories have a specific structure. In Version 7, file names were limited to 14 characters, so directories were a list of 16-byte entries: 2 bytes for an inode number and 14 bytes for a file name.

In 4.3BSD, file names are of variable length, up to 255 bytes, so directory entries are also of variable length. Each entry contains first the length of the entry, then the file name and the inode number. This variable-length entry makes the directory management and search routines more complex, but greatly improves the ability of users to choose meaningful names for their files and directories, with no practical limit on the length of the name.

The first two names in every directory are ".". and "..". New directory entries are added to the directory in the first space available, generally after the existing files. A linear search is used.

The user refers to a file by a path name, whereas the file system uses the inode as its definition of a file. Thus, the kernel has to map the supplied user path name to an inode. The directories are used for this mapping.

First, a starting directory is determined. If the first character of the path name is "/", the starting directory is the root directory. If the path name starts with any character other than a slash, the starting directory is the current directory of the current process. The starting directory is checked for proper file type and access permissions, and an error is returned if necessary. The inode of the starting directory is always available.

The next element of the path name, up to the next "/", or to the end of the path name, is a file name. The starting directory is searched for this name, and an error is returned if the name is not found. If there is yet another element in the path name, the current inode must refer to a directory, and an error is returned if it does not, or if access is denied. This directory is searched as was the previous one. This process continues until the end of the path name is reached and the desired inode is returned. This step-by-step process is needed because, at any directory, a mount point (or symbolic link) may be encountered, causing the translation to move to a different directory structure for continuation.

Hard links are simply directory entries like any other. We handle symbolic links for the most part by starting the search over with the path name taken from the contents of the symbolic link. We prevent infinite loops by counting the number of symbolic links encountered during a path-name search and returning an error when a limit (eight) is exceeded.

Nondisk files (such as devices) do not have data blocks allocated on the disk. The kernel notices these file types (as indicated in the inode) and calls appropriate drivers to handle I/O for them.

Once the inode is found by—for instance, by the open system call—a **file structure** is allocated to point to the inode. The file descriptor given to the user refers to this file structure. 4.3BSD added a **directory name cache** to hold recent directory-to-inode translations. This improvement greatly increased file-system performance.

20.7.4 Mapping of a File Descriptor to an Inode

System calls that refer to open files indicate the file by passing a file descriptor as an argument. The file descriptor is used by the kernel to index a table of open files for the current process. Each entry of the table contains a pointer to a file structure. This file structure in turn points to the inode; see Figure 20.7. The open file table has a fixed length that can be set only at boot time. Therefore, there is a fixed limit on the number of concurrently open files in a system.

The read and write system calls do not take a position in the file as an argument. Rather, the kernel keeps a *file offset*, which is updated by an appropriate amount after each read or write according to the number of data actually transferred. The offset can be set directly by the lseek system call. If the file descriptor indexed an array of inode pointers instead of file pointers, this offset would have to be kept in the inode. Because more than one process

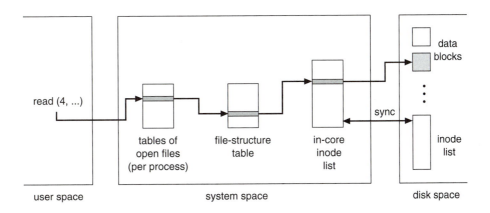

Figure 20.7 File-system control blocks.

may open the same file, and each such process needs its own offset for the file, keeping the offset in the inode is inappropriate. Thus, we use the file structure to contain the offset.

File structures are inherited by the child process after a fork, so several processes may share the *same* offset location for a file.

The **inode structure** pointed to by the file structure is an in-core copy of the inode on the disk. The in-core inode has a few extra fields, such as a reference count of how many file structures are pointing at it, and the file structure has a similar reference count for how many file descriptors refer to it. When a count becomes zero, the entry is no longer needed and may be reclaimed and reused.

20.7.5 Disk Structures

The file system that the user sees is supported by data on a mass-storage device —usually, a disk. The user ordinarily knows of only one file system, but this one logical file system may consist of several **physical file systems,** each on a different device. Because device characteristics differ, each separate hardware device defines its own physical file system. In fact, it is generally desirable to partition large physical devices, such as disks, into multiple **logical devices**. Each logical device defines a physical file system. Figure 20.8 illustrates how a directory structure is partitioned into file systems, which are mapped onto logical devices, which are partitions of physical devices. The sizes and locations of these partitions were coded into device drivers in earlier systems, but are maintained on the disk by 4.3BSD.

Partitioning a physical device into multiple file systems has several benefits. Different file systems can support different uses. Although most partitions would be used by the file system, at least one will be necessary for a swap area for the virtual-memory software. Reliability is improved, because software damage is generally limited to only one file system. We can improve efficiency by varying the file-system parameters (such as the block and fragment sizes) for each partition. Also, separate file systems prevent one program from using all available space for a large file, because files cannot be split across file systems. Finally, disk backups are done per partition, and it is faster to search a backup tape for a file if the partition is smaller. Restoring the full partition from tape is also faster.

The actual number of file systems on a drive varies according to the size of the disk and the purpose of the computer system as a whole. One file system, the **root file system,** is always available. Other file systems may be **mounted**— that is, integrated into the directory hierarchy of the root file system.

A bit in the inode structure indicates that the inode has a file system mounted on it. A reference to this file causes the **mount table** to be searched to find the device number of the mounted device. The device number is used to find the inode of the root directory of the mounted file system, and that inode is used. Conversely, if a path-name element is ".." and the directory being

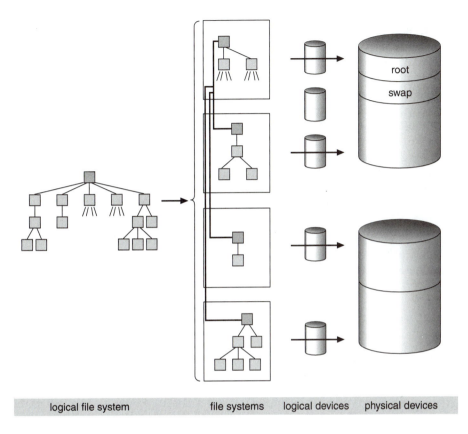

logical file system   file systems   logical devices   physical devices

Figure 20.8   Mapping of a logical file system to physical devices.

searched is the root directory of a file system that is mounted, the mount table is searched to find the inode it is mounted on, and that inode is used.

Each file system is a separate system resource and represents a set of files. The first sector on the logical device is the **boot block,** possibly containing a primary bootstrap program, which may be used to call a secondary bootstrap program residing in the next 7.5K. A system needs only one partition containing boot-block data, but duplicates can be installed via privileged programs by the systems manager, to allow booting when the primary copy is damaged. The **superblock** contains static parameters of the file system. These parameters include the total size of the file system, the block and fragment sizes of the data blocks, and assorted parameters that affect allocation policies.

20.7.6 Implementations

The user interface to the file system is simple and well defined, allowing the implementation of the file system itself to be changed without significant effect on the user. The file system was changed between Version 6 and Version 7, and again between Version 7 and 4BSD. For Version 7, the size of inodes doubled, the maximum file and file-system sizes increased, and the details of free-list handling and superblock information changed. At that time also, seek (with a 16-bit offset) became lseek (with a 32-bit offset), to allow specification of offsets in larger files, but few other changes were visible outside the kernel.

In 4.0BSD, the size of blocks used in the file system was increased from 512 bytes to 1024 bytes. Although this increased size produced increased internal fragmentation on the disk, it doubled throughput, due mainly to the greater number of data accessed on each disk transfer. This idea was later adopted by System V, along with a number of other ideas, device drivers, and programs.

4.3BSD added the Berkeley Fast File System, which increased speed, and was accompanied by new features. Symbolic links required new system calls. Long file names necessitated the new directory system calls to traverse the now-complex internal directory structure. Finally, the truncate calls were added. The Fast File System was a success; it is now found in most implementations of UNIX. Its performance is made possible by its layout and allocation policies, which we discuss next. In Section 11.6.4, we discussed changes made in SunOS to increase disk throughput.

20.7.7 Layout and Allocation Policies

The kernel uses a <*logical device number, inode number*> pair to identify a file. The logical device number defines the file system involved. The inodes in the file system are numbered in sequence. In the Version 7 file system, all inodes are located in an array immediately following a single superblock at the beginning of the logical device, with the data blocks following the inodes. The *inode number* is effectively just an index into this array.

With the Version 7 file system, a block of a file can be anywhere on the disk between the end of the inode array and the end of the file system. Free blocks are kept in a linked list in the superblock. Blocks are pushed onto the front of the free list, and are removed from the front as needed to serve new files or to extend existing files. Thus, the blocks of a file may be arbitrarily far from both the inode and one another. Furthermore, the more a file system of this kind is used, the more disorganized the blocks in a file become. We can reverse this process only by reinitializing and restoring the entire file system, which is not a convenient task to perform. This process was described in Section 11.10.2.

Another difficulty is that the reliability of the file system is suspect. For speed, the superblock of each mounted file system is kept in memory. Keeping the superblock in memory allows the kernel to access a superblock quickly, especially for using the free list. Every 30 seconds, the superblock is written to the disk, to keep the in-core and disk copies synchronized (by the update program, using the **sync** system call). However, it is not uncommon for system bugs or hardware failures to cause a system crash, which destroys the in-core superblock between updates to the disk. Then, the free list on disk does not reflect accurately the state of the disk; to reconstruct it, we must perform a lengthy examination of all blocks in the file system. Note that this problem still remains in the new file system.

The 4.3BSD file-system implementation is radically different from that of Version 7. The primary purpose of this reimplementation was to improve efficiency and robustness, and most such changes are invisible outside the kernel. There were other changes introduced at the same time, such as symbolic links and long file names (up to 255 characters), that are visible at both the system-call and the user levels. Most of the changes required for these features were not in the kernel, however, but rather were in the programs that use them.

Space allocation is especially different. The major new concept in 4.3BSD is the **cylinder group**. The cylinder group was introduced to allow localization of the blocks in a file. Each cylinder group occupies one or more consecutive cylinders of the disk, so that disk accesses within the cylinder group require minimal disk head movement. Every cylinder group has a superblock, a cylinder block, an array of inodes, and some data blocks (Figure 20.9).

The superblock is identical in each cylinder group, so that it can be recovered from any one of them in the event of disk corruption. The **cylinder block** contains dynamic parameters of the particular cylinder group. These include a bit map of free data blocks and fragments, and a bit map of free inodes. Statistics on recent progress of the allocation strategies also are kept here.

The header information in a cylinder group (the superblock, the cylinder block, and the inodes) is not always at the beginning of the cylinder group. If it were, the header information for every cylinder group might be on the same disk platter; a single disk head crash could wipe out all of them. Therefore, each cylinder group has its header information at a different offset from the beginning of the group.

It is common for the directory-listing command **ls** to read all the inodes of every file in a directory, making it desirable for all such inodes to be close together on the disk. For this reason, the inode for a file is usually allocated

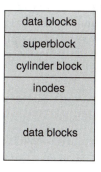

Figure 20.9   4.3BSD cylinder group.

from the same cylinder group as is the inode of the file's parent directory. Not everything can be localized, however, so an inode for a new directory is put in a cylinder group *different* from that of its parent directory. The cylinder group chosen for such a new directory inode is the one with the greatest number of unused inodes.

To reduce disk head seeks involved in accessing the data blocks of a file, we allocate blocks from the same cylinder group as often as possible. Because a single file cannot be allowed to take up all the blocks in a cylinder group, a file exceeding a certain size (such as 2 megabytes) has further block allocation redirected to a different cylinder group, the new group being chosen from among those having more than average free space. If the file continues to grow, allocation is again redirected (at each megabyte) to yet another cylinder group. Thus, all the blocks of a small file are likely to be in the same cylinder group, and the number of long head seeks involved in accessing a large file is kept small.

There are two levels of disk-block-allocation routines. The global policy routines select a desired disk block according to the considerations already discussed. The local policy routines use the specific information recorded in the cylinder blocks to choose a block near the one requested. If the requested block is not in use, it is returned. Otherwise, the block rotationally closest to the one requested in the same cylinder, or a block in a different cylinder but in the same cylinder group, is returned. If there are no more blocks in the cylinder group, a quadratic rehash is done among all the other cylinder groups to find a block; if that fails, an exhaustive search is done. If enough free space (typically 10 percent) is left in the file system, blocks usually are found where desired, the quadratic rehash and exhaustive search are not used, and performance of the file system does not degrade with use.

Because of the increased efficiency of the Fast File System, typical disks are now utilized at 30 percent of their raw transfer capacity. This percentage is a marked improvement over that realized with the Version 7 file system, which used about 3 percent of the bandwidth.

4.3BSD Tahoe introduced the Fat Fast File System, which allows the number of inodes per cylinder group, the number of cylinders per cylinder group, as well as the number of distinguished rotational positions, to be set when the file system is created. 4.3BSD used to set these parameters according to the disk hardware type.

20.8 ■ I/O System

One of the purposes of an operating system is to hide the peculiarities of specific hardware devices from the user. For example, the file system presents a simple consistent storage facility (the file) independent of the underlying disk hardware. In UNIX, the peculiarities of I/O devices are also hidden from the bulk of the kernel itself by the **I/O system**. The I/O system consists of a buffer caching system, general device driver code, and drivers for specific hardware devices. Only the device driver knows the peculiarities of a specific device. The major parts of the I/O system are diagrammed in Figure 20.10.

There are three main kinds of I/O in 4.3BSD: block devices, character devices, and the **socket** interface. The socket interface, with its protocols and network interfaces, will be treated in Section 20.9.1.

Block devices include disks and tapes. Their distinguishing characteristic is that they are directly addressable in a fixed block size—usually, 512 bytes. A block-device driver is required to isolate details of tracks, cylinders, and so on, from the rest of the kernel. Block devices are accessible directly through appropriate device special files (such as */dev/rp0*), but are more commonly accessed indirectly through the file system. In either case, transfers are buffered through the **block buffer cache,** and that process has a profound effect on efficiency.

Character devices include terminals and line printers, as well as almost everything else (except network interfaces) that does not use the block buffer cache. For instance, */dev/mem* is an interface to physical main memory, and */dev/null* is a bottomless sink for data and an endless source of end-of-file markers. Some devices, such as high-speed graphics interfaces, may have their own buffers or may always do I/O directly into the user's data space; because they do not use the block buffer cache, they are classed as character devices.

Terminals and terminal-like devices use **C-lists,** which are buffers smaller than those of the block buffer cache.

Block devices and **character** devices are the two main device classes. Device drivers are accessed by one of two arrays of entry points. One array is for block devices; the other is for character devices. A device is distinguished by a class (block or character) and a **device number**. The device number consists of two parts. The **major device number** is used to index the array for character or block devices to find entries into the appropriate device driver. The **minor**

system-call interface to the kernel					
socket	plain file	cooked block interface	raw block interface	raw tty interface	cooked TTY
protocols	file system				line discipline
network interface	block-device driver			character-device driver	
the hardware					

Figure 20.10   4.3BSD kernel I/O structure.

device number is interpreted by the device driver as, for example, a logical disk partition or a terminal line.

A device driver is connected to the rest of the kernel only by the entry points recorded in the array for its class, and by its use of common buffering systems. This segregation is important for portability, and also for system configuration.

20.8.1 Block Buffer Cache

The block devices use a block buffer cache. The buffer cache consists of a number of buffer headers, each of which can point to a piece of physical memory, as well as to a device number and a block number on the device. The buffer headers for blocks not currently in use are kept in several linked lists, one each for:

- Buffers recently used, linked in LRU order (the LRU list)

- Buffers not recently used, or without valid contents (the AGE list)

- EMPTY buffers with no physical memory associated with them

The buffers in these lists are also hashed by device and block number for search efficiency.

When a block is wanted from a device (a read), the cache is searched. If the block is found, it is used, and no I/O transfer is necessary. If it is not found, a buffer is chosen from the AGE list, or the LRU list if AGE is empty. Then the device number and block number associated with it are updated, memory is found for it if necessary, and the new data are transferred into it from the device. If there are no empty buffers, the LRU buffer is written to its device (if it is modified) and the buffer is reused.

On a write, if the block in question is already in the buffer cache, the new data are put in the buffer (overwriting any previous data), the buffer header is marked to indicate that the buffer has been modified, and no I/O is immediately necessary. The data will be written when the buffer is needed for other data. If the block is not found in the buffer cache, an empty buffer is chosen (as with a read) and a transfer is done to this buffer.

Writes are periodically forced for dirty buffer blocks to minimize potential file-system inconsistencies after a crash.

The number of data in a buffer in 4.3BSD is variable, up to a maximum over all file systems, usually 8K. The minimum size is the paging-cluster size, usually 1024 bytes. Buffers are page-cluster aligned, and any page cluster may be mapped into only one buffer at a time, just as any disk block may be mapped into only one buffer at a time. The EMPTY list holds buffer headers which are used if a physical memory block of 8K is split to hold multiple, smaller blocks. Headers are needed for these blocks and are retrieved from EMPTY.

The number of data in a buffer may grow as a user process writes more data following those already in the buffer. When this increase in the data occurs, a new buffer large enough to hold all the data is allocated, and the original data are copied into it, followed by the new data. If a buffer shrinks, a buffer is taken off the empty queue, excess pages are put in it, and that buffer is released to be written to disk.

Some devices, such as magnetic tapes, require blocks to be written in a certain order, so facilities are provided to force a synchronous write of buffers to these devices, in the correct order. Directory blocks are also written synchronously, to forestall crash inconsistencies. Consider the chaos that could occur if many changes were made to a directory, but the directory entries themselves were not updated.

The size of the buffer cache can have a profound effect on the performance of a system, because, if it is large enough, the percentage of cache hits can be high and the number of actual I/O transfers low.

There are interesting interactions among the buffer cache, the file system, and the disk drivers. When data are written to a disk file, they are buffered in the cache, and the disk driver sorts its output queue according to disk address. These two actions allow the disk driver to minimize disk head seeks and to write data at times optimized for disk rotation. Unless synchronous writes are required, a process writing to disk simply writes into the buffer cache, and the system asynchronously writes the data to disk when convenient. The user process sees very fast writes. When data are read from a disk file, the block I/O system does some read-ahead; however, writes are much nearer to asynchronous than are reads. Thus, output to the disk through the file system is often faster than is input for large transfers, counter to intuition.

20.8.2 Raw Device Interfaces

Almost every block device also has a character interface, and these are called **raw device interfaces**. Such an interface differs from the **block interface** in that the block buffer cache is bypassed.

Each disk driver maintains a queue of pending transfers. Each record in the queue specifies whether it is a read or a write, a main memory address for the transfer (usually in 512-byte increments), a device address for the transfer (usually the address of a disk sector), and a transfer size (in sectors). It is simple to map the information from a block buffer to what is required for this queue.

It is almost as simple to map a piece of main memory corresponding to part of a user process's virtual address space. This mapping is what a raw disk interface, for instance, does. Unbuffered transfers directly to or from a user's virtual address space are thus allowed. The size of the transfer is limited by the physical devices, some of which require an even number of bytes.

The kernel accomplishes transfers for swapping and paging simply by putting the appropriate request on the queue for the appropriate device. No special swapping or paging device driver is needed.

The 4.3BSD file-system implementation was actually written and largely tested as a user process that used a raw disk interface, before the code was moved into the kernel. In an interesting about-face, the Mach operating system has no file system per se. File systems can be implemented as user-level tasks.

20.8.3 C-Lists

Terminal drivers use a character buffering system, which keeps small blocks of characters (usually 28 bytes) in linked lists. There are routines to enqueue and dequeue characters for such lists. Although all free-character buffers are kept in a single free list, most device drivers that use them limit the number of characters that may be queued at one time for any given terminal line.

A `write` system call to a terminal enqueues characters on a list for the device. An initial transfer is started, and interrupts cause dequeuing of characters and further transfers.

Input is similarly interrupt driven. Terminal drivers typically support *two* input queues, however, and conversion from the first, raw queue to the other, canonical queue is triggered by the interrupt routine putting an end-of-line character on the raw queue. The process doing a read on the device is then awakened, and its system phase does the conversion; the characters thus put on the canonical queue are then available to be returned to the user process by the read.

It is also possible to have the device driver bypass the canonical queue and return characters directly from the raw queue. This mode of operation is known as **raw mode**. Full-screen editors, and other programs that need to react to every keystroke, use this mode.

20.9 ▪ Interprocess Communication

Many tasks can be accomplished in isolated processes, but many others require interprocess communication. Isolated computing systems have long served for many applications, but networking is increasingly important. With the increasing use of personal workstations, resource sharing is becoming more common. Interprocess communication has not traditionally been one of UNIX's strong points.

Most UNIX systems have not permitted shared memory because the PDP-11 hardware did not encourage it. System V does support a shared-memory facility, and one was planned for 4.3BSD, but was not implemented due to time constraints. Solaris 2 supports shared memory, as do many other current versions of UNIX. In any case, shared memory presents a problem in a networked environment, because network accesses can never be as fast as memory accesses on the local machine. Although we could, of course, pretend that memory was shared between two separate machines by copying data across a network transparently, the major benefit of shared memory (speed) would be lost.

20.9.1 Sockets

The **pipe** (discussed in Section 20.4.3) is the IPC mechanism most characteristic of UNIX. A pipe permits a reliable unidirectional byte stream between two processes. It is traditionally implemented as an ordinary file, with a few exceptions. It has no name in the file system, being created instead by the pipe system call. Its size is fixed, and when a process attempts to write to a full pipe, the process is suspended. Once all data previously written into the pipe have been read out, writing continues at the beginning of the file (pipes are not true circular buffers). One benefit of the small size (usually 4096 bytes) of pipes is that pipe data are seldom actually written to disk; they usually are kept in memory by the normal block buffer cache.

In 4.3BSD, pipes are implemented as a special case of the **socket** mechanism. The socket mechanism provides a general interface not only to facilities such as pipes, which are local to one machine, but also to networking facilities. Even on the same machine, a pipe can be used only by two processes related through use of the fork system call. The socket mechanism can be used by unrelated processes.

A socket is an endpoint of communication. A socket in use usually has an address bound to it. The nature of the address depends on the **communication domain** of the socket. A characteristic property of a domain is that processes communicating in the same domain use the same **address format**. A single socket can communicate in only one domain.

The three domains currently implemented in 4.3BSD are the UNIX domain (AF_UNIX), the Internet domain (AF_INET), and the XEROX Network Services (NS) domain (AF_NS). The address format of the UNIX domain is ordinary file-system path names, such as */alpha/beta/gamma*. Processes communicating in the Internet domain use DARPA Internet communications protocols (such as TCP/IP) and Internet addresses, which consist of a 32-bit host number and a 32-bit port number (representing a rendezvous point on the host).

There are several **socket types,** which represent classes of services. Each type may or may not be implemented in any communication domain. If a type is implemented in a given domain, it may be implemented by one or more protocols, which may be selected by the user:

- **Stream sockets:** These sockets provide reliable, duplex, sequenced data streams. No data are lost or duplicated in delivery, and there are no record boundaries. This type is supported in the Internet domain by the TCP protocol. In the UNIX domain, pipes are implemented as a pair of communicating stream sockets.

- **Sequenced packet sockets:** These sockets provide data streams like those of stream sockets, except that record boundaries are provided. This type is used in the XEROX AF_NS protocol.

- **Datagram sockets:** These sockets transfer messages of variable size in either direction. There is no guarantee that such messages will arrive in the same order they were sent, or that they will be unduplicated, or that they will arrive at all, but the original message (record) size is preserved in any datagram that does arrive. This type is supported in the Internet domain by the UDP protocol.

- **Reliably delivered message sockets:** These sockets transfer messages that are guaranteed to arrive, and that otherwise are like the messages transferred using datagram sockets. This type is currently unsupported.

- **Raw sockets:** These sockets allow direct access by processes to the protocols that support the other socket types. The protocols accessible include not only the uppermost ones, but also lower-level protocols. For example, in the Internet domain, it is possible to reach TCP, IP beneath that, or an Ethernet protocol beneath that. This capability is useful for developing new protocols.

The socket facility has a set of system calls specific to it. The `socket` system call creates a socket. It takes as arguments specifications of the communication domain, the socket type, and the protocol to be used to support that type. The value returned by the call is a small integer called a **socket descriptor,** which is in the same name space as file descriptors. The socket descriptor indexes the array of open "files" in the **u** structure in the kernel, and has a file structure allocated for it. The 4.3BSD file structure may point to a **socket** structure instead of to an inode. In this case, certain socket information (such as the socket's type, message count, and the data in its input and output queues) is kept directly in the socket structure.

For another process to address a socket, the socket must have a name. A name is bound to a socket by the `bind` system call, which takes the socket descriptor, a pointer to the name, and the length of the name as a byte string. The contents and length of the byte string depend on the address format. The `connect` system call is used to initiate a connection. The arguments are syntactically the same as those for `bind`; the socket descriptor represents the local socket and the address is that of the foreign socket to which the attempt to connect is made.

Many processes that communicate using the socket IPC follow the **client–server model**. In this model, the **server** process provides a **service** to the **client** process. When the service is available, the server process listens on a well-known address, and the client process uses **connect,** as described previously, to reach the server.

A server process uses `socket` to create a socket and `bind` to bind the well-known address of its service to that socket. Then, it uses the `listen` system call to tell the kernel that it is ready to accept connections from clients, and to specify how many pending connections the kernel should queue until the server can service them. Finally, the server uses the `accept` system call to accept individual connections. Both `listen` and `accept` take as an argument the socket descriptor of the original socket. `Accept` returns a new socket descriptor corresponding to the new connection; the original socket descriptor is still open for further connections. The server usually uses `fork` to produce a new process after the `accept` to service the client while the original server process continues to listen for more connections.

There are also system calls for setting parameters of a connection and for returning the address of the foreign socket after an `accept`.

When a connection for a socket type such as a stream socket is established, the addresses of both endpoints are known and no further addressing information is needed to transfer data. The ordinary `read` and `write` system calls may then be used to transfer data.

The simplest way to terminate a connection and to destroy the associated socket is to use the `close` system call on its socket descriptor. We may also wish to terminate only one direction of communication of a duplex connection; the `shutdown` system call can be used for this purpose.

Some socket types, such as datagram sockets, do not support connections; instead, their sockets exchange datagrams that must be addressed individually. The system calls `sendto` and `recvfrom` are used for such connections. Both take as arguments a socket descriptor, a buffer pointer and the length, and an address-buffer pointer and length. The address buffer contains the address to send to for `sendto` and is filled in with the address of the datagram just received by `recvfrom`. The number of data actually transferred is returned by both system calls.

The `select` system call can be used to multiplex data transfers on several file descriptors and/or socket descriptors. It can even be used to allow one server process to listen for client connections for many services and to `fork` a process for each connection as the connection is made. The server does a `socket`, `bind`, and `listen` for each service, and then does a `select` on all the socket descriptors. When `select` indicates activity on a descriptor, the server does an `accept` on it and forks a process on the new descriptor returned by `accept`, leaving the parent process to do a `select` again.

20.9.2 Network Support

Almost all current UNIX systems support the UUCP network facilities, which are mostly used over dial-up telephone lines to support the UUCP mail network and the USENET news network. These are, however, rudimentary networking facilities, as they do not support even remote login, much less remote procedure call or distributed file systems. These facilities are also almost completely implemented as user processes, and are not part of the operating system proper.

4.3BSD supports the DARPA Internet protocols UDP, TCP, IP, and ICMP on a wide range of Ethernet, token-ring, and ARPANET interfaces. The framework in the kernel to support this is intended to facilitate the implementation of further protocols, and all protocols are accessible via the socket interface. The first version of the code was written by Robert Gurwitz of BBN as an add-on package for 4.1BSD.

The International Standards Organization's (ISO) Open System Interconnection (OSI) Reference Model for networking prescribes seven layers of network protocols and strict methods of communication between them. An implementation of a protocol may communicate only with a peer entity speaking the same protocol at the same layer, or with the protocol–protocol interface of a protocol in the layer immediately above or below in the same system. The ISO networking model is implemented in 4.3BSD Reno and 4.4BSD.

The 4.3BSD networking implementation, and to a certain extent the socket facility, is more oriented toward the ARPANET Reference Model (ARM). The ARPANET in its original form served as a proof of concept for many networking concepts, such as packet switching and protocol layering. The ARPANET was retired in 1988 because the hardware that supported it was no longer up to date. Its successors, such as the NSFNET and the Internet, are even larger, and serve as a communications utility for researchers and as a testbed for Internet gateway research. The ARM predates the ISO model; the ISO model was in large part inspired by the ARPANET research.

Although the ISO model is often interpreted as requiring a limit of one protocol communicating per layer, the ARM allows several protocols in the same layer. There are only four protocol layers in the ARM, plus

- *Process/Applications:* This layer subsumes the application, presentation, and session layers of the ISO model. Such user-level programs as the File Transfer Protocol (FTP) and Telnet (remote login) exist at this level.

- *Host–Host:* This layer corresponds to ISO's transport and the top part of its network layers. Both the Transmission Control Protocol (TCP) and the Internet Protocol (IP) are in this layer, with TCP on top of IP. TCP corresponds to an ISO transport protocol, and IP performs the addressing functions of the ISO network layer.

- *Network Interface:* This layer spans the lower part of the ISO network layer and all of the data-link layer. The protocols involved here depend on the physical network type. The ARPANET uses the IMP-Host protocols, whereas an Ethernet uses Ethernet protocols.

- *Network Hardware:* The ARM is primarily concerned with software, so there is no explicit network hardware layer; however, any actual network will have hardware corresponding to the ISO physical layer.

The networking framework in 4.3BSD is more generalized than is either the ISO model or the ARM, although it is most closely related to the ARM; see Figure 20.11.

User processes communicate with network protocols (and thus with other processes on other machines) via the socket facility, which corresponds to the ISO Session layer, as it is responsible for setting up and controlling communications.

Sockets are supported by one or several protocols, layered one on another. A protocol may provide services such as reliable delivery, suppression of duplicate transmissions, flow control, or addressing, depending on the socket type being supported and on the services required by any higher protocols.

A protocol may communicate with another protocol or with the network interface that is appropriate for the network hardware. There is little restriction in the general framework on what protocols may communicate with what other protocols, or on how many protocols may be layered on top of one another. The user process may, by means of the raw socket type, directly access any layer of protocol from the uppermost used to support one of the other socket types, such as streams, down to a raw network interface. This capability is used by routing processes and also for new protocol development.

There tends to be one **network-interface driver** per network controller type. The network-interface driver is responsible for handling characteristics specific to the local network being addressed. This arrangement ensures that the protocols using the interface do not need to be concerned with these characteristics.

The functions of the network interface depend largely on the **network hardware,** which is whatever is necessary for the network to which it is connected.

ISO reference model	ARPANET reference model	4.2BSD layers	example layering
application	process applications	user programs and libraries	telnet
presentation	process applications	user programs and libraries	telnet
session	process applications	sockets	sock_stream
transport	host–host	protocol	TCP
network	host–host	protocol	IP
data link	network interface	network interfaces	Ethernet driver
hardware	network interface	network interfaces	Ethernet driver
	network hardware	network hardware	interlan controller

Figure 20.11   Network reference models and layering.

Some networks may support reliable transmission at this level, but most do not. Some networks provide broadcast addressing, but many do not.

The socket facility and the networking framework use a common set of memory buffers, or **mbuf**s. These are intermediate in size between the large buffers used by the block I/O system and the C-lists used by character devices. An **mbuf** is 128 bytes long, 112 bytes of which may be used for data; the rest is used for pointers to link the **mbuf** into queues and for indicators of how much of the data area is actually in use.

Data are ordinarily passed between layers (socket-protocol, protocol-protocol, or protocol-network interface) in **mbuf**s. This ability to pass the buffers containing the data eliminates some data copying, but there is still frequently a need to remove or add protocol headers. It is also convenient and efficient for many purposes to be able to hold data that occupy an area the size of the memory-management page. Thus, it is possible for the data of an **mbuf** to reside not in the **mbuf** itself, but rather elsewhere in memory. There is an **mbuf** page table for this purpose, as well as a pool of pages dedicated to **mbuf** use.

20.10 ■ Summary

The early advantages of UNIX were that this system was written in a high-level language, was distributed in source form, and had provided powerful operating-system primitives on an inexpensive platform. These advantages led to UNIX's popularity at educational, research, and government institutions, and eventually in the commercial world. This popularity first produced many strains of UNIX with variant and improved facilities. Market pressures are currently leading to the consolidation of these versions. One of the most influential versions is 4.3BSD, developed at Berkeley for the VAX, and later ported to many other platforms.

UNIX provides a file system with tree-structured directories. Files are supported by the kernel as unstructured sequences of bytes. Direct access and sequential access are supported through system calls and library routines.

Files are stored as an array of fixed-size data blocks with perhaps a trailing fragment. The data blocks are found by pointers in the inode. Directory entries point to inodes. Disk space is allocated from cylinder groups to minimize head movement and to improve performance.

UNIX is a multiprogrammed system. Processes can easily create new processes with the `fork` system call. Processes can communicate with pipes or, more generally, sockets. They can be grouped into jobs that can be controlled with signals.

Processes are represented by two structures: the process structure and the user structure. CPU scheduling is a priority algorithm with dynamically computed priorities that reduces to round-robin scheduling in the extreme case.

4.3BSD memory management is swapping supported by paging. A *pagedaemon* process uses a modified second-chance page-replacement algorithm to keep enough free frames to support the executing processes.

Page and file I/O uses a block buffer cache to minimize the amount of actual I/O. Terminal devices use a separate character buffering system.

Networking support is one of the most important features in 4.3BSD. The socket concept provides the programming mechanism to access other processes, even across a network. Sockets provide an interface to several sets of protocols.

■ Exercises

20.1 What are the major differences between 4.3BSD UNIX and SYSVR3? Is one system "better" than the other? Explain your answer.

20.2 How were the design goals of UNIX different from those of other operating systems during the early stages of UNIX development?

20.3 Why are there many different versions of UNIX currently available? Name two ways in which is this diversity an advantage to UNIX. Name two ways in which is it a disadvantage.

20.4 What are the advantages and disadvantages of writing an operating system in a high-level language, such as C?

20.5 In what circumstances is the system-call sequence `fork` `execve` most appropriate? When is `vfork` preferable?

20.6 Does 4.3BSD UNIX give scheduling priority to I/O or CPU-bound processes? For what reason does it differentiate between these categories, and why is one given priority over the other? How does it know which of these categories fits a given process?

20.7 Early UNIX systems used swapping for memory management, whereas 4.3BSD used paging and swapping. Discuss the relative advantages and disadvantages of the two memory methods.

20.8 Describe the modifications to a file system that the 4.3BSD kernel makes when a process requests the creation of a new file */tmp/foo* and writes to that file sequentially until the file size reaches 20K.

20.9 Directory blocks in 4.3BSD are written synchronously when they are changed. Consider what would happen if they were written asynchronously. Describe the state of the file system if a crash occurred after all the files in a directory were deleted but before the directory entry was updated on disk.

20.10 Describe the process that is needed to recreate the free list after a crash in 4.1BSD.

20.11 What effects on system performance would the following changes to 4.3BSD have? Explain your answers.

    a. Merging the block buffer cache and the process paging space

    b. Clustering disk I/O into larger chunks

    c. Implementing and using shared memory to pass data between processes, rather than using RPC or sockets

    d. Using the ISO seven-layer networking model, rather than the ARM network model

20.12 What socket type should you use to implement an intercomputer file-transfer program? What type should you use for a program that periodically tests to see whether another computer is up on the network? Explain your answer.

Bibliographical Notes

The best general description of the distinctive features of UNIX is still that presented by Ritchie and Thompson [1974]. Much of the history of UNIX was given in Ritchie [1979].

Possibly the best book on general programming under UNIX, especially on the use of the shell and facilities such as **yacc** and **sed,** is that by Kernighan and Pike [1984]. The programming language of choice under UNIX is C [Kernighan and Ritchie 1988]. C is also the system's implementation language.

The set of documentation that comes with UNIX systems is called the *UNIX Programmer's Manual* (UPM) and is traditionally organized in two volumes. Volume 1 contains short entries for every command, system call, and subroutine package in the system, and is also available on-line on UNIX systems via the **man** command. Volume 2, *Supplementary Documents* (usually divided into Volumes 2A and 2B for convenience of binding), contains assorted papers relevant to the system and manuals for those commands or packages too complex to describe in one or two pages. Berkeley systems add Volume 2C to contain documents concerning Berkeley-specific features.

A description of the UNIX operating-system security was given by Grampp and Morris [1984] and by Wood and Kochan [1985].

The Internet and its protocols were described in Comer [1991], and Comer and Stevens [1991, 1993]. UNIX network programming was described thoroughly in Stevens [1990]. The general state of networks was explored by Quarterman [1990].

Several textbooks describing variants of the UNIX system are those by Holt [1983], discussing the Tunis operating system; by Comer [1984, 1987], discussing the Xinu operating system; and by Tanenbaum and Woodhull [1997], describing the Minix operating system.

Chapter 21

THE LINUX SYSTEM

Chapter 20 discussed the internal workings of the 4.3BSD operating system. BSD is just one of the UNIX-like systems. Linux is another UNIX-like system that has gained popularity in recent years. In this chapter, we look at the history and development of Linux, and cover the user and programmer interfaces that Linux presents—interfaces that owe a great deal to the UNIX tradition. We also discuss the internal methods by which Linux implements these interfaces. However, since Linux has been designed to run as many standard UNIX applications as possible, it has much in common with existing UNIX implementations. We do not duplicate the basic description of UNIX given in the previous chapter.

Linux is a rapidly evolving operating system. This chapter describes specifically the Linux 2.0 kernel, which was released in June 1996.

21.1 ■ History

Linux looks and feels much like any other UNIX system; indeed, UNIX compatibility has been a major design goal of the Linux project. However, Linux is much younger than most UNIX systems. Its development began in 1991, when a Finnish student, Linus Torvalds, wrote and christened Linux, a small but self-contained kernel for the 80386 processor, the first true 32-bit processor in Intel's range of PC-compatible CPUs.

Early in its development, the Linux's source code was made available for free on the Internet. As a result, Linux's history has been one of collaboration by many users from all around the world, corresponding almost exclusively over the Internet. From an initial kernel that partially implemented a small subset of the UNIX system services, the Linux system has grown to include much UNIX functionality.

In its early days, Linux development revolved largely around the central operating-system kernel—the core, privileged executive that manages all system resources and that interacts directly with the hardware. We need much more than this kernel to produce a full operating system, of course. It is useful to make the distinction between the Linux kernel and a Linux system: The **Linux kernel** is an entirely original piece of software developed from scratch by the Linux community; the **Linux system,** as we know it today, includes a multitude of components, some written from scratch, others borrowed from other development projects or created in collaboration with other teams.

The basic Linux system is a standard environment for applications and for user programming, but it does not enforce any standard means of managing the available functionality as a whole. As Linux has matured, there has been a need for another layer of functionality on top of the Linux system. A Linux **distribution** includes all the standard components of the Linux system, plus a set of administrative tools to simplify the initial installation and subsequent upgrading of Linux, and to manage installation and deinstallation of other packages on the system. A modern distribution also typically includes tools for management of file systems, creation and management of user accounts, administration of networks, and so on.

21.1.1 The Linux Kernel

The first Linux kernel released to the public was Version 0.01, dated May 14, 1991. It had no networking, ran on only 80386-compatible Intel processors and PC hardware, and had extremely limited device-driver support. The virtual-memory subsystem was also fairly basic, and included no support for memory-mapped files; however, even this early incarnation supported shared pages with copy-on-write. The only file system supported was the Minix file system —the first Linux kernels were cross-developed on a Minix platform. However, the kernel did implement proper UNIX processes with protected address spaces.

It was not until March 14, 1994, that the next milestone version, Linux 1.0, was released. This release culminated three years of rapid development of the Linux kernel. Perhaps the single biggest new feature was networking: 1.0 included support for UNIX's standard TCP/IP networking protocols, as well as a BSD-compatible socket interface for networking programming. Device-driver support was added for running IP over an Ethernet or (using PPP or SLIP protocols) over serial lines or modems.

The 1.0 kernel also included a new, much enhanced file system without the limitations of the original Minix file system, and supported a range of SCSI controllers for high-performance disk access. The developers extended the virtual-memory subsystem to support paging to swap files and memory mapping of arbitrary files (but only read-only memory mapping was implemented in 1.0).

A range of extra hardware support was also included in this release. Although still restricted to the Intel/PC platform, hardware support had grown to include floppy-disk and CD-ROM devices, as well as sound cards, a range of mice, and international keyboards. Floating-point emulation was also provided in the kernel for 80386 users who had no 80387 math coprocessor, and System V UNIX-style interprocess communication (IPC), including shared memory, semaphores, and message queues, was implemented. Simple support for dynamically loadable and unloadable kernel modules was also provided.

At this point, development started on the 1.1 kernel stream, but numerous bug-fix patches were released subsequently against 1.0. This pattern was adopted as the standard numbering convention for Linux kernels: Kernels with an odd minor-version number such as 1.1, 1.3, or 2.1 are development kernels; even-numbered minor-version numbers are stable, production kernels. Updates against the stable kernels are intended as only remedial versions, whereas the development kernels may include newer and relatively untested functionality.

In March 1995, the 1.2 kernel was released. This release did not offer nearly the same improvement in functionality as the 1.0 release, but it did include support for a much wider variety of hardware, including the new PCI hardware bus architecture. Developers added another PC-specific feature—support for the 80386 CPU's virtual 8086 mode—to allow emulation of the DOS operating system for PC computers. They updated the networking stack to provide support for the IPX protocol, and made the IP implementation more complete by including accounting and firewalling functionality.

The 1.2 kernel also was the final PC-only Linux kernel. The source distribution for Linux 1.2 included partially implemented support for SPARC, Alpha, and MIPS CPUs, but full integration of these other architectures did not begin until after the 1.2 stable kernel was released.

The Linux 1.2 release concentrated on wider hardware support and more complete implementations of existing functionality. Much new functionality was under development at the time, but integration of the new code into the main kernel source code had been deferred until after the stable 1.2 kernel had been released. As a result, the 1.3 development stream saw a great deal of new functionality added to the kernel.

This work was finally released as Linux 2.0 in June 1996. This release was given a major version-number increment on account of two major new capabilities: support for multiple architectures, including a fully 64-bit native Alpha port, and support for multiprocessor architectures. Linux distributions based on 2.0 are also available for the Motorola 68000-series processors and for Sun's SPARC systems. A derived version of Linux running on top of the Mach Microkernel also runs on PC and PowerMac systems.

The changes in 2.0 did not stop there. The memory-management code was substantially improved, to provide a unified cache for file-system data independent of the caching of block devices. As a result of this change, the kernel offered greatly increased file-system and virtual-memory performance. For the first time, file-system caching was extended to networked file systems, and writable memory-mapped regions also were supported.

The 2.0 kernel also included much improved TCP/IP performance, and a number of new networking protocols were added, including AppleTalk, AX.25 amateur radio networking, and ISDN support. The ability to mount remote Netware and SMB (Microsoft LanManager) network volumes was added.

Other major improvements in 2.0 were support for internal kernel threads, for handling dependencies between loadable modules, and for automatic loading of modules on demand. Dynamic configuration of the kernel at run time was much improved through a new, standardized configuration interface. Additional, unrelated new features included file-system quotas and POSIX-compatible real-time process-scheduling classes.

21.1.2 The Linux System

In many ways, the Linux kernel forms the core of the Linux project, but other components make up the complete Linux operating system. Whereas the Linux kernel is composed entirely of code written from scratch specifically for the Linux project, much of the supporting software that makes up the Linux system is not exclusive to Linux, but rather is common to a number of UNIX-like operating systems. In particular, Linux uses many tools developed as part of Berkeley's BSD operating system, MIT's X Window System, and the Free Software Foundation's GNU project.

This sharing of tools has worked in both directions. The main system libraries of Linux were originally started by the GNU project, but much effort was expended by the Linux community in improving the libraries to address omissions, inefficiencies, and bugs. Other components such as the GNU C compiler, **gcc,** were already of sufficiently high quality to be used directly in Linux. The networking-administration tools under Linux were derived from code first developed for 4.3BSD, but more recent BSD derivatives such as FreeBSD have borrowed code from Linux in return, such as the Intel floating-point–emulation math library and the PC sound-hardware device drivers.

The Linux system as a whole is maintained by a loose network of developers collaborating over the Internet, with small groups or individuals having responsibility for maintaining the integrity of specific components. A small number of public Internet file-transfer protocol (ftp) archive sites act as de facto standard repositories for these components. The *File System Hierarchy Standard* document is also maintained by the Linux community as a means of keeping compatibility across the various different system components. This standard specifies the overall layout of a standard Linux file system; it determines under which directory names configuration files, libraries, system binaries, and run-time data files should be stored.

21.1.3 Linux Distributions

In theory, anybody can install a Linux system by fetching the latest revisions of the necessary system components from the ftp sites and compiling them. In Linux's early days, this operation was often precisely the one that a Linux user had to carry out. As Linux has matured, however, various individuals and groups have attempted to make this job less painful, by providing a standard, precompiled set of packages for easy installation.

These collections, or distributions, include much more than just the basic Linux system. They typically include extra system-installation and management utilities, as well as precompiled and ready-to-install packages of many of the common UNIX tools, such as news servers, web browsers, text-processing and editing tools, and even games.

The first distributions managed these packages by simply providing a means of unpacking all the files into the appropriate places. One of the important contributions of modern distributions, however, is advanced package management. Today's Linux distributions include a package-tracking database that allows packages to be installed, upgraded, or removed painlessly.

In the early days of Linux, the SLS distribution was the first collection of Linux packages that was recognizable as a complete distribution. Although it could be installed as a single entity, SLS lacked the package-management tools now expected of Linux distributions. The **Slackware** distribution represented a great improvement in overall quality (despite also having poor package management); it is still one of the most widely installed distributions in the Linux community.

Since Slackware's release, a large number of commercial and noncommercial Linux distributions have become available. **Red Hat** and **Debian** are particularly popular distributions from a commercial Linux support company and from the free-software Linux community, respectively. Other commercially supported Linuxes include distributions from **Caldera, Craftworks,** and **Work-Group Solutions**. A large Linux following in Germany has resulted in several dedicated German-language distributions, including versions from **SuSE** and **Unifix**. There are too many Linux distributions in current circulation for us to list here. The variety of distributions available does not prohibit compatibility across Linux distributions. The *RPM* package file format is used, or at least understood, by the majority of distributions, and commercial applications distributed in this format can be installed and run on any distribution that can accept RPM files.

21.1.4 Linux Licensing

The Linux kernel is distributed under the GNU General Public License (GPL), the terms of which are set out by the Free Software Foundation. Linux is not public-domain software: *Public domain* implies that the authors have waived copyright over the software, but copyright over Linux code is still held by the code's various authors. Linux is *free* software, however: It is free in the sense that people can copy it, modify it, use it in any manner they want, and give away their own copies without any restrictions.

The main implications of Linux's licensing terms are that anybody using Linux, or creating her own derivative of Linux (a legitimate exercise), cannot make the derived product proprietary. Software released under the GPL cannot be redistributed as a binary-only product. If you release software that includes any GPLed components, then, under the GPL, you must make source code available alongside any binary distributions. (This restriction does not prohibit making—or even selling—binary-only software distributions, as long as anybody who receives binaries is also given the opportunity to get source code too, for a reasonable distribution charge.)

21.2 ■ Design Principles

In its overall design, Linux resembles any other traditional, nonmicrokernel UNIX implementation. It is a multiuser, multitasking system with a full set of UNIX-compatible tools. Linux's file system adheres to traditional UNIX semantics, and the standard UNIX networking model is implemented fully. The internal details of Linux's design have been influenced heavily by the history of this operating system's development.

Although Linux runs on a wide variety of platforms, in its early days it was developed exclusively on PC architecture. A great deal of that early development was carried out by individual enthusiasts, rather than by well-funded development or research facilities, so from the start Linux attempted to squeeze as much functionality as possible from limited resources. Today, Linux can run happily on a multiprocessor machine with hundreds of megabytes of main memory and many gigabytes of disk space, but it is still capable of operating usefully in under 4 MB of RAM.

As PCs became more powerful and as memory and hard disks became cheaper, the original, minimalist Linux kernels grew to implement more UNIX functionality. Speed and efficiency are still important design goals, but much of the recent and current work on Linux has concentrated on a third major design goal: standardization. One of the prices paid for the diversity of UNIX implementations currently available is that source code written for one flavor may not necessarily compile or run correctly on another. Even when the same system calls are present on two different UNIX systems, they do not necessarily behave in exactly the same way. The POSIX standards comprise a set of specifications of different aspects of operating-system behavior. There are POSIX documents for common operating-system functionality and for extensions such as process threads and real-time operations. Linux is designed to be compliant with the relevant POSIX documents; at least two Linux distributions have achieved official POSIX certification.

Because it presents standard interfaces to both the programmer and the user, Linux presents few surprises to anybody familiar with UNIX. We do not detail these interfaces under Linux. The sections on the programmer interface (Section 20.3) and user interface (Section 20.4) of 4.3BSD in Chapter 20 apply equally well to Linux. By default, however, the Linux programming interface adheres to SVR4 UNIX semantics, rather than to BSD behavior. A separate set of libraries is available to implement BSD semantics in places where the two behaviors are significantly different.

There are many other standards in the UNIX world, but full certification of Linux against them is sometimes slowed because they are often available only for a fee, and there is a substantial expense involved in certifying an operating system's compliance with most standards. However, supporting a wide base of applications is important for any operating system, so implementation of standards is a major goal for Linux development even if the implementation is not formally certified. In addition to the basic POSIX standard, Linux currently supports the POSIX threading extensions and a subset of the POSIX extensions for real-time process control.

21.2.1 Components of a Linux System

The Linux system is composed of three main bodies of code, in line with most traditional UNIX implementations:

1. The **kernel** is responsible for maintaining all the important abstractions of the operating system, including such things as virtual memory and processes.

2. The **system libraries** define a standard set of functions through which applications can interact with the kernel, and which implement much of the operating-system functionality that does not need the full privileges of kernel code.

3. The **system utilities** are programs that perform individual, specialized management tasks. Some system utilities may be invoked just once to initialize and configure some aspect of the system; others (known as *daemons* in UNIX terminology) may run permanently, handling such tasks as responding to incoming network connections, accepting logon requests from terminals, or updating log files.

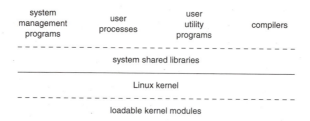

Figure 21.1   Components of the Linux system.

Figure 21.1 illustrates the various components that make up a full Linux system. The most important distinction here is between the kernel and everything else. All the kernel code executes in the processor's privileged mode with full access to all the physical resources of the computer. Linux refers to this privileged mode as **kernel mode,** equivalent to the monitor mode described in Section 2.5.1. Under Linux, no user-mode code is built into the kernel. Any operating-system–support code that does not need to run in kernel mode is placed into the system libraries instead.

Although various modern operating systems have adopted a message-passing architecture for their kernel internals, Linux retains UNIX's historical model: The kernel is created as a single, monolithic binary. The main reason is to improve performance: Because all kernel code and data structures are kept in a single address space, no context switches are necessary when a process calls an operating-system function or when a hardware interrupt is delivered. Not only the core scheduling and virtual-memory code occupies this address space; *all* kernel code, including all device drivers, file systems, and networking code, is present in the same single address space.

Just because all the kernel shares this same melting pot does not mean that there is no scope for modularity. In just the same way that user applications can load shared libraries at run time to pull in a needed piece of code, so the Linux kernel can load (and unload) modules dynamically at run time. The kernel does not necessarily need to know in advance which modules may be loaded—they are truly independent loadable components.

The Linux kernel forms the core of the Linux operating system. It provides all the functionality necessary to run processes, and it provides system services to give arbitrated and protected access to hardware resources. The kernel implements all the features that are required to qualify as an operating system. On its own, however, the operating system provided by the Linux kernel looks nothing like a UNIX system. It is missing many of the extra features of UNIX, and the features that it does provide are not necessarily in the format in which a UNIX application expects them to appear. The operating-system interface visible to running applications is not maintained directly by the kernel. Rather, applications make calls to the system libraries, which in turn call the operating-system services as necessary.

The system libraries provide many types of functionality. At the simplest level, they allow applications to make kernel system service requests. Making a system call involves transferring control from unprivileged user mode to privileged kernel mode; the details of this transfer vary from architecture to architecture. The libraries take care of collecting together the system-call arguments and, if necessary, arranging those arguments in the special form necessary to make the system call.

The libraries may also provide more complex versions of the basic system calls. For example, the C language's buffered file-handling functions are all implemented in the system libraries, providing more advanced control of file I/O than the basic kernel system calls provide. The libraries also provide routines that do not correspond to system calls at all, such as sorting algorithms, mathematical functions, and string-manipulation routines. All the functions that are necessary to support the running of UNIX or POSIX applications are implemented here in the system libraries.

The Linux system includes a wide variety of user-mode programs—both system utilities and user utilities. The system utilities include all the programs necessary to initialize the system, such as those to configure network devices or to load kernel modules. Continually running server programs also count as system utilities; such programs handle user login requests, incoming network connections, and the printer queues.

Not all the standard utilities serve key system-administration functions. The UNIX user environment contains a large number of standard utilities to do simple everyday tasks, such as listing directories, moving around and deleting files, or displaying the contents of a file. More complex utilities can perform text-processing functions, such as sorting textual data or performing pattern searches on input text. Together, these utilities form a standard toolset that users can expect to see on any UNIX system; although they do not perform any operating-system function, they are still an important part of the basic Linux system.

21.3 ■ Kernel Modules

The Linux kernel has the ability to load and unload arbitrary sections of kernel code on demand. These loadable kernel modules run in privileged kernel mode, and as a consequence have full access to all the hardware capabilities of the machine on which they run. In theory, there is no restriction on what a kernel module is allowed to do; typically, a module might implement a device driver, a file system, or a networking protocol.

There are several reasons why it is convenient to have kernel modules. Linux's source code is free, so anybody wanting to write kernel code is able to compile a modified kernel and to reboot to load that new functionality; however, recompiling, relinking, and reloading the entire kernel is a cumbersome cycle to undertake when you are developing a new driver. If you use kernel modules, you do not have to make a new kernel to test a new driver—the driver may be compiled on its own and loaded into the already-running kernel. Of course, once a new driver is written, it can be distributed as a module so that other users can benefit from it without having to rebuild their kernels.

This latter point has another implication. Because it is covered by the GPL license, the Linux kernel cannot be released with proprietary components added to it, unless those new components are also released under the GPL and the source code for them is made available on demand. The kernel's module interface allows third parties to write and distribute, on their own terms, device drivers or file systems that could not be distributed under the GPL.

Kernel modules allow a Linux system to be set up with a standard, minimal kernel, without any extra device drivers built in. Any device drivers that the user needs can be either loaded explicitly by the system at startup, or loaded automatically by the system on demand and unloaded when not in use. For example, a CD-ROM driver might be loaded when a CD is mounted, and the driver unloaded again from memory when the CD is dismounted from the file system.

There are three components to the module support under Linux:

1. The **module management** allows modules to be loaded into memory and to talk to the rest of the kernel.

2. The **driver registration** allows modules to tell the rest of the kernel that a new driver has become available.

3. A **conflict-resolution mechanism** allows different device drivers to reserve hardware resources and to protect those resources from accidental use by another driver.

21.3.1 Module Management

Loading a module requires more than just loading its binary contents into kernel memory. The system must also make sure that any references that the module makes to kernel symbols or entry points get updated to point to the correct locations in the kernel's address space. Linux deals with this reference updating by splitting the job of module loading into two separate sections: the management of sections of module code in kernel memory, and the handling of symbols that modules are allowed to reference.

Linux maintains an internal symbol table in the kernel. This symbol table does not contain the full set of symbols defined in the kernel during the latter's compilation: rather, a symbol must be exported explicitly by the kernel. The set of exported symbols constitutes a well-defined interface by which a module may interact with the kernel.

Although exporting symbols from a kernel function requires an explicit request by the programmer, no special effort is needed to import those symbols into a module. A module writer just uses the standard external linkage of the C language: Any external symbols referenced by the module but not declared by it are simply marked as unresolved in the final module binary produced by the compiler. When a module is to be loaded into the kernel, a system utility first scans the module for these unresolved references. All symbols that still need to be resolved are looked up in the kernel's symbol table, and the correct addresses of those symbols in the currently running kernel are substituted into the module's code. Only then is the module passed to the kernel for loading. If the system utility cannot resolve any references in the module by looking them up in the kernel's symbol table, then the module is rejected.

The loading of the module is performed in two stages. First, the module-loader utility asks the kernel to reserve a continuous area of virtual kernel memory for the module. The kernel returns the address of the memory allocated, and the loader utility can use this address to relocate the module's machine code to the correct loading address. A second system call then passes the module, plus any symbol table that the new module wants to export, to the kernel. The module itself is now copied verbatim into the previously allocated space, and the kernel's symbol table is updated with the new symbols for possible use by other modules not yet loaded.

The final module-management component is the module requestor. The kernel defines a communication interface to which a module-management program can connect. With this connection established, the kernel will inform the management process whenever a process requests a device driver, file system, or network service that is not currently loaded, and will give the manager the opportunity to load that service. The original service request will complete once the module is loaded. The manager process regularly queries the kernel to see whether a dynamically loaded module is still in use, and unloads that module when it is no longer actively needed.

21.3.2 Driver Registration

Once a module is loaded, it remains no more than an isolated region of memory unless it lets the rest of the kernel know what new functionality it provides. The kernel maintains dynamic tables of all known drivers, and provides a set of routines to allow drivers to be added to or removed from these tables at any time. The kernel makes sure that it calls a module's startup routine when that module is loaded, and calls the module's cleanup routine before that module is unloaded: It is these routines that are responsible for registering the module's functionality.

There are many types of driver that a module may register. A single module may register drivers on any or all these types, and may register more than one driver if it wishes. For example, a device driver might want to register two separate mechanisms for accessing the device. Registration tables include the following items:

- *Device drivers:* These drivers include character devices (such as printers, terminals, or mice), block devices (including all disk drives), and network interface devices.

- *File systems:* The file system may be anything that implements Linux's virtual-file-system calling routines. It might implement a format for storing files on a disk, but it might equally well be a network file system such as NFS, or a virtual file system whose contents are generated on demand, such as Linux's **proc** file system.

- *Network protocols:* A module may implement an entire networking protocol, such as IPX, or simply a new set of packet-filtering rules for a network firewall.

- *Binary format:* This format specifies a way of recognizing, and loading, a new type of executable file.

In addition, a module can register a new set of entries in the **sysctl** and **/proc** tables, to allow that module to be configured dynamically (see Section 21.7.3).

21.3.3 Conflict Resolution

Commercial UNIX implementations usually are sold to run on a vendor's own hardware. One advantage of a single-supplier solution is that the software vendor has a good idea about what hardware configurations are possible. IBM PC hardware, on the other hand, comes in a vast number of configurations, with large numbers of different possible drivers for devices such network cards, SCSI controllers, and video display adapters. The problem of managing the hardware configuration becomes more severe when modular device drivers are supported, since the currently active set of devices becomes dynamically variable.

Linux provides a central conflict-resolution mechanism to help arbitrate access to certain hardware resources. Its aims are as follows:

- To prevent modules from clashing over access to hardware resources

- To prevent **autoprobes** (device-driver probes that auto-detect device configuration) from interfering with existing device drivers

- To resolve conflicts among multiple drivers that are trying to access the same hardware; for example, the parallel printer driver and PLIP (parallel-line IP) network driver might both try to talk to the parallel printer port

To these ends, the kernel maintains lists of allocated hardware resources. The PC has only a limited number of possible I/O ports (addresses in its hardware I/O address space), interrupt lines, and DMA channels; when any device driver wants to access such a resource, it is expected to reserve the resource with the kernel database first. This requirement incidentally allows the system administrator to determine exactly which resources have been allocated by which driver at any given point.

A module is expected to use this mechanism to reserve in advance any hardware resources that it expects to use. If the reservation is rejected, because the resource is not present or is already in use, then it is up to the module to decide how to proceed. It may fail its initialization and request that it be unloaded if it cannot continue, or it may carry on, using alternative hardware resources.

21.4 ■ Process Management

A **process** is the basic context within which all user-requested activity is serviced within the operating system. To be compatible with other UNIX systems, Linux must necessarily use a process model similar to those of other UNIXes. There are a few key places where Linux operates differently, however. In this section, we review the traditional UNIX process model from Section 20.3.2, and introduce Linux's own threading model.

21.4.1 The Fork/Exec Process Model

The basic principle of UNIX process management is to separate two distinct operations: the creation of processes and the running of a new program. A new process is created by the fork system call, and a new program is run after a call to execve. These are two distinctly separate functions. A new process may be created with fork without a new program being run—the new subprocess simply continues to execute exactly the same program that the first, parent process was running. Equally, running a new program does not require that a new process be created first: Any process may call execve at any time. The currently running program is immediately terminated, and the new program starts executing in the context of the existing process.

This model has the advantage of great simplicity. Rather than having to specify every detail of the environment of a new program in the system call that runs that program, new programs simply run in their existing environment. If a parent process wishes to modify the environment in which a new program is to be run, it can fork and then, still running the original program in a child process, make any system calls it requires to modify that child process before finally executing the new program.

Under UNIX, then, a process encompasses all the information that the operating system must maintain to track the context of a single execution of a single program. Under Linux, we can break down this context into a number of specific sections. Broadly, process properties fall into three groups: the process's identity, environment, and context.

21.4.1.1 Process Identity

A process's identity consists mainly of the following items:

- *Process ID (PID):* Each process has a unique identifier. PIDs are used to specify processes to the operating system when an application makes a system call to signal, modify, or wait for another process. Additional identifiers associate the process with a process group (typically, a tree of processes forked by a single user command) and login session.

- *Credentials:* Each process must have an associated user ID and one or more group IDs (user groups are discussed in Section 11.4.2; process groups are not) that determine the process's rights to access system resources and files.

- *Personality:* Process personalities are not traditionally found on UNIX systems, but under Linux each process has an associated personality identifier that can modify slightly the semantics of certain system calls. Personalities are primarily used by emulation libraries to request that system calls be compatible with certain specific flavors of UNIX.

Most of these identifiers are under limited control of the process itself. The process's group and session identifiers can be changed if the process wants to start a new group or session. Its credentials can be changed, subject to appropriate security checks. However, the primary PID of a process is unchangeable and uniquely identifies that process until termination.

21.4.1.2 Process Environment

A process's environment is inherited from that process's parent, and is composed of two null-terminated vectors: the argument vector and the environment vector. The **argument vector** simply lists the command-line arguments used to invoke the running program, and conventionally starts with the name of the program itself. The **environment vector** is a list of "NAME=VALUE" pairs that associates named environment variables with arbitrary textual values. The environment is not held in kernel memory, but rather is stored in the process's own user-mode address space as the first datum at the top of the process's stack.

The argument and environment vectors are not altered when a new process is created: The new child process will inherit the same environment that its parent possesses. However, a completely new environment is set up when a new program is invoked. On calling execve, a process must supply the environment for the new program. These environment variables are passed by the kernel to the next program, replacing the process's current environment. The environment and command-line vectors are otherwise left alone by the kernel —their interpretation is left entirely to the user-mode libraries and applications.

The passing of environment variables from one process to the next, and the inheriting of these variables by a process's children, provide flexible ways to pass information to different components of the user-mode system software. Various important environment variables have conventional meanings to related parts of the system software. For example, the TERM variable is set up to name the type of terminal connected to a user's login session; many different programs use this variable to determine how to perform operations on the user's display, such as moving the cursor or scrolling a region of text. Programs with multilingual support use the LANG variable to determine in which language to display system messages for programs that have been programmed with multilingual support.

The important feature of the environment-variable mechanism is that it custom tailors the operating system on a per-process basis, rather than for the system as a whole. Users can choose their own languages or select their own preferred editors independent of one another.

21.4.1.3 Process Context

The process's identity and environment are usually properties that are set up when a process is created, and that are not changed until that process exits. A process may choose to change some aspects of its identity if it needs to do so, or may alter its environment. Process context, on the other hand, is the state of the running program at any one point in time; it changes constantly.

- *Scheduling context*: The most important part of the process context is its scheduling context: the information that the scheduler needs to suspend and restart the process. This information includes saved copies of all the process's registers. Floating-point registers are stored separately, and are restored only when needed, so that processes that do not use floating-point arithmetic do not incur the overhead of saving that state. The scheduling context also includes information about scheduling priority and about any outstanding signals waiting to be delivered to the process. A key part of the scheduling context is the process's kernel stack: a separate area of kernel memory reserved for use exclusively by kernel-mode code. Both system calls and interrupts that occur while the process is executing will use this stack.

- *Accounting*: The kernel maintains information about the resources currently being consumed by each process, and the total resources consumed by the process in its entire lifetime so far.

- *File table*: The file table is an array of pointers to kernel file structures. When making file I/O system calls, processes refer to files by their index into this table.

- *File-system context*: Whereas the file table lists the existing open files, the file-system context applies to requests to open new files. The current root and default directories to be used for new file searches are stored here.

- *Signal-handler table*: UNIX systems can deliver asynchronous signals to a process in response to various external events. The signal-handler table defines the routine in the process's address space to be called when specific signals arrive.

- *Virtual-memory context*: The virtual-memory context describes the full contents of a process's private address space; we discuss it in Section 21.6.

21.4.2 Processes and Threads

Most modern operating systems support both processes and threads. Although the precise difference between the two often varies from implementation to implementation, we distinguish them as follows: *Processes* represent the execution of single programs, whereas *threads* represent separate, concurrent execution contexts within a single process running a single program.

Any two separate processes have their own independent address spaces, even if they are using shared memory to share some (but not all) of the contents of their virtual memory. In contrast, two threads within the same process will share *the same* (rather than *similar*) address spaces. They do not simply share similar address spaces. Any change to the virtual-memory layout made by one thread will be visible immediately to other threads in process, because there is in reality only one address space in which they are all running.

There are several different ways in which threads can be implemented. A thread may be implemented in the operating system's kernel as an object owned by a process, or it may be a fully independent entity. It may not be implemented in the kernel at all—threads may be implemented purely within application or library code with the help of kernel-supplied timer interruptions.

The Linux kernel deals simply with the difference between processes and threads: It uses exactly the same internal representation for each. A thread is just a new process that happens to share the same address space as its parent. The distinction between a process and a thread is made only when a new thread is created, by the `clone` system call. Whereas `fork` creates a new process that has its own entirely new process context, `clone` creates a new process that has own identity, but that is allowed to share the data structures of its parent.

This distinction can be accomplished because Linux does not hold all a process's context within the main process data structure; rather, it holds context within independent subcontexts. A process's file-system context, file-descriptor table, signal-handler table, and virtual-memory context are held in separate data structures. The process data structure simply contains pointers to these other structures, so any number of processes can easily share one of these subcontexts by pointing to the same subcontexts as appropriate.

The `clone` system call accepts an argument that tells it which subcontexts to copy, and which to share, when it creates the new process. The new process always is given a new identity and a new scheduling context; according to the arguments passed, however, it may either create new subcontext data structures initialized to be a copy of the parent's, or set up the new process to use the same subcontext data structure being used by the parent. The `fork` system call is nothing more than a special case of `clone` that copies all subcontexts, sharing none. Using `clone` gives an application fine-grained control over exactly what is shared between two threads.

The POSIX working groups have defined a programming interface, specified in the POSIX.1c standard, to allow applications to run multiple threads. The Linux system libraries support two separate mechanisms that implement this single standard in different ways. An application may choose to use either Linux's user-mode–based thread package or its kernel-based one. The user-mode thread library avoids the overhead of kernel scheduling and kernel system calls when threads interact, but is limited by the fact that all threads run in a single process. The kernel-supported thread library uses the `clone` system call to implement the same programming interface, but, since multiple scheduling contexts are created, it has the advantage of allowing an application to run threads on multiple processors at once on a multiprocessor system. It also allows multiple threads to be executing kernel system calls simultaneously.

21.5 ■ Scheduling

Scheduling is the job of allocating CPU time to different tasks within an operating system. Normally, we think of scheduling as being the running and interrupting of processes, but there is another aspect of scheduling that is important to Linux: the running of the various kernel tasks. Kernel tasks encompass both tasks that are requested by a running process and tasks that execute internally on behalf of a device driver.

21.5.1 Kernel Synchronization

The way that the kernel schedules its own operations is fundamentally different from the way that it does process scheduling. There are two ways in which a request for kernel-mode execution can occur. A running program may request an operating-system service, either explicitly via a system call, or implicitly —for example, when a page fault occurs. Alternatively, a device driver may deliver a hardware interrupt that causes the CPU to start executing a kernel-defined handler for that interrupt.

The problem posed to the kernel is that these various tasks may all try to access the same internal data structures. If one kernel task is in the middle of accessing some data structure when an interrupt service routine executes, then that service routine cannot access or modify the same data without risking data corruption. This fact relates to the idea of critical sections: portions of code that access shared data and that must not be allowed to execute concurrently.

As a result, kernel synchronization involves much more than just process scheduling. A framework is required that will allow the kernel's critical sections to run without interruption by another critical section.

The first part of Linux's solution to this problem lies in making normal kernel code nonpreemptible. Usually, when a timer interrupt is received by the kernel, it invokes the process scheduler, potentially so that it can suspend execution of the currently running process and resume running another one—the natural time sharing of any UNIX system. However, when a timer interrupt is received while a process is executing a kernel-system service routine, the rescheduling does not take place immediately; rather, the kernel's **need_resched** flag is set to tell the kernel to run the scheduler after the system call has completed and control is about to be returned to user mode.

Once a piece of kernel code starts running, it can guarantee that it will be the only kernel code running until one of the following actions occurs:

- An interrupt

- A page fault

- A kernel-code call to the scheduler function itself

Interrupts are a problem only if they contain critical sections themselves. Timer interrupts never directly cause a process reschedule; they just request that a reschedule be performed later, so any incoming interrupts cannot affect the execution order of noninterrupt kernel code. Once the interrupt service is finished, execution will simply return to the same kernel code that was running when the interrupt was taken.

Page faults are a potential problem; if a kernel routine tries to read or write to user memory, it may incur a page fault that requires disk I/O to complete, and the running process will be suspended until the I/O completes. Similarly, if a system-call service routine calls the scheduler while it is in kernel mode, either explicitly by making a direct call to the scheduling code or implicitly by calling a function to wait for I/O to complete, then the process will be suspended and a reschedule will occur. When the process becomes runnable again, it will continue to execute in kernel mode, continuing at the instruction after the call to the scheduler.

Kernel code can thus make the assumptions that it will never be preempted by another process and that no special care must be taken to protect critical sections. The only requirement is that critical sections do not contain references to user memory or waits for I/O completions.

The second protection technique that Linux uses applies to critical sections that occur in interrupt service routines. The basic tool is the processor's interrupt-control hardware. By disabling interrupts during a critical section, the kernel guarantees that it can proceed without the risk of concurrent access of shared data structures.

There is a penalty for disabling interrupts. On most hardware architectures, interrupt enable and disable instructions are expensive. Furthermore, as long as interrupts remain disabled, all I/O is suspended, and any device waiting for servicing will have to wait until interrupts are reenabled, so performance degrades. Linux's kernel uses a synchronization architecture that allows long critical sections to run for their entire duration without having interrupts disabled. This ability is especially useful in the networking code: An interrupt in a network device driver can signal the arrival of an entire network packet, which may result in a great deal of code being executed to disassemble, route, and forward that packet within the interrupt service routine.

Linux implements this architecture by separating interrupt service routines into two sections: the top half and bottom half. The **top half** is a normal interrupt service routine, and runs with recursive interrupts disabled (interrupts of a higher priority may interrupt the routine, but interrupts of the same or lower priority are disabled). The **bottom half** of a service routine is run, with all interrupts enabled, by a miniature scheduler that ensures that bottom halves never interrupt themselves. The bottom-half scheduler is invoked automatically whenever an interrupt service routine exits.

This separation means that any complex processing that has to be done in response to an interrupt can be completed by the kernel without the kernel worrying about being interrupted itself. If another interrupt occurs while a bottom half is executing, then that interrupt can request that the same bottom half executes, but the execution will be deferred until the currently running one completes. Each execution of the bottom half can be interrupted by a top half, but can never be interrupted by a similar bottom half.

The top-half bottom-half architecture is completed by a mechanism for disabling selected bottom halves while executing normal, foreground kernel code. The kernel can code critical sections easily using this system: Interrupt handlers can code their critical sections as bottom halves, and when the foreground kernel wants to enter a critical section, it can disable any relevant bottom halves to prevent any other critical sections from interrupting it. At the end of the critical section, the kernel can reenable the bottom halves and run any bottom-half tasks that have been queued by top-half interrupt service routines during the critical section.

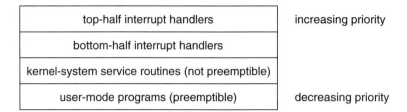

Figure 21.2   Interrupt protection levels.

Figure 21.2 summarizes the various levels of interrupt protection within the kernel. Each level may be interrupted by code running at a higher level, but will never be interrupted by code running at the same or a lower level (except for user-mode code, user processes can always be preempted by another process when a time-sharing scheduling interrupt occurs).

21.5.2 Process Scheduling

Once the kernel has reached a rescheduling point—either a rescheduling interrupt has occurred or a running kernel process has blocked waiting for some wakeup signal—it must decide what process to run next. Linux has two separate process-scheduling algorithms. One is a time-sharing algorithm for fair preemptive scheduling among multiple processes; the other is designed for real-time tasks where absolute priorities are more important than fairness.

Part of every process's identity is a scheduling class, which defines which of these algorithms to apply to the process. The scheduling classes used by Linux are defined in the POSIX standard's extensions for real-time computing (POSIX.4, now known as POSIX.1b).

For time-sharing processes, Linux uses a prioritized, **credit-based** algorithm. Each process possesses a certain number of scheduling credits; when a new task must be chosen to run, the process with the most credits is selected. Every time that a timer interrupt occurs, the currently running process loses one credit; when its credits reaches zero, it is suspended and another process is chosen.

If no runnable processes have any credits, then Linux performs a recrediting operation, adding credits to *every* process in the system (rather than to just the runnable ones), according to the following rule:

$$\text{credits} = \frac{\text{credits}}{2} + \text{priority}$$

This algorithm tends to mix two factors: the process's history and the process's priority. One-half of the credits that a process still holds since the previous recrediting operation will be retained after the algorithm has been applied, retaining some history of the process's recent behavior. Processes that are running all the time tend to exhaust their credits rapidly, but processes that spend much of their time suspended can accumulate credits over multiple recreditings and consequently end up with a higher credit count after a recredit. This crediting system automatically gives high priority to interactive or I/O-bound processes, for which a rapid response time is important.

The use of a process priority in calculating new credits allows the priority of a process to be fine tuned. Background batch jobs can be given a low priority; they will automatically receive fewer credits than interactive users' jobs, and hence will receive a smaller percentage of the CPU time than will similar jobs that have higher priorities. Linux uses this priority system to implement the standard UNIX **nice** process-priority mechanism.

Linux's real-time scheduling is simpler still. Linux implements the two real-time scheduling classes required by POSIX.1b: first in, first out (FIFO), and round-robin (Sections 6.3.1 and 6.3.4, respectively). In both cases, each process has a priority in addition to its scheduling class. In time-sharing scheduling, however, processes of different priorities can still compete with one another to some extent; in real-time scheduling, the scheduler always runs the process with the highest priority. Among processes of equal priority, it runs the process that has been waiting longest. The only difference between FIFO and round-robin scheduling is that FIFO processes continue to run until they either exit or block, whereas a round-robin process will be preempted after a while and will be moved to the end of the scheduling queue, so round-robin processes of equal priority will automatically time share among themselves.

Note that Linux's real-time scheduling is soft—rather than hard—real time. The scheduler offers strict guarantees about the relative priorities of real-time processes, but the kernel does not offer any guarantees about how quickly a real-time process will be scheduled once that process becomes runnable. Remember that Linux kernel code cannot ever be preempted by user-mode code. If an interrupt arrives that wakes up a real-time process while the kernel is already executing a system call on behalf of another process, the real-time process will just have to wait until the currently running system call completes or blocks.

21.5.3 Symmetric Multiprocessing

The Linux 2.0 kernel was the first stable Linux kernel to support **symmetric multiprocessor (SMP)** hardware. Separate processes or threads can execute in parallel on separate processors. However, to preserve the nonpreemptible synchronization requirements of the kernel, the implementation of SMP in this kernel imposes the restriction that only one processor at a time can be executing kernel-mode code. SMP uses a single kernel spinlock to enforce this rule. This spinlock does not pose a problem for computation-bound tasks, but tasks that involve a lot of kernel activity can become seriously bottlenecked.

A major project in the Linux 2.1 development kernel is making the SMP implementation more scalable, by splitting the single kernel spinlock into multiple locks that each protect against reentrance only a small subset of the kernel's data structures. By using such techniques, the latest development kernels do allow multiple processors to be executing kernel-mode code simultaneously.

21.6 ■ Memory Management

There are two components to memory management under Linux. The first deals with allocating and freeing physical memory: pages, groups of pages, and small blocks of memory. The second handles virtual memory, which is memory mapped into the address space of running processes.

We describe these two components, and then examine the mechanisms by which the loadable components of a new program are brought into a process's virtual memory in response to an **exec** system call.

21.6.1 Management of Physical Memory

The primary physical-memory manager in the Linux kernel is the **page allocator**. This allocator is responsible for allocating and freeing all physical pages, and is capable of allocating ranges of physically contiguous pages on request. The allocator uses a **buddy-heap** algorithm to keep track of available physical pages. A buddy-heap allocator pairs adjacent units of allocatable memory together; hence its name. Each allocatable memory region has an adjacent partner, or buddy, and whenever two allocated partner regions are both freed up, they are combined to form a larger region. That larger region also has a partner, with which it can combine to form a still larger free region. Alternatively, if a small memory request cannot be satisfied by allocation of an existing small free region, then a larger free region will be subdivided into two partners to satisfy the request. Separate linked lists are used to record the free memory regions of each allowable size; under Linux, the smallest size allocatable under this mechanism is a single physical page. Figure 21.3 shows an example of buddy-heap allocation: A 4-kilobyte region is being allocated, but the smallest available region is 16 kilobytes. The region is broken up recursively until a piece of the desired size is available.

Ultimately, all memory allocations in the Linux kernel either occur statically, by drivers that reserve a contiguous area of memory during system boot time, or dynamically, by the page allocator. However, kernel functions do not necessarily have to use the basic allocator to reserve memory. Several specialized memory-management subsystems use the underlying page allocator to manage their own pool of memory. The most important are the virtual-memory system, described in Section 21.6.2; the **kmalloc** variable-length allocator; and the kernel's two persistent data caches, the buffer cache and the page cache.

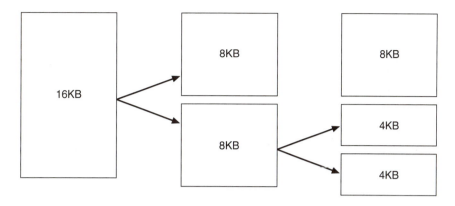

Figure 21.3 Splitting of memory in a buddy heap.

Many components of the Linux operating system need to allocate entire pages at will, but often smaller blocks of memory are required. The kernel provides an additional allocator for arbitrary-sized requests, where the size of a request is not necessarily known in advance and may be only a few bytes, rather than an entire page. Analogous to the C language's **malloc** function, this **kmalloc** service allocates entire pages on demand, but then splits them into smaller pieces. The kernel maintains a set of lists of pages in use by the **kmalloc** service, where all the pages on a given list have been split into pieces of a specific size. Allocating memory involves working out the appropriate list and either taking the first free piece available on the list or allocating a new page and splitting it up.

Both the page and **kmalloc** allocators are interrupt safe. A function that wants to allocate memory passes a request priority to the allocation function. Interrupt routines use an atomic priority that guarantees that the request either is satisfied or, if there is no more memory, fails immediately. In contrast, normal user processes that require a memory allocation will start attempting to find existing memory to free, and will stall until memory becomes available. The allocation priority can also be used for specifying that the memory is required for DMA, for use on architectures such as the PC where certain DMA requests are not supported on all pages of physical memory.

Memory regions claimed by the **kmalloc** system are allocated permanently until they are freed explicitly. The **kmalloc** system cannot relocate or reclaim these regions in response to memory shortages.

The other three main subsystems that do their own management of physical pages are closely related. These are the buffer cache, the page cache, and the virtual-memory system. The **buffer cache** is the kernel's main cache for block-oriented devices such as disk drives, and is the main mechanism through which I/O to these devices is performed. The **page cache** caches entire pages of file contents, and is not limited to block devices; it can also cache networked data, and is used both by the native Linux disk-based file systems and the NFS networked file system. The **virtual-memory system** manages the contents of each process's virtual address space.

These three systems interact closely with one another. Reading a page of data into the page cache requires going temporarily through the buffer cache; pages in the page cache can also be mapped into the virtual-memory system if a process has mapped a file into its address space. The kernel maintains a reference count on each page of physical memory, so that pages that are shared by two or more of these subsystems can be released when they are no longer in use anywhere.

21.6.2 Virtual Memory

The Linux virtual-memory system is responsible for maintaining the address space visible to each process. It creates pages of virtual memory on demand, and manages the loading of those pages from disk or their swapping back out to disk as required. Under Linux, the virtual-memory manager maintains two separate views of a process's address space: as a set of separate regions, and as a set of pages.

The first view of an address space is the logical view, describing instructions that the virtual-memory system has received concerning the layout of the address space. In this view, the address space consists of a set of nonoverlapping regions, each region representing a continuous, page-aligned subset of the address space. Each region is described internally by a single **vm_area_struct** structure, which defines the properties of the region, including the process's read, write, and execute permissions in the region, and information about any files associated with the region. The regions for each address space are linked into a balanced binary tree to allow fast lookup of the region corresponding to any virtual address.

The kernel also maintains a second, physical view of each address space. This view is stored in the hardware page tables for the process. The page-table entries determine the exact current location of each page of virtual memory, whether it is on disk or in physical memory. The physical view is managed by a set of routines that is invoked from the kernel's software-interrupt handlers whenever a process tries to access a page that is not currently present in the page tables. Each **vm_area_struct** in the address-space description contains a field that points to a table of functions that implement the key page-management functions for any given virtual-memory region. All requests to read or write an unavailable page are eventually dispatched to the appropriate handler in **vm_area_struct**'s function table, so that the central memory-management routines do not have to know the details of managing each possible type of memory region.

21.6.2.1 Virtual-Memory Regions

Linux implements a number of different types of virtual-memory regions. The first property that characterizes a type of virtual memory is the backing store for the region: This store describes from where the pages for a region come. Most memory regions are backed either by a file, or by nothing. A region that is backed by nothing is the simplest type of virtual memory. Such a region represents **demand-zero memory:** When a process tries to read a page in such a region, it is simply given back a page of memory filled with zeros.

A region backed by a file acts as a viewport onto a section of that file: Whenever the process tries to access a page within that region, the page table is filled with the address of a page within the kernel's page cache corresponding to the appropriate offset in the file. The same page of physical memory is used both by the page cache and by the process's page tables, so any changes made to the file by the file system are immediately visible to any processes that have mapped that file into their address space. Any number of different processes can map the same region of the same file, and they will all end up using the same page of physical memory for the purpose.

A virtual-memory region is also defined by its reaction to writes. The mapping of a region into the process's address space can be either **private** or **shared**. If a process writes to a privately mapped region, then the pager detects that a copy-on-write is necessary to keep the changes local to the process. On the other hand, writes to a shared region result in the object mapped into that region being updated, so that the change will be visible immediately to any other process that is mapping that object.

21.6.2.2 Lifetime of a Virtual Address Space

There are exactly two situations where the kernel will create a new virtual address space: When a process runs a new program with the **exec** system call, and on creation of a new process by the `fork` system call. The first case is easy: When a new program is executed, the process is given a new, completely empty virtual address space. It is up to the routines for loading the program to populate the address space with virtual-memory regions.

In the second case, creating a new process with `fork` involves creating a complete copy of the existing process's virtual address space. The kernel copies the parent process's **vm_area_struct** descriptors, then creates a new set of page tables for the child. The parent's page tables are copied directly into the child's, with the reference count of each page covered being incremented; thus, after the fork, the parent and child share the same physical pages of memory in their address spaces.

A special case occurs when the copying operation reaches a virtual-memory region that is mapped privately. Any pages to which the parent process has written within such a region are private, and subsequent changes to these pages by either the parent or the child must not update the page in the other process's address space. When the page-table entries for such regions are copied, they are set to be read only and are marked for copy-on-write. As long as these pages are not modified by either process, the two processes share the same page of physical memory. However, if either process tries to modify a copy-on-write page, the reference count on the page is checked. If the page is still shared, then the process copies the page's contents to a brand-new page of physical memory and uses its copy instead. This mechanism ensures that private data pages are shared between processes whenever possible; copies are made only when absolutely necessary.

21.6.2.3 Swapping and Paging

An important task for a virtual-memory system is to relocate pages of memory from physical memory out to disk when that memory is needed. Early UNIX systems performed this relocation by swapping out the contents of entire processes at once, but modern UNIXes rely more on **paging:** the movement of individual pages of virtual memory between physical memory and disk. Linux does not implement whole-process swapping; it uses the newer paging mechanism exclusively.

The paging system can be divided into two sections. First, there is the **policy algorithm,** which decides which pages to write out to disk, and when to write them. Second, there is the **paging mechanism,** which carries out the transfer, and which pages data back into physical memory when they are needed again.

Linux's pageout policy uses a modified version of the standard clock (second-chance) algorithm described in Section 10.3.5.2. Under Linux, a multiple-pass clock is used, and every page has an *age* that is adjusted on each pass of the clock. The age is more precisely a measure of the page's youthfulness, or how much activity the page has seen recently. Frequently accessed pages will attain a higher age value, but the age of infrequently accessed pages will drop toward zero with each pass. This age valuing allows the pager to select pages to page out based on a least frequently used (LFU) policy.

The paging mechanism supports paging both to dedicated swap devices and partitions, and to normal files, although swapping to a file is significantly slower due to the extra overhead incurred by the file system. Blocks are allocated from the swap devices according to a bitmap of used blocks, which is maintained in physical memory at all times. The allocator uses a next-fit algorithm to try to write out pages to continuous runs of disk blocks for improved performance. The allocator records the fact that a page has been paged out to disk by using a feature of the page tables on modern processors: The page-table entry's page-not-present bit is set, allowing the rest of the page-table entry to be filled with an index identifying to where the page has been written.

21.6.2.4 Kernel Virtual Memory

Linux reserves for its own internal use a constant, architecture-dependent region of the virtual address space of every process. The page-table entries that map to these kernel pages are marked as protected, so that the pages are not visible or modifiable when the processor is running in user mode. This kernel virtual-memory area contains two regions. The first section is a static area that contains page-table references to every available physical page of memory in the system, so that there is a simple translation from physical to virtual addresses when kernel code is run. The core of the kernel, plus all pages allocated by the normal page allocator, reside in this region.

The remainder of the kernel's reserved section of address space is not reserved for any specific purpose. Page-table entries in this address range can be modified by the kernel to point to any other areas of memory as desired. The kernel provides a pair of facilities that allow processes to use this virtual memory. The vmalloc function allocates an arbitrary number of physical pages of memory, and maps them into a single region of kernel virtual memory, allowing allocation of large contiguous memory chunks even if there are not sufficient adjacent free physical pages to satisfy the request. The vremap function maps a sequence of virtual addresses to point to an area of memory used by a device driver for memory-mapped I/O.

21.6.3 Execution and Loading of User Programs

The Linux kernel's execution of user programs is triggered by a call to the exec system call. This call commands the kernel to run a new program within the current process, completely overwriting the current execution context with the initial context of the new program. The first job of this system service is to verify that the calling process has permission rights to the file being executed. Once that matter has been checked, the kernel invokes a loader routine to start running the program. The loader does not necessarily load the contents of the program file into physical memory, but it does at least set up the mapping of the program into virtual memory.

There is no single routine in Linux for loading a new program. Instead, Linux maintains a table of possible loader functions, and it gives each such function the opportunity to try loading the given file when an exec system call is made. The initial reason for this loader table was that, between the release of the 1.0 and 1.2 kernels, the standard format for Linux's binary files was changed. Older Linux kernels understood the a.out format for binary files —a relatively simple format common on older UNIX systems. Newer Linux systems use the more modern ELF format, now supported by most current UNIX implementations. ELF has a number of advantages over a.out, including flexibility and extensibility: New sections can be added to an ELF binary (for example, to add extra debugging information), without the loader routines becoming confused. By allowing registration of multiple loader routines, Linux can easily support the ELF and a.out binary formats in a single running system.

In Sections 21.6.3.1 and 21.6.3.2, we concentrate exclusively on the loading and running of ELF-format binaries. The procedure for loading a.out binaries is simpler, but is similar in operation.

21.6.3.1 Mapping of Programs into Memory

The loading of a binary file into physical memory is not performed by the binary loader under Linux. Rather, the pages of the binary file are mapped into regions of virtual memory. Only when the program tries to access a given page will a page fault result in the loading of that page into physical memory.

It is the responsibility of the kernel's binary loader to set up the initial memory mapping. An ELF-format binary file consists of a header followed by several page-aligned sections. The ELF loader works by reading the header and mapping the sections of the file into separate regions of virtual memory.

Figure 21.4 shows the typical layout of memory regions set up by the ELF loader. In a reserved region at one end of the address space sits the kernel, in its own privileged region of virtual memory inaccessible to normal user-mode programs. The rest of virtual memory is available to applications, which can use the kernel's memory-mapping functions to create regions that map a portion of a file or that are available for application data.

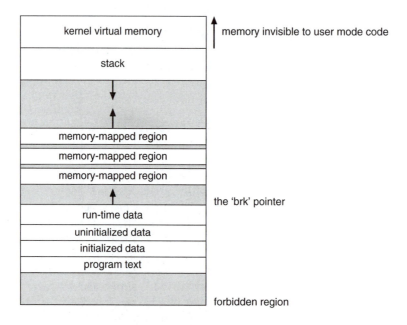

Figure 21.4   Memory layout for ELF programs.

The loader's job is to set up the initial memory mapping to allow the execution of the program to start. The regions that need to be initialized include the stack and the program's text and data regions.

The stack is created at the top of the user-mode virtual memory; it grows downward toward lower-numbered addresses. It includes copies of the arguments and environment variables given to the program in the exec system call. The other regions are created near the bottom end of virtual memory. The sections of the binary file that contain program text or read-only data are mapped into memory as a write-protected region. Writable initialized data are mapped next; then any uninitialized data are mapped in as a private demand-zero region.

Directly beyond these fixed-sized regions is a variable-sized region that programs can expand as needed to hold data allocated at run time. Each process has a pointer, *brk*, which points to the current extent of this data region, and processes can extend or contract their *brk* region with a single system call.

Once these mappings have been set up, the loader initializes the process's program-counter register with the starting point recorded in the ELF header, and the process can be scheduled.

21.6.3.2 Static and Dynamic Linking

Once the program has been loaded and has started running, all the necessary contents of the binary file have been loaded into the process's virtual address space. However, most programs also need to run functions from the system libraries, and these library functions also need to be loaded. In the simplest case, when a programmer builds an application, the necessary library functions are embedded directly in the program's executable binary file. Such a program is **statically linked** to its libraries, and statically linked executables can commence running as soon as they are loaded.

The main disadvantage of static linkage is that every program generated must contain copies of exactly the same common system library functions. It is much more efficient, in terms of both physical memory and disk-space usage, to load the system libraries into memory only once. **Dynamic linking** allows this single loading to happen.

Linux implements dynamic linking in user mode through a special linker library. Every dynamically linked program contains a small statically linked function that is called when the program starts. This static function just maps the link library into memory and runs the code that the function contains. The link library reads a list of the dynamic libraries required by the program and the names of the variables and functions needed from those libraries by reading the information contained in sections of the ELF binary. It then maps the libraries into the middle of virtual memory, and resolves the references to the symbols contained in those libraries. It does not matter exactly where in memory these shared libraries get mapped: They are compiled into position-independent code (PIC), which can run at any address in memory.

21.7 ■ File Systems

Linux retains UNIX's standard file-system model. In UNIX, a file does not necessarily have to be an object stored on disk or fetched over a network from a remote file server. Rather, UNIX files can be anything capable of handling the input or output of a stream of data. Device drivers can appear as files, and interprocess-communication channels or network connections also look like files to the user.

The Linux kernel handles all these various different types of file by hiding the implementation details of any single file type behind a layer of software, the **virtual file system** (VFS).

21.7.1 The Virtual File System

The Linux VFS is designed around object-oriented principles. It has two components: a set of definitions that define what a file object is allowed to look like, and a layer of software to manipulate those objects. The three main object types defined by the VFS are the **inode-object** and the **file-object** structures, which represent individual files, and the **file-system object,** which represents an entire file system.

For each of these three types of object, the VFS defines a set of operations that must be implemented by that structure. Every object of one of these types contains a pointer to a function table. The function table lists the addresses of the actual functions that implement those operations for that particular object. Thus, the VFS software layer can perform an operation on one of these objects by calling the appropriate function from that object's function table, without having to know in advance exactly with what kind of an object it is dealing. The VFS does not know, or care, whether an inode represents a networked file, a disk file, a network socket, or a directory file—the appropriate function for that file's **read data** operation will always be at the same place in its function table, and the VFS software layer will call that function without caring how the data are actually read.

The file-system object represents a connected set of files that forms a self-contained directory hierarchy. The operating-system kernel maintains a single file-system object for each disk device mounted as a file system and for each networked file system currently connected. The file-system object's main responsibility is to give access to inodes. The VFS identifies every inode by a unique (file-system–inode number) pair, and it finds the inode corresponding to a particular inode number by asking the file-system object to return the inode with that number.

The inode and file objects are the mechanisms used to access files. An inode object represents the file as a whole, and a file object represents a point of access to the data in the file. A process cannot access an inode's data contents without first obtaining a file object pointing to the inode. The file object keeps track of where in the file the process is currently reading or writing, to keep track of sequential file I/O. It also remembers whether the process asked for write permissions when the file was opened, and keeps track of the process's activity if necessary to perform adaptive read-ahead (fetching file data into memory in advance of the process requesting it, to improve performance).

File objects typically belong to a single process, but inode objects do not. Even once a file is no longer being used by any processes, its inode object may still be cached by the VFS to improve performance if the file is used again in the near future. All cached file data are linked onto a list in the file's inode object. The inode also maintains standard information about each file, such as the owner, size, and time most recently modified.

Directory files are dealt with slightly differently from other files. The UNIX programming interface defines a number of operations on directories, such as creating, deleting, and renaming a file in a directory. Unlike reading and writing data, for which a file must first be opened, the system calls for these directory operations do not require that the user open the files concerned. The VFS therefore defines these directory operations in the inode object, rather than in the file object.

21.7.2 The Linux ext2fs File System

The standard on-disk file system used by Linux is called **ext2fs**, for historical reasons. Linux was originally programmed with a Minix-compatible file system, to ease exchanging data with the Minix development system, but that file system was severely restricted by 14-character file-name limits and the maximum file-system size of 64 megabytes. The Minix file system was superseded by a new file system, which was christened the **extended file system, extfs.** A later redesign of this file system to improve performance and scalability and to add a few missing features led to the **second extended file system, ext2fs.**

ext2fs has much in common with the BSD Fast File System (ffs) (described in Section 20.7.7). It uses a similar mechanism for locating the data blocks belonging to a specific file, storing data-block pointers in indirect blocks throughout the file system with up to three levels of indirection. As they are in ffs, directory files are stored on disk just like normal files, although their contents are interpreted differently. Each block in a directory file consists of a linked list of entries, where each entry contains the length of the entry, the name of a file, and the inode number of the inode to which that entry refers.

The main differences between ext2fs and ffs lie in the disk-allocation policies. In ffs, the disk is allocated to files in blocks of 8 kilobytes, with blocks being subdivided into fragments of 1 kilobyte to store small files or partially filled blocks at the end of a file. In contrast, ext2fs does not use fragments at all, but rather performs all its allocations in smaller units. The default block size on ext2fs is 1 kilobyte, although 2-kilobyte and 4-kilobyte blocks are also supported.

To maintain high performance, the operating system must try to perform I/Os in large chunks whenever possible, by **clustering** physically adjacent I/O requests. Clustering reduces the per-request overhead incurred by device drivers, disks, and disk-controller hardware. A 1 kilobyte I/O request size is too small to maintain good performance, so ext2fs uses allocation policies designed to place logically adjacent blocks of a file into physically adjacent blocks on disk, so that it can submit an I/O request for several disk blocks as a single operation.

The ext2fs allocation policy comes in two parts. As in ffs, an ext2fs file system is partitioned into multiple **block groups**. ffs uses the similar concept of **cylinder groups,** where each group corresponds to a single cylinder of a physical disk. However, modern disk-drive technology packs sectors onto the disk at different densities, and thus with different cylinder sizes, depending on how far the disk head is from the center of the disk, so fixed-sized cylinder groups do not necessarily correspond to the disk's geometry.

When allocating a file, ext2fs must first select the block group for that file. For data blocks, it attempts to choose the same block group as that in which the file's inode has been allocated. For inode allocations, it selects the same block group as the file's parent directory, for nondirectory files. Directory files are not kept together, but rather are dispersed throughout the available block groups. These policies are designed to keep related information within the same block group, but also to spread out the disk load among the disk's block groups to reduce the fragmentation of any one area of the disk.

Within a block group, ext2fs tries to keep allocations physically contiguous if possible, reducing fragmentation if it can. It maintains a bitmap of all free blocks in a block group. When allocating the first blocks for a new file, it starts searching for a free block from the beginning of the block group; when extending a file, it continues the search from the block most recently allocated to the file. The search is performed in two stages. First, it searches for an entire free byte in the bitmap; if it fails to find one, it looks for any free bit. The search for free bytes aims to allocate disk space in chunks of at least eight blocks where possible.

Once a free block has been identified, the search is extended backward until an allocated block is encountered. When a free byte is found in the bitmap, this backward extend prevents ext2fs from leaving a hole between the most recently allocated block in the previous nonzero byte and the zero byte found. Once the next block to be allocated has been thus found by either bit or byte search, ext2fs extends the allocation forward for up to eight blocks and **preallocates** these extra blocks to the file. This preallocation helps to reduce fragmentation during interleaved writes to separate files, and also reduces the CPU cost of disk allocation by allocating multiple blocks simultaneously. The preallocated blocks are returned to the free-space bitmap when the file is closed.

Figure 21.5 illustrates the allocation policies. Each row represents a sequence of set and unset bits in an allocation bitmap, representing used and

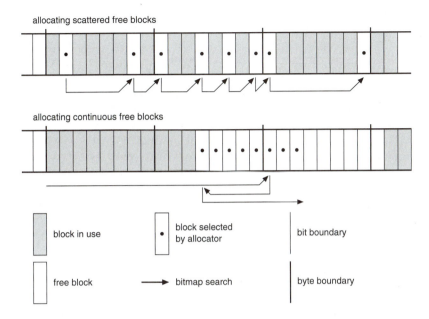

Figure 21.5   ext2fs block-allocation policies.

free blocks on disk. In the first case, if we can find any free blocks sufficiently near the start of the search, then we allocate them no matter how fragmented they may be. The fragmentation is partially compensated by the fact that the blocks are close together and can probably all be read without any disk seeks being incurred, and allocating them all to one file is better in the long run than is allocating isolated blocks to separate files once large free areas become scarce on disk. In the second case, we have not immediately found a free block close by, so we search forward for an entire free byte in the bitmap. If we allocated that byte as a whole, we would end up creating a fragmented area of free space before it, so before allocating we back up to make this allocation flush with the allocation preceding it, and then we allocate forward to satisfy the default allocation of eight blocks.

21.7.3 The Linux Proc File System

The Linux VFS is sufficiently flexible that it is possible to implement a file system that does not store data persistently at all, but rather simply provides an interface to some other functionality. The Linux **process file system,** known as the proc file system, is an example of a file system whose contents are not actually stored anywhere, but are rather computed on demand according to user file I/O requests.

A proc file system is not unique to Linux. SVR4 UNIX introduced a proc file system as an efficient interface to the kernel's process debugging support:

Each subdirectory of the file system corresponded not to a directory on any disk, but rather to an active process on the current system. A listing of the file system reveals one directory per process, with the directory name being the ASCII decimal representation of the process's unique process identifier (PID).

Linux implements such a proc file system, but extends it greatly by adding a number of extra directories and text files under the file system's root directory. These new entries correspond to various statistics about the kernel and the associated loaded drivers. The proc file system provides a way for programs to access this information as plain text files, which the standard UNIX user environment provides powerful tools to process. For example, in the past, the traditional UNIX **ps** command for listing the states of all running processes has been implemented as a privileged process that reads the process state directly from the kernel's virtual memory. Under Linux, this command is implemented as an entirely unprivileged program that simply parses and formats the information from **proc**.

The proc file system must implement two things: a directory structure, and the file contents within. Given that a UNIX file system is defined as a set of file and directory inodes identified by their inode numbers, the proc file system must define a unique and persistent inode number for each directory and the associated files. Once such a mapping exists, it can use this inode number to identify just what operation is required when a user tries to read from a particular file inode or to perform a lookup in a particular directory inode. When data are read from one of these files, the proc file system will collect the appropriate information, format it into textual form, and place it into the requesting process's read buffer.

The mapping from inode number to information type splits the inode number into two fields. In Linux, a PID is 16 bits wide, but an inode number is 32 bits. The top 16 bits of the inode number are interpreted as a PID, and the remaining bits define what type of information is being requested about that process.

A PID of zero is not valid, so a zero PID field in the inode number is taken to mean that this inode contains global—rather than process-specific—information. Separate global files exist in proc to report information such as the kernel version, free memory, performance statistics, and drivers currently running.

Not all the inode numbers in this range are reserved: The kernel can allocate new proc inode mappings dynamically, maintaining a bitmap of allocated inode numbers. It also maintains a tree data structure of registered global proc file-system entries: Each entry contains the file's inode number, file name, access permissions, and the special functions used to generate the file's contents. Drivers can register and deregister entries in this tree at any time, and a special section of the tree (appearing under the /proc/sys directory) is reserved for kernel variables. Files under this tree are dealt with by a set of common handlers that allow both reading and writing of these variables, so a system administrator can tune the value of kernel parameters simply by writing the new desired values out in ASCII decimal to the appropriate file.

To allow efficient access to these variables from within applications, the */proc/sys* subtree is made available through a special system call, `sysctl`, which reads and writes the same variables in binary, rather than in text, without the overhead of the file system. `sysctl` is not an extra facility; it simply reads the `proc` dynamic entry tree to decide to which variables the application is referring.

21.8 ■ Input and Output

To the user, the I/O system in Linux looks much like it does in any UNIX. That is, to the extent possible, all device drivers appear as normal files. A user can open an access channel to a device in the same way as she can open any other file—devices can appear as objects within the file system. The system administrator can create special files within a file system that contain references to a specific device driver, and a user opening such a file will be able to read from and write to the device referenced. By using the normal file-protection system, which determines who can access which file, the administrator can set access permissions for each device.

Linux splits all devices into three classes: block devices, character devices, and network devices. Figure 21.6 illustrates the overall structure of the device-driver system. **Block devices** include all devices that allow random access to completely independent, fixed-sized blocks of data, including hard disks, floppy disks, and CD-ROMs. Block devices are typically used to store file systems, but direct access to a block device is also allowed so that programs can create and repair the file system that the device contains. Applications can also access these block devices directly if they wish; for example, a database application may prefer to perform its own, fine-tuned laying out of data onto the disk, rather than using the general-purpose file system.

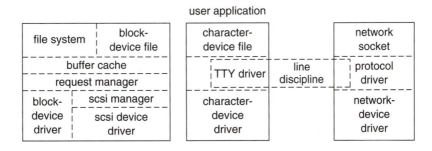

Figure 21.6   Device-driver block structure.

Character devices include most other devices, with the main exception of network devices. Character devices do not need to support all the functionality of regular files. For example, a loudspeaker device would allow data to be written to it, but would not support reading of data back from it. Similarly, seeking to a certain position in the file might be supported for a magnetic-tape device, but would make no sense to a pointing device such as a mouse.

Network devices are dealt with differently from block and character devices. Users cannot directly transfer data to network devices, but must instead communicate indirectly by opening a connection to the kernel's networking subsystem. We discuss the interface to network devices separately in Section 21.10.

21.8.1 Block Devices

Block devices provide the main interface to all disk devices in a system. Performance is particularly important for disks, and the block-device system must provide functionality to ensure that disk access is as fast as possible. This functionality is achieved through the use of two system components: the **block buffer cache** and the **request manager**.

21.8.1.1 The Block Buffer Cache

The Linux **block buffer cache** serves two main purposes: It acts as both a pool of buffers for active I/O, and a cache for completed I/O. The buffer cache consists of two parts. First, there are the buffers themselves: a dynamically sized set of pages allocated directly from the kernel's main memory pool. Each page is split up into a number of equally sized buffers. Second, there is a set of corresponding buffer descriptors, the **buffer_heads**—one for each buffer in the cache.

The **buffer_heads** contain all the information that the kernel maintains about the buffers. The primary information is the buffer's identity. Each buffer is identified by a 3-tuple: the block device to which the buffer belongs, the offset of the data within that block device, and the size of the buffer. Buffers are also held on a number of lists. There are separate lists for clean, dirty, and locked buffers, plus a list of free buffers. Buffers enter the free list by being placed there either by a file system (for example, when a file is deleted), or by a **refill_freelist** function, which is called whenever the kernel needs more buffers. The kernel fills the free list by expanding the pool of buffers or by recycling existing buffers, according to whether sufficient free memory is available. Finally, each buffer not on the free list is indexed by a hash function on its device and block number, and is linked onto a corresponding hash lookup list.

The kernel's buffer management automatically deals with the writing of dirty buffers back to disk. Two background daemons assist. One simply wakes up at a regular interval and requests that all data be written back to disk if it has been dirty for longer than a certain interval. The other is a kernel thread that is woken up whenever the **refill_freelist** function finds that too high a proportion of the buffer cache is dirty.

21.8.1.2 The Request Manager

The request manager is the layer of software that manages the reading and writing of buffer contents to and from a block-device driver. The request system revolves around a function, **ll_rw_block**, which performs low-level read and write of block devices. This function takes a list of **buffer_head** buffer descriptors and a read–write flag as its argument, and sets the I/O in progress for all those buffers. It does not wait for that I/O to complete.

Outstanding I/O requests are recorded in **request** structures. A **request** represents an outstanding I/O request for the read or write of a contiguous range of sectors on a single block device. Since more than one buffer may be involved in the transfer, the **request** contains a pointer to the first in a linked list of **buffer_heads** to be used for the transfer.

A separate list of requests is kept for each block-device driver, and these requests are scheduled according to a unidirectional elevator (C-SCAN) algorithm, which exploits the order in which requests are inserted and removed from the per-device lists. The request lists are maintained in sorted order of increasing starting-sector number. When a request is accepted for processing by a block-device driver, it is not removed from the list. It is removed only after the I/O is complete, at which point the driver continues with the next request in the list, even if new requests have been inserted into the list before the active request.

As new I/O requests are made, the request manager attempts to merge requests in the per-device lists. Passing a single, large request, instead of many smaller requests, is often much more efficient in terms of the overhead of the underlying devices. All the **buffer_heads** in such an aggregate request are locked as soon as the initial I/O request is made. As the request is processed by a device driver, the individual **buffer_heads** constituting the aggregate request are unlocked one at a time; there is no need for a process waiting on one buffer to wait for all the other buffers in the request to become unlocked, too. This factor is particularly important because it ensures that read-ahead can be performed efficiently.

One final feature of the request manager is that I/O requests can be made that bypass the buffer cache entirely. The low-level page I/O function, **brw_page**, creates a set of temporary **buffer_heads** to label the contents of a page of memory for the purpose of submitting I/O requests to the request manager. However, these temporary **buffer_heads** are not linked into the buffer cache, and once the final buffer on the page has completed its I/O, the entire page is unlocked and the **buffer_heads** are discarded.

This cache-bypassing mechanism is used in the kernel whenever the caller is doing independent caching of data, or whenever the data are known to be no longer cachable. The page cache fills its pages in this way, to avoid unnecessary caching of the same data in both the page cache and the buffer cache. The virtual-memory system also bypasses the cache when performing I/O to swap devices.

21.8.2 Character Devices

A character-device driver can be almost any device driver that does not offer random access to fixed blocks of data. Any character-device drivers registered to the Linux kernel must also register a set of functions that implements the various file I/O operations that the driver can handle. The kernel performs almost no preprocessing of a file read or write request to a character device, but rather simply passes on the request to the device in question, and lets the device deal with the request.

The main exception to this rule is the special subset of character-device drivers that implement terminal devices. The kernel maintains a standard interface to these drivers by means of a set of **tty_struct** structures. Each of these structures provides buffering and flow control on the data stream from the terminal device and feeds those data to a line discipline.

A **line discipline** is an interpreter for the information from the terminal device. The most common line discipline is the **tty** discipline, which glues the terminal's data stream onto the standard input and output streams of a user's running processes, allowing those processes to communicate directly with the user's terminal. This job is complicated by the fact that more than one such process may be running simultaneously, and the **tty** line discipline is responsible for attaching and detaching the terminal's input and output from the various processes connected to it as those processes are suspended or are woken up by the user.

Other line disciplines also are implemented that have nothing to do with I/O to a user process. The PPP and SLIP networking protocols are ways of encoding a networking connection over a terminal device such as a serial line. These protocols are implemented under Linux as drivers that at one end appear to the terminal system as line disciplines, and at the other end appear to the networking system as a network-device driver. After one of these line disciplines has been enabled on a terminal device, any data appearing on that terminal will be routed directly to the appropriate network device driver.

21.9 ■ Interprocess Communication

UNIX provides a rich environment for allowing processes to communicate with each other. Communication may be just a matter of letting another process know that some event has occurred, or it may involve transferring data from one process to another.

21.9.1 Synchronization and Signals

The standard UNIX mechanism for informing a process that an event has occurred is the **signal**. Signals can be sent from any process to any other (with restrictions on signals sent to processes owned by another user), but there is only a limited number of signals available and they cannot carry information: Only the fact that a signal occurred is available to a process. Signals do not need to be generated by another process. The kernel also generates signals internally; for example, it can send a signal to a server process when data arrive on a network channel, to a parent process when a child terminates, or when a timer expires.

Internally, the Linux kernel does not use signals to communicate with processes that are running in kernel mode: If a kernel-mode process is expecting an event to occur, it will not normally use signals to receive notification of that event. Rather, communication about incoming asynchronous events within the kernel is performed through the use of scheduling states and **wait_queue** structures. These mechanisms allow kernel-mode processes to inform one another about relevant events, and also allow events to be generated by device drivers or by the networking system. Whenever a process wants to wait for some event to complete, it places itself on a **wait_queue** associated with that event and tells the scheduler that it is no longer eligible for execution. Once the event has completed, it will wake up every process on the **wait_queue**. This procedure allows multiple processes to wait for a single event. For example, if several processes are trying to read a file from a disk, then they will all be woken up once the data have been read into memory successfully.

Although signals have always been the main mechanism for communicating asynchronous events among processes, Linux also implements the semaphore mechanism of System V UNIX. A process can wait on a semaphore as easily as it can wait for a signal, but semaphores have the advantages that large numbers of semaphores can be shared among multiple independent processes, and that operations on multiple semaphores can be performed atomically. Internally, the standard Linux **wait_queue** mechanism synchronizes processes that are communicating with semaphores.

21.9.2 Passing of Data Among Processes

Linux offers several mechanisms for passing data among processes. The standard UNIX **pipe** mechanism allows a child process to inherit a communication channel to its parent; data written to one end of the pipe can be read at the other. Under Linux, pipes appear as just another type of inode to virtual-file-system software, and each pipe has a pair of **wait_queue**s to synchronize the reader and writer. UNIX also defines a set of networking facilities that can send streams of data to both local and remote processes. Networking is covered in Section 21.10.

Two other methods of sharing data among processes are available. First, shared memory offers an extremely fast way to communicate large or small numbers of data; any data written by one process to a shared memory region can be read immediately by any other process that has mapped that region into its address space. The main disadvantage of shared memory is that, on its own, it offers no synchronization: A process can neither ask the operating system whether a piece of shared memory has been written to, nor suspend execution until such a write occurs. Shared memory becomes particularly powerful when used in conjunction with another interprocess-communication mechanism that provides the missing synchronization.

A shared-memory region in Linux is a persistent object that can be created or deleted by processes. Such an object is treated as though it were a small independent address space: The Linux paging algorithms can elect to page out to disk shared-memory pages, just as they can page out a process's data pages. The shared-memory object acts as a backing store for shared-memory regions, just as a file can act as a backing store for a memory-mapped memory region. When a file is mapped into a virtual-address-space region, then any page faults that occur cause the appropriate page of the file to be mapped into virtual memory. Similarly, shared-memory mappings direct page faults to map in pages from a persistent shared-memory object. Also just as for files, shared-memory objects remember their contents even if no processes are currently mapping them into virtual memory.

21.10 ■ Network Structure

Networking is a key area of functionality for Linux. Not only does Linux support the standard Internet protocols used for most UNIX-to-UNIX communications, but also it implements a number of protocols native to other, non-UNIX operating systems. In particular, since Linux was originally implemented primarily on PCs, rather than on large workstations or on server class systems, it supports many of the protocols typically used on PC networks, such as AppleTalk and IPX.

Internally, networking in the Linux kernel is implemented by three layers of software:

1. The socket interface

2. Protocol drivers

3. Network-device drivers

User applications perform all networking requests through the socket interface. This interface is designed to look like the BSD4.3 socket layer, so that any programs designed to make use of Berkeley sockets will run on Linux without any source-code changes. This interface is described in Section 20.9.1. One of the important features of the BSD socket interface is that it is sufficiently general purpose to represent network addresses for a wide range of different networking protocols. This single interface is used in Linux to access not just those protocols implemented on standard BSD systems, but rather all the protocols supported by the system.

The next layer of software is the protocol stack, which is similar in organization to BSD's own framework. Whenever any networking data arrive at this layer, either from an application's socket or from a network-device driver, the data are expected to have been tagged with an identifier specifying which network protocol they contain. Protocols can communicate with one another if they desire; for example, within the Internet protocol set, there are separate protocols to manage routing, error reporting, and reliable retransmission of lost data.

The protocol layer may rewrite packets, create new packets, split or reassemble packets into fragments, or simply discard incoming data. Ultimately, once it has finished processing a set of packets, it passes them on, either up to the socket interface if the data are destined for a local connection or downward to a device driver if the packet needs to be transmitted remotely. It is up to the protocol layer to decide to which socket or device to send the packet.

All communication between the layers of the networking stack is performed by passing single **skbuff** structures. An **skbuff** contains a set of pointers into a single continuous area of memory, representing a buffer inside which network packets can be constructed. The valid data in an **skbuff** do not need to start at the beginning of the **skbuff**'s buffer, and do not need to run to the end: The networking code can add data to or trim data from either end of the packet, as long as the result still fits into the **skbuff**. This capacity is especially important on modern microprocessors where improvements in CPU speed have far outstripped the performance of main memory: The **skbuff** architecture allows flexibility in manipulating packet headers and checksums while avoiding any unnecessary data copying.

The most important set of protocols in the Linux networking system is the Internet protocol (IP) suite. This suite comprises a number of separate protocols. The IP protocol implements routing between different hosts anywhere on the network. On top of the routing protocol are built the UDP, TCP, and ICMP protocols. The UDP protocol carries arbitrary individual datagrams between hosts; the TCP protocol implements reliable connections between hosts with guaranteed in-order delivery of packets and automatic retransmission of lost data. The ICMP protocol is used to carry various error and status messages between hosts.

Packets (**skbuffs**) arriving at the networking stack's protocol software are expected to be already tagged with an internal identifier indicating to which protocol the packet is relevant. Different networking-device drivers encode the protocol type in different ways over their communications media; thus, identifying the protocol for incoming data must be done in the device driver. The device driver uses a hash table of known networking-protocol identifiers to look up the appropriate protocol, and passes the packet to that protocol. New protocols can be added to the hash table as kernel-loadable modules.

Incoming IP packets are delivered to the IP driver. The job of this layer is to perform routing: It decides where the packet is destined and forwards the packet to the appropriate internal protocol driver to be delivered locally, or injects the packet back into a selected network-device-driver queue to be forwarded to another host. It performs the routing decision using two tables: the persistent forwarding information base (FIB), and a cache of recent routing decisions. The FIB holds routing-configuration information and can specify routes based either on a specific destination address or on a wildcard representing multiple destinations. The FIB is organized as a set of hash tables indexed by destination address; the tables representing the most specific routes are always searched first. Successful lookups from this table are added to the route-caching table, which caches routes only by specific destination; no wildcards are stored in the cache, so lookups can be made quickly. An entry in the route cache expires after a fixed period with no hits.

At various stages, the IP software passes packets to a separate section of code for **firewall management:** selective filtering of packets according to arbitrary criteria, usually for security purposes. The firewall manager maintains a number of separate **firewall chains,** and allows an **skbuff** to be matched against any chain. Separate chains are reserved for separate purposes: One is used for forwarded packets, one for packets being input to this host, and one for data generated at this host. Each chain is held as an ordered list of rules, where a rule specifies one of a number of possible firewall-decision functions plus some arbitrary data to match against.

Two other functions performed by the IP driver are disassembly and reassembly of large packets. If an outgoing packet is too large to be queued to a device, it is simply split up into smaller **fragments,** which are all queued to the driver. At the receiving host, these fragments must be reassembled. The IP driver maintains an **ipfrag** object for each fragment awaiting reassembly, and a **ipq** for each datagram being assembled. Incoming fragments are matched against each known **ipq**. If a match is found, the fragment is added to it; otherwise, a new **ipq** is created. Once the final fragment has arrived for a **ipq,** a completely new **skbuff** is constructed to hold the new packet, and this packet is passed back into the IP driver.

Packets that are matched by the IP as destined for this host are passed on to one of the other protocol drivers. The UDP and TCP protocols share a means of associating packets with source and destination sockets: Each connected pair of sockets is uniquely identified by its source and destination addresses and by the source and destination **port** numbers. The socket lists are linked onto hash tables keyed on these four address–port values for socket lookup on incoming packets. The TCP protocol has to deal with unreliable connections, so it maintains ordered lists of unacknowledged outgoing packets to retransmit after a timeout, and of incoming out-of-order packets to be presented to the socket when the missing data have arrived.

21.11 ■ Security

Linux's security model is closely related to typical UNIX security mechanisms. The security concerns can be classified in two groups:

1. *Authentication:* Making sure that nobody can access the system without first proving that she has entry rights

2. *Access control:* Providing a mechanism for checking whether a user has the right to access a certain object, and preventing access to objects as required

21.11.1 Authentication

Authentication in UNIX has typically been performed through the use of a publicly readable password file. A user's password is combined with a random "salt" value and the result is encoded with a one-way transformation function and is stored in the password file. The use of the one-way function means that it is not possible to deduce the original password from the password file except by trial and error. When a user presents a password to the system, the password is recombined with the salt value stored in the password file and is passed through the same one-way transformation. If the result matches the contents of the password file, then the password is accepted.

Historically, UNIX implementations of this mechanism have had several problems. Passwords were often limited to eight characters, and the number of possible salt values was so low that an attacker could easily combine a dictionary of commonly used passwords with every possible salt value and have a good chance of matching one or more passwords in the password file, gaining unauthorized access to any accounts compromised as a result. Extensions to the password mechanism have been introduced that keep the encrypted password secret in a file that is not publicly readable, that allow longer passwords, or that use more secure methods of encoding the password. Other authentication mechanisms have been introduced that limit the times during which a user is permitted to connect to the system or to distribute authentication information to all the related systems in a network.

A new security mechanism has been developed by UNIX vendors to address these issues. The **pluggable authentication modules** (PAM) system is based on a shared library that can be used by any system component that needs to authenticate users. An implementation of this system is available under Linux. PAM allows authentication modules to be loaded on demand as specified in a systemwide configuration file. If a new authentication mechanism is added at a later date, it can be added to the configuration file and all system components will immediately be able to take advantage of it. PAM modules can specify authentication methods, account restrictions, session-setup functions, or password-changing functions (so that, when users change their passwords, all the necessary authentication mechanisms can be updated at once).

21.11.2 Access Control

Access control under UNIX systems, including Linux, is performed through the use of unique numeric identifiers. A **user identifier** (**uid**) identifies a single user or a single set of access rights. A **group identifier (gid)** is an extra identifier that can be used to identify rights belonging to more than one user.

Access control is applied to various objects in the system. Every file available in the system is protected by the standard access-control mechanism. In addition, other shared objects, such as shared-memory sections and semaphores, employ the same access system.

Every object in a UNIX system that is under user and group access control has a single uid and a single gid associated with it. User processes also have a single uid, but they may have more than one gid. If a process's uid matches the uid of an object, then the process has **user rights** or **owner rights** to that object; if the uids do not match but any of the process's gids match the object's gid, then **group rights** are conferred; otherwise, the process has **world** rights to the object.

Linux performs access control by assigning objects a **protection mask**, which specifies which access modes—read, write, or execute—are to be granted to processes with owner, group, or world access. Thus, the owner of an object might have full read, write, and execute access to a file; other users in a certain group might be given read access but denied write access; and everybody else might be given no access at all.

The only exception is the privileged **root** uid. A process with this special uid is granted automatic access to any object in the system, bypassing normal access checks. Such processes are also granted permission to perform privileged operations such as reading any physical memory or opening reserved network sockets. This mechanism allows the kernel to prevent normal users from accessing these resources: Most of the kernel's key internal resources are implicitly owned by this root uid.

Linux implements the standard UNIX **setuid** mechanism described in Section 20.3.2. This mechanism allows a program to run with privileges different from those of the user running the program: For example, the **lpr** program (which submits a job onto a print queue) has access to the system's print queues even if the user running that program does not. The UNIX implementation of **setuid** distinguishes between a process's **real** and **effective** uid: The real uid is that of the user running the program; the effective uid is that of the file's owner.

Under Linux, this mechanism is augmented in two ways. First, Linux implements the POSIX specification's **saved user-id** mechanism, which allows a process to drop and reacquire its effective uid repeatedly; for security reasons, a program may want to perform most of its operations in a safe mode, waiving the privileges granted by its **setuid** status, but may wish to perform selected operations with all its privileges. Standard UNIX implementations achieve this capacity only by swapping the real and effective uids; the previous effective uid is remembered but the program's real uid does not always correspond to the uid of the user running the program. Saved uids allow a process to set its effective uid to its real uid and then back to the previous value of its effective uid, without having to modify the real uid at any time.

The second enhancement provided by Linux is the addition of a process characteristic that grants just a subset of the rights of the effective uid. The **fsuid** and **fsgid** process properties are used when access rights are granted to files, and are set every time the effective uid or gid are set. However, the fsuid and fsgid can be set independently of the effective ids, allowing a process to access files on behalf of another user without taking on the identity of that other user in any other way. Specifically, server processes can use this mechanism to serve files to a certain user without the process becoming vulnerable to being killed or suspended by that user.

Linux provides another mechanism that has become common in modern UNIXes for flexible passing of rights from one program to another. When a local network socket has been set up between any two processes on the system, either of those processes may send to the other process a file descriptor for one of its open files; the other process receives a duplicate file descriptor for the same file. This mechanism allows a client to pass access to a single file selectively to some server process, without granting that process any other privileges. For example, it is no longer necessary for a print server to be able to read all the files of a user who submits a new print job; the print client could simply pass the server file descriptors for any files to be printed, denying the server access to any of the user's other files.

21.12 ■ Summary

Linux is a modern, free operating system based on UNIX standards. It has been designed to run efficiently and reliably on common PC hardware; it also runs on a variety of other platforms. It provides a programming interface and user interface compatible with standard UNIX systems, and can run a large number of UNIX applications, including an increasing number of commercially supported applications.

Linux has not evolved in a vacuum. A complete Linux system includes many components that were developed independently of Linux. The core Linux operating-system kernel is entirely original, but it allows much existing free UNIX software to run, resulting in an entire UNIX-compatible operating system free from proprietary code.

The Linux kernel is implemented as a traditional monolithic kernel for performance reasons, but is modular enough in design to allow most drivers to be dynamically loaded and unloaded at run time.

Linux is a multiuser system, providing protection between processes and running multiple processes according to a time-sharing scheduler. Newly created processes can share selective parts of their execution environment with their parent processes, allowing multithreaded programming. Interprocess communication is supported by both System V mechanisms—message queues, semaphores, and shared memory—and BSD's socket interface. Multiple networking protocols can be accessed simultaneously through the socket interface.

To the user, the file system appears as a hierarchical directory tree that obeys UNIX semantics. Internally, Linux uses an abstraction layer to manage multiple different file systems. Device-oriented, networked, and virtual file systems are supported. Device-oriented file systems access disk storage through two caches: Data are cached in the page cache that is unified with the virtual-memory system, and metadata are cached in the buffer cache—a separate cache indexed by physical disk block.

The memory-management system uses page sharing and copy-on-write to minimize the duplication of data shared by different processes. Pages are loaded on demand when they are first referenced, and are paged back out to backing store according to an LFU algorithm if physical memory needs to be reclaimed.

■ Exercises

21.1 Linux runs on a variety of hardware platforms. What steps must the Linux developers take to ensure that the system is portable to different processors and memory-management architectures, and to minimize the amount of architecture-specific kernel code?

21.2 Dynamically loadable kernel modules give flexibility when drivers are added to a system. Do they also have disadvantages? Under what circumstances would a kernel be compiled into a single binary file? When would it be better to keep it split into modules? Explain your answers.

21.3 Multithreading is a commonly used programming technique. Describe three different ways that threads could be implemented. Explain how these ways compare to the Linux clone mechanism. When might each alternative mechanism be better or worse than using clones?

21.4 What are the extra costs incurred by the creation and scheduling of a process, as compared to the cost of a cloned thread?

21.5 The Linux scheduler implements *soft* real-time scheduling. What features are missing that are necessary for certain real-time programming tasks? How might they be added to the kernel?

21.6 The Linux kernel does not allow paging out of kernel memory. What effect does this restriction have on the kernel's design? What are two advantages and two disadvantages of this design decision?

21.7 In Linux, shared libraries perform many operations central to the operating system. What is the advantage of keeping this functionality out of the kernel? Are there any drawbacks? Explain your answer.

21.8 What are three advantages of dynamic (shared) linkage of libraries compared to static linkage? What are two cases where static linkage is preferable?

21.9 Compare the use of networking sockets with the use of shared memory as a mechanism for communicating data between processes on a single computer. Name two of the advantages of each method. When might each be preferred?

21.10 UNIX systems used to use disk-layout optimizations based on the rotation position of disk data, but modern implementations, including Linux, simply optimize for sequential data access. Why do they do so? Of what hardware characteristics does sequential access take advantage? Why is rotational optimization no longer so useful?

21.11 The Linux source code is freely and widely available over the Internet or from CD-ROM vendors. What are three implications of this availability for the security of the Linux system?

Bibliographical Notes

The Linux system is a product of the Internet; as a result, most of the available documentation on Linux is available in some form on the Internet. The following key sites reference most of the useful information available:

- The Linux Cross-Reference Pages at http://lxr.linux.no/ maintain current listings of the Linux kernel, browsable via the Web and fully cross-referenced.

- Linux-HQ at http://www.linuxhq.com/ hosts a large amount of information relating to the Linux 2.0 and Linux 2.1 kernels. This site also includes links to the home pages of most Linux distributions, as well as archives of the major mailing lists.

- The Linux Documentation Project at http://sunsite.unc.edu/linux/ lists many books on Linux that are available in source format as part of the Linux Documentation Project. The project also hosts the Linux *How-To* guides, which contain a series of hints and tips relating to aspects of Linux.

- The *Kernel Hackers' Guide* is an Internet-based guide to kernel internals in general. This constantly expanding site is located at http://www.redhat.com:8080/HyperNews/get/khg.html.

In addition, there are many mailing lists devoted to Linux. The most important are maintained by a mailing-list manager that can be reached at the e-mail address majordomo@vger.rutgers.edu. Send e-mail to this address with the single line "help" in the mail's body for information on how to access the list server and to subscribe to any lists.

The one book that currently describes the internal details of the Linux kernel—*Linux Kernel Internals* by Beck and colleagues 1996—deals with only Linux 1.2.13. For further reading on UNIX in general, a good place to start is Vahalia's *Unix Internals: The New Frontiers* [Vahalia 1996].

Finally, the Linux system itself can be obtained over the Internet. Complete Linux distributions can be obtained from the home sites of the companies concerned, and the Linux community also maintains archives of current system components at several places on the Internet. The most important are these:

- ftp://tsx-11.mit.edu/pub/linux/

- ftp://sunsite.unc.edu/pub/Linux/

- ftp://linux.kernel.org/pub/linux/

Chapter 22

WINDOWS NT

The Microsoft Windows NT operating system is a 32-bit preemptive multitasking operating system for modern microprocessors. NT is portable to a variety of processor architectures. One or more versions of NT have been ported to Intel 386 and higher, MIPS R4000, DEC Alpha, and the PowerPC. Key goals for the system are portability, security, Portable Operating System Interface (POSIX) or IEEE Std. 1003.1 compliance, multiprocessor support, extensibility, international support, and compatibility with MS-DOS and MS-Windows applications. NT uses a micro-kernel architecture (like Mach), so enhancements can be made to one part of the operating system without greatly affecting other parts of the system. NT (through Version 4) is not a multiuser operating system.

The two versions of NT are Windows NT Workstation and Windows NT Server. They use the same kernel and operating-system code, but NT Server is configured for client–server applications and can act as an application server on NetWare and Microsoft LANs. Version 4.0 of NT Server incorporates Internet web-server software and the Windows 95 user interface. In 1996, more NT Server licenses were sold than all versions of UNIX licenses.

22.1 ■ History

In the mid-1980s, Microsoft and IBM cooperated to develop the OS/2 operating system, which was written in assembly language for single-processor Intel 80286 systems. In 1988, Microsoft decided to make a fresh start, and to develop a "new technology" (NT) portable operating system that supported both the

OS/2 and POSIX application programming interfaces (APIs). In October 1988, Dave Cutler, the architect of the DEC VAX/VMS operating system, was given the charter of building this new operating system. Originally, NT was supposed to use the OS/2 API as its native environment; during development, however, NT was changed to use the 32-bit Windows API or Win32 API, reflecting the popularity of Windows 3.0. The first versions of NT were Windows NT 3.1 and Windows NT 3.1 Advanced Server. (At that time, 16-bit Windows was at Version 3.1.) In Version 4.0, NT adopted the Windows 95 user interface and incorporated Internet web-server and browser software. In addition, several user-interface routines and graphics code were moved into the kernel to improve performance, with the side effect of decreased system reliability.

22.2 ■ Design Principles

The design goals that Microsoft has stated for NT include extensibility, portability, reliability, compatibility, performance, and international support.

Extensibility is an important property of any operating system whose developers hope to keep up with advancements in computing technology. So that changes are facilitated over time, NT is implemented with a layered architecture. The NT executive, which runs in kernel or protected mode, provides the basic system services. On top of the executive, several server subsystems operate in user mode. Among these are **environmental subsystems** that emulate different operating systems. Thus, programs written for MS-DOS, Microsoft Windows, and POSIX can all run on NT in the appropriate environment. (See Section 22.5 for more information on environmental subsystems.) Because of the modular structure, additional environmental subsystems can be added without affecting the executive. In addition, NT uses loadable drivers in the I/O system, so that new file systems, new kinds of I/O devices, and new kinds of networking can be added while the system is running. NT uses a client–server model like that of the Mach operating system, and supports distributed processing by remote procedure calls (RPCs) as defined by the Open Software Foundation.

An operating system is *portable* if it can be moved from one hardware architecture to another with relatively few changes. NT is designed to be portable. As is true of UNIX, the majority of the system is written in C and C++. All processor-dependent code is isolated in a dynamic link library (DLL), called the **hardware abstraction layer (HAL)**. A DLL is a file that gets mapped into a process's address space such that any functions in the DLL appear as though they are part of the process. The upper layers of NT depend on HAL, rather than on the underlying hardware, and that helps NT to be portable. The HAL manipulates hardware directly, isolating the rest of NT from hardware differences among the platforms on which it runs.

Reliability is the ability to handle error conditions, including the ability of the operating system to protect itself and its users from defective or malicious software. NT resists defects and attacks by using hardware protection for virtual memory, and software protection mechanisms for operating-system resources. Also, NT comes with a file system, called the **native NT file system** (**NTFS**), that recovers automatically from many kinds of file-system errors after a system crash. NT Version 3.51 has a C-2 security classification from the U.S. government, which signifies a moderate level of protection from defective software and malicious attacks.

NT provides source-level *compatibility* to applications that follow the IEEE 1003.1 (POSIX) standard. Thus, they can be compiled to run on NT without changes beng made to the source code.

In addition, NT can run the executable binaries for many programs compiled for Intel 80X86 architectures running MS-DOS, 16-bit Windows, OS/2, Lan Manager, and 32-bit Windows. It does so via two mechanisms. First, versions of NT for non-Intel processors provide 80X86 instruction-set emulation in software. Second, the system calls for MS-DOS, 32-bit Windows, and so on are handled by the environmental subsystems mentioned earlier. These environmental subsystems support a variety of file systems, including the MS-DOS FAT file system, the OS/2 HPFS file system, the ISO9660 CD file system, and NTFS. NT's binary compatibility, however, is not perfect. In MS-DOS, for example, applications can access hardware ports directly. For reliability and security, NT prohibits such access.

NT is designed to afford good *performance*. The subsystems that comprise NT can communicate with one another efficiently by a local-procedure-call facility that provides high-performance message passing. Except for the kernel, threads in the subsystems of NT can be preempted by higher-priority threads. Thus, the system can respond quickly to external events. In addition, NT is designed for symmetrical multiprocessing: On a multiprocessor computer, several threads can run at the same time. The current scalability of NT is limited, compared to that of UNIX. As of 1997, NT supported systems with up to eight CPUs; Solaris ran on systems with up to 64 processors.

NT is also designed for *international* use. It provides support for different locales via the national language support (NLS) API. NLS API provides specialized routines to format dates, time, and money in accordance with various national customs. String comparisons are specialized to account for varying character sets. UNICODE is NT's native character code, although NT supports ANSI characters by converting them to UNICODE characters before manipulating them (8-bit to 16-bit conversion).

22.3 ▪ System Components

The architecture of NT is a layered system of modules. Figure 22.1 shows the architecture of NT Version 4. The main layers are the hardware abstraction

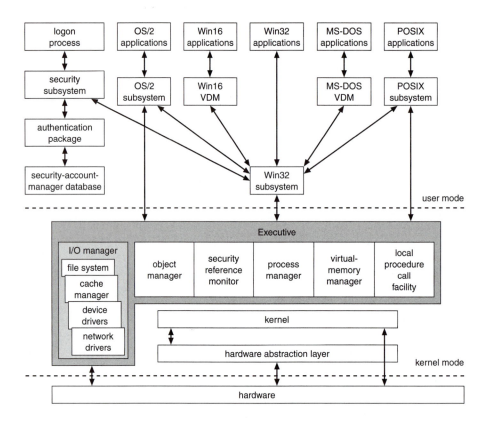

Figure 22.1 Windows NT block diagram.

layer, the kernel and the executive that run in protected mode, and a large collection of subsystems that run in user mode. There are two categories of user-mode subsystems: The **environmental subsystems** emulate different operating systems, and the **protection subsystems** provide security functions. One of the chief advantages of this architecture is that interactions between modules can be kept simple. The remainder of this chapter describes these layers and subsystems.

22.3.1 Hardware Abstraction Layer

The **hardware abstraction layer** (**HAL**) is a layer of software that hides hardware differences from upper levels of the operating system, to help make NT portable. HAL exports a virtual-machine interface that is used by the kernel, the executive, and the device drivers. One advantage of this approach is that only a single version of each device driver is needed—it can run on all hardware platforms without porting of the driver code. HAL also provides support for symmetric multiprocessing. For performance reasons, I/O drivers (and graphics drivers in NT 4.0) may access the hardware directly.

22.3.2 Kernel

The kernel of NT provides the foundation for the executive and the subsystems. The kernel is never paged out of memory, and its execution is never preempted. It has four main responsibilities: thread scheduling, interrupt and exception handling, low-level processor synchronization, and recovery after a power failure.

The kernel is object oriented. An **object type** in NT is a system-defined data type that has a set of attributes (data values) and a set of methods (functions or operations). An **object** is just an instance of a particular object type. The kernel performs its job by using a set of kernel objects whose attributes store the kernel data, and whose methods perform the kernel activities.

The kernel uses two sets of objects. The first set comprises **dispatcher objects,** which control dispatching and synchronization in the system. Examples of these objects are events, mutants, mutexes, semaphores, threads, and timers. The **event object** is used to record an event occurrence and to synchronize the latter with some action. The **mutant** provides kernel-mode or user-mode mutual exclusion with the notion of ownership. The **mutex,** which is available in only kernel mode, provides deadlock-free mutual exclusion. A **semaphore object** acts as a counter or gate to control the number of threads that access some resource. The **thread object** is the entity that is run by the kernel and is associated with a **process object**. **Timer objects** keep track of the time and signal time outs when operations take too long and need to be interrupted.

The second set of kernel objects comprises the **control objects**. These objects include asynchronous procedure calls, interrupts, power notify, power status, process, and profile objects. The **asynchronous procedure call** breaks into an executing thread and calls a procedure. The **interrupt object** binds an interrupt service routine to an interrupt source. The **power-notify object** calls a specified routine automatically after a power failure, and the **power-status object** checks whether the power has failed. A **process object** represents the virtual address space and control information necessary to execute the set of threads associated with a process. Finally, the **profile object** measures the amount of time used by a block of code.

As do many modern operating systems, NT has the notions of processes and threads for executable code. The **process** has a virtual-memory-address space, and information such as a base priority and an affinity for one or more processors. Each process has one or more **threads,** which are the units of execution dispatched by the kernel. Each thread has its own state, including a priority, processor affinity, and accounting information.

The six possible thread states are ready, standby, running, waiting, transition, and terminated. **Ready** means waiting to run. The highest-priority ready thread is moved to the **standby** state, which means that it will be the next thread to run. In a multiprocessor system, one thread is kept in the standby state for each processor. A thread is **running** when it is executing on a processor. It will run until it is preempted by a higher-priority thread, until it terminates, until its time quantum ends, or until it calls a blocking system call, such as for I/O. A thread is in the **waiting** state when it is waiting for a signal, such as an I/O completion. A new thread is in the **transition** state while it is waiting for the resources necessary for execution. A thread enters the **terminated** state when it finishes execution.

The dispatcher uses a 32-level priority scheme to determine the order of thread execution. Priorities are divided into two classes: the *real-time class* contains threads with priorities ranging from 16 to 31, and the *variable class* contains threads with priorities ranging from 0 to 15. The dispatcher uses a queue for each scheduling priority, and traverses the set of queues from highest to lowest until it finds a thread that is ready to run. If a thread has a particular processor affinity but that processor is not available, the dispatcher will skip past it, and will continue looking for a thread that is ready to run. If no ready thread is found, the dispatcher will execute a special thread called the *idle thread*.

When a thread's time quantum runs out, the thread is interrupted; if the thread is in the variable-priority class, its priority is lowered. The priority is never lowered below the base priority, however. Lowering the thread's priority tends to limit the CPU consumption of compute-bound threads. When a variable-priority thread is released from a wait operation, the dispatcher boosts its priority. The amount of the boost depends on for what it was waiting. A thread that is waiting for keyboard I/O gets a large priority increase, whereas a thread that is waiting for a disk operation gets a moderate one. This strategy tends to give good response times to interactive threads that are using the mouse and windows, and enables I/O-bound threads to keep the I/O devices busy, while permitting compute-bound threads to use spare CPU cycles in the background. This strategy is used by several time-sharing operating systems, including UNIX. In addition, the current window with which the user is interacting also receives a priority boost to enhance its response time.

Scheduling can occur when a thread enters the ready or wait state, when a thread terminates, or when an application changes a thread's priority or processor affinity. If a higher-priority real-time thread becomes ready while a lower-priority thread is running, the lower-priority thread will be preempted. This preemption gives a real-time thread preferential access to the CPU when the thread needs such access. NT is not a hard real-time operating system, however, because it does not guarantee that a real-time thread will start to execute within any particular time limit.

The kernel also provides trap handling for exceptions and interrupts that are generated by hardware or software. NT defines several architecture-independent exceptions, including memory-access violation, integer overflow, floating-point overflow or underflow, integer divide by zero, floating-point divide by zero, illegal instruction, data misalignment, privileged instruction, page read error, guard-page violation, paging-file quota exceeded, debugger breakpoint, and debugger single step.

Exceptions that are simple can be handled by the trap handler; others are handled by the kernel's **exception dispatcher**. The exception dispatcher creates an exception record that contains the reason for the exception, and that finds an exception handler that can deal with the exception.

When an exception occurs in kernel mode, the exception dispatcher simply calls a routine to locate the exception handler. If no handler is found, a fatal system error occurs and the user is left with the infamous "blue screen of death" that signifies system failure.

Exception handling is more complex for user-mode processes, because an environmental subsystem (such as the POSIX system) can set up a debugger port and an exception port for every process that it creates. If a debugger port is registered, the exception handler sends the exception to the debugger. If the debugger port is not found or does not handle that exception, the dispatcher then attempts to find an appropriate exception handler. If a handler is not found, the debugger is called again so that it can catch the error for debugging. If a debugger is not running, a message is then sent to the process's exception port to give the environmental subsystem a chance to translate the exception. For example, the POSIX environment translates NT exception messages into POSIX signals before sending them to the thread that caused the exception. Finally, if nothing else works, the kernel simply terminates the process containing the thread that caused the exception.

The interrupt dispatcher in the kernel handles interrupts by calling either an interrupt service routine (such as in a device driver) or an internal kernel routine. The interrupt is represented by an interrupt object that contains all the information needed to handle the interrupt. Using an interrupt object makes it easy to associate interrupt service routines with an interrupt without having to access the interrupt hardware directly.

Various processor architectures, such as Intel or DEC Alpha, have different types and numbers of interrupts. For portability, the interrupt dispatcher maps the hardware interrupts into a standard set. The interrupts are prioritized and are serviced in priority order. There are 32 interrupt request levels (IRQLs) in NT. Eight are reserved for the use of the kernel; the other 24 represent hardware interrupts via the HAL. The NT interrupts are defined in Figure 22.2.

The kernel uses an **interrupt dispatch table** to bind each interrupt level to a service routine. In a multiprocessor computer, NT keeps a separate interrupt dispatch table for each processor, and each processor's IRQL can be set independently to mask out interrupts. All interrupts that occur at a level equal to or less than the IRQL of a processor get blocked until the IRQL is lowered by a kernel-level thread. NT takes advantage of this property to use software interrupts to perform system functions. For instance, the kernel uses soft-

Interrupt levels	Types of interrupts
31	machine check or bus error
30	power fail
29	interprocessor notification (request another processor to act; e.g., dispatch a process or update the TLB)
28	clock (used to keep track of time)
12–27	traditional PC IRQ hardware interrupts
4–11	dispatch and deferred procedure call (by the kernel)
3	software debugger
0–2	software interrupts (used by device drivers)

Figure 22.2   NT interrupts.

ware interrupts to start a thread dispatch, to handle timers, and to support asynchronous operations.

The kernel uses the dispatch interrupt to control thread context switching. When the kernel is running, it raises the IRQL on the processor to a level above the dispatch level. When the kernel determines that a thread dispatch is required, the kernel generates a dispatch interrupt, but this interrupt is blocked until the kernel finishes what it is doing and lowers the IRQL. At that point, the dispatch interrupt can be serviced, so the dispatcher chooses a thread to run.

When the kernel decides that some system function should be executed eventually, but not immediately, it queues a **deferred procedure call** (**DPC**) object that contains the address of the function to be executed, and generates a DPC interrupt. When the IRQL of the processor drops low enough, the DPC objects are executed. The IRQL of the DPC interrupt is typically higher than that of user threads, so DPCs will interrupt the execution of user threads. To avoid problems, DPCs are restricted to be fairly simple. They cannot modify a thread's memory; create, acquire, or wait on objects; call system services; or generate page faults.

The **asynchronous procedure call** (**APC**) mechanism is similar to the DPC mechanism, but is designed for more general use. The APC mechanism enables threads to set up a procedure call that will happen out of the blue at some future time. For instance, many system services accept a user-mode routine as a parameter. Instead of invoking a synchronous system call that will block the thread until the system call completes, a user thread can call an asynchronous system call and supply an APC. The user thread will continue running. When the system service finishes, the user thread will be interrupted to run the APC spontaneously.

An APC can be queued on either a system thread or a user thread, although a user-mode APC will be executed only if the thread has declared itself to be **alertable**. An APC is more powerful than a DPC, in that it can acquire and wait on objects, cause page faults, and call system services. Since an APC executes in the address space of the target thread, the NT executive uses APCs extensively for I/O processing.

NT can run on symmetric multiprocessor machines, so the kernel must prevent two of its threads from modifying a shared data structure at the same time. The kernel uses spinlocks that reside in global memory to achieve multiprocessor mutual exclusion. Because all activity on a processor stops when a thread is attempting to acquire a spinlock, a thread that holds a spinlock is not preempted, so it can finish and release the lock as quickly as possible.

A power-fail interrupt, which has the second highest priority, notifies the operating system whenever a power loss is detected. The *power-notify object* provides a way for a device driver to register a routine that will be called on power restoration and ensures that devices get set to the proper state on recovery. For systems backed up with a battery, the *power-status object* determines the power status. A driver examines the power-status object to determine whether or not the power has failed before it begins a critical operation. If the driver determines that power has not failed, it raises the IRQL of its processor to powerfail, performs the operation, and resets the IRQL. This sequence of actions blocks the powerfail interrupt until after the critical operation completes.

22.4 ■ Executive

The NT executive provides a set of services that all environmental subsystems can use. The services are in the following groups: object manager, virtual-memory manager, process manager, local-procedure-call facility, I/O manager, and security reference monitor.

22.4.1 Object Manager

As an object-oriented system NT uses objects for all its services and entities. Examples of objects are directory objects, symbolic link objects, semaphore objects, event objects, process and thread objects, port objects, and file objects. The job of the object manager is to supervise the use of all objects. When a thread wants to use an object, it calls the object manager's open method to get a **handle** to the object. Handles are a standardized interface to all kinds of objects. Like a file handle, an object handle is an identifier unique to a process that gives a process the ability to access and manipulate a system resource.

Since the object manager is the only entity that can generate an object handle, it is the natural place to check security. For instance, the object manager checks whether a process has the right to access an object when the process tries to open that object. The object manager can also enforce quotas, such as the maximum amount of memory that a process may allocate.

The object manager can also keep track of which processes are using each object. Each object header contains a count of the number of processes that have handles to that object. When the counter goes to zero, the object is deleted from the name space if it is a temporary object name. Since NT itself often uses pointers (instead of handles) to access objects, the object manager also maintains a reference count that it increments when NT gains access to an object and decrements the count when the object is no longer needed. When the reference count of a temporary object goes to zero, the object is deleted from memory. Permanent objects represent physical entities, such as disk drives, and are not deleted when the reference count and the open handle counter go to zero.

The objects are manipulated by a standard set of methods: create, open, close, delete, query name, parse, and security. The final three need explanation:

- query name is called when a thread has a handle to an object, but wants to know the object's name.

- parse is used by the object manager to search for an object given the object's name.

- security is called when a process opens or changes the protection of an object.

22.4.2 Naming of Objects

The NT executive allows any object to be given a name. The name space is global, so one process can create a named object, and a second process can then open a handle to the object and share it with the first process. A process opening a named object can ask for the search to be either case sensitive or case insensitive.

A name can be either permanent or temporary. A **permanent name** represents an entity, such as a disk drive, that remains even if no process is accessing it. A **temporary name** exists only while some process holds a handle to that object.

Although the name space is not directly visible across a network, a process uses the object manager's parse method to help it to access a named object on another system. When a process attempts to open an object that resides on a remote computer, the object manager calls the parse method, which then calls a network redirector to find the object.

Object names are structured like file-path names in MS-DOS and in UNIX. Directories are represented by a **directory object** that contains the names of all the objects in that directory. The object name space can grow by the addition of **object domains,** which are self-contained sets of objects. Examples of object domains are floppy disks and hard drives. It is easy to see how the name space gets extended when a floppy disk is added to the system—the floppy has its own name space that is grafted onto the existing name space.

UNIX file systems have **symbolic links,** so multiple nicknames or aliases can refer to the same file. Similarly, NT implements a **symbolic link object**. One way that NT uses symbolic links is to map drive names to the standard MS-DOS drive letters. The drive letters are just symbolic links that may be remapped to suit the user's preferences.

A process gets an object handle by creating an object, by opening an existing one, by receiving a duplicated handle from another process, or by inheriting a handle from a parent process. This approach is similar to the way a UNIX process can get a file descriptor. These handles are all stored in the process's **object table**. An entry in the object table contains the object's access rights and states whether the handle should be inherited by child processes. When a process terminates, NT automatically closes all the process's open handles.

When a user is authenticated by the logon process, an access-token object is attached to the user's process. The access token contains information such as the security id, group ids, privileges, primary group, and default access-control list. These attributes determine which services and objects the user can use.

In NT, each object is protected by an **access-control list**. This list contains the security ids and the set of access rights granted to each process. When a process attempts to access an object, the system compares the security id in the process's access token with the object's access control list to determine whether access should be permitted. This check is done only when an object is opened, so internal NT services that use pointers rather than opening a handle to an object bypass the access check.

Generally, the creator of the object determines the access-control list for that object. If none is supplied explicitly, one may be inherited from the creator object, or a default list may be obtained from the user's access token object.

One field in the access token controls auditing of the object. Operations that are being audited get logged to the system's audit log with an identification of the user. The audit field can watch this log to discover attempts to break into the system or to access protected objects.

22.4.3 Virtual-Memory Manager

The virtual-memory portion of the NT executive is the **virtual-memory (VM) manager**. The design of the VM manager assumes that the underlying hardware supports virtual-to-physical mapping, a paging mechanism, and transparent cache coherence on multiprocessor systems, and allows multiple page-table entries to map to the same page frame. The VM manager in NT uses a page-based management scheme with a page size of 4 kilobytes. Pages of data that are assigned to a process but are not in physical memory are stored in the **paging file** on disk.

The VM manager uses 32-bit addresses, so each process has a 4-gigabyte virtual address space. The upper 2 gigabytes are always the same for all processes, and are used by NT in kernel mode. The lower 2 gigabytes are distinct for every process, and are accessible by both user- and kernel-mode threads.

The NT VM manager uses a two-step process to allocate memory. The first step **reserves** a portion of the process's address space. The second step **commits** the allocation by assigning space in the NT paging file. NT can limit the amount of paging file space that a process consumes by enforcing a quota on committed memory. A process can uncommit memory that it is no longer using to free up its paging quota. Since memory is represented by objects, when one process (the *parent*) creates a second process (the *child*), the parent can maintain the ability to access the virtual memory of the child. That is how environmental subsystems can manage the memory of their client processes. For performance, the VM manager allows a privileged process to lock selected pages in physical memory, thus ensuring that the pages will not be swapped out to the paging file.

Two processes can share memory by getting handles to the same memory object, but this approach can be inefficient since the entire memory space of that object would need to be committed before either process could access that object. NT provides an alternative called a **section object** to represent a block of shared memory. After getting a handle to a section object, a process can map only the needed portion of the memory. This portion is called a **view**. The view mechanism also enables a process to access an object that is too large to fit into the process's paging-file quota. The system can use the view to walk through the address space of the object, one piece at a time.

A process can control the use of a shared-memory section object in many ways. The maximum size of a section can be bounded. The section can be backed either by disk space in the system paging file or by a regular file (called a **memory-mapped** file). A section can be based: It appears at the same virtual address for all processes that access it. The memory protection of pages in the section can be set to read only, read–write, execute only, guard page, and copy-on-write. A guard page raises an exception if accessed; the exception can be used (for example) to check whether a faulty program iterates beyond the end of an array. The copy-on-write mechanism allows the VM manager to save memory. When two processes want independent copies of an object, the VM manager places only one shared copy into physical memory, but the VM manager sets the copy-on-write property on that region of memory. If one of the processes tries to modify data in a copy-on-write page, the VM manager first makes a private copy of the page for that process to use.

The virtual address translation in NT uses several data structures. Each process has a **page directory** that contains 1,024 **page-directory entries** of size 4 bytes. Typically the page directory is private, but it could be shared among processes if the environment required. Each page-directory entry points to a **page table** that contains 1,024 **page-table entries** (PTEs) of size 4 bytes. Each

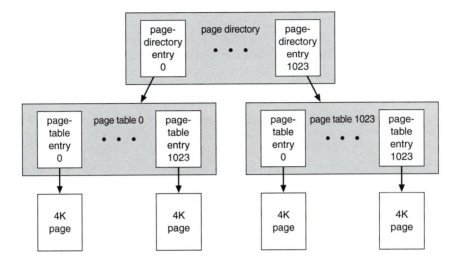

Figure 22.3 Virtual-memory layout.

PTE points to a 4-kilobyte **page frame** in physical memory. The total size of all the page tables for a process is 4 megabytes, so the VM manager will swap out these tables to disk when necessary. See Figure 22.3 for a diagram of this structure.

A 10-bit integer can represent all the values from 0 to 1023. Thus, a 10-bit integer can select any entry in the page directory, or in a page table. This property is used when a virtual-address pointer is translated to a byte address in physical memory. A 32-bit virtual-memory address is split into three integers, as shown in Figure 22.4. The first 10 bits of the virtual address are used as a subscript in the page directory. This address selects one page-directory entry, which points to a page table. The next 10 bits of the virtual address are used to select a PTE from that page table. The PTE points to a page frame in physical memory. The remaining 12 bits of the virtual address point to a specific byte in that page frame. A pointer to that specific byte in physical memory is made by concatenating 20 bits from the PTE with the lower 12 bits from the virtual address. Thus, the 32-bit PTE has 12 bits left over; these bits are used to describe the page. The first 5 bits specify the page protection, such

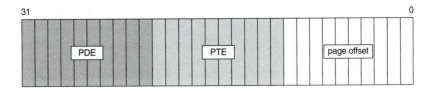

Figure 22.4 Virtual-to-physical address translation.

as PAGE_READONLY or PAGE_READWRITE. The next 4 bits specify which paging file backs the page of memory. The final 3 bits specify the state of the page in memory. For more general information on paging schemes, see Section 9.4.

A page can be in one of six states: valid, zeroed, free, standby, modified, and bad. A **valid page** is in use by an active process. A **free page** is a page that is not referenced in a PTE. A **zeroed page** is a free page that has been zeroed out and is ready for immediate use. A **standby page** has been removed from the working set of a process. A **modified page** has been written to, but not yet flushed to disk. The final page type is the **bad page**; it is unusable because a hardware error has been detected.

The actual structure of the PTE is shown in Figure 22.5. The PTE contains 5 bits for page protection, 20 bits for page-frame address, 4 bits to select a paging file, and 3 bits that describe the page state. If the page is not in memory, the 20 bits of page-frame address hold an offset into the paging file, instead. Since executable code and memory-mapped files already have a copy on disk, they do not need space in a paging file. If one of these pages is not in physical memory, the PTE structure is as follows: The most significant bit is used to specify the page protection, the next 28 bits are used to index into a system data structure that indicates a file and offset within the file for the page, and the lower 3 bits specify the page state.

It is difficult to share a page between processes if every process has its own set of page tables, because each process will have its own PTE for the page frame. When a shared page is faulted in to physical memory, the physical address will have to be stored in the PTEs belonging to each process sharing the page. The protection bits and page state bits in these PTEs will all need to be set and updated consistently. To avoid these problems, NT uses indirection. For every page that is shared, the process has a PTE that points to a **prototype page-table entry,** rather than to the page frame. The prototype PTE contains the page-frame address and the protection and state bits. Thus, the first access by a process to a shared page generates a page fault. After the first access, further accesses are performed in the normal manner. If the page is marked read only, the VM manager does a copy-on-write and the process effectively does not have

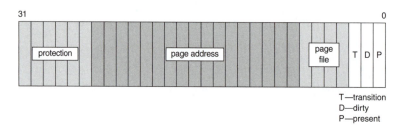

Figure 22.5   Standard page-table entry.

a shared page any longer. Shared pages never appear in the pagefile, but are instead found in the filesystem.

The VM manager keeps track of all pages of physical memory in a **page-frame database**. There is one entry for every page frame. The entry points to the PTE that points to the page frame, so the VM manager can maintain the state of the page. Page frames are linked to form (for instance) the list of zeroed pages, and the list of free pages.

When a page fault occurs, the VM manager faults in the missing page, placing that page into the first frame on the free list. But it does not stop there. Research shows that the memory referencing of a thread tends to have a property termed **locality:** When a page is used, it is likely that adjacent pages will be referenced in the near future. (Think of iterating over an array, or fetching sequential instructions that form the executable code for a thread.) Because of locality, when the VM manager faults in a page, it also faults in a few adjacent pages. This **adjacent faulting** tends to reduce the total number of page faults. For more information on locality, see Section 10.5.1.

If no page frames are available on the free list, NT uses a per-process FIFO replacement policy to take pages from processes that are using more than their minimum working-set size. NT monitors the page faulting of each process that is at its minimum working-set size, and adjusts the working-set size accordingly. In particular, when a process is started under NT, it is assigned a default working-set size of 30 pages. NT periodically tests this size by stealing a valid page from the process. If the process continues executing without generating a page fault for the stolen page, the working-set of the process is reduced by 1, and the page is added to the list of free pages.

22.4.4 Process Manager

The NT process manager provides services for creating, deleting, and using threads and processes. It has no knowledge about parent–child relationships or process hierarchies—those refinements are left to the particular environmental subsystem that owns the process.

An example of process creation in the Win32 environment is as follows. When a Win32 application calls `CreateProcess`, a message is sent to the Win32 subsystem, which calls the process manager to create a process. The process manager calls the object manager to create a process object, and then returns the object handle to Win32. Win32 calls the process manager again to create a thread for the process, and finally Win32 returns handles to the new process and thread.

22.4.5 Local-Procedure-Call Facility

The **local-procedure-call** (**LPC**) facility is used to pass requests and results between client and server processes within a single machine. In particular, it is used to request services from the various NT subsystems. It is similar in many respects to the remote-procedure-call (RPC) mechanisms that are used by many operating systems for distributed processing across networks, but LPC is optimized for use within one NT system.

LPC is a message-passing mechanism. The server process publishes a globally visible connection-port object. When a client wants services from a subsystem, it opens a handle to the subsystem's connection-port object, and then sends a connection request to that port. The server creates a channel and returns a handle to the client. The channel consists of a pair of private communication ports: one for client-to-server messages, and the other for server-to-client messages. Communication channels support a callback mechanism, so the client and server can accept requests when they would normally be expecting a reply.

When an LPC channel is created, one of three types of message-passing techniques must be specified. The first type is suitable for small (up to 256-byte) messages. In this case, the port's message queue is used as intermediate storage, and the messages are copied from one process to the other. The second type is for larger messages. In this case, a shared-memory section object is created for the channel. Messages sent through the port's message queue contain a pointer and size information that refer to the section object. Thus, the need to copy large messages is avoided: The sender places data into the shared section, and the receiver can view them directly.

The third method of LPC message passing, called **quick LPC**, is used by graphical display portions of the Win32 subsystem. When a client asks for a connection that will use quick LPC, the server sets up three objects: a dedicated server thread to handle requests, a 64-kilobyte section object, and an event-pair object. An **event-pair object** is a synchronization object that is used by the Win32 subsystem to provide notification when the client thread has copied a message to the Win32 server, or vice versa. LPC messages are passed in the section object, and synchronization is performed by the event-pair object. The section object eliminates message copying, since it represents a region of shared memory. Using the event-pair object for synchronization eliminates the overhead of using the port object to pass messages containing pointers and lengths. The dedicated server thread eliminates the overhead of determining which client thread is calling the server, since there is one server thread per client thread. Also, the kernel gives scheduling preference to these dedicated server threads to improve performance further. The drawback is that quick LPC uses more resources than do the other two methods, so the Win32 subsystem uses quick LPC for only the window-manager and graphics-device interfaces.

22.4.6 I/O Manager

The **I/O manager** is responsible for file systems, cache management, device drivers, and network drivers. It keeps track of which installable file systems are loaded, and manages buffers for I/O requests. It works with the VM manager to provide memory-mapped file I/O, and controls the NT cache manager, which handles caching for the entire I/O system. The I/O manager supports both synchronous and asynchronous operations, provides timeouts for drivers, and has mechanisms for one driver to call another.

The I/O manager converts the requests that it receives into a standard form called an **I/O request packet** (**IRP**). It then forwards the IRP to the correct driver for processing. When the operation is finished, the I/O manager receives the IRP from the driver that most recently performed an operation, and completes the request.

In many operating systems, caching is done by the file system. NT provides a centralized caching facility, instead. The cache manager provides cache services for all components under the control of the I/O manager, and works closely with the VM manager. The size of the cache changes dynamically, according to how much free memory is available in the system. Recall that the upper 2 gigabytes of a process's address space is the system area; it is identical for all processes. The VM manager allocates up to one-half of this space to the system cache. The cache manager maps files into this address space, and uses the capabilities of the VM manager to handle file I/O.

The cache is divided into blocks of 256 kilobytes. Each cache block can hold a view (that is, a memory-mapped region) of a file. Each cache block is described by a **virtual-address control block** (**VACB**) that stores the virtual address and file offset for that view, and also the number of processes that are using the view. The VACBs reside in a single array that is maintained by the cache manager.

For each open file, the cache manager maintains a separate VACB index array. This array has an element for each 256-kilobyte chunk of the file; so, for instance, a 2-megabyte file would have an 8-entry VACB index array. An entry in the VACB index array points to the VACB if that portion of the file is in the cache; it is null otherwise.

When it receives a user-level read request, the I/O manager sends an IRP to the cache manager (unless the request specifically asks for a noncached read). The cache manager calculates which entry of that file's VACB index array corresponds to the byte offset of the request. The entry either points to the view in the cache, or is null. If it is null, the cache manager allocates a cache block (and the corresponding entry in the VACB array), and maps the view into that cache block. The cache manager then attempts to copy data from the mapped file to the caller's buffer. If the copy succeeds, the operation is completed. If the copy fails, it does so because of a page fault, which causes the VM manager to send a noncached read request to the I/O manager. The I/O manager asks the appropriate device driver to read the data, and returns the data to the VM manager, which loads the data into the cache. The data, now in the cache, are copied to the caller's buffer, and the I/O request completes. Figure 22.6 shows how this operation proceeds.

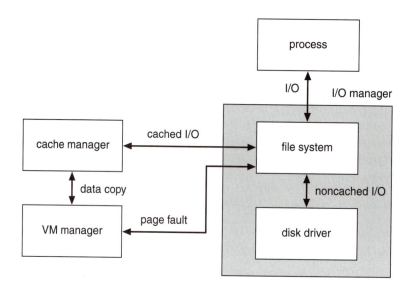

Figure 22.6   File I/O.

A kernel-level read operation is similar, except that the data can be accessed directly from the cache, rather than being copied to a buffer in user space. To use file-system **metadata**, or data structures that describe the file system, the kernel uses the cache manager's mapping interface to read the metadata. To modify the metadata, the file system uses the cache manager's pinning interface. **Pinning** a page locks the page into a physical-memory page frame, so the VM manager cannot move or swap out the page. After updating the metadata, the file system asks the cache manager to unpin the page. Since the page has been modified, it is marked dirty, so the VM manager will flush the page to disk.

To improve performance, the cache manager keeps a small history of read requests, and attempts to predict future requests. If the cache manager can find a pattern in the previous three requests, such as sequential access forward or backward, it can prefetch data into the cache before the next request is submitted by the application. Then, the application may find its data already in the cache, and may not need to wait for disk I/O. The Win32 API OpenFile and CreateFile functions can be passed the FILE_FLAG_SEQUENTIAL_SCAN flag, which is a hint to the cache manager to try to prefetch 192 kilobytes ahead of the thread's requests. Typically, NT performs I/O operations in chunks of 64 kilobytes or 16 pages; thus, this readahead is three times the normal amount.

The cache manager is also responsible for telling the VM manager to flush the contents of the cache. The cache manager's default behavior is write-back caching. The cache manager accumulates writes for 4 to 5 seconds, and then the writer thread wakes up. When write-through caching is needed, a process can set a flag when opening the file, or the process can call an explicit cache-flush function when needed.

A fast-writing process could potentially fill all the free cache pages before the cache-writer thread has a chance to wake up and to flush the pages to disk. To prevent a process from flooding the system in this way, when the amount of free cache memory gets low, the cache manager temporarily blocks processes that attempt to write data, and wakes the cache-writer thread to flush pages to disk. If the fast-writing process is actually a network redirector for a network file system, blocking it for too long could cause network transfers to time out and be retransmitted. This retransmission would waste network bandwidth. To prevent this waste, network redirectors can tell the cache manager not to let a large backlog of writes accumulate in the cache.

Because a network file system needs to move data between a disk and the network interface, the cache manager also provides a DMA interface to move the data directly. Moving data directly avoids copying data through an intermediate buffer.

22.4.7 Security Reference Monitor

The object-oriented nature of NT enables the use of a uniform mechanism to perform run-time access validation and audit checks for every entity in the system. Whenever a process opens a handle to an object, the security reference monitor checks the process's security token and the object's access-control list to see whether the process has the necessary rights.

22.5 ■ Environmental Subsystems

Environmental subsystems are user-mode processes layered over the native NT executive services to enable NT to run programs developed for other operating systems, including 16-bit Windows, MS-DOS, POSIX, and character-based applications for 16-bit OS/2. Each environmental subsystem provides one API or application environment.

NT uses the Win32 subsystem as the main operating environment, and Win32 is used to start all processes. When an application is executed, the Win32 subsystem calls the VM manager to load the application's executable code. The memory manager returns a status to Win32 that tells what kind of executable it is. If it is not a native Win32 executable, the Win32 environment checks whether the appropriate environmental subsystem is running; if the subsystem is not running, it is started as a user-mode process. Then, Win32 creates a process to run the application, and passes control to the environmental subsystem.

The environmental subsystem uses the NT local-procedure call facility to get kernel services for the process. This utilization helps NT to be robust, because the parameters passed to a system call can be checked for correctness before the actual kernel routine is invoked. NT prohibits applications from mixing API routines from different environments. For instance, a Win32 application cannot call a POSIX routine.

Since each subsystem is run as a separate user-mode process, a crash in one has no effect on the others. The exception is Win32, which provides all the keyboard, mouse, and graphical display capabilities. If it fails, the system is effectively disabled.

Win32 categorizes applications as either graphical or character based, where a character-based application is one that thinks that interactive output goes to an 80 by 24 ASCII display. Win32 transforms the output of a character-based application to a graphical representation in a window. This transformation is easy: Whenever an output routine is called, the environmental subsystem calls a Win32 routine to display the text. Since the Win32 environment performs this function for all character-based windows, it can transfer screen text between windows via the clipboard. This transformation works for MS-DOS applications, as well as for POSIX command-line applications.

22.5.1 MS-DOS Environment

MS-DOS does not have the complexity of the other NT environmental subsystems. It is provided by a Win32 application called the **virtual DOS machine** (**VDM**). Since the VDM is just a user-mode process, it is paged and dispatched like any other NT thread. The VDM has an **instruction-execution unit** to execute or emulate Intel 486 instructions. It also provides routines to emulate the MS-DOS ROM BIOS and "int 21" software-interrupt services, and has virtual device drivers for the screen, keyboard, and communication ports. The VDM is based on the MS-DOS 5.0 source code and gives the application at least 620 KB of memory.

The NT command shell is a program that creates a window that looks like an MS-DOS environment. It can run both 16-bit and 32-bit executables. When an MS-DOS application is run, the command shell starts a VDM process to execute the program.

If NT is running on an 80X86 processor, MS-DOS graphical applications run in full-screen mode, and character applications can run full screen or in a window. If NT is running on a different processor architecture, all MS-DOS applications run in windows. Some MS-DOS applications access the disk hardware directly, but they fail to run on NT because disk access is privileged to protect the file system. In general, MS-DOS applications that directly access hardware will fail to operate under NT.

Since MS-DOS is not a multitasking environment, some applications have been written that hog the CPU—for instance, by using busy loops to cause time delays or pauses in execution. The priority mechanism in the NT dispatcher detects such delays and automatically throttles the CPU consumption (and causes the offending application to operate incorrectly).

22.5.2 16-Bit Windows Environment

The Win16 execution environment is provided by a VDM that incorporates additional software called **Windows on Windows** that provides the Windows 3.1 kernel routines and stub routines for window manager and GDI functions. The stub routines call the appropriate Win32 subroutines, converting or **thunking** 16-bit addresses into 32-bit ones. Applications that rely on the internal structure of the 16-bit window manager or GDI may not work, because Windows on Windows does not really implement the 16-bit API.

Windows on Windows can multitask with other processes on NT, but it resembles Windows 3.1 in many ways. Only one Win16 application can run at a time, all applications are single threaded and reside in the same address space, and they all share the same input queue. These features imply that an application that stops receiving input will block all the other Win16 applications, just like in Windows 3.x, and one Win16 application can crash other Win16 applications by corrupting the address space.

22.5.3 Win32 Environment

The main subsystem in NT is the Win32 subsystem. It runs Win32 applications, and manages all keyboard, mouse, and screen I/O. Since it is the controlling environment, it is designed to be extremely robust. Several features of Win32 contribute to this robustness. Unlike the Win16 environment, each Win32 process has its own input queue. The window manager dispatches all input on the system to the appropriate process's input queue, so a failed process will not block input to other processes. The NT kernel also provides preemptive multitasking, which enables the user to terminate applications that have failed or are no longer needed. Win32 also validates all objects before using them, to prevent crashes that could otherwise occur if an application tried to use an invalid or wrong handle. The Win32 subsystem verifies the type of the object to which a handle points before using that object. The reference counts kept by the object manager prevent objects from being deleted while they are still being used, and prevent their use after they have been deleted.

22.5.4 POSIX Subsystem

The POSIX subsystem is designed to run POSIX applications following the POSIX.1 standard, which is based on the UNIX model. POSIX applications can be started by the Win32 subsystem or by another POSIX application. POSIX applications use the POSIX subsystem server PSXSS.EXE, the POSIX dynamic link library PSXDLL.DLL, and the POSIX console session manager POSIX.EXE.

Although the POSIX standard does not specify printing, POSIX applications can use printers transparently via the NT redirection mechanism. POSIX applications have access to any file system on the NT system; the POSIX environment enforces UNIX-like permissions on directory trees. Several Win32 facilities are not supported by the POSIX subsystem, including memory-mapped files, networking, graphics, and dynamic data exchange.

22.5.5 OS/2 Subsystem

Although NT was originally intended to provide a robust OS/2 operating environment, the success of Microsoft Windows led to a change, during the early development of NT: The Windows environment became the default. Consequently, NT provides only limited facilities in the OS/2 environmental subsystem. OS/2 1.x character-based applications can run on only NT on Intel 80X86 computers. Real-mode OS/2 applications can run on all platforms by using the MS-DOS environment. Bound applications, which are applications that have dual code for both MS-DOS and OS/2, run in the OS/2 environment unless the OS/2 environment is disabled.

22.5.6 Logon and Security Subsystems

Before a user can access objects on NT, that user must be authenticated by the logon subsystem. To be authenticated, a user must have an account and must provide the password for that account.

The security subsystem generates access tokens to represent users on the system. It calls an **authentication package** to perform authentication using information from the logon subsystem or network server. Typically, the authentication package simply looks up the account information in a local database and checks to see that the password is correct. The security subsystem then generates the access token for the user id containing the appropriate privileges, quota limits, and group ids. Whenever the user attempts to access an object in the system, such as by opening a handle to the object, the access token is passed to the security reference monitor, which checks privileges and quotas.

22.6 ■ File System

Historically, MS-DOS systems have used the **file-allocation table** (FAT) file system. The 16-bit FAT file system has several shortcomings, including internal fragmentation, a size limitation of 2 gigabytes, and a lack of access protection for files. The 32-bit FAT file system has solved the size and fragmentation problems, but the performance and features are still weak by comparison with modern file systems. The NTFS is much better. It was designed with many features, including data recovery, security, fault tolerance, large files and file systems, multiple data streams, UNICODE names, and file compression. For compatibility, NT provides support for the FAT and OS/2 HPFS file systems.

22.6.1 Internal Layout

The fundamental entity in NTFS is a **volume**. A volume is created by the NT disk-administrator utility, and is based on a logical disk partition. The volume may occupy a portion of a disk, may occupy an entire disk, or may span across several disks. In NTFS, all metadata—such as information about the volume—are stored in a regular file.

NTFS does not deal with individual sectors of a disk, but instead uses **clusters** as the unit of disk allocation. A cluster is a number of disk sectors that is a power of 2. The cluster size is configured when an NTFS file system is formatted. The default cluster size is the sector size for volumes up to 512 MB, 1 kilobyte for volumes up to 1 gigabyte, 2 kilobyte for volumes up to 2 gigabyte, and 4 kilobyte for larger volumes. This cluster size is much smaller than that for the 16-bit FAT file system, and the small size reduces the amount of internal fragmentation. As an example, consider a 1.6-gigabyte disk with 16,000 files. If you use a FAT-16 file system, 400 megabytes may be lost to internal fragmentation because the cluster size is 32 kilobytes. Under NTFS, only 17 megabytes would be lost when the same files are stored.

NTFS uses **logical cluster numbers** (**LCNs**) as disk addresses. It assigns them by numbering clusters from the beginning of the disk to the end. Using this scheme, the system can calculate a physical disk offset (in bytes) by multiplying the LCN by the cluster size.

A file in NTFS is not a simple byte stream, as it is in MS-DOS or UNIX; rather, it is a structured object consisting of **attributes**. Each attribute of a file is an independent byte stream that can be created, deleted, read, and written. Some attributes are standard for all files, including the file name (or names, if the file has aliases), the creation time, and the security descriptor that specifies access control. Other attributes are specific to certain kinds of files. For instance, Macintosh files have two data attributes: the resource fork and the data fork. A directory has attributes that implement an index for the file names in the directory. Most traditional data files have an *unnamed* data attribute that contains all that file's data. Some attributes are small, and others are large.

Every file in NTFS is described by one or more records in an array stored in a special file called the **master file table** (**MFT**). The size of a record is determined when the file system is created; it ranges from 1 to 4 kilobytes. Small attributes are stored in the MFT record itself, and are called **resident attributes**. Large attributes, such as the unnamed bulk data, called **nonresident attributes,** are stored in one or more contiguous **extents** on the disk, and a pointer to each extent is stored in the MFT record. For a tiny file, even the data attribute may fit inside the MFT record. If a file has many attributes, or if it is highly fragmented and therefore many pointers are needed to point to all the fragments, one record in the MFT might not be large enough. In this case, the file is described by a record called the **base file record,** which contains pointers to overflow records that hold the additional pointers and attributes.

Each file in an NTFS volume has a unique ID called a **file reference**. The file reference is a 64-bit quantity that consists of a 48-bit file number and a 16-bit sequence number. The file number is the record number (that is, the array slot) in the MFT that describes the file. The sequence number is incremented every time that an MFT entry is reused. This incrementation enables NTFS to perform internal consistency checks, such as catching a stale reference to a deleted file after the MFT entry has been reused for a new file.

As in MS-DOS and UNIX, the NTFS name space is organized as a hierarchy of directories. Each directory uses a data structure called a *B+ tree* to store an index of the file names in that directory. A B+ tree is used because it eliminates the cost of reorganizing the tree and has the property that the length of every path from the root of the tree to a leaf is the same. The **index root** of a directory contains the top level of the B+ tree. For a large directory, this top level contains pointers to disk extents that hold the remainder of the tree. Each entry in the directory contains the name and file reference of the file, and also a copy of the update timestamp and file size taken from the file's resident attributes in the MFT. Copies of this information are stored in the directory, so it is efficient to generate a directory listing—all the file names, sizes, and update times are available from the directory itself, so there is no need to gather these attributes from the MFT entries for each of the files.

The NTFS volume's metadata are all stored in files. The first file is the MFT. The second file, which is used during recovery if the MFT is damaged, contains a copy of the first 16 entries of the MFT. The next few files are also special. They are called the log file, volume file, attribute-definition table, root directory, bitmap file, boot file, and bad-cluster file. The *log file*, described in Section 22.6.2, records all metadata updates to the file system. The *volume file* contains the name of the volume, the version of NTFS that formatted the volume, and a bit that tells whether the volume may have been corrupted and needs to be checked for consistency. The *attribute-definition table* indicates which attribute types are used in the volume, and what operations can be performed on each of them. The *root directory* is the top level directory in the file-system hierarchy. The *bitmap file* indicates which clusters on a volume are allocated to files, and which are free. The *boot file* contains the startup code for NT and must be located at a particular disk address so that it can be found easily by a simple ROM bootstrap loader. The boot file also contains the physical address of the MFT. Finally, the *bad-cluster file* keeps track of any bad areas on the volume that NTFS uses for error recovery.

22.6.2 Recovery

In many simple file systems, a power failure at the wrong time can damage the file-system data structures so severely that the entire volume is scrambled. Many versions of UNIX store redundant metadata on the disk, and recover from crashes using the fsck program to check all the file-system data structures, and to restore them forcibly to a consistent state. Restoring them often involves deleting damaged files and freeing data clusters that had been written with user data but have not been properly recorded in the file system's metadata structures. This checking can be a slow process, and can lose significant numbers of data.

NTFS takes a different approach to file-system robustness. In NTFS, all file-system data-structure updates are performed inside **transactions**. Before a data structure is altered, the transaction writes a log record that contains redo and undo information; after the data structure has been changed, a commit record is written to the log to signify that the transaction succeeded. After a crash, the system can restore the file-system data structures to a consistent state by processing the log records, first redoing the operations for committed transactions, then undoing the operations for transactions that did not commit successfully before the crash. Periodically (usually every 5 seconds), a checkpoint record is written to the log. The system does not need log records prior to the checkpoint to recover from a crash. They can be discarded, so the log file does not grow without bound. The first time that an NTFS volume is accessed after system startup, NTFS automatically performs file-system recovery.

This scheme does not guarantee that all the user-file contents are correct after a crash; it ensures only that the file-system data structures (the metadata files) are undamaged and reflect some consistent state prior to the crash. It would be possible to extend the transaction scheme to cover user files, but the overhead would impair the file-system performance.

The log is stored in the third metadata file at the beginning of the volume. It is created with a fixed maximum size when the file system is formatted. It has two sections: the *logging area*, which is a circular queue of log records, and the *restart area*, which holds context information, such as the position in the logging area where NTFS should start reading during a recovery. In fact, the restart area holds two copies of its information, so recovery is still possible if one copy is damaged during the crash.

The logging functionality is provided by the NT **log-file service**. In addition to writing the log records and performing recovery actions, the log-file service keeps track of the free space in the log file. If the free space gets too low, the log-file service queues pending transactions, and NTFS halts all new I/O operations. After the in-progress operations complete, NTFS calls the cache manager to flush all data, then resets the log file and performs the queued transactions.

22.6.3 Security

Security of an NTFS volume is derived from the NT object model. Each file object has a security-descriptor attribute stored in its MFT record. This attribute contains the access token of the owner of the file, and an access-control list that states the access privileges that are granted to each user that has access to the file.

22.6.4 Volume Management and Fault Tolerance

FtDisk is the fault-tolerant disk driver for NT. When installed, it provides several ways to combine multiple disk drives into one logical volume, to improve performance, capacity, or reliability.

One way to combine multiple disks is to concatenate them logically to form a large logical volume, as shown in Figure 22.7. In NT, this logical volume is called a **volume set;** it can consist of up to 32 physical partitions. A volume set that contains an NTFS volume can be extended without the data already stored in the file system being disturbed. The bitmap metadata on the NTFS volume are simply extended to cover the newly added space. NTFS continues to use the same LCN mechanism that it uses for a single physical disk, and the FtDisk driver supplies the mapping from a logical volume offset to the offset on one particular disk.

Another way to combine multiple physical partitions is to interleave their blocks in round-robin fashion to form what is called a **stripe set,** as shown in Figure 22.8. This scheme is also called **RAID level 0,** or **disk striping**. FtDisk uses a stripe size of 64 kilobytes: The first 64 kilobytes of the logical volume are stored in the first physical partition, the second 64 kilobytes of the logical volume are stored in the second physical partition, and so on, until each partition has contributed 64 kilobytes of space. Then, the allocation wraps around to the first disk, allocating the second 64-kilobyte block. A stripe set

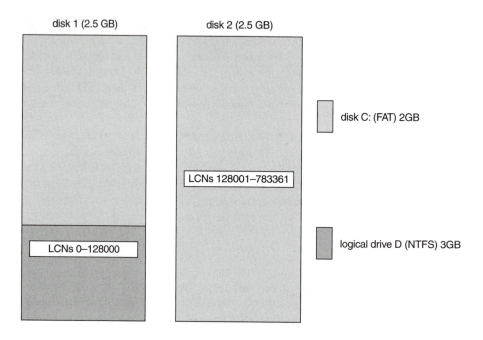

Figure 22.7   Volume set on two drives.

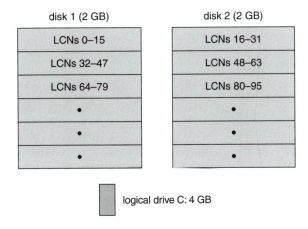

Figure 22.8   Stripe set on two drives.

forms one large logical volume, but the physical layout can improve the I/O
bandwidth, because, for a large I/O, all the disks can transfer data in parallel.

A variation of this idea is the **stripe set with parity,** which is shown in
Figure 22.9. This scheme is also called **RAIDlevel 5**. If the stripe set has eight
disks, then for each seven data stripes, on seven separate disks, there will be
a parity stripe on the eighth disk. The parity stripe contains the byte-wise
`exclusive or` of the data stripes. If any one of the eight stripes is destroyed,
the system can reconstruct the data by calculating the `exclusive or` of the
remaining seven. This ability to reconstruct data makes the disk array much
less likely to lose data in case of a disk failure. Notice that an update to one data

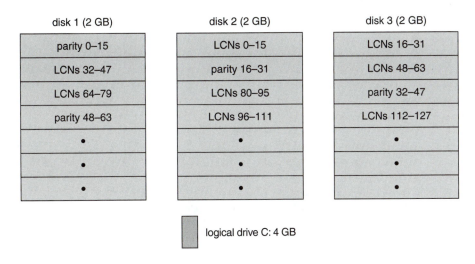

Figure 22.9   Stripe set with parity on three drives.

stripe also requires recalculation of the parity stripe. Seven concurrent writes to seven different data stripes thus would also require seven parity stripes to be updated. If the parity stripes were all on the same disk, that disk could have seven times the I/O load of the data disks. To avoid creating this bottleneck, we spread the parity stripes over all the disks, such as by assigning them round-robin. To build a stripe set with parity, we need a minimum of three equal-sized partitions located on three separate disks.

An even more robust scheme is **disk mirroring,** or **RAID level 1**; it is depicted in Figure 22.10. A **mirror set** comprises two equal-sized partitions on two disks, such that their data contents are identical. When an application writes data to a mirror set, FtDisk writes the data to both partitions. If one partition fails, FtDisk has another copy safely stored on the mirror. Mirror sets can also improve the performance, because read requests can be split between the two mirrors, giving each mirror one-half of the workload. To protect against the failure of a disk controller, we can attach the two disks of a mirror set to two separate disk controllers. This arrangement is called a **duplex set**.

To deal with disk sectors that go bad, FtDisk uses a hardware technique called **sector sparing,** and NTFS uses a software technique called **cluster remapping**. Sector sparing is a hardware capability provided by many disk drives. When a disk drive is formatted, it creates a map from logical block numbers to good sectors on the disk. It also leaves extra sectors unmapped, as spares. If a sector fails, FtDisk will instruct the disk drive to substitute a spare. Cluster remapping is a software technique performed by the file system. If a disk block

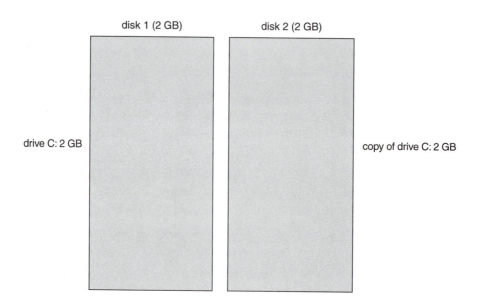

Figure 22.10   Mirror set on two drives.

goes bad, NTFS will substitute a different, unallocated block by changing any affected pointers in the MFT. NTFS also makes a note that the bad block should never be allocated to any file.

When a disk block goes bad, the usual outcome is a data loss. But sector sparing or cluster remapping can be combined with fault-tolerant volumes such as stripe sets to mask the failure of a disk block. If a read fails, the system reconstructs the missing data by reading the mirror or by calculating the exclusive or parity in a stripe set with parity. The reconstructed data are stored into a new location that is obtained by sector sparing or cluster remapping.

22.6.5 Compression

NTFS can perform data compression on individual files or on all data files in a directory. To compress a file, NTFS divides the file's data into **compression units,** which are blocks of 16 contiguous clusters. When each compression unit is written, a data-compression algorithm is applied. If the result fits into fewer than 16 clusters, the compressed version is stored. When reading, NTFS can determine whether data have been compressed, because if they have been then the length of the stored compression unit is less than 16 clusters. To improve performance when reading contiguous compression units, NTFS prefetches and decompresses ahead of the application requests.

For **sparse files,** or files that mostly contain zeros, NTFS uses another technique to save space. Clusters that contain all zeros are not allocated or stored on disk. Instead, gaps are left in the sequence of virtual-cluster numbers stored in the MFT entry for the file. When it is reading a file, if it finds a gap in the virtual-cluster numbers, NTFS just zero-fills that portion of the caller's buffer. This technique is also used by UNIX.

22.7 ■ Networking

NT supports both peer-to-peer and client–server networking. It also has facilities for network management. The networking components in NT provide data transport, interprocess communication, file sharing across a network, and the ability to send print jobs to remote printers.

NT supports many protocols that are used in computer networking; they are described in Section 22.7.1. In Section 22.7.2, we discuss the distributed-processing mechanisms of NT. A **redirector** in NT is an object that provides a uniform interface for files, whether they are local or remote; it is discussed in Section 22.7.3. A **domain** is a group of NT server machines that share a common security policy and user database, as described in Section 22.7.4. Finally, NT has mechanisms for **name resolution** that enable one computer to look up the address of another computer, given that other computer's name; Section 22.7.5 explains how these mechanisms work.

To describe networking in NT, we refer to two of the internal networking interfaces, called the **Network Device Interface Specification** (**NDIS**) and the **Transport Driver Interface** (**TDI**). The NDIS interface was developed in 1989 by Microsoft and 3Com to separate network adapters from the transport protocols so that either could be changed without the other being affected. NDIS resides at the interface between the data-link and media-access control layers in the OSI model and enables many protocols to operate over many different network adapters. In terms of the OSI model, the TDI is the interface between the transport layer (layer 4) and the session layer (layer 5). This interface enables any session-layer component to use any available transport mechanism. (Similar reasoning led to the **streams** mechanism in UNIX.) The TDI supports both connection-based and connectionless transport, and has functions to send any type of data.

22.7.1 Protocols

NT implements transport protocols as drivers. These drivers can be loaded and unloaded from the system dynamically, although in practice the system typically has to be rebooted after a change. NT comes with several networking protocols.

The **server message-block** (**SMB**) protocol was first introduced in MS-DOS 3.1. The protocol, which sends I/O requests over the network, has four message types. The `Session-control` messages are commands that start and end a redirector connection to a shared resource at the server. The `File` messages are used by a redirector to access files at the server. The `Printer` messages send data to a remote print queue and receive back status information. The `Message` message communicates with another workstation.

The **Network Basic Input/Output System** (**NetBIOS**) is a hardware-abstraction interface for networks, analogous to the BIOS hardware-abstraction interface devised for PCs running MS-DOS. NetBIOS was developed in the early 1980s, and has become a standard network-programming interface. NetBIOS establishes logical names on the network, establishes logical connections or **sessions** between two logical names on the network, and supports reliable data transfer for a session via either NetBIOS or SMB requests.

The **NetBIOS Extended User Interface** (**NetBEUI**) was introduced by IBM in 1985 as a simple, efficient networking protocol for up to 254 machines. It is the default protocol for Windows 95 peer networking and for Windows for Workgroups. NT uses NetBEUI to share resources with these networks. Among the limitations of NetBEUI are that it uses the actual name of a computer as the address, and that it does not support routing.

The TCP/IP protocol suite that is used on the Internet has become the de facto standard networking infrastructure, and is widely supported. Windows NT uses TCP/IP to connect to a wide variety of operating systems and hardware platforms. The NT TCP/IP package includes the simple network-management protocol (SNMP), dynamic host-configuration protocol (DHCP), Windows Internet name service (WINS), and NetBIOS support.

The *point-to-point tunneling protocol (PPTP)* is a new protocol provided by Windows NT 4.0 to communicate between remote-access server modules running on NT machines that are connected over the Internet. The remote-access servers can encrypt data sent over the connection, and they support multiprotocol virtual private networks over the Internet.

The Novell NetWare protocols (IPX datagram service on the SPX transport layer) are widely used for PC local-area networks. The NT NWLink protocol connects the NetBIOS to NetWare networks. In combination with a redirector, such as Microsoft's Client Service for Netware or Novell's NetWare Client for Windows NT, this protocol enables an NT client to connect to a NetWare server.

The *data-link control (DLC) protocol* accesses IBM mainframes and HP printers that are connected directly to the network. It is not otherwise used by NT systems.

The *AppleTalk protocol* was designed as a low-cost connection by Apple so that Macintosh computers could share files. NT systems can share files and printers with Macintosh computers via AppleTalk if an NT server on the network is running the Windows NT Services for Macintosh package.

22.7.2 Distributed-Processing Mechanisms

Although NT is not a distributed operating system, it does support distributed applications. Mechanisms that support distributed processing on NT include NetBIOS, named pipes and mailslots, windows sockets, remote procedure calls (RPCs), and network dynamic data exchange (NetDDE).

In NT, NetBIOS applications can communicate over the network using Net-BEUI, NWLink, or TCP/IP.

Named pipes are a connection-oriented messaging mechanism. Named pipes were originally developed as a high-level interface to NetBIOS connections over the network. A process can also use named pipes to communicate with other processes on the same machine. Since named pipes are accessed through the file-system interface, the security mechanisms used for file objects also apply to named pipes.

The name of a named pipe has a format called the **uniform naming convention (UNC)**. A UNC name looks like a typical remote file name. The format of a UNC name is \\server_name\share_name\x\y\z, where the server_name identifies a server on the network; a share_name identifies any resource that is made available to network users, such as directories, files, named pipes and printers; and the \x\y\z part is a normal file path name.

Mailslots are a connectionless messaging mechanism. Mailslots are unreliable, in that a message sent to a mailslot may be lost before the intended recipient receives it. Mailslots are used for broadcast applications, such as for finding components on the network. Mailslots are also used by the NT Computer Browser service.

Winsock is the Windows sockets API. Winsock is a session-layer interface that is largely compatible with UNIX sockets, with some Windows extensions. It provides a standardized interface to many transport protocols that may have different addressing schemes, so that any Winsock application can run on any Winsock-compliant protocol stack.

A **remote procedure call** (**RPC**) is a client–server mechanism that enables an application on one machine to make a procedure call to code on another machine. The client calls a local procedure—a **stub routine**—that packs its arguments into a message and sends them across the network to a particular server process. The client-side stub routine then blocks. Meanwhile, the server unpacks the message, calls the procedure, packs the return results into a message, and sends them back to the client stub. The client stub unblocks, receives the message, unpacks the results of the RPC, and returns them to the caller. This packing of arguments is sometimes called **marshaling**.

The NT RPC mechanism follows the widely used distributed-computing environment standard for RPC messages, so programs written to use NT RPCs are highly portable. The RPC standard is detailed. It hides many of the architectural differences between computers, such as the sizes of binary numbers and the order of bytes and bits in computer words, by specifying standard data formats for RPC messages.

NT can send RPC messages using NetBIOS, or Winsock on TCP/IP networks, or named pipes on Lan Manager networks. The LPC facility, discussed in Section 22.4.5, is similar to RPC, except that the messages are passed between two processes running on the same computer.

It is tedious and error-prone to write the code to marshal and transmit arguments in the standard format, to unmarshal and execute the remote procedure, to marshal and send the return results, and to unmarshal and return them to the caller. But much of this code can be generated automatically from a simple description of the arguments and return results.

NT provides the **Microsoft Interface Definition Language** to describe the remote procedure names, arguments, and results. The compiler for this language generates header files that declare the stubs for the remote procedures, and the data types for the argument and return-value messages. It also generates source code for the stub routines used at the client side, and for an unmarshaller and dispatcher at the server side. When the application is linked, the stub routines are included. When the application executes the RPC stub, the generated code handles the rest.

Dynamic Data Exchange (*DDE*) is a mechanism for interprocess communication that was developed for Microsoft Windows. NT has an extension called *Network DDE* that can be used over a network. It communicates over a pair of one-way pipes.

22.7.3 Redirectors and Servers

In NT, an application can use the NT I/O API to access files from a remote computer as though they were local, provided that the remote computer is running an MS-NET server, such as is provided by NT or Windows for Workgroups. A **redirector** is the client-side object that forwards I/O requests to remote files, where they are satisfied by a **server**. For performance and security, the redirectors and servers run in kernel mode.

Access to a remote file occurs as follows:

- The application calls the I/O manager to request that a file be opened with a file name in the standard UNC format.

- The I/O manager builds an I/O request packet, as described in Section 22.4.6.

- The I/O manager recognizes that the access is for a remote file, and calls a driver called a multiple universal-naming-convention provider (MUP).

- The MUP sends the I/O request packet asynchronously to all registered redirectors.

- A redirector that can satisfy the request responds to the MUP. To avoid asking all the redirectors the same question in the future, the MUP uses a cache to remember which redirector can handle this file.

- The redirector sends the network request to the remote system.

- The remote-system network drivers receive the request and pass it to the server driver.

- The server driver hands the request to the proper local file-system driver.

- The proper device driver is called to access the data.

- The results are returned to the server driver, which sends the data back to the requesting redirector. The redirector then returns the data to the calling application via the I/O manager.

A similar process occurs for applications that use the Win32 network API, rather than the UNC services, but a module called a multiprovider router is used, instead of a MUP.

For portability, redirectors and servers use the TDI API for network transport. The requests themselves are expressed in a higher-level protocol, which by default is the SMB protocol mentioned in Section 22.7.1. The list of redirectors is maintained in the system registry database.

22.7.4 Domains

Many networked environments have natural groups of users, such as students in a computer laboratory at a school, or employees in one department in a business. Frequently, we want all the members of the group to be able to access shared resources on the computers in the group. To manage the global access rights within such groups, NT uses the concept of a domain. (This term has no relation to the Domain Name System that maps Internet host names to IP addresses.) Specifically, an NT *domain* is a group of NT workstations and servers that share a common security policy and user database. One server in the domain acts as the primary domain controller that maintains the security databases for the domain. Other servers in the domain can act as backup domain controllers, and can also authenticate log-in requests. The workstations in the domain trust the primary domain controller to give correct information about the access rights of each user (via the user's access token). All users retain the ability to restrict access to their own workstations, no matter what any domain controller may say.

Because a business may have many departments, and a school has many classes, it is often necessary to manage multiple domains within a single organization. NT provides four domain models to do so. In the **single-domain model,** each domain is isolated from the others. In the **master-domain model,** one designated master domain is trusted by all the other domains. It maintains a global user account database, and provides authentication services to the other domains. This model provides centralized administration of multiple domains. A master domain can support up to 40,000 users. The **multiple–master-domain model** is designed for large organizations. It has more than one master domain, and all the masters trust one another. This trust enables a user who has an account in one master domain to access resources of another master domain— the master that has an account for the user can certify the user's privileges. In the **multiple-trust model,** there is no master domain. All domains manage their own users, but they also all trust one another.

So, if a user in domain A tried to access a resource in domain B, the interaction between domain B and the user would be as follows. In the single-domain model, domain B would say "I do not know anything about you. Go away." In the master-domain model, B would say "Let me ask the master whether you have permission." In the multiple–master-domain model, B would say "Let me ask my master whether any of the other masters say you have permission." In the multiple-trust model, B would say "Let me ask to see whether any domain says you have permission."

22.7.5 Name Resolution in TCP/IP Networks

On an IP network, **name resolution** is the process of converting a computer name to an IP address, such as resolving `www.bell-labs.com` to

135.104.1.14. NT provides several methods of name resolution, including Windows Internet Name Service (WINS), broadcast name resolution, domain name system (DNS), a hosts file, and an LMHOSTS file. Most of these methods are used by many operating systems, so we describe only WINS here.

Under WINS, two or more WINS servers maintain a dynamic database of name-to-IP address bindings, and client software to query the servers. At least two servers are used, so that the WINS service can survive a server failure, and so that the name resolution workload can be spread over multiple machines.

WINS uses the dynamic host-configuration protocol (DHCP). DHCP updates address configurations automatically in the WINS database, without user or administrator intervention, as follows. When a DHCP client starts up, it broadcasts a `discover` message. Each DHCP server that receives the message replies with an `offer` message that contains an IP address and configuration information for the client. The client then chooses one of the configurations and sends a `request` message to the selected DHCP server. The DHCP server responds with the IP address and configuration information it gave previously, and with a **lease** for that address. The lease gives the client the right to use that IP address for a specified period of time. When the lease time is half expired, the client attempts to renew the lease for that address. If the lease is not renewed, the client must get a new one.

22.8 ■ Programmer Interface

The Win32 API is the fundamental interface to the capabilities of NT. This section describes five main aspects of the Win32 API: the use of kernel objects, sharing of objects between processes, process management, interprocess communication, and memory management.

22.8.1 Access to Kernel Objects

The NT kernel provides many services that application programs can use. Application programs obtain these services by manipulating kernel objects. A process gains access to a kernel object named XXX by calling the `CreateXXX` function to open a **handle** to XXX. This handle is unique to that process. Depending on which object is being opened, if the `create` function fails, it may return 0, or it may return a special constant named `INVALID_HANDLE_VALUE`. A process can close any handle by calling the `CloseHandle` function, and the system may delete the object if the count of processes using the object drops to 0.

22.8.1.1 Sharing Objects

NT provides three ways to share objects between processes. The first way is for a child process to inherit a handle to the object. When the parent calls the `CreateXXX` function, the parent supplies a `SECURITIES_ATTRIBUTES` structure

```
...
SECURITY_ATTRIBUTES sa;
sa.nlength = sizeof(sa);
sa.lpSecurityDescriptor = NULL;
sa.bInheritHandle = TRUE;
Handlea_semaphore = CreateSemaphore(&sa,1,1,NULL);
char command_line[132];
ostrstream ostring(command_line,sizeof(command_line));
ostring << a_semaphore << ends;
 CreateProcess("another_process.exe",
                command_line,NULL,NULL,TRUE, ... );
...
```

Figure 22.11   Code for a child to share an object by inheriting a handle.

with the bInheritHandle field set to TRUE. This field creates an inheritable handle. Then, the child process can be created, passing a value of TRUE to the CreateProcess function's bInheritHandle argument. Figure 22.11 shows a code sample that creates a semaphore handle that is inherited by a child process.

Assuming that the child process knows which handles are shared, the parent and child can achieve interprocess communication through the shared objects. In the example in Figure 22.11, the child process would get the value of the handle from the first command-line argument, and could then share the semaphore with the parent process.

The second way to share objects is for one process to give the object a name when that object is created, and for the second process to open that name. This method has two drawbacks. One is that NT does not provide a way to check whether an object with the chosen name already exists. A second drawback is that the object namespace is global, without regard to the object type. For instance, two applications may create an object named "pipe" when two distinct (and possibly different) objects are desired.

```
// process A
...
Handle a_semaphore = CreateSemaphore(NULL,1,1,"MySEM1");
...
// process B
...
Handle b_semaphore = OpenSemaphore(SEMAPHORE_ALL_ACCESS,FALSE,
    "MySEM1");
...
```

Figure 22.12   Code for sharing an object by name lookup.

The advantage of named objects is that unrelated processes can readily share them. The first process would call one of the CreateXXX functions and supply a name in the lpszName parameter. The second process can get a handle to share this object by calling OpenXXX (or CreateXXX) with the same name, as shown in the example of Figure 22.12.

The third way to share objects is via the DuplicateHandle function. This method requires some other method of interprocess communication to pass the duplicated handle. Given a handle to a process, and the value of a handle within that process, a second process can get a handle to the same object, and thus share it. An example of this method is shown in Figure 22.13.

22.8.2 Process Management

In NT, a **process** is an executing instance of an application, and a **thread** is a unit of code that can be scheduled by the operating system. Thus, a process contains one or more threads. A process is started when some other process calls the CreateProcess routine. This routine loads any dynamic link libraries that are used by the process, and creates a **primary thread**. Additional threads can be created by the CreateThread function. Each thread is created with its own stack, which defaults to one MB unless specified otherwise in an argument to CreateThread. Because certain C run-time functions maintain state in static variables, such as errno, a multithread application needs to guard against unsynchronized access. The wrapper function beginthreadex provides appropriate synchronization.

```
...
// process A wants to give process B access to a semaphore
// process A
Handle a_semaphore = CreateSemaphore(NULL,1,1,NULL);
// send the value of the semaphore to process B
// using a message or shared memory
...
// process B
Handle process_a = OpenProcess(PROCESS_ALL_ACCESS,FALSE,
    process_id_of_A);
Handle b_semaphore; DuplicateHandle(process_a,a_semaphore,
    GetCurrentProcess(),&b_semaphore,
    0,FALSE,DUPLICATE_SAME_ACCESS);
// use b_semaphore to access the semaphore
...
```

Figure 22.13   Code for sharing an object by passing a handle.

Every dynamic link library or executable file that is loaded into the address space of a process is identified by an **instance handle**. The value of the instance handle is actually the virtual address where the file is loaded. An application can get the handle to a module in its address space by passing the name of the module to GetModuleHandle. If NULL is passed as the name, the base address of the process is returned. The lowest 64K of the address space is not used, so a faulty program that tries to dereference a NULL pointer will get an access violation.

Priorities in the Win32 environment are based on the NT scheduling model, but not all priority values may be chosen. Win32 uses four priority classes: IDLE_PRIORITY_CLASS (priority level 4), NORMAL_PRIORITY_CLASS (level 8), HIGH_PRIORITY_CLASS (level 13) and REALTIME_PRIORITY_CLASS (level 24). Processes are typically members of the NORMAL_PRIORITY_CLASS unless the parent of the process was of the IDLE_PRIORITY_CLASS, or another class was specified when CreateProcess was called. The priority class of a process can be changed with the SetPriorityClass function, or by an argument being passed to the START command. For example, the command START /REALTIME cbserver.exe would run the cbserver program in the REAL-TIME_PRIORITY_CLASS. Note that only users with the **increase-scheduling-priority** privilege can move a process into the REALTIME_PRIORITY_CLASS. Administrators and power users have this privilege by default.

When a user is running an interactive program, the system needs to provide especially good performance for that process. For this reason, NT has a special scheduling rule for processes in the NORMAL_PRIORITY_CLASS. NT distinguishes between the **foreground process** that is currently selected on the screen, and the **background processes** that are not currently selected. When a process moves into the foreground, NT increases the scheduling quantum by a set factor— typically of 3. (This factor can be changed via the performance option in the system section of the control panel). This increase gives the foreground process three times longer to run before a timesharing preemption occurs.

A thread starts with an initial priority determined by its class, but the priority can be altered by the SetThreadPriority function. This function takes an argument that specifies a priority relative to the base priority of its class:

- THREAD_PRIORITY_LOWEST: base − 2

- THREAD_PRIORITY_BELOW_NORMAL: base − 1

- THREAD_PRIORITY_NORMAL: base + 0

- THREAD_PRIORITY_ABOVE_NORMAL: base + 1

- THREAD_PRIORITY_HIGHEST: base + 2

Two other designations also adjust the priority. Recall from Section 22.3.2 that the kernel has two priority classes: 16 to 31 for the real-time class, and 0 to 15 for the variable-priority class. THREAD_PRIORITY_IDLE sets the priority to 16 for real-time threads, and to 1 for variable-priority threads. THREAD_PRIORITY_TIME_CRITICAL sets the priority to 31 for real-time threads, and to 15 for variable-priority threads.

As we discussed in Section 22.3.2, the kernel adjusts the priority of a thread dynamically depending on whether that thread is I/O bound or CPU bound. The Win32 API provides a method to disable this adjustment, via SetProcessPriorityBoost and SetThreadPriorityBoost functions.

A thread can be created in a **suspended** state: The thread will not execute until another thread makes it eligible via the ResumeThread function. The SuspendThread function does the opposite. These functions set a counter, so if a thread is suspended twice, it must be resumed twice before it can run.

To synchronize the concurrent access to shared objects by threads, the kernel provides synchronization objects, such as semaphores and mutexes. In addition, threads can synchronize by using the WaitForSingleObject or WaitForMultipleObjects functions. Another method of synchronization in the Win32 API is the *critical section*. A critical section is a synchronized region of code that can be executed by only one thread at a time. A thread establishes a critical section by calling InitializeCriticalSection. The application must call EnterCriticalSection before the critical section, and LeaveCriticalSection after exiting the critical section. These two routines guarantee that, if multiple threads attempt to enter the critical section concurrently, only one thread at a time will be permitted to proceed, and the others will wait in the EnterCriticalSection routine. The critical-section mechanism is slightly faster than the kernel-synchronization objects.

A **fiber** is user-mode code that gets scheduled according to a user-defined scheduling algorithm. A process may have multiple fibers in it, just as it can have multiple threads. A major difference between threads and fibers is that threads can execute concurrently, but only one fiber at a time is permitted to execute, even on multiprocessor hardware. This mechanism is included in NT to facilitate the porting of those legacy UNIX applications that were written for a fiber-execution model.

The system creates a fiber by calling either ConvertThreadToFiber or CreateFiber. The primary difference between these functions is that CreateFiber does not begin executing the fiber that was created. To do that, the application must call SwitchToFiber. The application can terminate a fiber by calling DeleteFiber.

22.8.3 Interprocess Communication

One way that Win32 applications can implement interprocess communication is by sharing kernel objects. Another way is by passing messages—a particularly popular solution for Windows GUI applications.

One thread can send a message to another thread or to a window by calling `PostMessage`, `PostThreadMessage`, `SendMessage`, `SendThreadMessage`, or `SendMessageCallback`. The difference between *posting* a message and *sending* a message is that the post routines are asynchronous: They return immediately, and the calling thread does not know when the message is actually delivered. The send routines are synchronous: They block the caller until the message has been delivered and processed.

In addition to sending a message, a thread can also send data with the message. Since processes have separate address spaces, the data must be copied. The system copies them by calling `SendMessage` to send a message of type `WM_COPYDATA` with a `COPYDATASTRUCT` data structure that contains the length and address of the data to be transferred. When the message is sent, NT copies the data to a new block of memory and gives the virtual address of the new block to the receiving process.

Unlike in the 16-bit Windows environment, every Win32 thread has its own input queue from which the thread receives messages. (All input is received via messages.) This structure is more reliable than the shared input queue of 16-bit Windows, because, with separate queues, one stuck application cannot block input to the other applications. If a Win32 application does not call `GetMessage` to handle events on its input queue, the queue will fill up, and after about 5 seconds the system will mark the application as "Not Responding."

22.8.4 Memory Management

The Win32 API provides several ways for an application to use memory: virtual memory, memory-mapped files, heaps, and thread-local storage.

An application calls `VirtualAlloc` to reserve or commit virtual memory, and `VirtualFree` to decommit or release the memory. These functions enable

```
...
// allocate 16 MB at the top of our address space
void *buf = VirtualAlloc(0,0×1000000,MEM_RESERVE | MEM_TOP_DOWN,
    PAGE_READWRITE);
// commit the upper 8 MB of the allocated space
VirtualAlloc(buf + 0×800000,0×800000,MEM_COMMIT,PAGE_READWRITE);
// do some stuff with it
// decommit
VirtualFree(buf + 0×800000,0×800000,MEM_DECOMMIT);
// release all the allocated address space
VirtualFree(buf,0,MEM_RELEASE);
...
```

Figure 22.14   Code fragments for allocating virtual memory.

the application to specify the virtual address at which the memory is allocated. They operate on multiples of the memory page size, and the starting address of an allocated region must be greater than $0 \times 10,000$. Examples of these functions appear in Figure 22.14.

A process may lock some of its committed pages into physical memory by calling `VirtualLock`. The maximum number of pages that a process can lock is 30, unless the process first calls `SetProcessWorkingSetSize` to increase the minimum working set size.

Another way for an application to use memory is by memory mapping a file into its address space. Memory mapping is also a convenient way for two processes to share memory—both processes map the same file into their virtual memory. Memory mapping is a multistage process, as you can see in the example of Figure 22.15.

If a process wants to map some address space just to share a memory region with another process, no file is needed. The process can call `Create-FileMapping` with a file handle of 0xffffffff and a particular size. The resulting file-mapping object can be shared by inheritance, by name lookup, or by duplication.

A **heap** in the Win32 environment is just a region of reserved address space. When a Win32 process is initialized, it is created with a 1MB **default heap**. Since many Win32 functions use the default heap, access to the heap is synchronized so that the heap's space-allocation data structures are protected from damage by concurrent updates by multiple threads. Win32 provides several heap-

```
...
// open the file or create it if it does not exist
HANDLE hfile = CreateFile("somefile",GENERIC_READ | GENERIC_WRITE,
    FILE_SHARE_READ | FILE_SHARE_WRITE,NULL,OPEN_ALWAYS,
    FILE_ATTRIBUTE_NORMAL,
    NULL);
// create the file mapping 8 MB in size
HANDLE hmap = CreateFileMapping(hfile,PAGE_READWRITE,
    SEC_COMMIT,0,0×800000,"SHM_1");
// get a view to the space mapped
void *buf = MapViewOfFile(hmap,FILE_MAP_ALL_ACCESS,0,0,0×800000);
// do some stuff with it
// unmap the file
UnmapViewOfFile(buf);
CloseHandle(hmap);
CloseHandle(hfile);
...
```

Figure 22.15   Code fragments for memory mapping of a file.

```
// reserve a slot for a variable
DWORD var_index = TlsAlloc();
// set it to some value
TlsSetValue(var_index,10);
// get the value back
int var = TlsGetValue(var_index);
// release the index
TlsFree(var_index);
```

Figure 22.16   Code for dynamic thread-local storage.

management functions so that a process can allocate and manage a private heap. These functions are HeapCreate, HeapAlloc, HeapRealloc, HeapSize, HeapFree, and HeapDestroy. The Win32 API also provides the HeapLock and HeapUnlock functions to enable a thread to gain exclusive access to a heap. Unlike VirtualLock, these functions perform only synchronization; they do not lock pages into physical memory

Functions that rely on global or static data typically fail to work properly in a multithreaded environment. For instance, the C runtime function strtok uses a static variable to keep track of its current position while parsing a string. To execute strtok correctly, two concurrent threads must have separate "current position" variables. The thread-local storage mechanism allocates global storage on a per-thread basis. The thread-local storage mechanism provides both dynamic and static methods of creating thread-local storage. The dynamic method is illustrated by the example in Figure 22.16.

To use a thread-local static variable, so that every thread has its own private copy, the application declares the variable as follows:

__declspec(thread) DWORD cur_pos = 0;

22.9 ■ Summary

Microsoft designed NT to be an extensible, portable operating system, able to take advantage of new techniques and hardware. NT supports multiple operating environments and symmetric multiprocessing. The use of kernel objects to provide basic services, and the support for client–server computing, enable NT to support a wide variety of application environments. For instance, NT can run programs compiled for MS-DOS, Win16, Windows 95, NT, and POSIX. It provides virtual memory, integrated caching, and preemptive scheduling. NT supports a security model stronger than those of previous Microsoft operating systems, and includes internationalization features. NT runs on a wide variety of computers, so users can choose and upgrade hardware to match their budgets and performance requirements, without needing to alter the applications that they run.

■ **Exercises**

22.1 Discuss why moving the graphics code in NT from user mode to kernel mode would decrease the reliability of the system. How does this degradation of reliability violate the original design goals for NT?

22.2 The NT VM manager uses a two-stage process to allocate memory. Why is this approach beneficial?

22.3 Discuss the advantages and disadvantages of the particular page-table structure used in NT.

22.4 What is the maximum number of page faults that could occur in the access of a virtual address and of a shared virtual address? What hardware mechanism is provided by most processors to decrease these numbers?

22.5 What is the purpose of a prototype page-table entry in NT?

22.6 What steps must the cache manager take to copy data into and out of the cache?

22.7 What are the problems involved in running 16-bit Windows applications in a VDM? What are the solutions chosen by NT? What are the drawbacks of these solutions?

22.8 What changes would be needed for NT to run a process that uses a 64-bit address space?

22.9 NT has a centralized cache manager. What are the advantages and disadvantages of this cache manager?

22.10 NT uses a packet-driven I/O system. Discuss the pros and cons of the packet-driven approach to I/O.

22.11 Consider a main-memory database of 1 TB. What mechanisms in NT could you use to access it?

Bibliographical Notes

Solomon [1998] gives an overview of NT and provides considerable technical detail about the system internals and components. Custer [1994] describes the NTFS in great detail. The Microsoft Windows *NT Resource Kit: Resource Guide* [1993] gives an overview of the operation and components of NT. The Microsoft Windows *NT Workstation Resource Kit* [1996] is the version that was updated for NT 4.0. Ivens and Hallberg [1996] describe features of Windows NT 4.0. The *Microsoft Developer Network Library* is issued quarterly. It provides a wealth of information on NT and other Microsoft products. Richter [1997] gives a detailed discussion on writing programs to use the Win32 API. Silberschatz and colleagues [1997] present a good discussion of B+ trees.

Chapter 23

WINDOWS 2000

The Microsoft Windows 2000 operating system is a 32-bit preemptive multitasking operating system for Intel Pentium and later microprocessors. The successor to the Windows NT operating system, it was previously named Windows NT Version 5.0. Key goals for the system are portability, security, Portable Operating System Interface (POSIX or IEEE Std. 1003.1) compliance, multiprocessor support, extensibility, international support, and compatibility with MS-DOS and Microsoft Windows applications. In this chapter, we discuss the key goals for this system, the layered architecture of the system that makes it so easy to use, the file system, networks, and the programming interface.

23.1 ■ History

In the mid-1980s, Microsoft and IBM cooperated to develop the OS/2 operating system, which was written in assembly language for single-processor Intel 80286 systems. In 1988, Microsoft decided to make a fresh start and to develop a "new technology" (or NT) portable operating system that supported both the OS/2 and POSIX application-programming interfaces (APIs). In October, 1988, Dave Cutler, the architect of the DEC VAX/VMS operating system, was hired and given the charter of building this new operating system.

Originally, the team planned for NT to use the OS/2 API as its native environment, but during development, Windows NT was changed to use the 32-bit Windows API (or Win32 API), reflecting the popularity of Windows 3.0. The first versions of NT were Windows NT 3.1 and Windows NT 3.1 Advanced

Server. (At that time, 16-bit Windows was at Version 3.1.) Windows NT version 4.0 adopted the Windows 95 user interface and incorporated Internet web-server and web-browser software. In addition, user-interface routines and graphics code were moved into the kernel to improve performance, with the side effect of decreased system reliability. Although previous versions of NT had been ported to other microprocessor architectures, Windows 2000 discontinues that practice due to marketplace factors. Thus, *portability* now refers to portability among Intel architecture systems. Windows 2000 uses a microkernel architecture (like Mach), so enhancements can be made to one part of the operating system without greatly affecting other parts. With the addition of Terminal Services, Windows 2000 is a multiuser operating system.

Windows 2000 was released in 2000 and incorporated significant changes. It adds an X.500-based directory service, better networking support, support for Plug-and-Play devices, a new file system with support for hierarchical storage, and a distributed file system, as well as support for more processors and more memory.

There are four versions of Windows 2000. The Professional version is intended for desktop use. The other three are server versions: Server, Advanced Server, and Datacenter Server. These differ primarily in the amount of memory and number of processors that they support. They use the same kernel and operating-system code, but Windows 2000 Server and Advanced Server versions are configured for client–server applications and can act as application servers on NetWare and Microsoft LANs. Windows 2000 Datacenter Server now supports up to 32 processors and up to 64 GB of RAM.

In 1996, more Windows NT Server licenses were sold than all versions of UNIX licenses. Interestingly, the code base for Windows 2000 is on the order of 30 million lines of code. Compare this size with the code base of Windows NT version 4.0: about 18 million lines of code.

23.2 ■ Design Principles

The design goals that Microsoft has stated for Windows 2000 include extensibility, portability, reliability, compatibility, performance, and international support.

Extensibility refers to the capacity of an operating system to keep up with advances in computing technology. So that changes are facilitated over time, the developers implemented Windows 2000 using a layered architecture. The Windows 2000 executive, which runs in kernel or protected mode, provides the basic system services. On top of the executive, several server subsystems operate in user mode. Among them are *environmental subsystems* that emulate different operating systems. Thus, programs written for MS-DOS, Microsoft Windows, and POSIX can all run on Windows 2000 in the appropriate environment. (See Section 23.4 for more information on environmental subsystems.)

Because of the modular structure, additional environmental subsystems can be added without affecting the executive. In addition, Windows 2000 uses loadable drivers in the I/O system, so new file systems, new kinds of I/O devices, and new kinds of networking can be added while the system is running. Windows 2000 uses a client–server model like the Mach operating system, and supports distributed processing by remote procedure calls (RPCs) as defined by the Open Software Foundation.

An operating system is *portable* if it can be moved from one hardware architecture to another with relatively few changes. Windows 2000 is designed to be portable. As is true of the UNIX operating system, the majority of the system is written in C and C++. All processor-dependent code is isolated in a dynamic link library (DLL) called the *hardware-abstraction layer (HAL)*. A DLL is a file that gets mapped into a process' address space such that any functions in the DLL appear to be part of the process. The upper layers of Windows 2000 depend on HAL, rather than on the underlying hardware, and that helps Windows 2000 to be portable. HAL manipulates hardware directly, isolating the rest of Windows 2000 from hardware differences among the platforms on which it runs.

Reliability is the ability to handle error conditions, including the ability of the operating system to protect itself and its users from defective or malicious software. Windows 2000 resists defects and attacks by using hardware protection for virtual memory, and software protection mechanisms for operating-system resources. Also, Windows 2000 comes with a native file system—the *NTFS file system*—that recovers automatically from many kinds of file-system errors after a system crash. Windows NT Version 4.0 has a C-2 security classification from the U.S. government, which signifies a moderate level of protection from defective software and malicious attacks. Windows 2000 is currently under evaluation by the government for that classification as well.

Windows 2000 provides source-level *compatibility* to applications that follow the IEEE 1003.1 (POSIX) standard. Thus, they can be compiled to run on Windows 2000 without changes to the source code. In addition, Windows 2000 can run the executable binaries for many programs compiled for Intel X86 architectures running MS-DOS, 16-bit Windows, OS/2, LAN Manager, and 32-bit Windows, by using the environmental subsystems mentioned earlier. These environmental subsystems support a variety of file systems, including the MS-DOS FAT file system, the OS/2 HPFS file system, the ISO9660 CD file system, and NTFS. Windows 2000' binary compatibility, however, is not perfect. In MS-DOS, for example, applications can access hardware ports directly. For reliability and security, Windows 2000 prohibits such access.

Windows 2000 is designed to afford good *performance*. The subsystems that constitute Windows 2000 can communicate with one another efficiently by a local-procedure-call (LPC) facility that provides high-performance message passing. Except for the kernel, threads in the subsystems of Windows 2000 can be preempted by higher-priority threads. Thus, the system can respond quickly to external events. In addition, Windows 2000 is designed for symmetrical multiprocessing: On a multiprocessor computer, several threads can run at the same time. The current scalability of Windows 2000 is limited, compared to that of UNIX. As of late 2000, Windows 2000 supported systems with up to 32 CPUs, whereas Solaris ran on systems with up to 64 processors. Previous versions of NT supported only up to 8 processors.

Windows 2000 is also designed for *international use*. It provides support for different locales via the *national language support (NLS) API*. NLS API provides specialized routines to format dates, time, and money in accordance with various national customs. String comparisons are specialized to account for varying character sets. UNICODE is Windows 2000's native character code; Windows 2000 supports ANSI characters by converting them to UNICODE characters before manipulating them (8-bit to 16-bit conversion).

23.3 ■ System Components

The architecture of Windows 2000 is a layered system of modules, as shown in Figure 23.1. The main layers are the HAL, the kernel, and the executive, all of which run in protected mode, and a large collection of subsystems that run in user mode. The user-mode subsystems are in two categories. The environmental subsystems emulate different operating systems; the *protection subsystems* provide security functions. One of the chief advantages of this type of architecture is that interactions between modules can be kept simple. The remainder of this section describes these layers and subsystems.

23.3.1 Hardware-Abstraction Layer

HAL is the layer of software that hides hardware differences from upper levels of the operating system, to help make Windows 2000 portable. HAL exports a virtual-machine interface that is used by the kernel, the executive, and the device drivers. One advantage of this approach is that only a single version of each device driver is needed—it can run on all hardware platforms without porting the driver code. HAL also provides the support for symmetric multiprocessing. For performance reasons, I/O drivers (and graphics drivers in Windows 2000) can access the hardware directly.

23.3.2 Kernel

The kernel of Windows 2000 provides the foundation for the executive and the subsystems. The kernel is never paged out of memory, and its execution is never preempted. It has four main responsibilities: thread scheduling, interrupt and exception handling, low-level processor synchronization, and recovery after a power failure.

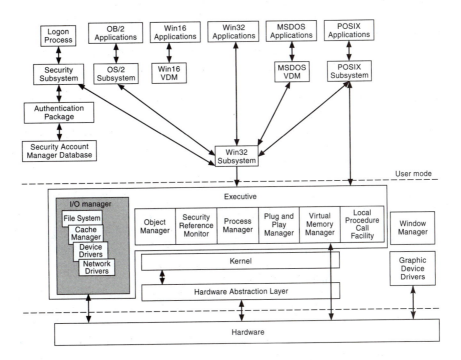

Figure 23.1   Windows 2000 block diagram.

The kernel is object oriented. An *object type* in Windows 2000 is a system-defined data type that has a set of attributes (or data values) and a set of methods (that is, functions or operations). An *object* is just an instance of a particular object type. The kernel performs its job by using a set of kernel objects whose attributes store the kernel data and whose methods perform the kernel activities.

The kernel uses two sets of objects. The first set comprises the dispatcher objects. *Dispatcher objects* control dispatching and synchronization in the system. Examples of these objects are events, mutants, mutexes, semaphores, threads, and timers. The *event object* is used to record an event occurrence and to synchronize the latter with some action. The *mutant* provides kernel-mode or user-mode mutual exclusion with the notion of ownership. The *mutex*, which is available only in kernel mode, provides deadlock-free mutual exclusion. A *semaphore object* acts as a counter or gate to control the number of threads that access some resource. The *thread object* is the entity that is run by the kernel and is associated with a *process object*. *Timer objects* are used to keep track of the time and to signal timeouts when operations take too long and need to be interrupted.

The second set of kernel objects comprises the *control objects*. These objects include asynchronous procedure calls, interrupts, power notify, power status, process, and profile objects. The system uses an asynchronous procedure call

(APC) to break into an executing thread and to call a procedure. The *interrupt object* binds an interrupt service routine to an interrupt source. The system uses the *power-notify object* to call a specified routine automatically after a power failure, and the *power-status object* to check whether the power has failed. A process object represents the virtual address space and control information necessary to execute the set of threads associated with a process. Finally, the system uses the *profile object* to measure the amount of time used by a block of code.

23.3.2.1 Threads and Scheduling

As do many modern operating systems, Windows 2000 uses the notions of processes and threads for executable code. The process has a virtual-memory address space, and information such as a base priority and an affinity for one or more processors. Each process has one or more threads, which are the units of execution dispatched by the kernel. Each thread has its own state, including a priority, processor affinity, and accounting information.

The six possible thread states are ready, standby, running, waiting, transition, and terminated. *Ready* means waiting to run. The highest-priority ready thread is moved to the *standby* state, which means that it will be the next thread to run. In a multiprocessor system, one thread is kept in the standby state for each processor. A thread is *running* when it is executing on a processor. It will run until it is preempted by a higher-priority thread, until it terminates, until its time quantum ends, or until it calls a blocking system call, such as for I/O. A thread is in the *waiting* state when it is waiting for a signal such as an I/O completion. A new thread is in the *transition* state while it is waiting for the resources necessary for execution. A thread enters the *terminated* state when it finishes execution.

The dispatcher uses a 32-level priority scheme to determine the order of thread execution. Priorities are divided into two classes: The variable class contains threads having priorities from 0 to 15, and the real-time class contains threads with priorities ranging from 16 to 31. The dispatcher uses a queue for each scheduling priority, and traverses the set of queues from highest to lowest until it finds a thread that is ready to run. If a thread has a particular processor affinity but that processor is not available, the dispatcher will skip past it, and will continue looking for a thread that is ready to run. If no ready thread is found, the dispatcher will execute a special thread called the idle thread.

When a thread's time quantum runs out, that thread is interrupted; if the thread is in the variable-priority class, its priority is lowered. The priority is never lowered below the base priority, however. Lowering the thread's priority tends to limit the CPU consumption of compute-bound threads. When a variable-priority thread is released from a wait operation, the dispatcher boosts the priority. The amount of the boost depends on for what the thread was waiting; for example, a thread that was waiting for keyboard I/O would get a large priority increase, whereas a thread waiting for a disk operation would get a moderate one. This strategy tends to give good response times to interactive threads that are using the mouse and windows, and enables I/O-bound threads to keep the I/O devices busy, while permitting compute-bound threads to use spare CPU cycles in the background. This strategy is used by several time-sharing operating systems, including UNIX. In addition, the current window with which the user is interacting also receives a priority boost to enhance its response time.

Scheduling can occur when a thread enters the ready or wait state, when a thread terminates, or when an application changes a thread's priority or processor affinity. If a higher-priority real-time thread becomes ready while a lower-priority thread is running, the lower-priority thread will be preempted. This preemption gives a real-time thread preferential access to the CPU when the thread needs such access. Windows 2000 is not a hard real-time operating system, however, because it does not guarantee that a real-time thread will start to execute within any particular time limit.

23.3.2.2   Exceptions and Interrupts

The kernel also provides trap handling for exceptions and interrupts that are generated by hardware or software. Windows 2000 defines several architecture-independent exceptions, including memory-access violation, integer overflow, floating-point overflow or underflow, integer divide by zero, floating-point divide by zero, illegal instruction, data misalignment, privileged instruction, page read error, guard-page violation, paging file quota exceeded, debugger breakpoint, and debugger single step.

The trap handler can handle simple exceptions; others are handled by the kernel's exception dispatcher. The *exception dispatcher* creates an exception record that contains the reason for the exception and finds an exception handler that can deal with it.

When an exception occurs in kernel mode, the exception dispatcher simply calls a routine to locate the exception handler. If no handler is found, a fatal system error occurs and the user is left with the infamous "blue screen of death" that signifies system failure.

Exception handling is more complex for user-mode processes, because an environmental subsystem (such as the POSIX system) can set up a debugger port and an exception port for every process that it creates. If a debugger port is registered, the exception handler sends the exception to that port. If the debugger port is not found or does not handle that exception, the dispatcher then attempts to find an appropriate exception handler. If a handler is not found, the debugger is called again so that it can catch the error for debugging. If a debugger is not running, a message is then sent to the process' exception port to give the environmental subsystem a chance to translate the exception. For example, the POSIX environment translates Windows 2000 exception messages into POSIX signals before sending them to the thread that caused the exception.

Finally, if nothing else works, the kernel simply terminates the process that contains the thread that caused the exception.

The interrupt dispatcher in the kernel handles interrupts by calling either an interrupt service routine (such as in a device driver) or an internal kernel routine. The interrupt is represented by an interrupt object that contains all the information needed to handle the interrupt. Using an interrupt object makes it easy to associate interrupt service routines with an interrupt without having to access the interrupt hardware directly.

Various processor architectures, such as Intel or DEC Alpha, have different types and numbers of interrupts. For portability, the interrupt dispatcher maps the hardware interrupts into a standard set. The interrupts are prioritized and are serviced in priority order. There are 32 interrupt levels (IRQLs) in Windows 2000. Eight are reserved for the use of the kernel; the other 24 represent hardware interrupts via the HAL (although most x86 systems use only 16 lines). The Windows 2000 interrupts are defined in Figure 23.2.

The kernel uses an *interrupt dispatch table* to bind each interrupt level to a service routine. In a multiprocessor computer, Windows 2000 keeps a separate interrupt dispatch table for each processor, and each processor's IRQL can be set independently to mask out interrupts. All interrupts that occur at a level equal to or less than the IRQL of a processor get blocked until the IRQL is lowered by a kernel-level thread. Windows 2000 takes advantage of this property to use software interrupts to perform system functions. For instance, the kernel uses software interrupts to start a thread dispatch, to handle timers, and to support asynchronous operations.

The kernel uses the dispatch interrupt to control thread context switching. When the kernel is running, it raises the IRQL on the processor to a level above the dispatch level. When the kernel determines that a thread dispatch is required, the kernel generates a dispatch interrupt, but this interrupt is blocked

interrupt levels	types of interrupts
31	machine check or bus error
30	power fail
29	interprocessor notification (request another processor to act; e.g., dispatch a process or update the TLB)
28	clock (used to keep track of time)
27	profile
3-26	traditional PC IRQ hardware interrupts
2	dispatch and deferred procedure call (DPC) (kernel)
1	asynchronous procedure call (APC)
0	passive

Figure 23.2   Windows 2000 interrupt request levels.

until the kernel finishes what it is doing and lowers the IRQL. At that point, the dispatch interrupt can be serviced, so the dispatcher chooses a thread to run.

When the kernel decides that some system function should be executed eventually, but not immediately, it queues a *deferred procedure call (DPC)* object that contains the address of the function to be executed, and generates a DPC interrupt. When the IRQL of the processor drops low enough, the DPC objects are executed. The IRQL of the DPC interrupt is typically higher than that of user threads, so DPCs will interrupt the execution of user threads. To avoid problems, DPCs are restricted to be fairly simple. They cannot modify a thread's memory; create, acquire, or wait on objects; call system services; or generate page faults.

23.3.2.3 Low-level Processor Synchronization

The third responsibility of the kernel is to provide low-level processor synchronization. The APC mechanism is similar to the DPC mechanism, but for more general use. The APC mechanism enables threads to set up a procedure call that will happen out of the blue at some future time. For instance, many system services accept a user-mode routine as a parameter. Instead of calling a synchronous system call that will block the thread until the system call completes, a user thread can call an asynchronous system call and supply an APC. The user thread will continue running. When the system service finishes, the user thread will be interrupted to run the APC spontaneously.

An APC can be queued on either a system thread or a user thread, although a user-mode APC will be executed only if the thread has declared itself to be *alertable*. An APC is more powerful than a DPC, in that it can acquire and wait on objects, cause page faults, and call system services. Since an APC executes in the address space of the target thread, the Windows 2000 executive uses APCs extensively for I/O processing.

Windows 2000 can run on symmetric multiprocessor machines, so the kernel must prevent two of its threads from modifying a shared data structure at the same time. The kernel uses spinlocks that reside in global memory to achieve multiprocessor mutual exclusion. Because all activity on a processor stops when a thread is attempting to acquire a spinlock, a thread that holds a spinlock is not preempted, so it can finish and release the lock as quickly as possible.

23.3.2.4 Recovery After a Power Failure

The fourth and final responsibility of the kernel is to provide recovery after a power failure. A power-fail interrupt, which has the second-highest priority, notifies the operating system whenever a power loss is detected. The power-notify object provides a way for a device driver to register a routine that will be called on power restoration and ensures that devices get set to the proper state on recovery. For battery–backed-up systems, the power-status object is useful.

Before it begins a critical operation, a driver examines the power-status object to determine whether or not the power has failed. If the driver determines that power has not failed, it raises the IRQL of its processor to powerfail, performs the operation, and resets the IRQL. This sequence of actions blocks the powerfail interrupt until after the critical operation completes.

23.3.3 Executive

The Windows 2000 executive provides a set of services that all environmental subsystems can use. The services are grouped as follows: object manager, virtual-memory manager, process manager, local-procedure-call facility, I/O manager, and security reference monitor.

23.3.3.1 Object Manager

As an object-oriented system, Windows 2000 uses objects for all its services and entities. Examples of objects are directory objects, symbolic link objects, semaphore objects, event objects, process and thread objects, port objects, and file objects. The job of the *object manager* is to supervise the use of all objects. When a thread wants to use an object, it calls the object manager's open method to get a handle to the object. *Handles* are a standardized interface to all kinds of objects. Like a file handle, an object handle is an identifier unique to a process that confers the ability to access and manipulate a system resource.

Since the object manager is the only entity that can generate an object handle, it is the natural place to check security. For instance, the object manager checks whether a process has the right to access an object when the process tries to open that object. The object manager can also enforce quotas, such as the maximum amount of memory that a process may allocate.

The object manager can keep track of which processes are using each object. Each object header contains a count of the number of processes that have handles to that object. When the counter goes to zero, the object is deleted from the name space if it is a temporary object name. Since Windows 2000 itself often uses pointers (instead of handles) to access objects, the object manager also maintains a reference count, which it increments when Windows 2000 gains access to an object and decrements when the object is no longer needed. When the reference count of a temporary object goes to zero, the object is deleted from memory. Permanent objects represent physical entities, such as disk drives, and are not deleted when the reference count and the open-handle counter go to zero.

The objects are manipulated by a standard set of methods: `create`, `open`, `close`, `delete`, `query name`, `parse`, and `security`. The latter three objects need explanation:

- `query name` is called when a thread has a handle to an object, but wants to know the object's name.

- `parse` is used by the object manager to search for an object given the object's name.

- `security` is called when a process opens or changes the protection of an object.

The Windows 2000 executive allows any object to be given a *name*. The name space is global, so one process may create a named object, and a second process can then open a handle to the object and share it with the first process. A process opening a named object can ask for the search to be either case sensitive or case insensitive.

A name can be either permanent or temporary. A permanent name represents an entity, such as a disk drive, that remains even if no process is accessing it. A temporary name exists only while some process holds a handle to that object.

Although the name space is not directly visible across a network, the object manager's `parse` method is used to help access a named object on another system. When a process attempts to open an object that resides on a remote computer, the object manager calls the parse method, which then calls a network redirector to find the object.

Object names are structured like file path names in MS-DOS and UNIX. Directories are represented by a *directory object* that contains the names of all the objects in that directory. The object name space can grow by the addition of *object domains*, which are self-contained sets of objects. Examples of object domains are floppy disks and hard drives. It is easy to see how the name space gets extended when a floppy disk is added to the system: The floppy has its own name space that is grafted onto the existing name space.

UNIX file systems have *symbolic links*, so multiple nicknames or aliases can refer to the same file. Similarly, Windows 2000 implements a *symbolic link object*. One way that Windows 2000 uses symbolic links is to map drive names to the standard MS-DOS drive letters. The drive letters are just symbolic links that can be remapped to suit the user's preferences.

A process gets an object handle by creating an object, by opening an existing object, by receiving a duplicated handle from another process, or by inheriting a handle from a *parent process*, similar to the way a UNIX process gets a file descriptor. These handles are all stored in the process' *object table*. An entry in the object table contains the object's access rights and states whether the handle should be inherited by *child processes*. When a process terminates, Windows 2000 automatically closes all the process' open handles.

When a user is authenticated by the login process, an access-token object is attached to the user's process. The access token contains information such as the security id, group ids, privileges, primary group, and default access control list. These attributes determine which services and objects can be used by a given user.

In Windows 2000, each object is protected by an access-control list that contains the security ids and access rights granted to each process. When a process attempts to access an object, the system compares the security id in the process' access token with the object's access-control list to determine whether access should be permitted. This check is done only when an object is opened, so internal Windows 2000 services that use pointers, rather than opening a handle to an object, bypass the access check.

Generally, the creator of the object determines the access-control list for that object. If none is supplied explicitly, one may be inherited from the creator object, or a default list may be obtained from the user's access-token object.

One field in the access token controls auditing of the object. Operations that are being audited get logged to the system's audit log with an identification of the user. The audit field can watch this log to discover attempts to break into the system or to access protected objects.

23.3.3.2 Virtual-Memory Manager

The virtual-memory portion of the Windows 2000 executive is the *virtual-memory (VM) manager*. The design of the VM manager assumes that the underlying hardware supports virtual-to-physical mapping, a paging mechanism, and transparent cache coherence on multiprocessor systems, and allows multiple page-table entries to map to the same page frame. The VM manager in Windows 2000 uses a page-based management scheme with a page size of 4 KB. Pages of data that are assigned to a process but are not in physical memory are stored in the *paging file* on disk.

The VM manager uses 32-bit addresses, so each process has a 4 GB virtual address space. The upper 2 GB are identical for all processes, and are used by Windows 2000 in kernel mode. The lower 2 GB are distinct for every process, and are accessible by both user- and kernel-mode threads. Note that certain configurations of Windows 2000 reserve only 1 GB for operating system use, allowing a process to use 3 GB of address space.

The Windows 2000 VM manager uses a two-step process to allocate memory. The first step *reserves* a portion of the process' address space. The second step *commits* the allocation by assigning space in the Windows 2000 paging file. Windows 2000 can limit the amount of paging file space that a process consumes by enforcing a quota on committed memory. A process can uncommit memory that it is no longer using to free up its paging quota. Since memory is represented by objects, when one process (the parent) creates a second process (the child), the parent can maintain the ability to access the virtual memory of the child. That is how environmental subsystems can manage the memory of their client processes. For performance, the VM manager allows a privileged process to lock selected pages in physical memory, thus ensuring that the pages will not be swapped out to the paging file.

Two processes can share memory by getting handles to the same memory object, but this approach can be inefficient since the entire memory space of an object must be committed before either process can access that object. Windows 2000 provides an alternative, called a *section object*, to represent a block of shared memory. After getting a handle to a section object, a process can map only the needed portion of the memory. This portion is called a *view*. The view mechanism also enables a process to access an object that is too large to fit into the process' paging file quota. The system can use the view to walk through the address space of the object, one piece at a time.

A process can control the use of a shared-memory section object in many ways. The maximum size of a section can be bounded. The section can be backed by disk space either in the system paging file or by a regular file (a *memory-mapped file*). A section can be *based*, meaning that the section appears at the same virtual address for all processes that access it. Finally, the memory protection of pages in the section can be set to read only, read–write, execute only, guard page, or copy on write. The last two of these protection settings need some explanation:

- A guard page raises an exception if accessed; the exception can be used, for example, to check whether a faulty program iterates beyond the end of an array.

- The copy-on-write mechanism allows the VM manager to save memory. When two processes want independent copies of an object, the VM manager places only one shared copy into physical memory, but it sets the copy-on-write property on that region of memory. If one of the processes tries to modify data in a copy-on-write page, the VM manager first makes a private copy of the page for that process to use.

The virtual-address translation in Windows 2000 uses several data structures. Each process has a *page directory* that contains 1,024 *page-directory entries* of size 4 bytes. Typically, the page directory is private, but it can be shared among processes if the environment so requires. Each page-directory entry points to a *page table* that contains 1,024 *page-table entries (PTEs)* of size 4 bytes. Each PTE points to a 4 KB *page frame* in physical memory. The total size of all the page tables for a process is 4 MB, so the VM manager will swap out these tables to disk when necessary. See Figure 23.3 for a diagram of this structure.

A 10-bit integer can represent all the values from 0 to 1,023. Thus, a 10-bit integer can select any entry in the page directory, or in a page table. This property is used when a virtual-address pointer is translated to a byte address in physical memory. A 32-bit virtual-memory address is split into three integers, as shown in Figure 23.4. The first 10 bits of the virtual address are used as a subscript in the page directory. This address selects one page-directory entry, which points to a page table. The memory management unit (MMU) uses the next 10 bits of the virtual address to select a PTE from that page table. The PTE points to a page frame in physical memory. The remaining 12 bits of the

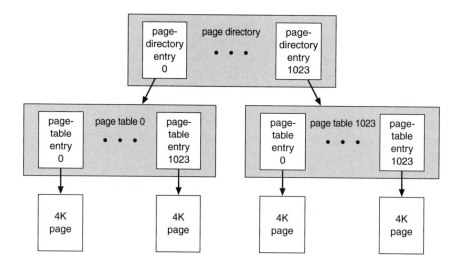

Figure 23.3   Virtual-memory layout.

virtual address point to a specific byte in that page frame. The MMU creates a pointer to that specific byte in physical memory by concatenating 20 bits from the PTE with the lower 12 bits from the virtual address. Thus, the 32-bit PTE has 12 bits left over; these bits describe the page. The Pentium PTE reserves 3 bits for the use of the operating system. The rest of the bits specify whether the page is dirty, accessed, cacheable, read only, write through, kernel mode, or valid; thus, they describe the state of the page in memory. For more general information on paging schemes, see Section 9.4.

A page can be in one of six states: valid, free, zeroed, standby, modified, or bad. A *valid* page is in use by an active process. A *free* page is a page that is not referenced in a PTE. A *zeroed* page is a free page that has been zeroed out and is ready for immediate use. A *standby* page has been removed from the working set of a process. A *modified* page has been written to, but not yet flushed to, disk. Standby and modified pages are considered to be *transition* pages. Finally, a *bad* page is unusable because a hardware error has been detected.

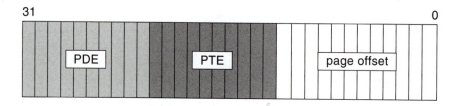

Figure 23.4   Virtual-to-physical address translation.

The actual structure of the page-file PTE is shown in Figure 23.5. The PTE contains 5 bits for page protection, 20 bits for page-file offset, 4 bits to select the paging file, and 3 bits that describe the page state. This page-file PTE would appear as an invalid page to the hardware. Since executable code and memory-mapped files already have a copy on disk, they do not need space in a paging file. If one of these pages is not in physical memory, the PTE structure is as follows. The most significant bit is used to specify the page protection, the next 28 bits are used to index into a system data structure that indicates a file and offset within the file for the page, and the lower 3 bits specify the page state.

It is difficult to share a page between processes if every process has its own set of page tables, because each process will have its own PTE for the page frame. When a shared page is faulted into physical memory, the physical address will have to be stored in the PTEs that belong to each process that shares the page. The protection bits and page-state bits in these PTEs will all need to be set and updated consistently. To avoid these problems, Windows 2000 uses an indirection. For every page that is shared, the process has a PTE that points to a *prototype page-table entry*, rather than to the page frame. The prototype PTE contains the page-frame address and the protection and state bits. Thus, the first access by a process to a shared page generates a page fault. After the first access, further accesses are performed in the normal manner. If the page is marked read-only, the VM manager does a copy-on-write and the process effectively does not have a shared page any longer. Shared pages never appear in the page file, but are instead found in the file system.

The VM manager keeps track of all pages of physical memory in a *page-frame database*. There is one entry for every page frame. The entry points to the PTE that points to the page frame, so the VM manager can maintain the state of the page. Page frames are linked to form, for instance, the list of zeroed pages and the list of free pages.

When a page fault occurs, the VM manager faults in the missing page, placing that page into the first frame on the free list. But it does not stop there. Research shows that the memory referencing of a thread tends to have a *locality* property: When a page is used, it is likely that adjacent pages will be referenced in the near future. (Think of iterating over an array, or fetching sequential instructions that form the executable code for a thread.) Because of locality, when the VM manager faults in a page, it also faults in a few adjacent pages.

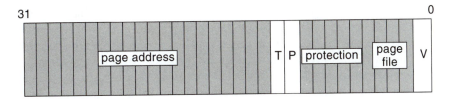

Figure 23.5   Page file page-table entry.

This adjacent faulting tends to reduce the total number of page faults. For more information on locality, see Section 10.5.1.

If no page frames are available on the free list, Windows 2000 uses a per-process FIFO replacement policy to take pages from processes that are using more than their minimum working-set size. Windows 2000 monitors the page faulting of each process that is at its minimum working-set size, and adjusts the working-set size accordingly. In particular, when a process is started under Windows 2000, it is assigned a default working-set size of 30 pages. Windows 2000 periodically tests this size by stealing a valid page from the process. If the process continues executing without generating a page fault for the stolen page, the working set of the process is reduced by 1, and the page is added to the list of free pages.

23.3.3.3 Process Manager

The Windows 2000 process manager provides services for creating, deleting, and using threads and processes. It has no knowledge about parent–child relationships or process hierarchies; those refinements are left to the particular environmental subsystem that owns the process.

An example of process creation in the Win32 environment is as follows. When a Win32 application calls CreateProcess, a message is sent to the Win32 subsystem, which calls the process manager to create a process. The process manager calls the object manager to create a process object, and then returns the object handle to Win32. Win32 calls the process manager again to create a thread for the process, and finally Win32 returns handles to the new process and thread.

23.3.3.4 Local-Procedure-Call Facility

The operating system uses the LPC facility to pass requests and results between client and server processes within a single machine. In particular, it uses LPC to request services from the various Windows 2000 subsystems. LPC is similar in many respects to the RPC mechanisms that are used by many operating systems for distributed processing across networks, but LPC is optimized for use within one Windows 2000 system.

LPC is a message-passing mechanism. The server process publishes a globally visible connection-port object. When a client wants services from a subsystem, it opens a handle to the subsystem's connection-port object, and then sends a connection request to that port. The server creates a channel and returns a handle to the client. The channel consists of a pair of private communication ports: one for client-to-server messages, and the other for server-to-client messages. Communication channels support a callback mechanism, so the client and server can accept requests when they would normally be expecting a reply.

When an LPC channel is created, one of three message-passing techniques must be specified.

1. The first technique is suitable for small messages (up to 256 bytes). In this case, the port's message queue is used as intermediate storage, and the messages are copied from one process to the other.

2. The second technique is for larger messages. In this case, a shared-memory section object is created for the channel. Messages sent through the port's message queue contain a pointer and size information that refer to the section object. Thus, the need to copy large messages is avoided: The sender places data into the shared section, and the receiver can view them directly.

3. The third technique of LPC message passing, called *quick LPC*, is used by graphical display portions of the Win32 subsystem. When a client asks for a connection that will use quick LPC, the server sets up three objects: a dedicated server thread to handle requests, a 64 KB section object, and an event-pair object. An *event-pair object* is a synchronization object that is used by the Win32 subsystem to provide notification when the client thread has copied a message to the Win32 server, or vice versa. LPC messages are passed in the section object, and synchronization is performed by the event-pair object. The LPC has several advantages. The section object eliminates message copying, since it represents a region of shared memory. The event-pair object eliminates the overhead of using the port object to pass messages containing pointers and lengths. The dedicated server thread eliminates the overhead of determining which client thread is calling the server, since there is one server thread per client thread. Finally, the kernel gives scheduling preference to these dedicated server threads to improve performance. The drawback is that quick LPC uses more resources than do the other two methods, so the Win32 subsystem uses quick LPC only for the window-manager and graphics-device interfaces.

23.3.3.5 I/O Manager

The *I/O manager* is responsible for file systems, cache management, device drivers, and network drivers. It keeps track of which installable file systems are loaded, and manages buffers for I/O requests. It works with the VM manager to provide memory-mapped file I/O, and controls the Windows 2000 cache manager, which handles caching for the entire I/O system. The I/O manager supports both synchronous and asynchronous operations, provides timeouts for drivers, and has mechanisms for one driver to call another.

The I/O manager converts the requests it receives into a standard form called an *I/O request packet (IRP)*. It then forwards the IRP to the correct driver for processing. When the operation is finished, the I/O manager receives the IRP from the driver that most recently performed an operation, and completes the request.

In many operating systems, caching is done by the file system. Windows 2000 provides a centralized caching facility, instead. The cache manager provides cache services for all components under the control of the I/O manager, and works closely with the VM manager. The size of the cache changes dynamically, according to how much free memory is available in the system. Recall that the upper 2 GB of a process' address space comprise the system area; it is identical for all processes. The VM manager allocates up to one-half of this space to the system cache. The cache manager maps files into this address space, and uses the capabilities of the VM manager to handle file I/O.

The cache is divided into blocks of 256 KB. Each cache block can hold a view (that is, a memory-mapped region) of a file. Each cache block is described by a *virtual-address control block (VACB)* that stores the virtual address and file offset for that view, as well as the number of processes that are using the view. The VACBs reside in a single array that is maintained by the cache manager.

For each open file, the cache manager maintains a separate VACB index array. This array has an element for each 256 KB chunk of the file; so, for instance, a 2 MB file would have an 8-entry VACB index array. An entry in the VACB index array points to the VACB if that portion of the file is in the cache; it is null otherwise.

When the I/O manager receives a user-level read request, the I/O manager sends an IRP to the cache manager (unless the request specifically asks for a noncached read). The cache manager calculates which entry of that file's VACB index array corresponds to the byte offset of the request. The entry either points to the view in the cache, or is null. If it is null, the cache manager allocates a cache block (and the corresponding entry in the VACB array), and maps the view into that cache block. The cache manager then attempts to copy data from the mapped file to the caller's buffer. If the copy succeeds, the operation is completed. If the copy fails, it does so because of a page fault, which causes the VM manager to send a noncached read request to the I/O manager. The I/O manager asks the appropriate device driver to read the data, and returns the data to the VM manager, which loads the data into the cache. The data, now in the cache, are copied to the caller's buffer, and the I/O request is completed. Figure 23.6 shows an overview of all these operations. When possible, for synchronous, cached, nonlocking I/O, I/O is handled by the *fast I/O mechanism*. This mechanism simply copies data to/from cache pages directly and utilizes the cache manager to perform any needed I/O.

A kernel-level read operation is similar, except that the data can be accessed directly from the cache, rather than being copied to a buffer in user space. To use file-system metadata, or data structures that describe the file system, the kernel uses the cache manager's mapping interface to read the metadata. To modify the metadata, the file system uses the cache manager's pinning interface. *Pinning* a page locks the page into a physical-memory page frame, so the VM manager cannot move or swap out the page. After updating the metadata, the file system asks the cache manager to unpin the page. Since the page has been modified, it is marked dirty, so the VM manager will flush the page to disk. Note that the metadata is actually stored in a regular file.

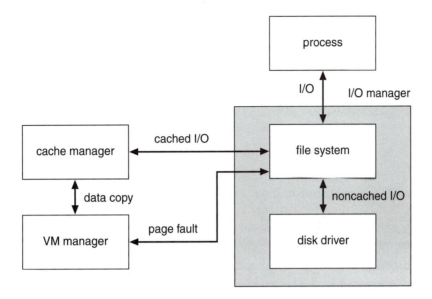

Figure 23.6   File I/O.

To improve performance, the cache manager keeps a small history of read requests, and attempts to predict future requests. If the cache manager can find a pattern in the previous three requests, such as sequential access forward or backward, it can prefetch data into the cache before the next request is submitted by the application. Then, the application may find its data already in the cache, and may not need to wait for disk I/O. The Win32 API OpenFile and CreateFile functions can be passed the FILE_FLAG_SEQUENTIAL_SCAN flag, which is a hint to the cache manager to try to prefetch 192 KB ahead of the thread's requests. Typically, Windows 2000 performs I/O operations in chunks of 64 KB or 16 pages; thus, this read-ahead is three times the normal amount.

The cache manager is also responsible for telling the VM manager to flush the contents of the cache. The cache manager's default behavior is write-back caching: it accumulates writes for 4 to 5 seconds, and then the cache-writer thread wakes up. When write-through caching is needed, a process can set a flag when opening the file, or the process can call an explicit cache-flush function when needed.

A fast-writing process could potentially fill all the free cache pages before the cache-writer thread has a chance to wake up and flush the pages to disk. The cache writer prevents a process from flooding the system in the following way: When the amount of free cache memory gets low, the cache manager temporarily blocks processes that attempt to write data, and wakes the cache-writer thread to flush pages to disk. If the fast-writing process is actually a network redirector for a network file system, blocking it for too long could cause network transfers to time out and be retransmitted. This retransmission would waste network bandwidth. To prevent this waste, network redirectors can tell the cache manager not to let a large backlog of writes accumulate in the cache.

Because a network file system needs to move data between a disk and the network interface, the cache manager also provides a DMA interface to move the data directly. Moving data directly avoids copying data through an intermediate buffer.

23.3.3.6 Security Reference Monitor

The object-oriented nature of Windows 2000 enables the use of a uniform mechanism to perform run-time access validation and audit checks for every entity in the system. Whenever a process opens a handle to an object, the *security reference monitor* checks the process' security token and the object's access-control list to see whether the process has the necessary rights.

23.3.3.7 Plug-and-Play Manager

The operating system uses the *plug-and-play (PnP) manager* to recognize and adapt to changes in the hardware configuration. For PnP to work, both the device and the driver must support the PnP standard. The PnP manager automatically recognizes installed devices and detects changes in devices as the system operates. The manager also keeps tracks of resources used by a device, as well as potential resources that could be used, and takes care of loading the appropriate drivers. This management of hardware resources— primarily interrupts and I/O memory ranges—has the goal of determining a hardware configuration in which all devices are able to operate. For example, if device B can use only interrupt 5 but device A could use 5 or 7, then the PnP manager could assign 5 to B and 7 to A. In previous versions, the user might have had to remove device A and reconfigure it to use interrupt 7, before installing device B. The user thus had to study system resources before installing new hardware, and to find out or remember which devices were using which hardware resources. The proliferation of PCCARD and USB devices also dictates that dynamic configuration of resources be supported.

The PnP manager handles this dynamic reconfiguration as follows. First, it gets a list of devices from each bus driver (for example, PCI, USB). It then loads the installed driver (or installs one, if necessary) and sends an `add-device` command to the appropriate driver for each device. The PnP manager figures out the optimal resource assignments and then sends a `start-device` command to each driver along with the resource assignment for that device. If a device needs to be reconfigured, the PnP manager sends a `query-stop` command, which asks the driver whether the device can be temporarily disabled. If the driver can disable the device, then all pending operations are completed and new operations are not allowed to be started. Next, the PnP manager sends a `stop` command; it can then reconfigure the device with another `start-`

device command. The PnP manager also supports other commands, such as query-remove. This command is used when the user is getting ready to eject a PCCARD device, and operates in a fashion similar to query-stop. The surprise-remove command is used when a device fails or, more likely, when a user removes a PCCARD device without using the PCCARD utility to stop it first. The remove command requests that the driver stop using the device and release all resources that have been allocated to the device.

23.4 ■ Environmental Subsystems

Environmental subsystems are user-mode processes layered over the native Windows 2000 executive services to enable Windows 2000 to run programs developed for other operating systems, including 16-bit Windows, MS-DOS, POSIX, and character-based applications for 16-bit OS/2. Each environmental subsystem provides one API or application environment.

Windows 2000 uses the Win32 subsystem as the main operating environment, and thus to start all processes. When an application is executed, the Win32 subsystem calls the VM manager to load the application's executable code. The memory manager returns a status to Win32 that tells what kind of executable the code is. If it is not a native Win32 executable, the Win32 environment checks whether the appropriate environmental subsystem is running; if the subsystem is not running, it is started as a user-mode process. Then, Win32 creates a process to run the application, and passes control to the environmental subsystem.

The environmental subsystem uses the Windows 2000 LPC facility to get kernel services for the process. This approach helps Windows 2000 to be robust, because the parameters passed to a system call can be checked for correctness before the actual kernel routine is invoked. Windows 2000 prohibits applications from mixing API routines from different environments. For instance, a Win32 application cannot call a POSIX routine.

Since each subsystem is run as a separate user-mode process, a crash in one has no effect on the others. The exception is Win32, which provides all the keyboard, mouse, and graphical display capabilities. If it fails, the system is effectively disabled.

The Win32 environment categorizes applications as either graphical or character based, where a *character-based application* is one that thinks that interactive output goes to an 80 by 24 ASCII display. Win32 transforms the output of a character-based application to a graphical representation in a window. This transformation is easy: Whenever an output routine is called, the environmental subsystem calls a Win32 routine to display the text. Since the Win32 environment performs this function for all character-based windows, it can transfer screen text between windows via the clipboard. This transformation works for MS-DOS applications, as well as for POSIX command-line applications.

23.4.1 MS-DOS Environment

The MS-DOS environment does not have the complexity of the other Windows 2000 environmental subsystems. It is provided by a Win32 application called the *virtual DOS machine (VDM)*. Since the VDM is just a user-mode process, it is paged and dispatched like any other Windows 2000 thread. The VDM has an *instruction-execution unit* to execute or emulate Intel 486 instructions. The VDM also provides routines to emulate the MS-DOS ROM BIOS and "int 21" software-interrupt services, and has virtual device drivers for the screen, keyboard, and communication ports. The VDM is based on the MS-DOS 5.0 source code; it gives the application at least 620 KB of memory.

The Windows 2000 command shell is a program that creates a window that looks like an MS-DOS environment. It can run both 16-bit and 32-bit executables. When an MS-DOS application is run, the command shell starts a VDM process to execute the program.

If Windows 2000 is running on an x86 processor, MS-DOS graphical applications run in full-screen mode, and character applications can run full screen or in a window. If Windows 2000 is running on a different processor architecture, all MS-DOS applications run in windows. Some MS-DOS applications access the disk hardware directly, but they fail to run on Windows 2000 because disk access is privileged to protect the file system. In general, MS-DOS applications that directly access hardware will fail to operate under Windows 2000.

Since MS-DOS is not a multitasking environment, some applications have been written that hog the CPU—for instance, by using busy loops to cause time delays or pauses in execution. The priority mechanism in the Windows 2000 dispatcher detects such delays and automatically throttles the CPU consumption (and causes the offending application to operate incorrectly).

23.4.2 16-Bit Windows Environment

The Win16 execution environment is provided by a VDM that incorporates additional software called *Windows on Windows* that provides the Windows 3.1 kernel routines and stub routines for window manager and GDI functions. The stub routines call the appropriate Win32 subroutines, converting, or *thunking*, 16-bit addresses into 32-bit ones. Applications that rely on the internal structure of the 16-bit window manager or GDI may not work, because Windows on Windows does not really implement the 16-bit API.

Windows on Windows can multitask with other processes on Windows 2000, but it resembles Windows 3.1 in many ways. Only one Win16 application can run at a time, all applications are single threaded and reside in the same address space, and they all share the same input queue. These features imply that an application that stops receiving input will block all the other Win16 applications, just as in Windows 3.x, and one Win16 application can crash other Win16 applications by corrupting the address space. Multiple

Win16 environments can coexist, however, by using the command *start /separate* win16application from the command line.

23.4.3 Win32 Environment

The main subsystem in Windows 2000 is the Win32 subsystem. It runs Win32 applications, and manages all keyboard, mouse, and screen I/O. Since it is the controlling environment, it is designed to be extremely robust. Several features of Win32 contribute to this robustness. Unlike the Win16 environment, each Win32 process has its own input queue. The window manager dispatches all input on the system to the appropriate process' input queue, so a failed process will not block input to other processes. The Windows 2000 kernel also provides preemptive multitasking, which enables the user to terminate applications that have failed or are no longer needed. Win32 also validates all objects before using them, to prevent crashes that could otherwise occur if an application tried to use an invalid or wrong handle. The Win32 subsystem verifies the type of the object to which a handle points before using that object. The reference counts kept by the object manager prevent objects from being deleted while they are still being used, and prevent their use after they have been deleted.

23.4.4 POSIX Subsystem

The POSIX subsystem is designed to run POSIX applications following the POSIX.1 standard, which is based on the UNIX model. POSIX applications can be started by the Win32 subsystem or by another POSIX application. POSIX applications use the POSIX subsystem server PSXSS.EXE, the POSIX dynamic link library PSXDLL.DLL, and the POSIX console session manager POSIX.EXE.

Although the POSIX standard does not specify printing, POSIX applications can use printers transparently via the Windows 2000 redirection mechanism. POSIX applications have access to any file system on the Windows 2000 system; the POSIX environment enforces UNIX-like permissions on directory trees. Several Win32 facilities are not supported by the POSIX subsystem, including memory-mapped files, networking, graphics, and dynamic data exchange.

23.4.5 OS/2 Subsystem

Although Windows 2000 was originally intended to provide a robust OS/2 operating environment, the success of Microsoft Windows led to a change; during the early development of Windows 2000, the Windows environment became the default. Consequently, Windows 2000 provides only limited facilities in the OS/2 environmental subsystem. OS/2 1.x character-based applications can run only on Windows 2000 on Intel x86 computers. Real-mode OS/2 applications can run on all platforms by using the MS-DOS environment. Bound applications, which have dual code for both MS-DOS and OS/2, run in the OS/2 environment unless the OS/2 environment is disabled.

23.4.6 Logon and Security Subsystems

Before a user can access objects on Windows 2000, that user must be authenticated by the logon subsystem. To be authenticated, a user must have an account and provide the password for that account.

The security subsystem generates access tokens to represent users on the system. It calls an *authentication package* to perform authentication using information from the logon subsystem or network server. Typically, the authentication package simply looks up the account information in a local database and checks to see that the password is correct. The security subsystem then generates the access token for the user id containing the appropriate privileges, quota limits, and group ids. Whenever the user attempts to access an object in the system, such as by opening a handle to the object, the access token is passed to the security reference monitor, which checks privileges and quotas. The default authentication package for Windows 2000 domains is Kerberos.

23.5 ■ File System

Historically, MS-DOS systems have used the file-allocation table (FAT) file system. The 16-bit FAT file system has several shortcomings, including internal fragmentation, a size limitation of 2 GB, and a lack of access protection for files. The 32-bit FAT file system has solved the size and fragmentation problems, but its performance and features are still weak by comparison with modern file systems. The NTFS file system is much better. It was designed to include many features, including data recovery, security, fault tolerance, large files and file systems, multiple data streams, UNICODE names, and file compression. For compatibility, Windows 2000 provides support for the FAT and OS/2 HPFS file systems.

23.5.1 Internal Layout

The fundamental entity in NTFS is a volume. A volume is created by the Windows 2000 disk administrator utility, and is based on a logical disk partition. The volume may occupy a portion of a disk, may occupy an entire disk, or may span across several disks.

NTFS does not deal with individual sectors of a disk, but instead uses clusters as the unit of disk allocation. A cluster is a number of disk sectors that is a power of 2. The cluster size is configured when an NTFS file system is formatted. The default cluster size is the sector size for volumes up to 512 MB, 1 KB for volumes up to 1 GB, 2 KB for volumes up to 2 GB, and 4 KB for larger volumes. This cluster size is much smaller than that for the 16-bit FAT file system, and the small size reduces the amount of internal fragmentation. As an example, consider a 1.6 GB disk with 16,000 files. If you use a FAT-16 file system, 400 MB may be lost to internal fragmentation because the cluster size is 32 KB. Under NTFS, only 17 MB would be lost when storing the same files.

NTFS uses *logical cluster numbers (LCNs)* as disk addresses. It assigns them by numbering clusters from the beginning of the disk to the end. Using this scheme, the system can calculate a physical disk offset (in bytes) by multiplying the LCN by the cluster size.

A file in NTFS is not a simple byte stream, as it is in MS-DOS or UNIX; rather, it is a structured object consisting of *attributes*. Each attribute of a file is an independent byte stream that can be created, deleted, read, and written. Some attributes are standard for all files, including the file name (or names, if the file has aliases), the creation time, and the security descriptor that specifies access control. Other attributes are specific to certain kinds of files. For instance, Macintosh files have two data attributes, the resource fork and the data fork. A directory has attributes that implement an index for the file names in the directory. In general, attributes may be added as necessary and are accessed using a *file-name:attribute* nomenclature. Most traditional data files have an *unnamed* data attribute that contains all that file's data. Note that NTFS only returns the size of the unnamed attribute in response to file-query operations, such as when running the `dir` command. Clearly, some attributes are small, and others are large.

Every file in NTFS is described by one or more records in an array stored in a special file called the master file table (MFT). The size of a record is determined when the file system is created; it ranges from 1 to 4 KB. Small attributes are stored in the MFT record itself, and are called *resident attributes*. Large attributes, such as the unnamed bulk data, called *nonresident attributes*, are stored in one or more contiguous *extents* on the disk, and a pointer to each extent is stored in the MFT record. For a tiny file, even the data attribute may fit inside the MFT record. If a file has many attributes, or if it is highly fragmented and therefore many pointers are needed to point to all the fragments, one record in the MFT might not be large enough. In this case, the file is described by a record called the *base file record*, which contains pointers to overflow records that hold the additional pointers and attributes.

Each file in an NTFS volume has a unique ID called a *file reference*. The file reference is a 64-bit quantity that consists of a 48-bit file number and a 16-bit sequence number. The file number is the record number (that is, the array slot) in the MFT that describes the file. The sequence number is incremented every time that an MFT entry is reused. This incrementation enables NTFS to perform internal consistency checks, such as catching a stale reference to a deleted file after the MFT entry has been reused for a new file.

As in MS-DOS and UNIX, the NTFS name space is organized as a hierarchy of directories. Each directory uses a data structure called a *B+ tree* to store an index of the file names in that directory. A B+ tree is used because it eliminates the cost of reorganizing the tree and has the property that the length of every path from the root of the tree to a leaf is the same. The *index root* of a directory contains the top level of the B+ tree. For a large directory, this top level contains pointers to disk extents that hold the remainder of the tree. Each entry in the directory contains the name and file reference of the file, as well as a copy of the update timestamp and file size taken from the file's resident attributes in the MFT. Copies of this information are stored in the directory, so it is efficient to generate a directory listing—all the file names, sizes, and update times are available from the directory itself, so there is no need to gather these attributes from the MFT entries for each of the files.

The NTFS volume's metadata are all stored in files. The first file is the MFT. The second file, which is used during recovery if the MFT is damaged, contains a copy of the first 16 entries of the MFT. The next few files are also special. They are called the log file, volume file, attribute-definition table, root directory, bitmap file, boot file, and bad-cluster file. The *log file* (Section 23.5.2) records all metadata updates to the file system. The *volume file* contains the name of the volume, the version of NTFS that formatted the volume, and a bit that tells whether the volume may have been corrupted and needs to be checked for consistency. The *attribute-definition table* indicates which attribute types are used in the volume, and what operations can be performed on each of them. The *root directory* is the top-level directory in the file-system hierarchy. The *bitmap file* indicates which clusters on a volume are allocated to files, and which are free. The *boot file* contains the startup code for Windows 2000 and must be located at a particular disk address so that it can be found easily by a simple ROM bootstrap loader. The boot file also contains the physical address of the MFT. Finally, the *bad-cluster file* keeps track of any bad areas on the volume; NTFS uses this record for error recovery.

23.5.2 Recovery

In many simple file systems, a power failure at the wrong time can damage the file-system data structures so severely that the entire volume is scrambled. Many versions of UNIX store redundant metadata on the disk, and they recover from crashes using the `fsck` program to check all the file-system data structures, and to restore them forcibly to a consistent state. Restoring them often involves deleting damaged files and freeing data clusters that had been written with user data but have not been properly recorded in the file system's metadata structures. This checking can be a slow process, and can lose significant numbers of data.

NTFS takes a different approach to file-system robustness. In NTFS, all file-system data-structure updates are performed inside transactions. Before a data structure is altered, the transaction writes a log record that contains redo and undo information; after the data structure has been changed, the transaction writes a commit record to the log to signify that the transaction succeeded. After a crash, the system can restore the file-system data structures to a consistent state by processing the log records, first redoing the operations for committed transactions, then undoing the operations for transactions that did not commit successfully before the crash. Periodically (usually every 5 seconds), a checkpoint record is written to the log. The system does not need log records prior to the checkpoint to recover from a crash. They can be discarded, so the log file does not grow without bound. The first time after system startup that an NTFS volume is accessed, NTFS automatically performs file-system recovery.

This scheme does not guarantee that all the user-file contents are correct after a crash; it ensures only that the file-system data structures (the metadata files) are undamaged and reflect some consistent state that existed prior to the crash. It would be possible to extend the transaction scheme to cover user files, but the overhead would impair the file-system performance.

The log is stored in the third metadata file at the beginning of the volume. It is created with a fixed maximum size when the file system is formatted. It has two sections: the *logging area*, which is a circular queue of log records, and the *restart area*, which holds context information, such as the position in the logging area where NTFS should start reading during a recovery. In fact, the restart area holds two copies of its information, so recovery is still possible if one copy is damaged during the crash.

The logging functionality is provided by the Windows 2000 *log-file service*. In addition to writing the log records and performing recovery actions, the log-file service keeps track of the free space in the log file. If the free space gets too low, the log-file service queues pending transactions, and NTFS halts all new I/O operations. After the in-progress operations complete, NTFS calls the cache manager to flush all data, then resets the log file and performs the queued transactions.

23.5.3 Security

The security of an NTFS volume is derived from the Windows 2000 object model. Each file object has a security-descriptor attribute stored in its MFT record. This attribute contains the access token of the owner of the file, and an access-control list that states the access privileges granted to each user having access to the file.

23.5.4 Volume Management and Fault Tolerance

FtDisk is the fault-tolerant disk driver for Windows 2000. When installed, it provides several ways to combine multiple disk drives into one logical volume, so as to improve performance, capacity, or reliability.

One way to combine multiple disks is to concatenate them logically to form a large logical volume, as shown in Figure 23.7. In Windows 2000, this logical

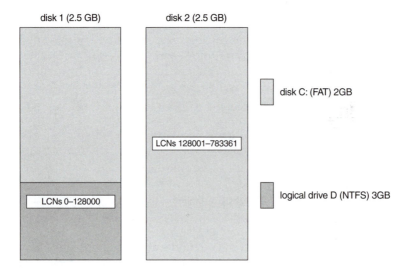

disk 1 (2.5 GB)   disk 2 (2.5 GB)

disk C: (FAT) 2GB

LCNs 128001–783361

LCNs 0–128000

logical drive D (NTFS) 3GB

Figure 23.7   Volume set on two drives.

volume is called a *volume set*, which can consist of up to 32 physical partitions.
A volume set that contains an NTFS volume can be extended without the data
already stored in the file system being disturbed. The bitmap metadata on
the NTFS volume are simply extended to cover the newly added space. NTFS
continues to use the same LCN mechanism that it uses for a single physical disk,
and the FtDisk driver supplies the mapping from a logical volume offset to the
offset on one particular disk.

Another way to combine multiple physical partitions is to interleave their
blocks in round-robin fashion to form what is called a *stripe set*, as shown in
Figure 23.8. This scheme is also called RAID level 0, or *disk striping*. FtDisk
uses a stripe size of 64 KB: The first 64 KB of the logical volume are stored in
the first physical partition, the second 64 KB of the logical volume are stored
in the second physical partition, and so on, until each partition has contributed
64 KB of space. Then, the allocation wraps around to the first disk, allocating
the second 64 KB block. A stripe set forms one large logical volume, but the
physical layout can improve the I/O bandwidth, because, for a large I/O, all the
disks can transfer data in parallel. For more information on RAID, see Section
13.5.

A variation of this idea is the *stripe set with parity*, which is shown in Figure
23.9. This scheme is also called RAID level 5. If the stripe set has eight disks,
then, for each of the seven data stripes, on seven separate disks, there will
be a parity stripe on the eighth disk. The parity stripe contains the byte-wise
exclusive or of the data stripes. If any one of the eight stripes is destroyed,
the system can reconstruct the data by calculating the exclusive or of the
remaining seven. This ability to reconstruct data makes the disk array much

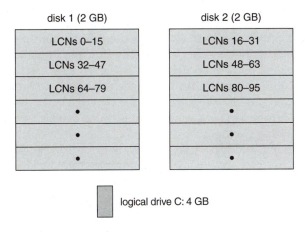

Figure 23.8 Stripe set on two drives.

less likely to lose data in case of a disk failure. Notice that an update to one data stripe also requires recalculation of the parity stripe. Seven concurrent writes to seven different data stripes thus would also require seven parity stripes to be updated. If the parity stripes were all on the same disk, that disk could have seven times the I/O load of the data disks. To avoid creating this bottleneck, we spread the parity stripes over all the disks, such as by assigning them round-robin. To build a stripe set with parity, we need a minimum of three equal-sized partitions located on three separate disks.

An even more robust scheme is called *disk mirroring* or RAID level 1; it is depicted in Figure 23.10. A *mirror set* comprises two equal-sized partitions on

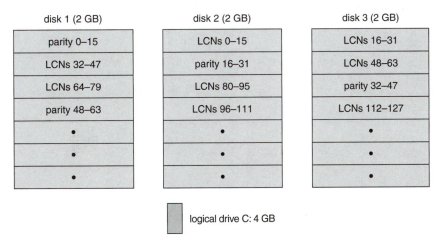

Figure 23.9 Stripe set with parity on three drives.

two disks, such that their data contents are identical. When an application writes data to a mirror set, FtDisk writes the data to both partitions. If one partition fails, FtDisk has another copy safely stored on the mirror. Mirror sets can also improve the performance, because read requests can be split between the two mirrors, giving each mirror half of the workload. To protect against the failure of a disk controller, we can attach the two disks of a mirror set to two separate disk controllers. This arrangement is called a *duplex set*.

To deal with disk sectors that go bad, FtDisk uses a hardware technique called sector sparing, and NTFS uses a software technique called cluster remapping. Sector sparing is a hardware capability provided by many disk drives. When a disk drive is formatted, it creates a map from logical block numbers to good sectors on the disk. It also leaves extra sectors unmapped, as spares. If a sector fails, FtDisk will instruct the disk drive to substitute a spare. *Cluster remapping* is a software technique performed by the file system. If a disk block goes bad, NTFS will substitute a different, unallocated block by changing any affected pointers in the MFT. NTFS also makes a note that the bad block should never be allocated to any file.

When a disk block goes bad, the usual outcome is a data loss. But sector sparing or cluster remapping can be combined with fault-tolerant volumes such as stripe sets to mask the failure of a disk block. If a read fails, the system reconstructs the missing data by reading the mirror or by calculating the exclusive or parity in a stripe set with parity. The reconstructed data are stored into a new location that is obtained by sector sparing or cluster remapping.

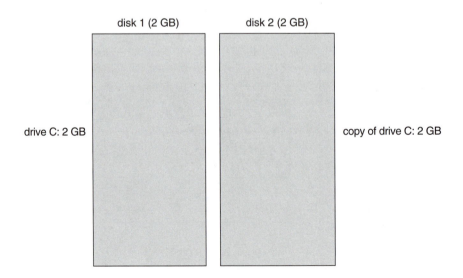

Figure 23.10   Mirror set on two drives.

23.5.5 Compression

NTFS can perform data compression on individual files or on all data files in a directory. To compress a file, NTFS divides the file's data into *compression units*, which are blocks of 16 contiguous clusters. When each compression unit is written, a data-compression algorithm is applied. If the result fits into fewer than 16 clusters, the compressed version is stored. When reading, NTFS can determine whether data have been compressed: If they have been, the length of the stored compression unit is less than 16 clusters. To improve performance when reading contiguous compression units, NTFS prefetches and decompresses ahead of the application requests.

For sparse files or files that mostly contain zeros, NTFS uses another technique to save space. Clusters that contain all zeros are not actually allocated or stored on disk. Instead, gaps are left in the sequence of virtual-cluster numbers stored in the MFT entry for the file. When reading a file, if it finds a gap in the virtual-cluster numbers, NTFS just zero-fills that portion of the caller's buffer. This technique is also used by UNIX.

23.5.6 Reparse Points

Reparse points are a new feature in the file system that in effect return an error code when accessed. The reparse data then tell the I/O manager what to do.

Mount points are another feature added to Windows 2000; they are a form of reparse points. Unlike UNIX systems, previous Windows versions provided no way to do a logical join of partitions. Each partition was assigned a drive letter that was distinct from every other partition. This meant that, among other things, that if a file system filled, the directory structure would need to be changed to add more space. Mount points would allow you to create a new volume on another drive, move the old data to the new volume, and then mount the new volume in the original place. The data would then still be usable by installed programs, since the data would appear to be in the same place as before. The mount point is implemented as a reparse point with reparse data that contains the true volume name.

The *remote storage services* facility also uses reparse points. When a file is moved to offline storage, the original file data are replaced with a reparse point that contains information about where that file is. When the file is accessed later, the file is retrieved and the reparse point is replaced with the data from the file. For more information about hierarchical storage, see Section 13.7.1.

23.6 ■ Networking

Windows 2000 supports both peer-to-peer and client–server networking. It also has facilities for network management. The networking components in Windows 2000 provide data transport, interprocess communication, file sharing across a network, and the ability to send print jobs to remote printers.

To describe networking in Windows 2000, we will refer to two of the internal networking interfaces called the *network device interface specification (NDIS)* and the *transport driver interface (TDI)*. The NDIS interface was developed in 1989 by Microsoft and 3Com to separate network adapters from the transport protocols, so that either could be changed without affecting the other. NDIS resides at the interface between the data-link control and media-access-control layers in the OSI model and enables many protocols to operate over many different network adapters. In terms of the OSI model, the TDI is the interface between the transport layer (layer 4) and the session layer (layer 5). This interface enables any session-layer component to use any available transport mechanism. (Similar reasoning led to the streams mechanism in UNIX.) The TDI supports both connection-based and connectionless transport, and has functions to send any type of data.

23.6.1 Protocols

Windows 2000 implements transport protocols as drivers. These drivers can be loaded and unloaded from the system dynamically, although in practice the system typically has to be rebooted after a change. Windows 2000 comes with several networking protocols.

The *server message-block (SMB)* protocol was first introduced in MS-DOS 3.1. The system uses the protocol to send I/O requests over the network. The SMB protocol has four message types. The `Session control` messages are commands that start and end a redirector connection to a shared resource at the server. A redirector uses `File` messages to access files at the server. The system uses `Printer` messages to send data to a remote print queue and to receive back status information, and the `Message` message is used to communicate with another workstation.

The *network basic input/output system (NetBIOS)* is a hardware-abstraction interface for networks, analogous to the BIOS hardware-abstraction interface devised for PCs running MS-DOS. NetBIOS, developed in the early 1980s, has become a standard network-programming interface. NetBIOS is used to establish logical names on the network, to establish logical connections or *sessions* between two logical names on the network, and to support reliable data transfer for a session via either NetBIOS or SMB requests.

The *NetBIOS extended user interface (NetBEUI)* was introduced by IBM in 1985 as a simple, efficient networking protocol for up to 254 machines. It is the default protocol for Windows 95 peer networking and for Windows for Workgroups. Windows 2000 uses NetBEUI when it wants to share resources with these networks. Among the limitations of NetBEUI are that it uses the actual name of a computer as the address, and that it does not support routing.

The TCP/IP protocol suite that is used on the Internet has become the de facto standard networking infrastructure; it is widely supported. Windows 2000 uses TCP/IP to connect to a wide variety of operating systems and hardware platforms. The Windows 2000 TCP/IP package includes the simple network-management protocol (SNMP), dynamic host-configuration protocol (DHCP), Windows Internet name service (WINS), and NetBIOS support.

The *point-to-point tunneling protocol (PPTP)* is a protocol provided by Windows 2000 to communicate between remote-access server modules running on Windows 2000 Server machines and other client systems that are connected over the Internet. The remote-access servers can encrypt data sent over the connection, and they support multiprotocol virtual private networks over the Internet.

The Novell NetWare protocols (IPX datagram service on the SPX transport layer) are widely used for PC LANs. The Windows 2000 NWLink protocol connects the NetBIOS to NetWare networks. In combination with a redirector (such as Microsoft's Client Service for Netware or Novell's NetWare Client for Windows 2000), this protocol enables a Windows 2000 client to connect to a NetWare server.

Windows 2000 uses the *data-link control (DLC) protocol* to access IBM mainframes and HP printers that are connected directly to the network. This protocol is not otherwise used by Windows 2000 systems.

The *AppleTalk protocol* was designed as a low-cost connection by Apple to allow Macintosh computers to share files. Windows 2000 systems can share files and printers with Macintosh computers via AppleTalk if a Windows 2000 server on the network is running the Windows 2000 Services for Macintosh package.

23.6.2 Distributed-Processing Mechanisms

Although Windows 2000 is not a distributed operating system, it does support distributed applications. Mechanisms that support distributed processing on Windows 2000 include NetBIOS, named pipes and mailslots, windows sockets, RPCs, and network dynamic data exchange (NetDDE).

In Windows 2000, NetBIOS applications can communicate over the network using NetBEUI, NWLink, or TCP/IP.

Named pipes are a connection-oriented messaging mechanism. Named pipes were originally developed as a high-level interface to NetBIOS connections over the network. A process can also use named pipes to communicate with other processes on the same machine. Since named pipes are accessed through the file-system interface, the security mechanisms used for file objects also apply to named pipes.

The name of a named pipe has a format called the *uniform naming convention (UNC)*. A UNC name looks like a typical remote file name. The format of a UNC name is \\server_name\share_name\x\y\z, where the server_name identifies a server on the network; a share_name identifies any resource that is made available to network users, such as directories, files, named pipes and printers; and the \x\y\z part is a normal file path name.

Mailslots are a connectionless messaging mechanism. They are unreliable, in that a message sent to a mailslot may be lost before the intended recipient receives it. Mailslots are used for broadcast applications, such as for finding components on the network; they are also used by the Windows 2000 Computer Browser service.

Winsock is the Windows 2000 sockets API. Winsock is a session-layer interface that is largely compatible with UNIX sockets, with some Windows 2000 extensions. It provides a standardized interface to many transport protocols that may have different addressing schemes, so that any Winsock application can run on any Winsock-compliant protocol stack.

An RPC is a client–server mechanism that enables an application on one machine to make a procedure call to code on another machine. The client calls a local procedure—a *stub routine*—that packs its arguments into a message and sends them across the network to a particular server process. The client-side stub routine then blocks. Meanwhile, the server unpacks the message, calls the procedure, packs the return results into a message, and sends them back to the client stub. The client stub unblocks, receives the message, unpacks the results of the RPC, and returns them to the caller. This packing of arguments is sometimes called *marshalling*.

The Windows 2000 RPC mechanism follows the widely used distributed-computing environment standard for RPC messages, so programs written to use Windows 2000 RPCs are highly portable. The RPC standard is detailed. It hides many of the architectural differences between computers, such as the sizes of binary numbers and the order of bytes and bits in computer words, by specifying standard data formats for RPC messages.

Windows 2000 can send RPC messages using NetBIOS, or Winsock on TCP/IP networks, or named pipes on LAN Manager networks. The LPC facility, discussed earlier, is similar to RPC, except that in the LPC case the messages are passed between two processes running on the same computer.

It is tedious and error-prone to write the code to marshal and transmit arguments in the standard format, to unmarshal and execute the remote procedure, to marshal and send the return results, and to unmarshal and return them to the caller. Fortunately, however, much of this code can be generated automatically from a simple description of the arguments and return results.

Windows 2000 provides the *Microsoft Interface Definition Language* to describe the remote procedure names, arguments, and results. The compiler for this language generates header files that declare the stubs for the remote procedures, and the data types for the argument and return-value messages. It also generates source code for the stub routines used at the client side, and for an unmarshaller and dispatcher at the server side. When the application is linked, the stub routines are included. When the application executes the RPC stub, the generated code handles the rest.

COM is a mechanism for interprocess communication that was developed for Windows. COM objects provide a well defined interface to manipulate the data in the object. Windows 2000 has an extension called *DCOM* that can be used over a network utilizing the RPC mechanism to provide a transparent method of developing distributed applications.

23.6.3 Redirectors and Servers

In Windows 2000, an application can use the Windows 2000 I/O API to access files from a remote computer as though they were local, provided that the remote computer is running an MS-NET server, such as is provided by Windows 2000 or Windows for Workgroups. A *redirector* is the client-side object that forwards I/O requests to remote files, where they are satisfied by a server. For performance and security, the redirectors and servers run in kernel mode.

In more detail, access to a remote file occurs as follows:

- The application calls the I/O manager to request that a file be opened with a file name in the standard UNC format.

- The I/O manager builds an I/O request packet, as described in Section 23.3.3.5.

- The I/O manager recognizes that the access is for a remote file, and calls a driver called a *multiple universal-naming-convention provider (MUP)*.

- The MUP sends the I/O request packet asynchronously to all registered redirectors.

- A redirector that can satisfy the request responds to the MUP. To avoid asking all the redirectors the same question in the future, the MUP uses a cache to remember which redirector can handle this file.

- The redirector sends the network request to the remote system.

- The remote-system network drivers receive the request and pass it to the server driver.

- The server driver hands the request to the proper local file-system driver.

- The proper device driver is called to access the data.

- The results are returned to the server driver, which sends the data back to the requesting redirector. The redirector then returns the data to the calling application via the I/O manager.

A similar process occurs for applications that use the Win32 network API, rather than the UNC services, except that a module called a multiprovider router is used, instead of a MUP.

For portability, redirectors and servers use the TDI API for network transport. The requests themselves are expressed in a higher-level protocol, which by default is the SMB protocol mentioned in Section 23.6.1. The list of redirectors is maintained in the system registry database.

23.6.4 Domains

Many networked environments have natural groups of users, such as students in a computer laboratory at school, or employees in one department in a business. Frequently, we want all the members of the group to be able to access shared resources on their various computers in the group. To manage the global access rights within such groups, Windows 2000 uses the concept of a domain. Previously, these domains had no relationship whatsoever to the domain name system DNS that maps Internet host names to IP addresses; now, however, they are closely related. Specifically, a Windows 2000 domain is a group of Windows 2000 workstations and servers that shares a common security policy and user database. Since Windows 2000 now uses the Kerberos protocol for trust and authentication, a Windows 2000 domain is the same thing as a Kerberos realm. Previous versions of NT used the idea of primary and backup domain controllers; now all servers in a domain are domain controllers. In addition, previous versions required the setup of one-way trusts between domains. Windows 2000 utilizes uses a hierarchical approach based on DNS, and allows transitive trusts that can flow up and down the hierarchy. This approach reduces the number of trusts required for n domains from $n * (n - 1)$ to $O(n)$. The workstations in the domain trust the domain controller to give correct information about the access rights of each user (via the user's access token). All users retain the ability to restrict access to their own workstations, no matter what any domain controller may say.

Because a business may have many departments and a school may have many classes, it is often necessary to manage multiple domains within a single organization. A *domain tree* is a contiguous DNS naming hierarchy. For example, *bell-labs.com* might be the root of the tree, with *research.bell-labs.com* and *pez.bell-labs.com* as children—domains *research* and *pez*. A *forest* is a set of non-contiguous names. An example would be the trees *bell-labs.com* and/or *lucent.com*. A forest may be comprised of only one domain tree, however.

Trust relationships may be set up between domains in three ways, one-way, transitive, and cross-link. Versions of NT through Version 4.0 allowed only one-way trusts to be set up. A *one-way trust* is exactly what its name implies: Domain A is told it can trust domain B. However, B would not trust A unless another relationship is configured. Under a *transitive trust*, if A trusts B and B trusts C, then A, B, and C all trust one another since transitive trusts are two-way by default. Transitive trusts are enabled by default for new domains in a tree and can be configured only among domains within a forest. The third type, a *cross-link trust*, is useful to cut down on authentication traffic. Suppose that domains A and B are leaf nodes, and that users in A often use resources in B. If a standard transitive trust is used, authentication requests must traverse up to the common ancestor of the two leaf nodes; but if A and B have a cross-linking trust established, the authentications would be sent directly to the other node.

23.6.5 Name Resolution in TCP/IP Networks

On an IP network, *name resolution* is the process of converting a computer name to an IP address, such as resolving *www.bell-labs.com* to 135.104.1.14. Windows 2000 provides several methods of name resolution, including Windows Internet Name Service (WINS), broadcast name resolution, domain name system (DNS), a hosts file, and an LMHOSTS file. Most of these methods are used by many operating systems, so we describe only WINS here.

Under WINS, two or more WINS servers maintain a dynamic database of name-to-IP address bindings, and client software to query the servers. At least two servers are used, so that the WINS service can survive a server failure, and so that the name-resolution workload can be spread over multiple machines.

WINS uses the dynamic host-configuration protocol (DHCP). DHCP updates address configurations automatically in the WINS database, without user or administrator intervention, as follows. When a DHCP client starts up, it broadcasts a `discover` message. Each DHCP server that receives the message replies with an `offer` message that contains an IP address and configuration information for the client. The client then chooses one of the configurations and sends a `request` message to the selected DHCP server. The DHCP server responds with the IP address and configuration information it gave previously, and with a *lease* for that address. The lease gives the client the right to use that IP address for a specified period of time. When the lease time is half expired, the client will attempts to renew the lease for that address. If the lease is not renewed, the client must get a new one.

23.7 ■ Programmer Interface

The Win32 API is the fundamental interface to the capabilities of Windows 2000. This section describes five main aspects of the Win32 API: access to kernel objects, sharing of objects between processes, process management, interprocess communication, and memory management.

23.7.1 Access to Kernel Objects

The Windows 2000 kernel provides many services that application programs can use. Application programs obtain these services by manipulating kernel objects. A process gains access to a kernel object named XXX by calling the `CreateXXX` function to open a handle to XXX. This handle is unique to that process. Depending on which object is being opened, if the `create` function fails, it may return 0, or it may return a special constant named

INVALID_HANDLE_VALUE. A process can close any handle by calling the Close-Handle function, and the system may delete the object if the count of processes using the object drops to 0.

Windows 2000 provides three ways to share objects between processes. The first way is for a child process to inherit a handle to the object. When the parent calls the CreateXXX function, the parent supplies a SECURITIES_ATTRIBUTES structure with the bInheritHandle field set to TRUE. This field creates an inheritable handle. Then, the child process can be created, passing a value of TRUE to the CreateProcess function's bInheritHandle argument. Figure 23.11 shows a code sample that creates a semaphore handle that is inherited by a child process.

Assuming that the child process knows which handles are shared, the parent and child can achieve interprocess communication through the shared objects. In the example in Figure 23.11, the child process would get the value of the handle from the first command-line argument, and could then share the semaphore with the parent process.

The second way to share objects is for one process to give the object a name when that object is created, and for the second process to open that name. This method has two drawbacks. One is that Windows 2000 does not provide a way to check whether an object with the chosen name already exists. A second drawback is that the object name space is global, without regard to the object type. For instance, two applications may create an object named *pipe* when two distinct—and possibly different—objects are desired.

Named objects have the advantage that unrelated processes can share them readily. The first process would call one of the CreateXXX functions and supply a name in the lpszName parameter. The second process can get a handle to share this object by calling OpenXXX (or CreateXXX) with the same name, as shown in the example of Figure 23.12.

```
...
SECURITY_ATTRIBUTES sa;
sa.nlength = sizeof(sa);
sa.lpSecurityDescriptor = NULL;
sa.bInheritHandle = TRUE;
Handle a_semaphore = CreateSemaphore(&sa,1,1,NULL);
char command_line[132] ;
ostrstream ostring(command_line,sizeof(command_line));
ostring << a_semaphore << ends;
CreateProcess("another_process.exe",command_line,
              NULL,NULL,TRUE, ... );
...
```

Figure 23.11   Code for a child to share an object by inheriting a handle.

```
// process A
...
Handle a_semaphore = CreateSemaphore(NULL,1,1,"MySEM1");
...
// process B
...
Handle b_semaphore = OpenSemaphore(SEMAPHORE_ALL_ACCESS,
                                   FALSE, "MySEM1");
...
```

Figure 23.12   Code for sharing an object by name lookup.

The third way to share objects is via the `DuplicateHandle` function. This method requires some other method of interprocess communication to pass the duplicated handle. Given a handle to a process and the value of a handle within that process, a second process can get a handle to the same object, and thus share it. An example of this method is shown in Figure 23.13.

23.7.2 Process Management

In Windows 2000, a process is an executing instance of an application, and a thread is a unit of code that can be scheduled by the operating system. Thus, a process contains one or more threads. A process is started when some other process calls the `CreateProcess` routine. This routine loads any dynamic link libraries that are used by the process, and creates a *primary thread*. Additional

```
...
// process A wants to give process B access to a semaphore
// process A
Handle a_semaphore = CreateSemaphore(NULL,1,1,NULL);
// send the value of the semaphore to process B
// using a message or shared memory
...
// process B
Handle process_a = OpenProcess(PROCESS_ALL_ACCESS,FALSE,
                               process_id_of_A);
Handle b_semaphore;
DuplicateHandle(process_a,a_semaphore,
   GetCurrentProcess(),&b_semaphore,
   0,FALSE,DUPLICATE_SAME_ACCESS);
// use b_semaphore to access the semaphore
...
```

Figure 23.13   Code for sharing an object by passing a handle.

threads can be created by the CreateThread function. Each thread is created with its own stack, which defaults to 1 MB unless specified otherwise in an argument to CreateThread. Because some C run-time functions maintain state in static variables, such as errno, a multithread application needs to guard against unsynchronized access. The wrapper function beginthreadex provides appropriate synchronization.

Every dynamic link library or executable file that is loaded into the address space of a process is identified by an *instance handle*. The value of the instance handle is actually the virtual address where the file is loaded. An application can get the handle to a module in its address space by passing the name of the module to GetModuleHandle. If NULL is passed as the name, the base address of the process is returned. The lowest 64 KB of the address space are not used, so a faulty program that tries to dereference a NULL pointer will get an access violation.

Priorities in the Win32 environment are based on the Windows 2000 scheduling model, but not all priority values may be chosen. Win32 uses four priority classes: IDLE_PRIORITY_CLASS (priority level 4), NOR-MAL_PRIORITY_CLASS (priority level 8), HIGH_PRIORITY_CLASS (priority level 13) and REALTIME_PRIORITY_CLASS (priority level 24). Processes are typically members of the NORMAL_PRIORITY_CLASS unless the parent of the process was of the IDLE_PRIORITY_CLASS, or another class was specified when CreateProcess was called. The priority class of a process can be changed with the SetPriorityClass function, or by an argument being passed to the START command. For example, the command START /REALTIME cbserver.exe would run the cbserver program in the REALTIME_PRIORITY_CLASS. Note that only users with the increase scheduling priority privilege can move a process into the REALTIME_PRIORITY_CLASS. Administrators and power users have this privilege by default.

When a user is running an interactive program, the system needs to provide especially good performance for that process. For this reason, Windows 2000 has a special scheduling rule for processes in the NORMAL_PRIORITY_CLASS. Windows 2000 distinguishes between the foreground process that is currently selected on the screen, and the background processes that are not currently selected. When a process moves into the foreground, Windows 2000 increases the scheduling quantum by some factor—typically by 3. (This factor can be changed via the performance option in the system section of the control panel.) This increase gives the foreground process three times longer to run before a timesharing preemption occurs.

A thread starts with an initial priority determined by its class, but the priority can be altered by the SetThreadPriority function. This function takes an argument that specifies a priority relative to the base priority of its class:

- THREAD_PRIORITY_LOWEST: base − 2

- THREAD_PRIORITY_BELOW_NORMAL: base − 1

- THREAD_PRIORITY_NORMAL: base + 0

- THREAD_PRIORITY_ABOVE_NORMAL: base + 1

- THREAD_PRIORITY_HIGHEST: base + 2

Two other designations are also used to adjust the priority. Recall from Section 23.3.2 that the kernel has two priority classes: 16–31 for the real-time class, and 0–15 for the variable-priority class. THREAD_PRIORITY_IDLE sets the priority to 16 for real-time threads, and to 1 for variable-priority threads. THREAD_PRIORITY_TIME_CRITICAL sets the priority to 31 for real-time threads, and to 15 for variable-priority threads.

As we discussed in Section 22.3.2, the kernel adjusts the priority of a thread dynamically depending on whether the thread is I/O bound or CPU bound. The Win32 API provides a method to disable this adjustment, via SetProcessPriorityBoost and SetThreadPriorityBoost functions.

A thread can be created in a *suspended state*: The thread will not execute until another thread makes it eligible via the ResumeThread function. The SuspendThread function does the opposite. These functions set a counter, so if a thread is suspended twice, it must be resumed twice before it can run.

To synchronize the concurrent access to shared objects by threads, the kernel provides synchronization objects, such as semaphores and mutexes. In addition, synchronization of threads can be achieved by using the WaitFor-SingleObject or WaitForMultipleObjects functions. Another method of synchronization in the Win32 API is the critical section. A critical section is a synchronized region of code that can be executed by only one thread at a time. A thread establishes a critical section by calling InitializeCritical-Section. The application must call EnterCriticalSection before entering the critical section, and LeaveCriticalSection after exiting the critical section. These two routines guarantee that, if multiple threads attempt to enter the critical section concurrently, only one thread at a time will be permitted to proceed, and the others will wait in the EnterCriticalSection routine. The critical-section mechanism is slightly faster than the kernel-synchronization objects.

A *fiber* is user-mode code that gets scheduled according to a user-defined scheduling algorithm. A process may have multiple fibers in it, just as it can have multiple threads. A major difference between threads and fibers is that threads can execute concurrently, but only one fiber at a time is permitted to execute, even on multiprocessor hardware. This mechanism is included in Windows 2000 to facilitate the porting of those legacy UNIX applications that were written for a fiber-execution model.

The system creates a fiber by calling either ConvertThreadToFiber or CreateFiber. The primary difference between these functions is that Create-Fiber does not begin executing the fiber that was created. To begin execution, the application must call `SwitchToFiber`. The application can terminate a fiber by calling `DeleteFiber`.

23.7.3 Interprocess Communication

One way that Win32 applications can do interprocess communication is by sharing kernel objects. Another way is by passing messages, an approach that is particularly popular for Windows GUI applications.

One thread can send a message to another thread or to a window by calling `PostMessage`, `PostThreadMessage`, `SendMessage`, `SendThreadMessage`, or `SendMessageCallback`. The difference between *posting* a message and *sending* a message is that the post routines are asynchronous: They return immediately, and the calling thread does not know when the message is actually delivered. The send routines are synchronous—they block the caller until the message has been delivered and processed.

In addition to sending a message, a thread can also send data with the message. Since processes have separate address spaces, the data must be copied. The system copies them by calling `SendMessage` to send a message of type `WM_COPYDATA` with a `COPYDATASTRUCT` data structure that contains the length and address of the data to be transferred. When the message is sent, Windows 2000 copies the data to a new block of memory and gives the virtual address of the new block to the receiving process.

Unlike the 16-bit Windows environment, every Win32 thread has its own input queue from which the thread receives messages. (All input is received via messages.) This structure is more reliable than the shared input queue of 16-bit windows, because, with separate queues, one stuck application cannot block input to the other applications. If a Win32 application does not call `GetMessage` to handle events on its input queue, the queue will fill up, and after about 5 seconds the system will mark the application as "Not Responding."

23.7.4 Memory Management

The Win32 API provides several ways for an application to use memory: virtual memory, memory-mapped files, heaps, and thread-local storage.

An application calls `VirtualAlloc` to reserve or commit virtual memory, and `VirtualFree` to decommit or release the memory. These functions enable the application to specify the virtual address at which the memory is allocated. They operate on multiples of the memory page size, and the starting address of an allocated region must be greater than 0x10000. Examples of these functions appear in Figure 23.14.

A process may lock some of its committed pages into physical memory by calling `VirtualLock`. The maximum number of pages that a process can lock is 30, unless the process first calls `SetProcessWorkingSetSize` to increase the maximum working-set size.

```
...
// allocate 16 MB at the top of our address space
void *buf = VirtualAlloc(0,0x1000000,MEM_RESERVE | MEM_TOP_DOWN,
            PAGE_READWRITE);
// commit the upper 8 MB of the allocated space
VirtualAlloc(buf + 0x800000,0x800000,MEM_COMMIT,PAGE_READWRITE);
// do some stuff with it
// decommit
VirtualFree(buf + 0x800000,0x800000,MEM_DECOMMIT);
// relcase all the allocated address space
VirtualFree(buf,0,MEM_RELEASE);
...
```

Figure 23.14   Code fragments for allocating virtual memory.

Another way for an application to use memory is by memory mapping a file into its address space. Memory mapping is also a convenient way for two processes to share memory: Both processes map the same file into their virtual memory. Memory mapping is a multistage process, as you can see in the example of Figure 23.15.

If a process wants to map some address space just to share a memory region with another process, no file is needed. The process can call Create-FileMapping with a file handle of 0xffffffff and a particular size. The resulting file-mapping object can be shared by inheritance, by name lookup, or by duplication.

```
...
// open the file or create it if it does not exist
HANDLE hfile = CreateFile("somefile",GENERIC_READ | GENERIC_WRITE,
    FILE_SHARE_READ | FILE_SHARE_WRITE,NULL,OPEN_ALWAYS,
    FILE_ATTRIBUTE_NORMAL,
    NULL);
// create the file mapping 8 MB in size
HANDLE hmap = CreateFileMapping(hfile,PAGE_READWRITE,
    SEC_COMMIT,0,0x800000,"SHM_1");
// get a view to the space mapped
void *buf = MapViewOfFile(hmap,FILE_MAP_ALL_ACCESS,0,0,0×800000);
// do some stuff with it
// unmap the file
UnmapViewOfFile(buf);
CloseHandle(hmap);
CloseHandle(hfile); ...
```

Figure 23.15   Code fragments for memory mapping of a file.

```
// reserve a slot for a variable
DWORD var_index = TlsAlloc();
// set it to some value
TlsSetValue(var_index,10);
// get the value back
int var = TlsGetValue(var_index);
// release the index
TlsFree(var_index);
```

Figure 23.16   Code for dynamic thread-local storage.

The third way for applications to use memory is a heap. A heap in the Win32 environment is just a region of reserved address space. When a Win32 process is initialized, it is created with a 1 MB *default heap*. Since many Win32 functions use the default heap, access to the heap is synchronized to protect the heap's space-allocation data structures from being damaged by concurrent updates by multiple threads. Win32 provides several heap-management functions so that a process can allocate and manage a private heap. These functions are HeapCreate, HeapAlloc, HeapRealloc, HeapSize, HeapFree, and HeapDestroy. The Win32 API also provides the HeapLock and HeapUnlock functions to enable a thread to gain exclusive access to a heap. Unlike VirtualLock, these functions perform only synchronization; they do not lock pages into physical memory.

The fourth way for applications to use memory is a thread-local storage mechanism. Functions that rely on global or static data typically fail to work properly in a multithreaded environment. For instance, the C run-time function strtok uses a static variable to keep track of its current position while parsing a string. For two concurrent threads to execute strtok correctly, they need separate *current position* variables. The thread-local storage mechanism allocates global storage on a per-thread basis. It provides both dynamic and static methods of creating thread-local storage. The dynamic method is illustrated in Figure 23.16.

To use a thread-local static variable, the application would declare the variable as follows to ensure that every thread has its own private copy:

```
__declspec(thread) DWORD cur_pos = 0;
```

23.8 ■ Summary

Microsoft designed Windows 2000 to be an extensible, portable operating system—one able to take advantage of new techniques and hardware. Windows 2000 supports multiple operating environments and symmetric multiprocessing. The use of kernel objects to provide basic services, and the support for client–server computing, enable Windows 2000 to support a wide variety of application environments. For instance, Windows 2000 can run programs compiled for MS-DOS, Win16, Windows 95, Windows 2000, and/or POSIX. It provides virtual memory, integrated caching, and preemptive scheduling. Windows 2000 supports a security model stronger than those of previous Microsoft operating systems, and includes internationalization features. Windows 2000 runs on a wide variety of computers, so users can choose and upgrade hardware to match their budgets and performance requirements, without needing to alter the applications that they run.

■ Exercises

23.1 What are some reasons why moving the graphics code in Windows NT from user mode to kernel mode might decrease the reliability of the system? Which of the original design goals for Windows NT does this degradation violate?

23.2 The Windows 2000 VM manager uses a two-stage process to allocate memory. Identify several ways in which this approach is beneficial.

23.3 Discuss some advantages and some disadvantages of the particular page-table structure used in Windows 2000.

23.4 What is the maximum number of page faults that could occur in the access of (a) a virtual address, and (b) a shared virtual address? What hardware mechanism do most processors provide to decrease these numbers?

23.5 What is the purpose of a prototype page-table entry in Windows 2000?

23.6 What are the steps the cache manager must take to copy data into and out of the cache?

23.7 What are the main problems involved in running 16-bit Windows applications in a VDM? Identify the solutions chosen by Windows 2000 for each of these problems. For each solution, name at least one drawback.

23.8 What changes would be needed for Windows 2000 to run a process that uses a 64-bit address space?

23.9 Windows 2000 has a centralized cache manager. What are the advantages and disadvantages of this cache manager?

23.10 Windows 2000 uses a packet-driven I/O system. Discuss the pros and cons of the packet-driven approach to I/O.

23.11 Consider a main-memory database of 1 terabytes. What mechanisms in Windows 2000 could you use to access this database?

Bibliographical Notes

Solomon and Russinovich [2000] gives an overview of Windows 2000 and considerable technical detail about the system internals and components. Tate [2000] is a good reference on using Windows 2000. The Microsoft Windows 2000 Server Resource Kit (Microsoft [2000b]) is a six-volume set helpful for using and deploying Windows 2000. The Microsoft Developer Network Library (Microsoft [2000a]) is issued quarterly. It provides a wealth of information on Windows 2000 and other Microsoft products. Iseminger [2000] provides a good reference on the Windows 2000 Active Directory. Richter [1997] gives a detailed discussion on writing programs that use the Win32 API. Silberschatz et al. [2001] contains a good discussion of B+ trees.

Chapter 24

WINDOWS XP

The Microsoft Windows XP operating system is a 32/64-bit preemptive multitasking operating system for AMD K6/K7, Intel IA32/IA64 and later microprocessors. The successor to Windows NT/2000, Windows XP is also intended to replace the Windows 95/98 operating system. Key goals for the system are security, reliability, ease-of-use, Windows and POSIX application compatibility, high performance, extensibility, portability and international support. In this chapter, we discuss the key goals for Windows XP, the layered architecture of the system that makes it so easy to use, the file system, networks, and the programming interface.

24.1 ■ History

In the mid-1980s, Microsoft and IBM cooperated to develop the OS/2 operating system, which was written in assembly language for single-processor Intel 80286 systems. In 1988, Microsoft decided to make a fresh start and to develop a "new technology" (or NT) portable operating system that supported both the OS/2 and POSIX application-programming interfaces (APIs). In October, 1988, Dave Cutler, the architect of the DEC VAX/VMS operating system, was hired and given the charter of building this new operating system.

Originally, the team planned for NT to use the OS/2 API as its native environment, but during development, NT was changed to use the 32-bit Windows API (or Win32 API), reflecting the popularity of Windows 3.0. The first versions of NT were Windows NT 3.1 and Windows NT 3.1 Advanced Server.

(At that time, 16-bit Windows was at Version 3.1.) Windows NT version 4.0 adopted the Windows 95 user interface and incorporated Internet web-server and web-browser software. In addition, user-interface routines and all graphics code were moved into the kernel to improve performance, with the side effect of decreased system reliability. Although previous versions of NT had been ported to other microprocessor architectures, the Windows 2000 version, released in February 2000, discontinued support for other than Intel (and compatible) processors due to marketplace factors. Windows 2000 incorporated significant changes over Windows NT. It added Active Directory (an X.500-based directory service), better networking and laptop support, support for plug-and-play devices, a distributed file-system, and support for more processors and more memory.

In October 2001 Windows XP was released as both an update to the Windows 2000 desktop operating system and a replacement for Windows 95/98. In 2002 the server versions of Windows XP will be available (to be called Windows .Net Server). Windows XP updates the graphical user interface with a visual design that takes advantage of more recent hardware advances and many new *ease-of-use* features. Numerous features have been added to automatically repair problems in applications and the operating system itself. Windows XP provides better networking and device experience (including zero-configuration wireless, instant messaging, streaming media, digital photography/video), dramatic performance improvements both for the desktop and large multiprocessors, and better reliability and security than even Windows 2000.

Windows XP uses a client–server architecture (like Mach) to implement multiple operating system personalities, such as Win32 and POSIX, with user-level processes called subsystems. The subsystem architecture allows enhancements to be made to one operating system personality without affecting the other's application compatibility.

Windows XP is a multi-user operating system, supporting simultaneous access through distributed services, or through multiple instances of the graphical user interface (GUI) via the Windows terminal server. The server versions of Windows XP support simultaneous terminal server sessions from Windows desktop systems. The desktop versions of terminal server multiplex the keyboard, mouse, and monitor between virtual terminal sessions for each logged-on user. This feature, called fast-user switching, allows users to preempt each other at the console of a PC without having to log off and on the system.

Windows XP is the first version of Windows to ship a 64-bit version. The native NT File System (NTFS) and many of the Win32 APIs have always used 64-bit integers where appropriate—so the major extension to 64-bit in Windows XP is support for large addresses.

There are two desktop versions of Windows XP. Windows XP Professional is the premium desktop system for power users at work and at home. For home users migrating from Windows 95/98, Windows XP Personal provides the reliability and ease-of-use of Windows XP, but without the more advanced features needed to work seamlessly with Active Directory or run POSIX applications.

The members of the Windows .Net Server family use the same core components as the desktop versions, but add a range of features needed for uses such as webserver farms, print/file servers, clustered systems, and large datacenter machines. The large datacenter machines can reach to 64 GB of memory and 32 processors on IA32 systems, and 128 GB and 64 processors on IA64 systems.

24.2 ■ Design Principles

Microsoft's design goals for Windows XP include security, reliability, Windows and POSIX application compatibility, high performance, extensibility, portability and international support.

24.2.1 Security

Windows XP *security* goals required more than just adherence to the design standards that enabled Windows NT4.0 to receive C-2 security classification from the U.S. government (which signifies a moderate level of protection from defective software and malicious attacks). Extensive code review and testing were combined with sophisticated automatic analysis tools to identify and investigate potential defects that might represent security vulnerabilities.

24.2.2 Reliability

Windows 2000 was the most reliable, stable operating system Microsoft ever shipped to that point. Much of this reliability came from maturity in the source code, extensive stress testing of the system, and automatic detection of many serious errors in drivers. The *reliability* requirements for Windows XP were even more stringent. Microsoft used extensive manual and automatic code review to identify over 63,000 lines in the source files that might contain issues not detected by testing, and set about reviewing each area to verify that the code was indeed correct.

Windows XP extends driver verification to catch more subtle bugs, improves the facilities for catching programming errors in user-level code, subjects third party applications, drivers, and devices to a rigorous certification process. Furthermore, Windows XP adds new facilities for monitoring the health of the PC including downloading fixes for problems before they are encountered by users. The perceived reliability of Windows XP was also improved by making the graphical user interface easier to use through better visual design, simpler menus, and measured improvements in the discoverability of how to perform common tasks.

24.2.3 Windows and Posix Application Compatibility

Windows XP is not only an update of Windows 2000; it is a replacement for Windows 95/98. Windows 2000 focused primarily on compatibility for business applications. The requirements for Windows XP include a much higher compatibility with consumer applications that run on Windows 95/98. *Application compatibility* is difficult to achieve because each application checks for a particular version of Windows, may have dependence on the quirks of the implementation of APIs, may have latent application bugs that were masked in the previous system, and other similar dependencies.

Windows XP introduces a compatibility layer that falls between applications and the Win32 APIs. This layer makes Windows XP look (almost) bug-for-bug compatible with previous versions of Windows. Windows XP, like earlier NT releases, maintains support for running many 16-bit applications using a thunking layer that translates 16-bit API calls into equivalent 32-bit calls. Similarly the 64-bit version of Windows XP provides a thunking layer that translates 32-bit API calls into native 64-bit calls. Posix support in Windows XP is much improved. A new POSIX subsystem called Interix is now available. Most available UNIX-compatible software compiles and runs under Interix without modification.

24.2.4 High Performance

Windows XP is designed to provide *high performance* on desktop systems (which are largely constrained by I/O performance), server systems (where CPU is often the bottleneck), and large multi-threaded and multi-processor environments (where locking and cache-line management are key to scalability). High performance has been an increasingly important goal for Windows XP. Windows 2000 with SQL 2000 on Compaq hardware achieved top TPC-C numbers at the time it shipped.

To satisfy performance requirements NT uses a variety of techniques such as asynchronous I/O, optimized protocols for networks (e.g. optimistic locking of distributed data, batching of requests), kernel-based graphics, and sophisticated caching of file-system data. The memory management and synchronization algorithms are designed with an awareness of the performance considerations related to cache-lines and multiprocessors.

Windows XP has further improved performance by reducing the code-path length in critical functions, using better algorithms and per-processor data structures, using memory coloring for NUMA (Non-Uniform Memory Access) machines, and implementing more scalable locking protocols, such as queued spinlocks. The new locking protocols help reduce system bus cycles, lock-free lists and queues, use of atomic read-modify-write operations (like interlocked increment), and other advanced locking techniques.

The subsystems that constitute Windows XP communicate with one another efficiently by a local procedure call (LPC) facility that provides high-performance message passing. Except while executing in the kernel dispatcher, threads in the subsystems of Windows XP can be preempted by higher-priority threads. Thus, the system responds quickly to external events. In addition, Windows XP is designed for symmetrical multiprocessing; on a multiprocessor computer, several threads can run at the same time.

24.2.5 Extensibility

Extensibility refers to the capacity of an operating system to keep up with advances in computing technology. So that changes are facilitated over time, the developers implemented Windows XP using a layered architecture. The Windows XP executive runs in kernel or protected mode and provides the basic system services. On top of the executive, several server subsystems operate in user-mode. Among them are *environmental subsystems* that emulate different operating systems. Thus, programs written for MS-DOS, Microsoft Windows, and POSIX all run on Windows XP in the appropriate environment. (See Section 24.4 for more information on environmental subsystems.) Because of the modular structure, additional environmental subsystems can be added without affecting the executive. In addition, Windows XP uses loadable drivers in the I/O system, so new file systems, new kinds of I/O devices, and new kinds of networking can be added while the system is running. Windows XP uses a client–server model like the Mach operating system, and supports distributed processing by remote procedure calls (RPCs) as defined by the Open Software Foundation.

24.2.6 Portability

An operating system is *portable* if it can be moved from one hardware architecture to another with relatively few changes. Windows XP is designed to be portable. As is true of the UNIX operating system, the majority of the system is written in C and C++. Most processor-dependent code is isolated in a dynamic link library (DLL) called the *hardware-abstraction layer* (**HAL**). A DLL is a file that gets mapped into a process' address space such that any functions in the DLL appear to be part of the process. The upper layers of Windows XP kernel depend on the HAL interfaces rather than on the underlying hardware, bolstering Windows XP portability. The HAL manipulates hardware directly, isolating the rest of Windows XP from hardware differences among the platforms on which it runs.

Although for market reasons Windows 2000 only shipped on Intel IA32 compatible platforms, it was also tested on IA32 and DEC Alpha platforms until just prior to release to ensure portability. Windows XP runs on IA32-compatible and IA64 processors. Microsoft recognizes the importance of multi-platform development and testing, since, as a practical matter, maintaining portability is a matter of *use it or lose it.*

24.2.7 International Support

Windows XP is also designed for *international* and *multinational* use. It provides support for different locales via the *national language support (NLS) API*. The NLS API provides specialized routines to format dates, time, and money in accordance with various national customs. String comparisons are specialized to account for varying character sets. UNICODE is Windows XP's native character code. Windows XP supports ANSI characters by converting them to UNICODE characters before manipulating them (8-bit to 16-bit conversion). System text strings are kept in resource files that can be replaced to localize the system for different languages. Multiple locales can be used concurrently, which is important to multilingual individuals and businesses.

24.3 ■ System Components

The architecture of Windows XP is a layered system of modules, as shown in Figure 24.1. The main layers are the HAL, the kernel, and the executive, all of which run in protected mode, and a collection of subsystems and services that run in user-mode. The user-mode subsystems fall into two categories. The environmental subsystems emulate different operating systems; the *protection subsystems* provide security functions. One of the chief advantages of this type of architecture is that interactions between modules are kept simple. The remainder of this section describes these layers and subsystems.

24.3.1 Hardware-Abstraction Layer

The HAL is the layer of software that hides hardware differences from upper levels of the operating system, to help make Windows XP portable. The HAL exports a virtual-machine interface that is used by the kernel dispatcher, the executive, and the device drivers. One advantage of this approach is that only a single version of each device driver is required—it runs on all hardware platforms without porting the driver code. The HAL also provides support for symmetric multiprocessing. Device drivers map devices and access them directly, but the administrative details of mapping memory, configuring I/O busses, setting up DMA and coping with motherboard-specific facilities is all provided by the HAL interfaces.

24.3.2 Kernel

The kernel of Windows XP provides the foundation for the executive and the subsystems. The kernel remains in memory, and its execution is never preempted. It has four main responsibilities: thread scheduling, interrupt and exception handling, low-level processor synchronization, and recovery after a power failure .

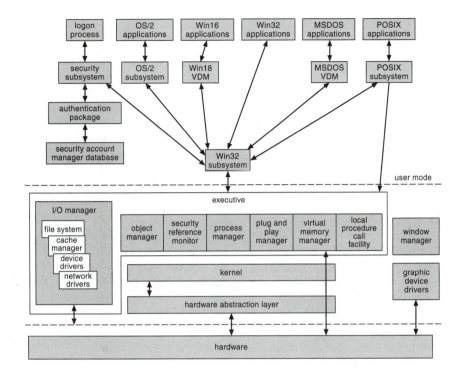

Figure 24.1 Windows XP block diagram.

The kernel is object-oriented. An *object type* in Windows 2000 is a system-defined data type that has a set of attributes (data values) and a set of methods (for example, functions or operations). An *object* is an instance of an object type. The kernel performs its job by using a set of kernel objects whose attributes store the kernel data, and whose methods perform the kernel activities.

24.3.2.1 Kernel Dispatcher

The kernel dispatcher provides the foundation for the executive and the subsystems. Most of the dispatcher is never paged out of memory, and its execution is never preempted. Its main responsibilities are thread scheduling, implementation of synchronization primitives, timer management, software interrupts (Asynchronous and Deferred Procedure Calls), and exception dispatching.

24.3.2.2 Threads and Scheduling

As do many modern operating systems, Windows XP uses the concepts of processes and threads for executable code. The process has a virtual-memory address space, and information used to initialize each thread, such as a base priority and an affinity for either one or more processors. Each process has one or more threads, each of which is an executable unit dispatched by the kernel.

Each thread has its own scheduling state, including actual priority, processor affinity, and CPU usage information.

The six possible thread states are ready, standby, running, waiting, transition, and terminated. *Ready* indicates waiting to run. The highest-priority ready thread is moved to the *standby* state, which means it is the next thread to run. In a multiprocessor system, each process keeps one thread in a standby state. A thread is *running* when it is executing on a processor. It runs until it is preempted by a higher-priority thread, it terminates, its alloted execution time (*quantum*) ends, or it blocks on a dispatcher object, such as an event signaling I/O completion. A thread is in the *waiting* state when it is waiting for a dispatcher object to be signaled. A new thread is in the *transition* state while it waits for resources necessary for execution. A thread enters the *terminated* state when it finishes execution.

The dispatcher uses a 32-level priority scheme to determine the order of thread execution. Priorities are divided into two classes: variable class and real-time class. The variable class contains threads having priorities from 0 to 15, and the real-time class contains threads with priorities ranging from 16 to 31. The dispatcher uses a queue for each scheduling priority, and traverses the set of queues from highest to lowest until it finds a thread that is ready to run. If a thread has a particular processor affinity but that processor is not available, the dispatcher skips past it, and continues looking for a ready thread that is willing to run on the available processor. If no ready thread is found, the dispatcher executes a special thread called the idle thread.

When a thread's time quantum runs out, the clock interrupt queues a quantum-end DPC to the processor in order to reschedule the processor. If the preempted thread is in the variable-priority class, its priority is lowered. The priority is never lowered below the base priority. Lowering the thread's priority tends to limit the CPU consumption of compute-bound threads. When a variable- priority thread is released from a wait operation, the dispatcher boosts the priority. The amount of the boost depends on the device for which the thread was waiting; for example, a thread that was waiting for keyboard I/O would get a large priority increase, whereas a thread waiting for a disk operation would get a moderate one. This strategy tends to give good response times to interactive threads using a mouse and windows, and enables I/O-bound threads to keep the I/O devices busy, while permitting compute-bound threads to use spare CPU cycles in the background. This strategy is used by several time-sharing operating systems, including UNIX. In addition, the thread associated with the user's active GUI window receives a priority boost to enhance its response time.

Scheduling occurs when a thread enters the ready or wait state, when a thread terminates, or when an application changes a thread's priority or processor affinity. If a higher-priority real-time thread becomes ready while a lower-priority thread is running, the lower-priority thread is preempted. This preemption gives a real-time thread preferential access to the CPU when the thread needs such access. Windows XP is not a hard real-time operating system, however, because it does not guarantee that a real-time thread will start to execute within a particular time limit.

24.3.2.3 Implementation of Synchronization Primitives

Key operating system data structures are managed as objects using common facilities for allocation, reference counting, and security. *Dispatcher objects* control dispatching and synchronization in the system. Examples of these objects are events, mutants, mutexes, semaphores, processes, threads, and timers. The *event object* is used to record an event occurrence and to synchronize the latter with some action. Notification events signal all waiting threads, and synchronization events signal a single waiting thread. The *mutant* provides kernel-mode or user-mode mutual exclusion with the notion of ownership. The *mutex*, available only in kernel-mode, provides deadlock-free mutual exclusion. A *semaphore object* acts as a counter or gate to control the number of threads that access a resource. The *thread object* is the entity that is scheduled by the kernel dispatcher and is associated with a *process object* which encapsulates a virtual address space. *Timer objects* are used to keep track of time and to signal timeouts when operations take too long and need to be interrupted, or a periodic activity needs to be scheduled.

Many of the dispatcher objects are accessed from user-mode via an open operation that returns a handle. The user-mode code polls and/or waits on handles to synchronize with other threads as well as the operating system (See section 24.7.1).

24.3.2.4 Software Interrupt: Asynchronous Procedure Calls

The dispatcher implements two types of software interrupts: asynchronous procedure calls and deferred procedure calls. Asynchronous procedure calls (APCs) break into an executing thread and call a procedure. APCs are used to begin execution of a new thread, terminate processes, and deliver notification that an asynchronous I/O has completed. APCs are queued to specific threads, and allow the system to execute both system and user code within a process' context.

24.3.2.5 Software Interrupt: Deferred Procedure Calls

Deferred procedure calls (DPCs) are used to postpone interrupt processing. After handling all blocked device interrupt processes, the interrupt service routine (ISR) schedules the remaining processing by queuing a DPC. The dispatcher schedules software interrupts at a lower priority than the device interrupts so that DPCs do not block other ISRs.

In addition to deferring device interrupt processing, the dispatcher uses DPCs to process timer expirations and to preempt thread execution at the end of the scheduling quantum.

Execution of DPCs prevent threads from being scheduled on the current processor, and also keeps APCs from signaling the completion of I/O. This is done so DPC routines do not take an extended amount of time to complete. As an alternative, the dispatcher maintains a pool of worker threads. ISRs and DPCs queue work items to the worker threads. DPC routines are restricted such that they cannot take page faults, call system services, or take any other action that might possibly result in an attempt to block execution on a dispatcher object. Unlike APCs, DPC routines make no assumptions about what process context the processor is executing.

24.3.2.6 Exceptions and Interrupts

The kernel dispatcher also provides trap handling for exceptions and interrupts generated by hardware or software. Windows XP defines several architecture-independent exceptions, including: memory-access violation, integer overflow, floating-point overflow or underflow, integer divide by zero, floating-point divide by zero, illegal instruction, data misalignment, privileged instruction, page read error, access violation, paging file quota exceeded, debugger breakpoint, and debugger single step.

The trap handlers deal with simple exceptions. Elaborate exception handling is performed by the kernel's exception dispatcher. The *exception dispatcher* creates an exception record containing the reason for the exception and finds an exception handler to deal with it.

When an exception occurs in kernel-mode, the exception dispatcher simply calls a routine to locate the exception handler. If no handler is found, a fatal system error occurs and the user is left with the infamous "blue screen of death" that signifies system failure.

Exception handling is more complex for user-mode processes, because an environmental subsystem (such as the POSIX system) sets up a debugger port and an exception port for every process it creates. If a debugger port is registered, the exception handler sends the exception to the port. If the debugger port is not found or does not handle that exception, the dispatcher attempts to find an appropriate exception handler. If a handler is not found, the debugger is called again to catch the error for debugging. If a debugger is not running, a message is sent to the process' exception port to give the environmental subsystem a chance to translate the exception. For example, the POSIX environment translates Windows XP exception messages into POSIX signals before sending them to the thread that caused the exception. Finally, if nothing else works, the kernel simply terminates the process that contains the thread that caused the exception.

The interrupt dispatcher in the kernel handles interrupts by calling either an interrupt service routine (ISR) supplied by a device driver, or a kernel trap handler routine. The interrupt is represented by an interrupt object that contains all the information needed to handle the interrupt. Using an interrupt object makes it easy to associate interrupt service routines with an interrupt without having to access the interrupt hardware directly.

Various processor architectures, such as Intel or DEC Alpha, have different types and numbers of interrupts. For portability, the interrupt dispatcher maps the hardware interrupts into a standard set. The interrupts are prioritized and are serviced in priority order. There are 32 interrupt request levels (**IRQLs**) in Windows XP. Eight are reserved for use by the kernel; the remaining 24 represent hardware interrupts via the HAL (although most IA32 systems use only 16). The Windows XP interrupts are defined in Figure 24.2.

The kernel uses an *interrupt dispatch table* to bind each interrupt level to a service routine. In a multiprocessor computer, Windows XP keeps a separate interrupt dispatch table for each processor, and each processor's IRQL can be set independently to mask-out interrupts. All interrupts that occur at a level equal to or less than the IRQL of a processor get blocked until the IRQL is lowered by a kernel-level thread or by an ISR returning from interrupt processing. Windows XP takes advantage of this property and uses software interrupts to deliver APCs and DPCs, to perform system functions such as synchronizing threads with I/O completion, to start thread dispatches and to handle timers.

24.3.3 Executive

The Windows XP executive provides a set of services that all environmental subsystems use. The services are grouped as follows: object manager, virtual-memory manager, process manager, local procedure call facility, I/O manager, security reference monitor, plug-and-play and security managers, registry, and booting.

interrupt levels	types of interrupts
31	machine check or bus error
30	power fail
29	interprocessor notification (request another processor to act; e.g., dispatch a process or update the TLB)
28	clock (used to keep track of time)
27	profile
3-26	traditional PC IRQ hardware interrupts
2	dispatch and deferred procedure call (DPC) (kernel)
1	asynchronous procedure call (APC)
0	passive

Figure 24.2 Windows XP interrupt request levels.

24.3.3.1 Object Manager

Windows XP uses a generic set of interfaces for managing the kernel-mode entities that is manipulated by user-mode programs. Windows XP calls these entities *objects*, and the executive component that manipulates them is the *object manager*. Each process has an object table containing entries that track the objects used by the process. User-mode code accesses these objects using an opaque value called a *handle* that is returned by many APIs. Object Handles can also be created by duplicating an existing handle, either from the same process or a different process.

Examples of objects are semaphores, mutexes, events, processes and threads. These are all *dispatcher objects*. Threads can block in the kernel dispatcher waiting for any of these objects to be signaled. The process, thread, and virtual memory APIs use process and thread handles to identify the process or thread to be operated on. Other examples of objects include files, sections, ports, and various internal I/O objects. File objects are used to maintain the open state of files and devices. Sections are used to map files. Open files are described in terms of file objects. Local communication endpoints are implemented as port objects.

The object manager maintains the Windows XP internal namespace. In contrast to UNIX which roots the system namespace in the file system, Windows XP uses an abstract namespace and connects the file-systems as devices.

The object manager provides interfaces for defining both object types and object instances, translating names to objects, maintaining the abstract namespace (through internal directories and symbolic links), and managing object creation and deletion. Objects are typically managed using reference counts in protected- mode code and handles in user-mode. However, some kernel-mode components use the same APIs as user-mode code and thus use handles to manipulate objects. If a handle needs to exist beyond the lifetime of the current process, it is marked as a kernel handle and stored in the object table for the system process. The abstract namespace does not persist across reboots, but is built up from configuration information stored in the system registry, plug-and-play device discovery, and creation of objects by system components.

The Windows XP executive allows any object to be given a *name*. One process may create a named object, while a second process opens a handle to the object and shares it with the first process. Processes can also share objects by duplicating handles between processes, in which case the objects need not be named.

A name can be either permanent or temporary. A permanent name represents an entity, such as a disk drive, that remains even if no process is accessing it. A temporary name exists only while a process holds a handle to the object.

Object names are structured like file path names in MS-DOS and UNIX. Namespace directories are represented by a *directory object* that contains the names of all the objects in the directory. The object namespace is extended by the addition of device objects representing volumes containing file systems.

Objects are manipulated by a set of virtual functions with implementations provided for each object type: `create`, `open`, `close`, `delete`, `query name`, `parse`, and `security`. The latter three objects need explanation:

- `query name` is called when a thread has a reference to an object, but wants to know the object's name.

- `parse` is used by the object manager to search for an object given the object's name.

- `security` is called to make security checks on all object operations, such as when a process opens or closes an object, makes changes to the security descriptor, or duplicates a handle for an object.

The parse procedure is used to extend the abstract namespace to include files. The translation of a pathname to a file object begins at the root of the abstract namespace. Pathname components are separated by whack characters ('\') rather than the slashes ('/') used in UNIX. Each component is looked up in the current parse directory of the namespace. Internal nodes within the namespace are either directories or symbolic links. If a leaf object is found and there are no pathname components remaining, the leaf object is returned. Otherwise the leaf object's parse procedure is invoked with the remaining pathname.

Parse procedures are only used with a small number of objects belonging to the Windows GUI, the configuration manager (registry), and— most notably —device objects representing file systems.

The parse procedure for the device object-type allocates a file object and initiates an open or create I/O operation on the file-system. If successful, the file object fields are filled in to describe the file.

In summary, the pathname to a file is used to traverse the object manager namespace, translating the original absolute pathname into a (device object, relative pathname) pair. This pair is then passed to the file system via the I/O manager, which fills in the file object. The file object itself has no name, but is referred to by a handle.

UNIX file systems have *symbolic links*, permitting multiple nicknames or aliases for the same file. The *symbolic link object* implemented by the Windows XP object manager is used within the abstract namespace, not to alias files on a file-system. Even so, symbolic links are still very useful. They are used to organize the namespace, similar to the organization of the /Devices directory in UNIX. They are also used to map standard MS-DOS drive letters to drive names. Drive letters are symbolic links that can be remapped to suit the convenience of the user or administrator.

Drive letters are one place where the abstract namespace in Windows XP is not global. Each logged-on user has their own set of drive letters so they avoid interfering with one another. On the other hand, terminal server sessions share all processes within a session. `BaseNamedObjects` contain the named objects created by most applications.

Although the namespace is not directly visible across a network, the object manager's `parse` method is used to help access a named object on another system. When a process attempts to open an object that resides on a remote computer, the object manager calls the parse method for the device object corresponding to a network redirector. This results in an I/O operation which accesses the file across the network.

Objects are instances of an *object type*. The object type specifies how instances are to be allocated, the definitions of the data fields, and the implementation of the standard set of virtual functions used for all objects. These functions implement operations such as mapping names to objects, closing and deleting, and applying security.

The object manager keeps track of two counts for each object. The pointer count is the number of distinct references made to an object. Protected-mode code that refers to objects must keep a reference on the object to ensure the object isn't deleted while in use. The handle count is the number of handle table entries referring to an object. Each handle is also reflected in the reference count.

When a handle for an object is closed, the object's close routine is called. In the case of file objects this call causes the I/O manager to do a cleanup operation at the close of the last handle. The cleanup operation tells the file system that the file is no longer accessed by user-mode so it removes sharing restrictions, range locks, and other states specific to the corresponding open routine.

Each handle close removes a reference from the pointer count, but internal system components may retain additional references. When the final reference is removed, the object's delete procedure is called. Again using file objects as an example, the delete procedure causes the I/O manager to send the file system a close operation on the file object. This causes the file system to deallocate any internal data structures that were allocated for the file object.

After the delete procedure for a temporary object completes, the object is deleted from memory. Objects can be made permanent (at least with respect to the current boot of the system) by asking the object manager to take an extra reference against the object. Thus permanent objects are not deleted even when the last reference outside the object manager is removed. When a permanent object is made temporary again, the object manager removes the extra reference. If this was the last reference, the object is deleted. Permanent objects are rare, used mostly for devices, drive letter mappings and the directory and symbolic link objects.

The job of the *object manager* is to supervise the use of all managed objects. When a thread wants to use an object, it calls the object manager's `open` method to get a reference to the object. If the object is being opened from a user-mode API, the reference is inserted into the process' object table and a handle is returned.

A process gets a handle by creating an object, by opening an existing object, by receiving a duplicated handle from another process, or by inheriting a handle from a *parent process*, similar to the way a UNIX process gets a file descriptor. These handles are all stored in the process' *object table*. An entry in the object table contains the object's access rights and states whether the handle should be inherited by *child processes*. When a process terminates, Windows XP automatically closes all the process' open handles.

Handles are a standardized interface to all kinds of objects. Like a file descriptor in UNIX an object handle is an identifier unique to a process that confers the ability to access and manipulate a system resource. Handles can be duplicated within a process, or between processes. The latter case is used when creating child processes or implementing out-of-process execution contexts.

Since the object manager is the only entity that generates object handles, it is the natural place to check security. The object manager checks whether a process has the right to access an object when the process tries to open the object. The object manager also enforces quotas, such as the maximum amount of memory a process may use, by charging a process for the memory occupied by all its referenced objects and refusing to allocate more memory when the accumulated charges exceed the process' quota.

When the login process authenticates a user, an access-token is attached to the user's process. The access token contains information such as the security id, group ids, privileges, primary group, and default access control list. The services and objects a user can access are determined by these attributes.

The token that controls access is associated with the thread making the access. Normally the thread token is missing and defaults to the process token, but services often need to execute code on behalf of their client. Windows XP allows threads to temporarily impersonate by using a client's token. Thus, the thread token is not necessarily the same as the process token.

In Windows XP, each object is protected by an access-control list that contains the security ids and access rights granted. When a thread attempts to access an object, the system compares the security id in the thread's access token with the object's access-control list to determine whether access should be permitted. The check is performed only when an object is opened, so it is not possible to deny access after the open occurs. Operating system components executing in kernel-mode bypass the access check, since kernel-mode code is assumed to be trusted. Therefore, kernel-mode code must avoid security vulnerabilities, such as leaving checks disabled while creating a user-mode accessible handle in an untrusted process.

Generally, the creator of the object determines the access-control list for the object. If none is explicitly supplied, one may be set to a default by the object-type's open routine, or a default list may be obtained from the user's access-token object.

The access token has a field that controls auditing of object accesses. Operations that are being audited get logged to the system's security log with an identification of the user. An administrator monitors this log to discover attempts to break into the system or to access protected objects.

24.3.3.2 Virtual-Memory Manager

The executive component that manages the virtual address space, physical memory allocation, and paging is the *virtual-memory (VM) manager*. The design of the VM manager assumes that the underlying hardware supports virtual-to-physical mapping, a paging mechanism, transparent cache coherence on multiprocessor systems, and allows multiple page-table entries to map to the same physical page frame. The VM manager in Windows XP uses a page- based management scheme with a page size of 4 KB on IA32compatible processors and 8 KB on the IA64. Pages of data allocated to a process that are not in physical memory are stored in either the *paging files* on disk or mapped directly to a regular file on a local or remote file- system. Pages can also be marked zero-on-demand.

On IA32 processors each process has a 4 GB virtual address space. The upper 2 GB are mostly identical for all processes, and are used by Windows XP in kernel mode to access the operating system code and data structures. Key areas of the kernel-mode region that are not identical in each process are the *page table self-map*, *hyperspace* and *session space*. The hardware references a process' page tables using physical page-frame numbers. The VM manager maps the page tables into a single 4 MB region in the process' address space so they are accessed through virtual addresses. Hyperspace maps the current process' working set information into the kernel-mode address space.

Session space is used to share the win32k and other session-specific drivers between all the processes in the same terminal-server session rather than with all the processes in the system. The lower 2 GB are specific to every process, and are accessible by both user- and kernel-mode threads. Certain configurations of Windows XP reserve only 1 GB for operating system use, allowing a process to use 3 GB of address space. Running the system in /3GB mode drastically reduces the amount of data caching in the kernel. However, for large applications that manage their own I/O such as SQL databases, the advantage of a larger user-mode address space may be worth the loss of caching.

The Windows XP VM manager uses a two-step process to allocate user memory. The first step *reserves* a portion of the process' virtual address space. The second step *commits* the allocation by assigning virtual memory space (physical memory or space in the paging files). Windows XP limits the amount of virtual memory space a process consumes by enforcing a quota on committed memory. A process decommits memory that it is no longer using to free up virtual memory for use by other processes. The APIs used to reserve virtual addresses and commit virtual memory take a handle on a process object as a parameter. This allows one process to control the virtual memory of another. This is how environmental subsystems manage the memory of their client processes.

For performance, the VM manager allows a privileged process to lock selected pages in physical memory, thus ensuring the pages are not paged out to the paging file. Processes also allocate raw physical memory and then map regions into its virtual address space. IA32 processors with the Physical Address Extension (PAE) feature can have up to 64GB of physical memory on a system. This memory cannot all be mapped in a process' address space at once, but Windows XP makes it available using the Address Windowing Extension (AWE) APIs that allocate physical memory and then map regions of virtual addresses in the process' address space onto part of the physical memory. The AWE facility is primarily used by very large applications such as the SQL database.

Windows XP implements shared memory by defining a *section object*. After getting a handle to a section object, a process maps the memory portion it needs into its address space. This portion is called a *view*. A process redefines its view of an object to gain access to the entire object, one region at a time.

A process can control the use of a shared-memory section object in many ways. The maximum size of a section can be bounded. The section can be backed by disk space either in the system-paging file or by a regular file (a *memory-mapped file*). A section can be *based*, meaning the section appears at the same virtual address for all processes attempting to access it. Finally, the memory protection of pages in the section can be set to read–only, read–write, read–write–execute, execute–only, no access, or copy–on–write. The last two of these protection settings need some explanation:

- A no-access page raises an exception if accessed; the exception is used, for example, to check whether a faulty program iterates beyond the end of an array. Both the user-mode memory allocator and the special kernel allocator used by the device verifier can be configured to map each allocation onto the end of a page followed by a no-access page in order to detect buffer overruns.

- The copy-on-write mechanism increases the efficient use of physical memory by the VM manager. When two processes want independent copies of an object, the VM manager places a single shared copy into virtual memory and activates the copy-on-write property for that region of memory. If one of the processes tries to modify data in a copy-on-write page, the VM manager makes a private copy of the page for the process.

The virtual-address translation in Windows XP uses a multi-level page table. For IA32 processors, without the Physical Address Extensions enabled, each process has a *page directory* that contains 1024 *page-directory entries* (PDEs) of size 4 bytes. Each PDE points to a *page table* that contains 1024 *page-table entries* (PTEs) of size 4 bytes. Each PTE points to a 4 KB *page frame* in physical memory. The total size of all page tables for a process is 4 MB, so the VM manager pages out individual tables to disk when necessary. See Figure 24.3 for a diagram of this structure.

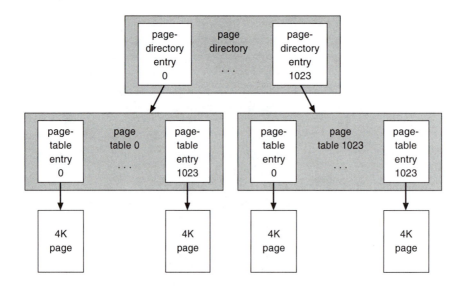

Figure 24.3   Page table layout.

The page-directory and page-tables are referenced by the hardware via physical addresses. To improve performance the VM manager self-maps the page directory and page tables into a 4 MB region of virtual addresses. The self-map allows the VM manager to translate a virtual address into the corresponding PDE or PTE without additional memory accesses. When a process context is changed, a single page-directory entry needs to be changed to map the new process' page tables. For a variety of reasons the hardware requires that each page directory or page table occupy a single page. Thus the number of PDEs or PTEs that fit in a page determine how virtual addresses are translated.

The following describes how virtual addresses are translated into physical addresses on IA32 compatible processors (without PAE enabled). A 10-bit value can represent all the values from 0 to 1023. Thus, a 10-bit value can select any entry in the page directory, or in a page table. This property is used when a virtual-address pointer is translated to a byte address in physical memory. A 32-bit virtual-memory address is split into three values, as shown in Figure 24.4. The first 10 bits of the virtual address are used as an index into the page directory. This address selects one page-directory entry (PDE), which contains the physical page frame of a page table. The memory management unit (MMU) uses the next 10 bits of the virtual address to select a PTE from the page table. The PTE specifies a page frame in physical memory. The remaining 12 bits of the virtual address are the offset of a specific byte in the page frame. The MMU creates a pointer to the specific byte in physical memory by concatenating the 20 bits from the PTE with the lower 12 bits from the virtual address. Thus, the 32-bit PTE has 12 bits to describe the state of the physical page. The IA32 hardware reserves 3 bits for use by the operating system. The rest of the bits

31   0

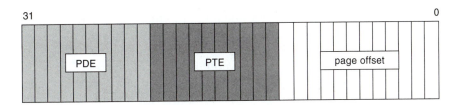

Figure 24.4   Virtual-to-physical address translation on IA32.

specify whether the page has been accessed or written, the caching attributes, the access mode, if the page is global, and whether the PTE is valid.

IA32 processors running with PAE enabled use 64-bit PDEs and PTEs in order to represent the larger 24 bit page-frame number field. Thus the second level page directories and the page tables contain only 512 PDEs and PTEs, respectively. To provide 4 GB of virtual address space requires an extra level of page directory containing four PDEs. Translation of a 32-bit virtual address uses 2 bits for the top-level directory index, and 9 bits for each of the second-level page directories and the page tables.

To avoid the overhead of translating every virtual address by looking up the PDE and PTE, processors use a *translation-lookaside buffer* (TLB) which contains an associative memory cache for mapping virtual pages to PTEs. Unlike the IA32 architecture where the TLB is maintained by the hardware MMU, the IA64 invokes a software-trap routine to supply translations missing from the TLB. This gives the VM manager flexibility in choosing the data structures to use. In Windows XP a three-level tree structure is chosen for mapping user-mode virtual addresses on the IA64.

On IA64 processors the page size is 8 KB, but the PTEs occupy 64- bits, so a page still only contain 1024 (10 bits worth) of PDEs or PTEs. Therefore, with 10 bits worth of top-level PDEs, 10 bits of second-level, 10 bits of page table, and 13 bits of page offset, the user portion of the process' virtual address space for Windows XP on the IA64 is 8 TB (43 bits worth). The 8 TB limitation in the current version of Windows XP is less than the capabilities of the IA64 processor, but represents a trade-off between the number of memory references required to handle TLB misses and the size of the user-mode address space supported.

A physical page can be in one of six states: valid, free, zeroed, standby, modified, bad, or in transition. A *valid* page is in use by an active process. A *free* page is a page that is not referenced in a PTE. A *zeroed* page is a free page that has been zeroed out and is ready for immediate use to satisfy zero-on-demand faults. A *modified* page is one that has been written by a process, and must be sent to the disk before it is allocated for another process. *Standby* pages are copies of information already stored on disk. They can be pages that were not modified, modified pages that have already been written to the disk, or pages that were pre-fetched to exploit locality. A *bad* page is unusable because a hardware error has been detected. Finally, a *transition* page is one that is on its way in from disk to a page frame allocated in physical memory.

When the valid bit in a PTE is zero, the VM manager defines the format of the other bits. Invalid pages can have a number of states represented by bits in the PTE. Page-file pages that have not ever been faulted in are marked zero-on-demand. Files mapped through section objects encode a pointer to that section object. Pages that have been written to the page file contain enough information to find the page on disk, etc.

The actual structure of the page-file PTE is shown in Figure 24.5. The PTE contains 5 bits for page protection, 20 bits for page-file offset, 4 bits to select the paging file, and 3 bits that describe the page-state. A page-file PTE is marked to be an invalid virtual address to the MMU. Since executable code and memory-mapped files already have a copy on disk, they do not need space in a paging file. If one of these pages is not in physical memory, the PTE structure is as follows. The most significant bit is used to specify the page protection, the next 28 bits are used to index into a system data structure that indicates a file and offset within the file for the page, and the lower 3 bits specify the page-state.

Invalid virtual addresses can also be in a number of temporary states that are part of the paging algorithms. When a page is removed from a process working set it is moved to either the modified list (to be written to disk) or directly to the standby list. If written to the standby list, the page is reclaimed without reading from disk if it is needed again before it is moved to the free list. When possible, the VM manager uses idle CPU cycles to zero pages on the free list and move them to the zeroed list. Transition pages have been allocated a physical page, and are awaiting the completion of the paging I/O before the PTE is marked as valid.

Windows XP uses section objects to describe pages that are sharable between processes. Each process has its own set of virtual page tables, but the section object also contains a set of page tables containing the master (or prototype) PTEs. When a PTE in a process page table is marked valid it points at the physical page frame containing the page, as it must on IA32 processors where the hardware MMU reads the page tables directly from memory. But when a shared page is made invalid, the PTE is edited to point to the prototype PTE associated with the section object.

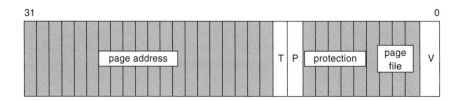

Figure 24.5   Page file page-table entry. The Valid bit is zero.

The page tables associated with a section object are virtual so far as they are created and trimmed as needed. The only prototype PTEs needed are those that describe pages for which there is a currently mapped view. This greatly improves performance and allows more efficient use of kernel virtual addresses.

The prototype PTE contains the page-frame address and the protection and state bits. Thus, the first access by a process to a shared page generates a page fault. After the first access, further accesses are performed in the normal manner. If a process writes to a copy-on-write page marked read-only in the PTE, the VM manager makes a copy of the page, marks the PTE writable and the process effectively does not have a shared page any longer. Shared pages never appear in the page file, but are instead found in the file- system.

The VM manager keeps track of all pages of physical memory in a *page-frame database*. There is one entry for every page of physical memory in the system. The entry points to the PTE which in turn points to the page frame, so the VM manager can maintain the state of the page. Page frames not referenced by a valid PTE are linked to lists according to page type such as zeroed, modified, free, etc.

If a shared physical page is marked as valid for any process, the page cannot be removed from memory. The VM manager keeps a count of valid PTEs for each page in the page frame database. When the count goes to zero the physical page can be reused once its contents have been written back to disk (if it was marked dirty).

When a page fault occurs, the VM manager finds a physical page to hold the data. For zero-on-demand pages the first choice is to find a page that has already been zeroed. If none is available, a page from the free list or standby list is chosen and the page is zeroed before proceeding.If the faulted page has been marked as in transition, it is either already being read in from disk, or has been unmapped or trimmed and is still available on the standby or modified list. The thread either waits for the I/O to complete or, in the latter cases, reclaims the page from the appropriate list.

Otherwise, an I/O must be issued to read the page in from the paging file or file-system. The VM manager tries to allocate an available page from either the free list or the standby list. Pages in the modified list cannot be used until they have been written back to disk and transferred to the standby list. If no pages are available, the thread blocks until the working set manager trims pages from memory, or a page in physical memory is unmapped by a process.

Windows XP uses a per-process First In First Out (FIFO) replacement policy to take pages from processes that are using more than their minimum working-set size. Windows XP monitors the page faulting of each process that is at its minimum working-set size, and adjusts the working-set size accordingly. When a process is started, it is assigned a default minimum working-set size of 50 pages. The VM manager replaces and trims pages in the working set of a process according to their age. The age of a page is determined by counting how many trimming cycles have occurred without the PTE. Trimmed pages are moved to the standby or modified list, depending on whether the modified bit is set in the page's PTE.

The VM manager does not fault-in only the page immediately needed. Research shows that the memory referencing of a thread tends to have a *locality* property; when a page is used, it is likely that adjacent pages will be referenced in the near future. (Think of iterating over an array, or fetching sequential instructions that form the executable code for a thread.) Because of locality, when the VM manager faults in a page, it also faults in a few adjacent pages. This prefetching tends to reduce the total number of page faults. Writes are also clustered to reduce the number of independent I/O operations.

In addition to managing committed memory, the VM manager manages each process' reserved memory, or virtual address space. Each process has an associated splay tree that describes the ranges of virtual addresses in use, and what the use is. This allows the VM manager to fault in page tables as needed. If the PTE for a faulting address does not exist, the VM manager searches for the address in the process' tree of *virtual address descriptors* (VADs), and uses this information to fill in the missing PTE and retrieve the page. In some cases a page-table page itself may not exist and must be transparently allocated and initialized by the VM manager.

24.3.3.3 Process Manager

The Windows XP process manager provides services for creating, deleting, and using processes, threads and jobs. It has no knowledge about parent–child relationships or process hierarchies; those refinements are left to the particular environmental subsystem that owns the process. The process manager is also not involved in the scheduling of processes, other than setting the priorities and affinities in processes and threads when they are created. Thread scheduling takes place in the kernel dispatcher.

Processes contain one or more threads. Processes themselves can be collected together into large units called *job objects* which allow limits on CPU usage, working-set size, and processor affinities which control multiple processes at once. Job objects are used to manage large datacenter machines.

An example of process creation in the Win32 environment is as follows. When a Win32 application calls `CreateProcess`, a message is sent to the Win32 subsystem to notify it that the process is being created. `CreateProcess` in the original process then calls an API in the process manager of the NT executive to actually create the process. The process manager calls the object manager to create a process object, and returns the object handle to Win32. Win32 calls the process manager again to create a thread for the process, and returns handles to the new process and thread.

The Windows XP APIs for manipulating virtual memory, threads, and duplicating handles take a process handle so subsystems can perform operations on behalf of a new process without having to directly execute in the new process' context. Once a new process is created, the initial thread is created and an APC is delivered to the thread to prompt the start of execution at the user-mode image loader. The loader is an ntdll.dll, which is a link library automatically mapped into every newly created process. Windows XP also supports a UNIX fork() style of process creation in order to support the POSIX environmental subsystem. Although the Win32 environment calls the process manager from the client process, POSIX uses the cross-process nature of the Windows XP APIs to create the new process from within the subsystem process.

The process manager also implements the queuing and delivery of asynchronous procedure calls (APCs) to threads. APCs are used by the system to initiate thread execution, complete I/O, terminate threads and processes, and attach debuggers. User-mode code can also queue an APC to a thread for delivery of signal-like notifications. To support POSIX the process manager provides APIs that send alerts to threads to unblock them from system calls.

The debugger support in the process manager includes the capability to suspend and resume threads, and create threads that begin in a suspended mode. There are also process manager APIs that get and set a thread's register context and access another process' virtual memory.

Threads can be created in the current process; they can also be injected into another process. Within the executive, existing threads can temporarily attach to another process. This method is used by worker threads that need to execute in the context of the process orininating a work request.

The process manager also supports impersonation. A thread running in a process with a security token belonging to one user can set a thread-specific token belonging to another user. This facility is fundamental to the client–server computing model where services need to act on behalf of a variety of clients with different security ids.

24.3.3.4 Local Procedure Call Facility

The implementation of Windows XP uses a client–server model. The environmental subsystems are servers that implement particular operating system personalities. The client–server model is used for implementing a variety of operating system services besides the environmental subsystems. Security management, printer spooling, web services, network file-systems, plug-and-play, and many other features are implemented using this model. To reduce the memory footprint, multiple services are often collected together into a few processes, which then rely on the user-mode threadpool facilities to share threads and wait for messages (See section 24.3.3.3).

The operating system uses the local procedure call (LPC) facility to pass requests and results between client and server processes within a single machine. In particular, LPC is used to request services from the various Windows XP subsystems. LPC is similar in many respects to the RPC mechanisms that are used by many operating systems for distributed processing across networks, but LPC is optimized for use within a single system. The

Windows XP implementation of Open Software Foundation (OSF) RPC often uses LPC as a transport on the local machine.

LPC is a message-passing mechanism. The server process publishes a globally visible connection-port object. When a client wants services from a subsystem, it opens a handle to the subsystem's connection-port object, and sends a connection request to the port. The server creates a channel and returns a handle to the client. The channel consists of a pair of private communication ports: one for client-to-server messages, and the other for server-to-client messages. Communication channels support a callback mechanism, so the client and server can accept requests when they would normally be expecting a reply.

When an LPC channel is created, one of three message-passing techniques must be specified.

1. The first technique is suitable for small messages (up to a couple hundred bytes). In this case, the port's message queue is used as intermediate storage, and the messages are copied from one process to the other.

2. The second technique is for larger messages. In this case, a shared-memory section object is created for the channel. Messages sent through the port's message queue contain a pointer and size information refering to the section object. This avoids the need to copy large messages. The sender places data into the shared section, and the receiver views them directly.

3. The third technique of LPC message passing uses the APIs that read/write directly into a process' address space. The LPC provides functions and synchronization so a server can access the data in a client.

The Win32 window manager uses its own form of message passing that is independent of the executive LPC facilities. When a client asks for a connection that uses window manager messaging, the server sets up three objects: a dedicated server thread to handle requests, a 64 KB section object, and an event-pair object. An *event-pair object* is a synchronization object that is used by the Win32 subsystem to provide notification when the client thread has copied a message to the Win32 server, or vice versa. The section object passes the messages and the event-pair object performs synchronization. Window manager messaging has several advantages. The section object eliminates message copying, since it represents a region of shared memory. The event-pair object eliminates the overhead of using the port object to pass messages containing pointers and lengths. The dedicated server thread eliminates the overhead of determining which client thread is calling the server, since there is one server thread per client thread. Finally, the kernel gives scheduling preference to these dedicated server threads to improve performance.

24.3.3.5   I/O Manager

The **I/O** *manager* is responsible for file-systems, device drivers, and network drivers. It keeps track of which device drivers, filter drivers and file-systems are loaded, and also manages buffers for I/O requests. It works with the VM manager to provide memory-mapped file I/O, and controls the Windows XP cache manager, which handles caching for the entire I/O system. The I/O manager is fundamentally asynchronous. Synchronous I/O is provided by explicitly waiting for an I/O operation to complete. The I/O manager provides several models of asynchronous I/O completion including setting events, delivering APCs to the initiating thread, and I/O completion ports which allow a single thread to process I/O completions from many other threads.

Device drivers are arranged as a list for each device (called a driver or I/O stack because of how device drivers are added). The I/O manager converts the requests it receives into a standard form called an **I/O** *request packet (IRP)*. It then forwards the IRP to the first driver in the stack for processing. After each driver processes the IRP it calls the I/O manager to either forward it to the next driver in the stack, or if all processing is finished, to complete the operation on the IRP.

Completions may occur in a different context than the original I/O request. For example, if a driver is performing its part of an I/O operation and is forced to block for an extended time, it may queue the IRP to a worker thread to continue processing in the system context. In the original thread the driver returns a status indicating the I/O request is pending so the thread can continue executing in parallel with the I/O operation. IRPs may also be processed in interrupt service routines, and completed in an arbitrary context. Because some final processing may need to happen in the context that initiated the I/O, the I/O manager uses an APC to do final I/O completion processing in the context of the originating thread.

The device stack model is very flexible. As a driver stack is built, various drivers have the opportunity to insert themselves into the stack as *filter drivers*. Filter drivers have the opportunity to examine and potentially modify each I/O operation. Mount management, partition management and disk striping/mirroring are all examples of functionality implemented using filter drivers that execute beneath the file system in the stack. File-system filter drivers execute above the file system, and have been used to implement functionality such as hierarchical storage management, single instancing of files for remote boot, and dynamic format conversion. Third parties also use file-system filter drivers to implement virus detection.

Device drivers for Windows XP are written to the Windows Driver Model specification (WDM). This model lays out all the requirements for device drivers including how to layer filter drivers, share common code for handling power and plug-and-play requests, build correct cancellation logic, etc.

Because of the richness of the WDM, it can be an excessive amount of work to write a full WDM device driver for each new hardware device. Fortunately it is unnecessary because of the port/miniport model. For similar classes of devices, such as audio drivers, SCSI devices, and ethernet controllers, each instance of a device in a class shares a common driver for that class called a *port driver*. The port driver implements the standard operations for the class and then calls device-specific routines in the device's *mini-port driver* to implement device-specific functionality.

24.3.3.6 Cache Manager

In many operating systems, caching is done by the file-system. Instead, Windows XP provides a centralized caching facility. The *cache manager* works closely with the VM manager to provide cache services for all components under the control of the I/O manager. Caching in Windows XP is based on files rather than raw blocks.

The size of the cache changes dynamically, according to how much free memory is available in the system. Recall that the upper 2 GB of a process' address space comprise the system area; it is available in the context of all processes. The VM manager allocates up to one-half of this space to the system cache. The cache manager maps files into this address space, and uses the capabilities of the VM manager to handle file I/O.

The cache is divided into blocks of 256 KB. Each cache block can hold a view (that is, a memory-mapped region) of a file. Each cache block is described by a *virtual-address control block (VACB)* that stores the virtual address and file offset for the view, as well as the number of processes using the view. The VACBs reside in a single array maintained by the cache manager.

For each open file, the cache manager maintains a separate VACB index array that describes the caching for the entire file. This array has an entry for each 256 KB chunk of the file; so, for instance, a 2 small MB file would have an 8-entry VACB index array. An entry in the VACB index array points to the VACB, if that portion of the file is in the cache; it is null otherwise. When the I/O manager receives a file's user-level read request the I/O manager sends an IRP to the device-driver stack on which the file resides. The file-system attempts to lookup the requested data in the cache manager (unless the request specifically asks for a non-cached read). The cache manager calculates which entry of that file's VACB index array corresponds to the byte offset of the request. The entry either points to the view in the cache, or is invalid. If it is invalid, the cache manager allocates a cache block (and the corresponding entry in the VACB array), and maps the view into the cache block. The cache manager then attempts to copy data from the mapped file to the caller's buffer. If the copy succeeds, the operation is completed.

If the copy fails, it does so because of a page fault, which causes the VM manager to send a non-cached read request to the I/O manager. The I/O manager sends another request down the driver stack, this time requesting a *paging* operation, which bypasses the cache manager and reads the data from the file directly into the page allocated for the cache manager. Upon completion the VACB is set to point at the page. The data, now in the cache, is copied to the

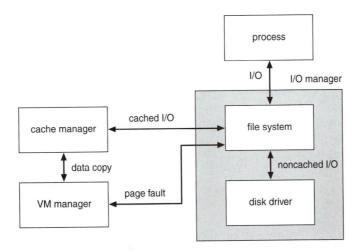

Figure 24.6   File I/O.

caller's buffer, and the original I/O request is completed. Figure 24.6 shows an overview of these operations.

When possible, for synchronous operations on cached files, I/O is handled by the *fast I/O mechanism*. This mechanism parallels the normal IRP-based I/O but calls into the driver stack directly rather than passing down an IRP. Because there is no IRP involved, the operation should not block for an extended period of time and cannot be queued to a worker thread. Therefore, when the operation reaches the file-system and it calls the cache manager, the operation fails if the information is not already in cache. The I/O manager then attempts the operation using the normal IRP path.

A kernel-level read operation is similar, except that the data can be accessed directly from the cache, rather than being copied to a buffer in user space. To use file-system metadata (data structures that describe the file-system) the kernel uses the cache manager's mapping interface to read the metadata. To modify the metadata, the file system uses the cache manager's pinning interface. *Pinning* a page locks the page into a physical-memory page frame, so the VM manager cannot move or page-out the page. After updating the metadata, the file system asks the cache manager to unpin the page. A modified page is marked dirty, and so the VM manager flushes the page to disk. The metadata is stored in a regular file.

To improve performance, the cache manager keeps a small history of read requests, and from this history attempts to predict future requests. If the cache manager finds a pattern in the previous three requests, such as sequential access forward or backward, it prefetches data into the cache before the next request is submitted by the application. In this way the application finds its data already cached, and does not need to wait for disk I/O. The Win32 API OpenFile and CreateFile functions can be passed the FILE_FLAG_SEQUENTIAL_SCAN flag, which is a hint to the cache manager to try to prefetch 192 KBs ahead of the thread's requests. Typically, Windows XP performs I/O operations in chunks of 64 KB or 16 pages; thus, this read-ahead is three times the normal amount.

The cache manager is also responsible for telling the VM manager to flush the contents of the cache. The cache manager's default behavior is write-back caching: it accumulates writes for 4 to 5 seconds, and then wakes up the cache-writer thread. When write-through caching is needed, a process can set a flag when opening the file, or the process can call an explicit cache-flush function.

A fast-writing process could potentially fill all the free cache pages before the cache-writer thread has a chance to wake up and flush the pages to disk. The cache writer prevents a process from flooding the system in the following way. When the amount of free cache memory gets low, the cache manager temporarily blocks processes attempting to write data, and wakes the cache-writer thread to flush pages to disk. If the fast-writing process is actually a network redirector for a network file-system, blocking it for too long could cause network transfers to time out and be retransmitted. This retransmission would waste network bandwidth. To prevent such waste, network redirectors can instruct the cache manager to limit the backlog of writes in the cache.

Because a network file-system needs to move data between a disk and the network interface, the cache manager also provides a DMA interface to move the data directly. Moving data directly avoids copying data through an intermediate buffer.

24.3.3.7 Security Reference Monitor

Centralizing management of system entities in the object manager enables the use of a uniform mechanism to perform run-time access validation and audit checks for every user-accessible entity in the system. Whenever a process opens a handle to an object, the *security reference monitor* (SRM) checks the process' security token and the object's access-control list to see whether the process has the necessary rights.

The SRM is also responsible for manipulating the privileges in security tokens. Special privileges are required for users to perform backup or restore operations on file-systems, overcome certain checks as an administrator, debug processes, etc. Tokens can also be marked as being restricted in their privileges so they cannot access objects that are available to most users. Restricted tokens are primarily used to restrict the damage that can be done by execution of untrusted code.

Another responsibility of the SRM is logging security audit events. A C2 security rating requires that the system have the ability to detect and log all attempts to access system resources so that it is easier to trace attempts at unauthorized access. Because the SRM is responsible for making access checks, it generates most of the audit records in the security event log.

24.3.3.8 Plug-and-Play and Power Managers

The operating system uses the *plug-and-play* (**PnP**) **manager** to recognize and adapt to changes in the hardware configuration. For PnP to work, both the device and driver must support the PnP standard. The PnP manager automatically recognizes installed devices and detects changes in devices as the system operates. The manager also keeps tracks of resources used by a device, as well as potential resources that could be used, and takes care of loading the appropriate drivers. This management of hardware resources—primarily interrupts and I/O memory ranges—has the goal of determining a hardware configuration in which all devices are able to operate.

For example, if device B can use interrupt 5 and device A can use 5 or 7, then the PnP manager will assign 5 to B and 7 to A. In previous versions, the user might have had to remove device A and reconfigure it to use interrupt 7, before installing device B. The user thus had to study system resources before installing new hardware, and to find out or remember which devices were using which hardware resources. The proliferation of PCMCIA cards, laptop docks, USB, IEEE 1394, Infiniband, and other hot-pluggable devices also dictates the support of dynamically configurable resources.

The PnP manager handles this dynamic reconfiguration as follows. First, it gets a list of devices from each bus driver (for example, PCI, USB). It loads the installed driver (or installs one, if necessary) and sends an add-device request to the appropriate driver for each device. The PnP manager figures out the optimal resource assignments and sends a start-device request to each driver along with the resource assignment for the device. If a device needs to be reconfigured, the PnP manager sends a query-stop request, which asks the driver whether the device can be temporarily disabled. If the driver can disable the device, then all pending operations are completed and new operations are prevented from starting. Next, the PnP manager sends a stop request; it can then reconfigure the device with another start-device request.

The PnP manager also supports other requests, such as query-remove. This request is used when the user is getting ready to eject a PCCARD device, and operates in a fashion similar to query-stop. The surprise-remove request is used when a device fails or, more likely, when a user removes a PCCARD device without stopping it first. The remove request tells the driver to stop using the device and release all resources allocated to it.

Windows XP supports sophisticated power management. Although these facilities are useful for home systems to reduce power consumption, their primary application is for ease-of-use (quicker access) and extending the battery life of laptops. The system and individual devices can be moved to low-power mode (called standby or sleep mode) when not in use, so the battery is primarily directed at physical memory (RAM) data retention. The system can turn itself back on when packets are received from the network, a phone line to a modem rings, or a user opens a laptop or pushes a soft power button. Windows XP can also hibernate a system by storing physical memory contents to disk and completely shutting down the machine, then restoring the system at a later point before execution continues.

Further strategies for reducing power consumption are supported. Rather than spinning in a processor loop when the CPU is idle, Windows XP moves the system to a state requiring lower power consumption. If the CPU is underutilized, Windows XP reduces the CPU clock speed, which can save significant power.

24.3.3.9 Registry

Windows XP keeps much of its configuration information in an internal database called *the registry*. A registry database is called a *hive*. There are separate hives for system information, default user-preferences, software installation, and security. Because the information in the *system hive* is required in order to boot the system, the registry manager is implemented as a component of the executive.

Every time the system successfully boots it saves the system hive as *last-known-good*. If the user installs software, such as a device driver, that produces a system hive configuration that will not boot, the user can usually boot using the last-known-good configuration.

Damage to the system hive from installing third party applications and drivers is so common that Windows XP has a component called *system restore* which periodically saves the hives, as well as other software states like driver executables and configuration files, so that the system can be restored to a previously working state in cases where the system boots, but no longer operates as expected.

24.3.3.10 Booting

The booting of a Windows XP PC begins when the hardware powers on and the BIOS begins executing from ROM. The BIOS identifies the *system device* to be booted, and loads and executes the bootstrap loader from the front of the disk. This loader knows enough about the file-system format to load the NTLDR program from the root directory of the system device. NTLDR is used to determine which *boot device* contains the operating system. Next the NTLDR loads in the HAL library, the kernel, and the system hive from the boot device. From the system hive it determines what device drivers are needed to boot the system (the *boot drivers*) and loads them. Finally NTLDR begins kernel execution.

The kernel initializes the system and creates two processes. The *system process* contains all the internal worker threads, and never executes in user-mode. The first user-mode process created is SMSS, which is similar to the INIT (initialization) process in UNIX. SMSS does further initialization of the system, including establishing the paging files and loading device drivers, and creates the WINLOGON and CSRSS processes. CSRSS is the Win32 subsystem.

WINLOGON brings up the rest of the system, including the LSASS security subsystem and the remaining services needed to run the system.

The system optimizes the boot process by pre-loading files from disk based on previous boots of the system. Disk access patterns at boot are also used to re-layout system files on disk to reduce the number of I/O operations required. The processes required to start the system is reduced by grouping services into one process. All of these approaches contribute to a dramatic reduction in system boot time.

On the other hand, the sleep and hibernation capabilities of Windows XP allow users to power down their computer and then quickly resume where they left off, making system boot time less important than it once was.

24.4 ■ Environmental Subsystems

Environmental subsystems are user-mode processes layered over the native Windows XP executive services to enable Windows XP to run programs developed for other operating systems, including 16-bit Windows, MS-DOS, and POSIX. Each environmental subsystem provides a single application environment.

Windows XP uses the Win32 subsystem as the main operating environment, and thus it starts all processes. When an application is executed, the Win32 subsystem calls the VM manager to load the application's executable code. The memory manager returns a status to Win32 indicating the type of executable. If it is not a native Win32 executable, the Win32 environment checks whether the appropriate environmental subsystem is running; if the subsystem is not running, it is started as a user-mode process. The subsystem then takes control over the application start up.

The environmental subsystems use the LPC facility to provide operating system services to client processes. The Windows XP subsystem architecture keeps applications from mixing API routines from different environments. For instance, a Win32 application cannot make a POSIX system call because only one environmental subsystem can be associated with each process.

Since each subsystem is run as a separate user-mode process, a crash in one has no effect on other processes. The exception is Win32 which provides all keyboard, mouse, and graphical display capabilities. If it fails, the system is effectively disabled and requires a reboot.

The Win32 environment categorizes applications as either graphical or character based, where a *character-based application* is one that thinks interactive output goes to a character-based (command) window. Win32 transforms the output of a character-based application to a graphical representation in the command window. This transformation is easy: whenever an output routine is called, the environmental subsystem calls a Win32 routine to display the text. Since the Win32 environment performs this function for all character-based windows, it can transfer screen text between windows via the clipboard. This transformation works for MS-DOS applications, as well as for POSIX command-line applications.

24.4.1 MS-DOS Environment

The MS-DOS environment does not have the complexity of the other Windows XP environmental subsystems. It is provided by a Win32 application called the *virtual* **DOS** *machine (VDM)*. Since the VDM is a user-mode process, it is paged and dispatched like any other Windows XP application. The VDM has an *instruction-execution unit* to execute or emulate Intel 486 instructions. The VDM also provides routines to emulate the MS-DOS ROM BIOS and "int 21" software-interrupt services, and has virtual device drivers for the screen, keyboard, and communication ports. The VDM is based on the MS-DOS 5.0 source code; it allocates at least 620 KB of memory to the application.

The Windows XP command shell is a program that creates a window that looks like an MS-DOS environment. It can run both 16-bit and 32-bit executables. When an MS-DOS application is run, the command shell starts a VDM process to execute the program.

If Windows XP is running on a IA32 compatible processor, MS-DOS graphical applications run in full-screen mode, and character applications can run full screen or in a window. Not all MS-DOS applications run under the VDM. For example, some MS-DOS applications access the disk hardware directly, so they fail to run on Windows XP because disk access is restricted to protect the file-system. In general, MS-DOS applications that directly access hardware will fail to operate under Windows XP.

Since MS-DOS is not a multitasking environment, some applications have been written in such a way as to hog the CPU. For instance, the use of busy loops can cause time delays or pauses in execution. The scheduler in the kernel dispatcher detects such delays and automatically throttles the CPU usage, but this may cause the offending application to operate incorrectly.

24.4.2 16-Bit Windows Environment

The Win16 execution environment is provided by a VDM that incorporates additional software called *Windows on Windows* (WOW32 for 16-bit applications) that provides the Windows 3.1 kernel routines and stub routines for window manager and graphical device interface (GDI) functions. The stub routines call the appropriate Win32 subroutines, converting, or *thunking*, 16-bit addresses into 32-bit addresses. Applications that rely on the internal structure of the 16-bit window manager or GDI may not work, because the underlying Win32 implementation is, of course, different than in true 16-bit Windows.

WOW32 can multitask with other processes on Windows XP, but it resembles Windows 3.1 in many ways. Only one Win16 application can run at a time, all applications are single threaded and reside in the same address space, and they all share the same input queue. These features imply that an application that stops receiving input will block all the other Win16 applications, just as in Windows 3.x, and one Win16 application can crash other Win16 applications by corrupting the address space. Multiple Win16 environments can coexist, however, by using the command *start /separate* win16application from the command line.

There are relatively few 16-bit applications that users need to continue to run on Windows XP, but some of them include common installation (setup) programs. Thus, the WOW32 environment continues to exist primarily because a number of 32-bit applications cannot be installed on Windows XP without it.

24.4.3 32-Bit Windows Environment on IA64

The native environment for Windows on IA64 uses 64-bit addresses and the native IA64 instruction set. To execute IA32 programs in this environment requires a thunking layer to translate 32-bit Win32 calls into the corresponding 64-bit calls—just as 16-bit applications require on IA32 systems. Thus 64-bit Windows supports the WOW64 environment. The implementations of 32-bit and 64-bit Windows are essentially identical, and the IA64 processor provides direct execution of IA32 instructions, so WOW64 achieves a higher level of compatibility than WOW32.

24.4.4 Win32 Environment

The main subsystem in Windows XP is the Win32. It runs Win32 applications, and manages all keyboard, mouse, and screen I/O. Since it is the controlling environment, it is designed to be extremely robust. Several features of Win32 contribute to this robustness. Unlike the Win16 environment, each Win32 process has its own input queue. The window manager dispatches all input on the system to the appropriate process' input queue, so a failed process does not block input to other processes.

The Windows XP kernel also provides preemptive multitasking, which enables the user to terminate applications that have failed or are no longer needed. Win32 also validates all objects before using them, to prevent crashes that could otherwise occur if an application tried to use an invalid or wrong handle. The Win32 subsystem verifies the type of the object to which a handle points before using the object. The reference counts kept by the object manager prevent objects from being deleted while they are still being used, and prevent their use after they have been deleted.

To achieve a high level of compatibility with Windows 95/98 systems, Windows XP allows users to specify that individual applications be run using a *shim layer* which modifies the Win32 APIs to better approximate the behavior expected by old applications. For example some applications expect to see a particular version of the system, and fail on new versions. Frequently applications have latent bugs that become exposed due to changes in the implementation. For example, using memory after freeing it may only cause corruption if the order of memory reuse by the heap changes, or an application may make assumptions about which errors can be returned by a routine, or the number of valid bits in an address. Running an application with the Windows 95/98 shims enabled causes the system to provide behavior much closer to Windows 95/98— though with reduced performance and limited interoperability with other applications.

24.4.5 POSIX Subsystem

The POSIX subsystem is designed to run POSIX applications written to follow the POSIX standard, which is based on the UNIX model. POSIX applications can be started by the Win32 subsystem or by another POSIX application. POSIX applications use the POSIX subsystem server PSXSS.EXE, the POSIX dynamic link library PSXDLL.DLL, and the POSIX console session manager POSIX.EXE.

Although the POSIX standard does not specify printing, POSIX applications can use printers transparently via the Windows XP redirection mechanism. POSIX applications have access to any file system on the Windows XP system; the POSIX environment enforces UNIX-like permissions on directory trees.

Due to scheduling issues, the POSIX system in Windows XP does not ship with the system, but is available separately for professional desktop systems and servers. It provides a much higher-level of compatibility with UNIX applications than in previous versions of NT}. Of the commonly available UNIX applications, most compile and run without change with the latest version of Interix.

24.4.6 Logon and Security Subsystems

Before a user can access objects on Windows XP, that user must be authenticated by the logon service, WINLOGON. WINLOGON is responsible for responding to the secure attention sequence (Control-Alt-Delete). The secure attention sequence is a required mechanism for keeping an application from acting as a trojan horse. Only WINLOGON can intercept this sequence in order to put up a logon screen, change passwords, and lock the workstation. To be authenticated, a user must have an account and provide the password for that account. Alternatively, a user logs on by using a smart-card and personal identification number, subject to the security policies in effect for the domain.

The local security authority subsystem (LSASS) is the process that generates access tokens to represent users on the system. It calls an *authentication package* to perform authentication using information from the logon subsystem or network server. Typically, the authentication package simply looks up the account information in a local database and checks to see that the password is correct. The security subsystem then generates the access token for the user ID containing the appropriate privileges, quota limits, and group IDs. Whenever the user attempts to access an object in the system, such as by opening a handle to the object, the access token is passed to the security reference monitor, which checks privileges and quotas. The default authentication package for Windows XP domains is Kerberos. LSASS also has the responsibility for implementing security policy such as strong passwords, authenticating users, and performing encryption of data and keys.

24.5 ■ File System

Historically, MS-DOS systems have used the file-allocation table (FAT) file-system. The 16-bit FAT file system has several shortcomings, including internal fragmentation, a size limitation of 2 GB, and a lack of access protection for files. The 32-bit FAT file system has solved the size and fragmentation problems, but its performance and features are still weak by comparison with modern file systems. The NTFS file system is much better. It was designed to include many features, including data recovery, security, fault tolerance, large files and file systems, multiple data streams, UNICODE names, sparse files, encryption, journaling, volume shadow copies, and file compression.

Windows 2000XP continues to use FAT16, however, to read floppies and other removable media. And despite the advantages of NTFS, FAT32 continues to be important for interoperability of media with Windows 95/98 systems. Windows XP supports additional file-system types for the common formats used for CD and DVD media.

24.5.1 NTFS Internal Layout

The fundamental entity in NTFS is a volume. A volume is created by the Windows XP logical disk management utility, and is based on a logical disk partition. A volume may occupy a portion of a disk, may occupy an entire disk, or may span across several disks.

NTFS does not deal with individual sectors of a disk, but instead uses clusters as the unit of disk allocation. A *cluster* is a number of disk sectors that is a power of 2. The cluster size is configured when an NTFS file system is formatted. The default cluster size is the sector size for volumes up to 512 MBs, 1 KB for volumes up to 1 GB, 2 KBs for volumes up to 2 GBs, and 4 KBs for larger volumes. This cluster size is much smaller than that for the 16-bit FAT file system, and the small size reduces the amount of internal fragmentation. As an example, consider a 1.6 GB disk with 16,000 files. If you use a FAT-16 file system, 400 MBs may be lost to internal fragmentation because the cluster size is 32 KBs. Under NTFS, only 17 MBs would be lost when storing the same files.

NTFS uses *logical cluster numbers (LCNs)* as disk addresses. It assigns them by numbering clusters from the beginning of the disk to the end. Using this scheme, the system can calculate a physical disk offset (in bytes) by multiplying the LCN by the cluster size.

A file in NTFS is not a simple byte stream as it is in MS-DOS or UNIX; rather, it is a structured object consisting of typed *attributes*. Each attribute of a file is an independent byte stream that can be created, deleted, read, and written. Some attribute types are standard for all files, including the file name (or names, if the file has aliases such as an MS-DOS shortname), the creation time, and the security descriptor that specifies access control. User data is stored in *data attributes*.

Most traditional data files have an *unnamed* data attribute that contains all the file's data. However additional data streams can be created with explicit names. For instance, Macintosh files stored on a Windows XP server put the resource fork as a named data stream. The IProp interfaces of the Common Object Model (COM) use a named data stream to store properties on ordinary files, including thumbnails of images. In general, attributes may be added as necessary and are accessed using a *file-name:attribute* syntax. NTFS only returns the size of the unnamed attribute in response to file-query operations, such as when running the `dir` command.

Every file in NTFS is described by one or more records in an array stored in a special file called the master file table (MFT). The size of a record is determined when the file system is created; it ranges from 1 to 4 KBs. Small attributes are stored in the MFT record itself, and are called *resident attributes*. Large attributes, such as the unnamed bulk data, called *nonresident attributes*, are stored in one or more contiguous *extents* on the disk, and a pointer to each extent is stored in the MFT record. For a small file, even the data attribute may fit inside the MFT record. If a file has many attributes, or if it is highly fragmented and therefore many pointers are needed to point to all the fragments, one record in the MFT might not be large enough. In this case, the file is described by a record called the *base file record*, which contains pointers to overflow records that hold the additional pointers and attributes.

Each file in an NTFS volume has a unique ID called a *file reference*. The file reference is a 64-bit quantity that consists of a 48-bit file number and a 16-bit sequence number. The file number is the record number (that is, the array slot) in the MFT that describes the file. The sequence number is incremented every time that an MFT entry is reused. The sequence number enables NTFS to perform internal consistency checks, such as catching a stale reference to a deleted file after the MFT entry has been reused for a new file.

24.5.1.1 NTFS B+ Tree

As in MS-DOS and UNIX, the NTFS namespace is organized as a hierarchy of directories. Each directory uses a data structure called a *B+ tree* to store an index of the file names in that directory. A B+ tree is used because it eliminates the cost of reorganizing the tree and has the property that the length of every path from the root of the tree to a leaf is the same. The *index root* of a directory contains the top level of the B+ tree. For a large directory, this top level contains pointers to disk extents that hold the remainder of the tree. Each entry in the directory contains the name and file reference of the file, as well as a copy of the update timestamp and file size taken from the file's resident attributes in the MFT. Copies of this information are stored in the directory, so it is efficient to generate a directory listing. All the file names, sizes, and update times are available from the directory itself, so there is no need to gather these attributes from the MFT entries for each of the files.

24.5.1.2 NTFS Metadata

The NTFS volume's metadata are all stored in files. The first file is the MFT. The second file, which is used during recovery if the MFT is damaged, contains a copy of the first 16 entries of the MFT. The next few files are also special in purpose. They include the log file, volume file, attribute-definition table, root directory, bitmap file, boot file, and bad-cluster file. The *log file* records all metadata updates to the file-system. The *volume file* contains the name of the volume, the version of NTFS that formatted the volume, and a bit that tells whether the volume may have been corrupted and needs to be checked for consistency. The *attribute-definition table* indicates which attribute types are used in the volume, and what operations can be performed on each of them.

The *root directory* is the top-level directory in the file-system hierarchy. The *bitmap file* indicates which clusters on a volume are allocated to files, and which are free. The *boot file* contains the startup code for Windows XP and must be located at a particular disk address so that it can be found easily by a simple ROM bootstrap loader. The boot file also contains the physical address of the MFT. Finally, the *bad- cluster file* keeps track of any bad areas on the volume; NTFS uses this record for error recovery.

24.5.2 Recovery

In many simple file systems, a power failure at the wrong time can damage the file-system data structures so severely that the entire volume is scrambled. Many versions of UNIX store redundant metadata on the disk, and they recover from crashes using the `fsck` program to check all the file-system data structures, and to restore them forcibly to a consistent state. Restoring them often involves deleting damaged files and freeing data clusters that had been written with user data but have not been properly recorded in the file-system's metadata structures. This checking can be a slow process, and can lose significant amounts of data.

24.5.2.1 NTFS Log File

NTFS takes a different approach to file-system robustness. In NTFS, all file-system data-structure updates are performed inside transactions. Before a data structure is altered, the transaction writes a log record that contains redo and undo information; after the data structure has been changed, the transaction writes a commit record to the log to signify that the transaction succeeded.

After a crash, the system can restore the file-system data structures to a consistent state by processing the log records, first redoing the operations for committed transactions, then undoing the operations for transactions that did not commit successfully before the crash. Periodically (usually every 5 seconds), a checkpoint record is written to the log. The system does not need log records prior to the checkpoint to recover from a crash. They can be discarded, so the log file does not grow without bounds. The first time after system startup that an NTFS volume is accessed, NTFS automatically performs file-system recovery.

This scheme does not guarantee that all the user-file contents are correct after a crash; it ensures only that the file-system data structures (the metadata files) are undamaged and reflect some consistent state that existed prior to the crash. It would be possible to extend the transaction scheme to cover user files and Microsoft may do so in the future.

The log is stored in the third metadata file at the beginning of the volume. It is created with a fixed maximum size when the file system is formatted. It has two sections: the *logging area*, which is a circular queue of log records, and the *restart area*, which holds context information, such as the position in the logging area where NTFS should start reading during a recovery. In fact, the restart area holds two copies of its information, so recovery is still possible if one copy is damaged during the crash.

The logging functionality is provided by the Windows XP *log-file service*. In addition to writing the log records and performing recovery actions, the log-file service keeps track of the free space in the log file. If the free space gets too low, the log-file service queues pending transactions, and NTFS halts all new I/O operations. After the in-progress operations complete, NTFS calls the cache manager to flush all data, then resets the log file and performs the queued transactions.

24.5.3 Security

The security of an NTFS volume is derived from the Windows XP object model. Each NTFS file references a security descriptor which contains the access token of the owner of the file, and an access-control list that states the access privileges granted to each user having access to the file.

In normal operation, NTFS does not enforce permissions on traversal of directories in file pathnames. However, for compatibility with POSIX} these checks can be enabled. Traversal checks are inherently more expensive since modern parsing of file pathnames uses prefix matching rather than component-by- component opening of directory names.

24.5.4 Volume Management and Fault Tolerance

FtDisk is the fault-tolerant disk driver for Windows XP. When installed, it provides several ways to combine multiple disk drives into one logical volume, so as to improve performance, capacity, or reliability.

24.5.4.1 Volume Set

One way to combine multiple disks is to concatenate them logically to form a large logical volume, as shown in Figure 24.7. In Windows XP, this logical volume is called a *volume set*, which can consist of up to 32 physical partitions. A volume set that contains an NTFS volume can be extended without the data already stored in the file system being disturbed. The bitmap metadata on the NTFS volume are simply extended to cover the newly added space. NTFS continues to use the same LCN mechanism that it uses for a single physical disk, and the FtDisk driver supplies the mapping from a logical volume offset to the offset on one particular disk.

24.5.4.2 Stripe Set

Another way to combine multiple physical partitions is to interleave their blocks in round-robin fashion to form what is called a *stripe set*, as shown in Figure 24.8. This scheme is also called RAID level 0, or *disk striping*. FtDisk uses a stripe size of 64 KBs: The first 64 KBs of the logical volume are stored in the first physical partition, the second 64 KBs of the logical volume are stored in the second physical partition, and so on, until each partition has contributed 64 KBs of space. Then, the allocation wraps around to the first disk, allocating

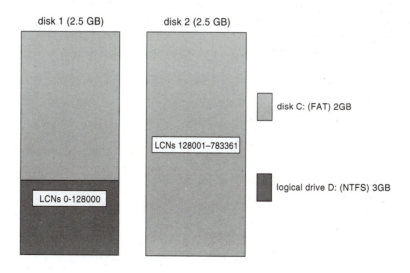

Figure 24.7   Volume set on two drives.

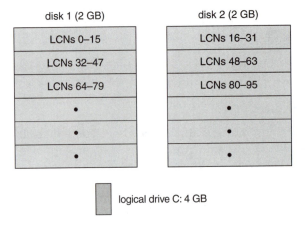

Figure 24.8   Stripe set on two drives.

the second 64 KB block. A stripe set forms one large logical volume, but the physical layout can improve the I/O bandwidth, because, for a large I/O, all the disks can transfer data in parallel.

24.5.4.3 Stripe Set with Parity

A variation of this idea is the *stripe set with parity*, which is shown in Figure 24.9. This scheme is also called RAID level 5. If the stripe set has eight disks, then, for each of the seven data stripes, on seven separate disks, there is a parity stripe on the eighth disk. The parity stripe contains the byte-wise `exclusive or` of the data stripes. If any one of the eight stripes is destroyed, the system can reconstruct the data by calculating the `exclusive or` of the remaining seven.

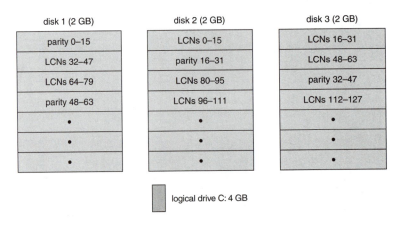

Figure 24.9   Stripe set with parity on three drives.

This ability to reconstruct data makes the disk array much less likely to lose data in case of a disk failure.

Notice that an update to one data stripe also requires recalculation of the parity stripe. Seven concurrent writes to seven different data stripes thus would also require seven parity stripes to be updated. If the parity stripes were all on the same disk, that disk could have seven times the I/O load of the data disks. To avoid creating this bottleneck, we spread the parity stripes over all the disks, by assigning them in round-robin style. To build a stripe set with parity, we need a minimum of three equal-sized partitions located on three separate disks.

24.5.4.4 Disk Mirroring, Mirror Sets, RAID and Duplex Sets

An even more robust scheme is called *disk mirroring* or RAID level 1; it is depicted in Figure 24.10. A *mirror set* comprises two equal-sized partitions on two disks, such that their data contents are identical. When an application writes data to a mirror set, FtDisk writes the data to both partitions. If one partition fails, FtDisk has another copy safely stored on the mirror. Mirror sets can also improve the performance, because read requests can be split between the two mirrors, giving each mirror half of the workload. To protect against the failure of a disk controller, we can attach the two disks of a mirror set to two separate disk controllers. This arrangement is called a *duplex set*.

24.5.4.5 Sector Sparing and Cluster Remapping

To deal with disk sectors that go bad, FtDisk uses a hardware technique called sector sparing, and NTFS uses a software technique called cluster remapping.

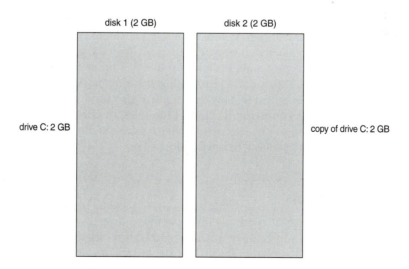

Figure 24.10   Mirror set on two drives.

Sector sparing is a hardware capability provided by many disk drives. When a disk drive is formatted, it creates a map from logical block numbers to good sectors on the disk. It also leaves extra sectors unmapped, as spares. If a sector fails, FtDisk instructs the disk drive to substitute a spare. *Cluster remapping* is a software technique performed by the file system. If a disk block goes bad, NTFS substitutes a different, unallocated block by changing any affected pointers in the MFT. NTFS also makes a note that the bad block should never be allocated to any file.

When a disk block goes bad, the usual outcome is a data loss. But sector sparing or cluster remapping can be combined with fault-tolerant volumes to mask the failure of a disk block. If a read fails, the system reconstructs the missing data by reading the mirror or by calculating the exclusive or parity in a stripe set with parity. The reconstructed data are stored into a new location that is obtained by sector sparing or cluster remapping.

24.5.5 Compression and Encryption

NTFS can perform data compression on individual files or on all data files in a directory. To compress a file, NTFS divides the file's data into *compression units*, which are blocks of 16 contiguous clusters. When each compression unit is written, a data-compression algorithm is applied. If the result fits into fewer than 16 clusters, the compressed version is stored. When reading, NTFS can determine whether data have been compressed: if they have been, the length of the stored compression unit is less than 16 clusters. To improve performance when reading contiguous compression units, NTFS prefetchs and decompresses ahead of the application requests.

For sparse files or files that contain mostly zeros, NTFS uses another technique to save space. Clusters that contain all zeros due to never having been written are not actually allocated or stored on disk. Instead, gaps are left in the sequence of virtual-cluster numbers stored in the MFT entry for the file. When reading a file, if it finds a gap in the virtual-cluster numbers, NTFS just zero-fills that portion of the caller's buffer. This technique is also used by UNIX.

NTFS supports encryption of files. Individual files, or entire directories, can be specified for encryption. The security system manages the keys used, and a key recovery service is available to retrieve lost keys.

24.5.6 Mount Points

Mount points are a form of symbolic link specific to directories on NTFS. They provide a more flexible mechanism for administrators to organize disk volumes than simply providing global names (like drive letters). Mount points are implemented as a symbolic link with associated data that contain the true volume name. Ultimately, mount points will supplant drive letters completely, but there will be a long transition due to the dependence of many applications on the drive letter scheme.

24.5.7 Change Journal

NTFS keeps a journal describing all changes that have been made to the file system. User-mode services can receive notifications of changes to the journal, and then identify what files have changed. The content indexing service uses this to identify files that need to be re-indexed. The file replication service uses the change journal to identify files that need to be replicated across the network.

24.5.8 Volume Shadow Copies

Windows XP implements the capability of bringing a volume to a known state and then creating a shadow copy which can be used to backup a consistent view of the volume. Making a shadow copy of a volume is a form of copy-on-write, where blocks modified after the shadow copy is created have their original contents stashed in the copy. To achieve a consistent state for the volume requires the cooperation of applications since the system cannot know when the data used by the application is in a stable state from which the application could be safely restarted.

The server version of Windows XP uses shadow copies to efficiently maintain old versions of files stored on file servers. This allows users to see documents stored on file servers as they existed at earlier points in time. The user can use this feature to recover files that were accidentally deleted, or simply look at a previous version of the file, all without pulling out a backup tape.

24.6 ■ Networking

Windows XP supports both peer-to-peer and client–server networking. It also has facilities for network management. The networking components in Windows XP provide data transport, interprocess communication, file sharing across a network, and the ability to send print jobs to remote printers.

24.6.1 Network Interfaces

To describe networking in Windows XP, reference is made to two of the internal networking interfaces called the *network device interface specification (NDIS)* and the *transport driver interface (TDI)*. The NDIS interface was developed in 1989 by Microsoft and 3Com to separate network adapters from the transport protocols, so that either could be changed without affecting the other. NDIS resides at the interface between the data-link control and media-access-control layers in the OSI model and enables many protocols to operate over many different network adapters. In terms of the OSI model, the TDI is the interface between the transport layer (layer 4) and the session layer (layer 5). This interface enables any session-layer component to use any available transport mechanism. (Similar reasoning led to the streams mechanism in UNIX.) The TDI supports both connection-based and connectionless transport, and has functions to send any type of data.

24.6.2 Protocols

Windows XP implements transport protocols as drivers. These drivers can be loaded and unloaded from the system dynamically, although in practice the system typically has to be rebooted after a change. Windows XP comes with several networking protocols.

24.6.2.1 Server Message Block

The *server message-block (SMB)* protocol was first introduced in MS-DOS 3.1. The system uses the protocol to send I/O requests over the network. The SMB protocol has four message types. The `Session control` messages are commands that start and end a redirector connection to a shared resource at the server. A redirector uses `File` messages to access files at the server. The system uses `Printer` messages to send data to a remote print queue and to receive back status information, and the `Message` message is used to communicate with another workstation. The SMB protocol was published as the *Common Internet File System* (CIFS), and is supported on a number of operating systems.

24.6.2.2 Network Basic Input/Output System

The *network basic input/output system (NetBIOS)* is a hardware-abstraction interface for networks, analogous to the BIOS hardware-abstraction interface devised for PCs running MS-DOS. NetBIOS, developed in the early 1980s, has become a standard network-programming interface. NetBIOS is used to establish logical names on the network, to establish logical connections or *sessions* between two logical names on the network, and to support reliable data transfer for a session via either NetBIOS or SMB requests.

24.6.2.3 Net BIOS Extended User Interface

The *NetBIOS extended user interface (NetBEUI)* was introduced by IBM in 1985 as a simple, efficient networking protocol for up to 254 machines. It is the default protocol for Windows 95 peer networking and for Windows for Workgroups. Windows XP uses NetBEUI when it wants to share resources with these networks. Among the limitations of NetBEUI are that it uses the actual name of a computer as the address, and that it does not support routing.

24.6.2.4 Transmission Control Protocol/Internet Protocol

The Transmission Control Protocol/Internet Protocol (TCPIP) suite that is used on the Internet has become the de facto standard networking infrastructure.

Windows XP uses TCP/IP to connect to a wide variety of operating systems and hardware platforms. The Windows XP TCP/IP package includes the simple network-management protocol (SNMP), dynamic host-configuration protocol (DHCP), Windows Internet name service (WINS), and NetBIOS support.

24.6.2.5 Point-to-Point Tunneling Protocol

The *point-to-point tunneling protocol (PPTP)* is a protocol provided by Windows XP to communicate between remote-access server modules running on Windows XP Server machines and other client systems that are connected over the Internet. The remote-access servers can encrypt data sent over the connection, and they support multi-protocol *virtual private networks* (VPNs) over the Internet.

24.6.2.6 Novell NetWare Protocols

The Novell NetWare protocols (IPX datagram service on the SPX transport layer) are widely used for PC LANs. The Windows XP NWLink protocol connects the NetBIOS to NetWare networks. In combination with a redirector (such as Microsoft's Client Service for Netware or Novell's NetWare Client for Windows), this protocol enables a Windows XP client to connect to a NetWare server.

24.6.2.7 Web Distributed Authoring and Versioning Protocol

Web Distributed Authoring and Versioning (WebDAV) is a http-based protocol for collaborative authoring across the network. Windows XP builds a WebDAV redirector into the file system. By building WebDAV support directly into the file-system, it can work with other features, such as encryption. Personal files can now be stored securely in a public place.

24.6.2.8 AppleTalk Protocol

The *AppleTalk protocol* was designed as a low-cost connection by Apple to allow Macintosh computers to share files. Windows XP systems can share files and printers with Macintosh computers via AppleTalk if a Windows XP server on the network is running the Windows' Services for Macintosh package.

24.6.3 Distributed-Processing Mechanisms

Although Windows XP is not a distributed operating system, it does support distributed applications. Mechanisms that support distributed processing on Windows XP include NetBIOS, named pipes and mailslots, windows sockets, RPCs, and network dynamic data exchange (NetDDE).

24.6.3.1 Net BIOS

In Windows XP, NetBIOS applications can communicate over the network using NetBEUI, NWLink, or TCP/IP.

24.6.3.2 Named Pipes

Named pipes are a connection-oriented messaging mechanism. Named pipes were originally developed as a high-level interface to NetBIOS connections over the network. A process can also use named pipes to communicate with other processes on the same machine. Since named pipes are accessed through the file-system interface, the security mechanisms used for file objects also apply to named pipes.

The name of a named pipe has a format called the *uniform naming convention (UNC)*. A UNC name looks like a typical remote file name. The format of a UNC name is \\server_name\share_name\x\y\z, where the server_name identifies a server on the network; a share_name identifies any resource that is made available to network users, such as directories, files, named pipes and printers; and the \x\y\z part is a normal file path name.

24.6.3.3 Mailslots

Mailslots are a connectionless messaging mechanism. They are unreliable when accessed across the network, in that a message sent to a mailslot may be lost before the intended recipient receives it. Mailslots are used for broadcast applications, such as finding components on the network; they are also used by the Windows Computer Browser service.

24.6.3.4 Winsock

Winsock is the Windows XP sockets API. Winsock is a session-layer interface that is largely compatible with UNIX sockets, but with some added Windows XP extensions. It provides a standardized interface to many transport protocols that may have different addressing schemes, so that any Winsock application can run on any Winsock-compliant protocol stack.

24.6.3.5 Remote Procedure Call

A remote procedure call RPC is a client–server mechanism that enables an application on one machine to make a procedure call to code on another machine. The client calls a local procedure—a *stub routine*—that packs its arguments into a message and sends them across the network to a particular server process. The client-side stub routine then blocks. Meanwhile, the server unpacks the message, calls the procedure, packs the return results into a message, and sends them back to the client stub. The client stub unblocks, receives the message, unpacks the results of the RPC, and returns them to the caller. This packing of arguments is sometimes called *marshalling*. The

Windows XP RPC mechanism follows the widely used distributed computing environment standard for RPC messages, so programs written to use Windows XP RPCs are highly portable. The RPC standard is detailed. It hides many of the architectural differences between computers, such as the sizes of binary numbers and the order of bytes and bits in computer words, by specifying standard data formats for RPC messages.

Windows XP can send RPC messages using NetBIOS, or Winsock on TCP/IP networks, or named pipes on LAN Manager networks. The LPC facility, discussed earlier, is similar to RPC, except that in the LPC case the messages are passed between two processes running on the same computer.

24.6.3.6 Microsoft Interface Definition Language

It is tedious and error-prone to write the code to marshal and transmit arguments in the standard format, to unmarshal and execute the remote procedure, to marshal and send the return results, and to unmarshal and return them to the caller. Fortunately, however, much of this code can be generated automatically from a simple description of the arguments and return results.

Windows XP provides the *Microsoft Interface Definition Language* to describe the remote procedure names, arguments, and results. The compiler for this language generates header files that declare the stubs for the remote procedures, and the data types for the argument and return-value messages. It also generates source code for the stub routines used at the client side, and for an unmarshaller and dispatcher at the server side. When the application is linked, the stub routines are included. When the application executes the RPC stub, the generated code handles the rest.

24.6.3.7 Common Object Model

The *component object model* (COM) is a mechanism for interprocess communication that was developed for Windows. COM objects provide a well-defined interface to manipulate the data in the object. For instance, COM is the infrastructure used by Microsoft's *object linking and embedding* (OLE) technology for inserting spreadsheets into WORD documents. Windows XP has a distributed extension called *DCOM* that can be used over a network utilizing RPC to provide a transparent method of developing distributed applications.

24.6.4 Redirectors and Servers

In Windows XP, an application can use the Windows XP I/O API to access files from a remote computer as though they were local, provided that the remote computer is running a CIFS server, such as is provided by Windows XP or earlier Windows systems. A *redirector* is the client-side object that forwards I/O requests to remote files, where they are satisfied by a server. For performance and security, the redirectors and servers run in kernel-mode.

In more detail, access to a remote file occurs as follows:

- The application calls the I/O manager to request that a file be opened with a file name in the standard UNC format.

- The I/O manager builds an I/O request packet, as described in Section 24.3.3.5.

- The I/O manager recognizes that the access is for a remote file, and calls a driver called a *multiple universal-naming-convention provider (MUP)*.

- The MUP sends the I/O request packet asynchronously to all registered redirectors.

- A redirector that can satisfy the request responds to the MUP. To avoid asking all the redirectors the same question in the future, the MUP uses a cache to remember which redirector can handle this file.

- The redirector sends the network request to the remote system.

- The remote-system network drivers receive the request and pass it to the server driver.

- The server driver hands the request to the proper local file-system driver.

- The proper device driver is called to access the data.

- The results are returned to the server driver, which sends the data back to the requesting redirector. The redirector then returns the data to the calling application via the I/O manager.

A similar process occurs for applications that use the Win32 network API, rather than the UNC services, except that a module called a multi-provider router is used, instead of a MUP.

For portability, redirectors and servers use the TDI API for network transport. The requests themselves are expressed in a higher-level protocol, which by default is the SMB protocol mentioned in Section 24.6.2. The list of redirectors is maintained in the system registry database.

24.6.4.1 Distributed File System

The UNC names are not always convenient because multiple file servers may be available to serve the same content, and UNC names explicitly include the name of the server. Windows XP supports a *Distributed File System* (DFS) protocol that allows a network administrator to serve up files from multiple servers using a single distributed namespace.

24.6.4.2 Folder Redirection and Client-Side Caching

To improve the PC experience for business users who frequently switch between computers, Windows XP allows administrators to give users *roaming profiles* which keep the user's preferences and other settings on servers. *Folder redirection* is then used to automatically store a user's documents and other files on a server. This works well until one of the computers is no longer attached to the network, such as a laptop on an airplane. To give users off-line access to their redirected files, Windows XP uses *client-side caching* (CSC). CSC is used when on-line to keep copies of the server files on the local machine for better performance. The files are pushed up to the server as they are changed. If the computer becomes disconnected, the files are still available, and the update of the server is deferred until the next time the computer is on-line with a suitably performing network link.

24.6.5 Domains

Many networked environments have natural groups of users, such as students in a computer laboratory at school, or employees in one department in a business. Frequently, we want all the members of the group to be able to access shared resources on their various computers in the group. To manage the global access rights within such groups, Windows XP uses the concept of a domain. Previously, these domains had no relationship whatsoever to the domain name system DNS that maps Internet host names to IP addresses. Now, however, they are closely related.

Specifically, a Windows XP domain is a group of Windows XP workstations and servers that shares a common security policy and user database. Since Windows XP now uses the Kerberos protocol for trust and authentication, a Windows XP domain is the same thing as a Kerberos realm. Previous versions of NT used the idea of primary and backup domain controllers; now all servers in a domain are domain controllers. In addition, previous versions required the setup of one-way trusts between domains. Windows XP uses a hierarchical approach based on DNS, and allows transitive trusts that can flow up and down the hierarchy. This approach reduces the number of trusts required for n domains from $n * (n - 1)$ to $O(n)$. The workstations in the domain trust the domain controller to give correct information about the access rights of each user (via the user's access token). All users retain the ability to restrict access to their own workstations, no matter what any domain controller may say.

24.6.5.1 Domain Trees and Forests

Because a business may have many departments and a school may have many classes, it is often necessary to manage multiple domains within a single organization. A *domain tree* is a contiguous DNS naming hierarchy. For example, *bell-labs.com* might be the root of the tree, with *research.bell-labs.com* and *pez.bell-labs.com* as children—domains *research* and *pez*. A *forest* is a set of non-contiguous names. An example would be the trees *bell-labs.com* and/or *lucent.com*. A forest may be comprised of only one domain tree, however.

24.6.5.2 Trust Relationships

Trust relationships may be set up between domains in three ways, one-way, transitive, and cross-link. Versions of NT through Version 4.0 allowed only one-way trusts. A *one-way trust* is exactly what its name implies: domain A is told it can trust domain B. However, B would not trust A unless another relationship is configured. Under a *transitive trust*, if A trusts B and B trusts C, then A, B, and C all trust one another since transitive trusts are two-way by default. Transitive trusts are enabled by default for new domains in a tree and can be configured only among domains within a forest. The third type, a *cross-link trust*, is useful to cut down on authentication traffic. Suppose that domains A and B are leaf nodes, and that users in A often use resources in B. If a standard transitive trust is used, authentication requests must traverse up to the common ancestor of the two leaf nodes; but if A and B have a cross-linking trust established, the authentications would be sent directly to the other node.

24.6.6 Active Directory

Active Directory is the Windows XP implementation of *lightweight directory access protocol* (LDAP) services. Active Directory stores the topology information about the domain, keeps the domain-based user and group accounts and passwords, and provides a domain-based store for technologies like *group policies* and *intellimirror*.

Administrators use group policies to establish standards for desktop preferences and software. For many corporate information technology groups, uniformity drastically reduces the cost of computing. Intellimirror is used in conjunction with group policies to specify what software should be available to each class of user, even automatically installing it on demand from a corporate server.

24.6.7 Name Resolution in TCP/IP Networks

On an IP network, *name resolution* is the process of converting a computer name to an IP address, such as resolving *www.bell-labs.com* to 135.104.1.14. Windows XP provides several methods of name resolution, including Windows Internet Name Service (WINS), broadcast name resolution, domain name system (DNS), a hosts file, and an LMHOSTS file. Most of these methods are used by many operating systems, so we describe only WINS here.

Under WINS, two or more WINS servers maintain a dynamic database of name-to-IP address bindings, and client software to query the servers. At least two servers are used, so that the WINS service can survive a server failure, and so that the name-resolution workload can be spread over multiple machines.

24.6.7.1 Dynamic Host Configuration Protocol

WINS uses the dynamic host-configuration protocol (DHCP). DHCP updates address configurations automatically in the WINS database, without user or administrator intervention, as follows. When a DHCP client starts up, it broadcasts a `discover` message. Each DHCP server that receives the message replies with an `offer` message that contains an IP address and configuration information for the client. The client chooses one of the configurations and sends a `request` message to the selected DHCP server. The DHCP server responds with the IP address and configuration information it gave previously, and with a *lease* for that address. The lease gives the client the right to use the IP address for a specified period of time. When the lease time is half expired, the client attempts to renew the lease for the address. If the lease is not renewed, the client must obtain a new one.

24.7 ■ Programmer Interface

The Win32 API is the fundamental interface to the capabilities of Windows XP. This section describes five main aspects of the Win32 API: access to kernel objects, sharing of objects between processes, process management, interprocess communication, and memory management.

24.7.1 Access to Kernel Objects

The Windows XP kernel provides many services that application programs can use. Application programs obtain these services by manipulating kernel objects. A process gains access to a kernel object named XXX by calling the `CreateXXX` function to open a handle to XXX. This handle is unique to the process. Depending on which object is being opened, if the `create` function fails, it may return 0, or it may return a special constant named `INVALID_HANDLE_VALUE`. A process can close any handle by calling the `Close-Handle` function, and the system may delete the object if the count of processes using the object drops to 0.

24.7.2 Sharing Objects Between Processes

Windows XP provides three ways to share objects between processes. The first way is for a child process to inherit a handle to the object. When the parent calls the `CreateXXX` function, the parent supplies a `SECURITIES_ATTRIBUTES` structure with the `bInheritHandle` field set to TRUE. This field creates an inheritable handle. Next the child process is created, passing a value of TRUE

```
...
SECURITY_ATTRIBUTES sa;
sa.nlength = sizeof(sa);
sa.lpSecurityDescriptor = NULL;
sa.bInheritHandle = TRUE;
Handle a_semaphore = CreateSemaphore(&sa,1,1,NULL);
char command_line[132] ;
ostrstream ostring(command_line,sizeof(command_line));
ostring << a_semaphore << ends;
CreateProcess("another_process.exe",command_line,
              NULL,NULL,TRUE, ... );
...
```

Figure 24.11   Code for a child to share an object by inheriting a handle.

to the CreateProcess function's bInheritHandle argument. Figure 24.11 shows a code sample that creates a semaphore handle inherited by a child process.

Assuming the child process knows which handles are shared, the parent and child can achieve interprocess communication through the shared objects. In the example in Figure 24.11, the child process gets the value of the handle from the first command-line argument, and then shares the semaphore with the parent process.

The second way to share objects is for one process to give the object a name when the object is created, and for the second process to open the name. This method has two drawbacks: Windows XP does not provide a way to check whether an object with the chosen name already exists, and the object namespace is global, without regard to the object type. For instance, two applications may create an object named *pipe* when two distinct—and possibly different—objects are desired.

Named objects have the advantage that unrelated processes can readily share them . The first process calls one of the CreateXXX functions and supplies

```
// process A
...
Handle a_semaphore = CreateSemaphore(NULL,1,1,"MySEM1");
...
// process B
...
Handle b_semaphore = OpenSemaphore(SEMAPHORE_ALL_ACCESS,
                     FALSE, "MySEM1");
...
```

Figure 24.12   Code for sharing an object by name lookup.

```
...
// process A wants to give process B access to a semaphore
// process A
Handle a_semaphore = CreateSemaphore(NULL,1,1,NULL);
// send the value of the semaphore to process B
// using a message or shared memory
...
// process B
Handle process_a = OpenProcess(PROCESS_ALL_ACCESS,FALSE,
                      process_id_of_A);
Handle b_semaphore;
DuplicateHandle(process_a,a_semaphore,
   GetCurrentProcess(),&b_semaphore,
   0,FALSE,DUPLICATE_SAME_ACCESS);
// use b_semaphore to access the semaphore
...
```

Figure 24.13   Code for sharing an object by passing a handle.

a name in the `lpszName` parameter. The second process gets a handle to share the object by calling `OpenXXX` (or `CreateXXX`) with the same name, as shown in the example of Figure 24.12.

The third way to share objects is via the `DuplicateHandle` function. This method requires some other method of interprocess communication to pass the duplicated handle. Given a handle to a process and the value of a handle within that process, a second process can get a handle to the same object, and thus share it. An example of this method is shown in Figure 24.13.

24.7.3 Process Management

In Windows XP, a *process* is an executing instance of an application, and a *thread* is a unit of code that can be scheduled by the operating system. Thus, a process contains one or more threads. A process is started when some other process calls the `CreateProcess` routine. This routine loads any dynamic link libraries used by the process, and creates a *primary thread*. Additional threads can be created by the `CreateThread` function. Each thread is created with its own stack, which defaults to 1 MB unless specified otherwise in an argument to `CreateThread`. Because some C run-time functions maintain state in static variables, such as `errno`, a multithread application needs to guard against unsynchronized access. The wrapper function `beginthreadex` provides appropriate synchronization.

24.7.3.1 Instance Handles

Every dynamic link library or executable file loaded into the address space of a process is identified by an *instance handle*. The value of the instance handle is actually the virtual address where the file is loaded. An application can get the handle to a module in its address space by passing the name of the module to GetModuleHandle. If NULL is passed as the name, the base address of the process is returned. The lowest 64 KBs of the address space are not used, so a faulty program that tries to dereference a NULL pointer gets an access violation.

Priorities in the Win32 environment are based on the Windows XP scheduling model, but not all priority values may be chosen. Win32 uses four priority classes: IDLE_PRIORITY_CLASS (priority level 4), NOR-MAL_PRIORITY_CLASS (priority level 8), HIGH_PRIORITY_CLASS (priority level 13), and REALTIME_PRIORITY_CLASS (priority level 24). Processes are typically members of the NORMAL_PRIORITY_CLASS unless the parent of the process was of the IDLE_PRIORITY_CLASS, or another class was specified when CreateProcess was called. The priority class of a process can be changed with the SetPriorityClass function, or by an argument being passed to the START command. For example, the command START /REALTIME cbserver.exe would run the cbserver program in the REALTIME_PRIORITY_CLASS. Only users with the *increase scheduling priority* privilege can move a process into the REALTIME_PRIORITY_CLASS. Administrators and power users have this privilege by default.

24.7.3.2 Scheduling Rule

When a user is running an interactive program, the system needs to provide especially good performance for the process. For this reason, Windows XP has a special scheduling rule for processes in the NORMAL_PRIORITY_CLASS. Windows XP distinguishes between the foreground process that is currently selected on the screen, and the background processes that are not currently selected. When a process moves into the foreground, Windows XP increases the scheduling quantum by some factor—typically by 3. (This factor can be changed via the performance option in the system section of the control panel.) This increase gives the foreground process three times longer to run before a time-sharing preemption occurs.

24.7.3.3 Thread Priorities

A thread starts with an initial priority determined by its class. The priority can be altered by the SetThreadPriority function. This function takes an argument that specifies a priority relative to the base priority of its class:

- THREAD_PRIORITY_LOWEST: base − 2
- THREAD_PRIORITY_BELOW_NORMAL: base − 1
- THREAD_PRIORITY_NORMAL: base + 0
- THREAD_PRIORITY_ABOVE_NORMAL: base + 1
- THREAD_PRIORITY_HIGHEST: base + 2

Two other designations are also used to adjust the priority. Recall from Section 24.3.2.1 that the kernel has two priority classes: 16–31 for the real-time class, and 0–15 for the variable-priority class. THREAD_PRIORITY_IDLE sets the priority to 16 for real-time threads, and to 1 for variable-priority threads. THREAD_PRIORITY_TIME_CRITICAL sets the priority to 31 for real-time threads, and to 15 for variable-priority threads.

As we discussed in Section 24.3.2.1, the kernel adjusts the priority of a thread dynamically depending on whether the thread is I/O bound or CPU bound. The Win32 API provides a method to disable this adjustment, via SetProcessPriorityBoost and SetThreadPriorityBoost functions.

24.7.3.4 Thread Synchronization

A thread can be created in a *suspended state*: the thread does not execute until another thread makes it eligible via the ResumeThread function. The SuspendThread function does the opposite. These functions set a counter, so if a thread is suspended twice, it must be resumed twice before it can run. To synchronize the concurrent access to shared objects by threads, the kernel provides synchronization objects, such as semaphores and mutexes.

In addition, synchronization of threads can be achieved by using the WaitForSingleObject or WaitForMultipleObjects functions. Another method of synchronization in the Win32 API is the critical section. A critical section is a synchronized region of code that can be executed by only one thread at a time. A thread establishes a critical section by calling InitializeCriticalSection. The application must call EnterCriticalSection before entering the critical section, and LeaveCriticalSection after exiting the critical section. These two routines guarantee that, if multiple threads attempt to enter the critical section concurrently, only one thread at a time is permitted to proceed, and the others wait in the EnterCriticalSection routine. The critical-section mechanism is faster than using kernel-synchronization objects because it avoids allocation of kernel objects until it first encounters contention for the critical section.

24.7.3.5 Fibers

A *fiber* is user-mode code that gets scheduled according to a user-defined scheduling algorithm. A process may have multiple fibers in it, just as it can have multiple threads. A major difference between threads and fibers is that threads can execute concurrently, but only one fiber at a time is permitted to execute, even on multiprocessor hardware. This mechanism is included in Windows XP to facilitate the porting of those legacy UNIX applications that were written for a fiber-execution model.

The system creates a fiber by calling either ConvertThreadToFiber or CreateFiber. The primary difference between these functions is that CreateFiber does not begin executing the fiber that was created. To begin execution,

the application must call SwitchToFiber. The application can terminate a
fiber by calling DeleteFiber.

Repeated creation/deletion of threads can be expensive for applications
and services that perform small amounts of work in each. The threadpool
provides user-mode programs with three services: a queue to which work
requests may be submitted (via the QueueUserWorkItem API), an API (Reg-
isterWaitForSingleObject) which can be used to bind callbacks to waitable handles and APIs to bind callbacks to timeouts (CreateTimerQueue and
CreateTimerQueueTimer).

The threadpool's goal is to increase performance. Threads are relatively
expensive, and a processor can only be executing one thing at a time no matter
how many threads are used. The threadpool attempts to reduce the number
of outstanding threads by slightly delaying work requests (reusing each thread
for many requests), while providing enough threads to effectively utilize the
machine's CPUs.

The wait and timer callback APIs allow the threadpool to further reduce the
number of threads in a process, using far fewer threads than would be necessary
if a process were to devote one thread to servicing each waitable handle or
timeout.

24.7.4 Interprocess Communication

One way Win32 applications handle interprocess communication is by sharing
kernel objects. Another way is by passing messages, an approach that is particularly popular for Windows GUI applications. One thread can send a message
to another thread or to a window by calling PostMessage, PostThreadMes-
sage, SendMessage, SendThreadMessage, or SendMessageCallback. The
difference between *posting* a message and *sending* a message is that the post
routines are asynchronous: they return immediately, and the calling thread
does not know when the message is actually delivered. The send routines are
synchronous—they block the caller until the message has been delivered and
processed.

In addition to sending a message, a thread can also send data with the
message. Since processes have separate address spaces, the data must be
copied. The system copies them by calling SendMessage to send a message
of type WM_COPYDATA with a COPYDATASTRUCT data structure that contains the
length and address of the data to be transferred. When the message is sent,
Windows XP copies the data to a new block of memory and gives the virtual
address of the new block to the receiving process.

24.7.4.1 Individual Input Queues

Unlike the 16-bit Windows environment, every Win32 thread has its own input
queue from which the thread receives messages. (All input is received via
messages.) This structure is more reliable than the shared input queue of 16-bit

```
...
// allocate 16 MB at the top of our address space
void *buf = VirtualAlloc(0,0x1000000,MEM_RESERVE | MEM_TOP_DOWN,
           PAGE_READWRITE);
// commit the upper 8 MB of the allocated space
VirtualAlloc(buf + 0x800000,0x800000,MEM_COMMIT,PAGE_READWRITE);
// do some stuff with it
// decommit
VirtualFree(buf + 0x800000,0x800000,MEM_DECOMMIT);
// release all the allocated address space
VirtualFree(buf,0,MEM_RELEASE);
...
```

Figure 24.14   Code fragments for allocating virtual memory.

windows, because, with separate queues, one stuck application cannot block input to the other applications. If a Win32 application does not call `GetMessage` to handle events on its input queue, the queue fills up, and after about 5 seconds the system marks the application as "Not Responding."

24.7.5 Memory Management

The Win32 API provides several ways for an application to use memory: virtual memory, memory-mapped files, heaps, and thread-local storage.

24.7.5.1 Virtual Memory

An application calls `VirtualAlloc` to reserve or commit virtual memory, and `VirtualFree` to decommit or release the memory. These functions enable the application to specify the virtual address at which the memory is allocated. They operate on multiples of the memory page size, and the starting address of an allocated region must be greater than 0x10000. Examples of these functions appear in Figure 24.14.

A process may lock some of its committed pages into physical memory by calling `VirtualLock`. The maximum number of pages a process can lock is 30, unless the process first calls `SetProcessWorkingSetSize` to increase the maximum working-set size.

24.7.5.2 Memory-Mapping Files

Another way for an application to use memory is by memory mapping a file into its address space. Memory mapping is also a convenient way for two processes to share memory: both processes map the same file into their virtual memory. Memory mapping is a multistage process, as you can see in the example of Figure 24.15.

```
...
// open the file or create it if it does not exist
HANDLE hfile = CreateFile("somefile",GENERIC_READ | GENERIC_WRITE,
    FILE_SHARE_READ | FILE_SHARE_WRITE,NULL,OPEN_ALWAYS,
    FILE_ATTRIBUTE_NORMAL,
    NULL);
// create the file mapping 8 MB in size
HANDLE hmap = CreateFileMapping(hfile,PAGE_READWRITE,
    SEC_COMMIT,0,0x800000,"SHM_1");
// get a view to the space mapped
void *buf = MapViewOfFile(hmap,FILE_MAP_ALL_ACCESS,0,0,0 times800000);
// do some stuff with it
// unmap the file
UnmapViewOfFile(buf);
CloseHandle(hmap);
CloseHandle(hfile); ...
```

Figure 24.15   Code fragments for memory mapping of a file.

If a process wants to map some address space just to share a memory region with another process, no file is needed. The process calls `CreateFileMapping` with a file handle of 0xffffffff and a particular size. The resulting file-mapping object can be shared by inheritance, by name lookup, or by duplication.

24.7.5.3 Heaps

The third way for applications to use memory is a heap. A heap in the Win32 environment is a region of reserved address space. When a Win32 process is initialized, it is created with a 1 MB *default heap*. Since many Win32 functions use the default heap, access to the heap is synchronized to protect the heap's space-allocation data structures from being damaged by concurrent updates by multiple threads.

Win32 provides several heap-management functions so a process can allocate and manage a private heap. These functions are `HeapCreate`, `HeapAlloc`, `HeapRealloc`, `HeapSize`, `HeapFree`, and `HeapDestroy`. The Win32 API also provides the `HeapLock` and `HeapUnlock` functions to enable a thread to gain exclusive access to a heap. Unlike `VirtualLock`, these functions perform only synchronization; they do not lock pages into physical memory.

24.7.5.4 Thread-Local Storage

The fourth way for applications to use memory is a thread-local storage mechanism. Functions that rely on global or static data typically fail to work properly in a multithreaded environment. For instance, the C run-time function `strtok`

```
// reserve a slot for a variable
DWORD var_index = TlsAlloc();
// set it to some value
TlsSetValue(var_index,10);
// get the value back
int var = TlsGetValue(var_index);
// release the index
TlsFree(var_index);
```

Figure 24.16   Code for dynamic thread-local storage.

uses a static variable to keep track of its current position while parsing a string. For two concurrent threads to execute strtok correctly, they need separate *current position* variables. The thread-local storage mechanism allocates global storage on a per-thread basis. It provides both dynamic and static methods of creating thread-local storage. The dynamic method is illustrated in Figure 24.16.

To use a thread-local static variable, the application declares the variable as follows to ensure that every thread has its own private copy:

```
__declspec(thread) DWORD cur_pos = 0;
```

24.8 ■ Summary

Microsoft designed Windows XP to be an extensible, portable operating system—one able to take advantage of new techniques and hardware. Windows XP supports multiple operating environments and symmetric multiprocessing, including both 32-bit and 64-bit processors, and NUMA computers. The use of kernel objects to provide basic services, and the support for client–server computing, enable Windows XP to support a wide variety of application environments. For instance, Windows XP can run programs compiled for MS-DOS, Win16, Windows 95, Windows XP, and/or POSIX. It provides virtual memory, integrated caching, and preemptive scheduling. Windows XP supports a security model stronger than those of previous Microsoft operating systems, and includes internationalization features. Windows XP runs on a wide variety of computers, so users can choose and upgrade hardware to match their budgets and performance requirements without needing to alter the applications they run.

■ Exercises

24.1 What type of operating system is Windows XP? Describe two of its major features.

24.2 List the design goals of Windows XP. Describe two in detail.

24.3 Describe the booting process for a Windows XP system.

24.4 Describe the three main architectural layers of Windows XP.

24.5 What is the job of the object manager?

24.6 What is a handle, and how does a process obtain a handle?

24.7 Describe the management scheme of the virtual memory manager. How does the VM manager improve performance?

24.8 What types of services does the process manager provide? What is a local procedure call?

24.9 What are the responsibilities of the I/O manager?

24.10 What manages cache in Windows XP? How is cache managed?

24.11 Does Windows XP offer any user-mode processes that enable Windows XP to run programs developed for other operating systems? Describe two of these subsystems.

24.12 What types of networking does Windows XP support? How does Windows XP implement transport protocols? Describe two networking protocols.

24.13 How is the NTFS namespace organized? Describe.

24.14 How does NTFS handle data structures? How does NTFS recover from a system crash? What is guaranteed after a recovery takes place?

24.15 What is a process, and how is it managed in Windows XP?

24.16 How does Windows XP allocate user memory?

24.17 Describe some of the ways an application can use memory via the Win32 API.

Bibliographical Notes

Solomon and Russinovich [2000] gives an overview of Windows XP and considerable technical detail about the system internals and components. Tate [2000] is a good reference on using Windows XP. The Microsoft Windows XP Server Resource Kit (Microsoft [2000b]) is a six-volume set helpful for using and deploying Windows XP. The Microsoft Developer Network Library (Microsoft [2000a]) is issued quarterly. It provides a wealth of information on Windows XP and other Microsoft products.

Iseminger [2000] provides a good reference on the Windows XP Active Directory. Richter [1997] gives a detailed discussion on writing programs that use the Win32 API. Silberschatz et al. [2001] contains a good discussion of B+ trees.

Appendix A

JAVA PRIMER

In this appendix, we present a primer for people who are unfamiliar with the Java language. This introduction is intended to allow you to develop the Java skills necessary to understand the programs in this text. It is not a complete Java reference; for a more thorough coverage of Java, consult the Bibliographical Notes. We do not assume that you are familiar with object-oriented principles, such as classes, objects, and encapsulation, although some knowledge of these topics would be helpful. If you are already familiar with C or C++, the transition to Java will be smooth, because much Java syntax is based on C/C++.

A.1 ■ Basics

In this section, we cover basics such as the structure of a basic program, control statements, methods, classes, objects, and arrays.

A.1.1 A Simple Program

A Java program consists of one or more classes. One class must contain the `main()` method. (A method is equivalent to a function in C/C++.) Program execution begins in this main method. Figure A.1 illustrates a simple program that outputs a message to the terminal. The `main()` method must be defined as `public static void main(String args[])`, where `String args[]` are optional parameters that may be passed on the command line. Output to the

```
/*
The first simple program
*/
public class First
{
    public static void main(String args[]) {
        // output a message to the screen
        System.out.println("Java Primer Now Brewing!");
    }
}
```

Figure A.1   A first Java program.

screen is done via the call to the method System.out.println(). Note that
Java supports the C++ style of comments, including

```
// This string is a comment
```

for single-line comments and

```
/* And this string
too is
a comment */
```

for multiline comments.

The name of the file containing the main() method must match the class
name in which it appears. In this instance, the main() method is in the class
First. Therefore, the name of this file must be **First.java**. To compile this
program using the Java Development Kit (JDK) command line compiler, enter

```
javac First.java
```

on the command line. This will result in the generation of the file *First.class*. To
run this program, type the following on the command line

```
java First
```

Note that java commands and file names are case sensitive.

A.1.2   Methods

A program usually consists of other methods in addition to main(). Figure A.2
illustrates the use of a separate method to output the message *Java Primer Now
Brewing!* In this instance, the String is passed to the static method printIt(),
where it is printed. Note that both the main() and printIt() methods return
void. Later examples throughout this chapter will use methods that return
values. We will also explain the meaning of the keywords public and static
in Section A.1.6.

```
public class Second
{
    public static void printIt(String message) {
        System.out.println(message);
    }

    public static void main(String args[]) {
        printIt("Java Primer Now Brewing!");
    }
}
```

Figure A.2   The use of methods.

A.1.3 Operators

Java uses the + - * / operators for addition, subtraction, multiplication, and division, and the & operator for the remainder. Java also provides the C++ autoincrement and autodecrement operators ++ and --. The statement ++T; is equivalent to T = T + 1. In addition, Java provides shortcuts for all the binary arithmetic operators. For example, the += operator allows the statement T = T + 5; to be written as T += 5.

The relational operators are == for equality and != for inequality. For example, the statement 4 == 4 is true, whereas 4 != 4 is false. Other relational operators include < <= >= >. Java uses && as the and operator and || as the or operator.

Unlike C++, Java does not allow operator overloading. However, you can use the + operator to append strings. For example, the statement

```
System.out.println("Can you hear " + "me?");
```

appends me? to Can you hear.

A.1.4 Statements

In this section, we cover the basic statements for controlling the flow of a program.

A.1.4.1 The for statement

The format of the **for** loop is as follows:

```
for (initialization; test; increment) {
    // body of for loop
}
```

For example, the following for loop prints out the numbers from 1 to 25.

```java
int i;
for (i = 1; i <= 25; i++) {
    System.out.println("i = " + i);
}
```

Note that, when the body of the for loop consists of only one line, the braces of the loop can be eliminated. Also, the index of the for loop can be declared within the for statement, rather than prior to the statement. Therefore, the previous loop could have been written as follows:

```java
for (int i = 1; i <= 25; i++)
    System.out.println("i = " + i);
```

When the index is declared in the for loop, the scope of the index is only within the for statement. The index of a for loop must be an integer (int). Java data types are discussed in Section A.1.5.

A.1.4.2 The while statement

The format of the **while** loop is as follows:

```java
while (boolean condition is true) {
    // body of loop
}
```

The format of the **do-while** loop is as follows:

```java
do {
    // body of loop
} while (boolean condition is true);
```

As is the case for the for loop, if the body of either the while or the do-while loops is only one statement, the braces can be eliminated.

A.1.4.3 The if statement

The format of the **if** statement is as follows:

```java
if (boolean condition is true) {
    // statement(s)
}
else if (boolean condition is true) {
    // other statement(s)
}
else {
    // even other statement(s)
}
```

If there is only a single statement to be performed if the Boolean expression is true, then the braces can be eliminated.

A.1.5 Data Types

Java provides two different varieties of data types: primitive and reference (or nonprimitive). Primitive data types include boolean, char, byte, short, int, long, float, and double. Reference data types include objects and arrays.

A.1.6 Classes and Objects

Objects are at the heart of Java programming. An object consists of data and methods that access (and possibly manipulate) the data. An object also has a state, which consists of the values for the object's data at a particular time. Objects are modeled with classes. Figure A.3 is a class for a Point. The data

```java
class Point
{
    // constructor to initialize the object
    public Point(int i, int j) {
        xCoord = i;
        yCoord = j;
    }

    // exchange the values of xCoord and yCoord
    public void swap() {
        int temp;
        temp = xCoord;
        xCoord = yCoord;
        yCoord = temp;
    }

    public void printIt() {
        System.out.println("X coordinate = " + xCoord);
        System.out.println("Y coordinate = " + yCoord);
    }

    // class data
    private int xCoord; // X coordinate
    private int yCoord; // Y coordinate
}
```

Figure A.3   A point.

```
public Point() {
    xCoord = 0;
    yCoord = 0;
}
```

Figure A.4   Default constructor for the Point class.

for this class are the *x* and *y* coordinates for the point. An object—which is an instance of this class—can be created with the new statement. For example, the statement

```
Point ptA = new Point(0,15);
```

creates an object with the name ptA of type Point. Furthermore, the state of this object is initialized to $x = 0$ and $y = 15$. We initilize objects using a constructor. A constructor looks like an ordinary method except that it has no return value and it must have the same name as the name of the class. The constructor is called when the object is created with the new statement. In the statement Point ptA = new Point(0,15);, the values 0 and 15 are passed as parameters to the constructor, where they are assigned to the data xCoord and yCoord.

   With the Point class written the way it is, we could not create a point using the statement

```
Point ptA = new Point();
```

because there is no constructor that has an empty parameter list. If we wanted to allow the creation of such an object, we have to create a matching constructor. For example, we could add the constructor shown in Figure A.4 to the class Point. Doing so allow us to create an object using the statement Point ptA = new Point();. In this case, the *x* and *y* coordinates for the point are initialized to 0.

   Having two constructors in the Point class leads to an interesting issue. In some ways, a constructor behaves like an ordinary method. Two constructors for this class essentially means two methods with the same name. This feature of object-oriented languages is known as **method overloading**. A class may contain one or more methods with the same name, as long as the data types in the parameter list are different.

   The Point class has two other methods: swap() and printIt(). Note that these methods are not declared as static; unlike the printIt() method in Figure A.2. These methods can be invoked with the statements

```
ptA.swap();
ptA.printIt();
```

   The difference between static and instance (nonstatic) methods is that static methods do not require being associated with an object, and we can call them by merely invoking the name of the method. Instance methods can be invoked only by being associated with an instance of an object. That is, they can be called with only the notation `object-name.method`. Also, an object containing the instance methods must be instantiated with `new` before its instance methods can be called. In this example, we must first create `ptA` to call the instance methods `swap()` and `printIt()`.

Also notice that we declare the methods and data belonging to the class `Point` using either the `public` or `private` modifiers. A public declaration allows the method or data to be accessed from *outside* the class. Private declaration allows the data or methods to be accessed from only *within* the class. Typically, we design classes by declaring class data as private. Thus, the data for the class are accessible through only those methods that are defined within the class. Declaring data as private prevents the data from being manipulated from outside the class. In Figure A.3, only the `swap()` and `printIt()` methods can access the class data. These methods are defined as public, meaning that they can be called by code outside the class. Therefore, the designer of a class can determine how the class data are accessed and manipulated by restricting access to private class data through public methods. (In Section A.4, we look at the `protected` modifier.)

Note that there are instances where data may be declared as public and methods as private. Data constants may be declared as public if access from outside the class is desired. We declare constants using the keywords `static final`. For example, a class consisting of mathematical functions may publicly declare the constant pi as

```
public static final double PI = 3.14159;
```

Also, if a method is to be used only within the class, it is appropriate to define that method as private.

Objects are treated by reference in Java. When the program creates an instance of an object, that instance is assigned a reference to the object. Figure A.5 shows two objects of class `Point`: `ptA` and `ptB`. These objects are unique; each has its own state. However, the statement

```
Point ptC = ptB;
```

assigns `ptC` a reference to object `ptB`. In essence, both `ptB` and `ptC` now refer to the same object, as shown in Figure A.6. The statement

```
ptC.swap();
```

alters the value of this object, calling the `swap()` method, which exchanges the values of `xCoord` and `yCoord`. Calling the `printIt()` method for `ptB` and `ptC` illustrates the change in the state for the object, showing that now the x coordinate is -25 and the y coordinate is -15.

Whenever objects are passed as parameters to methods, they are passed by reference. Thus, the local parameter is a reference to the argument being passed. If the method alters the state of the local parameter, it also changes the state of

```
public class Third
{
    public static void main(String args[]) {
        // create 2 points and initialize them
        Point ptA = new Point(5,10);
        Point ptB = new Point(-15,-25);

        // output their values
        ptA.printIt();
        ptB.printIt();

        // now exchange values for first point
        ptA.swap();
        ptA.printIt();

        // ptC is a reference to ptB
        Point ptC = ptB;
        // exchange the values for ptC
        ptC.swap();

        // output the values
        ptB.printIt();
        ptC.printIt();
    }
}
```

Figure A.5   Objects as references.

the argument that it was passed. In Figure A.7, the object ptD is passed to the method change(), where the swap() method is called. When they return from change(), the values of the *x* and *y* parameters for ptD are exchanged.

The Java keyword this provides an object a reference to itself. The this reference is useful when an object needs to pass a reference of itself to another object.

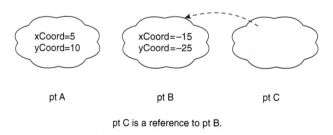

pt C is a reference to pt B.

Figure A.6   ptC is a reference to ptB.

```
public static void change(Point tmp) {
    tmp.swap();
}

Point ptD = new Point(0,1);
change(ptD);
ptD.printIt();
```

Figure A.7   Object parameters are passed by reference.

A.1.7 Arrays

Arrays are reference data types in Java; thus, they are created just like any other type of object. The syntax for creating an array of 10 bytes is

```
byte[] numbers = new byte[10];
```

Arrays can also be created and initialized in the same step. The following code fragment initializes an array to the first five prime numbers.

```
int[] primeNums = {3,5,7,11,13};
```

Note that neither is the size of the array specified nor is the new statement used when an array is initialized.

When we create an array of objects, we must first allocate the array with the new statement *and* we must allocate each object using new. The statement

```
Point[] pts = new Point[5];
```

creates an array to hold five *references* to Point objects. The statements

```
for (int i = 0; i < 5; i++) {
    pts[i] = new Point(i,i);
    pts[i].printIt();
}
```

create the five *objects*, assigning a reference to each object to the appropriate array element.

Java performs default array initialization. Primitive numeric data types are initialized to zero, and arrays of objects are initialized to null.

A.1.8 Packages

Many of the core classes for Java are gathered into packages. We do not teach you how to create packages, but we do show how to use the different packages that consistute the core Java application programming interface (API). A package is simply a set of related classes. The naming convention for the core Java packages is *java.<package name>.<class name>*. The standard package for the core API is java.lang. Many of the more commonly used classes belong to this package, including String and Thread. Therefore, the fully qualified names for these classes are java.lang.String and java.lang.Thread. Classes that belong to java.lang are so common that we can refer to them by their class name, omitting the preceding package name. However, there are many other classes that belong to packages other than java.lang, and they do not follow this rule. In these instances, the fully qualified package name must be used. For example, the Vector class belongs to the package java.util (we look at vectors in Section A.3). To use a Vector, therefore, we must use the following syntax

```
java.util.Vector items = new java.util.Vector();
```

This requirement obviously can lead to cumbersome syntax. The less verbose solution is for the program to declare that it is using a class in a certain package by issuing the following statement at the top (before any class definitions.)

```
import java.util.Vector;
```

Now, we could declare the Vector using the easier style:

```
Vector items = new Vector();
```

However, the most common style people use when they are using packages is

```
import java.util.*;
```

This approach allows the program to use *any* class in the package java.util. The JavaSoft web site (http://www.javasoft.com) includes a complete listing of all packages in the core API.

A.2 ■ Exception Handling

An exception is an occurrence of an unusual event during the operation of a program. Java allows a program to catch exceptions and to handle them in a graceful manner. When an exception occurs within a method, that method can throw the exception to the code that called it. For example, the API for the wait() method for the class Object appears as

```
public final void wait() throws InterruptedException;
```

Thus, calling the wait() could result in an InterruptedException occurring. Exceptions can be handled by being caught. The syntax for catching and handling exceptions is as follows:

```
try {
    // call some method(s) that
    // may result in an exception.
}
catch(theException e) {
    // now handle the exception
}
finally {
    // perform this whether the
    // exception occurred or not.
}
```

All code that may cause an exception is enclosed within a try block. If an exception that is specified in the catch statement occurs, the exception is caught and handled within the catch block. (When an exception is thrown, any following code in the try block is not executed.) An optional finally clause allows the program to run code whether or not the exception occurred. The program shown in Figure A.8 illustrates the use of these statements. This program generates randomly either 0 or 1 using the static method random()

```
public class TestExcept
{
    public static void main(String args[]) {
        int num, recip;

        // generate a random number 0 or 1
        // random() returns a double, type-cast to int
        num = (int) (Math.random() * 2);

        try {
            recip = 1 / num;
            System.out.println("The reciprocal is " + recip);
        }
        catch (ArithmeticException e) {
            // output the exception message
            System.out.println(e);
        }
        finally {
            System.out.println("The number was " + num);
        }
    }
}
```

Figure A.8   Testing exceptions.

from the class java.lang.Math, and produces the reciprocal of this number. If this random number is 0, an arithmetic exception for divide by 0 is thrown. This exception is handled by outputting the exception message. The finally clause prints out the random number that was generated.

If an exception is not caught, it propagates up through the call stack until it reaches the main() method. For example, one such exception is an array out of bounds (java.lang.ArrayIndexOutOfBoundsException). The following code example illustrates how such an exception could occur:

```
int[] nums = {5,10,15,20,25};

for (int i = 0; i < 6; i++)
    System.out.println(nums[i]);
```

Since this exception is not caught within a try-catch block, it propagates all the way up through the original call to main(), where it causes program termination and an error message.

A.3 ■ Inheritance

Java is considered a pure object-oriented language. A feature of such languages is that they are able to extend the functionality of an existing class. In object-oriented terms, this extension is **inheritance**. In general, it works as follows.

```
public class Person
{
    public Person(String n, int a, String s) {
        name = n;
        age = a;
        ssn = s;
    }

    public void printPerson() {
        System.out.println("Name:   " + name);
        System.out.println("Age:   " + age);
        System.out.println("Social Security:   " + ssn);
    }

    private String name;
    private int age;
    private String ssn;
}
```

Figure A.9   A person.

Assume that there exists a class that has almost all the functionality that is needed for a particular application. Rather than developing from scratch a new class that contains all the necessary functionality, we can use inheritance to add to the existing class whatever is needed. For example, assume that an application must keep track of student records. A student is distinguished by her name, age, social-security number, major, and grade-point average (GPA). If another class already exists that represents people using name, age, and social-security number, we can create a student class by extending it, adding a major and GPA. The class being inherited from is the base class; the extended class is the derived class.

The code for the Person class is shown in Figure A.9. The class Student is shown in Figure A.10. What is new in this class definition is the keyword extends. The Java syntax for a derived class to inherit from a base class is

```
derived-class extends base-class
```

Also note that the constructor in the Student class has a call to super(n, a, s). When an object of class Student is created, the constructor for the base class is not normally called. By invoking the super() method, the derived class can call the constructor in the base class.

```
public class Student extends Person
{
    public Student(String n, int a, String s,
            String m, double g) {
        // call the constructor in the
        // parent (Person) class
        super(n, a, s);
        major = m;
        GPA = g;
    }

    public void studentInfo() {
        // call this method in the parent class
        printPerson();

        System.out.println("Major:   " + major);
        System.out.println("GPA: " + GPA);
    }

    private String major;
    private double GPA;
}
```

Figure A.10   A student.

Java makes extensive use of inheritance throughout the core API. For example, many of the classes in the packages `java.awt` (used for creating graphical programs) and `java.io` (provides I/O facilities) are part of an inheritance hierarchy. In addition, one of the ways of creating a thread (described in Chapter 5) is to define a class that extends the `Thread` class.

By default, all Java classes are derived from a common class called `Object`. We can exploit this feature by using the `Vector` class from the package `java.util`. A vector is a collection class: It contains a collection of objects. A vector behaves like a dynamic array: It grows and shrinks as needed. The method

```
addElement(Object obj)
```

of the `Vector` class inserts the `Object` obj at the end of the vector. Since all classes are derived from `Object`, this allows us to insert any class into a vector. The following statements illustrate how to insert three separate strings into a vector:

```
String first = "The first element";
String second = "The second element";
String third = "The third element";

// insert the strings into the vector
Vector items = new Vector();
items.addElement(first);
items.addElement(second);
items.addElement(third);
```

Note that, although these objects are `String` objects being inserted into the vector, they could be objects of any class.

Retrieving objects from a vector works similarly. The `elementAt()` method returns the `Object` at a specified index in the vector, as shown in the following statements.

```
String element;
element = (String) items.elementAt(0);
System.out.println(element);
element = (String) items.elementAt(1);
System.out.println(element);
element = (String) items.elementAt(2);
System.out.println(element);
```

Since the return type for this method is `Object`, the value being returned must be typecast to its appropriate data type. The ability to create collection classes— such as vectors, hashtables, stacks, and queues—that contain the type `Object` allows a programer to provide a generic data structure that works with all objects.

```
public interface Shape
{
    public double area();
    public double circumference();

    public static final double PI = 3.14159;
}
```

Figure A.11   Shape interface.

A.4 ■ Interfaces and Abstract Classes

Another feature of pure object-oriented languages is the ability to define the behavior of an object without specifying how that behavior is to be implemented. Java gives us this ability through interfaces and abstract classes.

In Java, an **interface** is similar to a class definition, except that it only contains a list of methods and their parameters while omitting the implementation of each method. Furthermore, interfaces may not contain any class data apart from constants. Figure A.11 provides an example of an interface for a shape. This interface merely specifies two methods that are common to shapes—the

```
public class Circle implements Shape
{
    // initialize the radius of the circle
    public Circle(double r) {
        radius = r;
    }

    // calculate the area of a circle
    public double area() {
        return PI * radius * radius;
    }

    // calculate the circumference of a circle
    public double circumference() {
        return 2 * PI * radius;
    }

    private double radius;
}
```

Figure A.12   Circle implementation of Shape interface.

```
public class Rectangle implements Shape
{
    public Rectangle(double h, double w) {
      height = h;
      width = w;
    }

    // calculate the area of a rectangle
    public double area() {
      return height * width;
    }

    // calculate the circumference of a rectangle
    public double circumference() {
      return 2 * (height + width);
    }

    private double height;
    private double width;
}
```

Figure A.13   Rectangle implementation of Shape interface.

area and circumference for the shape. Note that these methods are not defined; it is up to the class that implements this interface to define the body of these methods.

```
public class TestShapes
{
    public static void display(Shape figure) {
      System.out.println("The area is " + figure.area());
      System.out.println("The circumference is " +
        figure.circumference());
    }

    public static void main(String args[]) {
      Shape figOne = new Circle(3.5);
      display(figOne);

      figOne = new Rectangle(3,4);
      display(figOne);
    }
}
```

Figure A.14   Program to test the Circle and Rectangle shapes.

Two possible shapes that could implement this interface are a circle and rectangle. The implementation of the Shape interface for a circle is shown in Figure A.12 (on page 775).

When a class implements an interface, it must define the methods as specified by that interface. In this case, the Circle class must implement the area() and circumference() methods. The implementation of the interface for a rectangle is shown in Figure A.13. Since the area and circumference are determined differently for each Shape, the implementation of these methods is left up to classes that implement the interface.

Figure A.14 illustrates how we can use these classes. The interesting feature of this program is that the object reference figOne is declared as type Shape and is first used as a Circle object and next as a Rectangle. We are allowed to do this because the Circle and Rectangle classes both implement the Shape interface. Thus, they are both shapes. Thus, any object declared as type Shape CAN be an instance of any class that implements the Shape interface. Polymorphism is the ability to take on more than one form; in this example, figOne is considered a polymorphic reference, because it is first an instance of a Circle and then an instance of a Rectangle.

The methods shown in the Shape interface are considered to be abstract, in that they are not defined. In fact, we could have put the keyword abstract as

```
public abstract class Employee
{
    public Employee(String n, String t, double s) {
        name = n;
        title = t;
        salary = s;
    }

    public void printInfo() {
        System.out.println("Name:   " + name);
        System.out.println("Title:  " + title);
        System.out.println("Salary:  $ " + salary);
    }

    public abstract void computeRaise();
    private String name;
    private String title;
    protected double salary;
}
```

Figure A.15   Abstract class for an employee.

```
public class Manager extends Employee
{
    public Manager(String n, String t, double s) {
        super(n, t, s);
    }

    public void computeRaise() {
        salary += salary * .05 + BONUS;
    }

    private static final double BONUS = 2500;
}
```

Figure A.16   A manager.

follows, when we defined the interface:

```
public abstract double area();
public abstract double circumference();
```

The use of the keyword abstract is optional in an interface. If it is absent, it is implied.

Another special type of class is an **abstract class**. An abstract class is similar to an interface, but it may contain both abstract methods and defined methods. In an interface, all methods must be abstract. Figure A.15, shown on page 777, illustrates an abstract class to model an employee.

To use an abstract class, we extend the class using inheritance, as described in Section A.3. Figure A.16 provides an example of a class that extends Employee for managers. This class must implement the abstract method com-

```
public class Developer extends Employee
{
    public Developer(String n, String t,
        double s, int np) {
      super(n, t, s);
      numOfPrograms = np;
    }

    public void computeRaise() {
        salary += salary * .05 + numOfPrograms * 25;
    }

    private int numOfPrograms;
}
```

Figure A.17   A developer.

```
Employee[] worker = new Employee[3];

worker[0] = new Manager("Pat", "Supervisor", 30000);
worker[1] = new Developer("Tom", "Java Tech", 28000, 20);
worker[2] = new Developer("Jay", "Java Intern", 26000, 8);

for (int i = 0; i < 3; i++) {
    worker[i].computeRaise();
    worker[i].printInfo();
}
```

Figure A.18   Use of the Manager and Developer classes.

puteRaise(). We calculate the raise for managers by giving them a 5% salary increase in addition to a bonus. Figure A.17 illustrates a class for developers. Program developers are given a salary raise of 3% plus $25 for every program that they write. Figure A.18 shows an example that uses the Manager and Developer classes.

In Section A.1.6, we discussed what the private and public modifiers are and how we can use them to control access to data and methods from outside a class definition. However, the salary data in the Employee abstract class have been declared as protected. The protected modifier allows data to be accessed from within the class in which they are defined, in addition to any classes that are derived from that class. This scheme prevents access to data from code outside the class definition, but allows subclasses to access the data.

Neither interfaces nor abstract classes can be instantiated. Objects can be created only from classes that either implement the interface or extend the abstract class.

In addition to using inheritance, the core Java API also makes heavy use of interfaces and abstract classes. For example, event handling (for mouse clicks, key presses, and so on) in the package java.awt.event is done through implementation of interfaces. Also, a second way of creating threads (described in Section 5.6) implements the Runnable interface.

A.5 ▪ Applications and Applets

A Java program can be either a standalone application or an applet. The programs that we have shown thus far in this primer are standalone applications. An applet is a Java program that runs embedded within a web page. Because an applet is part of a web page, running an applet requires using either a web browser or the software appletviewer that comes with the Java Development Kit (JDK). Because this text deals primarily with applications, this primer has focused on the development of standalone applications. We cover the structure of applets briefly in this section.

```
import java.applet.*;
import java.awt.*;

public class FirstApplet extends Applet
{
    public void init() {
        // initialization code goes here
    }

    public void paint(Graphics g) {
        g.drawString("Java Primer Now Brewing!", 15, 15);
    }
}
```

Figure A.19   A simple applet.

A simple applet that displays a message is shown in Figure A.19. Note that creating an applet requires extending the Applet class, which is part of the package java.applet. Further note that there is no main() method, unlike in standalone applications. In standalone applications, control first begins in main(). Because an applet is part of a web page, it is the browser that starts the applet and thus fulfills the role of main(). In addition, applets do not have constructors. Used in their place is the init() method, which is called when the applet is first created. All initialization that is typically done in a constructor is done in this method. Because an applet provides a graphical display for output, rather than using System.out.println(), output must be sent to a graphical window. This primer does not cover graphics programming; consult the Bibliographical Notes for a good source. We do describe the method public void paint(), because it provides a mechanism for an applet to perform output. The paint() method is called asynchronously whenever the applet's window needs to be redrawn (for example, when the window is first displayed). The Graphics object (which is part of the package java.awt) that is passed to paint() is in fact the window that is displaying the applet. The method drawString(str, x, y) of the Graphics class will display a string str at the x and y coordinates of the window.

As mentioned, an applet runs embedded within a web page. Therefore, running an applet requires having an associated Hypertext Markup Language (HTML) file. (Web pages are written in HTML.) The HTML file shown in Figure A.20 displays the applet FirstApplet. The width and height of the web page is specified in this file in addition to the name of the class file where the applet is to begin execution. By convention, the name of the HTML file is the name of the applet. Therefore, to demonstrate how to run this applet, we assume the name of the file shown in Figure A.20 is FirstApplet.html. We run this applet by loading FirstApplet.html into a web browser or by using the appletviewer

```
<applet
    code = FirstApplet.class
    width = 400
    height = 200>
</applet>
```

Figure A.20   HTML file for `FirstApplet`.

program that comes with the JDK. We can run this applet using the appletviewer by entering

```
appletviewer FirstApplet.html
```

on the commend line.

A.6 ■ Summary

In this appendix, we provided an introduction to the Java language that should prepare a person unfamiliar with Java to read through the programs in this book. A Java program consists of one or more classes. Classes are used to model objects. An object consists of data and methods that may access the data. One class in a Java program must contain a `main()` method. Program execution starts from this `main()` method. Java treats access to objects by reference. Thus, a reference is assigned when an object is created. In addition to providing support for creating objects, Java also provides inheritance, interfaces, and abstract classes. Inheritance allows us to create a new class from an existing class. Interfaces and abstract classes are similar in that they are both classes and neither can be instantiated. Interfaces are like custom data types in that they define the behavior of an object, without specifying how that behavior is to be implemented. Interfaces consist of abstract methods that are not defined. When a class implements an interface, the class must implement the abstract methods. An abstract class also consists of abstract methods, but it may also contain defined methods. Abstract classes must be extended with inheritance. A Java program can be either a standalone application or an applet, which is a program that runs embedded within a web browser.

Bibliographical Notes

The specification for the Java language is provided in Gosling and colleagues [1996]. Excellent general-purpose books on Java programming include Horstmann and Cornell [1998a, 1998b], Flanagan [1997], Niemeyer and Peck [1997], and van der Linden [1999]. Campione and Walrath [1998] provide an introduction to Java using a tutorial approach. This tutorial is also available at the JavaSoft web site [http://www.javasoft.com]. A complete listing of the packages in the core Java API is also available at the JavaSoft web site. Although it does not refer to Java, Booch's [1994] presentation of object-oriented design principles is relevant. Grand [1998] presents several object-oriented design patterns in Java.

BIBLIOGRAPHY

[**Abbot 1984**] C. Abbot, "Intervention Schedules for Real-Time Programming," *IEEE Transactions on Software Engineering*, Volume SE-10, Number 3 (May 1984), pages 268–274.

[**Accetta et al. 1986**] M. Accetta, R. Baron, W. Bolosky, D. B. Golub, R. Rashid, A. Tevanian, Jr., and M. Young, "Mach: A New Kernel Foundation for UNIX Development," *Proceedings of the Summer 1986 USENIX Conference* (June 1986), pages 93–112.

[**Agrawal and El Abbadi 1991**] D. P. Agrawal and A. El Abbadi, "An Efficient and Fault-Tolerant Solution of Distributed Mutual Exclusion," *ACM Transactions on Computer Systems*, Volume 9, Number 1 (February 1991), pages 1–20.

[**Akyurek and Salem 1993**] S. Akyurek and K. Salem, "Adaptive Block Rearrangement," *Proceedings of the Ninth International Conference on Data Engineering* (April 1993), pages 182–189.

[**Alt 1993**] H. Alt, "Removable Media in Solaris," *Proceedings of the Winter 1993 USENIX Conference* (January 1993), pages 281–287.

[**Anderson et al. 1989**] T. E. Anderson, E. D. Lazowska, and H. M. Levy, "The Performance Implications of Thread Management Alternatives for Shared-Memory Multiprocessors," *IEEE Transactions on Computers*, Volume 38, Number 12 (December 1989), pages 1631–1644.

[Apple 1987] Apple Computer Inc., *Apple Technical Introduction to the Macintosh Family*, Addison-Wesley, Reading, MA (1987).

[Apple 1991] Apple Computer Inc., *Inside Macintosh, Volume VI*, Addison-Wesley, Reading, MA (1991).

[Artsy 1989] Y. Artsy, "Designing a Process Migration Facility: The Charlotte Experience," *Computer*, Volume 22, Number 9 (September 1989), pages 47–56.

[Asthana and Finkelstein 1995] P. Asthana and B. Finkelstein, "Superdense Optical Storage," *IEEE Spectrum*, Volume 32, Number 8 (August 1995), pages 25–31.

[AT&T 1986] AT&T, Steven V. Earhart (Editor), *UNIX Programmer's Manual*, Holt, Rinehart, and Winston, New York, NY (1986).

[Bach 1987] M. J. Bach, *The Design of the UNIX Operating System*, Prentice-Hall, Englewood Cliffs, NJ (1987).

[Balkovich et al. 1985] E. Balkovich, S. R. Lerman, and R. P. Parmelee, "Computing in Higher Education: The Athena Experience," *Communications of the ACM*, Volume 28, Number 11 (November 1985), pages 1214–1224.

[Barrera 1991] J. S. Barrera, "A Fast Mach Network IPC Implementation," *Proceedings of the USENIX Mach Symposium* (November 1991), pages 1–12.

[Belady 1966] L. A. Belady, "A Study of Replacement Algorithms for a Virtual-Storage Computer," *IBM Systems Journal*, Volume 5, Number 2 (1966), pages 78–101.

[Belady et al. 1969] L. A. Belady, R. A. Nelson, and G. S. Shedler, "An Anomaly in Space-Time Characteristics of Certain Programs Running in a Paging Machine," *Communications of the ACM*, Volume 12, Number 6 (June 1969), pages 349–353.

[Ben-Ari 1990] M. Ben-Ari, *Principles of Concurrent and Distributed Programming*, Prentice-Hall, Englewood Cliffs, NJ (1990).

[Benjamin 1990] C. D. Benjamin, "The Role of Optical Storage Technology for NASA's Image Storage and Retrieval Systems," *Proceedings Storage and Retrieval Systems and Applications* (February 1990), pages 10–17.

[Bershad et al. 1990] B. N. Bershad, T. E. Anderson, E. D. Lazowska, and H. M. Levy, "Lightweight Remote Procedure Call," *ACM Transactions on Computer Systems*, Volume 8, Number 1 (February 1990), pages 37–55.

[Birrell and Nelson 1984] A. D. Birrell and B. J. Nelson, "Implementing Remote Procedure Calls," *ACM Transactions on Computer Systems*, Volume 2, Number 1 (February 1984), pages 39–59.

[**Black 1990**] D. L. Black, "Scheduling Support for Concurrency and Parallelism in the Mach Operating System," *IEEE Computer* (May 1990), pages 35–43.

[**Black et al. 1988**] D. L. Black, D. B. Golub, R. F. Rashid, A. Tevanian, Jr., and M. Young, "The Mach Exception Handling Facility," Technical Report, Carnegie-Mellon University, Pittsburgh, PA (April 1988).

[**Black et al. 1992**] D. L. Black, D. B. Golub, D. P. Julin, R. F. Rashid, R. P. Draves, R. W. Dean, A. Forin, J. Barrera, H. Tokadu, G. Malan, and D. Bohman, "Microkernel Operating System Architecture and Mach," *Proceedings of the USENIX Workshop on Micro-Kernels and Other Kernel Architectures* (April 1992), pages 11–30.

[**Booch 1994**] G. Booch, *Object-Oriented Analysis and Design*, Second Edition, Benjamin/Cummings, Redwood City, CA (1994).

[**Boykin and Langerman 1990**] J. Boykin and A. B. Langerman, "Mach/ 4.3BSD: A Conservative Approach to Parallelization," *Computing Systems*, Volume 3, Number 1 (Winter 1990).

[**Boykin et al. 1993**] J. Boykin, D. Kirschen, A. B. Langerman, and S. LoVerso, *Programming under Mach*, Addison-Wesley, Reading, MA (1993).

[**Brereton 1986**] O. P. Brereton, "Management of Replicated Files in a UNIX Environment," *Software—Practice and Experience*, Volume 16 (August 1986), pages 771–780.

[**Brinch Hansen 1970**] P. Brinch Hansen, "The Nucleus of a Multiprogramming System," *Communications of the ACM*, Volume 13, Number 4 (April 1970), pages 238–241 and 250.

[**Brinch Hansen 1973**] P. Brinch Hansen, *Operating System Principles*, Prentice-Hall, Englewood Cliffs, NJ (1973).

[**Beveridge and Wiener 1997**] J. Beveridge and R. Wiener, *Mutlithreading Applications in Win32*, Addison-Wesley, Reading, MA (1997).

[**Buhr et al. 1995**] P. A. Buhr, M. Fortier, and M. H. Coffin, "Monitor Classification", ACM Computing Surveys, Volume 27, Number 1 (March 1995), pages 63–107.

[**Burns 1978**] J. E. Burns, "Mutual Exclusion with Linear Waiting Using Binary Shared Variables," *SIGACT News*, Volume 10, Number 2 (Summer 1978), pages 42–47.

[**Burns and Davies 1993**] A. Burns and G. Davies, *Concurrent Programming*, Addison-Wesley, Reading, MA (1993).

[**Campione and Walrath 1998**] M. Campione and K. Walrath, *The Java Tutorial: Object-Oriented Programming for the Internet*, Second Edition, Sun Microsystems Press, Upper Saddle River, NJ (1998).

[**Carvalho and Roucairol 1983**] O. S. Carvalho and G. Roucairol, "On Mutual Exclusion in Computer Networks," *Communications of the ACM*, Volume 26, Number 2 (February 1983), pages 146–147.

[**Carr and Hennessy 1981**] W. R. Carr and J. L. Hennessy, "WSClock—A Simple and Effective Algorithm for Virtual Memory Management," *Proceedings of the Eighth Symposium on Operating Systems Principles* (December 1981), pages 87–95.

[**Caswell and Black 1989**] D. Caswell and D. Black, "Implementing a Mach Debugger for Multithreaded Applications," Technical Report, Carnegie-Mellon University, Pittsburgh, PA (November 1989).

[**Chang 1980**] E. Chang, "N-Philosophers: An Exercise in Distributed Control," *Computer Networks*, Volume 4, Number 2 (April 1980), pages 71–76.

[**Chang and Mergen 1988**] A. Chang and M. F. Mergen, "801 Storage: Architecture and Programming," *ACM Transactions on Computer Systems*, Volume 6, Number 1 (February 1988), pages 28–50.

[**Chen et al. 1994**] P. M. Chen, E. K. Lee, G. A. Gibson, R. H. Katz, and D. A. Patterson, "RAID: High-Performance, Reliable Secondary Storage," *ACM Computing Surveys*, Volume 26, Number 2 (June 1994), pages 145–185.

[**Cheriton and Zwaenepoel 1983**] D. R. Cheriton and W. Z. Zwaenepoel, "The Distributed V Kernel and Its Performance for Diskless Workstations," *Proceedings of the Ninth Symposium on Operating Systems Principles* (October 1983), pages 129–140.

[**Cheung and Loong 1995**] W. H. Cheung and A. H. S. Loong, "Exploring Issues of Operating Systems Structuring: From Microkernel to Extensible Systems," *Operating Systems Review*, Volume 29 (October 1995), pages 4–16.

[**Chi 1982**] C. S. Chi, "Advances in Computer Mass Storage Technology," *Computer*, Volume 15, Number 5 (May 1982), pages 60–74.

[**Chow and Abraham 1982**] T. C. K. Chow and J. A. Abraham, "Load Balancing in Distributed Systems," *IEEE Transactions on Software Engineering*, Volume SE-8, Number 4 (July 1982), pages 401–412.

[**Coffman et al. 1971**] E. G. Coffman, M. J. Elphick, and A. Shoshani, "System Deadlocks," *Computing Surveys*, Volume 3, Number 2 (June 1971), pages 67–78.

[**Comer 1984**] D. Comer, *Operating System Design: The Xinu Approach*, Prentice-Hall, Englewood Cliffs, NJ (1984).

[Comer 1991] D. Comer, *Internetworking with TCP/IP, Volume I,* Second Edition, Prentice-Hall, Englewood Cliffs, NJ (1991).

[Comer and Stevens 1991] D. Comer and D. L. Stevens, *Internetworking with TCP/IP, Volume II,* Prentice-Hall, Englewood Cliffs, NJ (1991).

[Cooper and Draves 1987] E. C. Cooper and R. P. Draves, "C Threads," Technical Report, Carnegie-Mellon University, Pittsburgh, PA (July 1987).

[Corbato and Vyssotsky 1965] F. J. Corbato and V. A. Vyssotsky, "Introduction and Overview of the MULTICS System," *Proceedings of the AFIPS Fall Joint Computer Conference* (1965), pages 185–196.

[Corbato et al. 1962] F. J. Corbato, M. Merwin-Daggett, and R. C. Daley, "An Experimental Time-Sharing System," *Proceedings of the AFIPS Fall Joint Computer Conference* (1962), pages 335–344.

[Courtois et al. 1971] P. J. Courtois, F. Heymans, and D. L. Parnas, "Concurrent Control with 'Readers' and 'Writers'," *Communications of the ACM,* Volume 14, Number 10 (October 1971), pages 667–668.

[CSRG 1986] Computer Systems Research Group—University of California at Berkeley, *BSD UNIX Reference Manuals,* six volumes, USENIX Association (1986).

[Custer 1994] H. Custer, *Inside the Windows NT File System,* Microsoft Press, Redmond, WA (1994).

[Davcev and Burkhard 1985] D. Davcev and W. A. Burkhard, "Consistency and Recovery Control for Replicated Files," *Proceedings of the Tenth Symposium on Operating Systems Principles,* Volume 19, Number 5 (December 1985), pages 87–96.

[deBruijn 1967] N. G. deBruijn, "Additional Comments on a Problem in Concurrent Programming and Control," *Communications of the ACM,* Volume 10, Number 3 (March 1967), pages 137–138.

[Deitel 1990] H. M. Deitel, *An Introduction to Operating Systems,* Second Edition, Addison-Wesley, Reading, MA (1990).

[Deitel and Kogan 1992] H. M. Deitel and M. S. Kogan, *The Design of OS/2,* Addison-Wesley, Reading, MA (1992).

[Denning 1968] P. J. Denning, "The Working Set Model for Program Behavior," *Communications of the ACM,* Volume 11, Number 5 (May 1968), pages 323–333.

[Denning 1980] P. J. Denning, "Working Sets Past and Present," *IEEE Transactions on Software Engineering,* Volume SE-6, Number 1 (January 1980), pages 64–84.

[Dennis 1965] J. B. Dennis, "Segmentation and the Design of Multiprogrammed Computer Systems," *Journal of the ACM*, Volume 12, Number 4 (October 1965), pages 589–602.

[Dennis and Van Horn 1966] J. B. Dennis and E. C. Van Horn, "Programming Semantics for Multiprogrammed Computations," *Communications of the ACM*, Volume 9, Number 3 (March 1966), pages 143–155.

[Diffie and Hellman 1976] W. Diffie and M. E. Hellman, "New Directions in Cryptography," *IEEE Transactions on Information Theory*, Volume 22, Number 6 (November 1976), pages 644–654.

[Dijkstra 1965a] E. W. Dijkstra, "Cooperating Sequential Processes," Technical Report EWD-123, Technological University, Eindhoven, the Netherlands (1965); reprinted in **[Genuys 1968]**, pages 43–112.

[Dijkstra 1965b] E. W. Dijkstra, "Solution of a Problem in Concurrent Programming Control," *Communications of the ACM*, Volume 8, Number 9 (September 1965), page 569.

[Dijkstra 1968] E. W. Dijkstra, "The Structure of the THE Multiprogramming System," *Communications of the ACM*, Volume 11, Number 5 (May 1968), pages 341–346.

[Douglis and Ousterhout 1987] F. Douglis and J. Ousterhout, "Process Migration in the Sprite Operating System," *Proceedings of the Seventh IEEE International Conference on Distributed Computing Systems* (1987), pages 18–25.

[Douglis et al. 1991] F. Douglis, M. F. Kaashoek, and A. S. Tanenbaum, "A Comparison of Two Distributed Systems: Amoeba and Sprite," *Computing Systems*, Volume 4 (Fall 1991).

[Draves et al. 1989] R. P. Draves, M. B. Jones, and M. R. Thompson, "MIG— The MACH Interface Generator," Technical Report, Carnegie-Mellon University, Pittsburgh, PA (November 1989).

[Draves et al. 1991] R. P. Draves, B. N. Bershad, R. F. Rashid, and R. W. Dean, "Using Continuations to Implement Thread Management and Communication in Operating Systems," *Proceedings of the Thirteenth ACM Symposium on Operating Systems Principles* (October 1991), pages 122–136.

[DSS 1994] FIPS 186, Digital Signature Standard. Federal Information Processing Standards Publication 186, U.S. Department of Commerce/N.I.S.T., National Technical Information Service, Springfield, VA, 1994.

[Eisenberg and McGuire 1972] M. A. Eisenberg and M. R. McGuire, "Further Comments on Dijkstra's Concurrent Programming Control Problem," *Communications of the ACM*, Volume 15, Number 11 (November 1972), page 999.

[Eykholt et al. 1992] J. R. Eykholt, S. R. Kleiman, S. Barton, S. Faulkner, A. Shivalingiah, M. Smith, D. Stein, J. Voll, M. Weeks, and D. Williams, "Beyond Multiprocessing: Multithreading the SunOS Kernel," *Proceedings of the Summer 1992 USENIX Conference* (June 1992), pages 11–18.

[Farley 1998] J. Farley, *Java Distributed Computing*, O'Reilly & Associates, Sebastopol, CA (1998).

[Feitelson and Rudolph 1990] D. Feitelson and L. Rudolph, "Mapping and Scheduling in a Shared Parallel Environment Using Distributed Hierarchical Control," *Proceedings of the 1990 International Conference on Parallel Processing* (August 1990).

[Ferguson et al. 1988] D. Ferguson, Y. Yemini, and C. Nikolaou, "Microeconomic Algorithms for Load Balancing in Distributed Computer Systems," *Proceedings of the Eighth IEEE International Conference on Distributed Computing Systems* (1988), pages 491–499.

[Finkel 1988] R. A. Finkel, *Operating Systems Vade Mecum*, Second Edition, Prentice-Hall, Englewood Cliffs, NJ (1988).

[Flanagan 1997] D. Flanagan, *Java in a Nutshell*, Second Edition, O'Reilly & Associates, Sebastopol, CA (1997).

[Fortier 1989] P. J. Fortier, *Handbook of LAN Technology*, McGraw-Hill, New York, NY (1989).

[Freedman 1983] D. H. Freedman, "Searching for Denser Disks," *Infosystems* (September 1983), page 56.

[Fujitani 1984] L. Fujitani, "Laser Optical Disk: The Coming Revolution in On-Line Storage," *Communications of the ACM*, Volume 27, Number 6 (June 1984), pages 546–554.

[Gait 1988] J. Gait, "The Optical File Cabinet: A Random-Access File System for Write-On Optical Disks," *Computer*, Volume 21, Number 6 (June 1988).

[Garcia-Molina 1982] H. Garcia-Molina, "Elections in Distributed Computing Systems," *IEEE Transactions on Computers*, Volume C-31, Number 1 (January 1982).

[Genuys 1968] F. Genuys (Editor), *Programming Languages*, Academic Press, London, England (1968).

[Goldman 1989] P. Goldman, " Mac VM Revealed," *Byte* (September 1989).

[Gong et al. 1997] L. Gong, M. Mueller, H. Prafullchandra, and R. Schemers, "Going Beyond the Sandbox: An Overview of the New Security Architecture in the Java Development Kit 1.2," *Proceedings of the USENIX Symposium on Internet Technologies and Systems* (December 1997).

[Gosling et al. 1996] J. Gosling, B. Joy, and G. Steele, *The Java Language Specification*, Addison-Wesley, Reading, MA (1996).

[Graham 1995] J. Graham, *Solaris 2.X Internals and Architecture*, McGraw-Hill, New York, NY (1995).

[Grampp and Morris 1984] F. T. Grampp and R. H. Morris, "UNIX Operating-System Security," *AT&T Bell Laboratories Technical Journal*, Volume 63 (October 1984), pages 1649–1672.

[Grand 1998] M. Grand, *Patterns in Java: Volume 1. A Catalog of Reusable Design Patterns Illustrated with UML*, John Wiley and Sons, New York, NY (1998).

[Gray 1997] J. Gray, *Interprocess Communications in UNIX: The Nooks and Crannies*, Prentice-Hall, Upper Saddle River, NJ (1997).

[Grosshans 1986] D. Grosshans, *File Systems Design and Implementation*, Prentice-Hall, Englewood Cliffs, NJ (1986).

[Gupta and Franklin 1978] R. K. Gupta and M. A. Franklin, "Working Set and Page Fault Frequency Replacement Algorithms: A Performance Comparison," *IEEE Transactions on Computers*, Volume C-27, Number 8 (August 1978), pages 706–712.

[Habermann 1969] A. N. Habermann, "Prevention of System Deadlocks," *Communications of the ACM*, Volume 12, Number 7 (July 1969), pages 373–377 and 385.

[Hagmann 1989] R. Hagmann, "Comments on Workstation Operating Systems and Virtual Memory," *Proceedings of the Second Workshop on Workstation Operating Systems* (September 1989).

[Halsall 1992] F. Halsall, *Data Communications, Computer Networks, and Open Systems*, Addison-Wesley, Reading, MA (1992).

[Harker et al. 1981] J. M. Harker, D. W. Brede, R. E. Pattison, G. R. Santana, and L. G. Taft, "A Quarter Century of Disk File Innovation," *IBM Journal of Research and Development*, Volume 25, Number 5 (September 1981), pages 677–689.

[Harrison et al. 1976] M. A. Harrison, W. L. Ruzzo, and J. D. Ullman, "Protection in Operating Systems," *Communications of the ACM*, Volume 19, Number 8 (August 1976), pages 461–471.

[Hartley 1998] S. Hartley, *Concurrent Programming: The Java Programming Language*, Oxford University Press, New York, NY (1998).

[Havender 1968] J. W. Havender, "Avoiding Deadlock in Multitasking Systems," *IBM Systems Journal*, Volume 7, Number 2 (1968), pages 74–84.

[Hendricks and Hartmann 1979] E. C. Hendricks and T. C. Hartmann, "Evolution of a Virtual Machine Subsystem," *IBM Systems Journal,* Volume 18, Number 1 (1979), pages 111–142.

[Hennessy and Patterson 1996] J. L. Hennessy and D. A. Patterson, *Computer Architecture: A Quantitative Approach,* Second Edition, Morgan Kaufmann Publishers, Palo Alto, CA (1996).

[Henry 1984] G. Henry, "The Fair Share Scheduler," *AT&T Bell Laboratories Technical Journal* (October 1984).

[Hoagland 1985] A. S. Hoagland, "Information Storage Technology—A Look at the Future," *Computer,* Volume 18, Number 7 (July 1985), pages 60–68.

[Hoare 1974] C. A. R. Hoare, "Monitors: An Operating System Structuring Concept," *Communications of the ACM,* Volume 17, Number 10 (October 1974), pages 549–557; Erratum in *Communications of the ACM,* Volume 18, Number 2 (February 1975), page 95.

[Holt 1971] R. C. Holt, "Comments on Prevention of System Deadlocks," *Communications of the ACM,* Volume 14, Number 1 (January 1971), pages 36–38.

[Holt 1972] R. C. Holt, "Some Deadlock Properties of Computer Systems," *Computing Surveys,* Volume 4, Number 3 (September 1972), pages 179–196.

[Holt 1983] R. C. Holt, *Concurrent Euclid, the UNIX System, and Tunis,* Addison-Wesley, Reading, MA (1983).

[Horstmann and Cornell 1998a] C. Horstmann and G. Cornell, *Core Java 1.2, Volume I: Fundamentals,* Prentice-Hall, Upper Saddle River, NJ (1998).

[Horstmann and Cornell 1998b] C. Horstmann and G. Cornell, *Core Java 1.1, Volume II: Advanced Features,* Prentice-Hall, Upper Saddle River, NJ (1998).

[Howard et al. 1988] J. H. Howard, M. L. Kazar, S. G. Menees, D. A. Nichols, M. Satyanarayanan, and R. N. Sidebotham, "Scale and Performance in a Distributed File System," *ACM Transactions on Computer Systems,* Volume 6, Number 1 (February 1988), pages 55–81.

[Howarth et al. 1961] D. J. Howarth, R. B. Payne, and F. H. Sumner, "The Manchester University Atlas Operating System, Part II: User's Description," *Computer Journal,* Volume 4, Number 3 (October 1961), pages 226–229.

[Hyman 1985] D. Hyman, *The Columbus Chicken Statute, and More Bonehead Legislation,* S. Greene Press, Lexington, MA (1985).

[Iacobucci 1988] E. Iacobucci, *OS/2 Programmer's Guide,* Osborne McGraw-Hill, Berkeley, CA (1988).

[IBM 1983] IBM Corporation, *Technical Reference,* IBM (1983).

[Iliffe and Jodeit 1962] J. K. Iliffe and J. G. Jodeit, "A Dynamic Storage Allocation System," *Computer Journal,* Volume 5, Number 3 (October 1962), pages 200–209.

[Intel 1986] Intel Corporation, *iAPX 386 Programmer's Reference Manual,* Intel Corporation, Santa Clara, CA (1986).

[Intel 1993] Intel Corporation, *Pentium Processor User's Manual, Volume 3: Architecture and Programming Manual,* Intel Corporation, Mt. Prospect, IL (1993).

[Iseminger 2000] D. Iseminger, *Active Directory Services for Microsoft Windows 2000. Technical Reference,* Microsoft Press, Redmond, WA (2000).

[ITSEC 1991] ITSEC Working Group. *ITSEC: Information Technology Security Evaluation Criteria,* version 1.2, September 1991.

[Ivens and Hallberg 1996] K. Ivens and B. Hallberg, *Inside Windows NT Workstation 4,* New Riders Publishing, Indianapolis, IN (1996).

[Jacob and Mudge 1998a] B. Jacob and T. Mudge, "Virtual Memory: Issues of Implementation," *IEEE Computer Magazine,* Volume 31 (June 1998), pages 33–43.

[Jacob and Mudge 1998b] B. Jacob and T. Mudge, "Virtual Memory in Contemporary Microprocessors," *IEEE Micro Magazine,* Volume 18 (July/August 1998), pages 60–75.

[Java Report 1998] *Java Report,* Volume 3, Number 8 (August 1998).

[Jones and Liskov 1978] A. K. Jones and B. H. Liskov, "A Language Extension for Expressing Constraints on Data Access," *Communications of the ACM,* Volume 21, Number 5 (May 1978), pages 358–367.

[Jul et al. 1988] E. Jul, H. Levy, N. Hutchinson, and A. Black, "Fine-Grained Mobility in the Emerald System," *ACM Transactions on Computer Systems,* Volume 6, Number 1 (February 1988), pages 109–133.

[Kay and Lauder 1988] J. Kay and P. Lauder, "A Fair Share Scheduler," *Communications of the ACM,* Volume 31, Number 1 (January 1988), pages 44–55.

[Kenville 1982] R. F. Kenville, "Optical Disk Data Storage," *Computer,* Volume 15, Number 7 (July 1982), pages 21–26.

[Kernighan and Pike 1984] B. W. Kernighan and R. Pike, *The UNIX Programming Environment,* Prentice-Hall, Englewood Cliffs, NJ (1984).

[Kernighan and Ritchie 1988] B. W. Kernighan and D. M. Ritchie, *The C Programming Language,* Second Edition, Prentice-Hall, Englewood Cliffs, NJ (1988).

[Kessels 1977] J. L. W. Kessels, "An Alternative to Event Queues for Synchronization in Monitors," *Communications of the ACM*, Volume 20, Number 7 (July 1977), pages 500–503.

[Kieburtz and Silberschatz 1978] R. B. Kieburtz and A. Silberschatz, "Capability Managers," *IEEE Transactions on Software Engineering*, Volume SE-4, Number 6 (November 1978), pages 467–477.

[Kilburn et al. 1961] T. Kilburn, D. J. Howarth, R. B. Payne, and F. H. Sumner, "The Manchester University Atlas Operating System, Part I: Internal Organization," *Computer Journal*, Volume 4, Number 3 (October 1961), pages 222–225.

[King 1990] R. P. King, "Disk Arm Movement in Anticipation of Future Requests," *ACM Transactions on Computer Systems*, Volume 8, Number 3 (August 1990), pages 214–229.

[Kleiman et al. 1996] S. Kleiman, D. Shah, and B. Smaalders, *Programming with Threads*, Sunsoft Press, Upper Saddle River, NJ (1996).

[Kleinrock 1975] L. Kleinrock, *Queueing Systems, Volume II: Computer Applications*, Wiley-Interscience, New York, NY (1975).

[Knuth 1966] D. E. Knuth, "Additional Comments on a Problem in Concurrent Programming Control," *Communications of the ACM*, Volume 9, Number 5 (May 1966), pages 321–322.

[Knuth 1973] D. E. Knuth, *The Art of Computer Programming, Volume 1: Fundamental Algorithms*, Second Edition, Addison-Wesley, Reading, MA (1973).

[Kogan and Rawson 1988] M. S. Kogan and F. L. Rawson, "The Design of Operating System/2," *IBM Systems Journal*, Volume 27, Number 2 (1988), pages 90–104.

[Kosaraju 1973] S. Kosaraju, "Limitations of Dijkstra's Semaphore Primitives and Petri Nets," *Operating Systems Review*, Volume 7, Number 4 (October 1973), pages 122–126.

[Krakowiak 1988] S. Krakowiak, *Principles of Operating Systems*, MIT Press, Cambridge, MA (1988).

[Lamport 1974] L. Lamport, "A New Solution of Dijkstra's Concurrent Programming Problem," *Communications of the ACM*, Volume 17, Number 8 (August 1974), pages 453–455.

[Lamport 1977] L. Lamport, "Concurrent Reading and Writing," *Communications of the ACM*, Volume 20, Number 11 (November 1977), pages 806–811.

[**Lamport 1978a**] L. Lamport, "Time, Clocks, and the Ordering of Events in a Distributed System," *Communications of the ACM*, Volume 21, Number 7 (July 1978), pages 558–565.

[**Lamport 1978b**] L. Lamport, "The Implementation of Reliable Distributed Multiprocess Systems," *Computer Networks*, Volume 2, Number 2 (April 1978), pages 95–114.

[**Lamport 1986**] L. Lamport, "The Mutual Exclusion Problem," *Journal of the ACM*, Volume 33, Number 2 (1986), pages 313–348.

[**Lampson 1969**] B. W. Lampson, "Dynamic Protection Structures," *Proceedings of the AFIPS Fall Joint Computer Conference* (1969), pages 27–38.

[**Lampson 1973**] B. W. Lampson, "A Note on the Confinement Problem," *Communications of the ACM*, Volume 10, Number 16 (October 1973), pages 613–615.

[**Lea 1997**] D. Lea, *Concurrent Programming in Java*, Addison-Wesley, Reading, MA (1997).

[**Leffler et al. 1989**] S. J. Leffler, M. K. McKusick, M. J. Karels, and J. S. Quarterman, *The Design and Implementation of the 4.3BSD UNIX Operating System*, Addison-Wesley, Reading, MA (1989).

[**Lehmann 1987**] F. Lehmann, "Computer Break-Ins," *Communications of the ACM*, Volume 30, Number 7 (July 1987), pages 584–585.

[**Le Lann 1977**] G. Le Lann, "Distributed Systems—Toward a Formal Approach," *Proceedings of the IFIP Congress 77* (1977), pages 155–160.

[**Lett and Konigsford 1968**] A. L. Lett and W. L. Konigsford, "TSS/360: A Time-Shared Operating System," *Proceedings of the AFIPS Fall Joint Computer Conference* (1968), pages 15–28.

[**Leutenegger and Vernon 1990**] S. Leutenegger and M. Vernon, "The Performance of Multiprogrammed Multiprocessor Scheduling Policies," *Proceedings of the Conference on Measurement and Modeling of Computer Systems* (May 1990).

[**Letwin 1988**] G. Letwin, *Inside OS/2*, Microsoft Press, Redmond, WA (1988).

[**Levin et al. 1975**] R. Levin, E. S. Cohen, W. M. Corwin, F. J. Pollack, and W. A. Wulf, "Policy/Mechanism Separation in Hydra," *Proceedings of the Fifth ACM Symposium on Operating Systems Principles* (1975), pages 132–140.

[**Levy and Lipman 1982**] H. M. Levy and P. H. Lipman, "Virtual Memory Management in the VAX/VMS Operating System," *Computer*, Volume 15, Number 3 (March 1982), pages 35–41.

[Lewis and Berg 1998] B. Lewis and D. Berg, *Multithreaded Programming with Pthreads*, Sun Microsystems Press, Upper Saddle River, NJ (1998).

[Lichtenberger and Pirtle 1965] W. W. Lichtenberger and M. W. Pirtle, "A Facility for Experimentation in Man-Machine Interaction," *Proceedings of the AFIPS Fall Joint Computer Conference* (1965), pages 589–598.

[Lindholm and Yellin 1998] T. Lindholm and F. Yellin, *The Java Virtual Machine Specification*, Addison-Wesley, Reading, MA (1998).

[Lions 1977] J. Lions, "A Commentary on the UNIX Operating System," Technical Report, Department of Computer Science, The University of South Wales (November 1977).

[Lipner 1975] S. Lipner, "A Comment on the Confinement Problem," *Operating Systems Review*, Volume 9, Number 5 (November 1975), pages 192–196.

[Lipton 1974] R. Lipton, "On Synchronization Primitive Systems," PhD. Thesis, Carnegie-Mellon University, Pittsburgh, PA (1974).

[Litzkow et al. 1988] M. J. Litzkow, M. Livny, and M. W. Mutka, "Condor— A Hunter of Idle Workstations," *Proceedings of the Eighth IEEE International Conference on Distributed Computing Systems* (1988), pages 104–111.

[Loepere 1992] K. Loepere, "Mach 3 Kernel Principles," Technical Report, Open Software Foundation, Boston, MA (January 1992).

[Loucks and Sauer 1987] L. K. Loucks and C. H. Sauer, "Advanced Interactive Executive (AIX) Operating System Overview," *IBM Systems Journal*, Volume 26, Number 4 (1987), pages 326–345.

[MacKinnon 1979] R. A. MacKinnon, "The Changing Virtual Machine Environment: Interfaces to Real Hardware, Virtual Hardware, and Other Virtual Machines," *IBM Systems Journal*, Volume 18, Number 1 (1979), pages 18–46.

[Maekawa 1985] M. Maekawa, "A Square Root Algorithm for Mutual Exclusion in Decentralized Systems," *ACM Transactions on Computer Systems*, Volume 3, Number 2 (May 1985), pages 145–159.

[Maher et al. 1994] C. Maher, J. S. Goldick, C. Kerby, and Bill Zumach, "The Integration of Distributed File Systems and Mass Storage Systems," *Proceedings of the Thirteenth IEEE Symposium on Mass Storage Systems* (June 1994), pages 27–31.

[Massalin and Pu 1989] H. Massalin and C. Pu, "Threads and Input/Output in the Synthesis Kernel," *Proceedings of the 12th Symposium on Operating Systems Principles* (December 1989), pages 191–200.

[Mattson et al. 1970] R. L. Mattson, J. Gecsei, D. R. Slutz, and I. L. Traiger, "Evaluation Techniques for Storage Hierarchies," *IBM Systems Journal,* Volume 9, Number 2 (1970), pages 78–117.

[McGraw and Andrews 1979] J. R. McGraw and G. R. Andrews, "Access Control in Parallel Programs," *IEEE Transactions on Software Engineering,* Volume SE-5, Number 1 (January 1979), pages 1–9.

[McKusick et al. 1984] M. K. McKusick, W. N. Joy, S. J. Leffler, and R. S. Fabry, "A Fast File System for UNIX," *ACM Transactions on Computer Systems,* Volume 2, Number 3 (August 1984), pages 181–197.

[McKusick et al. 1996] M. K. McKusick, K. Bostic, M. J. Karels, and J. S. Quarterman, *The Design and Implementation of the 4.4 BSD UNIX Operating System,* Addison-Wesley, Reading, MA (1996).

[McNamee and Armstrong 1990] D. McNamee and K. Armstrong, "Extending the Mach External Pager Interface to Accommodate User-Level Page-Replacement Policies," *Proceedings of the USENIX MACH Workshop,* Burlington, VT (October 1990).

[McVoy and Kleiman 1991] L. W. McVoy and S. R. Kleiman, "Extent-like Performance from a UNIX File System," *Proceedings of the Winter 1991 USENIX Conference* (January 1991), pages 33–44.

[Menasce and Muntz 1979] D. Menasce and R. R. Muntz, "Locking and Deadlock Detection in Distributed Data Bases," *IEEE Transactions on Software Engineering,* Volume SE-5, Number 3 (May 1979), pages 195–202.

[Menezes et al. 1997] A. J. Menezes, P. C. van Oorschot, and S. A. Vanstone, *Handbook of Applied Cryptography,* CRC Press (1997).

[Meyer and Downing 1997] J. Meyer and T. Downing, *Java Virtual Machine,* O'Reilly & Associates, Sebastopol, CA (1997).

[Microsoft 1986] Microsoft Corporation, *Microsoft MS-DOS User's Reference* and *Microsoft MS-DOS Programmer's Reference,* Microsoft Press, Redmond, WA (1986).

[Microsoft 1989] Microsoft Corporation, *Microsoft Operating System/2 Programmer's Reference,* 3 Volumes, Microsoft Press, Redmond, WA (1989).

[Microsoft (2000a)] *Microsoft Developer Network Development Library.* Microsoft Press, Redmond, WA (2000).

[Microsoft (2000b)] *Microsoft Windows 2000 Server Resource Kit.* Microsoft Press, Redmond, WA (2000).

[**Miller and Katz 1993**] E. L. Miller and R. H. Katz, "An Analysis of File Migration in a UNIX Supercomputing Environment," *Proceedings of the Winter 1993 USENIX Conference* (January 1993), pages 421-434.

[**Morris 1973**] J. H. Morris, "Protection in Programming Languages," *Communications of the ACM*, Volume 16, Number 1 (January 1973), pages 15–21.

[**Morris et al. 1986**] J. H. Morris, M. Satyanarayanan, M. H. Conner, J. H. Howard, D. S. H. Rosenthal, and F. D. Smith, "Andrew: A Distributed Personal Computing Environment," *Communications of the ACM*, Volume 29, Number 3 (March 1986), pages 184–201.

[**Morris and Thompson 1979**] R. Morris and K. Thompson, "Password Security: A Case History," *Communications of the ACM*, Volume 22, Number 11 (November 1979), pages 594–597.

[**Morshedian 1986**] D. Morshedian, "How to Fight Password Pirates," *Computer*, Volume 19, Number 1 (January 1986).

[**Motorola 1989a**] Motorola Inc., *MC68000 Family Reference*, Second Edition, Prentice-Hall, Englewood Cliffs, NJ (1989).

[**Motorola 1989b**] Motorola Inc., *MC68030 Enhanced 32-Bit Microprocessor User's Manual*, Second Edition, Prentice-Hall, Englewood Cliffs, NJ (1989).

[**Motorola 1993**] Motorola Inc., *PowerPC 601 RISC Microprocessor User's Manual*, Motorola, Phoenix, AZ (1993).

[**Mullender 1993**] S. Mullender (Editor), *Distributed Systems*, Second Edition, ACM Press, New York, NY (1993).

[**Mullender et al. 1990**] S. J. Mullender, G. Van Rossum, A. S. Tanenbaum, R. van Renesse, and H. Van Staveren, "Amoeba: A Distributed-Operating System for the 1990s," *IEEE Computer*, Volume 23, Number 5 (May 1990), pages 44–53.

[**Mutka and Livny 1987**] M. W. Mutka and M. Livny, "Scheduling Remote Processor Capacity in a Workstation-Processor Bank Network," *Proceedings of the Seventh IEEE International Conference on Distributed Computing Systems* (1987).

[**Needham and Walker 1977**] R. M. Needham and R. D. H. Walker, "The Cambridge CAP Computer and Its Protection System," *Proceedings of the Sixth Symposium on Operating Systems Principles* (November 1977), pages 1–10.

[**Nelson et al. 1988**] M. Nelson, B. Welch, and J. K. Ousterhout, "Caching in the Sprite Network File System," *ACM Transactions on Computer Systems*, Volume 6, Number 1 (February 1988), pages 134–154.

[**Nichols 1987**] D. A. Nichols, "Using Idle Workstations in a Shared Computing Environment," *Proceedings of the Eleventh ACM Symposium on Operating Systems Principles* (October 1987), pages 5–12.

[**Niemeyer and Peck 1997**] P. Niemeyer and J. Peck, *Exploring Java*, Second Edition, O'Reilly & Associates, Sebastopol, CA (1997).

[**Norton 1986**] P. Norton, *Inside the IBM PC*, Revised and Enlarged, Brady Books, New York, NY (1986).

[**Norton and Wilton 1988**] P. Norton and R. Wilton, *The New Peter Norton Programmer's Guide to the IBM PC & PS/2*, Microsoft Press, Redmond, WA (1988).

[**Oaks 1998**] S. Oaks, *Java Security*, O'Reilly & Associates, Sebastopol, CA (1998).

[**Oaks and Wong 1999**] S. Oaks and H. Wong, *Java Threads*, Second Edition, O'Reilly & Associates, Sebastopol, CA (1999).

[**O'Leary and Kitts 1985**] B. T. O'Leary and D. L. Kitts, "Optical Device for a Mass Storage System," *Computer*, Volume 18, Number 7 (July 1985).

[**Obermarck 1982**] R. Obermarck, "Distributed Deadlock Detection Algorithm," *ACM Transactions on Database Systems*, Volume 7, Number 2 (June 1982), pages 187–208.

[**Olsen and Kenley 1989**] R. P. Olsen and G. Kenley, "Virtual Optical Disks Solve the On-Line Storage Crunch," *Computer Design*, Volume 28, Number 1 (January 1989), pages 93–96.

[**Organick 1972**] E. I. Organick, *The Multics System: An Examination of Its Structure*, MIT Press, Cambridge, MA (1972).

[**OSF 1989**] Open Software Foundation, *Mach Technology: A Series of Ten Lectures*, OSF Foundation, Cambridge, MA (Fall 1989).

[**Ousterhout et al. 1985**] J. K. Ousterhout, H. Da Costa, D. Harrison, J. A. Kunze, M. Kupfer, and J. G. Thompson, "A Trace-Driven Analysis of the UNIX 4.2 BSD File System," *Proceedings of the Tenth ACM Symposium on Operating Systems Principles* (December 1985), pages 15–24.

[**Ousterhout et al. 1988**] J. K. Ousterhout, A. R. Cherenson, F. Douglis, M. N. Nelson, and B. B. Welch, "The Sprite Network-Operating System," *IEEE Computer*, Volume 21, Number 2 (February 1988), pages 23–36.

[**Parnas 1975**] D. L. Parnas, "On a Solution to the Cigarette Smokers' Problem Without Conditional Statements," *Communications of the ACM*, Volume 18, Number 3 (March 1975), pages 181–183.

[Patil 1971] S. Patil, "Limitations and Capabilities of Dijkstra's Semaphore Primitives for Coordination Among Processes," Technical Report, MIT (1971).

[Patterson and Hennessy 1998] D. A. Patterson and J. Hennessy, *Computer Organization and Design—The Hardware/Software Interface*, Second Edition, Morgan Kaufmann Publishers, San Francisco, CA (1998).

[Patterson et al. 1988] D. A. Patterson, G. Gibson, and R. H. Katz, "A Case for Redundant Arrays of Inexpensive Disks (RAID)," *Proceedings of the ACM SIGMOD International Conference on the Management of Data* (1988).

[Peacock 1992] J. K. Peacock, "File System Multithreading in System V Release 4 MP," *Proceedings of the Summer 1992 USENIX Conference* (June 1992), pages 19–29.

[Pechura and Schoeffler 1983] M. A. Pechura and J. D. Schoeffler, "Estimating File Access Time of Floppy Disks," *Communications of the ACM*, Volume 26, Number 10 (October 1983), pages 754–763.

[Peterson 1981] G. L. Peterson, "Myths About the Mutual Exclusion Problem," *Information Processing Letters*, Volume 12, Number 3 (June 1981).

[Pham and Garg 1996] T. Pham and P. Garg, *Multithreaded Programming with Windows NT*, Prentice-Hall, Upper Saddle River, NJ (1996).

[Pinkert and Wear 1989] J. Pinkert and L. Wear, *Operating Systems: Concepts, Policies, and Mechanisms*, Prentice-Hall, Englewood Cliffs, NJ (1989).

[Popek and Walker 1985] G. Popek and B. Walker (Editors), *The LOCUS Distributed System Architecture*, MIT Press, Cambridge, MA (1985).

[Powell et al. 1991] M. L. Powell, S. R. Kleiman, S. Barton, D. Shaw, D. Stein, and M. Weeks, "SunOS Multi-threaded Architecture," *Proceedings of the Winter 1991 USENIX Conference* (January 1991), pages 65–80.

[Prieve and Fabry 1976] B. G. Prieve and R. S. Fabry, "VMIN—An Optimal Variable Space Page-Replacement Algorithm," *Communications of the ACM*, Volume 19, Number 5 (May 1976), pages 295–297.

[Psaltis and Mok 1995] D. Psaltis and F. Mok, "Holographic Memories," *Scientific American*, Volume 273, Number 5 (November 1995), pages 70–76.

[Quarterman 1990] J. S. Quarterman, *The Matrix Computer Networks and Conferencing Systems Worldwide*, Digital Press, Bedford, MA (1990).

[Quarterman and Hoskins 1986] J. S. Quarterman and H. C. Hoskins, "Notable Computer Networks," *Communications of the ACM*, Volume 29, Number 10 (October 1986), pages 932–971.

[Quinlan 1991] S. Quinlan, "A Cached WORM File System," *Software–Practice and Experience,* Volume 21, Number 12 (December 1991), pages 1289–1299.

[Rashid 1986] R. F. Rashid, "From RIG to Accent to Mach: The Evolution of a Network-Operating System," *Proceedings of the ACM/IEEE Computer Society, Fall Joint Computer Conference* (1986).

[Rashid and Robertson 1981] R. Rashid and G. Robertson, "Accent: A Communication Oriented Network-Operating System Kernel," *Proceedings of the Eighth Symposium on Operating Systems Principles* (December 1981).

[Raynal 1986] M. Raynal, *Algorithms for Mutual Exclusion,* MIT Press, Cambridge, MA (1986).

[Reed and Kanodia 1979] D. P. Reed and R. K. Kanodia, "Synchronization with Eventcounts and Sequences," *Communications of the ACM,* Volume 22, Number 2 (February 1979), pages 115–123.

[Reid 1987] B. Reid, "Reflections on Some Recent Widespread Computer Break-Ins," *Communications of the ACM,* Volume 30, Number 2 (February 1987), pages 103–105.

[Ricart and Agrawala 1981] G. Ricart and A. K. Agrawala, "An Optimal Algorithm for Mutual Exclusion in Computer Networks," *Communications of the ACM,* Volume 24, Number 1 (January 1981), pages 9–17.

[Richards 1990] A. E. Richards, "A File System Approach for Integrating Removable Media Devices and Jukeboxes," *Optical Information Systems,* Volume 10, Number 5 (September 1990), pages 270–274.

[Richter 1997] J. Richter, *Advanced Windows,* Third Edition, Microsoft Press, Redmond, WA (1997).

[Ritchie 1979] D. Ritchie, "The Evolution of the UNIX Time-Sharing System," *Language Design and Programming Methodology, Lecture Notes on Computer Science,* Volume 79, Springer-Verlag, Berlin (1979).

[Ritchie and Thompson 1974] D. M. Ritchie and K. Thompson, "The UNIX Time-Sharing System," *Communications of the ACM,* Volume 17, Number 7 (July 1974), pages 365–375; a later version appeared in *Bell System Technical Journal,* Volume 57, Number 6 (July-August 1978), pages 1905–1929.

[Rivest et al. 1978] R. L. Rivest, A. Shamir, and L. Adleman, "On Digital Signatures and Public Key Cryptosystems," *Communications of the ACM,* Volume 21, Number 2 (February 1978), pages 120–126.

[Rosenkrantz et al. 1978] D. J. Rosenkrantz, R. E. Stearns, and P. M. Lewis, "System Level Concurrency Control for Distributed Database Systems," *ACM Transactions on Database Systems,* Volume 3, Number 2 (June 1978), pages 178–198.

[**Ruemmler and Wilkes 1991**] C. Ruemmler and J. Wilkes, "Disk Shuffling," Technical Report HPL-CSP-91-30, Hewlett-Packard Laboratories, Palo Alto, CA (October 1991).

[**Ruemmler and Wilkes 1993**] C. Ruemmler and J. Wilkes, "UNIX Disk Access Patterns," *Proceedings of the Winter 1993 USENIX Conference* (January 1993), pages 405–420.

[**Ruemmler and Wilkes 1994**] C. Ruemmler and J. Wilkes, "An Introduction to Disk Drive Modeling," *IEEE Computer*, Volume 27, Number 3 (March 1994), pages 17–29.

[**Sandberg 1987**] R. Sandberg, *The Sun Network File System: Design, Implementation, and Experience*, Sun Microsystems, Inc., Mountain View, CA (1987).

[**Sandberg et al. 1985**] R. Sandberg, D. Goldberg, S. Kleiman, D. Walsh, and B. Lyon, "Design and Implementation of the Sun Network File System," *Proceedings of the 1985 USENIX Summer Conference* (June 1985), pages 119–130.

[**Sargent and Shoemaker 1995**] M. Sargent and R. Shoemaker, *The Personal Computer from the Inside Out*, Third Edition, Addison-Wesley, Reading, MA (1995).

[**Sarisky 1983**] L. Sarisky, "Will Removable Hard Disks Replace the Floppy?" *Byte* (March 1983), pages 110–117.

[**Satyanarayanan 1990**] M. Satyanarayanan, "Scalable, Secure, and Highly Available Distributed File Access," *Computer*, Volume 23, Number 5 (May 1990), pages 9–21.

[**Schlichting and Schneider 1982**] R. D. Schlichting and F. B. Schneider, "Understanding and Using Asynchronous Message Passing Primitives," *Proceedings of the Symposium on Principles of Distributed Computing* (August 1982), pages 141–147.

[**Schneider 1982**] F. B. Schneider, "Synchronization in Distributed Programs," *ACM Transactions on Programming Languages and Systems*, Volume 4, Number 2 (April 1982), pages 125–148.

[**Schrage 1967**] L. E. Schrage, "The Queue M/G/I with Feedback to Lower Priority Queues," *Management Science*, Volume 13 (1967), pages 466–474.

[**Schultz 1988**] B. Schultz, "VM: The Crossroads of Operating Systems," *Datamation*, Volume 34, Number 14 (July 1988), pages 79–84.

[**Schwartz and Weissman 1967**] J. I. Schwartz and C. Weissman, "The SDC Time-Sharing System Revisited," *Proceedings of the ACM National Meeting* (August 1967), pages 263–271.

[Schwartz et al. 1964] J. I. Schwartz, E. G. Coffman, and C. Weissman, "A General Purpose Time-Sharing System," *Proceedings of the AFIPS Spring Joint Computer Conference* (1964), pages 397–411.

[Seely 1989] D. Seely, "Password Cracking: A Game of Wits," *Communications of the ACM*, Volume 32, Number 6 (June 1989), pages 700–704.

[Shrivastava and Panzieri 1982] S. K. Shrivastava and F. Panzieri, "The Design of a Reliable Remote Procedure Call Mechanism," *IEEE Transactions on Computers*, Volume C-31, Number 7 (July 1982), pages 692–697.

[Silberschatz et al. 2001] A. Silberschatz, H. F. Korth, and S. Sudarshan, *Database System Concepts,* Fourth Edition, McGraw-Hill, New York, NY (2001).

[Sincerbox 1994] G. T. Sincerbox (Editor), *Selected Papers on Holographic Storage,* Number MS 95, SPIE Milestone Series, SPIE Optical Engineering Press, Bellingham, WA (1994).

[Smith 1982] A. J. Smith, "Cache Memories," *ACM Computing Surveys*, Volume 14, Number 3 (September 1982), pages 473–530.

[Smith 1988] A. J. Smith, "A Survey of Process Migration Mechanisms," *Operating Systems Review,* Volume 22, Number 3 (July 1988).

[Solomon 1998] D. A. Solomon, *Inside Windows NT,* Second Edition, Microsoft Press, Redmond, WA (1998).

[Solomon and Russinovich (2000)] D. A. Solomon and M. E. Russinovich, *Inside Microsoft Windows 2000,* Third Edition, Microsoft Press, Redmond, WA (1998)(2000).

[Spafford 1989] E. H. Spafford, "The Internet Worm: Crisis and Aftermath," *Communications of the ACM,* Volume 32, Number 6 (June 1989), pages 678–687.

[Garfinkel and Spafford 1996] S. Garfinkel and G. Spafford, *Practical UNIX & Internet Security,* O'Reilly & Associates, Sebastopol, CA (1996).

[Stallings 1992] W. Stallings, *Operating Systems,* Macmillan, New York, NY (1992).

[Stankovic 1982] J. S. Stankovic, "Software Communication Mechanisms: Procedure Calls Versus Messages," *Computer,* Volume 15, Number 4 (April 1982).

[Stankovic and Ramamrithan 1989] J. S. Stankovic and K. Ramamrithan, "The Spring Kernel: A New Paradigm for Real-Time Operating Systems," *Operating Systems Review*, Volume 23, Number 3 (July 1989).

[Staunstrup 1982] J. Staunstrup, "Message Passing Communication versus Procedure Call Communication," *Software—Practice and Experience,* Volume 12, Number 3 (March 1982), pages 223–234.

[Stein and Shaw 1992] D. Stein and D. Shaw, "Implementing Lightweight Threads," *Proceedings of the Summer 1992 USENIX Conference* (June 1992), pages 1–9.

[Stevens 1990] W. R. Stevens, *UNIX Network Programming,* Prentice-Hall, Englewood Cliffs, NJ (1990).

[Strachey 1959] C. Strachey, "Time Sharing in Large Fast Computers," *Proceedings of the International Conference on Information Processing* (June 1959), pages 336–341.

[Sun Microsystems 1990] Sun Microsystems, *Network Programming Guide,* Sun Microsystems, Inc., Mountain View, CA (1990), pages 168–186.

[Sunsoft 1995] *Solaris Multithreaded Programming Guide,* Sunsoft Press, Upper Saddle River, NJ (1995).

[Svobodova 1984] L. Svobodova, "File Servers for Network-Based Distributed Systems," *ACM Computing Surveys,* Volume 16, Number 4 (December 1984), pages 353–398.

[Tanenbaum 1990] A. S. Tanenbaum, *Structured Computer Organization,* Third Edition, Prentice-Hall, Englewood Cliffs, NJ (1990).

[Tanenbaum 1992] A. S. Tanenbaum, *Modern Operating Systems,* Prentice-Hall, Englewood Cliffs, NJ (1992).

[Tanenbaum 1996] A. Tanenbaum, *Computer Networks,* Third Edition, Prentice-Hall, Upper Saddle River, NJ (1996).

[Tanenbaum and van Renesse 1985] A. S. Tanenbaum and R. van Renesse, "Distributed-Operating Systems," *ACM Computing Surveys,* Volume 17, Number 4 (December 1985), pages 419–470.

[Tanenbaum and Woodhull 1997] A. S. Tanenbaum and A. S. Woodhull, *Operating System Design and Implementation,* Second Edition, Prentice-Hall, Englewood Cliffs, NJ (1997).

[Tanenbaum et al. 1990] A. S. Tanenbaum, R. van Renesse, H. Van Staveren, G. J. Sharp, S. J. Mullender, J. Jansen, and G. Van Rossum, "Experiences with the Amoeba Distributed-Operating System," *Communications of the ACM,* Volume 33, Number 12 (December 1990), pages 46–63.

[Tate (2000)] S. Tate, *Windows 2000 Essential Reference,* New Riders (2000).

[Tay and Ananda 1990] B. H. Tay and A. L. Ananda, "A Survey of Remote Procedure Calls," *Operating Systems Review,* Volume 24, Number 3 (July 1990), pages 68–79.

[TCSEC 1985] "Department of Defense Trusted Computer System Evaluation Criteria," *Department of Defense,* DoD 5200.28-STD (December 1985).

[Teorey and Pinkerton 1972] T. J. Teorey and T. B. Pinkerton, "A Comparative Analysis of Disk Scheduling Policies," *Communications of the ACM,* Volume 15, Number 3 (March 1972), pages 177–184.

[Tevanian et al. 1987a] A. Tevanian, Jr., R. F. Rashid, D. B. Golub, D. L. Black, E. Cooper, and M. W. Young, "Mach Threads and the UNIX Kernel: The Battle for Control," *Proceedings of the Summer 1987 USENIX Conference* (July 1987).

[Tevanian et al. 1987b] A. Tevanian, Jr., R. F. Rashid, M. W. Young, D. B. Golub, M. R. Thompson, W. Bolosky, and R. Sanzi, "A UNIX Interface for Shared Memory and Memory Mapped Files Under Mach," Technical Report, Carnegie-Mellon University, Pittsburgh, PA (July 1987).

[Tevanian and Smith 1989] A. Tevanian, Jr. and B. Smith, "Mach: The Model for Future UNIX," *Byte* (November 1989).

[Tucker and Gupta 1989] A. Tucker and A. Gupta, "Process Control and Scheduling Issues for Multiprogrammed Shared-Memory Multiprocessors," *Proceedings of the Twelfth ACM Symposium on Operating Systems Principles* (December 1989).

[USENIX 1990] USENIX Association, *Proceedings of the Mach Workshop,* Burlington, VT (October 1990).

[USENIX 1991] USENIX Association, *Proceedings of the USENIX Mach Symposium,* Monterey, CA (November 1991).

[USENIX 1992b] USENIX Association, *Proceedings of the USENIX Workshop on Micro-kernels and Other Kernel Architectures,* Seattle, WA (April 1992).

[Vahalia 1996] U. Vahalia, *UNIX Internals: The New Frontiers,* Prentice-Hall, Englewood Cliffs, NJ (1996).

[van der Linden 1999] P. van der Linden, *Just Java 1.2,* Sun Microsystems Press, Upper Saddle River, NJ (1999).

[Venners 1998] B. Venners, *Inside the Java Virtual Machine,* McGraw Hill, New York, NY (1998).

[Wah 1984] B. W. Wah, "File Placement on Distributed Computer Systems," *Computer,* Volume 17, Number 1 (January 1984), pages 23–32.

[**Waldo 1998**] J. Waldo, "OO Systems," *IEEE Concurrency*, Volume 16, Number 3 (July-September 1998).

[**Walmer and Thompson 1989**] L. R. Walmer and M. R. Thompson, "A Programmer's Guide to the Mach System Calls," Technical Report, Carnegie-Mellon University, Pittsburgh, PA (December 1989).

[**Windows NT Resource Kit 1993**] *Microsoft Windows NT Resource Kit: Volume 1, Windows NT Resource Guide*, Microsoft Press, Redmond, WA (1993).

[**Windows NT Workstation Resource Kit 1996**] *Microsoft Windows NT Workstation Resource Kit*, Microsoft Press, Redmond, WA (1996).

[**Wood and Kochan 1985**] P. Wood and S. Kochan, *UNIX System Security*, Hayden, Hasbrouck Heights, NJ (1985).

[**Woodside 1986**] C. Woodside, "Controllability of Computer Performance Tradeoffs Obtained Using Controlled-Share Queue Schedulers," *IEEE Transactions on Software Engineering*, Volume SE-12, Number 10 (October 1986), pages 1041–1048.

[**Worthington et al. 1994**] B. L. Worthington, G. R. Ganger, and Y. N. Patt, "Scheduling Algorithms for Modern Disk Drives," *Proceedings of the 1994 ACM Sigmetrics Conference on Measurement and Modeling of Computer Systems* (May 1994), pages 241–251.

[**Worthington et al. 1995**] B. L. Worthington, G. R. Ganger, Y. N. Patt, and J. Wilkes, "On-Line Extraction of SCSI Disk Drive Parameters," *Proceedings of the 1995 ACM Sigmetrics Conference on Measurement and Modeling of Computer Systems* (May 1995), pages 146–156.

[**Wulf 1969**] W. A. Wulf, "Performance Monitors for Multiprogramming Systems," *Proceedings of the Second ACM Symposium on Operating Systems Principles* (October 1969), pages 175–181.

[**Wulf et al. 1981**] W. A. Wulf, R. Levin, and S. P. Harbison, *Hydra/C. mmp: An Experimental Computer System*, McGraw-Hill, New York, NY (1981).

[**Zahorjan and McCann 1990**] J. Zahorjan and C. McCann, "Processor Scheduling in Shared Memory Multiprocessors," *Proceedings of the Conference on Measurement and Modeling of Computer Systems* (May 1990).

[**Zayas 1987**] E. R. Zayas, "Attacking the Process Migration Bottleneck," *Proceedings of the Eleventh ACM Symposium on Operating Systems Principles* (October 1987), pages 13–24.

[**Zhao 1989**] W. Zhao (Editor), Special Issue on Real-Time Operating Systems, *Operating Systems Review*, Volume 23, Number 3 (July 1989).

CREDITS

Figure 3.9: From Iaccobucci, *OS/2 Programmer's Guide*, ©1988, McGraw-Hill, Inc., New York, New York. Figure 1.7, p. 20. Reprinted with permission of the publisher.

Figure 6.8: From Khanna/Sebree/Zolnowsky, "Realtime Scheduling in SunOS 5.0," Proceedings of Winter USENIX, January 1992, San Francisco, California. Derived with permission of the authors.

Figure 6.9 adapted with permission from Sun Microsystems, Inc.

Figure 9.20: From *80386 Programmer's Reference Manual*, Figure 5-12, p. 5-12. Reprinted by permission of Intel Corporation, Copyright / Intel Corporation 1986.

Figure 10.15: From *IBM Systems Journal*, Vol. 10, No. 3, ©1971, International Business Machines Corporation. Reprinted by permission of IBM Corporation.

Figure 11.9: From Leffler/McKusick/Karels/Quarterman, *The Design and Implementation of the 4.3BSD UNIX Operating System*, ©1989 by Addison-Wesley Publishing Co., Inc., Reading, Massachusetts. Figure 7.6, p. 196. Reprinted with permission of the publisher.

Figure 12.4: From *Pentium Processor User's Manual: Architecture and Programming Manual*, Volume 3, Copyright 1993. Reprinted by permission of Intel Corporation.

Figures 14.4, 14.5, and 14.7: From Halsall, *Data Communications, Computer Networks, and Open Systems, Third Edition*, ©1992, Addison-Wesley Publishing Co., Inc., Reading, Massachusetts. Figure 1.9, p. 14, Figure 1.10, p. 15, and Figure 1.11, p. 18. Reprinted with permission of the publisher.

Figure 20.1: From Quarterman/Wilhelm, *UNIX, POSIX and Open Systems: The Open Standards Puzzle*, ©1993, by Addison-Wesley Publishing Co., Inc. Reading, Massachusetts. Figure 2.1, p. 31. Reprinted with permission of the publisher.

Timeline information for the back end papers was assembled: From a variety of sources, which include "The History of Electronic Computing," compiled and edited by Marc Rettig, Association for Computing Machinery, Inc. (ACM), New York, New York, and Shedroff/Hutto/Fromm, *Understanding Computers*, ©1992, Vivid Publishing, distributed by SYBEX, San Francisco, California.

Index